Delphi In Depth

Cary Jensen
Loy Anderson
Joseph Fung
Ann Lynnworth
Mark Ostroff
Martin Rudy
Robert Vivrette

Osborne **McGraw-Hill**

Berkeley New York St. Louis San Francisco
Auckland Bogotá Hamburg London Madrid
Mexico City Milan Montreal New Delhi Panama City
Paris São Paulo Singapore Sydney
Tokyo Toronto

Osborne **McGraw-Hill**
2600 Tenth Street
Berkeley, California 94710
U.S.A.

For information on translations or book distributors outside the U.S.A., or to arrange bulk purchase discounts for sales promotions, premiums, or fundraisers, please contact Osborne **McGraw-Hill** at the above address.

Delphi In Depth

1234567890 DOC 99876

ISBN 0-07-882211-4

Acquisitions Editor
Megg Bonar

Project Editor
Claire Splan

Copy Editor
Amy R. Marks

Proofreaders
Sally Engelfried
Pat Mannion

Coordinating Editors
Cary Jensen
Loy Anderson

Technical Editor
Cary Jensen

Computer Designer
Richard Whitaker

Illustrator
Leslee Bassin

Cover Design
Ted Mader Associates

Quality Control Specialist
Joe Scuderi

This book is for my wife for her love, support, and patience.

—Cary Jensen

To my husband and best friend for his love, and for his willingness to put up with the late nights and non-existent weekends that working on this book required.

—Loy Anderson

I would like to thank Veronica Stone, Ph. D. for all of her love and support.

—Joseph Fung

To my business partner, Michael Ax, author of TPack and WebHub.

—Ann Lynnworth

To the one person here on earth who best exemplifies unswerving loyalty, complete commitment, and unconditional love—my wife, Janet.

—Mark Ostroff

To my family—Terri, Matthew, and Rachel—for letting me take the time to write and for their patience, support, and love.

—Martin Rudy

To my loving wife and best friend Lorna, whose patience, love, and kindness have truly made every day the happiest one in my life.

—Robert Vivrette

About the Authors

Cary Jensen, Ph.D., is a Contributing Editor and columnist of *Delphi Informant Magazine*, the leading publication for Delphi developers. He has co-authored 16 computer books, including *Programming Paradox 5 for Windows* (Sybex, Inc., 1995), a two-time winner of the *Paradox Informant Magazine* Readers' Choice Award for best Paradox book, and *The Latte Handbook* (Osborne/McGraw-Hill, 1996). Cary is the lead Delphi trainer for Softbite International, winner of *Delphi Informant Magazine* Readers' Choice Award for best Delphi training organization, and author of the Borland/Softbite Delphi World Tour and Borland/Softbite Delphi 2 World Tour seminar materials. He is an internationally-recognized trainer who has spoken extensively on Delphi in the U.S. and Europe. Cary is an advisory board chairperson for the 1996 Borland Developer's Conference.

Loy Anderson, Ph.D., is an award-winning, best-selling author of more than a dozen computer books. She has served as Associated Editor of *Paradox Informant Magazine*, and is Vice President of Jensen Data Systems, Inc., a leading provider of Delphi application development and training. She has a Ph.D. in Human Factors Psychology, specializing in human-computer interaction.

Joseph C. Fung is Director of Technology and Tools at PCSI, a leading Client/Server and Internet consulting and development firm. He writes for *Delphi Informant Magazine* and *Databased Advisor* and is the author of *Paradox for Windows Essential Power Programming* (Prima). Mr. Fung is the architect of AppExpert and ScriptView, perennial winners of the *Databased Advisor* Readers' Choice Award and *Paradox Informant Magazine* Readers' Choice Award. Recently, Mr. Fung chaired an advisory board for the Borland Developer Conference. PCSI, Professional Computer Solutions, Inc., is the leader in developing SQL applications using Delphi, Visual Basic, and Access, and using Microsoft SQL Server, Sybase, and Oracle server technologies. PCSI is a Borland Connections Partner and Microsoft Solution Provider at the Partner level.

Ann Lynnworth, a pioneer on the World Wide Web, has been leading the Delphi tools wave for Web developers. Ann's new company, HREF Tools Corp., has been shipping a Delphi VCL product for the Web since October 1995. She is an active member of the Paradox and Delphi communities, with contributions to several magazines and papers presented at most of the Borland Developer conferences. Ann is co-founder of the Delphi Northbay SIG based in Petaluma, California.

Mark Ostroff has over 18 years experience in the computer industry. He began programming mini-computers for medical research and process control applications in Assembly, Fortran and C. Mark then moved to building PC database applications for the U.S. Navy and for IBM's COS Division. While working on the Navy project he stumbled across TurboPascal, which lead Mark to join Borland in 1989. Mark has presented several times at the Borland Developer's Conference, and has written articles for the *Informant* magazines. In addition, he was one of the volunteers who helped create the original Paradox-based "InTouch System" for the Friends of the Vietnam Veteran's Memorial. Mark also carries the distinction of being the only person who has sung at every Borland Developer's Conference held so far. He is currently employed by Borland as a Systems Engineer, specializing in client/server database applications.

Martin Rudy is CEO of Para/Matrix Solutions, Inc., a firm specializing in Delphi and Paradox application development, consulting, and training. He was the Paradox Advisory Board Chairman for the 1992 Borland Database Conference and a Paradox Advisory Board Member of the 1990, 1991, and 1996 Conferences. He as been a speaker at all of the Borland Conferences and two of the European Borland Conferences. Mr. Rudy is co-author with Greg Salcedo of IDG's Power Programming Secrets book series for Paradox DOS and Paradox for Windows.

Robert Vivrette is a Senior Programmer Analyst for Pacific Gas & Electric, working exclusively with Delphi since its release. He is Technical Editor of *Delphi Informant Magazine* and is the Publisher/Editor of the *Unofficial Newsletter for Delphi Users*, a free, electronic Delphi newsletter available on the Borland Delphi Forum. Since the release of Delphi, he has rarely had time to sleep.

Table of Contents

PART II
Techniques

PART IV

Appendixes

Foreword

In my ten years of computer experience I have never experienced a phenomenon quite like Delphi. In a little over a year, Delphi has taken the visual development segment of the personal computer market by storm. Software developers have rushed to experience firsthand what they have heard from the trade press and from colleagues. What they have heard is exciting. Delphi is a rich, robust development environment that brings unparalleled power and speed to the software developer.

There are few in the Delphi community with as much experience and expertise in Delphi as Cary Jensen and Loy Anderson. With a resume of dozens of book titles to their credit, Cary and Loy have teamed up with a group of Delphi experts to bring you *Delphi in Depth,* a no-nonsense tome that will not only provide you with Delphi programming fundamentals, but help you make the leap to more complex Delphi application development.

With *Delphi in Depth,* they demystify such Object Pascal topics as manipulating objects, using resource files, thread synchronization, and multithreading. Using sound and tested techniques, the authors provide an authoritative guide to the Delphi programming methodology.

Unlike other books that do little more than regurgitate the Object Pascal documentation, this book will open doors you previously found closed. Techniques or principles you found to be vague or poorly explained in other sources will suddenly make sense. *Delphi in Depth* takes you through the inner workings of Delphi. It will spur new ideas and insights and quite simply show you how to get the job done with Delphi.

The authors accomplish this through a number of solid, real-life examples. This hands-on approach results in a wonderfully clear tutorial and reference to an exciting new development environment. Based on their own experiences, the authors lead you through the Delphi basics. They then progress to more complex examples such as multithreading. By the book's end, you'll understand the fundamentals of Delphi programming. More importantly, you'll be ready to develop your own Delphi applications immediately.

If you haven't taken the dive into Delphi for lack of a clear path, this book eliminates the problem. I think you'll be pleased with the clarity and detail provided by *Delphi in Depth*. Moreover, you'll find it a valuable reference to keep by your side as you take your skills to the next level. I thoroughly enjoyed *Delphi in Depth* and I hope you do as well.

Mitchell Koulouris
Publisher
Delphi Informant Magazine

Acknowledgments

We want to extend our thanks and gratitude to the many individuals whose contributions and encouragement made this book possible. In particular, to Scott Rogers, Executive Editor at Osborne/McGraw-Hill, without whose dogged determination and commitment to this project, this book would never have been written. To Megg Bonar, Acquisitions Editor; Cindy Brown, Managing Editor; Claire Splan, Project Editor; and Daniela Dell'Orco, Senior Editorial Assistant; Amy R. Marks, Copyeditor; Sally Engelfried and Pat Mannion, Proofreaders; Richard Whitaker and Leslee Bassin in Production for their very hard work, insight, and dedication. Also, to the fine people at Borland International, including Nan Borreson, Zack Urlocker, Anders Hejlsberg, Diane Rogers, David Intersimone, Charles Calvert, Karen Giles, and too many more to name individually, for their technical support and assistance. We extend a special thanks to Kelly Welty, for the .AVI files of his delightful video productions that appear on the CD-ROM. Also thanks to the fine people at Informant Communications Group, including Mitchell Koulouris, for his assistance with the CD-ROM for this book and generous Foreword; Gary Praegitzer, for mastering the CD-ROM; Robert Muir, for his assistance; and Jerry Coffey, for his friendship and guidance during the initial stages of this project. We also want to thank Kevin Smith of Softbite International; Bill Todd, of the Database Group, Inc.; and Sue and Tony Bennett, of Desktop Associates, LTD; for their inspiration, support, and friendship. We would also like to thank Allan Lockert, for his input on QuickReport;

Richard Dominelli and Sean Wenzel, for their GIF2BMP unit; Nick Hodges, for TSmiley; Michael Ax, for his input and support; Corel Corporation, for the use of the PENPAPER.BMP and WORLD.BMP clipart files; and to the many individuals and companies who contributed material for the CD-ROM. Also, we wish to extend our thanks to the many fans of Delphi for sharing their enthusiasm for this absolutely incredible product. And finally, we wish to thank our talented co-authors, Joseph, Ann, Mark, Martin, and Robert, with whom it has been a great pleasure and honor to work.

—Cary Jensen and Loy Anderson

I would like to thank Gary Whizin, Anders Hejlsberg, Charles P. Jazdzewski, and Danny Thorpe for all their assistance in answering questions and helping me with my research.

—Joseph Fung

I'd like to thank Michael Ax for seeing the vision of this work and making it real; Cary Jensen for his gentle and clear guidance; Keith Bigelow at Borland for his encouragement and support; James Gleaves and Rob Martin for keeping HREF Tools Corp. going while I was writing; and my customers for tolerating long lapses in e-mail response time.

—Ann Lynnworth

My thanks to Jerry Coffey of the Informant Communications Group, who recommended me for this project. To Cary Jensen, who decided to take Jerry's advice and let me join this very special band of people. To Zack Urlocker, Anders Hejlsberg, and the entire Delphi team for putting the fun back into programming. To my fellow Borland Systems Engineers, particularly Louis Kleiman, Randy Haben, Phil Foti, Steve Segalewitz, Peter Marquez, Mike Destein, and David Pawloski. These guys have taught me a whole lot about the power of Delphi. To Fred Felman, the man who originally hired me at Borland and continues to provide an example of quiet leadership from within the Paradox group. To Bob Clemens, my boss at Borland who has always provided encouragement and support for my "extra projects." To my Borland Sales Reps, Brian Lantz and Darrin Christensen, who kept sending me out to potential ReportSmith customers and forced me to really get to know the product. And most importantly ... To my son, Michael, who keeps bringing me notes from the REAL world—and who keeps me humble by beating me embarrassingly well on my own computer games. To my daughter, Christine, who keeps reminding me what really matters—caring.

—Mark Ostroff

I want to thank Cary Jensen, for his comments and contributions, and to both Cary Jensen and Loy Anderson, for the effort that they put into this book.

—Martin Rudy

Special thanks to Dr. Adrian Bottoms for his work on loading audio data from resource files, and also to Guy R. Eddon whose excellent work on sprites and animation sparked several of the ideas for the animation components.

—Robert Vivrette

Introduction

Do you remember the first time you saw Delphi? If you were like us, your initial thoughts were ones of disbelief and wonder. Certainly, no tool could make Windows development so straightforward, so effortless, so easy. But Delphi appeared to do this.

But first impressions must eventually give way to reality. And herein lies the real test for a development tool. While the official demonstrations by a company's representatives always make the tool look easy to use, it is only through serious, applied use that you really begin to see the benefits and pitfalls of a product.

Fortunately, and remarkably, Delphi did not disappoint us. The more we work with it, and the more we ask of it, the more we like it. Clearly, Delphi is the truly groundbreaking product that it initially looked like. Even more importantly, a detailed look at the underlying architecture of Delphi reveals a sound foundation that provides for unlimited expansion. Delphi gives meaning to the word "elegant."

Now comes Delphi 2. It signifies a major leap forward, feature-wise. However, with the exception of it being compiled as a 32-bit application, Delphi 2 is, fundamentally, Delphi 1.0 with features added. This is very good. Again, using the solid foundation of Delphi 1.0, Delphi 2 builds on firm ground. There is no need to re-invent what is nearly perfect.

About this Book

This book covers Delphi—both Delphi 1.0 and Delphi 2 (and no doubt, will be applicable in many instances to future versions as well). Many of the basic techniques and overall approaches to application development apply equally to both versions. Consequently, most of the techniques covered here apply equally to both products. However, there are some capabilities that are unique to Delphi 2. Many of these are covered as well in this book, and are clearly identified as Delphi 2 only topics.

In addition to covering material applicable to both Delphi 1.0 and Delphi 2, this book was written to add something unique to the body of material already published on Delphi. We accomplished this by bringing together a team of talented and articulate Delphi developers, and asked them to write on their areas of particular interest. In doing so, we have produced a book that has something for every Delphi developer. If you are new to object-oriented programming, you will find an outstanding discussion of how this technology applies to Delphi. Whether you are a beginning database developer, or an advanced one, you will find extensive material that will satisfy you. If you have been curious about the Internet, an entire section of this book is devoted to the discussion of issues that you, as a developer, must concern yourself with. And the list goes on.

The techniques and code samples you find in the pages of this book are valuable. Even more valuable, however, is the general approach to Delphi development that pervades these examples. Here you will see how seasoned Delphi developers solve problems using Delphi, leveraging Delphi to produce functional, and maintainable, code.

Who Is This Book For?

This book is for every Delphi developer. This book assumes that you are already familiar with the basics of Delphi. Therefore, you will not find a tour of the component palette here, nor will you find a description of how to use the Delphi Editor. Instead, this book provides material that goes beyond the documentation that ships with Delphi.

This does not mean that you must be an advanced Delphi user to use this book. Indeed, whether you are new to Delphi, or already a seasoned expert, you will find insights, explanations, and examples that will improve the way you build Delphi applications.

About the Code

All of the code presented in this book is available on the CD-ROM that accompanies this book. This permits you to copy the code from the CD-ROM onto your hard disk, where you can compile and run these projects. Also, for the most part, the code discussed in each chapter is also listed there. While this may seem redundant, it permits you to inspect the code without having to resort to the CD-ROM.

The CD-ROM also contains more than just the code from this book. On it you will find a number of useful components, trial versions of software, three issues of *Delphi*

Informant Magazine, the Delphi PowerTools Catalog of third-party products and services, as well as a number of highly entertaining and fun .AVI files. You will find more information about using the CD-ROM for this book in Appendix A.

Where To Start

This book is divided into three parts. In Part One, you will find an introduction to the concepts critical to successful Delphi development. The chapters in this section are designed to introduce, or affirm, the principles and philosophy of Delphi. If you are already comfortable with the "how and why" of Delphi and are well grounded in the principles of object-oriented languages and how they apply to Delphi, you can advance directly to Part Two.

Part Two, Techniques, constitutes the majority of this book. In the chapters of this section you will find a variety of topics that are explained in detail, and numerous examples to backup these explanations. These topics range from designing property editors to using resource files, from the basics of building a database to using Delphi in a client/server environment, from using OLE automation servers to creating multithreaded applications. In short, this section includes a selection of topics that will interest nearly every Delphi developer and examines them in detail.

Part Three offers another perspective still. This section contains a case study—that is, an examination of development issues as they pertain to a specific implementation of Delphi. In this case, it is the commercial product WebHub, from HREF Tools Corporation, that is explored. Here you will see what considerations and solutions were required to take a Delphi application to market. No less interesting is the target market for this application—the World Wide Web. Consequently, this section looks both forward and backward. Backward in the sense of learning from the experiences gained from the successful deployment of an application, and forward in considering issues that pertain to the Internet, which may very well be the platform of tomorrow.

[illegible]

Where To Start

[illegible]

PART ONE

Foundations

Delphi is a revolutionary product, both in how it works and how you work with it. The focus of this section is on these issues.

In Chapter 1 you will learn about the underlying characteristics of Delphi's architecture and what benefits these provide. Here you will discover the real power of compiler technology and how applying it to a graphical environment gives you the best of all worlds.

The focus of Chapter 2 is on the proper approach to Delphi development. Here you will learn "developing the Delphi way." Developing the Delphi way defines a sound and consistent approach to building powerful and maintainable applications using Delphi. Even if you have been using Delphi for a while, you may very well find this chapter a refreshing affirmation of proper Delphi programming.

Chapter 3 tops off this section with an in depth look at object orientation. Here you will find a detailed discussion of what OOP (Object-Oriented Programming) is and how to benefit from it. You will also learn how to maximize the benefits of OOP with Delphi.

These issues, admittedly, are not for everyone. If you are already well versed in Delphi, you may want to be selective about which chapters you read in this section. For example, if you are already very comfortable with the approach required by Delphi development, you still may want to consider reading Chapter 3 for a solid introduction to object-oriented programming. If you would otherwise find all three of these chapters a review, you should simply scan these three chapters, and then move on to Part Two.

Chapter One

Overview of Delphi for Developers

The code for the examples presented in this chapter can be found in the \CODE\CH01 subdirectory on the CD-ROM that accompanies this book. Please refer to Appendix A for information on using the code files for this chapter.

Delphi is a unique product. For the first time, a single tool supports rapid application development (RAD) with a visual graphical user interface (GUI) tool that makes no compromises. Delphi can be used to develop virtually anything a developer can think of, and the applications created are fast. Delphi is able to provide this "pedal to the metal" kind of power in a visually oriented RADtool because of its underlying architecture, which combines a compiler, visual design tools, and database capabilities all wrapped around a core of object-oriented programming (OOP) technologies.

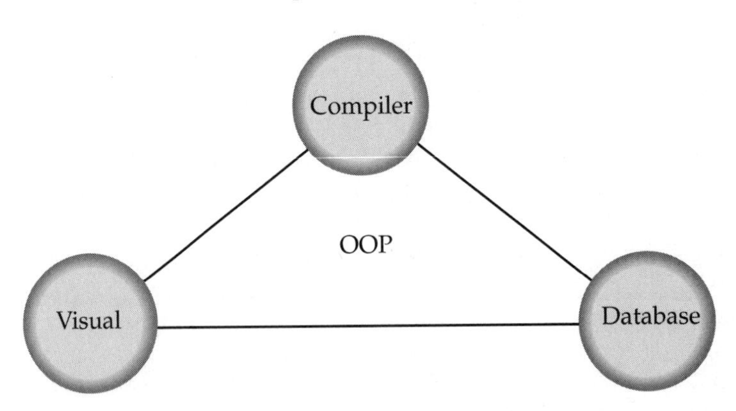

This architecture provides Delphi with its uniquely productive development style. Each of these elements is described in the following sections.

A Real Compiler

Unlike many other desktop development tools, Delphi is at its very core a world-class, optimizing, native code compiler. That is, the applications you build in Delphi are compiled to machine code that can be executed directly by your computer.

Other tools based on an interpreted language provide immediate feedback to the developer but at the cost of greatly decreased application performance. For example, in Paradox for Windows, a portion of an application can be modified without having to recompile the entire application.

Most interpreted environments also present limitations to the developer even if they do add a compiler as a back-end (separate) process. As long as the programmer only needs to do the tasks the tool developers included, the limitations are irrelevant.

However, as soon as a need arises that the tool developers did not anticipate, such as allowing read access to the CPU's (Central Processing Unit's) registers, interpreter-based environments force programmers to look outside their chosen tools for a solution.

Benefits of the Delphi Compiler

The Delphi compiler provides developers with several unique benefits that in many circles are considered absolute necessities for creating robust, modern applications. These are:

- **Performance**: Application speed is always "the unspoken requirement." No matter how slick the application is, it will be considered less than successful if end users become frustrated because of poor performance.
- **Unlimited Capabilities**: Developers can become frustrated, too. The programmer mindset is that the tool must be able to do everything that you need to do. Tools that provide this kind of open capability are justifiably preferred.
- **Robust Error Handling**: Experienced developers know that unexpected conditions should be expected. For example, any client/server application can expect to lose the server connection at some point in time. How the application responds to this predictable unexpected operating condition is crucial to the creation of mission-critical applications.

Performance

Applications compiled with the Delphi compiler execute fast—in many cases, as fast as those compiled in C/C++ (as measured in a performance test reported in *PC Week*, April 24, 1995). When execution speed is of the highest priority, you can also include assembly language code. With Delphi 2, it is even possible to link compiled code from object files (*.OBJ) into your applications.

In most cases, to produce lightning-fast code in Delphi, you simply need to use the compiler—no additional steps are necessary. This is especially true of Delphi 2, which includes many code-optimizing enhancements. The Delphi R&D team found that they improved performance of some of the Delphi 2 code by removing hand-coded assembly language from the source. This improvement occurred because the compiler generated machine code that was more efficient than that produced by manually generated assembly language.

When it comes to speed of execution, interpreted tools such as Visual Basic and PowerBuilder are no match for Delphi. *PC Week* (April, 1995) published test results on Delphi-based code that executed many times faster than code from Visual Basic and PowerBuilder.

But speed of code execution is not the only factor to consider when choosing a tool. Delphi's compiler compiles Delphi applications so fast that it can provide the same kind of immediate feedback as interpreted tools. Consequently, the apparent advantage of interpreted tools during development is inconsequential. To put it another way, Delphi provides the benefits of both worlds: instant feedback and fast execution.

Unlimited Capabilities

With a real compiler at its core, there are no limits to what you can create in Delphi. Delphi's compiler can easily handle:

- Creation of Windows DLLs (Dynamic Link Libraries) for use with any other applications (whether or not they are built using Delphi).
- Use of Windows DLLs created using Delphi or using any other tool that creates standard Windows DLLs.
- Use of inline assembly code, including compiler directives for creating single source code for both 16-bit and 32-bit Windows applications.
- Creation of Intel-standard *.OBJ files for inclusion in other compiler's projects, such as Borland C++ applications (in Delphi 2 only). This feature is not available in the 16-bit version of Delphi.

The following real-life example shows how Delphi's limits and performance benefits combine. An application was developed for a branch of the U.S. government in a popular interpreted development tool. This application had to regularly perform an ASCII import of downloaded mainframe data. The interpreted version of this application took 15 hours to perform the import on a 386 PC with 4MB of RAM. A Delphi version of the ASCII import routine was built as a Windows DLL and integrated into the original application in just four days. After conversion to Delphi, the application running on the same hardware took only 15 minutes to complete the same task. The import routine didn't need to run many times before the performance benefit exceeded the total development time.

As this example demonstrates, Delphi provides rapid development feedback without compromising application runtime performance. Furthermore, Delphi's ability to create DLLs makes it an ideal add-on tool for interpreted languages in situations where it may not be practical or politically acceptable to convert an entire project to Delphi.

Robust Error Handling

In general, good developers expect the unexpected. Runtime errors are a fact of life—especially in the world of Windows applications. Traditional programming tools use return codes to perform error checking on functional areas of an application. The typical logic sequence is to execute a routine, check the returned error code, and then process any error encountered by creating a large CASE statement that evaluates the error code. This sequence must be performed for *every* line of code in which you want error handling to take place. Traditional error checking is tedious to code and can greatly degrade system performance. As a result, most applications contain less error handling than is ideal. The lack of error checking in most programs is not a matter of lack of programming skill; rather, it is a consequence of using a tool that lacks structured exception handling.

Tools that support structured exception handling, like Delphi, provide a language construct and a runtime exception trapping system that eliminates the problems associated with traditional error handling. Structured exception handling provides a methodology whereby a programmer can include all the error handling an application needs without having to write an error-checking routine for each line of critical functional code and without degrading system performance. The following sections explain how exception handling works in Delphi.

THE TRY-EXCEPT BLOCK The programmer designates a block of critical code by creating a try-except block. Any error that occurs on *any* line in the try block automatically raises an exception (a special kind of object) and causes the application to jump to the first line of the except section. The built-in exception dispatch handler then compares the type of exception with each of the exception types called out in the except section. If a match is found, the block of exception handling code tied to that exception type is executed. Delphi then resumes execution at the first line of code following the try-except block. If a match is not found, the exception then pops out to the next higher try-except block until either a match is found or the exception arrives at the outermost layer of the application. If no match is found here, Delphi's built-in exception routine takes over and displays a message box that tells the user what type of error occurred.

The following code example shows how a try-except block can be used to check for any error in connecting to a remote SQL (Structured Query Language) database. This code attempts to activate two Table objects named DeptRemote and EmpRemote. Note that this code does not include separate error checks for these tables. If either connection fails, the try-except block construct ensures that the application will jump to the except section.

```
procedure TForm1.ShowData1Click(Sender: Tobject);
begin
   { Attempt to connect to the remote server }
   try
      begin
         DeptData.Dataset := DeptRemote ;
         EmpData.Dataset := EmpRemote ;
         DeptRemote.Active := true ;
         EmpRemote.Active := true ;
      end;
   except
      on EGPFault do             { Something really nasty happened }
                 MessageDlg('OOPS! That is an illegal operation.',
                 mtWarning, [mbIgnore], 0);

      on EDBEngineError do       { Failed to connect to remote server }
           if MessageDlg('Could not connect to remote server.'+#13+
                         'Close down application?', mtError,
                         [mbYes, mbNo], 0) = mrYes then Close;
   end;
end;
```

As the "bubble up" concept implies, try-except blocks can be nested within each other. This nesting can take place directly within the same code routine or a try-except block can be nested by including it in a subroutine called from within a try-except block in another procedure or function. The following code example expands on the first example by including a second, nested try-except block. This code provides a recovery mechanism for a lost server connection. However, nothing is assumed. The recovery routine (the outer except block) includes its own try-except block to ensure that the recovery occurs and doesn't create problems of its own.

```
procedure TForm1.ShowData1Click(Sender: TObject);
begin
  { Attempt to connect to the remote server }
   try
     begin
        DeptData.Dataset := DeptRemote ;
        EmpData.Dataset := EmpRemote ;
        DeptRemote.Active := true ;
        EmpRemote.Active := true ;
     end;
   except
     on EGPFault do              { Something really nasty happened }
              MessageDlg('OOPS! That is an illegal operation.',
              mtWarning, [mbIgnore], 0);

     on EDBEngineError do        { Failed to connect to remote server }
        begin
          if MessageDlg('Could not connect to remote server.'+#13+
                       'Do you want to use the local IB server instead?',
                       mtError, [mbYes, mbNo], 0) = mrYes then

            try          { Try connecting to Local InterBase instead }
              begin
                DeptData.Dataset := Depts;
                EmpData.Dataset := Emps;
                Depts.Active := true ;
                Emps.Active := true ;
              end;
            except
              on EDBEngineError do
                if MessageDlg('Could not connect to ANY server.'+#13+
                             'Close down application?', mtError,
                             [mbYes, mbNo], 0) = mrYes then Close;
            end;
        end;
   end;
end;
```

In reality, all exception handling routines you create are nested. The Delphi compiler automatically wraps your entire application within a global try-except block. This global try-except block provides default error handling even for runtime errors you did not anticipate. Your applications are protected automatically from any kind of error. Consequently, adding a custom exception routine for any newly discovered problem is very straightforward. Delphi's default error handler creates an error message box that reports the type of error and the module name in which the error occurred. Based on this information, you then add the appropriate test for that exception in the except block.

NOTE: You can attach your own code to the application-level exception handler. The Application component has an event property named OnException. An event handler assigned to this property is executed in response to an otherwise unhandled exception.

THE TRY-FINALLY BLOCK Structured exception handling can also be used to manage the release of resources through a try-finally language construct. It is similar in syntax to a try-except block. The try-finally block basically states to the program that, no matter what happens in the try block, the code in the finally section always gets executed. For example, the following code uses a try-finally block to set the cursor to the hourglass and then attempts to create a form on the fly and process some SQL code to determine what data to display in the created form. Whether or not the attempt succeeds, the code then makes sure that the form resource is freed and that the cursor is set back to the default.

```
procedure TForm1.ExecuteClick(Sender: TObject);
{OnClick exception handler for an object named Execute}
begin
  try
     try
       if not IB_Database.Connected then IB_Database.Open;
       Execute.Cursor := crHourGlass ;
       DisplayForm.Create ;
       SQLtoSend.Close ;
       SQLtoSend.SQL.Clear ;
       SQLtoSend.SQL.Add(SQLCode.Text) ;
       SQLtoSend.ExecSQL ;
       DisplayForm.Show ;
       CommitBtn.Enabled := true ;
       Execute.Enabled := false ;
     except
       on EGPFault do             { Something really nasty happened }
                  MessageDlg('OOPS! That is an illegal operation.',
                  mtWarning, [mbIgnore], 0);

       on EDBEngineError do       { Failed to connect to remote server }
           if MessageDlg('Could not connect to remote server.'+#13+
                         'Close down application?', mtError,
                         [mbYes, mbNo], 0) = mrYes then Close;
     end;
```

```
    finally
      DisplayForm.Free ;                { Now, free up the resources }
      Execute.Cursor := crDefault ;     { and reset the cursor }
    end;
  end;
```

Notice the use of a try-finally block that contains a nested try-except block. This nested construct provides both error handling and final clean-up processing.

Why Is Exception Handling Important?

Exceptions happen. For example, every client/server application can expect to lose the server connection from time to time, just as every Windows application has the potential to run out of available resources. The question is not whether an exception will occur, but rather, how your application will respond to the exception when it happens. You don't want your application to be the one that crashes in an inelegant fashion just because the server connection got dropped. Structured exception handling is the only way to provide the necessary error handling for creating robust mission-critical applications. That is why exception handling is not simply a nice-to-have feature. It is an absolute requirement.

A Modern Visual Development Environment

Delphi is a third generation language (3GL) that provides a visual integrated development environment (IDE) similar to many fourth generation language (4GL) products on the market today. Delphi's visual environment includes all the standard capabilities developers now expect, such as an integrated debugger, integrated version control, a programming editor, and a visual display of the application being created. At first glance, Delphi doesn't seem all that different. But it is.

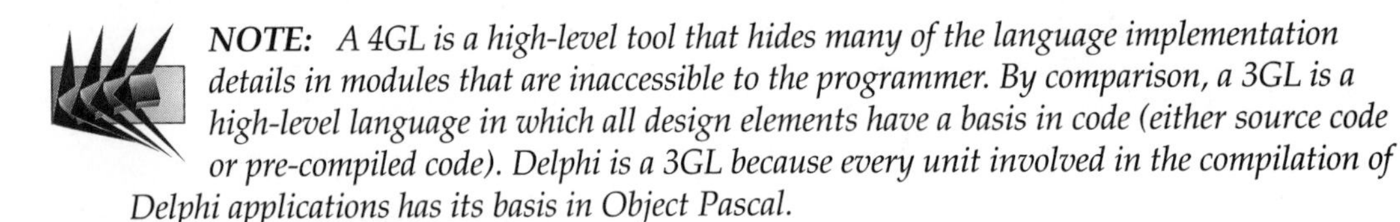

NOTE: A 4GL is a high-level tool that hides many of the language implementation details in modules that are inaccessible to the programmer. By comparison, a 3GL is a high-level language in which all design elements have a basis in code (either source code or pre-compiled code). Delphi is a 3GL because every unit involved in the compilation of Delphi applications has its basis in Object Pascal.

Tools and Materials

The opening chapter of the book *Pattern Languages of Programming Design* (James O. Coplien and Douglas C. Schmidt, eds., Addison-Wesley Publishing Company, 1995) discusses a metaphor for good application design that refers to tools and materials. Whenever you work with something in the real world, you use tools to operate on materials. The best tools allow you to focus on the materials and what you want to do with them. The tool itself gets out of the way of the creative process. You don't even consciously think about how to use the tool. In other words, you concentrate on the goal, not the process.

Take the use of a pencil as an example. You think about what you want to write. The words themselves are what you concentrate on. They are the material of writing. You never think about how the pencil applies graphite to the paper. Even when you make a mistake and use the pencil's eraser, you still concentrate on the proper word rather than the mechanism of using an eraser.

The same metaphor can be applied to computer software. The best software products are those that let you focus on the end result, not on how to operate the tool. Delphi is such a tool. Using the materials supplied in the Delphi Visual Component Library (VCL) and the Object Pascal language, the Delphi IDE gets out of your way. You'll find that Delphi's unique approach to application development allows you to think about what you want to create, not how to manipulate the tool.

Unique Benefits of the Delphi IDE

The Delphi IDE is a unique blend of tightly integrated features designed to meet the needs of the programmer who spends many hours each day with the tool. Developers don't want the IDE of their tool to make programming more difficult. The more seamlessly the environment lets them work, the better.

Delphi's visual development environment is different from other development tools because Delphi is built in itself. During the two years it took Borland to develop Delphi 1.0, the R&D team was, in effect, also running a two-year-long usability test lab while they built the product. This usability team was a bit different. The team had the power to fix what they didn't like about the product without having to support an installed base of prior versions. For Delphi 2 development, the feedback Borland received from the more than 250,000 Delphi 1.0 users was added to the R&D team's own experiences to fine-tune the Delphi IDE for version 2. This extensive usability testing shows in the day-to-day productivity of the Delphi IDE. The unique capabilities of the Delphi IDE are:

- An immediate feedback WYSBYGI (What-You-See-Before-You-Get-It) environment—in a compiled product
- A two-way development tool—to enhance productivity
- An easily extensible IDE—without ever leaving Delphi

Immediate Feedback

You get immediate feedback in Delphi's IDE precisely because Delphi knows how to deal with components created in itself at the moment you are designing your application. When you drop a Delphi component onto a form, Delphi actually calls the compiled component's constructor. This kind of WYSBYGI (pronounced "whiz-biggie") environment eliminates much of the lengthy envision-code-compile-run-debug-recode cycle of typical compiler products while simultaneously providing the immediate feedback more typical of interpreted tools.

Since Delphi is written in itself, you can even use the Delphi IDE for user interface ideas. Everything you see in the Delphi visual environment can be duplicated in your own applications. Standard user interface design concepts such as right-mouse click functionality and on-screen tips (called *hints* in Delphi) are supported through the setting of component properties.

A Two-Way Tool

Visual tools are generally very productive development environments. Sometimes, however, a particular application change could be implemented more easily in a straight coding environment. Many visual environments create code behind the visual designer; however, once you modify the code being produced, you are usually forced to continue in a coding-only development mode. Changing the generated code breaks the link between the code and the visual designer.

With Delphi, the visual design tools not only create code, but they also allow you to edit this code and then return to the visual designer for further development. The Delphi IDE automatically synchronizes any code changes into the visual representation of the application. Delphi provides for automatic translation of application components from visual representation to code and back again.

Where this two-way tool capability comes in really handy is when you discover that you need to use a different type of component than what you originally had selected. Let's say, for example, that you have placed an Edit component onto your Delphi form and named it MyEdit. You spend the next several hours changing properties, creating event handlers, and writing other pieces of code that reference the MyEdit component. Now you discover that you want to add an EditMask to your MyEdit component. The only problem is that the TEdit class does not have an EditMask property. That is a property of a TMaskEdit class component.

If Delphi was a traditional development tool, correcting this mistake could involve the tedious process of writing down all the property settings you had changed, all the event handler references you had defined, and various other pieces of information needed to recreate your hours of work. Some development tools even tightly tie the application code to the individual component itself, rather than using Delphi's more global approach of attaching the code to the application's form. With that type of tool you would also have to save all the code you had written so that you could paste it back in later. With Delphi's two-way capability, modifying an object is much simpler.

The following example shows how you could add an EditMask to your MyEdit component in Delphi. First, select the MyEdit component on your form and cut it to the Windows clipboard. Now switch over to a text editor, such as the Windows Notepad (the Delphi code editor will even do), and then paste your MyEdit component into it. Delphi automatically converts the visual representation of MyEdit into the correct Delphi code as shown in Figure 1-1.

Once the component has been pasted into the editor, simply change the component type from TEdit to TMaskEdit. The following code shows how the changed code might

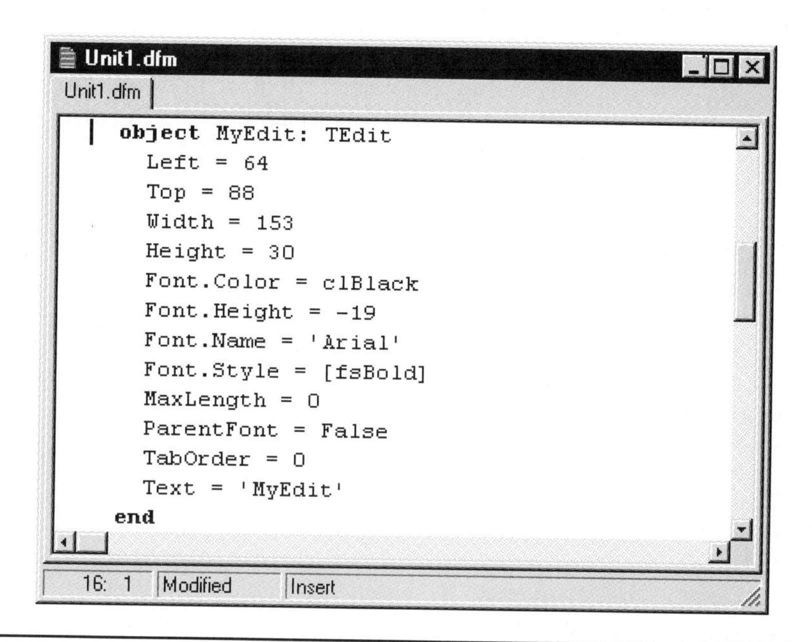


```
object MyEdit: TEdit
  Left = 64
  Top = 88
  Width = 153
  Height = 30
  Font.Color = clBlack
  Font.Height = -19
  Font.Name = 'Arial'
  Font.Style = [fsBold]
  MaxLength = 0
  ParentFont = False
  TabOrder = 0
  Text = 'MyEdit'
end
```

Figure 1-1. *An Edit component cut from a form and pasted into the Windows notepad*

look. Note that the MyEdit object is now declared to be a TMaskEdit instead of a TEdit (in the first line of code). Nothing else has changed.

```
object MyEdit: TMaskEdit
  Left = 64
  Top = 88
  Width = 153
  Height = 30
  Font.Color = clBlack
  Font.Height = -19
  Font.Name = 'Arial'
  Font.Style = [fsBold]
  ParentFont = False
  TabOrder = 4
  Text = 'MyEdit'
  OnChange = MyEditChange
  OnEnter = MyEditEnter
  OnExit = MyEditExit
end
```

Finally, highlight the component's code and cut it to the clipboard. Now switch back to the Delphi form designer, select the form, and paste in the new component. Delphi will automatically translate the code on the clipboard back into the proper visual representation on your form.

Since you did not change the name of your component, the other code that references MyEdit will still be able to find that object. You have preserved all your property changes and event handler designations as well. Now you can proceed with setting the EditMask property that now appears in the Object Inspector. MyEdit is now shown to be a TMaskEdit type object at the top of the Object Inspector, as shown in Figure 1-2. Since this TMaskEdit descendant is currently selected, the Object Inspector shows this object's properties.

TIP: Make sure you cut the code out of the editor, not simply copy it to the clipboard. Otherwise, you'll try to create two components with the same object name, and Delphi will produce an error message. Obviously, you also want to make sure that you cut every *line of the component's code to the clipboard.*

The two-way tool nature of Delphi even includes the ability to directly edit the code that is created for the visual representation of your form. One way is to simply save your form and then close it. Next, you select File | Open, change the desired file type to Delphi Form (*.dfm), and select your form. (It has the same filename as the form's unit.) In Delphi 2, it is even easier to switch between the form (the graphical view) and the code (the text view). Just right-click anywhere on the form and select View as Text. Alternatively, you can press ALT-F12 to toggle back and forth between the graphical form view and the text version of the .DFM file.

Delphi will automatically convert the DFM format to a code representation and open the form's object code in the programming editor. Any changes you make and

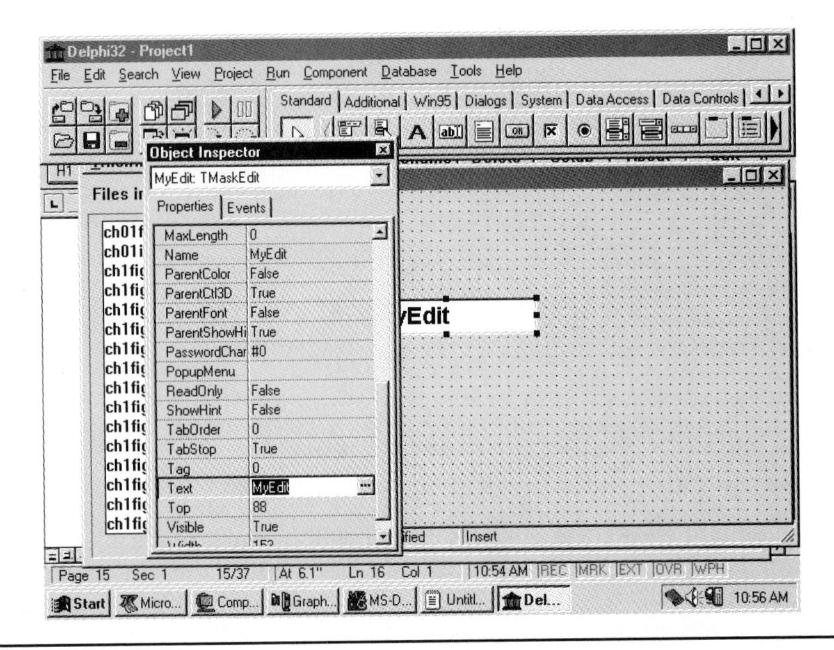

Figure 1-2. *Object Inspector showing the modified TEdit, now a TMaskEdit*

save will be reflected in the visual presentation of the form the next time you open the form designer.

NOTE: Viewing your form's properties in the DFM format permits you to see the containership organization of your form. If, for example, your form contains a Panel object with a number of SpeedButton objects contained within it, the SpeedButton definitions will be "nested" within the Panel definition. Opening a form in the Delphi code editor is also one of the easiest ways to alter the containership of an object. To do this, you move the object's definition outside the scope of the definition of its container object.

An Easily Extendible Environment

Since Delphi is written in Delphi, you can extend its development environment by creating custom components and adding them to your component palette. New components can either be created from scratch or built by inheriting from an existing component. The existing parent component can be a stock Delphi component, a custom Delphi component either you or a third-party vendor created, or a standard OCX component (usually created in C++). Delphi's support for true inheritance means that you can create an inherited child component whether or not you have a copy of the source code of the parent component.

You can even create complete applications that serve as programmer tools and add these to the Delphi IDE. The CopyToClipboard (CTC) program in file CTC_16B.EXE (Delphi 1.0) and CTC_V30.EXE (Delphi 2) in the CH01 subdirectory on the CD accompanying this book is an example of this kind of programmer utility. CTC makes use of the two-way tool nature of Delphi to allow you to access a database of Delphi components in the form of code routines. By pressing the CTC Copy button, you can copy the code to the clipboard and paste it into your Delphi application as a visual component.

You don't need to leave the Delphi environment to add additional features to Delphi and its environment. Delphi components that you create in Delphi code can have custom property editors, also written in Delphi code. (See Chapter 4 for information on creating custom property editors.) Delphi also includes tools for reading the help files you create for your custom components and integrating them directly into Delphi's help system. Delphi even provides a Tools API (Application Programming Interface) to tightly integrate programmer utilities such as alternate editors, version control systems, and additional experts into the IDE.

A Database Application Tool

Delphi's database capabilities are tightly integrated into the tool. All versions of Delphi 2 ship with an embedded version of the 32-bit Borland Database Engine (BDE), while version 1 products ship with the 16-bit version. All the capabilities of the stand-alone BDE (which can be purchased for C++ developers) are supported in this embedded version. A 32-bit version of the Local InterBase Server (LIBS) comes with the Developer and Client-Server editions of Delphi 2. The 32-bit version of LIBS is a vast improvement over the 16-bit version supplied with the first version of Delphi. In fact, the 32-bit LIBS is a fully functional single-user version of Borland's InterBase v. 4.0 for Windows NT. The inclusion of the 32-bit BDE and 32-bit LIBS provides Delphi 2 with some unique data-aware capabilities not found in any other product.

Benefits of Delphi's Database Capabilities

The inclusion of the Borland Database Engine and the Local InterBase Server provides Delphi with some unique data-aware capabilities not found in any other product. Among these are:

- Easy creation of completely scaleable applications
- Support for high-speed native API (Application Programming Interface) data access drivers as well as industry-standard ODBC (Open Database Connectivity) drivers
- The ability to treat set-oriented data as if it were record-oriented data and vice versa
- The ability to go from prototype to production with the same client/server application
- The ability to use Delphi to create n-tier applications through a variety of methods, such as:
    - Using third-party TP (Transaction Processing) Monitors to access existing n-tier development standards
    - Accessing system-level functionality such as Networked OLE (Object Linking and Embedding) to create distributed applications
    - Creating server-based user-defined functions (UDFs) for InterBase by linking Delphi DLLs into an InterBase database

Creating Scaleable Applications

It is not uncommon for data-intensive applications to outgrow available hard disk space. Consequently, application scalability is an important requirement.

Application scalability refers to two aspects—migrating the front-end application to different client configurations, and changing the location and/or type of the data being accessed. Each aspect affects the portability of a client/server application.

For example, how many different types of PCs will need to access your application? Can you ensure that all users of your application will be running Pentiums with 16MB or more of RAM? Probably not. Many aspects of client/server development can become dependent on specific client machine characteristics such as processor type or available RAM. Some development tools supply no built-in data buffering or require all data processing to take place in local RAM. Others rely solely on slower ODBC drivers or require massive amounts of RAM to operate efficiently. Thus, these tools produce applications that may run fine on the programmer's PC but perform unacceptably slow on end-user machines. The fewer restrictions that exist on the available deployment platform, the better.

The ideal data access scenario is for an organization to build a client/server application using prototype or sample data. The sample data typically does not reside on the production database's server, thus preventing any bugs created during development from bringing down mission-critical business processes. To facilitate this approach, the development tool must enable you to easily scale the data access of the application from the prototype data to the production data once the application is ready for deployment. The application's data access must be independent of any particular coding construct that would be data-type specific.

The Borland Database Engine included with Delphi provides many features (such as native API database drivers, automatic data buffering, database aliasing, and data table virtualization) that address both areas of scalability. Delphi 16-bit applications have run acceptably on client machines as lightweight as a 386 with 4MB of RAM. This was the platform mentioned earlier in this chapter in which the time to perform an import routine dropped from 15 hours to 15 minutes when converted to Delphi from another product. This dramatic performance improvement resulted in large part from the efficient native access database drivers and automatic data buffering of the BDE.

Database Aliases

Features such as database aliasing and data table virtualization provide easy scalability on the data access side as well. The BDE allows the developer to create database aliases (or nicknames) for any data source. The alias contains all the information needed to access the data such as data type (dBASE, Paradox, InterBase, Oracle, and so forth), physical location (for example, server name, database name, or directory), and communication protocol parameters. Your Delphi applications merely reference the alias name, not the specific connection information. If the data moves (for example, because the data grow beyond the capacity of the current server platform), you can change the definition of the alias with a configuration utility provided with Delphi. You do not need to change a single line of application code. You do not even need to recompile your application. The alias definitions reside in a separate configuration file outside of your application code and are read by the BDE at runtime.

Data Table Virtualization

What if your data not only changed location, but also changed type? Say, for example, that you originally used dBase tables and now want to convert the data to InterBase. Data table virtualization provides Delphi applications with a single standard coding method for accessing data, regardless of the data source in use at the time. First, you copy the data from dBASE to InterBase using the Data Pump Expert. (The Data Pump Expert is included with the Developer and Client-Server editions of Delphi 2. With Delphi 1.0, you can use the Copy utility of the Database Desktop.) Next, you delete the old alias definition that pointed to the dBASE data, and create a new InterBase alias with the same name as the dBASE alias that your application used before. The table virtualization features automatically take care of any specific data-handling differences.

For example, when deleting a record, dBASE just marks the record as no longer in use. InterBase and other SQL RDBMS (relational database management systems) servers eliminate the record—so long as you have sufficient rights to perform that action. In other words, the BDE will automatically handle record deletion in the proper manner based on the type of data being addressed. Furthermore, through Delphi's use of the BDE, any SQL RDBMS server error messages that may arise as a result of an operation will be automatically surfaced in Delphi as an exception.

High-Speed and Universal Data Access

Two different approaches have emerged for connecting to remote data: native API drivers and ODBC drivers. Native API drivers typically provide the best performance; however, they must be custom-built for each individual development tool. ODBC drivers, in contrast, provide a standardized way for many tools to reach a variety of data sources, although they often represent a compromise between performance, data-specific features, and universal connectivity. Fortunately, Delphi supports both drivers.

High-Speed Access: Native API Drivers

Delphi does not use specific proprietary API drivers that only Delphi applications can access. Instead, it uses the native API drivers available through the BDE for high-speed access to PC data stored in dBASE or Paradox format as well as SQL data stored in a variety of supported SQL RDBMS servers. This is the same database engine used by all Borland products, including Paradox, Visual dBASE, Borland C++, and ReportSmith. The BDE is also used by a number of other commercially available applications such as WordPerfect for Windows, PerForm Pro, E-Mail Connection, and GoldMine. For example, WordPerfect users can use as the source for a mail-merge operation the same table their Paradox application uses. WordPerfect's use of the BDE eliminates the need to translate the Paradox data into a separate mail-merge data file without using resource-intensive alternatives such as DDE (Dynamic Data Exchange) or OLE.

Since these products and tools all use the same core database engine, end users of these applications can safely access the data of any other BDE-based program across a network. The core BDE services supplied to every BDE application ensure that all multi-user concurrency issues will automatically be handled correctly—even though the users may be running entirely different applications. And since they all can make use of the native API drivers the BDE provides, SQL data access is always performed at the high speed available to native API drivers. As new drivers become available, all BDE-based applications can take advantage of the new connectivity options. As a result, Delphi's use of the BDE native drivers combines the best of native driver technology with the universality of a generally available database access engine.

Delphi 2 uses version 3.0 of the BDE. This 32-bit version of the Borland Database Engine provides separate direct native API drivers to connect to the following products:

Product	Version/System
InterBase	Versions 3.3 and 4.0
Oracle	Versions 6 and 7
Sybase	System 10 and 11 via CTLib
MS SQL Server	Versions 4 and 6 via DBLib
DB2, and so on	Any IBM SQL RDBMS that follows DRDA (IBM's Distributed Relational Database Access architecture) connecting via DDCS

NOTE: 32-bit native driver access to Informix databases did not ship with the initial release of Delphi 2 but will eventually be available. The current 16-bit drivers can still be used with Delphi 1.0 to create 16-bit applications that will run in Windows 95 and Windows NT.

Universal Access: ODBC Drivers

Many client/server development tools use standard ODBC drivers. Using ODBC drivers eliminates the need to build specific data access drivers. ODBC drivers provide universal connectivity to a huge range of data sources. If you can find an ODBC driver for your data, Delphi applications can use your data.

The primary concerns with selecting and using ODBC drivers are performance and standards compliance. Early ODBC drivers were notorious for poor performance. More modern ODBC drivers perform at much higher speeds. Some ODBC drivers are as fast or faster than some native API drivers; however, much variability still exists in the feature sets and speeds of even newer ODBC drivers. Consequently, you should first evaluate any ODBC drivers you plan to use with Delphi applications.

Three ODBC driver standards levels are available: level 0, level 1, and level 2. The higher the level, the more features an ODBC driver has. Many tools require that you use an ODBC driver that contains the features you want to use. If the ODBC driver is not of a high enough level, you won't get particular features.

The Borland Database Engine can use ODBC drivers of any of the three standards levels. The BDE includes support for all the data services needed, so it automatically queries the ODBC driver to see what features it supports. If the ODBC driver supports a feature, the BDE merely uses the driver. If you need a feature that your particular ODBC driver does not supply, then the BDE provides that service itself. In fact, the BDE can provide features (such as heterogeneous joins) that most other tools using ODBC drivers do not support. By using the ODBC socket in the BDE rather than just raw ODBC access, Delphi applications can take advantage of the general connectivity available through ODBC without compromising specific data access features that you may need.

Transparent Access Styles

Just as data connectivity can be split into two technologies, the style in which data is manipulated can also be performed in two very different ways: record-oriented data access and set-oriented data access. Most PC-oriented users are familiar with record-oriented data access. Common record-oriented operations include skipping ten records, navigating backwards, fetching a single record at a time, and so on. Most developers coming from an SQL server background are comfortable with SQL's set-oriented access. You define the parameters of the data you wish to see, and the server extracts a set of data rows that match that specification.

Both record-oriented and set-oriented access have their place in any database application. For example, set-oriented access by default assumes you know at least some of the particulars of the data in which you are interested. This kind of access, then, is ideal for portions of a database application where you want to select related rows or to exercise a certain amount of control over which data is presented to the user.

End users, however, typically prefer record-oriented access for ad hoc analysis and other "I'm not sure exactly what I want, but I'll know it when I see it" tasks. Record-orientation is ideal for these situations. The user only needs to know the type of data they want (for example, employee information, purchase orders, date ranges) without needing to know any specifics about the individual record desired.

Typically, however, the type of data access allowed is dependent on the type of data storage used. PC databases such as dBASE and Paradox use record-oriented storage and require record-oriented access. SQL database servers use set-oriented data access. Tools that operate based on the back-end capabilities alone require developers to either forego the use of the unsupported data access style or to simulate that access style in their own code.

For example, some tools perform all data access in a set-oriented manner, and the current data set must be able to reside fully in the local PC's memory. An application that accesses a large data set must then break the data access into more manageable chunks with a WHERE clause in the SQL used. When a different set of data is needed, the SQL query must be reissued with a different condition in the WHERE clause.

An example of an application that encountered this limit was one designed to look at information about various accounts that resided in different states. Since the development tool being used was entirely set-oriented, and the data set was too large to fit in local memory, record navigation from one state to another had to be programmed. The developer had to write a lot of code for handling the "simple" task of scrolling off the last account in one state and "automatically" fetching the first account in the next state.

Fortunately, Delphi's use of the BDE eliminates this problem. The table virtualization available to Delphi applications makes the type of data storage transparent to the application. The BDE makes record-oriented access available for SQL-based data sources and set-oriented access available for record-oriented data such as dBASE, Paradox, ASCII, and Btrieve. Applications that need both access styles become relatively simple to create in Delphi without regard for the data storage type used. This changeable access style is always available, whether you are using the BDE's own native API drivers or using a standard ODBC driver instead.

Prototyping and Deploying Client/Server Applications

It can be argued that application developers can no longer afford to take 12 to 24 months to develop an application. Consequently, developers have come to rely on RAD tools that produce applications more quickly through the use of interactive, interpreted technology. These tools can build an application rapidly and even operate in a prototype mode just fine. However, the performance limitations and RAM requirements mentioned earlier in this chapter make applications created with these same tools unsuitable for full-scale deployment. Regardless of what anyone says, application performance does count. Consequently, developers often have to recreate the prototype design in a compiler tool such as C++ to obtain the needed performance.

Delphi applications are compiled into .EXEs that produce performance often as good as applications built in C++. In addition, Delphi's strong support for RAD means that you can almost always create an application more rapidly than in C++. Consequently, you can quickly create an application as your prototype and still have enough performance and power to be deployed as your real-world implementation as well.

Creating N-Tier (Multi-Tier) Applications

Multi-tier development is, first and foremost, a logical model. Typically, client/server developers think of at least three tiers. The first tier is the data presentation. The middle tier is usually referred to as the business rules. The storage of the data is the third tier. As a developer, you need to think about all three aspects of your application and how to logically implement each tier.

What is N-Tier or Multi-Tier?

How the data appears to an end user is really independent (or should be) of any particulars of the business rules or data storage requirements of the application. After all, you don't want to require your data entry people to know the details of transaction processing or data normalization. Why should they? As a developer, that's your job. Also, the data storage medium should be independent of the application's data presentation or its business rules. After all, it's not uncommon for a database application on a LAN to get reorganized, or on a database server to get reoptimized. Ideally, you should not have to go back and change the source code in all your applications just to implement data storage changes.

You should also be able to update your business rules in one central location but in a manner independent of where the data is stored, in what format it is stored, and in the way the data is presented to end users. In fact, more than three logical divisions of labor could exist for any one application. As business process modeling becomes more of a standard practice, database application developers will need to think of more than just these three basic logical application layers. The number of logical divisions is limited only by the developer's imagination and by how closely the application needs to model real-world processes. This logical separation of tasks is what n-tier development is all about.

The logical division of labor should also be independent of where each tier is implemented. You should be able to separate the decision to use a logical n-tier model from the decision to implement n-tier hardware. For cost or performance reasons, you may want to select any number of physical implementations of an n-tier logical model. At least five physical implementations exist. (Strictly speaking, the first two are not n-tier implementations. They are included in the list merely for historical background and completeness.)

CLIENT ONLY This physical implementation is typical of most PC-based database applications. The data presentation, business rules, and data storage are all controlled by the data entry application running on the client machine. Even LAN-based PC applications fall into this category, since a LAN file server downloads the program and data files into the local client PC's active memory. No logic or data protection resides on the file server. It merely acts as a storage cabinet for the data and programs.

The advantage of this architecture is that knowledgeable users have the ability to create their own ad hoc data analysis. Direct access to data and logic at each client machine essentially eliminates most of the application backlog that had arisen prior to the advent of personal computers. The disadvantage is that most knowledgeable users have an incomplete understanding of data integrity and data normalization issues. Many are not formally trained programmers, either.

SERVER ONLY This implementation represents the bulk of mainframe applications in existence today. The server (that is, the mainframe) does all the work. The client machines are so-called *dumb terminals* that merely display on screen what the server tells them to display. Therefore, end users are bound by the capabilities and limitations of their mainframe. Information workers are not able to perform tasks that have not already been programmed.

The clear advantage of this approach is that only people conversant in database concepts and programming skills have access to the data and programs. This amount of centralized control provides great benefits in the areas of data integrity and security. Ad hoc analysis and the ability for business to "turn on a dime" are, however, sacrificed in the process.

CLIENT/SERVER: ONE TYPE OF COOPERATIVE DISTRIBUTED PROCESSING
Distributed processing had been relegated in the past to the realm of cooperating mainframes. The introduction of effective high-quality networks allowed distributed processing to move into the arena of heterogeneous platforms that combined the flexibility of PCs with the power and security of mainframes. The advent of true client/server architectures was designed to place the burden of each task area on the platform that was strongest in that task. PCs became the data presentation and

analysis platform. PC-based word processors and spreadsheets became the main presentation and analysis tools. The mini and mainframe computer still reigned supreme as high-speed data repositories. The missing piece was how to get the data entered. Knowledgeable users were familiar with the PC, so the natural evolution was to develop PC-based data entry/presentation systems that ran on the PC and accessed the data residing on the mainframe. Things got fuzzy, though, in the area of how to enforce business rules and processes.

One approach to Client/Sever is called the *fat client*. A fat client is a situation in which the client side of the application contains much of the business logic. These applications are easier to create since the same tool is used to define the business logic and the front-end application. These client/server applications make use of the better data storage capacity and security of a back-end database server.

However, many of the other problems that plague client-only applications still exist. Execution of application logic is distributed among all the client machines, but no centralized control exists for this logic. Basing the bulk of the logic at the client machine can also create very uneven performance characteristics if the client PCs cover a wide range of machine types and available RAM. Multiple applications that access the same data also become a code management nightmare when logic changes need to be made that affect all programs using that data.

Some developers found a solution to the fat client problems by migrating a portion of the business rules back to the server, making the back-end a *fat server*. The server-based business rules took the form of triggers and stored procedures. This approach centralizes the important business rules and allows multiple applications to use easily updated rules without having to maintain changes to the client applications.

Several problems can arise with this solution, too. Placing significant business logic at the database server can severely limit the scalability of the data side of the application. The logic becomes tightly tied to the physical implementation of the data storage. And as has already been noted, the need to scale the data as the application grows more useful is almost a universal given.

If the client-side tool creates applications that are slow, the developer may also be tempted to migrate too much logic to the server. This can degrade the server's performance and slow down all applications that use that server.

Another challenge is in the area of data-aware communication between the client logic and the server logic. The client-side application tool must provide a way for the client to invoke server-based stored procedures. Result sets returned from stored procedures can contain either single or multiple values. The client tool must support both types of return sets. If it doesn't, the ability to coordinate activity between the client and server machines can become too limited.

THREE-TIER CLIENT/SERVER The two-tier approaches (the client as one tier, and the server as the other) discussed previously address many issues but leave data scalability in a limited state. This condition prompted the development of a three-tier architecture. This physical implementation separates the application into three platforms. As with two-tier approaches, the presentation portion resides at the client PC and the data resides on a database server. The difference is that the major business logic resides on a third machine that sits between the other two. The logic remains in a single centralized location, so client application coordination is not an issue. The logic and data are on separate machines, so the presence of business logic does not degrade the performance of the database server. Thus, three-tier architectures provide the centralized logic control of two-tier implementations, while also preserving data scalability by having the logic tied to an independent middle tier rather than the database server itself.

Of course, there's no such thing as a free lunch. Communication between the various hardware pieces becomes more complex at the same time it becomes more crucial. These needs are often met by using RPCs (Remote Procedure Calls). However, since RPCs operate outside the realm of transaction control, they can create more problems than they solve. The combination of Delphi and InterBase, however, provides access to a technology called *event alerters.* InterBase event alerters are similar to RPCs except that they operate within the transaction context. Only when a transaction is posted does the related event alerter get sent. Delphi includes components that register an interest in and receive messages from InterBase event alerters. Because of the communication issues involved, three-tier architectures are best suited for intra-company distributed processing.

MULTI-TIER CLIENT/SERVER The complexities of today's business world often require more than three layers to properly implement a coherent application strategy. Some business processes require cooperative processing that reaches outside the organization. In these cases, the inability to force the use of specific standards makes three-tier architectures based on RPCs or proprietary communication services difficult to implement. Standardized, cooperative, distributed computing in the form of DCE (the Distributed Computing Environment) or CORBA (the Common Object Request Broker Architecture) is still in its infancy. Many different middleware implementations exist, but they all add yet another level of complexity that many organizations are not yet prepared to support.

Most middleware solutions can be placed in one of two general categories, RPC-based or messaging-based. RPC-based tools are generally more mature since RPCs have been in use for quite some time. The two major limitations of RPC-based middleware are:

- Dependence on specific hardware/software architectures that make portability difficult at best
- Lack of transaction control

RPCs are usually dependent on maintaining good communication connections between sender and receiver. If the communication link goes down, many applications can be affected. Recovery from lost communications can be difficult. RPCs are run outside the normal transaction control logic, which simply compounds the first problem. Extreme care must be taken when using RPCs to provide some mechanism for avoiding transaction-based anomalies.

Message-oriented middleware (MOM) was created to solve the issues that arise with RPC use. Technologies such as DCE- or CORBA-based products offer a measure of isolation from specific hardware and operating system issues. They also provide message queues that can maintain message-based actions even when the communications link is temporarily dropped. Using message queues can provide transaction-based levels of control for distributed processing. However, the same hardware/OS (operating system) isolation that makes these products suitable for inter-company applications also adds a much greater level of complexity to any application architecture that uses them.

In fact, many computer technology analysts caution that n-tier architectures are not the silver bullet many think they are. N-tier architectures are not suitable for many (some would say most) applications and should be considered only for situations in which obvious benefits exist. Others suggest that developers wait, if feasible, for both RPC and MOM products to mature further before implementing them.

Delphi: A Logical Multi-Tier Architecture

Delphi's way of handling creation of data-aware applications is a naturally multi-tier approach. Delphi provides separate components for data presentation, data validation, and data access. This separation of the functional parts of an application lends itself very easily to a logical implementation of an n-tier application architecture. Figure 1-3 shows a layout of the logical components that comprise a typical Delphi database application. The fact that Delphi provides various component-level constructs means that migration from a single-tier to a 2-tier to an n-tier architecture is a relatively easy process.

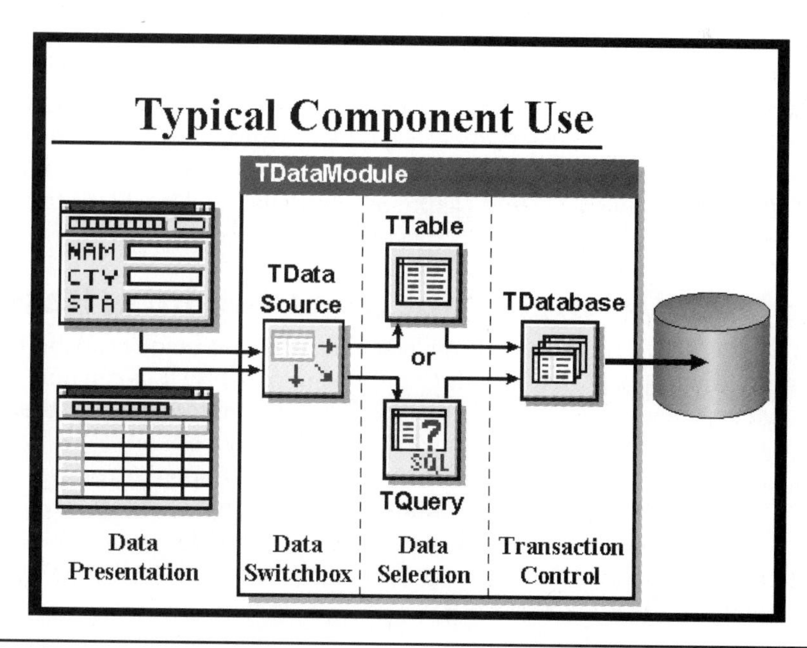

Figure 1-3. *How Delphi organizes a data-aware application*

Accessing Existing N-Tier Development Standards

A variety of n-tier development products already exists in the marketplace. Companies such as Novell, Transarc, and others sell TP Monitors, which have become standards in n-tier development. Other companies provide RPC support for Delphi applications. Several products are available for Delphi developers to hook their applications directly into a number of n-tier architecture implementations. The following list is a representative sample of the standard n-tier support products in existence for Delphi:

- **Communications Integrator** from Covia. Offers synchronous and asynchronous messaging services to enable application interoperability in a heterogeneous environment.
- **Connection Encina** from OpenHorizon. Provides an ODBC connection to Transarc's Encina TP monitor, which allows a Delphi application to create an n-tier application using standard Delphi data-aware components.
- **QuickApp** from Attachmate. Allows a Delphi application to integrate existing mainframe applications.
- **TopEnd** from AT&T GIS. A server middleware product that provides much of the functionality of a standard TP monitor plus messaging queue support.
- **EzRPC** from NobleNet. Provides support for RPC messaging across heterogeneous environments.

Accessing System-Level N-Tier Functionality

Visual Basic 4.0 (VB4) introduced the concept of Remote OLE, which is a systems-level feature implemented in a set of standard Windows DLLs. VB4 merely provides access to the functionality contained in these system-level DLLs. Since Delphi includes the ability to access DLL functions, Delphi applications can also take advantage of this kind of system-wide functionality. Networked OLE is expected to be available within Delphi 2 within a year of this version's release. Delphi's complete support of Windows system-level functionality means that Delphi programmers will be able to take advantage of this new feature as soon as it becomes available.

Creating User-Defined Functions for InterBase

The 32-bit version of Delphi now gives developers a new and unique capability. Function routines written in Delphi 2 and compiled into 32-bit DLLs can now be used from within an InterBase database. The InterBase system is told to register the functions contained in the Delphi DLL, making these functions available as User-Defined Functions (UDFs) in the database. This combination provides a completely native Delphi solution for creating true distributed n-tier applications in the 32-bit Windows environment. Because of Delphi's capabilities, it is an ideal RAD solution for creating high-performance compiled n-tier applications that include robust exception handling for server safety.

NOTE: A demo version of UDFLib, a third-party library of UDFs, can be found in the \UTILS\UDF_LIB directory on the CD-ROM that accompanies this book.

If You Are New to Delphi

Developers who are new to Delphi face several challenges. Fortunately, all of them are easily overcome. This section addresses two of the questions most commonly asked by new Delphi developers. (Developers new to Delphi should be sure to read Chapter 2 before proceeding to the more advanced topics covered in the rest of the book.)

How Do I Learn Object Pascal?

Developers coming from a DOS background frequently ask this question. Among the developers who fall into this category are those proficient in Fortran, Cobol, Paradox, and xBASE. What is interesting is that these people aren't new to development—most have already programmed in at least two or three tools prior to Delphi.

When it comes down to it, it's not Object Pascal that tends to trip up these developers, since they already know the fundamentals of one or more programming languages. Instead, it is the Windows development environment that is novel. These developers think they need help in learning Object Pascal because the approach to application development in the other languages was centered around the programming language itself. Delphi changes that.

Of course, a Delphi developer needs to learn the Object Pascal language. But this represents an easier learning curve for most developers. The typical developer is already familiar with the principles behind the for loop and the case statement. But a Delphi developer needs to realize that the actual language used is only a part of what Delphi development is all about.

Nonetheless, one area of Object Pascal tends to pose a greater challenge than others for new Delphi programmers. The Pascal language is a strongly-typed language, which means that every variable must be declared. If you are new to Delphi, you should pay special attention to data types, as these will play an important role in your code development. Here is one place where the online help can be very useful. (See Chapter 2 for useful tips on getting the most out of the Help system.) Also, the Object Pascal Language Reference, which is included in all versions of Delphi 2 as well as sold separately for Delphi 1.0, is an important resource for gaining an in-depth understanding of data types in particular and the Object Pascal language in general.

How Do I Get My Program to Do Anything?

This question is also one usually voiced by developers with backgrounds in traditional procedural programming environments. These developers are accustomed to building applications in which the programmer is in total control. The event-driven nature of the Windows environment changes all the rules. To highlight the task that lies before DOS programmers making the move to Windows, consider how each operating environment affects the nature of applications built for each.

DOS programs have the following design characteristics:

- Character-based
- Procedure-driven
- Sequential logic
- Sequencing under program control

Windows programs have the following characteristics:

- Graphical-based
- Event-driven
- Non-sequential logic
- Sequencing under end-user control

The very nature of event-driven environments in general, and Windows in particular, requires a mental transition on the part of developers unfamiliar with these issues.

The key is to understand the event-driven quality of Windows applications. Everything that happens in a Windows program is triggered by some kind of event. Furthermore, the end user is often the cause of that event. In other words, your program has to respond to its users rather than control them. Logic sequencing is no longer totally under program control. But this is not a Delphi issue; it's a Windows issue.

Fortunately, Delphi makes the transition to event-driven programming relatively painless. The idle loop that all Windows applications must have while waiting to recognize an event, the recognition of events, and the dispatching of those events to the affected component are all encapsulated within Delphi applications automatically. The only thing you have to be concerned with in Delphi development is which events you want to respond to with custom code, and what you want that code to do when the event occurs. (Chapter 2 covers how to choose which events to respond to.)

But another issue faces DOS developers who are making the transition to Windows development. In short, these developers must take the time to understand what makes a Windows application act like a Windows application. Merely developing the application with a tool like Delphi (or any other Windows-based development tool) is not enough. Windows applications have a specific look and feel that is achieved by intentionally designing the application to have these features. For example, a Windows application menu bar always has a File menu, and buttons are generally located at the bottom or right-hand side of a form. New Windows developers are strongly encouraged to look at how application features are presented in commercial Windows applications and to duplicate these conventions as much as possible.

Where to Go From Here

This chapter provides a general overview of the Delphi architecture and a glimpse of Object Pascal code as it appears in Delphi units. Chapter 2 discusses how you solve programming problems using Delphi.

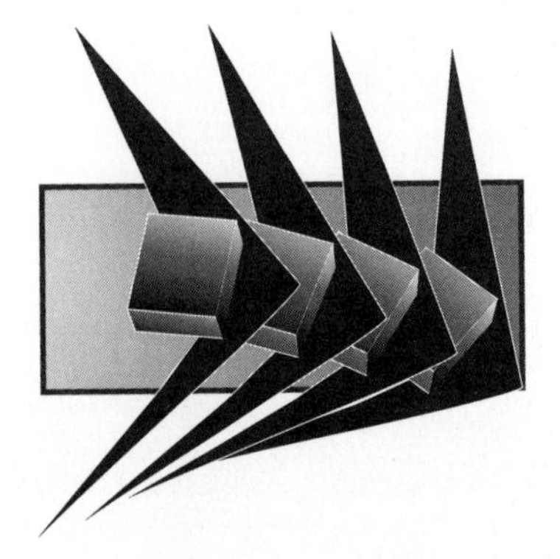

Chapter Two

Developing the Delphi Way

The code for the examples presented in this chapter can be found in the \CODE\CH02 subdirectory on the CD-ROM that accompanies this book. Please refer to Appendix A for information on using the code files for this chapter.

Like all complex development environments, effective use of Delphi requires that you take the proper approach. While it is possible to create a working application without knowing "the best way," such applications are less efficient and are more difficult to maintain. This chapter is designed to introduce you to the best approach to developing applications in Delphi—in other words, the Delphi way.

If you are already experienced in developing applications with Delphi, you may choose to skip this chapter altogether. However, even experienced Delphi developers may find the principles listed here to be a useful reminder of the characteristics that make Delphi development special. If you are new to Delphi development, this chapter will provide you with a sound foundation in the principles underlying this powerful tool.

There are two parts in this chapter. The first, and most important, discusses the importance of selecting the correct object for the task at hand. The second covers the primary support tools for building Delphi applications, including Delphi's extensive online help system.

Leverage Objects

Delphi is an object-oriented development tool and requires an object-centric approach to developing applications. (For a detailed explanation of object orientation with respect to Delphi, see Chapter 3.) Although in procedural languages you typically write code that presents an interface and responds to user interactions, in Delphi you must think about choosing and controlling objects. This task can be reduced to two essential points: choosing the appropriate object and controlling the default behaviors of the object.

Choosing the Correct Objects

It is essential to choose the correct object, since this is the starting point for everything that you do. When you choose the appropriate object, far less work needs to be performed by your code. In some cases, no code or other manipulation needs to be performed at all—the object does all the work for you.

For example, imagine that you are writing an application that permits a user to write a file to disk. One of the features that such an application must have is a way to permit the user to select the drive to which the file will be written. There are many alternative ways to provide this feature. For example, you could use an Edit component, which is a simple data-entry box, and request that the user type in a drive letter. This approach, however, requires that you write additional code to verify that the entered value is a valid drive letter.

But there is a better solution. Delphi includes a component that does everything you need. It is called the DriveComboBox component, and its default behaviors satisfy every need of your application. Specifically, when this component is created, it checks to see which drives are available and populates the combo box list with the valid entries. Furthermore, the entry field of the combo box is initialized to the default drive. If the user wishes to select a drive other than the default, he or she can click on the drop-down arrow of the combo box, and then select from one of the other valid drives.

You can demonstrate this effect yourself. Create a new form, and then place a DriveComboBox component onto the form (this component is located on the System page of the Visual Component Palette). Next, run this form and open the drop-down menu for this combo box. Your form should look something like the one shown here:

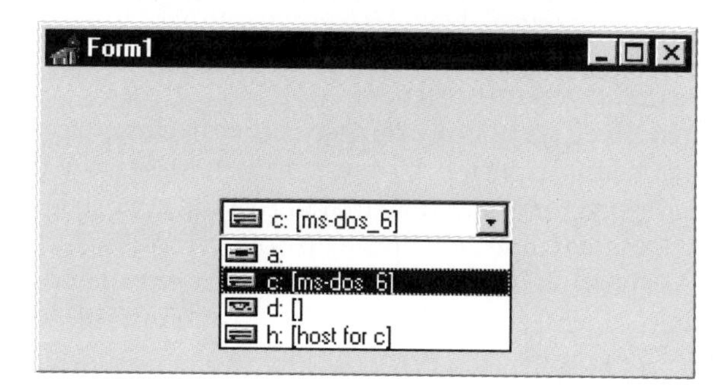

Notice that without having made any modifications to the component, it displays the current drives available on your machine.

Controlling Default Behaviors

Components that, without any modification, provide for all of your user's needs are very nice but are not always available. In most instances, there are a number of elements of the default behavior that are either unwelcome or simply inappropriate for your application. In these cases, you must either modify the object or enhance its default behaviors. The two primary means of making these adjustments are:

- changing the properties of the object
- writing event handlers

Programming by Properties

The most common mistake made by novice Delphi developers, especially those coming from a procedural programming background, is to write code in order to modify an object. As you will learn later in this chapter, writing code is a valid (and often essential) technique for modifying an object's behavior. However, code should be relied upon only when no other technique for controlling the object can be found. In many cases, especially with well-designed objects, custom code plays a minor role.

To put it simply, both Delphi's visual development environment and its programming language are centered around the concept of programming by properties. If you find yourself writing a lot of code to perform a simple task, you are most likely thinking "code" instead of "properties." Let's take a look at a simple example to demonstrate how this works.

CENTERING A FORM Imagine that you want your application's form to be centered on the screen when the application starts. Traditional procedural programmers may produce this result by writing code to measure the size of the form, detect the current screen resolution, calculate the necessary position of the upper left corner of the form to produce a centered form, and then move the form to this position. Although such a code segment is not rocket science, it can be time consuming to write. More important, it is completely unnecessary because Delphi forms provide a property that affects where a form will be displayed on-screen.

If you created the DriveComboBox example earlier in this chapter, return to that form and display the Object Inspector (by pressing F11). Make sure that the form is selected in the Object Inspector. Now, note that one of the properties for the form is named Position. Click in the value side of the Position property and display the drop-down menu. As shown in Figure 2-1, notice that one of the possible values of the Position property is poScreenCenter. If you set the Position property to this

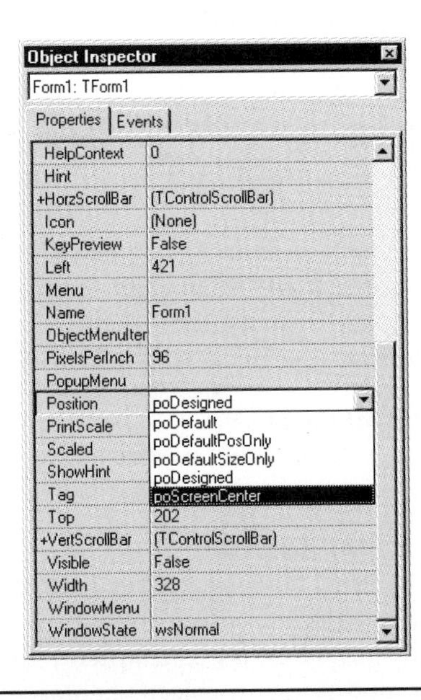

Figure 2-1. *Setting the Position property for a form at design time*

pre-defined value, the form will automatically be placed in the center of the user's screen at startup.

NOTE: The preceding example demonstrates how to control default behaviors by changing properties at design time. This is not meant to imply that you cannot change properties of objects while your application is running. In fact, using code to change properties at runtime is one of the most fundamental techniques that you will use in Delphi and is part of its incredible power. More is said about this issue later in this chapter.

PREDEFINED BITBUTTONS Centering a form is just one example of property-based functionality that typically requires procedural code in other tools. Many functional areas of a Delphi application are activated by setting a property. The BitBtn component includes a property named Kind. The default value of this property is bkCustom, which allows you to define the caption text, displayed bitmap, and default OnClick event behavior of the button. If you wish to invoke some standard kind of button, such as a Cancel button, the BitBtn's Kind property also can be set to one of a variety of predefined values. Each value automatically sets the button's caption text, displayed bitmap, and OnClick functionality.

Since properties can also be set at runtime, the Kind property allows your application to change the action of a button merely by changing the value of the button's Kind property. For example, setting Kind to bkClose sets the caption text to "Close" (with a predefined hot key of ALT-C), sets the bitmap to be an exit door, and sets the OnClick functionality to be that of closing the form on which the button resides. Figure 2-2 shows a form with a variety of BitBtn components on it, each one varying only by its Kind property setting. The label next to each BitBtn lists the Kind setting for that button.

Using Properties to Coordinate Application Changes

Changes to the value of an object's property can sometimes have a major impact on other objects as well. For example, changing the font of a group of objects on a form at runtime is a task that traditionally required a lot of code. But the design of Delphi's components makes font changes much easier to apply across the various objects on a form.

Every Delphi component that has a Font property also has a logical property named ParentFont (a Form component does not have the ParentFont property). In most cases, a component's parent is the form on which it appears. If ParentFont is True, the component will use the font designated in its parent component's Font property. If ParentFont is False, the component uses the values in its own Font property. Simply setting all the ParentFont properties to True (the default) means that any font change made for the form will cascade automatically throughout all the font-based components on that form.

Other properties also provide this cascading behavior. ParentColor, ParentCtl3D, and ParentShowHint properties are defined for components that can use them. These properties all control some aspect of your application's visual presentation. The ability

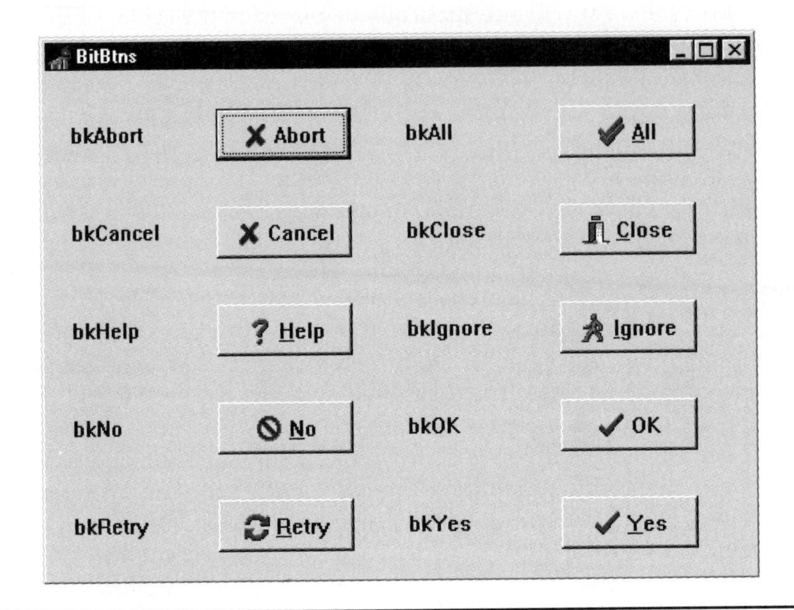

Figure 2-2. *This form displays a number of BitBtn components*

to set a property that cascades changes throughout a form makes it easy to create applications that allow end users to set their own display preferences.

COORDINATED PROPERTIES EXAMPLE Earlier in this chapter, you learned that you can place a DriveComboBox component on a form that will automatically display all available drive letters. Delphi also includes components that will automatically display a directory (folder) tree, a file list, and a file type list. Furthermore, these objects all have properties that permit these components to coordinate their display, without the need for additional code.

The form shown in Figure 2-3 is part of a project named FILELIST. It contains only four objects and no code. The four objects are a DirectoryListBox, a FileListBox, a DriveComboBox, and a FilterComboBox, all from the System palette. These objects work through the coordination of properties. The FileList property is set to the FileListBox, the *DirList* property of the DriveComboBox is set to the DirectoryListBox, and the FileList property of the FilterComboBox is set to the FileListBox. No code is required to keep these components synchronized.

When this form is run, the four components act in harmony. Changing the current directory in the DirectoryListBox causes the FileListBox contents to update its display of files available in the new directory. Changing the drive selected in the DriveComboBox updates the DirectoryListBox, which in turn updates the FileListBox, and so on.

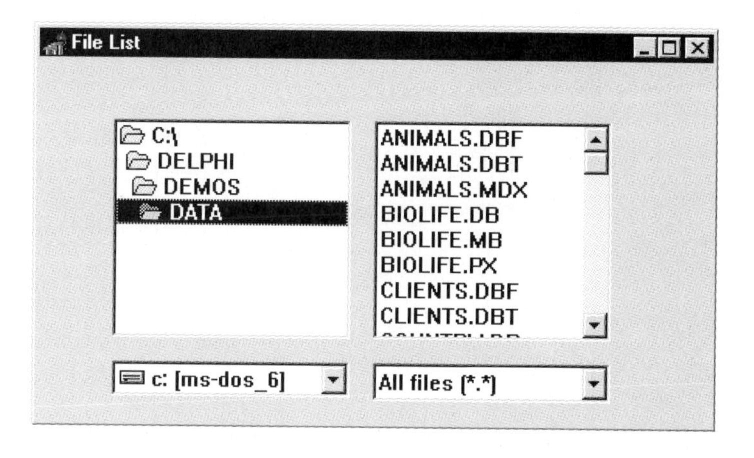

Figure 2-3. *The FILELIST project*

NOTE: You might be wondering how Delphi permits the change of one property to affect other properties of an object, such as in the case of a BitBtn, or even the properties of other objects, as demonstrated in the FILELIST project. This happens because changing a property can result in the execution of one or more methods of an object. Specifically, when a component writer designs a new component, he or she can associate a property with a method (specifically, a procedure method) of that object. Whenever a new value is assigned to the property, the method executes. The code within this method can then affect other properties of the object or even properties of other objects.

PROPERTIES CAN BE OBJECTS There are five categories of properties in Delphi: Simple, Enumerated, Set, Object, and Array. That a property can be an object has an important impact on how you can use properties. But before discussing Object properties, let's briefly consider the other four property types.

Simple properties are those that permit you to enter their value directly into the Object Inspector, such as the Caption property of a form, which defines the form's title. Enumerated properties, in contrast, display a drop-down menu of possible values within the Object Inspector. The Position property of the Form component discussed earlier in this chapter is an example of an Enumerated property.

Set properties appear as a set in the Object Inspector. Specifically, within the value column of the Object Inspector, the set appears enclosed within brackets ([]). Furthermore, sets can be expanded to display the individual values of the set, each of which is a Boolean value. An example of a Set property is the BorderIcons property of a form. Shown below is the Object Inspector with this set expanded, displaying the three possible members of the set and their current values.

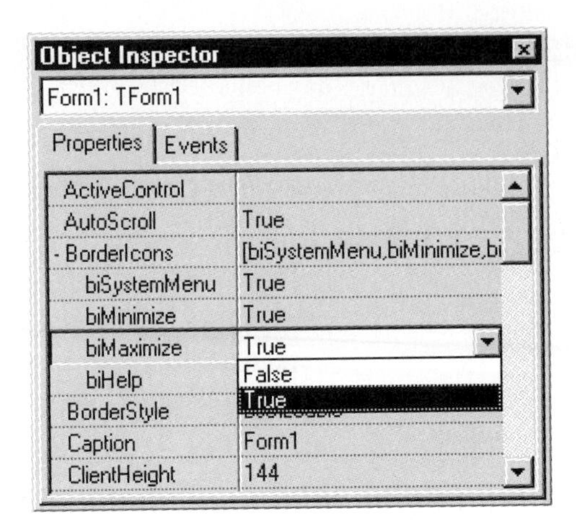

The value list of biMaximize is displayed, showing the two possible values.

Array properties are those with values defined by the contents of an array. Delphi does not support the direct manipulation of array properties—this is something that the component designer must do. All array properties have property editors. In other words, when you select the value column of one of these Array properties, an ellipsis (...) button appears, which you then click to access the property editor. Property editors are described in Chapter 4.

Object properties are properties that must be assigned an object. What makes Object properties so special is that they themselves often have properties. You might think that this would make their manipulation difficult, but the opposite is true. For example, a Label component has a Font property. The type of this property is TFont, which is an object class. Furthermore, a Font object has properties, such as Name, Pitch, Size, and so on. Consequently, modifying the size of the font for a label involves changing the Size property of the Font object. When done in code, it looks something like this:

```
Label1.Font.Size := 24;
```

This statement changes the size of the font used for the object Label1 to 24 point (assuming that the ParentFont property of this label is set to False). A project that controls the Font property of objects with code is presented later in this chapter.

Writing Event Handlers

Properties cannot provide for all changes that you may want to make to an object's default behavior. In some cases, you must add code. This code is always, either directly or indirectly, executed by event handlers. Another way to think of this is that all code is ultimately triggered by an event.

The Object Inspector contains two pages, the first labeled Properties and the second labeled Events. The Events page lists the various events that the selected object possesses. These events are actually properties; however, they are special properties in that you can only assign procedures to them. Furthermore, these procedures must be of a particular type, meaning that they must have a specific parameter list. The person who originally wrote the component decided which type of procedure a particular event property can be assigned.

Most of the event properties take a procedure of the type TNotifyEvent. The following is an example of a TNotifyEvent procedure, which in this case is an event handler that has been assigned to the OnClick event property for a button:

```
procedure TForm1.Button1Click(Sender: TObject);
begin
{This is a TNotifyEvent Procedure}
Close;
end;
```

This is an extremely simple example of an event handler—it has a single executable statement within it, a call to the Close method for a form. When this button is clicked, the Close method is executed, and the form closes. This procedure happens to be a TNotifyEvent procedure because of its parameter list, which contains a single parameter passed by reference. This parameter, named Sender, is an object. Specifically, it is an object of the type TObject, or a TObject descendant. (All objects in Delphi are TObject descendants.)

NOTE: *In a preceding discussion it was pointed out that if you set the Kind property of a BitBtn to bkClose, clicking this button will close the form. You may wonder why, in this case, an event handler that closes the form is even necessary, especially in light of the emphasis being placed on using properties in place of code whenever possible. The answer is that not all BitBtns close a form. For example, a BitBtn with its Kind property set to bkOK will not close a form. Consequently, if you want to close a form that uses this style of BitBtn or, alternatively, uses a button of the class Tbutton (this class does not supply a Kind property), you call the form's Close method.*

The obvious purpose of an event handler is to permit you, as the developer, to modify an object's response to an event. It might be easier to think of events if you consider that there are two general categories of events:

- messages
- state changes

A *message* specifically refers to a Windows message. A Windows message informs an object that it has been clicked, a key has been pressed, its image needs to be repainted, and so forth. In the case of those objects with which a user can interact, the component writer often publishes event properties that correspond to Windows messages, making it easy for the Delphi developer to execute custom code when one of these message is received. Message-related event properties are traditionally given names that begin with On, such as OnKeyDown, OnKeyUp, and OnMouseDown.

NOTE: An object can receive Windows messages only if it is a windowed control. Windowed controls are those objects that are assigned a window handle upon creation. Consequently, if an object is not a windowed control, it cannot have message-type events. In Delphi, windowed controls are descended from the TWinControl class. However, not all TWinControls have the same message-related event properties. Specifically, all message-related event properties are declared as Private in the TWinControl class. Only when these messages are redeclared as Published in a descendant class are the associated events available to the developer. If you want to associate code with a message-related event, but the corresponding component in the VCL (Visual Component Library) does not publish that event, you can descend a new object from the existing one and redeclare the event as Published in the new class.

A *state change* refers to a change in the underlying state of the object. In most cases, state changes occur in response to changes in one or more of an object's properties. A good example of this is the OnChange event property of an Edit component. When an event handler is assigned to this property, it is called when the component's Text property has been modified. The names of event properties associated with state changes are also sometimes named using On but also include Before and After, such as in the event properties OnChange, BeforePost, and AfterInsert.

MODIFYING OBJECTS USING EVENT HANDLERS Just as you should explore the use of properties before resorting to writing event handlers, the Delphi way also dictates a preferred approach to event handler code. In short, your code should attempt to exert its influence either by changing the properties of objects or by calling methods of objects. Only when either of these two techniques cannot be accomplished efficiently should you resort to other means. These other means include the use of operating system calls, calls to procedures and functions of external DLLs (Dynamic Link Library), or calls to custom functions and procedures.

The form shown in Figure 2-4 is part of a project named TYPEFACE.DPR. This project demonstrates the changing of properties at runtime using event handlers. This form has two Panel components, four Label components, one Checkbox component, and one Button component. Label1 and Label2 were drawn inside Panel1, as was the Checkbox component. As a result, Panel1 is the Parent object of these three objects. Label3 and Label4 were created inside of Panel2, making Panel2 their Parent object. The following code is the unit associated with this form:

```
unit Typefacu;

interface

  uses
  SysUtils, WinTypes, WinProcs,
  Messages, Classes, Graphics, Controls,
  Forms, Dialogs, StdCtrls, ExtCtrls;
```

```
type
  TForm1 = class(TForm)
    Panel1: TPanel;
    Panel2: TPanel;
    Label1: TLabel;
    Label2: TLabel;
    Label3: TLabel;
    Label4: TLabel;
    Button1: TButton;
    CheckBox1: TCheckBox;
    procedure Button1Click(Sender: TObject);
    procedure CheckBox1Click(Sender: TObject);
  private
    { Private declarations }
  public
    { Public declarations }
  end;

var
  Form1: TForm1;

implementation

{$R *.DFM}

procedure TForm1.Button1Click(Sender: TObject);
begin
if Button1.Caption = 'Use Ariel' then
  begin
    Form1.Font.Name := 'Ariel';
    Button1.Caption := 'Use System';
  end
else
  begin
    Form1.Font.Name := 'System';
    Button1.Caption := 'Use Ariel';
  end

end;

procedure TForm1.CheckBox1Click(Sender: TObject);
begin
Panel1.ParentFont := CheckBox1.Checked;
end;
end.
```

There are two event handlers on this form: one for the check box and one for the button. The code for the check box event handler is assigned to the OnChange event

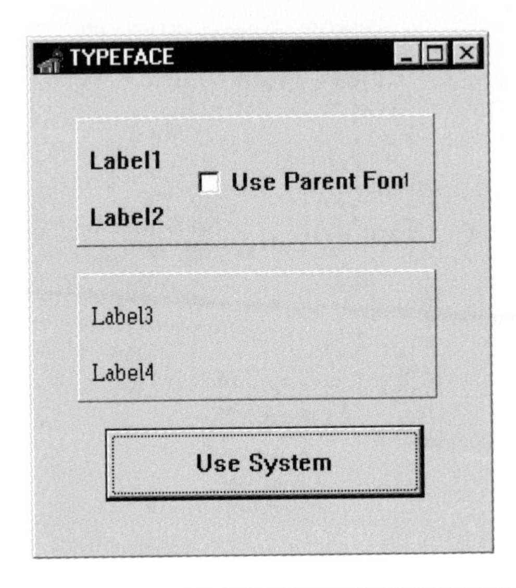

Figure 2-4. *The TYPEFACE project form*

property and, consequently, gets executed each time the value of the check box changes (each time a check is added or removed). The code within this event handler sets the ParentFont property of Panel1 to True when the check box is checked and False when it is not.

The second event handler, the one for Button1, changes the form's Font property, or more specifically, modifies the Name property of the form's Font property. When the check box is checked, this change affects all objects on the form. However, when the Use Parent Font check box is not checked, clicking on Button1 has no affect on the font used within Panel1 but does affect the fonts used for objects not contained within Panel1. Figure 2-4 shows the font changed for the form but not for the objects contained within Panel1.

NOTE: Although a Button component does have a ParentFont property, this property does not affect the font used for the button's caption. This is because a button is a standard windows control, and the label font is defined by Windows, not by Delphi.

More About Events as Properties

As pointed out earlier, an event is really just a property. Consequently, events can be manipulated at runtime like any other property. For example, when a form first initializes, you might have no event handler for a particular object. However, in response to some event that occurs on the form, you can assign an event handler (an appropriate procedure name) to an event property for that object, after which time that object behaves differently to the event.

Consider the form shown in Figure 2-5. This form displays a DBGrid in which the contents of the COUNTRY.DB table is displayed. Along the bottom of this form is a TabSet, which permits the user to navigate this table based on the first letter of the country name. This TabSet works through the use of an event handler assigned to the OnChange event property.

In most applications, the code for this event handler normally looks like this:

```
procedure TForm1.TabSet1Change(Sender: TObject; NewTab: Integer;
  var AllowChange: Boolean);
begin
Table1.FindNearest([TabSet1.Tabs[NewTab]]);
end;
```

However, the behavior of this event handler is somewhat inappropriate if the user selects a first letter for which the table has no corresponding country. For example, there is no country name beginning with the letter D in this database. Using the preceding event handler, once the user selects the letter D, focus within the DBGrid will shift to the country name Ecuador, but the letter D in the TabSet will still be selected.

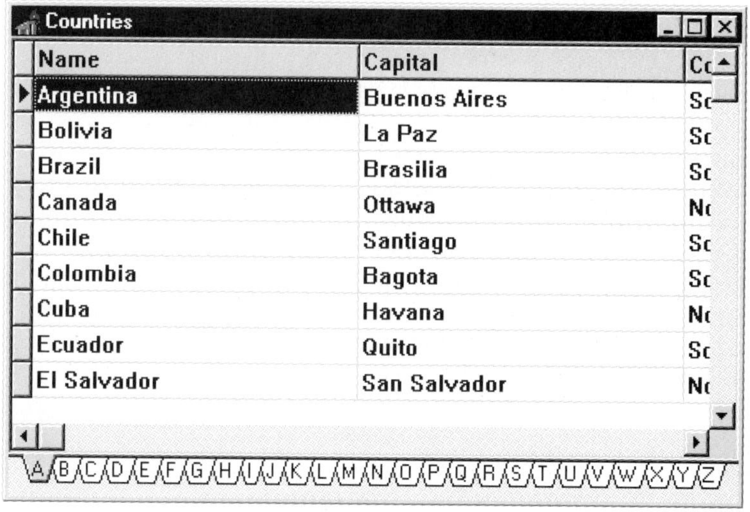

Figure 2-5. *The COUNTRY project table*

This inconsistency between the record found and the tab selected can be modified easily by updating the TabSet following the FindNearest method call so that the current tab will correspond to the found record. Such code might look like the following:

```
procedure TForm1.TabSet1Change(Sender: TObject; NewTab: Integer;
  var AllowChange: Boolean);
var
 S : String;
begin
Table1.FindNearest([TabSet1.Tabs[NewTab]]);
S := Copy(Table1.Fields[0].AsString,1,1);
AllowChange := False;
{The following line causes an infinite loop.}
TabSet1.TabIndex := Ord(S[1]) - 65;
end;
```

This event handler does almost everything right. It starts by locating the record that begins with the selected tab (the first character is calculated by adding 65 to the index of the selected tab. For example, if the first tab is selected, the calculated character is A). This code then copies the first letter of the located country name into the string variable S, sets the AllowChange parameter to False (so that the event handler will not update the displayed tab), and then assigns a value to the TabIndex property (which sets the displayed tab to the letter corresponding to the located country name).

But there is a serious problem with this code. The assignment of a new value to the TabIndex property (the property that controls which tab of the TabSet is selected) will cause a call to the OnChange event handler, which will assign a value to the TabIndex property, causing a call to the OnChange event handler, and so on. In other words, an infinite loop will result.

The solution to this recursive call to the OnChange event handler is to change the OnChange event property of the TabSet prior to making the assignment to the TabIndex property, setting it to a null value. This will prevent a call to OnChange when the TabIndex property is changed, since at the moment of the change there is no event handler assigned to OnChange. Once the TabIndex property has been modified, the original event handler can be assigned back to the OnChange event property. The following is the code for the unit associated with the COUNTRY project:

```
unit Countryu;

interface

uses
  SysUtils, WinTypes, WinProcs,
  Messages, Classes, Graphics, Controls,
  Forms, Dialogs, Tabs, Grids, DBGrids, DB, DBTables;
```

```
type
  TForm1 = class(TForm)
    DataSource1: TDataSource;
    Table1: TTable;
    DBGrid1: TDBGrid;
    TabSet1: TTabSet;
    procedure TabSet1Change(Sender: TObject; NewTab: Integer;
      var AllowChange: Boolean);
  private
    { Private declarations }
  public
    { Public declarations }
  end;

var
  Form1: TForm1;

implementation

{$R *.DFM}

procedure TForm1.TabSet1Change(Sender: TObject; NewTab: Integer;
  var AllowChange: Boolean);
var
 S            : String;
 OrigOnChange : TTabChangeEvent;
begin
  Table1.FindNearest([TabSet1.Tabs[NewTab]]);
  S := Copy(Table1.Fields[0].AsString,1,1);
  OrigOnChange := TabSet1.OnChange;     {Save original event handler}
  TabSet1.OnChange := nil;  {Clear event handler to prevent recursion}
  AllowChange := False;     {Prevent OnChange from changing TabIndex}
  TabSet1.TabIndex := Ord(S[1]) - 65;  {Set the value of TabIndex}
  TabSet1.OnChange := OrigOnChange;    {Restore original event handler}
end;
end.
```

Building Data Aware Applications

As you can see, the focus on using properties and events provides a simple yet powerful paradigm for building applications. This concept permeates every aspect of Delphi development, including how you build database applications.

For example, imagine that you want to create an application that permits the user to look at both current data and historical data using the same user interface. Delphi's programming by properties concept means that you don't have to create two identical forms. Instead, you can use a single form that can be used to display either of the data sets. For example, you can create a menu item that allows the user to toggle between the two data sets merely by changing a property in a data-aware component. The following is an example of code that can perform this task:

```
procedure TForm1.MnuHistDataClick(Sender: TObject);
begin
  MnuHistData.checked := not MnuHistData.checked;{Toggle the checkmark}
  if MnuHistData.checked then
    DBGrid1.DataSource := HistoricalData {Display the historical data}
  else
    DBGrid1.DataSource := CurrentData;   {Display the current data}
end;
```

Notice that Delphi uses properties to separate the data connection logic from the data presentation (or user interface). The user interface object, DBGrid1, does not connect directly to the data. Instead, it uses an intermediate object named a DataSource, which serves as a kind of data pipeline. In the preceding code, the items named CurrentData and HistoricalData are both these DataSource components that encapsulate all the data connection information. This permits the data-aware control, a DBGrid in this example, to switch between which of the two data sets is displayed, simply by changing the DataSource property. (For a complete discussion of DataSource, DataSet, and data-aware components, see "Basics for Connecting to Data" in Chapter 5.)

This separation of user interface from the data connection provides a powerful way to create flexible, robust database applications. Specifically, it permits you to isolate user interface changes from data logic changes for easier maintenance. Furthermore, separation also lets you share both data connections and data logic between multiple forms, and even multiple applications. In addition, you can easily change the type and location of the data being used without requiring massive code changes in the user interface portion of your applications. If you are accustomed to thinking of the user interface and the data as being one and the same, the Delphi way will require a shift in the way you think about how to build database applications. However, you'll find that the Delphi way offers you more power while requiring far less code than the alternative.

Getting to Know Your Objects

The examples given here make it obvious that a crucial step in becoming a good Delphi developer is to know your objects. This includes understanding which objects are available, what properties they have, what their methods are, and what events you can attach code to. Fortunately, Delphi's online help provides you with this detailed information. The section "The Online Help System" describes how to access this information.

If you are just beginning to learn Delphi, gaining an intimate knowledge of which objects are available, their properties, their legal values, and what those values represent in terms of functionality, should be your very *first* learning task. Don't be overly concerned with learning the specifics of the ObjectPascal programming

language. Since you are already a developer, learning the specifics of another language will likely be pretty easy for you. Furthermore, if you take the time to understand the objects, you won't have to learn a lot about Object Pascal to get started. In the end, you'll be writing a lot less Object Pascal code than you originally thought.
The following sections contain a few additional thoughts about objects.

What are Objects, Components, and Controls?

A common question that arises is what is the definition of an object? The answer is that an object is any instantiation of the TObject class, or the instantiation of any object descendant from that class. This means that everything on the component palette is an object.

You may have noticed that the objects that appear on the component palette are commonly referred to as components. A component is any object that is an instantiation of the TComponent class, or an instantiation of an object that descends from that class. Every object that appears on the component palette is a TComponent descendant, so referring to those objects as components is correct. However, the opposite is not true. That is, it is incorrect to assume that an object that does not appear on the component palette is not a component. Specifically, there are TComponent descendants that do not appear on the component palette. For example, the Application component, which is a component by virtue of being a TComponent descendant, does not appear on the component palette.

Controls are those objects that descend from the TControl class. Many of the components on the component palette are TControl descendants, and therefore can be referred to as either components or controls (as well as objects).

Not All Objects Appear on the Component Palettes

It is easy to be misled into thinking that all of the objects that you work with reside on the component palette, but as you might have gleaned from the preceding section, this is not the case. Although most of the components that you are most likely to use can be placed on a form from the component palette, there are more objects not on the component palette than there are on it. Consider this—an *exception* is an object. There are about 40 exception objects alone, and none of them appear on the component palette. By default, the component palette contains about 100 components (there are fewer in Delphi 1.0 and in the Desktop Edition of Delphi 2).

Some of these objects that do not appear on the component palette are still very important for your Delphi applications. For example, the Application and Screen components provide your Delphi applications with many important features, including the ability to create application-level exception handlers and determining which form of a multi-form application currently has focus.

While these non-component palette objects can be very important, they tend to be slightly more difficult to work with than those that appear on the component palette. This is because the objects that you place on a form from the component palette can be manipulated at design time. Non-component palette objects cannot be selected at design time; therefore, you cannot modify their properties or assign procedures to their event handlers at design time. (Yes, non-component palette objects may have event handlers.) The solution is to assign values to these objects at runtime, using the techniques presented earlier in this chapter. For example, if you want to create an application-level exception handler, you must first create an appropriate procedure manually. This procedure must be of the type TExceptionEvent, since this is the procedure type required by the Application component's corresponding event handler. You then assign the name of this procedure to the Application object's OnException event handler. The following code is the segment from a unit that defines this event handler and then assigns this event handler to the Application's OnException event property upon creation of the form associated with this unit:

```
procedure TForm1.AppException(Sender: TObject; E: Exception);
begin
  Application.ShowException(E);
end;
procedure TForm1.FormCreate(Sender: TObject);
begin
  Application.OnException := AppException;
end;
```

Objects Can be Created at Runtime

While the most common way to create an object is to place it on a form at design time, this is not the only technique available. It is also possible to create an object at runtime. In fact, for those objects that do not appear on the component palette and that are not created automatically by Delphi, this is your only solution. Note, however, that the Application and Screen components are created automatically by Delphi when an application is initialized, which means that not all non-VCL components need to be created explicitly.

NOTE: *Just because you can place an object from the component palette at design time does not mean that you cannot create one at runtime. Any object, whether or not it appears on the component palette, can be created at runtime.*

There are three steps to creating an object at runtime. First, you must ensure that the unit in which the object is declared is in a "uses" clause in the unit from which you will create the object. Second, you must define a variable of the object class. Finally, you must execute the Create method for the object.

Many developers add an additional step. Before they declare a variable of a given type, they declare a new type based on the existing type. They then declare their object variable to be of the new type. This approach has the added advantage of permitting the developer to make additional modifications to the descendant object without affecting the parent class.

The creation of an object is demonstrated in the following code. The object created here is an INI file, which does not appear on the component palette. Notice that the

IniFiles unit has been added to the "uses" clause, and a variable of the type TIniFile is declared in the FormCreate event handler. The code in this event handler extracts the path of the project's executable file name, and then creates an IniFile object, pointing to a file named CREATED.INI in the application directory. The code then uses the ReadString and WriteString method of the TIniFile class to read from, and write to, this INI file. The first time this project is run, the form's caption is set to "CREATED.INI has been created." Each additional time this application is run, the form's caption displays the date and time that the INI file was created.

```
unit Inifileu;

interface

uses
  SysUtils, WinTypes, WinProcs,
  Messages, Classes, Graphics, Controls,
  Forms, Dialogs, IniFiles, StdCtrls;

type
  TForm1 = class(TForm)
    Label1: TLabel;
    procedure FormCreate(Sender: TObject);
  private
    { Private declarations }
  public
    { Public declarations }
  end;

var
  Form1: TForm1;

implementation

{$R *.DFM}


procedure TForm1.FormCreate(Sender: TObject);
var
  MyIniFile  : TIniFile;
  CurrentDir : String;
begin
  CurrentDir := ExtractFilePath(Application.ExeName);
  MyIniFile := TIniFile.Create(CurrentDir + 'CREATED.INI');
  if MyIniFile.ReadString('CREATED','DATE','') = '' then
    begin
      MyIniFile.WriteString('CREATED','DATE',DateToStr(Date));
      MyIniFile.WriteString('CREATED','TIME',TimeToStr(Time));
      Self.Caption := 'CREATE.INI has been created';
```

```
      end
    else
        Self.Caption := 'Created at ' +
           MyIniFile.ReadString('CREATED','DATE',DateToStr(Date)) +
           ' : ' +
           MyIniFile.ReadString('CREATED','TIME',TimeToStr(Time));
MyIniFile.Free;
end;
end.
```

NOTE: Windows 95 discourages the use of INI files for storing application configuration information. In its place you are encouraged to use the Registry.

What If Delphi Doesn't Have the Object You Need?

In some cases, Delphi will not have exactly the object you need. In these instances, you have two choices. For most Delphi developers, it means obtaining the object from another source. There are innumerable World Wide Web sites, as well as other Internet sites, from which you can get all kinds of components. The Delphi forum on CompuServe is another great source for components. In addition, the PowerTools catalog on this book's CD-ROM contains a large list of valuable third-party components for sale. Most of the available components will cost you some money, although some freeware components are available.

The second solution is to build the object you need from scratch. This can be either a straightforward task or a major undertaking. Throughout this book you will find examples of components that are created to fill a gap.

Leveraging the Delphi Tools

Delphi has almost every capability that application developers need. To appreciate why this is the case, it helps to understand some of the history behind Delphi.

One of the remarkable facts about Delphi is that it was written in itself. Specifically, all the tools that constitute Delphi were produced by the Delphi Command-line Compiler (DCC.EXE). During this process, Borland's R&D team refined this compiler, providing it with additional capabilities to aid in the development of these tools. During the two years in which Delphi 1.0 was being developed, the R&D team was building a product as much for themselves as for the developer community at large. As they worked with Delphi to create Delphi, they came across problem areas that decreased their productivity. Some other parts of the emerging product didn't permit them to work the way they wanted to. This caused them to look for areas in which their initial design could be improved upon, even as Delphi took shape. When they found something they didn't like, they fixed it.

The success of this process is undeniable. Delphi is a developer's tool beyond comparison. The trick is to be aware of which tools are available and when they should be used. This section introduces you to some of the basic tools you will use with Delphi, including the Delphi SpeedMenus, Hints, the Delphi help system, and the Object Browser.

SpeedMenus

Whenever you use a windows-based Borland product, a basic training concept always applies: When in doubt, click the right mouse button. The advent of Windows 95 context menus makes this point seem trivial. However, Borland introduced the concept that many now take for granted. As a result, Delphi's context menus (called SpeedMenus) appear even in the 16-bit version. Furthermore, Delphi's SpeedMenus are not just generic right-mouse menus. They are specific to the functionality of the selected object.

For example, place a Table and a Query component on a form. Select each one in turn and click the right mouse button. You will notice that the displayed SpeedMenus are similar but not identical. Queries can have parameters defined, whereas tables cannot. These SpeedMenus are even sensitive to the edition of Delphi that you have. If you have the Client-Server edition, you'll see two extra menu items on a Query, as shown in Figure 2-6. One item will allow you to define parameters and the other will

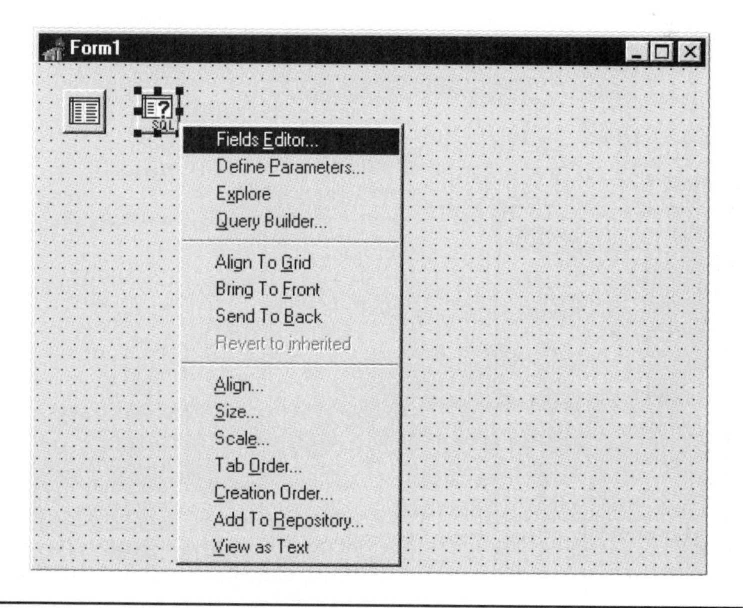

Figure 2-6. *A SpeedMenu for a Query component*

invoke the Visual Query Builder. Both Table and Query SpeedMenus provide access to the Fields Editor, where you can create and modify field-level components.

TIP: Many data validation options (such as EditMasks on data-aware components) require field-level control. However, Delphi does not create field-level components automatically, and they do not appear in the component palette. Simply right-click or double-click on any Query or Table component to bring up the Fields Editor. Then, using the Fields Editor, add field-level components for each field you need. Once you are done, the field components are created, permitting you to modify their properties and assign event handlers to their event properties.

Even more dramatic differences appear in the SpeedMenus when you select radically different items. Try switching to the program editor view and right-clicking on your code. You'll see an entirely different SpeedMenu. Now view the Watch window, by selecting View | Watches, and press the right mouse button on that area. Still another type of SpeedMenu appears.

Even the different parts of the Delphi IDE are sensitive to a right-click. For example, when you right-click on the Delphi Speedbar, a SpeedMenu appears that lets you configure it any way you like. The same can be done with the component palette.

If you view the Align dialog box, by selecting View | Alignment Palette, and then right-click it, you can choose whether or not this tool will float on top of all other IDE elements, as shown in Figure 2-7. The Object Inspector's SpeedMenu also provides the

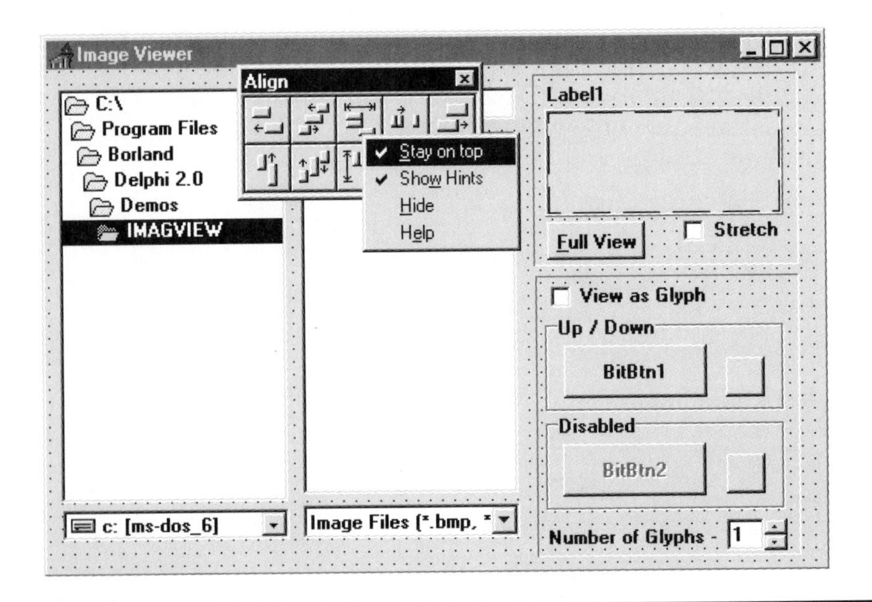

Figure 2-7. *Using a SpeedMenu to float the alignment palette on top*

same "Stay on top" capability as well. (Note that you must right-click on the body of these windows, not on their title bars.)

Remember, when in doubt (or even when you're just curious), hit the right mouse button. You'll discover all kinds of functionality you may have never realized was there.

Hints

Have you ever seen a new Windows development tool with all those icons and wondered if you had to take a class in Egyptian Hieroglyphics to understand them all? Windows 95 added the idea of pop-up "yellow sticky notes" to appear whenever you pause the mouse cursor over an icon. Once again, these pop-up notes, known in Delphi as "hints," appeared in Borland products (and other products as well) long before Windows 95 hit the scene. This means that you do not need to have Windows 95 to use hints in the Delphi IDE or to implement custom hints in your own applications. Even the 16-bit version of Delphi supports hints.

Hints appear all over the Delphi IDE. If they get too annoying, you can always turn them off once you become familiar with Delphi. Simply right-click on the area you are interested in and select Show Hints to uncheck that option. Hints will no longer appear for that item. If you want hints back, just right-click again and turn them on again.

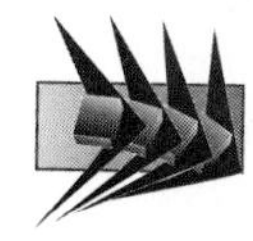

TIP: You can easily add hints to your own Delphi applications. Most objects have two properties that control this feature: ShowHint and Hint. When ShowHint is set to True, the value you assign to the Hint property will be displayed as a hint when the mouse pauses over the object on a running form.

The Online Help System

Delphi takes context-sensitive help to new heights. Whenever you need information about an item, just select it and press F1. For example, you can select a component on the component palette and press F1 to see that object's primary help screen. This standard Windows behavior applies throughout the Delphi IDE even in ways you may not anticipate.

Using the Help System with Delphi Code

Delphi provides you with context-sensitive help while you are writing code. For example, to get help about a particular object, place your cursor on the object name in the editor window and press F1. The help system displays the help topic about that object. For example, if you place your cursor on the object class name TInifile and then press F1, Delphi will display the help topic shown in Figure 2-8. If, instead, you position the cursor on the name of a property and press F1, Delphi displays a help topic about that property.

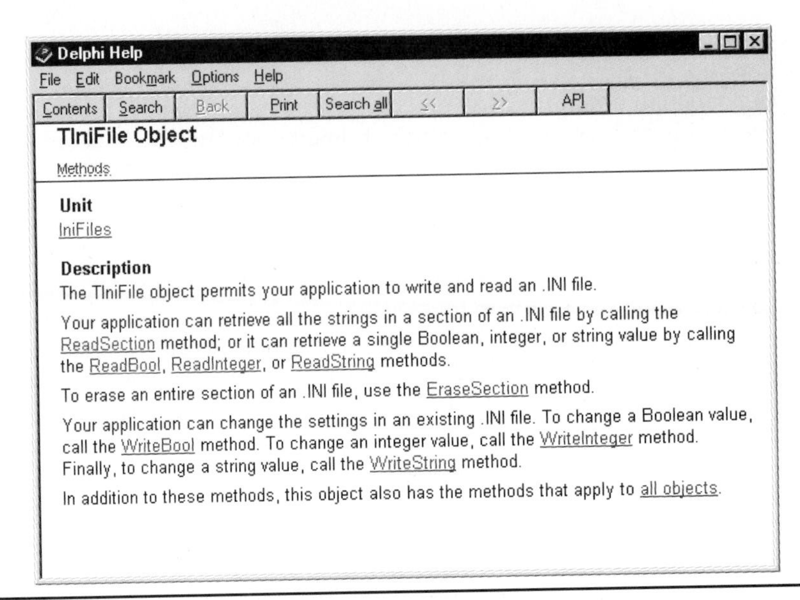

Figure 2-8. *Invoking context-sensitive help about your code*

NOTE: In Delphi 2, the context-sensitive help within the editor window is even more powerful. Whereas in Delphi 1.0 you must place your cursor on the name of a class before pressing F1, in Delphi 2 you can place your cursor on an instance of that class and press F1. The Delphi parser will determine the class type that your instance descended from and will display the help topic for the appropriate object.

Navigating the Help System Without Referencing Code

The context-sensitive help system even works when you don't have specific code to reference. For example, if you select a particular property from the Object Inspector and then press F1, Delphi will again display the corresponding help topic for that property. This also works on forms and on the component palette. Select an object on a form, or an object from the component palette, and then press F1. The Delphi help system is loaded, and the appropriate help topic is displayed.

The Object Help Topic

Every help topic for an object type is organized in a similar manner to the one shown in Figure 2-9. At the top of the help screen you'll notice a standard collection of hypertext jump points specifically designed for Delphi developer concerns. The Properties, Methods, Events and Tasks jump points appear on almost every object's help page. Many help pages, like the one shown in Figure 2-9, include a See Also reference of related topics or related components of possible interest.

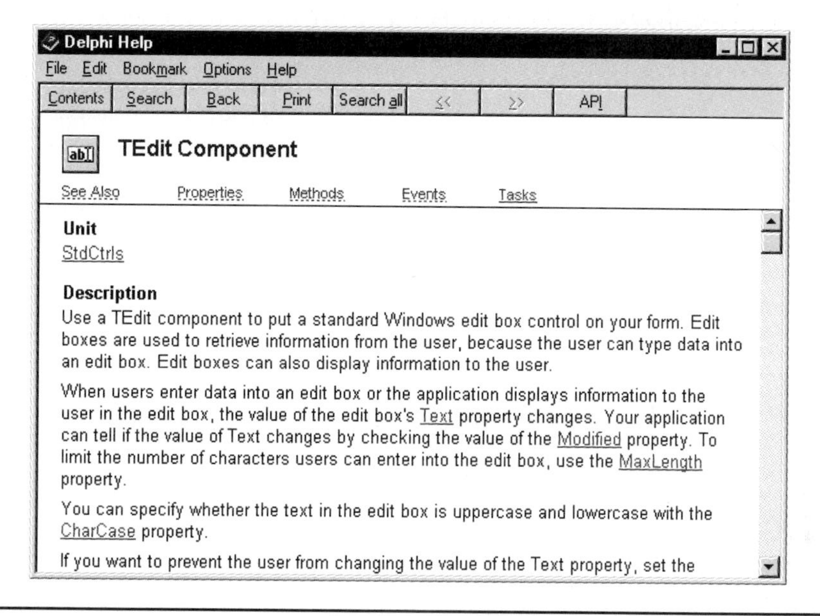

Figure 2-9. *The help topic page for the TEdit class*

Each of the hypertext jump points calls up an alphabetical listing of all the items of that particular type that apply to the selected object. For example, selecting Properties will display a list of the properties for that object, as shown in Figure 2-10. Some of the items listed have a bitmap of a key to the left of them. The entries so designated represent the key (important) items that you'll most likely need in your code. Also, some items are marked with a small triangle. This bitmap identifies those items that are available only at runtime. In other words, these properties do not appear in the Object Inspector at design time.

NOTE: A property that is identified as a run-time only property is one that has been declared as a Public property by the component designer. Properties that have been declared as Published, in contrast, can be modified either at runtime or at design time.

Each of the keywords in a methods, properties, or events list is a jump point to the help topic about that specific item. For example, selecting the Text property from the screen shown in Figure 2-10 displays the Text help topic shown in Figure 2-11. Each item help page has a See Also reference, and most have a hypertext jump to an Example reference as well. Selecting the Example reference calls up a sample code listing pertaining to the topic. Figure 2-12 displays the example associated with Text.

The examples can be particularly helpful since you can copy any portion of this code sample to the clipboard and then paste it into your own application code.

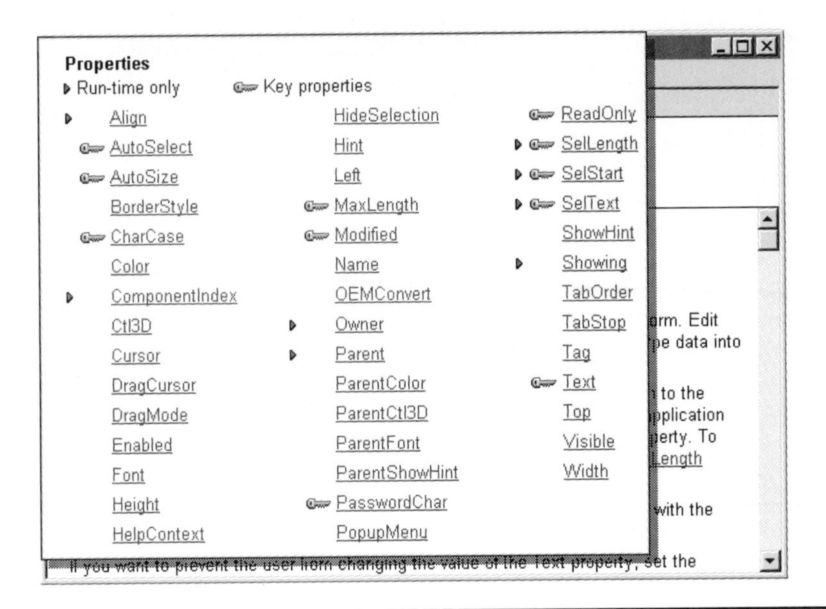

Figure 2-10. *List of properties for a selected object*

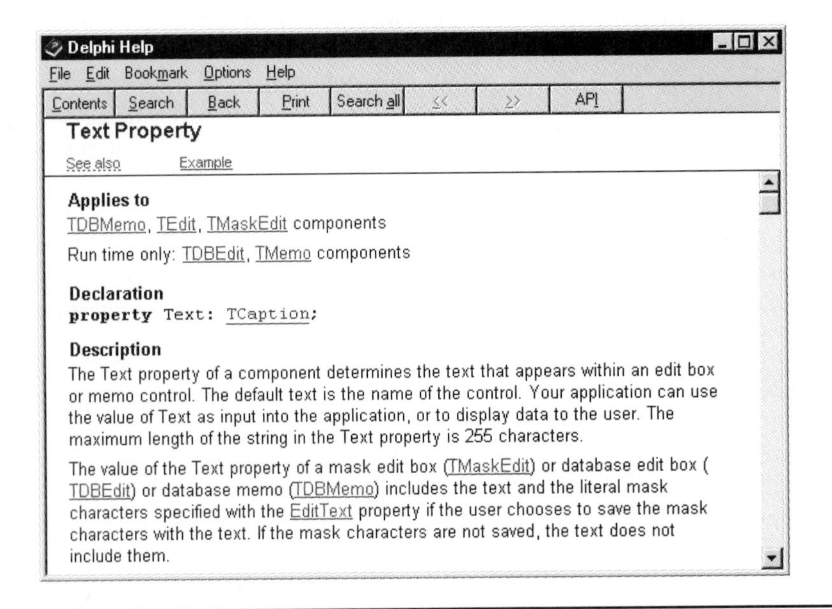

Figure 2-11. *The Text help topic screen*

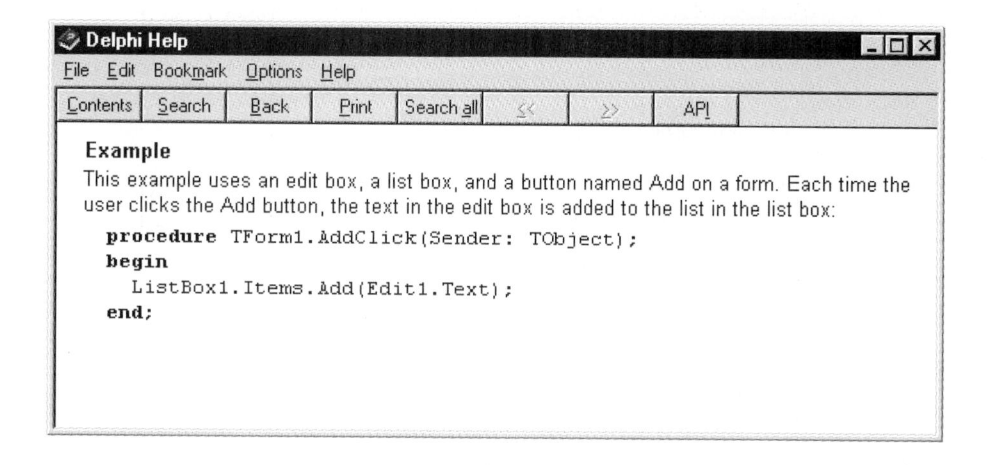

Figure 2-12. *Code example of using the Text property*

TIP: The help system in Windows 95 permits you to select text on any screen, not just the examples screen, and then copy it to the clipboard by selecting Edit | Copy, or by pressing CTRL-C or SHIFT-INS.

Using Help More Intelligently

You can improve your work with Delphi by making intelligent use of two help system features that are often overlooked: Bookmarks and Annotations. Bookmarks permit you to easily come back to a help topic you use over and over again. For example, if you frequently reference the help topic Building Applications, you can place a bookmark there to make it easier to find. You can try out this feature by selecting Help | Contents. Select Building Applications to move to this help topic. Once the help screen comes up, just use the help system Bookmark menu and select Define as shown in Figure 2-13. When you click OK, a new bookmark is established. Now, to go to this page, just select Bookmark and then select the name of the bookmark you placed.

To remove an existing bookmark, just call up help and use the bookmark to navigate to that location. Then select Bookmark | Define and click on the Delete button. The bookmark is now removed.

The ability to include your own custom notes can be extremely handy—especially when you have one of those "Ah, ha!" moments. You know, one of those times when you finally solved a problem. This is the perfect the time to select Edit | Annotate and put your insight into writing, as shown in Figure 2-14. When you select Save, a little paper clip appears at the top of the help topic. You then simply click this icon to display your previously entered annotations.

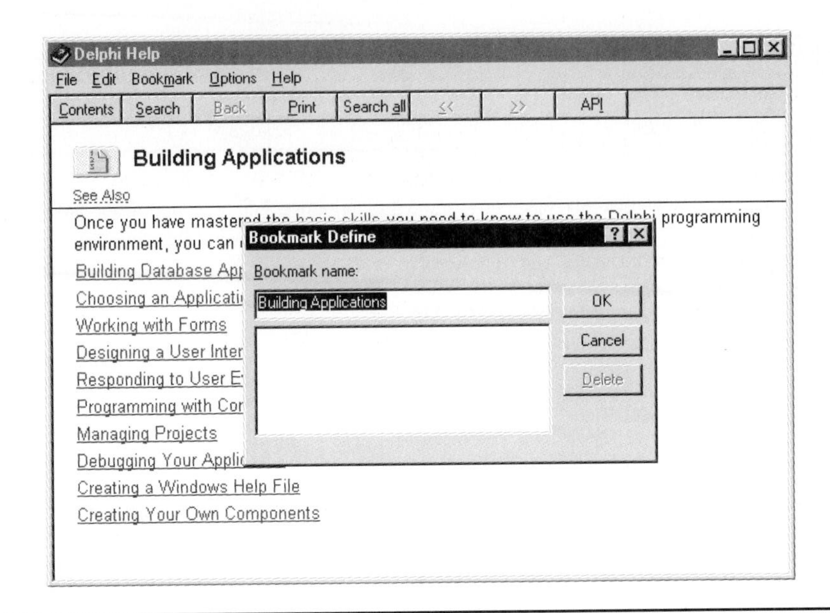

Figure 2-13. *Adding a bookmark to the Building Applications help topic*

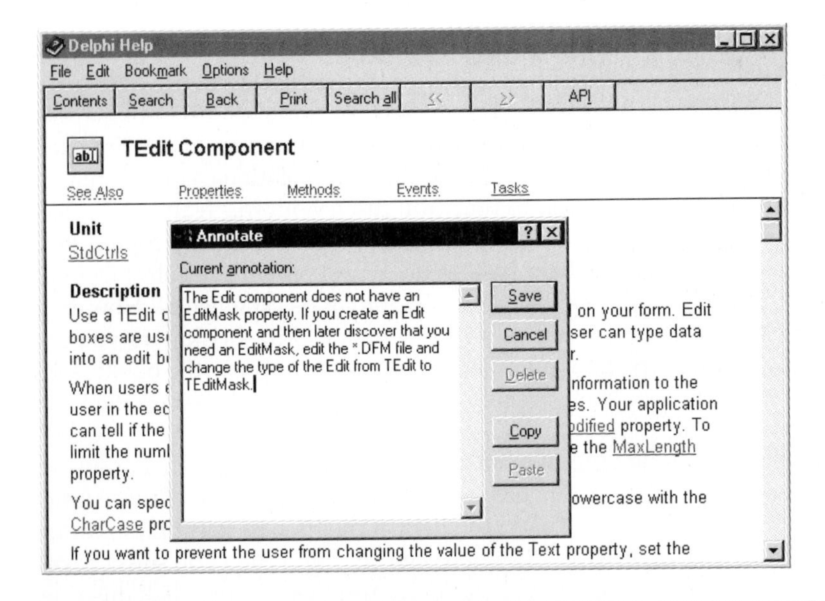

Figure 2-14. *Adding an annotation to a help topic*

The Object Browser

Although the help system is extremely useful, some pieces of information are better gleaned from the Object Browser. As noted previously, not all properties and methods are listed in the Object Inspector. Some aren't even listed within the help system. These two areas list items that are either Published or Public in scope. Also, some third-party components may not come with a complete help file, or they may not have a help file at all.

The Object Browser is especially helpful because its display is based on what actually exists in your application's code. Because documentation and help screens must be finalized long before a product is complete, last minute changes may not make it into these reference resources. The Object Browser, based on your actual code, will always be correct.

Viewing the Object Browser

The Object Browser's display is based on symbol information gathered by the Delphi compiler. Therefore, you must compile your application at least once to activate the Object Browser. Once you have successfully compiled your application, select View | Browser to call up the Object Browser display, as shown in Figure 2-15.

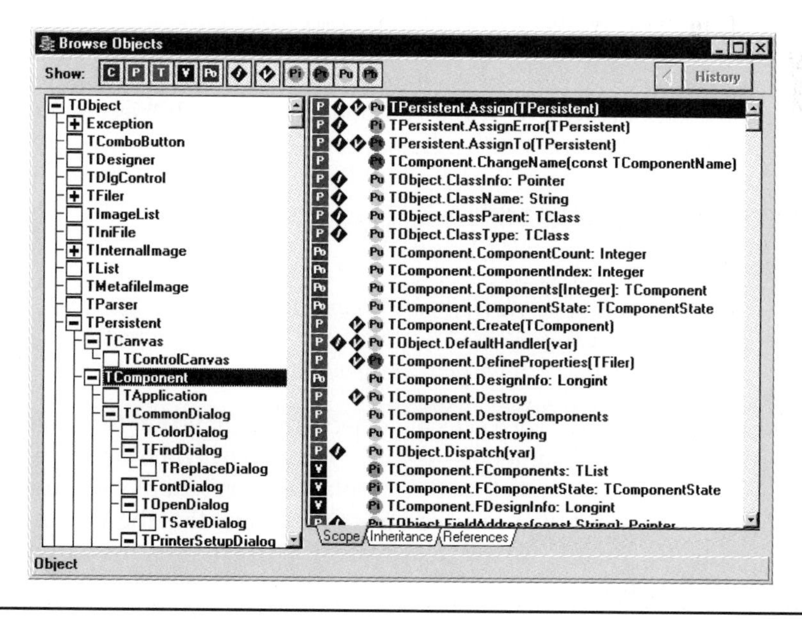

Figure 2-15. *The Object Browser*

NOTE: The image shown in Figure 2-15 is of the Delphi 1.0 Object Browser. Unfortunately, the version of the Object Browser that shipped with the initial release of Delphi 2 contained a bug that reduced the value of the Browser. Specifically, it did not display property types, the return types of function methods, nor the arguments of methods. This information, which is visible in the Delphi 1.0 Object Browser, is important for component users and absolutely essential for component writers. By the time this book is published, we anticipate that Borland will have released a patch for Delphi 2.0 and, furthermore, that this problem with the Delphi 2 Object Browser will be corrected in this patch. If such a patch is released and you install it, your view of the Object Browser in Delphi 2 will appear similar to the one in Figure 2-15.

You can control what symbol information is displayed in the Object Browser by using the Browser's SpeedMenus, as well as the buttons that appear on the Object Browser. In addition, you can use the Browser page of the Environment Preferences dialog box to set the default settings for the Object Browser. To do this, select Options | Environment, and then select the Browser page.

Leveraging the Browser's Information

As you can see in Figure 2-15, the Browser is divided into two main sections. The left side is called the Inspector Pane. It defaults to displaying the class inheritance hierarchy of your application. You can change what Delphi displays in the Inspector Pane by right-clicking the Browser and selecting from either Classes (the default), Units, or Symbols.

The right side of the Object Browser is called the Details Pane. It displays various pieces of information about the item that is currently highlighted in the Inspector Pane. You can navigate within the Browser's display by selecting an item in the desired pane and then starting to type the name of the item you want to find. For example, to find out information about the TDBNavigator component, click on TObject in the Inspector Pane and type **tdbn.** The Browser will automatically select the TDBNavigator entry in the Inspector Pane. The Details Pane will now reflect information about the properties, methods, constants, and so on of the TDBNavigator component.

TIP: You may want to right-click on the Details Pane and select Sort Always. This option displays the detail information in alphabetical order. When Sort Always is not selected, the symbols in the Details pane are displayed in order of declaration.

You control which elements of a selected object are displayed in the Object Browser by using the buttons that appear along the top of the screen. When a particular button is selected, the associated symbol element is displayed. For example, if you want to see which variables are declared for a selected object, make sure that the V button is selected. When the V button is not selected, symbols that are variables are suppressed from the Browser displayed.

TIP: To identify the symbol whose display is controlled by a particular button, pause your mouse cursor momentarily over the button. After a moment, a hint will be displayed, describing the button. If no hint is displayed, right-click the Object Browser and enable Show Hint.

The Browser is the most compact single source of technical information about your project within Delphi. The Object Inspector, by comparison, shows only properties that are declared as Published in scope. Likewise, the Delphi help system provides information about items that are either Published or Public in scope. By navigating to a particular component in the Browser, you can see properties and methods that don't show up in the Object Inspector or help system. You can even find out which properties are declared as Protected in scope. (This information is key to creating your own subclasses if you want to promote an inherited property to a broader scope level.)

You can also tell whether the detail items are inherited from some other class, or if they originate within that component's definition. To do so, right-click in the Object Browser and enable Qualified Symbols (a menu item is enabled when a check mark appears next to it). The name of the object that the particular symbol was declared in is displayed next to the symbol name.

TIP: Many times, you'll want to find all the properties and methods that are available to a particular type of component. Just turn off the C, T, and V buttons from the left-most grouping of five show buttons. This will leave only the P (procedures and functions) and Po (properties) buttons pressed in (that is, in the activated state).

USING THE BROWSER TO NAVIGATE YOUR CODE Wouldn't it be nice if there was a way of seeing in which units, and on which lines, a particular property was referenced? Fortunately, the Object Browser provides this assistance. Display in the Inspector Pane the symbol in which you are interested. Next, select the References tab in the Details Pane. The References page includes the unit and line number in which the selected symbol appears. For example, in Figure 2-16 the ReadSectionValues method of the TIniFile object is selected, and the Details Pane displays the locations where that method is called. You can then double-click on a reference item in the Details Pane and Delphi will automatically navigate you to that location in your source code.

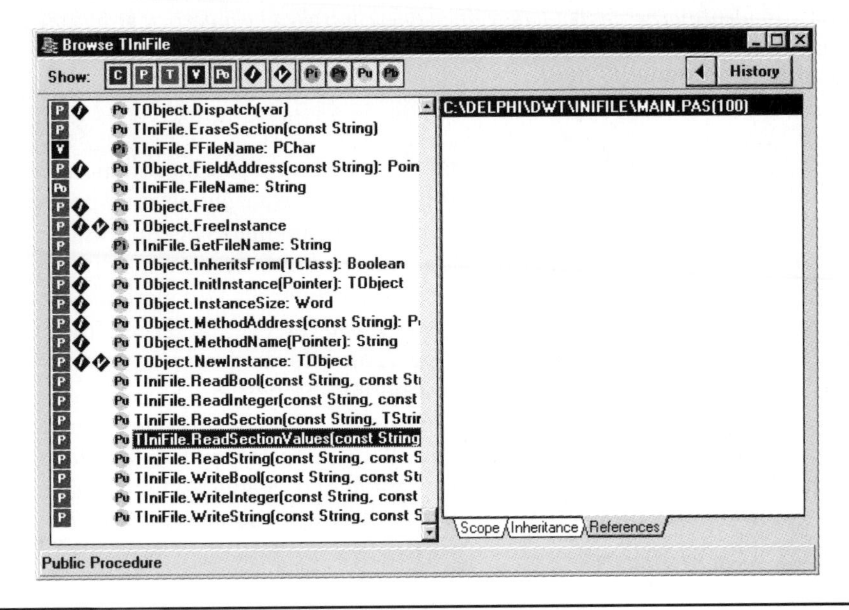

Figure 2-16. *Using the Object Browser to locate references to a particular symbol*

Conclusion

This chapter has introduced you to the basic approach to developing applications the Delphi way, as well as shown you some of the essential support tools provided by Delphi. In the next chapter, the underlying concepts of object-oriented programming in Delphi are discussed.

Chapter Three

Object Orientation in Delphi

The code for the examples presented in this chapter can be found in the \CODE\CH03 subdirectory on the CD-ROM that accompanies this book. Please refer to Appendix A for information on using the code files for this chapter.

A large part of Delphi's power comes from its robust support of object-oriented programming (OOP). This chapter introduces the basic concepts underlying OOP in general and how OOP concepts are applied to Delphi development.

You do not need to be familiar with object orientation. If you've heard all the talk about OOP and are wondering what it's all about, the first half of this chapter is the discussion you've been looking for. If you do have a grounding in object-oriented concepts, you can skip the earlier sections and go to the second half of this chapter, which covers the practical applications of OOP concepts as they apply to Delphi.

An OOP Primer

OOP technology lies at the heart of most modern programming languages. Development tools such as C++ and Delphi are OOP languages. Application environments such as Paradox for Windows and Access, while not OOP themselves, were created using OOP technology.

OOP in Delphi has an impact on several levels. First, if you become a component creator, it is essential that you understand and be able to apply the OOP philosophy. As a component user, understanding OOP is less critical though still important.

Let's start by considering a useful analogy that demonstrates some of the basic principles, as well as advantages, of object orientation.

A Hardware Analogy

You already use object orientation—in your PC hardware. Desktop computer systems certainly existed prior to the IBM PC. So why did personal computing take a quantum leap when the IBM PC was introduced? The PC revolution depended on the use of standard, off-the-shelf components. What made this system architecture so flexible and so successful was the ability to plug these ready-made components into a standard backplane. The standard framework of the original PC's ISA bus provided a context in which all kinds of components could be put together easily in a number of different, highly useful ways.

The IBM PC was the hardware equivalent of object orientation at its most fruitful. So let's examine this hardware example to learn a bit about the basic concepts involved in object orientation itself.

Upgrading a PC Video Board

Let's start with a familiar hardware example, that of upgrading the video in your PC. The video board is an object. You really don't care how it works. You're just interested in the results. Because a standard interface has been defined for all video board "objects," you can upgrade easily. You don't need to replace the entire PC. You don't have to become an electronics engineer and design your own board either. You simply replace the old video board with a better one.

Older desktop computer systems were highly flexible but required you to create your own configuration standards. The S-100 bus systems, for instance, had no established standards. You could add your own board—even build your own add-on board, and you had to determine all the I/O characteristics (including interrupt assignments). You certainly had a lot of power, but you couldn't take a board that worked in your system and assume that it would work in someone else's system.

Then came the IBM PC. A company with the clout of IBM was establishing standards that everyone could follow. At first, S-100 bus proponents lamented the loss of control that an externally imposed set of standards were thought to bring on. The reality was that these standards greatly broadened the appeal of desktop computing. With acceptance by business came a huge increase in the number of companies making add-on boards that took advantage of the IBM standard. A self-feeding cycle of new board development followed by broadening market acceptance had begun. Components had arrived in a big way to the computing hardware market.

Broadened appeal was a direct result of the fact that computer users could start to concentrate on what they wanted to do instead of how to get the hardware to do it. Another advantage of this component architecture was that you could now share components with other users. These components are reusable. For example, once you've upgraded your PC's video board, that same standard interface allows you to pass your old video board on to a coworker. Thus, a single upgrade can have a ripple effect throughout various parts of an organization.

A third advantage of components is in the area of the expertise required. Using a collection of standard components, you can build functional items without having to know how to build the individual parts yourself. The choice to build or buy is now available to you.

Finally, components provide easy support for maintenance. If a problem is discovered with your video board, you replace only the video board, not your entire PC.

This *plug-and-play* concept of creating reusable components is nothing new. It's the basis for the entire Industrial Revolution. What *is* new is the ability to apply these concepts to the world of software programming. The creation of reusable software components or *objects* is what object-oriented programming is all about.

Foundational Concepts of Object-Oriented Programming

Object-oriented programming is a methodology designed to bring the advantages of a component-based architecture into the software arena. OOP is based on three fundamental concepts. The technical terms for these three concepts are:

- Encapsulation
- Inheritance

- Polymorphism

Each of these concepts is discussed in the following sections.

Encapsulation

The idea behind *encapsulation* is that data structures and code routines are bound together, or encapsulated, into a single entity called an *object.* The public data structures of a Delphi object are known as *properties,* and the object's public code routines are called *methods.* Internal data and code are almost always a part of an object's definition as well. All access to the object's internal data structures and code routines must go through the object's interface, its properties, and methods as depicted in Figure 3-1. As shown in this figure, encapsulation means that an object can possess both code and data. It also permits one object to "hide" some or all of its data from another object. This ability of an object to hide its data, and even its code, is a crucial feature of encapsulation.

Relating encapsulation to the hardware analogy, a video board encapsulates all the I/O subroutines, internal data caches, and all the minute details of how to make a collection of dots appear on the screen. This one object embodies all those details so that you, the user of the board, don't have to be concerned with those internal details. You simply make use of the board's API (Application Programming Interface). For example, you simply want to instruct the computer to draw a circle and have it happen. You don't really care about how the electronics accomplish this task.

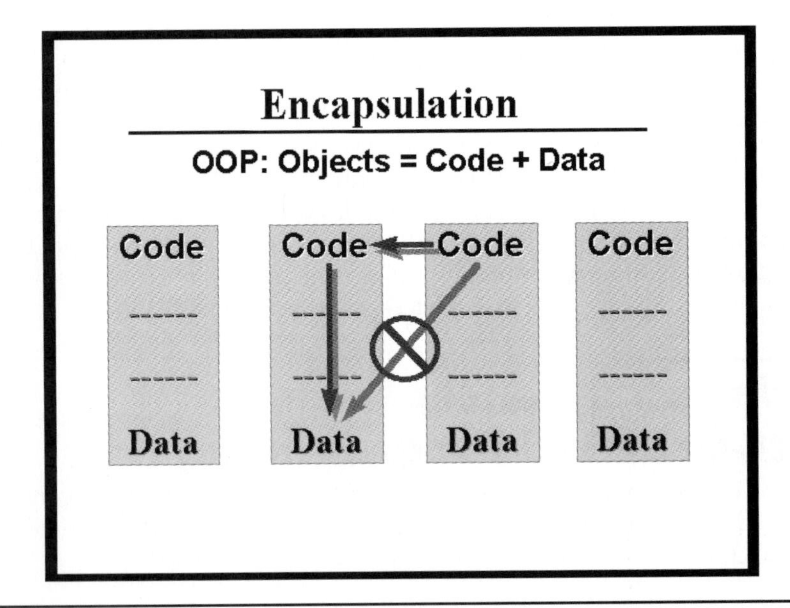

Figure 3-1. *Encapsulation means that an object can possess both code and data*

What are the main advantages of object encapsulation in the world of software? Consider this: most programming problems arise out of the issues of code re-entrance (the need to execute the same code from within multiple application contexts) and data access concurrency (the need to be able to have multiple pieces of code use the same data variables at the same time). Encapsulation by its very nature eliminates these areas as sources of programming glitches. Since similar objects can be created that use the same code routines encapsulated within themselves, all program code is re-entrant. Object encapsulation protects data access in such a way that concurrency never becomes an issue.

Encapsulation Versus Structured Programming

Prior to OOP, the standard accepted coding methodology involved a concept known as *structured programming.* Structured programming provided a clearly defined way for packaging code modules into subroutines and for defining the way each code routine interfaced with every other piece of code. The limitation of structured programming was that it provided no way to structure the data used by an application. So, although the code was structured, it sat atop a vast sea of unstructured data (see Figure 3-2). The programmer was responsible for ensuring that each routine treated this data sea in a well-behaved manner.

This lack of data access structure led to a commonly occurring problem, that of the ill-behaved routine. Since only the code was structured, an errant pointer or a memory glitch could send a routine off modifying data in use by other routines. This often led to mysterious and disastrous side effects, as shown in Figure 3-3. For example, have you ever fixed one routine in a large project only to find that your fix broke something else that was totally unrelated?

The most common example of this problem in the software world is in the improper setup of EMS (Expanded Memory Specification) memory managers. If your system has a video board with 1 MB of RAM, the EMS driver must be told explicitly not to use that extra video RAM for EMS page framing. (In most cases, you must tell the EMS manager to exclude the memory locations C000 to CFFF from use.) Windows provides its own EMS memory manager, so you still need to address this issue for Windows PCs. In Windows 3.x, you need to add a statement like the following to the [386Enh] section of your SYSTEM.INI file:

```
EMMExclude=C000-CFFF
```

If this is not done, the system may run fine—most of the time. However, when a software package that makes heavy use of video is invoked, both the graphic software and the EMS driver may try to use the same memory locations for different purposes.

First, let's say the graphics package draws a rich image on the screen. It stores video information in the C000 to CFFF range. Then, the EMS manager looks at the same range of data. Unfortunately, the EMS manager thinks this information is memory page frame data and tries to jump to a "memory location" that doesn't exist (since the data is really screen information, not address data). This often results in

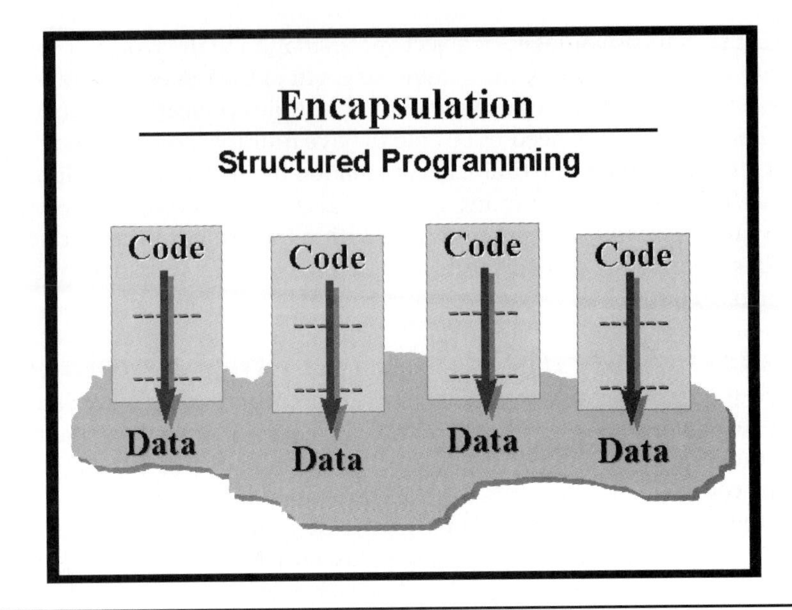

Figure 3-2. *In traditional structured programming, any one code segment may have access to any data element*

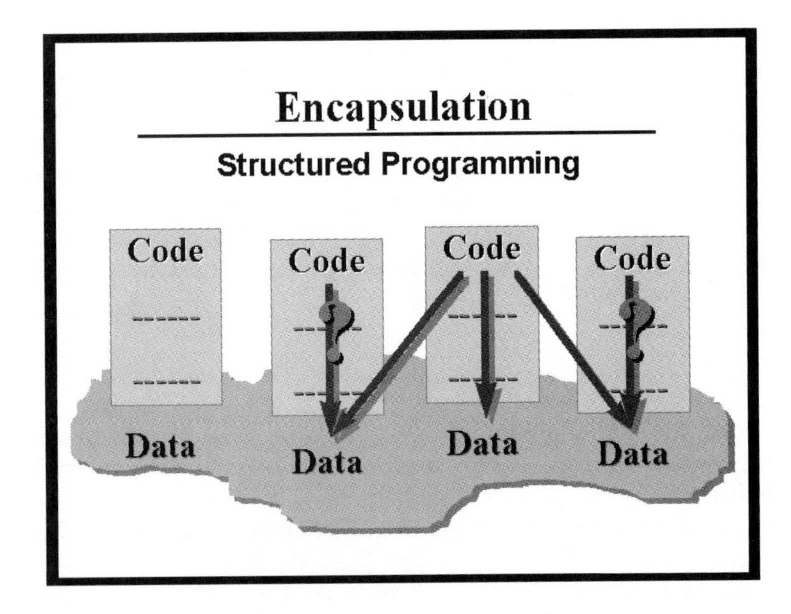

Figure 3-3. *In traditional structured programming, one misbehaved code segment can harm data that is used by many*

unexplainable system crashes. This problem is especially prevalent in systems like Windows, where multiple applications are almost always running in a shared memory environment. Thus, elimination of unwanted side effects is one of the design goals of encapsulation.

You can see the concept of encapsulation in Delphi's user interface as you build an application. When you look at the Object Inspector, you see a two-page dialog box with a tab for each page—one page labeled Properties and the other labeled Events. The Properties page for a Form object is shown in Figure 3-4. The visible published API of each object includes a set of data values called Properties and a set of possible code routines called Methods. The Object Inspector displays only properties. (The properties listed on the Events page of the Object Inspector are method pointer properties. You use these properties to point to procedures that you write that can be executed by the object.) Consequently, the Object Inspector could just as well have been called the Property Inspector.

To see the code routine of an object, you must use either the online help, the Object Browser, or the VCL (Visual Component Library) Reference Manual (this manual ships with the Developer and Client/Server editions of Delphi 2 and can be purchased as a separate manual for Delphi 1.0). To see these methods using the online help, select the object you are interested in on a form or in the component palette, and then press F1.

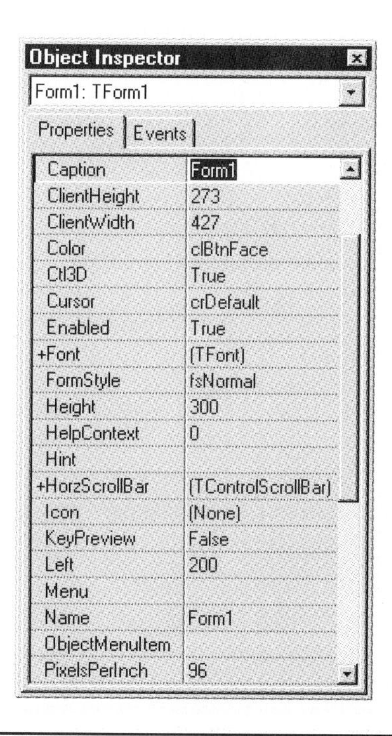

Figure 3-4. *The Properties page of the Object Inspector. The Object Inspector displays the published properties of a selected object*

This selection will take you to the main page for that object. Then, select the Methods hyperlink at the top of the page to display the public methods for that object. The public methods for the TForm class are shown in Figure 3-5. To see the public methods of an object, you select that object on a form or in the component palette, press F1, and then select the Methods hyperlink at the top of the displayed help page.

Beyond Strong Data Typing and Scoping

Encapsulation provides the structure needed to protect the data each routine uses from unexpected use by other routines. This structure is the mechanism whereby only code routines that belong to an object can modify the data within that object. Methods from any other object must make calls to the object's methods to view and modify the properties in that object.

Programmers usually think that they can accomplish the same results that OOP provides simply by using strong data typing, variable scoping, and careful coding. However, using strong data typing and variable scoping does not afford the same level of data protection. Strong typing only identifies what *type* of information can be stored in a variable. It can only tell you what doesn't belong somewhere. And data typing offers no information as to which code modules should be allowed access to the data.

Variable scoping provides some amount of access control, but it leaves many loopholes in providing data protection. For example, your program may need to perform some kind of data validation or automatically set other variables to preset values based on the value to which a particular data element is changed. If the variable scoping is set to allow such changes from different code modules, then nothing

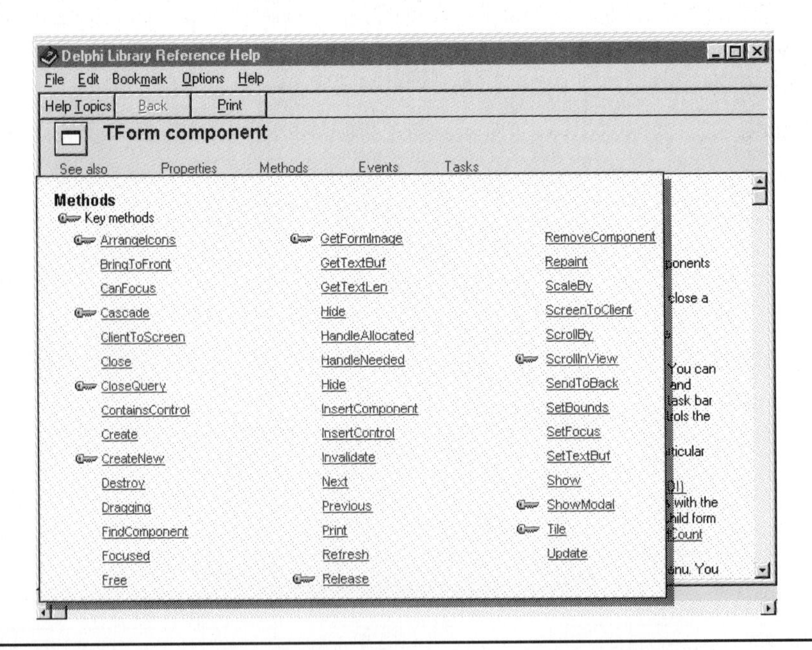

Figure 3-5. *This page displays the public methods of the TForm class*

prevents those same code modules from *directly* accessing those variables. Your data validation code could be easily circumvented. This kind of problem is fairly easy to avoid in single programmer projects. However, in team development, this problem happens all the time regardless of how careful the team is.

As a real-world example, think about making a cash withdrawal at the bank. We all hate waiting in lines, so why not let everyone simply go behind the counter and process their own transactions? Because that simply wouldn't be safe. What would prevent someone else from taking cash from your account, or from withdrawing more money than they had? That is why we need an intelligent agent behind the counter.

In a bank, access to certain routines needs to be restricted. The same idea applies to application development. Yet structured programming offers no way to hide program code modules from each other. OOP provides a way of creating scoping rules for your application's *code* as well as for your variables.

Let's return to the bank teller analogy. The idea of variable scoping can be seen in the control of account information. Each person can look at the information only in their own accounts. Code scoping can be seen in the control of how that data is accessed and modified. Bank customers have no idea what internal procedures the bank teller goes through to post a deposit to their account. That routine is scoped as being private to the "bank teller object."

In the same way, OOP encapsulation provides both data *and* method scoping capabilities. How does this work to provide added protection to your application? Let's say you need to create an object that has data you want to ensure never gets overwritten. You want other objects to be able to see this value, just not be able to change it. The following code sample demonstrates how to define such a "global" read-only data element using Delphi's encapsulation and scoping constructs. Simply put, the code declares the variable, named ROProp, to be private to the object class (and thus inaccessible from direct manipulation by other objects). The code also defines a public method for reading that "invisible" data. Other objects can read the value of the variable, but only by using the defined public method.

```
{**********************************************************************
               R O D E M O . P A S
***********************************************************************
This is a unit designed to demonstrate how the OOP concept of
encapsulation is more than just structured programming with a fancy
name. The code shown here demonstrates the use of a combination of
variable scoping and code scoping to create a "global" read-only
data element.

To see the effect of this VCL class, create a form with a
TRODemo object and a TButton object. Then attach the
following code to the OnClick event of the button:

procedure TForm1.Button1Click(Sender: TObject);
 begin
   Button1.Caption := RODemo1.GetROProp;
```

```
 end;
}
unit RODemo;

interface

uses
 SysUtils, WinTypes, WinProcs, Messages, Classes, Graphics, Controls,
 Forms, Dialogs, StdCtrls;

type
 TRODemo = class(TLabel)

 private
  { Private declarations - visible only to this class }
  ROProp : String;
  procedure SetROProp(ROValue: String);

 protected
  { Protected declarations - visible to this class and its descendants }

 public
  { Public declarations - visible to all classes }
  constructor Create(AOwner: TComponent); override;
  function GetROProp : String;

 published
  { Published declarations - visible to all classes, and displayed
    in the Delphi Object Inspector }
 end;

procedure Register;

implementation

constructor TRODemo.Create(AOwner: TComponent);
begin
 inherited Create(AOwner);   { Call the parent class' constructor }
{Set the default value of the R/O property }
SetROProp('This value is scoped to be hidden');
end;

procedure TRODemo.SetROProp(ROValue: String);
begin
  ROProp := ROValue;
end;

function TRODemo.GetROProp : String;
begin
```

```
  Result := ROProp;
end;

procedure Register;
begin
  RegisterComponents('Mine', [TRODemo]);
end;

end.
```

This unit defines a class called TRODemo. TRODemo has a single protected variable named ROProp, as well as two access methods, SetROProp and GetROProp. Like the variable ROProp, SetROProp is also private, meaning that other objects cannot call this method. In other words, only an RODemo object itself can set the value of its ROProp variable. Conversely, the GetROProp method is public. Public methods can be called by other objects. Consequently, other objects are permitted to see the value stored in the variable ROProp.

That is what encapsulation is all about. Your application uses multiple intelligent agents to get the job done. Thus, encapsulation is a safer way to structure both your code and your data.

Inheritance

The second OOP building block is called *inheritance*. Just like biological inheritance, OOP inheritance allows a programmer to create child object definitions, called *child classes*, that inherit the methods and data structures of the parent class.

Programming by Exception

One benefit of inheritance is that you can create a child class and then use the inherited methods and properties from the parent class without having to recreate them from scratch. You then code only the differences between the parent and child classes. This process is known as *programming by exception*. Your time is then free to concentrate on creating those methods and properties that are unique to the child class. Thus, inheritance allows developers to write less code. This process of programming by exception is depicted in Figure 3-6. In this figure, both the Rectangle and the Triangle inherit from Shape. Each child class then adds its own exception (methods and properties) to the Shape definition.

A second benefit to inheritance is that it affords easier maintainability. Inheritance provides a mechanism that permits you to make a change once, in the parent class. All classes that inherit from that parent will automatically pick up the change.

Along with encapsulation, inheritance can make debugging your applications more secure as well. Encapsulation provides the "firewalls" that prevent unwanted side effects. Inheritance then safely makes the job easier. If a bug is found in a particular routine that is used in a variety of places, fixing it in the parent class will automatically ripple that fix to all child classes.

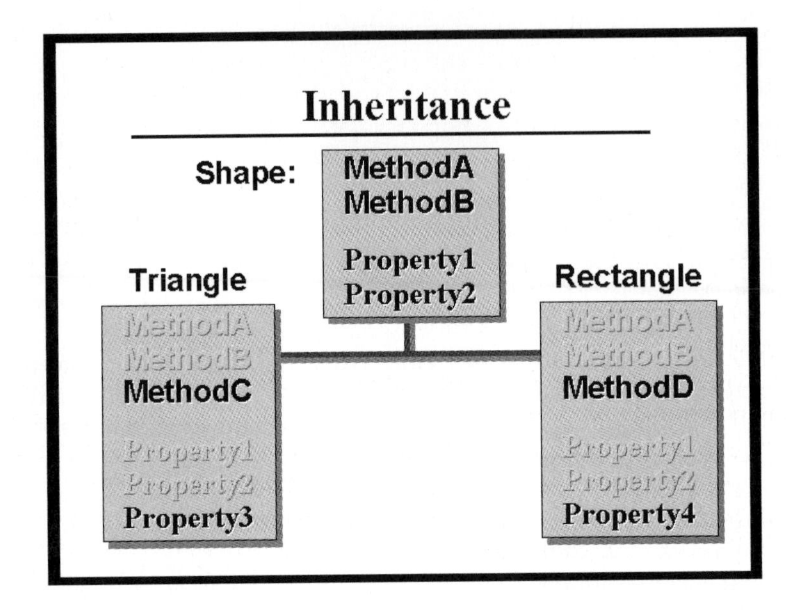

Figure 3-6. *Inheritance allows programming by exception*

Subclassing

Delphi fully supports the use of inheritance in every area of application development. You can create your own custom classes from scratch, or you can inherit from existing components. If there is a component that is already close to what you want, you don't need to reinvent the wheel. Instead, inherit from that component, and then program the differences.

This process is called *subclassing*, and Delphi makes it especially easy through the use of the Component Expert, shown in the next illustration. Select File | New Component from Delphi's File menu (Delphi 1.0) or select Component | New (Delphi 2) to launch the Component Expert. You use this form to assign your new component a class name, select an existing component from which to inherit, and define the component palette page on which you want your new component to appear. Delphi then builds the skeleton of your new component, ready for you to code the new properties, methods, and behaviors that are unique to your new component.

Component Expert

Class Name: TRODemo

Ancestor type: TLabel

Palette Page: Demos

OK Cancel Help

Delphi lets you inherit from more than just VCL components. Delphi 1.0 can use VBX (Visual Basic Extension) components and Delphi 2 can use OCX (OLE Control) controls. Delphi provides a VCL component wrapper for any VBX or OCX you install. This wrapper allows you to create component-type child classes that are based on your VBX or OCX components. Delphi 2 also adds a new TContainer class. The TContainer can act as a parent class that contains other components. Thus, child component classes will consist of all the parts contained within that parent. (The same containership effect can be created in Delphi 1.0, but the Delphi 2 TContainer class makes the process easier.) The TDBNavigator class is a good example of a container-based class. The TDBNavigator is actually a TPanel that contains a collection of SpeedButton objects.

The Object Repository provides another mechanism whereby you can inherit from classes that are less granular (low-level) than a single component. Forms, dialog boxes, and data modules can all serve as parent classes from which your project can inherit. In fact, efficient application design in Delphi 2 relies heavily on classes inherited through the Object Repository. Application maintenance and team development are much easier when you allow inheritance to automatically manage global application changes.

Once you compile your application, Delphi provides a visual display of the inheritance hierarchy used in your application. Select View | Browser to display Delphi's Object Browser, shown in Figure 3-7. The browser display is based on the actual code used in the currently open project. Figure 3-7 illustrates the Object Browser for an application that uses the RODemo object from the code sample shown previously. Notice that the display of the TRODemo class shows that its parent class is TLabel and that it contains only one variable (ROProp) that has not been inherited from TLabel.

You will find the Object Browser particularly useful in determining *all* the available properties and methods for an object class. The Object Inspector and Delphi's documentation will often tell you only what is surfaced (public or published) in the specific class you are looking at. Many other properties and methods may exist by virtue of inheritance from an ancestor class. Remember that the Object Browser is based on your actual code.

Polymorphism

Polymorphism is the third building block of OOP. All programming languages give you the ability to create a set of publicly available functions (known as *external methods* in the OOP world) for each object. These external methods make up the object's API. Polymorphism adds the ability to use the same method name to perform vastly different operations, based on the type of object that is being referenced by the method.

In real life, we make use of polymorphism all the time. We use the same word to mean different things based on the context. We can apply a single word such as "run" to a person, a nose, and a computer to get vastly different results without any need for additional language commands. If we then add a new type of object, say a faucet, we can still use the same "run" command. Now we have added yet another result for this

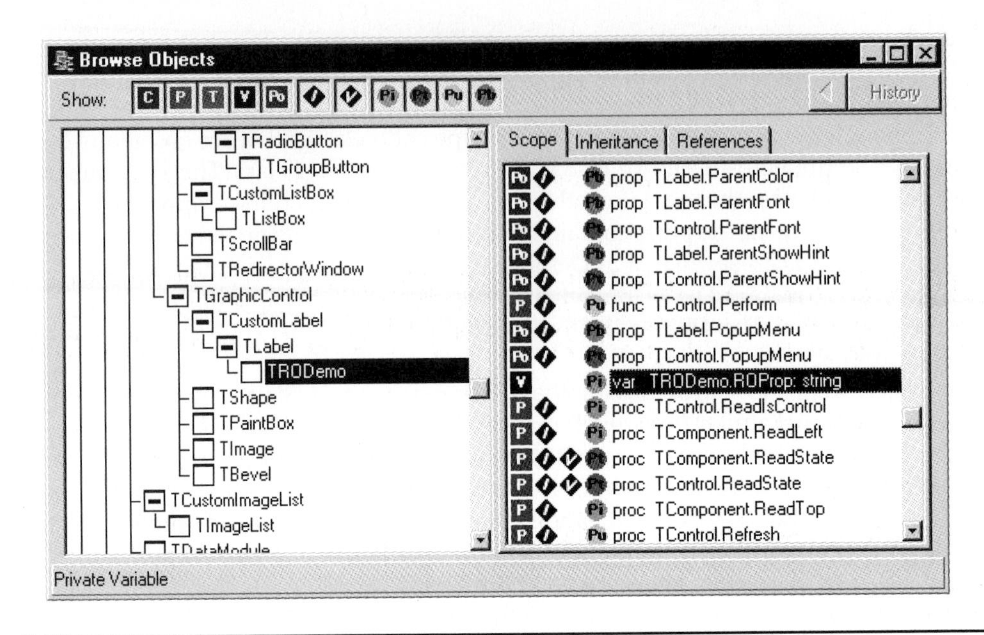

Figure 3-7. *Delphi's Object Browser displays VCL inheritance. The TRODemo class is selected in this display*

one word. The top-level "code" remains the same regardless of the type of object on which it is used.

Because of polymorphism, you can simply tell an object to perform a particular method without being concerned with any internal differences from one type of object to the next. Like the video hardware upgrader, you simply make use of the standard API of the object, its external methods. You can leave the details for the object to work out on its own.

Method Overloading

Returning to coding metaphors, let's take a look at the plus sign operator. Table 3-1 illustrates how a kind of polymorphism is used in the form of operator overloading. The plus sign performs a different function based on the objects upon which it is acting.

OOP applies the concept of polymorphism to more than simple operators. It can also be applied to entire code routines. Think of this concept as a kind of method overloading. Let's say you are creating a screen shape drawing package. You've defined a generic object class named Shape. From that parent, you have defined two child classes, Triangle and Rectangle, each with its own draw method defined.

The internal details of how to draw a triangle are very different from the details of how to draw a rectangle. Without polymorphism, you would have to create a DrawTriangle function, a DrawRectangle function, and so on. If you then wanted to add a new feature such as printing, you would have to create a whole new set of custom functions. You would then have a giant case statement to process the selection of the function to call based on the type of object.

Sample Code	Result	Operation Performed
5 + 7	12	Mathematical addition
"This is " + "a string."	"This is a string."	String concatenation
1/25/96 + 14	2/8/96	Date math

Table 3-1. *Polymorphism Illustrated in the Use of the Plus Sign (+)*

When it came time to develop a new version with a new type of object, you'd have to go back through all that old code to make sure everything still worked. You also would have to make sure that you added this new object type to every case statement in every code module where the object type needs to be referenced. This massive code maintenance task becomes even more complex when the application is being written by a team of programmers. To be totally successful, nearly every programmer on the project would need to know all the details about the project's entire code set.

Hiding Complexity

Polymorphism lets you ignore these details and simply say, "Object, draw thyself." (In the real world, you can tell both your friend and your dog, "Let's go for a walk." Your dog may scratch at the door, but your friend will simply open it.) This concept is depicted in Figure 3-8. The code shown in this figure simply tells each object to draw

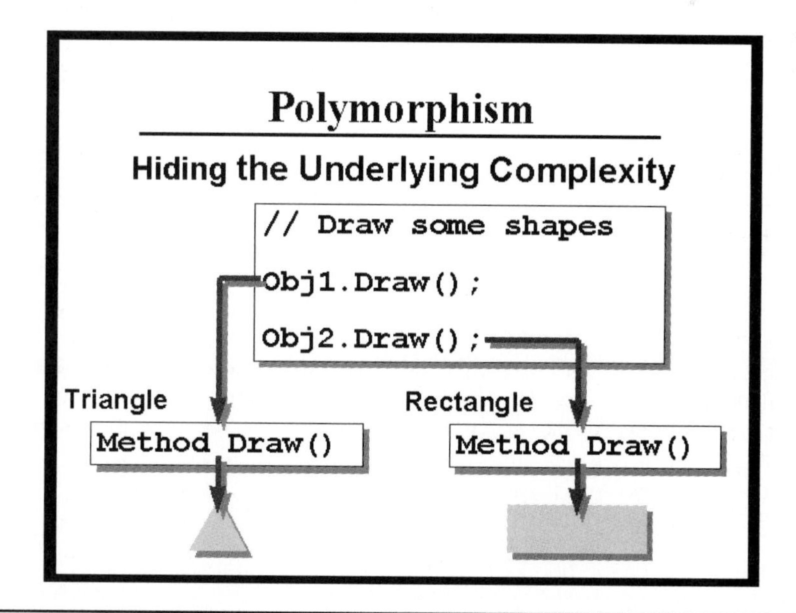

Figure 3-8. *Polymorphism allows the writing of simpler code*

itself. The small code segment in this figure depicts two objects, Obj1, which is a Triangle object, and Obj2, which is a Rectangle object. The same draw method can be used with each object, producing a result appropriate for that object. New types of objects can be added at any time and this same code will continue to work. As long as each new object type has some kind of draw method defined, the developer doesn't have to be concerned about exactly what the draw method does. Thus, polymorphism lets developers create simpler code by insulating them from internal complexities.

Delphi provides a simple way for supporting polymorphism, the override keyword. The code shown below creates a version of the DBNavigator control that defaults to being a simple record viewer. (It gets rather tedious to have to turn off a whole lot of properties every time you want to remove the insert, delete, and post buttons to create a read-only navigator.) This navigator also defaults to always show the help hints for the buttons used.

```
{*********************************************************************
                 N A V L I T E . P A S
*********************************************************************
This is a unit designed to demonstrate how the OOP concepts of
inheritance and polymorphism allow the developer to customize existing
classes to create new ones. This simple example uses a control that is
ALMOST what we want. However, this code will override the parent class'
constructor to set up THIS class the way we want it.

To see the effect of this VCL class, create a form and drop both a
DBNavigator and this new DBNavLite control onto it. You'll notice an
immediate difference in the display of the two controls, even though
both are calling their respective ObjName.Create methods.}

unit Navlite;

interface

uses
SysUtils, WinTypes, WinProcs, Messages, Classes, Graphics, Controls,
 Forms, Dialogs, ExtCtrls, DBCtrls;

type
 TDBNavLite = class(TDBNavigator) {Declare which class to inherit from}
 private
  { Private declarations - visible only to this class}
 protected
  { Protected declarations - visible to this class and its descendants}
 public
  { Public declarations - visible to all classes }
  constructor Create(AOwner: TComponent); override;
             { Polymorphism to produce a new effect }
 published
  { Published declarations - visible to all classes, and displayed
```

```
    in the Delphi Object Inspector }
  end;

procedure Register;

implementation

constructor TDBNavLite.Create(AOwner: TComponent);
begin
 inherited Create(AOwner);  { Call the parent class' constructor ,
               then set new default values }
 VisibleButtons := [nbFirst,nbPrior,nbNext,nbLast,nbRefresh] ;
 ShowHint := true;
 Width := 171;
end;

procedure Register;
begin
 RegisterComponents('Demos', [TDBNavLite]);
end;

end.
```

To build a read-only navigator, you create a new component (TDBNavLite) based on the TDBNavigator class and then override the DBNavigator.Create method (the class' constructor). In the new Create method, you merely call the parent's constructor and then manipulate the properties to set them the way you want inside NavLite's Create method. Polymorphism lets you instantiate either a DBNavigator or a DBNavLite object with the same code—ObjName.Create. The result you see will be determined by the type of object you are using, as shown in Figure 3-9. This figure shows a form with both a DBNavigator and a DBNavLite object displayed. The DBNavLite object has no buttons associated with editing and displays hints by default.

General OOP Terminology

Much of the confusion experienced by someone new to object-oriented programming is due in part to jargon, the sometimes obscure technical terms used to describe specific characteristics of object orientation. Unfortunately, many of these terms seem to be defined in almost the same way. The subtleties of the differences can elude even the most technically aware newcomer. Problems in coding can arise when the distinctions between the various terms are not kept clearly in mind.

Another factor adding to the confusion is that the terminology and its use are still evolving. Two experienced OOP developers may use the same terms but define them differently. Earlier discussions about object orientation use the words "class" and "object" interchangeably; however, there is a difference.

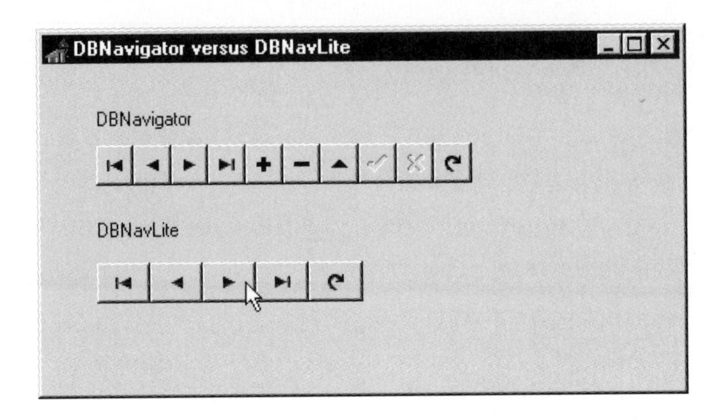

Figure 3-9. *A form with both a DBNavigator and a DBNavLite object displayed*

Other terms, such as "record" and "field," were holdovers from earlier versions of various OOP languages. These terms added to the confusion when database application tools started using object-oriented concepts. It was hard to keep straight whether you were talking about a database record or an OOP record (for example, a Pascal structure or code-less class); whether it was a database field or a data member of an OOP class. These terms created even more confusion when object-oriented databases started to appear. Were you discussing an OOP language that accessed a relational database, or an OOP tool that created an object-oriented database? Hence the use of some of these terms in an OOP context has been phased out to avoid this confusion.

The definitions below are as current as possible. They reflect the best way known to date of providing design information in the least confusing manner. All terms discussed here are defined in the context of Delphi development, except where noted otherwise.

Class

A *class* or *class definition* is the blueprint of the OOP world. It determines what the defined data elements and code routines will be for all objects created from that class. The class also defines the scope of those elements, determining which code routines will be external methods and which data variables will be properties. Just as the blueprint for a Chevy Nova is not an actual car itself, so the class is not an object itself. It merely defines how to build an object, and what its capabilities will be once it is created. In Delphi, the terms *type* and *class* are interchangeable (except in a class definition, which uses the type keyword).

Object

An *object* is an actual entity that is created at runtime and lives in active program memory. An object is created from a class definition, which determines what methods and properties it has, and can also define the initial values for those properties.

Once an object is created, it no longer refers back to the class from which it was created. Thus, any runtime changes made to an object have *no* effect on any other objects created from the same class. (In the same way that adding a ski rack to one Nova has no effect on any other cars made by GM.)

Delphi adds an interesting wrinkle to the definition of an object. What happens when you drop a VCL component onto your form in design mode? Do you have an object or a class? If you select a component and change one of its properties, do any other components on your form pick up that same change? No; therefore, you have an object on your form, not a class.

This is how it works: The component library (the actual DCL file Delphi is using) contains the entire class definition, in compiled form, of every component you see on the component palette. When you drop a component onto your form, Delphi calls the component class' constructor and creates an object with position properties set based on where you place the component on your form. In other words, when you click on a component in the component palette, you are *instantiating* (creating) an object.

Instantiation

Instantiation is the name given to the process of creating an in-memory object from a class definition. This process creates an *instance* of the class—hence the name. (An instance of a class is also referred to as an object of the class' type.)

Constructor

Each class definition has a section of code that tells the system how to create an object of that class. This instantiation code is called the *constructor.* The constructor is called to allocate memory for an object instance, initialize its properties, and perform any other startup tasks the object may require. Delphi's components use the Create method as their constructor.

Destructor

Just as a class definition needs a constructor method, it also needs a section of code that controls how to remove an object instance from memory. This clean-up code is referred to as the class' *destructor,* which should be defined to perform any "shutdown code" needed, and then release all resources associated with a particular object instance. The use of destructors is vitally important to the issue of resource management. Delphi components use the Destroy method as their destructor.

Instance Variable

A data element associated with an object is known as an *instance variable.* Although all objects within a particular class will have variables defined with the same names, each object will have separate memory storage for each of these variables. Thus, each *instance* of the class has its own copy of each *instance* variable. Rather than referencing the class' name, instance variables are always referenced with the following syntax:

```
ObjectName.VariableName
```

Instance variables are sometimes called field definitions, member fields (in earlier versions of Pascal), member variables, or data members (in C++).

Method

In Delphi applications, *methods* are the publicly available procedures and functions of a class. Methods are called member functions in C++.

Class Method

Most methods are associated with an instance of a class. You usually have to create an object to be able call an object's methods, since most methods will use some kind of variable storage. That storage usually takes place at the instance level, not at the class level, to avoid data collisions between different instances of the same class.

Delphi also supports the idea of a *class method,* a method that is associated with the class itself and not any particular instance of that class. Obviously, a class method cannot depend on any variable information that is determined at runtime. The Create method that is a part of every Delphi component class is actually an example of a class method.

Property

A *property* is a special kind of instance variable. Delphi properties provide the mechanism for protecting data elements from unwanted changes made by external code routines. A property is paired with a private or protected instance variable upon which the class' code routines will really operate. The property is used to control how data is retrieved from or written to that hidden instance variable. The general syntax for a Delphi property definition is as follows:

```
property VarName : VarType read HowToRead write HowToWrite;
```

HowToRead can be either an instance variable or a Delphi function. HowToWrite can be either an instance variable or a Delphi procedure. A Delphi property may or may not appear in the Object Inspector. Only properties scoped as published appear in Delphi's Object Inspector.

Subclassing

The process of creating a child class definition through inheritance from a parent class is called *subclassing*. Subclassing only has meaning in the context of the data elements and code routines inherited from the parent class. The child class thus created will, of course, have additional properties and methods defined, or will redefine one or more of the parent's methods (that is, use polymorphism), or both. After all, the whole idea behind subclassing is to create a new class from the building blocks of an existing one.

Ancestor Class

An *ancestor class* is a class from which data and code definitions are inherited. This ancestor class may not be the immediate parent from which a child class was defined.

It may be higher up on the inheritance hierarchy. For example, in Figure 3-7 TControl is an ancestor of TRODemo but is not its immediate parent.

Parent Class

A *parent class* is the immediate ancestor class from which data and code definitions are inherited to create a new child class definition. Thus, Shape is the parent class for our Rectangle class, TLabel is the parent class for TRODemo, and TDBNavigator is the parent class of TDBNavLite.

Abstract Class

A class usually inherits functionality from its parent class. In designing a flexible class hierarchy, you may need to create a generic parent class that acts as a "placeholder" class definition. Your applications will never really use this placeholder class. It merely reserves method names and instance variables for later surfacing by child classes. This kind of placeholder class is called an *abstract class.*

NOTE: The term virtual class is also often used. In fact, Delphi uses the keyword "virtual" to denote an abstract class.

The Delphi VCL makes extensive use of abstract classes. They not only provide structure to the various related groups of VCL components, but they also control the surfacing of various pieces of functionality. Look at the STDCTRLS.PAS source code file in the SOURCE\VCL subdirectory created during the Delphi installation. You will find that an abstract class called TCustomGroupBox contains the major functional pieces of all groupboxes that appear on the component palette. The TGroupBox class, which appears on the component palette, merely publishes a group of properties that are defined in its ancestor classes. The TRadioGroup class also descends from TCustomGroupBox but publishes a different set of properties defined in its parent class.

Descendant Class

Any class that has been defined based on inheritance from another class is known as a *descendant class* of that ancestor. The terms child class and descendant class are usually used interchangeably. A more strict definition would be that a descendant class is any class that inherits from an ancestor and may or may not be the immediate child of that ancestor. In other words, parent and child classes describe immediate inheritance relationships, whereas ancestor and descendant classes are their more general corollaries.

Classes Versus Objects

It is important to maintain a clear distinction between what a class is and what an object is. Although they are intimately related, code that is placed in a class will have radically different effects than will application code that operates on runtime objects. Table 3-2 shows the differences between class and object.

Programmers new to OOP often have complained that changes they made inexplicably disappeared or reset themselves when they exited their applications and then restarted them. They also become confused when changes to an object don't do what they thought they would. This confusion is especially apparent when these programmers want to make a copy of an object.

You need to ask yourself constantly whether you want to change the *object's blueprint* at design time, or change the *object* itself at runtime. For example, to make a copy of an object, you should instantiate a new object of the same class and then copy the values of the salient properties from the old object to the new instance. If instead you want to make a similar blueprint from which to instantiate objects, you should create a new class by subclassing the original.

How you code each (changing the object at design time or at runtime) is also subtly different. With a class definition, you should get into the habit of programming by exception—of programming only the differences. You accomplish this through the intelligent use of inheritance. Runtime coding of object behavior should be accomplished via a technique known as *programming by properties*. Your classes should be designed in such a way that runtime code can easily affect the behavior of an object instance simply by changing the values of its properties. In this fashion, properties become the way your code controls the current state of the object.

Single Versus Multiple Inheritance

Some OOP tools allow you to create a class definition that inherits from more than one parent class. This ability to have more than one parent class is called *multiple inheritance.* C++ tools typically support this type of inheritance; however, most OOP tools (including Delphi) only allow inheritance from a single parent. These tools are said to support *single inheritance.*

Multiple inheritance can indeed solve many problems, especially when you are modeling the real world in your application code. A component modeling a Foreman, for example, might usefully inherit from both the Employee class and the Manager class.

Class/Object	Use	Creation Process	Code Methodology
Class	Design-time blueprint	Subclassing	Programming by exception
Object	Runtime operation	Instantiation	Programming by properties

Table 3-2. *Classes and Objects*

Multiple inheritance can introduce a whole new variety of complex problems as well. If you create a CarBoat component inheriting from both the Boat class and the Automobile class, how do you steer the vehicle? Do you use a boat-style control panel or a car's? What kind of fuel do you use? What kind of engine? What do you do with the wheels when you are in the water?

As you can see, multiple inheritance can be a two-edged sword. Enough complexities exist in creating custom classes already. Programmers just starting to define custom classes should probably limit themselves to the single-inheritance model.

Debunking Some OOP Myths

Object orientation is not a magic bullet. The benefits come from a proper application of the three basic concepts of OOP. However, OOP is a significant advance from past technologies. As with any new idea, some people resist the change. Others find the change confusing. Still others find the idea stimulating and challenging, but have little guidance as to how to evaluate all the claims and counterclaims.

Making matters worse, the truth about OOP has often been obscured by a variety of half-truths, deceptions, and misleading statements. Let's examine some major myths about OOP and set the record straight.

Myth: Just a Fancy Name for Structured Programming

Some people suggest that OOP is nothing more than a fancy name for structured programming. This opinion fails to address the issues that OOP is designed to address. As you've seen, true object orientation involves a great deal more than just structured programming. True OOP is structured programming plus structured data plus structured access to that data. OOP also adds code scoping constructs to the existing variable scoping constructs seen in structured programming. The fundamental design issues that prompted the creation of OOP concepts were based on the idea of more closely modeling the real world. As shown in the examples given, OOP concepts are particularly apt in creating programmatic versions of real-world objects.

Myth: It Has To Be SmallTalk To Be OOP

Some purists claim that proper OOP can only be done in a language specifically designed for OOP from the beginning. In many cases, these purists will suggest a language such as SmallTalk.

This is patently absurd. If we make this assumption, then we would have to conclude that Delphi is not object-oriented, but it is. In fact, the single most popular object-oriented language today, C++, was not originally designed to be object-oriented.

What is important is that the implementation of object-oriented features in a language support the essential characteristics of object orientation. With Delphi, this is clearly the case.

Myth: OOP Applications Perform Poorly

Because the basic concepts of OOP involve creating class hierarchies that can reference long chains of inheritance, many people expect this overhead to result in poor application performance. In fact, early OOP development tools did create applications with poor performance characteristics.

However, the early OOP tools were not designed with performance in mind. They were simply created to prove the viability of OOP concepts on the design of applications. Many of the modern OOP tools that create slow applications are poor performers because they are interpreted systems. (Most SmallTalk tools are interpreted systems.) Interpreted systems do not compile the application code. Instead, the code is converted to something called *p-code,* which is then used to reference a runtime module when the application is executed. Such interpreted systems will always run slower than systems that create true machine-code executables through the use of a compiler.

Even compiled systems can be slow, however. The quality of an application's performance will be determined directly by the quality of the compiler technology used to translate your OOP source code into machine code ones and zeros.

Delphi, however, is fast. In fact, it is very fast, because of its underlying native code-optimizing compiler. Delphi demonstrates clearly that not all OOP tools are poor performers.

Myth: GUI's Make OOP Hard

Many claim that the paradigm shift to graphical user interfaces (GUIs) makes OOP development difficult for long-time developers. Unfortunately, the issue is really about GUI environments and not OOP itself. It's generally true that a graphical user interface poses a new challenge to procedurally-oriented programmers. The confusion arises because most modern GUI development tools are *also* object-oriented in nature. Condemning OOP because creating a good GUI is difficult is like discounting the skills of a world-class chef because that chef happens to cook a dish using your most hated vegetable.

Fortunately, OOP tools such as Delphi can make creating a GUI application much easier. GUI environments are designed around the concept of end-user manipulation of an application. OOP development treats code and data as if they were tangible objects with physical properties and abilities that can be manipulated. Thus, the OOP style of development fits in very well with creating GUI applications. The best GUI development tools support OOP precisely for this reason.

Myth: Anything that Has Objects Is OOP

Although possessing objects is a characteristic of OOP environments, it is not the defining characteristic. Any system that does not fully support the three major OOP concepts—inheritance, encapsulation, and polymorphism—is not truly object-oriented. Some development tools support one or two of the concepts but not all three. These environments are generally considered to be *object-based,* not object-oriented.

Some tools provide *no* support for OOP. They only have so-called on-screen objects that are merely visual representations; graphical widgets rather than true objects in the OOP sense. In fact, one of the biggest developments in Windows programming, Object

Linking and Embedding (OLE) and its related technologies (such as OLE controls), is not really object-oriented at all. OLE is merely *document-oriented.* There is no support for any kind of inheritance, nor any method encapsulation or true polymorphism. All coding capabilities reside in the OLE Server application, not in the object being used.

Good examples of object-based development tools for the PC are Paradox for Windows (no inheritance), Access (partial encapsulation and no inheritance), and Visual Basic (no true inheritance and limited encapsulation). Many consider PowerBuilder to be a true OOP system, but inheritance cannot be used on Data Windows. True OOP systems include C++, Delphi, Visual dBASE for Windows, SmallTalk, Logo, and ADA.

Creating an Object

Many people, even experienced programmers, feel somewhat daunted by the prospect of entering into this new world of programming in objects. The reality is that OOP is a natural extension of the use of structured data elements with which most programmers are already familiar. In C, structured data elements are known as STRUCTs. The ObjectPascal equivalent is a RECORD.

OOP Is a Natural Extension of What You Already Know

Let's say you wanted to create a data structure that held the program's user name and company name. You would define that structure in Delphi as a record this way:

```
Type
  UserInfo = record
    UserName : String;
    CompanyName : String;
  end;
```

The OOP concept of encapsulation states that an object is a collection of related data elements and code routines. To convert this UserInfo structure into an object is very simple. All you need to do is change the type declaration from record (data elements only) to class (data plus code) and add declarations for the related code routines. This is demonstrated in the following type declaration:

```
Type
  TUserInfo = class
    UserName : String;
    CompanyName : String;
    procedure WhoAmI;
  end;
```

This code follows the general Delphi convention of prefacing all type declaration names with a T.

You also need to add to the implementation section of the unit the actual code for each procedure and function declared as part of the class. Assuming that the user name will get set somewhere else, the following is an example of a possible definition of the WhoAmI procedure declared as part of TUserInfo. This code must appear in the implementation section of the same unit:

```
{ Who Am I procedure }
procedure TUserInfo.WhoAmI;
begin
 ShowMessage(UserName);
end;
```

You now have a structure that encapsulates both data and code—your first class. Actually, the declaration of TUserInfo as a class really creates it as a class of type TObject. Whenever you do not specify the name of the parent class, Delphi automatically assigns the new class to be a child of the generic TObject class. Thus, you could also have written the TUserInfo class declaration as

```
Type
  TUserInfo = class(TObject)
    UserName : String;
    CompanyName : String;
    procedure WhoAmI;
  end;
```

When you inherit from the TObject class, Delphi has already included a huge amount of functionality in your child class. Constructor and destructor routines have already been defined for your class. Delphi's TObject class provides a generic constructor (the Create method) and destructor (the Free method) routine.

Using Your New Class

To make use of this new class, in other words, to instantiate an instance of it, you create a variable of the appropriate type and then call the class constructor. Keep in mind that the design-time task of defining classes and variables is separate from the runtime task of instantiating objects of a particular class and then using those objects. Delphi does not automatically create an object instance when you declare a variable to be of type TUserInfo. The type declaration merely reserves certain information for the variable that may be created at runtime. Your code must explicitly call the class' Create method to create an instance of that class in memory. Thus, if you wanted your form to include a button that, when clicked, displays the user name, you might place the following code into your application:

```
var
 UI : TUserInfo;

{ Instantiate a TUserInfo object }
procedure TForm1.OnCreate(Sender: TObject);
begin
 UI := TUserInfo.create;
 UI.UserName := '<Your name goes here>';
end;

{ Use the TUserInfo object named UI }
procedure TForm1.Button1Click(Sender: TObject);
begin
 UI.WhoAmI;
end;
```

The code in the form's OnCreate event is where the object named UI (which stands for User Interface) is created. This object is an instance of the TUserInfo class. The object's UserName variable is then assigned a value that can be accessed through the WhoAmI procedure. Once the object named UI has been created by the form's OnCreate event, it is available to be used in the OnClick event of the button. (If you find yourself getting strange runtime Access Violation or GP Fault errors when you try to click on the button, you may have forgotten to call the class' Create method.) The following is the complete code for this unit:

```
unit class1;
{ S A M P L E 1
  The initial sample that converts a record
  into a true OOP class
}
interface

uses
Windows, Messages, SysUtils, Classes, Graphics, Controls, Forms,
 Dialogs, StdCtrls;

type
 TUserInfo = class(TObject)
  UserName : string;
  CompanyName : string;
  procedure WhoAmI;
 end;

 TForm1 = class(TForm)
  Button1: TButton;
  procedure FormCreate(Sender: TObject);
  procedure Button1Click(Sender: TObject);
```

```
  private
    { Private declarations }
  public
    { Public declarations }
  end;

var
  Form1: TForm1;
  UI : TUserInfo;

implementation

{$R *.DFM}

{ Instantiate a TUserInfo object }
procedure TForm1.FormCreate(Sender: TObject);
begin
  UI := TUserInfo.create;
  UI.UserName := '<Your name goes here>';
end;

{ Use the TUserInfo object named UI }
procedure TForm1.Button1Click(Sender: TObject);
begin
  UI.WhoAmI;
end;

{ TUserInfo's WhoAmI routine }
procedure TUserInfo.WhoAmI;
begin
  ShowMessage(UserName);
end;

end.
```

The Next Step: Access Control

Although the preceding example is of a true class, it is far from a complete implementation of all the benefits of object orientation. One of the key characteristics of good class design is the use of data hiding. True components hide the underlying details from objects that don't need to know them. Good OOP design also includes the concept of access control.

For example, you might want to create read-only data elements for your class. Or you might want to provide some internal validation code before you actually allow some code outside the class to write a value into a data element. (You might, for example, want to make sure a data value entered into an End Date variable was greater than or equal to the Start Date variable in the same class.) In Delphi, access control is performed by creating *properties* as described in the next section.

Properties: The Key to Control

You can add access control to the previous class example. For instance, you may want the TUserInfo class to read the registered user and company names from the Windows 95 Registry. You don't want to allow programmers that use TUserInfo to be able to change these values, but they do need to read them. So you'll need the access control offered through properties. Simple variable scoping won't provide the kind of controlled access you need.

You'll first need to modify the TUserInfo class definition to convert UserName and CompanyName into properties. Since you'll be fetching this information from the Registry, you'll also need to create a variable of type TRegistry and to define a couple of routines to fetch the requested Registry data.

```
type
 TUserInfo = class(TObject)
  Reg : TRegistry;
 private
  function GetUserName : String;
  function GetCompanyName : String;
 public
  property UserName : string read GetUserName;
  property CompanyName : string read GetCompanyName;
 end;

const
 Win95RegInfo = 'SOFTWARE\Microsoft\Windows\CurrentVersion\';
```

This code adds the private and public scoping keywords to begin providing some level of data and code hiding. Also note that the routines that fetch information from the Registry are scoped as private. This version of TUserInfo forces the user of TUserInfo to access all information in the class through the UserName and CompanyName properties. The previous WhoAmI procedure is not needed, and no direct calls to GetUserName or GetCompanyName are allowed. (The declaration of the Win95RegInfo constant is merely a convenience to make the coding of GetUserName and GetCompanyName easier.)

Since the UserName and CompanyName properties are declared as public, you can reference them directly in your form's code. To use them, you need to create an instance of TUserInfo and then just use the standard ObjectName.PropertyName syntax (called dot notation) to fetch the information out of the class. This code can be placed in the form's Button1Click routine as follows:

```
{ Use the TUserInfo object named UI }
procedure TForm1.Button1Click(Sender: TObject);
begin
 UI := TUserInfo.create;
 ShowMessage('User Name:    ' + UI.UserName + #13 +
       'Company Name: ' + UI.CompanyName);
end;
```

The form's Button1Click procedure is still fairly simple. The values of the properties UserName and CompanyName are concatenated into the string that constitutes the message. Importantly, the values of these properties are the return values of their corresponding read methods, which are GetUserName and GetCompanyName, respectively. Since these methods are scoped as private, no one can use these functions except by reading from the corresponding properties.

Hiding the Complexity

The heart of TUserInfo's functionality is provided by the read methods GetUserName and GetCompanyName. The following is the code for these methods:

```
{ Fetch registered user name from Win95 Registry }
function TUserInfo.GetUserName : String;
begin
 Reg := TRegistry.Create;
 with Reg do begin
  RootKey := HKEY_LOCAL_MACHINE;
  if KeyExists(Win95RegInfo) then begin
   OpenKey(Win95RegInfo, False);
   Result := ReadString('RegisteredOwner');
   end;
  Free;
 end; { with }
end;

{ Fetch registered company name from Win95 Registry }
function TUserInfo.GetCompanyName : String;
begin
 Reg := TRegistry.Create;
 with Reg do begin
  RootKey := HKEY_LOCAL_MACHINE;
  if KeyExists(Win95RegInfo) then begin
   OpenKey(Win95RegInfo, False);
   Result := ReadString('RegisteredOrganization');
   end;
  Free;
 end; { with }
end
```

These two private functions define exactly how TUserInfo gets the information from the Registry. Both routines use the new Delphi 2 TRegistry class to create an object named Reg. Reg is declared as a variable of type TRegistry in the initial TUserInfo class declaration. Once again, the Reg object isn't instantiated in memory until one of these routines is called. Since each routine is responsible for constructing the Reg object, each routine is also responsible for destroying it as well. That is why each function calls the TRegistry class' Create and Free methods at the appropriate time. This process provides the resource management needed to prevent memory resource leaks.

Putting It All Together

Putting it all together, the complete code of this second example class is as follows. Changes from the previous example are in boldface type.

```
unit class2;
{ S A M P L E 2
  Expanding the sample class to include properties that
  control the reading of the User and Company Name info
}
interface

uses

 Windows, Messages, SysUtils, Classes, Graphics, Controls, Forms,
 Dialogs,StdCtrls, Registry;
         { Use the Registry unit to fetch User/Company Name }

type
 TUserInfo = class(TObject)
  Reg : TRegistry;
 private
  function GetUserName : String;
  function GetCompanyName : String;
 public
  property UserName : string read GetUserName;
  property CompanyName : string read GetCompanyName;
 end;

 TForm1 = class(TForm)
  Button1: TButton;
  procedure Button1Click(Sender: TObject);
 private
  { Private declarations }
 public
  { Public declarations }
 end;

const
```

```
 Win95RegInfo = 'SOFTWARE\Microsoft\Windows\CurrentVersion\';

var
 Form1: TForm1;
 UI : TUserInfo;

implementation

{$R *.DFM}

{ Use the TUserInfo object named UI }
procedure TForm1.Button1Click(Sender: TObject);
begin
 UI := TUserInfo.create;
 ShowMessage('User Name:    ' + UI.UserName + #13 +
       'Company Name: ' + UI.CompanyName);
end;

{ Functional definition of TUserInfo code starts here }

{ Fetch registered user name from Win95 Registry }
function TUserInfo.GetUserName : String;
begin
 Reg := TRegistry.Create;
 with Reg do begin
  RootKey := HKEY_LOCAL_MACHINE;
  if KeyExists(Win95RegInfo) then begin
   OpenKey(Win95RegInfo, False);
   Result := ReadString('RegisteredOwner');
   end;
  Free;
 end; { with }
end;

{ Fetch registered company name from Win95 Registry }
function TUserInfo.GetCompanyName : String;
begin
 Reg := TRegistry.Create;
 with Reg do begin
  RootKey := HKEY_LOCAL_MACHINE;
  if KeyExists(Win95RegInfo) then begin
   OpenKey(Win95RegInfo, False);
   Result := ReadString('RegisteredOrganization');
   end;
  Free;
 end; { with }
end;

end.
```

Updating an Object: Making an Object 16-bit and 32-bit Compatible

One of the strengths of OOP is that subsequent changes to a class definition can have little or no effect on the component user. In other words, applications that use the component may not require any changes, other than recompilation, if the components they use are updated.

The key to this strength is in the class' original design. If the component designer has produced a flexible interface of published methods and properties and properly hidden the implementation details, the component can usually be changed, even radically, without any ramifications for the applications that use it.

The TUserInfo component was designed so that the component user does not need to know anything about where the user-related information is stored. As the component producer, however, you know that TUserInfo relies on the Registry for this information. Unfortunately, such a reliance makes this class of little use to those running Windows 3.x. This is because user information is stored in the file USER.EXE, which exports this information in the same fashion as a DLL (Dynamic Link Library).

The next sections describe how a major overhaul of this component can be achieved without affecting the application code. Fortunately, this modification will permit a detailed discussion of the differences between applications built with Delphi 2 and those built with Delphi 1.0.

Using Compiler Directives

To be able to create source code that can be compiled into either 16- or 32 -bit source code, you need to determine first whether there are any differences between the way Windows 3.x and Windows 95/NT operate in the areas affected by your application. The registered user and company name are stored and fetched very differently between the two platforms. In this case, you can use compiler directives to mark which pieces of code need to be used for 16-bit and which are used for 32-bit operations. Use the {$IFDEF WIN32}{ELSE}{$ENDIF} directives to perform this marking. This technique is demonstrated in the next code listing.

Declaring a Dual-mode Class

The class declaration for TUserInfo needs to have the use of the TRegistry class conditionalized. This results in the following code:

```
type
 TUserInfo = class(TObject)
{$IFDEF WIN32}
  Reg : TRegistry;
{$ENDIF}
 private
  function GetUserName : String;
  function GetCompanyName : String;
 public
```

```
  property UserName : string read GetUserName;
  property CompanyName : string read GetCompanyName;
 end;
```

The heart of the changes to this unit take place in the functions that retrieve the values for the UserName and CompanyName properties. These changes are shown in the following code:

```
{ Functional definition of TUserInfo code starts here }

function TUserInfo.GetUserName : String;
var
  fileHandle: THandle;
  fileBuffer: Array [0..29] of Char;
begin
{$IFDEF WIN32}
{ Fetch registered user name from Win95 Registry }
 Reg := TRegistry.Create;
 with Reg do begin
  RootKey := HKEY_LOCAL_MACHINE;
  if KeyExists(Win95RegInfo) then begin
   OpenKey(Win95RegInfo, False);
   Result := ReadString('RegisteredOwner');
   end;
  Free;
 end; { with }
{$ELSE}
{ Fetch registered user name from USER.DLL }
 fileHandle := LoadLibrary('USER');
 if fileHandle >= HINSTANCE_ERROR then begin
   If LoadString(fileHandle, 514, @fileBuffer, 30) <> 0 Then
    Result := fileBuffer;
   FreeLibrary(fileHandle);
 end;
{$ENDIF}
end;

function TUserInfo.GetCompanyName : String;
var
  fileHandle: THandle;
  fileBuffer: Array [0..29] of Char;
begin
{$IFDEF WIN32}
{ Fetch registered company name from Win95 Registry }
 Reg := TRegistry.Create;
 with Reg do begin
  RootKey := HKEY_LOCAL_MACHINE;
  if KeyExists(Win95RegInfo) then begin
```

```
      OpenKey(Win95RegInfo, False);
      Result := ReadString('RegisteredOrganization');
      end;
    Free;
  end; { with }
{$ELSE}
{ Fetch registered company name from USER.DLL }
 fileHandle := LoadLibrary('USER');
 if fileHandle >= HINSTANCE_ERROR then begin
   If LoadString(fileHandle, 515, @fileBuffer, 30) <> 0 Then
    Result := fileBuffer;
   FreeLibrary(fileHandle);
 end;
{$ENDIF}
end;
```

These changes instruct Delphi to retrieve the user information from the Registry if the application is compiled from Window 95 or Windows NT (in which case the resulting application will be a 32-bit application), and from a string resource if the application was compiled in Delphi 1.0 (resulting in a 16-bit application).

How Class Changes Affect the Rest of the Application

The code that performs the core of the functionality can be quite different, as you have seen from the preceding modifications. But how do these modifications affect the users of this TUserInfo class? Take a look at the Button1Click procedure for this dual 16/32-bit class:

```
{ Use the TUserInfo object named UI }
procedure TForm1.Button1Click(Sender: TObject);
begin
 UI := TUserInfo.create;
 ShowMessage('User Name:    '+UI.UserName+#13+
       'Company Name: '+UI.CompanyName);
end;
```

This code is exactly the same as before. That is one of the chief advantages of OOP—it permits you to use encapsulation, data hiding, and access control to simplify application maintenance. You are able to perform radical changes to the internals of the TUserInfo class without affecting the rest of the application's code.

Granted, this is a very simple example, yet hiding the underlying complexity of a class is exactly what makes OOP so productive. The class users merely access properties and public procedures/functions without worrying about how the underlying operations are performed. The result is greatly increased developer productivity.

Following is the entire code for this third example application. New changes to the code are shown in bold:

```
unit class3;
{ S A M P L E 3
  Expanding the sample class to include both 16-bit
  and 32-bit Windows support for reading of the
  User and Company Name info}

interface

{$IFDEF WIN32}
uses
 Windows, Messages, SysUtils, Classes, Graphics, Controls, Forms,
 Dialogs,StdCtrls, Registry;
        { Use the Registry unit to fetch User/Company Name }
{$ELSE}
uses
 WinTypes, WinProcs, Messages, SysUtils, Classes, Graphics, Controls,
 Forms, Dialogs, StdCtrls;
{$ENDIF}

type
 TUserInfo = class(TObject)
{$IFDEF WIN32}
  Reg : TRegistry;
{$ENDIF}
 private
  function GetUserName : String;
  function GetCompanyName : String;
 public
  property UserName : string read GetUserName;
  property CompanyName : string read GetCompanyName;
 end;

 TForm1 = class(TForm)
  Button1: TButton;
  procedure Button1Click(Sender: TObject);
 private
  { Private declarations }
 public
  { Public declarations }
 end;

const
 Win95RegInfo = 'SOFTWARE\Microsoft\Windows\CurrentVersion\';

var
 Form1: TForm1;
```

```
 UI : TUserInfo;

implementation

{$R *.DFM}

{ Use the TUserInfo object named UI }
procedure TForm1.Button1Click(Sender: TObject);
begin
 UI := TUserInfo.create;
 ShowMessage('User Name:     '+UI.UserName+#13+
       'Company Name: '+UI.CompanyName);
end;

{ Functional definition of TUserInfo code starts here }

function TUserInfo.GetUserName : String;
var
  fileHandle: THandle;
  fileBuffer: Array [0..29] of Char;
begin
{$IFDEF WIN32}
{ Fetch registered user name from Win95 Registry }
 Reg := TRegistry.Create;
 with Reg do begin
  RootKey := HKEY_LOCAL_MACHINE;
  if KeyExists(Win95RegInfo) then begin
   OpenKey(Win95RegInfo, False);
   Result := ReadString('RegisteredOwner');
   end;
  Free;
 end; { with }
{$ELSE}
{ Fetch registered user name from USER.DLL }
 fileHandle := LoadLibrary('USER');
 if fileHandle >= HINSTANCE_ERROR then begin
   If LoadString(fileHandle, 514, @fileBuffer, 30) <> 0 Then
    Result := fileBuffer;
   FreeLibrary(fileHandle);
 end;
{$ENDIF}
end;

function TUserInfo.GetCompanyName : String;
var
  fileHandle: THandle;
  fileBuffer: Array [0..29] of Char;
begin
{$IFDEF WIN32}
```

```
{ Fetch registered company name from Win95 Registry }
 Reg := TRegistry.Create;
 with Reg do begin
  RootKey := HKEY_LOCAL_MACHINE;
  if KeyExists(Win95RegInfo) then begin
   OpenKey(Win95RegInfo, False);
   Result := ReadString('RegisteredOrganization');
   end;
  Free;
 end; { with }
{$ELSE}
{ Fetch registered company name from USER.DLL }
 fileHandle := LoadLibrary('USER');
 if fileHandle >= HINSTANCE_ERROR then begin
   If LoadString(fileHandle, 515, @fileBuffer, 30) <> 0 Then
    Result := fileBuffer;
   FreeLibrary(fileHandle);
 end;
{$ENDIF}
end;

end.
```

Exceptions: Optimistic Error Handling

Well, so far, so good—unless you try to run the 32-bit version under Windows NT! The Registry Key for the user and company name information is different under Windows NT (in the directory SOFTWARE\Microsoft\WindowsNT\CurrentVersion\) than it is under Windows 95 (SOFTWARE\Microsoft\Windows\CurrentVersion\). The TUserInfo class has no error handling for this problem, so the SAMPLE3 application will crash—sort of. (If you are running Windows 95 and want to see what happens, just change the value of the Win95RegInfo constant to the Windows NT value and re-run the application.)

When this type of error occurs, Delphi generates a generic exception, and then traps it with its built-in exception handler, if it is not otherwise handled by the object user. When creating your own objects, it is often desirable to define custom exceptions. This permits the object user to more effectively handle the exception.

Declaring a Custom Exception

The first step toward adding custom exception handling is to declare a custom exception. This is demonstrated in the TUserInfo class as follows:

```
Type
 ERegInfoNotFound = class(Exception);
```

Delphi implements your custom exceptions as a child class of the generic Exception class included in Delphi. This works in much the same way that TUserInfo is a child of the TObject class.

Raising a Custom Exception

Just as with TUserInfo, the mere declaration of the ERegInfoNotFound class does not create the exception object in memory. Delphi's optimistic error handling assumes that all is running normally most of the time. The only time you need to create ERegInfoNotFound is when you come across an actual runtime error.

With regular classes, you instantiate an object of that class by calling the class' Create method. Exceptions are used slightly differently. You don't just create an exception object. You create it and then "raise" it, thereby triggering Delphi's exception handling routines. Raising the ERegInfoNotFound exception in the GetUserName function might look something like this:

```
function TUserInfo.GetUserName : String;
var
  fileHandle: THandle;
  fileBuffer: Array [0..29] of Char;
begin
{$IFDEF WIN32}
{ Fetch registered user name from Win95 Registry }
 Reg := TRegistry.Create;
 with Reg do begin
  RootKey := HKEY_LOCAL_MACHINE;
  if KeyExists(Win95RegInfo) then begin
   OpenKey(Win95RegInfo, False);
   Result := ReadString('RegisteredOwner');
   end
  else

   raise ERegInfoNotFound.Create('Could not locate
                                  registered user name');
  Free;
 end; { with }
{$ELSE}
{ Fetch registered user name from USER.DLL }
 fileHandle := LoadLibrary('USER');
 if fileHandle >= HINSTANCE_ERROR then begin
   If LoadString(fileHandle, 514, @fileBuffer, 30) <> 0 Then
    Result := fileBuffer;
   FreeLibrary(fileHandle);
   end
 else

   raise ERegInfoNotFound.Create('Could not locate
                                  registered user name');
{$ENDIF}
end;
```

The GetCompanyName function would include similar changes.

Handling the Exception

Once raised, the ERegInfoNotFound exception will bubble up through each level in the call stack of your application, looking for an exception handler routine. Once an exception handler is found, that handler checks the type of exception, sort of like a case statement. If the exception handler is designed to recognize an ERegInfoNotFound error, the exception processing stops there. (Unless the exception handler re-raises this or some other exception. Delphi exception handlers can be nested within each other.)

If the user of the TUserInfo class does nothing to trap the exception, it will continue to bubble up until it reaches the top of the Delphi call stack. At this point, the exception will be caught by the application-level exception handler that wraps around every Delphi application you build. In the case of the ERegInfoNotFound exception, the system will display a message box with the text of the exception's message shown inside.

The user of the object can also choose to handle the ERegInfoNotFound exception. This can be done by wrapping a try-except block around operations that work with the object. For example, the following code demonstrates how references to the UserName and UserCompany properties of the UserInfo object can be enclosed in an exception handler:

```
{ Use the TUserInfo object named UI }
procedure TForm1.Button1Click(Sender: TObject);
begin
 try
  UI := TUserInfo.create;
  ShowMessage('User Name:    '+UI.UserName+#13+
        'Company Name: '+UI.CompanyName);
 except
  on ERegInfoNotFound do
    ShowMessage(' An error was detected when' + #13 +
          'trying to fetch registration info.');
 end;
end;
```

TIP: *If you want to see the difference between what just raising the ERegInfoNotFound exception does and what this try-except block does, comment out the try keyword plus everything from the except to the first end, and run the application. Then restore the commented code and re-run the application.*

You could also nest this try-except block within a try-finally block. The finally portion will always execute, regardless of whether any errors occur in the try section. A finally block is especially useful for resource management. For example, even if you receive an ERegInfoNotFound exception, you'll still want to free up the TUserInfo object named UI. Thus you might change the code to create a try-finally wrapper around the try-except construct you had before.

```
{ Use the TUserInfo object named UI }
procedure TForm1.Button1Click(Sender: TObject);
begin
 try
  try
   UI := TUserInfo.create;
   ShowMessage('User Name:    '+UI.UserName+#13+
         'Company Name: '+UI.CompanyName);
  except
   on ERegInfoNotFound do
     ShowMessage(' An error was detected when' + #13 +
          'trying to fetch registration info.');
  end;
 finally
  UI.Free;
 end;
end;
```

The Final Class View

Following is the complete class definition that supports dual 16-/32-bit use along with custom exception handling. Changes from the previous version of this code are once again in bold.

```
unit class4;
{ S A M P L E 4
  Expanding the sample class to add structured
  Exception Handling within the form to trap
  and handle a runtime error.}

interface

{$IFDEF WIN32}
uses
Windows, Messages, SysUtils, Classes, Graphics, Controls, Forms,
 Dialogs,StdCtrls, Registry;
         { Use the Registry unit to fetch User/Company Name }
{$ELSE}
uses
 WinTypes, WinProcs, Messages, SysUtils, Classes, Graphics, Controls,
 Forms, Dialogs, StdCtrls;
{$ENDIF}

type
 ERegInfoNotFound = class(Exception);

 TUserInfo = class(TObject)
{$IFDEF WIN32}
```

```
    Reg : TRegistry;
  {$ENDIF}
   private
    function GetUserName : String;
    function GetCompanyName : String;
   public
    property UserName : string read GetUserName;
    property CompanyName : string read GetCompanyName;
   end;

   TForm1 = class(TForm)
    Button1: TButton;
    procedure Button1Click(Sender: TObject);
   private
    { Private declarations }
   public
    { Public declarations }
   end;

const
  Win95RegInfo = 'SOFTWARE\Microsoft\Windows\CurrentVersion\';

var
  Form1: TForm1;
  UI : TUserInfo;

implementation

{$R *.DFM}

{ Use the TUserInfo object named UI }
procedure TForm1.Button1Click(Sender: TObject);
begin
 try
  try
   UI := TUserInfo.create;
   ShowMessage('User Name:    '+UI.UserName+#13+
          'Company Name: '+UI.CompanyName);
  except
   on ERegInfoNotFound do
     ShowMessage(' An error was detected when' + #13 +
           'trying to fetch registration info.');
  end;
 finally
  UI.Free;
 end;
end;

{ Functional definition of TUserInfo code starts here }
```

```
function TUserInfo.GetUserName : String;
var
  fileHandle: THandle;
  fileBuffer: Array [0..29] of Char;
begin
{$IFDEF WIN32}
{ Fetch registered user name from Win95 Registry }
 Reg := TRegistry.Create;
 with Reg do begin
  RootKey := HKEY_LOCAL_MACHINE;
  if KeyExists(Win95RegInfo) then begin
   OpenKey(Win95RegInfo, False);
   Result := ReadString('RegisteredOwner');
   end
  else
   raise ERegInfoNotFound.Create('Could not locate '+
                              'registered user name');
  Free;
 end; { with }
{$ELSE}
{ Fetch registered user name from USER.DLL }
 fileHandle := LoadLibrary('USER');
 if fileHandle >= HINSTANCE_ERROR then begin
   If LoadString(fileHandle, 514, @fileBuffer, 30) <> 0 Then
    Result := fileBuffer;
   FreeLibrary(fileHandle);
   end
 else
   raise ERegInfoNotFound.Create('Could not locate '+
                              'registered user name');
{$ENDIF}
end;

function TUserInfo.GetCompanyName : String;
var
  fileHandle: THandle;
  fileBuffer: Array [0..29] of Char;
begin
{$IFDEF WIN32}
{ Fetch registered company name from Win95 Registry }
 Reg := TRegistry.Create;
 with Reg do begin
  RootKey := HKEY_LOCAL_MACHINE;
  if KeyExists(Win95RegInfo) then begin
   OpenKey(Win95RegInfo, False);
   Result := ReadString('RegisteredOrganization');
   end
  else
   raise ERegInfoNotFound.Create('Could not locate '+
```

```
                                        'registered company name');
  Free;
 end; { with }
{$ELSE}
{ Fetch registered company name from USER.DLL }
 fileHandle := LoadLibrary('USER');
 if fileHandle >= HINSTANCE_ERROR then begin
   If LoadString(fileHandle, 515, @fileBuffer, 30) <> 0 Then
    Result := fileBuffer;
   FreeLibrary(fileHandle);
   end
 else
   raise ERegInfoNotFound.Create('Could not locate '+
                                        'registered company name');

{$ENDIF}
end;

end.
```

Using Objects in Delphi

So far, you have seen how to create an object in Delphi. Up to this point, however, little has been said about how these objects are used in Delphi. As you will see, this is where Delphi really shines. Delphi makes it very easy to reuse objects.

In short, Delphi provides you with two basic mechanisms for reusing objects—the VCL and the Object Repository. The VCL is what immediately comes to mind for most developers when the issue of inheritance comes up. Any object that you define with a type declaration, as well as any component you add to the component palette, is part of the VCL.

The Object Repository offers an additional source of inheritance in Delphi 2. The inheritance supported by the Object Repository is based on the VCL but is accessed visually, making this type of inheritance very different from inheritance that uses VCL objects. Furthermore, the inheritance supported by the Object Repository is based on the concept of containers. Delphi 2 supplies two types of containers: visual and non-visual. Forms are visual containers, while data modules are non-visual containers.

This section begins with an introduction to inheritance based on the VCL, followed by the more special case of components that are placed on the component palette. Then, inheritance based on containers is discussed.

NOTE: *Although the Object Repository is a Delphi 2 feature, Delphi 1.0 provides a feature similar to the Object Repository in the form of templates in the Gallery.*

Using VCL Objects

The VCL defines the overall object hierarchy in Delphi. Every object declared in a type declaration is part of the VCL. However, as far as object usability is concerned, the VCL itself can be further divided into two groups: objects and components. The group of objects encompasses every object in the VCL. Components are a subset of objects. To be specific, a component is any object that descends from TComponent. The primary distinction here is that components can be placed onto the component palette, whereas non-component objects cannot.

The following section discusses how to use objects in general. This section is followed by a discussion of an alternative way of using components.

Using a VCL Object

You use a VCL object by declaring it in the interface section of a unit, and then adding this unit to the uses clause of another unit. Using this general technique, any unit can use any defined object.

To demonstrate this technique, the CLASS4.PAS unit that has been developed throughout this chapter will be used. However, this unit began as the unit for a form. The TUserInfo class does not require this form. Consequently, reference to the form, as well as the form's resource ({$R *.DFM}) must be removed. The following is the code for the CLASS5.PAS unit. The sole purpose of this unit is to define the TUserInfo object.

```
unit class5;
{ S A M P L E 5
  The complete definition of the TUserInfo
  object. This object can be used by any unit
  that includes this unit in its uses clause.}

interface

{$IFDEF WIN32}
uses
Windows, Messages, SysUtils, Classes, Graphics, Controls, Forms,
 Dialogs,StdCtrls, Registry;
         { Use the Registry unit to fetch User/Company Name }
{$ELSE}
uses
 WinTypes, WinProcs, Messages, SysUtils, Classes, Graphics, Controls,
 Forms, Dialogs, StdCtrls;
{$ENDIF}

type
 ERegInfoNotFound = class(Exception);

 TUserInfo = class(TObject)
{$IFDEF WIN32}
  Reg : TRegistry;
```

```
{$ENDIF}
 private
  function GetUserName : String;
  function GetCompanyName : String;
 public
  property UserName : string read GetUserName;
  property CompanyName : string read GetCompanyName;
 end;

const
 Win95RegInfo = 'SOFTWARE\Microsoft\Windows\CurrentVersion\';

implementation

{ Functional definition of TUserInfo code starts here }
function TUserInfo.GetUserName : String;
var
  fileHandle: THandle;
  fileBuffer: Array [0..29] of Char;
begin
{$IFDEF WIN32}
{ Fetch registered user name from Win95 Registry }
 Reg := TRegistry.Create;
 with Reg do begin
  RootKey := HKEY_LOCAL_MACHINE;
  if KeyExists(Win95RegInfo) then begin
   OpenKey(Win95RegInfo, False);
   Result := ReadString('RegisteredOwner');
   end
  else
   raise ERegInfoNotFound.Create('Could not locate ' +
                                 'registered user name');
  Free;
 end; { with }
{$ELSE}
{ Fetch registered user name from USER.DLL }
 fileHandle := LoadLibrary('USER');
 if fileHandle >= HINSTANCE_ERROR then begin
   If LoadString(fileHandle, 514, @fileBuffer, 30) <> 0 Then
    Result := fileBuffer;
   FreeLibrary(fileHandle);
   end
 else
   raise ERegInfoNotFound.Create('Could not locate '+
                                 'registered user name');
{$ENDIF}
end;

function TUserInfo.GetCompanyName : String;
```

```
var
  fileHandle: THandle;
  fileBuffer: Array [0..29] of Char;
begin
{$IFDEF WIN32}
{ Fetch registered company name from Win95 Registry }
 Reg := TRegistry.Create;
 with Reg do begin
  RootKey := HKEY_LOCAL_MACHINE;
  if KeyExists(Win95RegInfo) then begin
   OpenKey(Win95RegInfo, False);
   Result := ReadString('RegisteredOrganization');
   end
  else
   raise ERegInfoNotFound.Create('Could not locate '+
                                 'registered company name');
  Free;
 end; { with }
{$ELSE}
{ Fetch registered company name from USER.DLL }
 fileHandle := LoadLibrary('USER');
 if fileHandle >= HINSTANCE_ERROR then begin
   If LoadString(fileHandle, 515, @fileBuffer, 30) <> 0 Then
    Result := fileBuffer;
   FreeLibrary(fileHandle);
   end
 else
   raise ERegInfoNotFound.Create('Could not locate ' +
                                 'registered company name');
{$ENDIF}
end;

end.
```

Note that this unit declares two objects, the TUserInfo object as well as the exception object that it raises if a problem is encountered. It also declares the constant Win95RegInfo, which it uses to define the default location in the Registry for user information under Windows 95. This unit declares everything another unit needs if it wants to create an instance of the TUserInfo object.

Now that the CLASS5.PAS unit is defined, you are ready to use the TUserInfo class that it declares. To do so, add the CLASS5.PAS unit to the uses clause of any unit that needs it. For example, imagine that you have created a new application and want to be able to display user information when the user clicks on a button. The SHOWUI project does just this. It consists of a single form that includes a single button. This form is shown here:

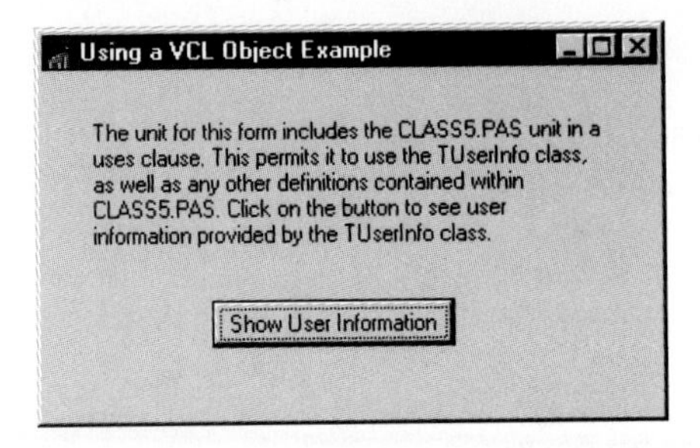

The following is the code for the SHOWUI.DPR project:

```
program showui;

uses
  Forms,
  showuiu in 'showuiu.pas' {Form1};

{$R *.RES}

begin
  Application.CreateForm(TForm1, Form1);
  Application.Run;
end.
```

The next code listing is the main form unit, SHOWUIU.PAS:

```
unit showuiu;

interface

uses
  WinProcs, WinTypes, Messages, SysUtils, Classes, Graphics, Controls,
  Forms, Dialogs, StdCtrls;

type
  TForm1 = class(TForm)
    Button1: TButton;
    procedure Button1Click(Sender: TObject);
  private
    { Private declarations }
  public
    { Public declarations }
  end;

var
  Form1: TForm1;

implementation
```

```
{$R *.DFM}

uses
  class5;

var
  UI: TUserInfo;

{ Use the TUserInfo object named UI }
procedure TForm1.Button1Click(Sender: TObject);
begin
 try
  try
   UI := TUserInfo.create;
   ShowMessage('User Name:     '+UI.UserName+#13+
         'Company Name: '+UI.CompanyName);
  except
   on ERegInfoNotFound do
     ShowMessage(' An error was detected when' + #13 +
          'trying to fetch registration info.');
  end;
 finally
  UI.Free;
 end;
end;

end.
```

For this unit to be able to create a UserInfo object, a uses clause is added to the implementation section of this unit, as well as a var declaration. A reference to Class5 is entered into this uses clause, and then a variable, UI, is declared of the type TUserInfo in the var statement. Within the button's OnClick event handler, the UI variable is used to instantiate a UserInfo object, which is then used. Once the UserInfo object is no longer needed, it is freed using the Free method. The following dialog box contains the UserName and UserCompany information returned by the UserInfo object of the TUserInfo class.

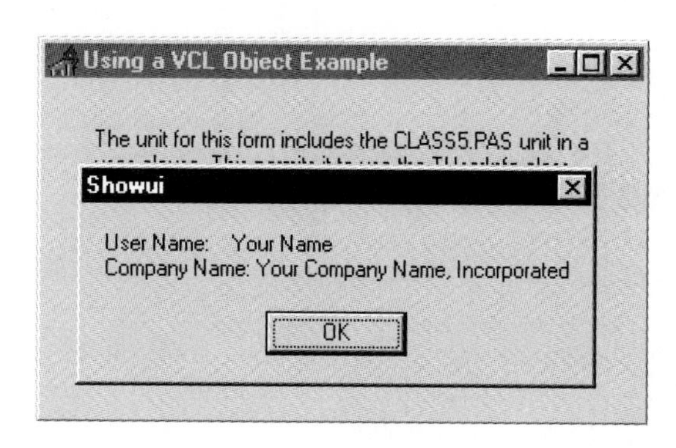

NOTE: The Class5 unit was added to a uses clause in the implementation section of the SHOWUIU.PAS unit. The Class5 unit could have been added to the interface uses clause instead, but this was not done here since only those elements in the implementation section of this unit need to reference the TUserInfo class. If an object, variable, or constant being declared in the interface section of SHOWUIU.PAS needed to use the TUserInfo definition, or any other definition that is part of CLASS5.PAS, Class5 would have been added to the uses clause in the interface section.

There are several important points to note about this technique. First, it can be used with any type definition, even with a TComponent descendant. Second, a single unit, such as CLASS5.PAS, can include many type definitions. Adding such a unit to the uses clause of another unit makes all of those type definitions available to the using unit. Finally, once you have added a unit to a project and compiled that project, the objects declared in the added unit become part of the VCL hierarchy depicted using the Object Browser. This is shown in Figure 3-10, in which the TUserInfo class appears in the Object Browser for the SHOWUI project.

Using VCL Components

As mentioned earlier, a component is any object whose ancestor (not necessarily whose parent) is a TComponent. The primary advantage of TComponent descendants is that they can be placed onto the component palette.

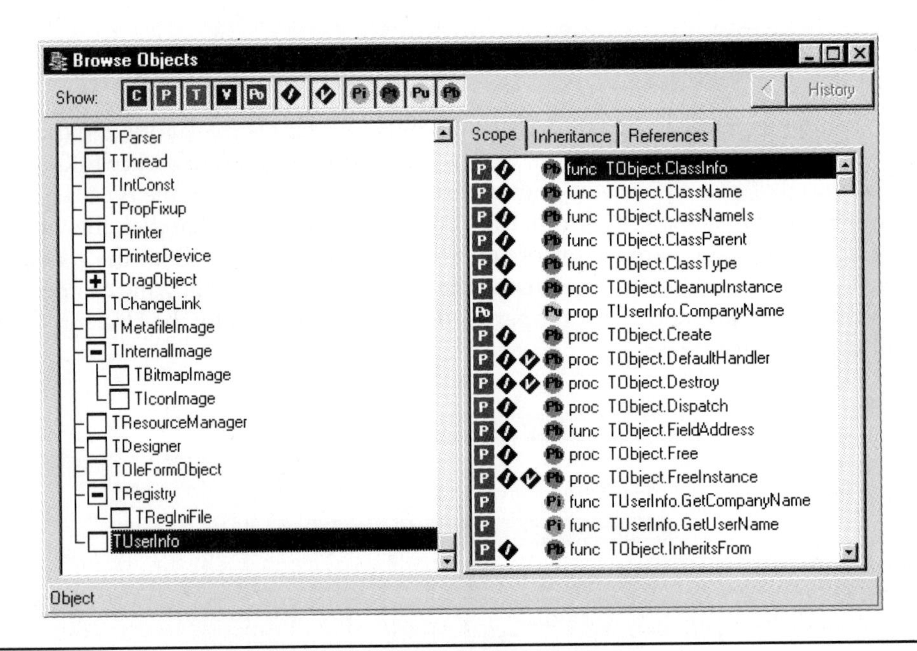

Figure 3-10. *The Object Browser shows that by adding a unit to a project, the objects declared in that unit become part of the VCL hierarchy*

You gain two major benefits by making a component available on the component palette. First, the component can be added to a form visually by clicking first on the component in the component palette and then on the form. Although it is not terribly difficult to add a unit to a uses clause, it is even easier to click on a form.

Second, the component can be manipulated at design time. In contrast, the technique for creating a VCL object (demonstrated in the preceding section) was limited to creating the object at runtime. As you learned in Chapter 2, sometimes the design-time manipulation of an object's properties make it unnecessary to perform any additional operations on the object at runtime. And because design-time manipulation of properties tends to be more visual, it is often much easier.

Adding a component to the component palette, although not that difficult, requires a number of steps. These include:

- Defining the object as a component
- Optionally overriding inherited methods
- Optionally redeclaring inherited properties
- Optionally defining new methods
- Optionally defining new properties
- Optionally implementing property access methods
- Optionally creating a component icon
- Optionally creating a help file for the component
- Creating a registration procedure
- Adding the component to the VCL

These steps include many facets, and most of these are covered in detail in the Delphi documentation, so they are not repeated here. The first step, however, deserves additional mention.

To add an object to the component palette, it must be a descendant of the TComponent class. This is achieved by changing the type declaration of TUserInfo from

```
TUserInfo = class(TObject)
```

to

```
TUserInfo = class(TComponent)
```

That's all it takes. Actually, it was not necessary to descend TUserInfo from TComponent itself. You could have descended it from one of the many other TComponent descendants, such as TPanel. Your selection of the component from which you descend TUserInfo depends on the types of properties and methods you want TUserInfo to inherit.

However, it is appropriate to point out here that not all objects lend themselves to being descended from TComponent. For example, if you want to inherit most or all of the functionality of the TRegistry object, your object cannot descend from TComponent (since TRegistry does not descend from TComponent). Consequently, not all objects that you create can be placed on the component palette.

The update of a VCL object to a component is demonstrated in the unit USRINFO.PAS. This unit, which was created from the CLASS5.PAS unit, includes the TUserInfo class redefined as a component, the addition of a published property that can be modified at design time, an overridden constructor, and a write access method for the published property. The following code is the USRINFO.PAS unit. The lines that have been added or modified appear in bold.

```
unit UsrInfo;

interface

{$IFDEF WIN32}
uses
 Windows, Messages, SysUtils, Classes, Graphics, Controls, Forms,
 Dialogs, StdCtrls, Registry; { Use the
                   Registry unit to fetch User/Company Name }
{$ELSE}
uses
 WinTypes, WinProcs, Messages, SysUtils, Classes, Graphics, Controls,
 Forms, Dialogs, StdCtrls;
{$ENDIF}

type
 ERegInfoNotFound = class(Exception);

 TUserInfo = class(TComponent)
{$IFDEF WIN32}
  Reg : TRegistry;
{$ENDIF}
 private
  { Private declarations }
  FPgmUser : String;
  function GetUserName : String;
  function GetCompanyName : String;
  procedure SetPgmUser(Value : String);
 protected
  { Protected declarations }
 public
  { Public declarations }
  property UserName : string read GetUserName;
  property CompanyName : string read GetCompanyName;
  constructor Create(AOwner: TComponent); override;
 published
```

```
  { Published declarations }
  property PgmUser : string read FPgmUser write SetPgmUser;
 end;

const
 Win95RegInfo = 'SOFTWARE\Microsoft\Windows\CurrentVersion\';

procedure Register;

implementation

{ Functional definition of TUserInfo code starts here }

constructor TUserInfo.Create(AOwner: TComponent);
begin
 inherited Create(AOwner);
 FPgmUser := GetUserName; {Set the default to be the registerd user}
end;

function TUserInfo.GetUserName : String;
{$IFNDEF WIN32}  {Avoid compiler warnings if not in Win16}
var
  fileHandle: THandle;
  fileBuffer: Array [0..29] of Char;
{$ENDIF}
begin
{$IFDEF WIN32}
{ Fetch registered user name from Win95 Registry }
 Reg := TRegistry.Create;
 with Reg do begin
  RootKey := HKEY_LOCAL_MACHINE;
  if KeyExists(Win95RegInfo) then begin
   OpenKey(Win95RegInfo, False);
   Result := ReadString('RegisteredOwner');
   end
  else
   raise ERegInfoNotFound.Create('Could not locate '+
                                 'registered user name');
  Free;
 end; { with }
{$ELSE}
{ Fetch registered user name from USER.DLL }
 fileHandle := LoadLibrary('USER');
 if fileHandle >= HINSTANCE_ERROR then begin
   If LoadString(fileHandle, 514, @fileBuffer, 30) <> 0 Then
    Result := fileBuffer;
   FreeLibrary(fileHandle);
   end
 else
```

```
    raise ERegInfoNotFound.Create('Could not locate '+
                                 'registered user name');
{$ENDIF}
end;

function TUserInfo.GetCompanyName : String;
{$IFNDEF WIN32}  {Avoid compiler warnings if not in Win16}
var
  fileHandle: THandle;
  fileBuffer: Array [0..29] of Char;
{$ENDIF}
begin
{$IFDEF WIN32}
{ Fetch registered company name from Win95 Registry }
 Reg := TRegistry.Create;
 with Reg do begin
  RootKey := HKEY_LOCAL_MACHINE;
  if KeyExists(Win95RegInfo) then begin
   OpenKey(Win95RegInfo, False);
   Result := ReadString('RegisteredOrganization');
   end
  else
   raise ERegInfoNotFound.Create('Could not locate '+
                                 'registered company name');
  Free;
 end; { with }
{$ELSE}
{ Fetch registered company name from USER.DLL }
 fileHandle := LoadLibrary('USER');
 if fileHandle >= HINSTANCE_ERROR then begin
   If LoadString(fileHandle, 515, @fileBuffer, 30) <> 0 Then
    Result := fileBuffer;
   FreeLibrary(fileHandle);
   end
 else
   raise ERegInfoNotFound.Create('Could not locate '+
                                 'registered company name');
{$ENDIF}
end;

procedure TUserInfo.SetPgmUser(Value : String);
begin
 if FPgmUser <> Value then
   if (Value = '') or
    not (csDesigning in ComponentState) then
    FPgmUser := Value
   else
    if Value <> GetUserName then
      if MessageDlg('"'+Value + '" does not match '+
```

```
                    'registered user name.'+#13+
              'Do you want to use "'+Value+'" anyway?',
              mtConfirmation, [mbYes, mbNo], 0) = mrYes then
       FPgmUser := Value;
end;

procedure Register;
begin
 RegisterComponents('Demos', [TUserInfo]);
end;

end.
```

Once you have completed the unit, you install it into the component palette. See the Component Writer's Guide that comes with Delphi (Appendix A also has steps for adding a component) for more information.

Using the New Component

Once your component is installed, it will appear in the VCL Palette tab that corresponds to the tab name you designated in the RegisterComponents functions. Figure 3-11 shows how the TUserInfo component you just installed should appear in Delphi.

Notice that the view of the Object Inspector in Figure 3-11 shows three properties including the PgmUser property you defined explicitly in TUserInfo. The other two published properties, Name and Tag, were inherited from the TComponent class. You

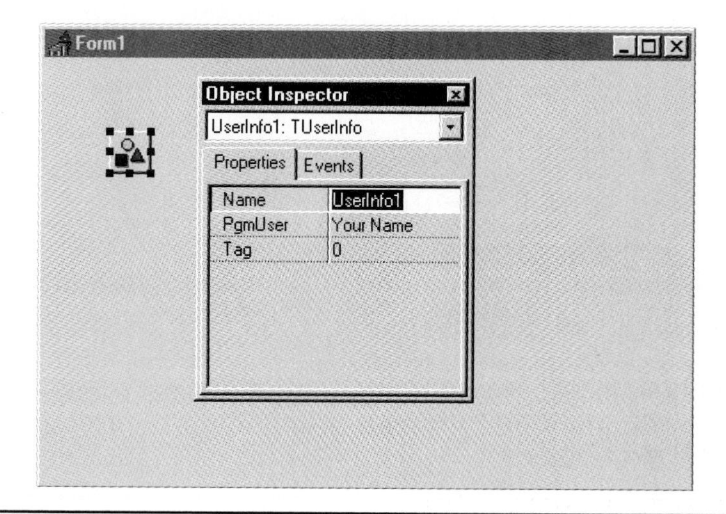

Figure 3-11. *The TUserInfo component installed and in use*

can also see that the PgmUser name is set automatically to your Windows registered user name as soon as you drop a TUserInfo component onto a form. If you make a change to PgmUser in the Object Inspector, the message box shown in Figure 3-12 appears in design mode.

Using Containers

A *container* is an object that can hold other objects inside itself. Delphi supports two types of containers: visual containers and non-visual containers.

Visual Containers

Forms and dialog boxes are visual containers. Your application's user interface will consist of a collection of these visual containers, each one containing a variety of UI-related (user-interface related) VCL components. These containers will also be the place where your UI processing logic will reside.

While VCL components are installed into your VCL Palette, you will install any reusable visual containers into Delphi's Object Repository, shown in Figure 3-13. The Object Repository is a Delphi 2 feature, but Delphi 1.0 has something similar, the Gallery. Both the Object Repository and the Gallery permit you to add new containers to them, as well as copy objects out of them. As with the DOS copy command, no tie exists between the copy and the original when you perform a copy operation.

In addition, the Object Repository in Delphi 2 provides the ability to inherit any of the containers stored there. Thus, you can choose whether to maintain a tie back to the original container. This tie is generally referred to as *visual form inheritance*. It is called visual because you can have the parent and child forms open in the IDE, make changes

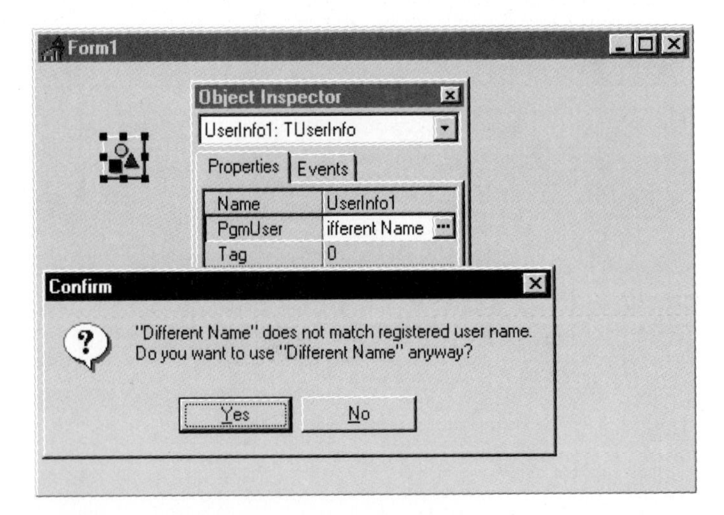

Figure 3-12. *Design-time Property Editor message*

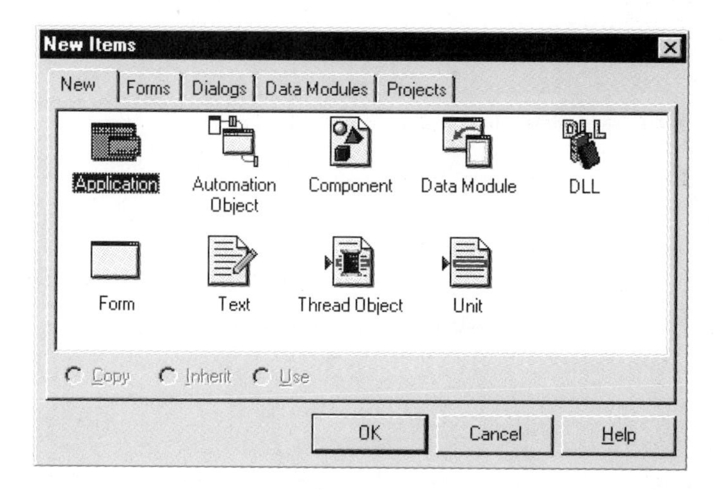

Figure 3-13. *The Delphi 2 Object Repository*

to the parent form and actually *see the changes* get inherited by the child form as you make the changes.

If you choose to use inheritance instead of a copy, any changes made to the container in the Object Repository will be reflected automatically in all projects that inherit that container. All you need to do is to recompile the project.

NOTE: Delphi 1 does not provide for visual form inheritance through the Gallery. It is possible, however, to use form inheritance in Delphi 1.0. This is achieved through the techniques described in the section "Using VCL Objects." The difference is that the object type you declare will be a TForm descendant and will include one or more additional components within itself.

Non-Visual Containers (Delphi 2 only)

New to Delphi 2 is the concept of the non-visual container. This concept is implemented in the form of *data modules.* Data modules are a special kind of non-visual form designed as a holding place for all your application's non-UI related items. Primary in the function of data modules is the storage of all the data connectivity components used by your application. Data modules provide the means to separate your data schema and business rule information in their own containers. This data isolation allows you to build reusable data-centric containers and then apply them to a variety of user interfaces. Creating and using data modules is discussed in Chapter 8.

Reusing Containers

There are two basic ways to reuse containers. Which technique you use depends on whether you want to reuse the container within a single application or across applications.

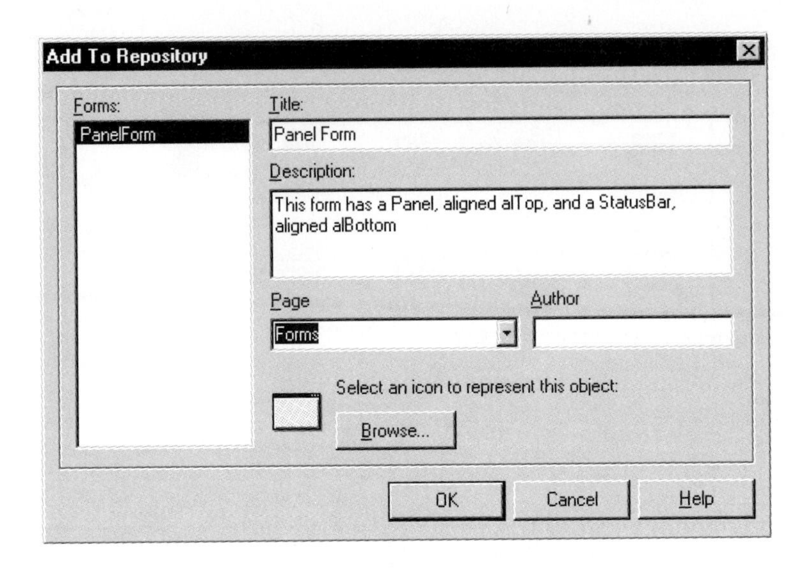

Figure 3-14. *Adding a container to the Object Repository*

To reuse a container across an application you add it to the Object Repository. To add a container to the Object Repository, select the form, dialog box, or data module and then right-click on it. When you select the Add to Repository SpeedMenu item, the screen shown in Figure 3-14 appears.

This screen allows you to name the class of object you are adding to the Object Repository, give a short description of its function, determine the page on which it will reside in the Object Repository, and even select a custom icon to display in the Object Repository. Once you have saved your new container class, everyone using that Object Repository can reuse your container.

In order to inherit the container, however, you must specifically select the Inherit radio button before selecting the container from the Object Repository. This button appears on every page of the Object Repository that permits inheritance. Once you have selected Inherit and then selected the object you want to inherit, a new container (form or data module) is created, and the name of the unit in which the container is defined is added to the uses clause of the new container's unit. The new container's type declaration will not be based on TForm. Instead, it will be based on the name of the container class defined in the unit in which this container is defined.

For example, image that you create a form that defines the basic look of all the forms you want to use in your application. This form, named PanelForm, contains a Panel component aligned to alTop and a StatusBar component aligned to alBottom. Furthermore, you have saved this form unit using the name PANFORM.PAS and then added the form to the Forms page of the Object Repository. If you inherit from this form, the new unit created from this inherited form will look like the following:

```
unit Unit2;

interface

uses
  Windows, Messages, SysUtils, Classes, Graphics, Controls, Forms,
  Dialogs, PANFORM, ExtCtrls, ComCtrls;

type
  TPanelForm2 = class(TPanelForm)
  private
    { Private declarations }
  public
    { Public declarations }
  end;

var
  PanelForm2: TPanelForm2;

implementation

{$R *.DFM}

end.
```

Notice that PANFORM.PAS was added to the uses clause, and the new form is descended from TPanelForm.

If you only need to reuse a container within an application, you do not need to do anything special—the container is already in the Object Repository. When a project is open, the Object Repository contains an additional page. This page has the same name as the project, and every container defined for that project appears on that page. Since all containers defined for a project automatically appear on this page, you can inherit from them easily. Figure 3-15 displays the Project1 page for a new project that contains two containers (a form and a data module) and has not yet been saved.

Conclusion

OOP is not magic. It is a well thought out methodology that provides specific benefits when used properly. Fortunately, Delphi not only permits you to use it properly, it encourages proper use.

References

To further your understanding of the issues involved in using object orientation, the following books will be valuable additions to your technical library. There are

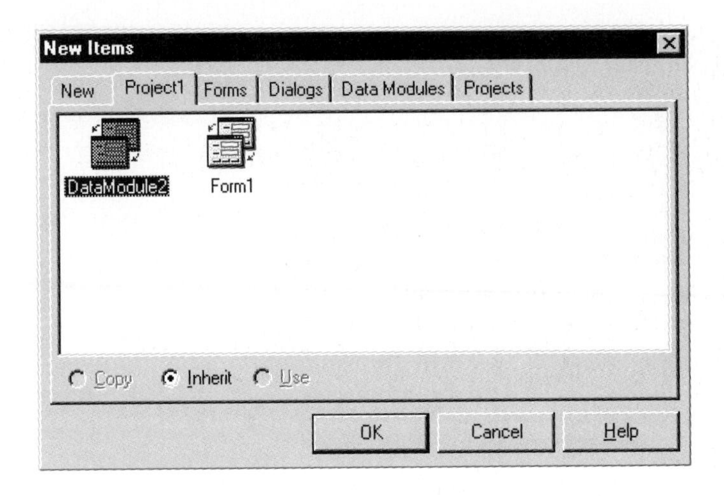

Figure 3-15. *The project-specific page of the Object Repository*

additional excellent books on object orientation, but these five should give you a good foundation from which to start.

- Booch, Grady, *Object-Oriented Analysis and Design with Application*, The Benjamin/Cummings Publishing Company, Inc., Redwood City, CA, 1991.
- Entsminger, Gary, *The Tao of Objects: A Beginner's Guide to Object-Oriented Programming (Second Edition)*, M&T Books, New York, NY, 1995.
- Konopka, Ray, *Developing Custom Delphi Components*, Coriolis Group Books, Scottsdale, AZ, 1996.
- Taylor, David A., *Object-Oriented Technology: A Manager's Guide*, Addison-Wesley Publishing Company, Reading, MA, 1994.
- Yourdon, Edward, *Object-Oriented Systems Design: An Integrated Approach*, Yourdon Press/PTR Prentice Hall, Englewood Cliffs, NJ, 1994.

PART TWO

Techniques

While Part One focused primarily on the philosophy of Delphi, Part Two takes aim directly at the tools and techniques that you use in day-to-day Delphi programming. Each chapter in Part Two focuses on a specific topic, providing you with an overview of the issues involved, followed by a demonstration of the various solutions that Delphi affords you.

Chapter 4 starts off with a look at property editors and how to define them. Here you will learn how you can extend the power of your own components, as well as improve the usability of those that ship with Delphi. This chapter concludes with the introduction of a powerful icon property editor that you can use to easily browse the icons, cursor, and other small bitmaps you have stored in your directories.

Chapters 5 through 8 focus on databases. In Chapter 5 you learn the fundamentals of data access in Delphi, including what components are involved and when they should be used. Chapter 6 continues this discussion with a look at a number of powerful solutions that you will want to include in many of your database applications. These techniques range from creating tables at runtime, to locating records, to using SQL statements to select and manipulate your data.

Chapter 7 is all about Delphi 2. Here you are introduced to the wealth of new database features introduced in the 32-bit version of Delphi, including filters, new components, cached updates, and much more. Chapter 8 rounds out the discussion of databases with a look at using Delphi in a client/server environment. Here you are introduced to the underlying technology involved, as well as how to perform many of the basic tasks required. These include a comparison between file server and client/server technologies, how to define an alias for a database server, how to control access to a remote server, how to implement transaction processing, as well as how to connect to a database server using an ODBC (Open Database Connectivity) driver.

Chapters 9 and 10 focus on reporting. Chapter 9 covers ReportSmith, the powerful and flexible reporting tool that ships with all versions of Delphi. This chapter begins by showing you how to create powerful ReportSmith reports, and then continues by showing you how to integrate them into your Delphi applications. In Chapter 10 you are introduced to QuickReports, the powerful report tool that permits you to compile reports directly into your .EXEs.

Chapters 11 and 12 focus on using graphics in Delphi. Topics covered in these chapters include how to create transparent objects, how to rotate text, and how to use masking. Most of these techniques are demonstrated using custom components that you can use in your own applications to display sophisticated graphical effects.

Chapter 13 gives you an in-depth look at resource files. Here you will learn how to use the Borland Resource Compiler to create resource files form strings, bitmaps, and almost any other type of data. You then learn how to compile and link these resources directly into your .EXEs, and then use them at runtime. Highlights include how to create multilanguage applications, as well as how to define custom cursors.

In Chapter 14 you learn how to exploit other applications from within Delphi using OLE Automation. This chapter also permits you to explore variants and variant arrays. It concludes with the demonstration of several useful OLE Automation examples, including how to fetch data and graphics from the World Wide Web.

If you are interested in creating multithreaded applications with Delphi 2, then you don't want to miss Chapters 15 and 16. In these two chapters you will find extensive details on what multithreading is, and how to use it safely. Topics covered here include creating new threads, how to properly suspend an executing thread, and how to synchronize two or more simultaneously executing threads.

Chapter Four

Property Editors

The code for the examples presented in this chapter can be found in the \CODE\CH04 subdirectory on the CD-ROM that accompanies this book. Please refer to Appendix A for information on using the code files for this chapter.

Property editors are one of the truly powerful elements of the Delphi programming environment. While many of the tips and techniques found in this book are aimed at adding new or interesting functionality to a program, property editors are designed to make your job, as a developer, easier. To put it simply, a property editor permits a component user to define the value of a property.

Delphi supplies a large number of default property editors that are automatically available for use by your components. In most cases, these default property editors provide everything your properties need. For example, text-based properties (such as a Caption or Text property) have a property editor that allows the user to key in text. A Boolean property editor manages the user's selection of True or False values for the property.

The Boolean property editor is demonstrated in the following example. The code in the unit BOOLPROP defines a new component that publishes a single Boolean property. The following is the code for this remarkably trivial component:

```
unit BoolProp;

interface

uses
  Windows, Messages, SysUtils, Classes, Graphics, Controls,
  Forms, Dialogs;

type
  TBoolProp = class(TComponent)
  private
    { Private declarations }
    FMyBool: Boolean;
  protected
    { Protected declarations }
  public
    { Public declarations }
  published
    { Published declarations }
    property MyBool: Boolean read FMyProp write FMyProp;
  end;

procedure Register;

implementation
```

```
procedure Register;
begin
  RegisterComponents('Samples', [TBoolProp]);
end;

end.
```

If you install this component into your component palette, place it on a form, and then select it using the Object Inspector, you will see that Delphi automatically provided a drop-down menu in the Object Inspector for the MyBool property. In addition, Delphi has provided default exception handling, displaying an error dialog box, like the one shown in Figure 4-1, if the component user tries to enter a non-Boolean value.

There are, however, times when the default property editors are not enough. For example, the default property editors are insufficient when you want to provide a custom drop-down menu similar to the one that Delphi provides for Boolean properties but that contains selections unique to your property. Likewise, the default property editors are not up to the task if your property is complex and does not lend itself to text-based or menu-based entry.

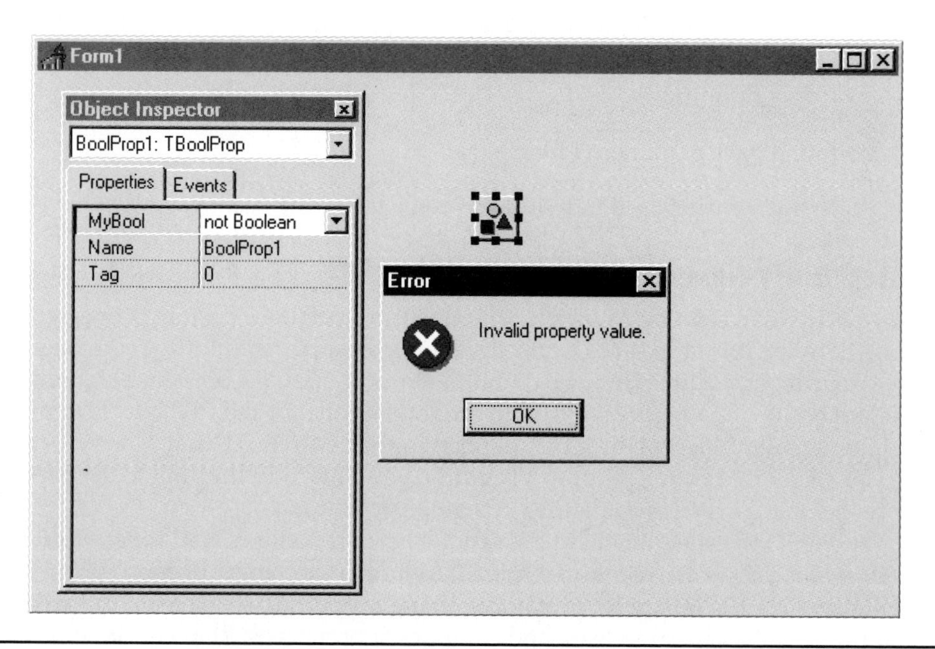

Figure 4-1. *A published Boolean property has a default property editor that provides a drop-down menu as well as exception handling if the component user enters an illegal property value*

The Delphi interface, as far as property editors are concerned, is wide open. Specifically, you can create custom property editors to permit a user to edit properties that you publish in components you build. In addition, you can even replace any of Delphi's existing property editors in order to provide one with greater functionality. This technique will be demonstrated later in this chapter, when you will learn how to create a new property editor for any object that has a Glyph property.

You can create two basic types of custom property editors: text-based property editors and dialog box–based property editors. Text-based property editors can be provided as long as the property can be handled as text. Dialog box–based property editors, in contrast, are more appropriate for situations in which complex properties, ones that do not have a textual representation, are involved.

This chapter begins with an overview of property editor creation. These techniques are then demonstrated by creating a text-based property editor. Finally, you will learn how to create dialog box–based property editors for those properties requiring a more complex solution.

Creating Property Editors

All property editors, whether text-based or dialog-based, are created using the same five steps. These are:

1. Deriving a property editor object
2. Writing the property editing routine
3. Specifying editor attributes
4. Registering the property editor
5. Updating the Component Library

Each of these steps is discussed individually in the following sections.

Deriving a Property Editor Object

Just as you do when creating a custom component, you create a custom property editor by deriving it from one of Delphi's predefined property editors. A complete hierarchy of property editors may be found in the VCL (Visual Component Library). The hierarchy shown in Figure 4-2 is from the source code for the DSGNINTF unit.

Delphi default property editors are defined in the DSGNINTF unit. Consequently, before you can derive your new property editor, you must add this unit to the uses clause of the unit in which you define your property editor.

As shown in Figure 4-2, the base class for all property editors is TPropertyEditor. The various subclasses are roughly divided into property editors appropriate for ordinal properties, floating point properties, string properties, set element properties, method properties, class properties, and component properties. Many of these property editors have additional descendants to handle the editing of special instances of that property type. For example, five property editors descend from the

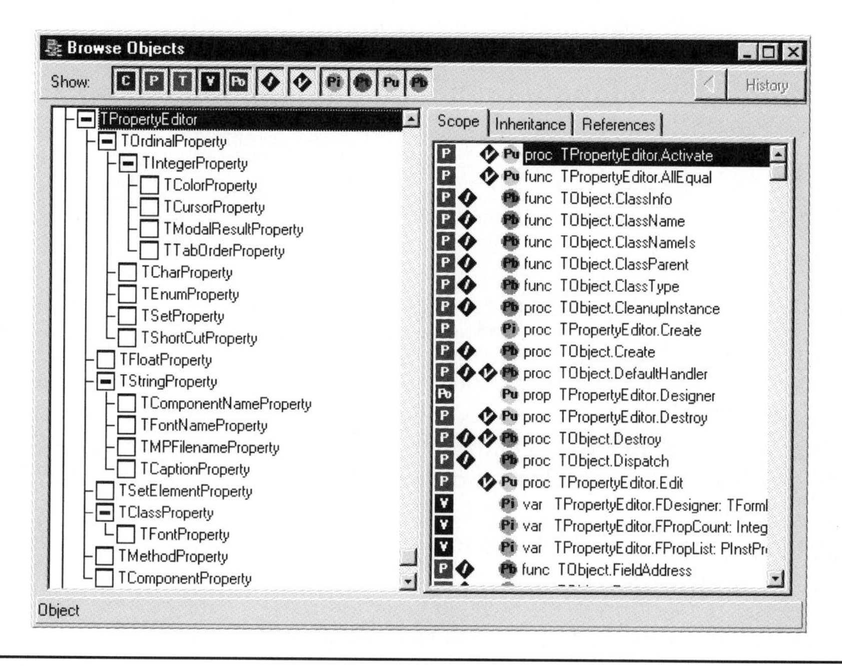

Figure 4-2. *The Property Editor hierarchy display in the Object Browser*

TOrdinalProperty property editor. Each of these editors is designed to handle a different type of ordinal property, such as Chars, Sets, and Integers.

The decision of which property editor you should descend your new property editor from is an important one. Each of the property editors inherits from its ancestors features that you can leverage in your custom property editor. For example, if you are creating a custom property editor to work with a Char property, you should derive your new property editor from the TCharProperty class. If, in contrast, you are creating a property editor to work with an object, you should derive it from TClassProperty.

You will use a type declaration to derive your property editor. In this declaration, you define the class from which you are descending the property editor, in addition to any member fields, variables, and methods you want for your editor. Furthermore, you will specify the ancestor methods you want to override. In many cases you will override the GetValue or SetValue methods of the ancestor class. You use these methods to write (Get) and read (Set) the value of the property in the Object Inspector from within your property editor.

Other methods that are commonly overridden include the GetAttributes and Edit methods. You override GetAttributes to change how the Object Inspector treats the property. Overriding this method is described in the section "Specifying Editor Attributes." You override the Edit method when you want to display a dialog box–based property editor. This technique is demonstrated in the section "A Simple Dialog Box–Based Property Editor." The following is an example of a property editor declaration:

```
TWordProperty = class(TIntegerProperty)
  public
    function GetAttributes: TPropertyAttributes; override;
    function GetValue: string; override;
    procedure SetValue(const Value: string); override;
  end;
```

Writing Property Editing Routines

The primary interface for writing your property editor routines are in the methods that you override when you derive your property editor. For example, to define a set of attributes that differs from the property editor from which you are deriving your property editor, you override the GetAttributes method of the ancestor. Table 4-1 contains a list of the virtual methods defined in the TPropertyEditor class that you can override.

Two of the more important methods to override are GetValue and SetValue. GetValue provides the Object Inspector with a text representation of the property value for display in the value column; the SetValue method retrieves the current value of the property. You usually override GetValue to call an appropriate Get method in order to convert a non-string property to a string representation. You override the SetValue method to call an appropriate Set method to convert the string representation of the property to the property type. The Get and Set methods, and the property types for which they are used, are shown in Table 4-2.

The following is a code segment depicting a property editor type declaration and the implementation of its overridden methods:

```
type
  TIntegerProperty = class(TOrdinalProperty)
  public
    function GetValue: string; override;
    procedure SetValue(const Value: string); override;
  end;

implementation
  function TIntegerProperty.GetValue: string;
  begin
    Result := IntToStr(GetOrdValue);
  end;

  procedure TIntegerProperty.SetValue(const Value: String);
  var
    E: Integer;
    L: Longint;
  begin
    L := StrToInt(Value);
    with GetTypeData(GetPropType)^ do
```

```
    if (L < MinValue) or (L > MaxValue) then
      raise EPropertyError.Create(
        FmtLoadStr(SOutOfRange, [MinValue, MaxValue]));
  SetOrdValue(L);
end;
```

This example shows how one of the base property editors provided with Delphi, TIntegerProperty, overrides two of its methods from the property editor from which it is indirectly derived, TPropertyEditor. The GetValue method is used to return a string

Method	Description
Activate	Called when the property is selected in the object inspector.
AllEqual	If GetAttributes returns paMultiSelect, this method is called when more than one component selected.
Edit	Called when the '...' button is clicked or when the property value field is double-clicked. Override this method when creating dialog box–based property editors.
GetAttributes	Returns a TPropertyAttributes set containing the editor's attributes.
GetEditLimit	Returns the maximum number of characters the user is allowed to enter into the value field for the property. Override this method to return a value smaller than the default of 255.
GetName	Returns the name of the property.
GetProperties	Called when paSubProperties is returned in GetAttributes.
GetValue	Returns the string value of the property to the Object Inspector. Override this method to call one of the Get methods to convert a non-string property to a string.
GetValues	Called when paValueList is returned in GetAttributes. Override this procedure to define the contents of a properties drop-down menu.
Initialize	Called after the property editor has been created but before it is used.
SetValue	Called to retrieve the string appearing in the value field of the Object Inspector. Override this method to call one of the Set methods when retrieving a non-string property.

Table 4-1. *Virtual Methods of the TPropertyEditor Class*

Property Type	Get Method	Set Method
Floating point	GetFloatValue	SetFloatValue
Method pointer (event)	GetMethodValue	SetMethodValue
Ordinal type	GetOrdValue	SetOrdValue
String	GetStrValue	SetStrValue

Table 4-2. *Get and Set Methods for the Corresponding Property Types*

representation of how the property is currently set. In this case, the property's integer value is converted into a string using the IntToStr function. That string value is then displayed in the Object Inspector. The SetValue method is overridden to provide safety checks. These checks prevent a user from entering a value that might exceed the capacity of the variable used to store the value. If the value entered exceeds these limits, this method will generate an exception message advising the user of the acceptable range of values for the property.

Specifying Editor Attributes

The GetAttributes method is used by the property editor to provide information about the property to the Object Inspector. You define the attributes of the property by overriding the GetAttributes method and returning a set of values of the type TPropertyAttributes. The possible members of the set TPropertyAttributes are shown in Table 4-3.

The following code sample demonstrates how to tell the Object Inspector that a property cannot be typed in directly by the user, but must be selected from a list:

```
function TMyPropEditor.GetAttributes: TPropertyAttributes;
begin
  Result := [paValueList,paReadOnly];
end;
```

Registering the Property Editor

For your property editor to be utilized by the Object Inspector you must register it. Registration is done using the RegisterPropertyEditor procedure, which must appear within a Register procedure. This is the same technique used to register a component, with the exception that you must execute a separate RegisterPropertyEditor statement for each property editor you are registering. By comparison, you can register more than one component in a single RegisterComponents statement.

Attribute	Description
paAutoUpdate	Calls the SetValue method after each change in the value, instead of after the entire value has been accepted.
paDialog	The editor can display a dialog box for editing the entire property. The Edit method opens the dialog box.
paMultiSelect	The property should appear when the user selects multiple components. Most property editors allow multiple selection. The notable exception is the editor for the Name property.
paReadOnly	The property is read-only in the Object Inspector. This is used for sets and fonts, which the user cannot type directly.
paSortList	The Object Inspector should sort the list of values alphabetically.
paSubProperties	The property is an object that has subproperties that can be displayed. The GetProperties method handles the subproperty lists.
paValueList	The editor can give a list of enumerated values. The GetValues method builds the list.

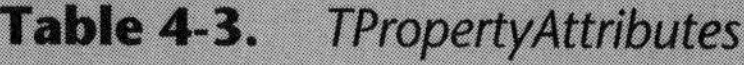

Table 4-3. *TPropertyAttributes*

NOTE: If a component and a property editor are defined in the same unit, both RegisterComponents and RegisterPropertyEditor will appear in the same Register procedure.

The RegisterPropertyEditor procedure has the following syntax:

```
RegisterPropertyEditor(PropertyType: PTypeInfo; ComponentClass: TClass;
    const PropertyName: string; EditorClass: TPropertyEditorClass);
```

As you can see, this procedure requires four parameters. The first parameter, PropertyType, is a record structure that points to the runtime type information (RTTI) for the data with which the property editor is designed to work. To pass this information correctly, you must use the function TypeInfo, to which you will pass the data type of the property that will be edited.

The second parameter is ComponentClass, which you use to specify the components that are allowed access to this particular property editor. By specifying a value for this parameter, you define where in the Object Hierarchy the property editor can be used. For example, if you are creating a property editor that you want to make available to any object descending from TComponent, you would pass TComponent as the second argument. If, in contrast, you wanted to restrict the use of your property editor to a single class named TMyOwnObject, for instance, you would pass TMyOwnObject in this parameter. If you supply nil as this parameter, the property editor will be available for all objects. This has the same effect as passing TComponent as the second argument.

The third parameter defines the name of the property for which this editor will be available. For example, if you write a replacement editor to be used for editing TFont properties, you would pass Font in this third parameter.

The final parameter is the name of your derived property editor class. For example, if you created a property editor class named TMyFontEditor, you would pass TMyFontEditor in this final parameter.

The following is an example of a registration procedure that makes a property editor named TWordProperty available for all objects of the class TWinControl that include an Integer property named Age:

```
procedure Register;
begin
  RegisterPropertyEditor(TypeInfo(Integer),
  TWinControl,'Age',TWordProperty);
end;
```

Updating the Component Library

The final step in creating a property editor is to add to the component library the unit that defines and registers the property editor. This step is done using the Install Components dialog box shown in Figure 4-3. You display this dialog box from Delphi 2 by selecting Components | Install. From Delphi 1.0 you select Options | Install Components.

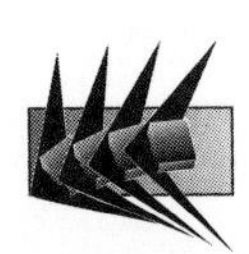

NOTE: The property editors installed by Delphi are registered by the STDREG.PAS unit.

A Text-Based Property Editor Example

The following example demonstrates how to create a text-based property editor. As mentioned earlier in this chapter, a text-based property editor is one that permits the user to edit the property directly in the Object Inspector (as opposed to displaying a dialog box for modifying the property).

The following code example creates a new component as well as a property editor designed for use with one of the component's properties. The component is a descendant of the TEdit class. The new property, NumFormat, is a string property that the user can use to define a numeric format for numbers entered into the component. The property editor is a descendant of the TStringProperty class and it provides a

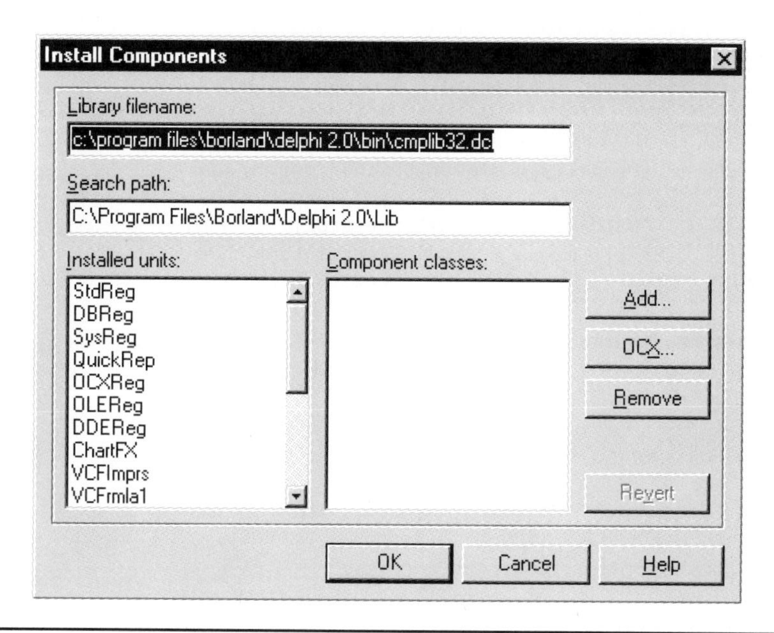

Figure 4-3. *Use the Install Components dialog box to add your property editors to the VCL*

drop-down menu for predefined formats. Both the component and the property editor are defined in the MYEDIT.PAS unit. The following is the code for this unit:

```
unit Myedit;

interface

uses
  SysUtils, WinTypes, WinProcs, Messages, Classes, Graphics, Controls,
  Forms, Dialogs, StdCtrls, DsgnIntF;

type
  TMyEdit = class(TEdit)
  private
    FFormat : String;
    FieldValue : Real;
    procedure SetFormat(Value: String);
    procedure CMEnter(var Message: TCMEnter);  message CM_ENTER;
    procedure CMExit(var Message: TCMExit);    message CM_EXIT;
  protected
    procedure UnformatText;
    procedure FormatText;
  published
```

```
    property NumFormat: String read FFormat write SetFormat;
  end;

  TNumericFormatsProperty = class(TStringProperty)
  public
    procedure GetValues(TheProc: TGetStrProc); override;
    function GetAttributes: TPropertyAttributes; override;
  end;

  procedure Register;

implementation

procedure Register;
begin
  RegisterComponents('Samples',[TMyEdit]);
  RegisterPropertyEditor(TypeInfo(String), TMyEdit,
    'NumFormat', TNumericFormatsProperty);
end;

{********************}
{* MyEdit Component *}
{********************}
procedure TMyEdit.UnFormatText;
var
  TmpText : String;
  Tmp     : Byte;
  IsNeg   : Boolean;
begin
  IsNeg := (Pos('-',Text) > 0) or (Pos('(',Text) > 0);
  TmpText := '';
  For Tmp := 1 to Length(Text) do
    if Text[Tmp] in ['0'..'9',DecimalSeparator] then
      TmpText := TmpText + Text[Tmp];
  try
    If TmpText='' Then TmpText := '0.00';
    FieldValue := StrToFloat(TmpText);
    if IsNeg then FieldValue := -FieldValue;
  except
    FieldValue := 0.0;
  end;
end;

procedure TMyEdit.FormatText;
begin
  try
    Text := FormatFloat(NumFormat,FieldValue)
  except
    Text := FormatFloat(NumFormat,0);
```

```
    end;
    if FieldValue < 0 then
      Font.Color := clRed
    else
      Font.Color := clBlack;
end;

procedure TMyEdit.SetFormat;
begin
  FFormat := Value;
  UnformatText;
  FormatText;
end;

procedure TMyEdit.CMEnter(var Message: TCMEnter);
begin
  SelectAll;
  inherited;
end;

procedure TMyEdit.CMExit(var Message: TCMExit);
begin
  UnformatText;
  FormatText;
  Inherited;
end;


{*************************}
{* NumericFormatsProperty *}
{*************************}
procedure TNumericFormatsProperty.GetValues(TheProc: TGetStrProc);
begin
  TheProc('0');
  TheProc('0.00');
  TheProc('#.##');
  TheProc('#,##0.00');
  TheProc('#,##0.00;(#,##0.00)');
  TheProc('#,##0.00;;Zero');
  TheProc('0.000E+00');
  TheProc('#.###E-0');
end;

function TNumericFormatsProperty.GetAttributes: TPropertyAttributes;
begin
  Result := [paValueList,paAutoUpdate,paMultiSelect];
end;

end.
```

The MyEdit component is simply a descendant of the TEdit class. The critical element is that it includes a published property named NumFormat. The property registration procedure is used to associate NumFormat with a custom property editor named NumericFormatsProperty:

```
RegisterPropertyEditor(TypeInfo(String), TMyEdit,'NumFormat',
                       TNumericFormatsProperty);
```

The call to RegisterPropertyEditor specifies that this property editor is associated with a property named NumFormat, of the class TMyEdit. In other words, this property editor will be available any time a developer works with the NumFormat property of an instantiation of the MyEdit class, or one of its descendants.

The definition of the TNumericFormatProperty class indicates that it is derived from the TStringProperty class. The declaration also overrides the GetValues and GetAttributes methods of the ancestor class, as shown in the following code segment:

```
TNumericFormatsProperty = class(TStringProperty)
  public
    procedure GetValues(TheProc: TGetStrProc); override;
    function GetAttributes: TPropertyAttributes; override;
  end;
```

The TNumericFormatsProperty class is quite simple to use. All it does is enhance the basic functionality of the TStringProperty class by adding a drop-down menu of numeric formats from which the user can select. This procedure requires two steps: first, the Object Inspector has to be informed that the property possesses a drop-down menu; and second, the list has to be populated when the Object Inspector asks for it (when the user clicks the button to display the drop-down menu).

Specifying that the property has a drop-down menu is done in the overridden GetAttributes function:

```
function TNumericFormatsProperty.GetAttributes: TPropertyAttributes;
begin
  Result := [paValueList,paAutoUpdate,paMultiSelect];
end;
```

This function returns a set of TPropertyAttributes flags. In the preceding example, three flags are set. The flag paValueList specifies that the property has a drop-down menu. The second flag, paAutoUpdate, tells the Object Inspector that it should update the property as the user types, rather than waiting until the user presses Enter, thus providing the program with a more dynamic feel. That is, users see the results in the MyEdit component as they key in the format specification. The third flag, paMultiSelect, tells the Object Inspector that this property can be displayed even if multiple components are selected at the same time.

The contents of the property editor are defined by the overridden GetValues procedure:

```
procedure TNumericFormatsProperty.GetValues(TheProc: TGetStrProc);
begin
  TheProc('0');
  TheProc('0.00');
  TheProc('#.##');
  TheProc('#,##0.00');
  TheProc('#,##0.00;(#,##0.00)');
  TheProc('#,##0.00;;Zero');
  TheProc('0.000E+00');
  TheProc('#.###E-0');
end;
```

This procedure contains a series of calls to a procedure pointer, passed by reference. This procedure, named TheProc in this example, is called once for each value that needs to be added to the drop-down menu, passing the value to display as a string. In this case, TheProc is called eight times, thereby producing a drop-down menu containing eight entries.

The rest of the work is performed by the MyEdit component. This component's methods define how it responds to the user changing the properties. You can see the effects of the property editor by adding the MyEdit unit to your component library, rebuilding the library, and then placing a MyEdit component on a form. Note that by compiling this unit into the component library, the MyEdit component will be added to the component palette, and the property editor TNumericFormatsProperty will be registered with the Object Inspector. Figure 4-4 displays what such a form might look like, as well as what the NumFormat property's property editor looks like.

This example has demonstrated a very easy technique for adding functionality to an existing property editor. The component user is provided with a predefined list of acceptable property values, but this property editor also allows the user to enter numeric formats that are not in the list. In addition, if the user double-clicks the NumFormat property, the property editor will cycle automatically to the next value in the drop-down menu.

A Simple Dialog Box–Based Property Editor

One of the more common properties that you may implement in a custom component is one that specifies a filename. For example, the component may need access to a filename for logging debugging output, or for specifying a .WAV file for a sound effect to be attached to a function of the control. The possibilities are endless.

There are several ways that you can permit your component user to define a filename. A simple approach would be to provide a string property, but a string

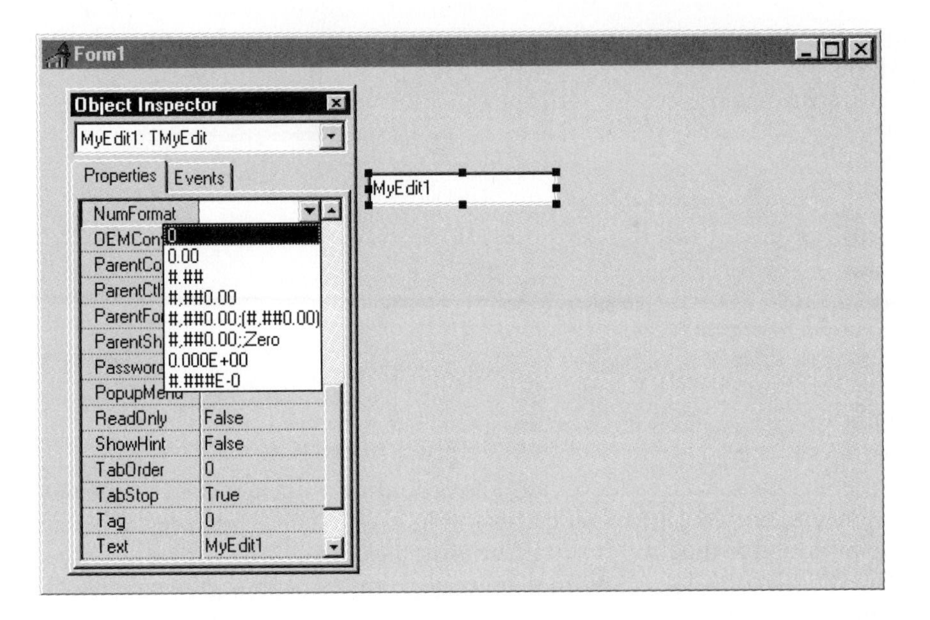

Figure 4-4. *The MyEdit component on a form. The drop-down menu for the NumFormat property is displayed in the Object Inspector*

property does not know that it is referring to a filename. As a result, you would also have to program error checking to verify that the user entered a valid path and name. Furthermore, what if the file the user wants to assign to this property is located in a deeply nested subdirectory (for instance, in a Windows 95 folder)? Are you really going to ask the user to type in something like:

```
C:\Program Files\Borland\Delphi 2.0\Images\Buttons\RARROW.BMP
```

That could get pretty tedious, even after entering only a few filenames. Fortunately, there are alternatives. One of the more powerful techniques available when designing property editors is to permit the display of a dialog box. This dialog box can be completely original, or it can be one of the dialog boxes available in Delphi. The next example shows how to create a powerful property editor by leveraging the OpenDialog component available in Delphi.

The following is the code from the TextEdit unit. This unit defines a dialog box-based property editor named TTextFileProperty.

```
unit Textedit;

interface

uses
  Forms, Classes, DsgnIntf, Dialogs;

type
  TTextFileProperty = class(TStringProperty)
  public
    procedure Edit; override;
    function GetAttributes: TPropertyAttributes; override;
  end;

  procedure Register;


implementation


procedure Register;
begin
  RegisterPropertyEditor(TypeInfo(string), nil,
   'TextFile',TTextFileProperty);
end;

{ TTextFileProperty }
procedure TTextFileProperty.Edit;
var
  FileOpen: TOpenDialog;
begin
  FileOpen := TOpenDialog.Create(Application);
  FileOpen.Filename := GetValue;
  FileOpen.Filter := 'Text files (*.txt)|*.TXT|'+
                     'INI Files (*.ini)|*.INI|'+
                     'Doc files (*.doc)|*.DOC|'+
                     'All files (*.*)|*.*';
  FileOpen.Options := FileOpen.Options + [ofPathMustExist,
                                          ofFileMustExist];
  try
    if FileOpen.Execute then SetValue(FileOpen.Filename);
  finally
    FileOpen.Free;
  end;
end;
```

```
function TTextFileProperty.GetAttributes: TPropertyAttributes;
begin
  Result := [paDialog,paMultiSelect];
end;

end.
```

This property editor is as simple as the TNumericFormatProperty class. Like that property editor, only two methods were overriden:

```
TTextFileProperty = class(TStringProperty)
  public
    procedure Edit; override;
    function GetAttributes: TPropertyAttributes; override;
  end;
```

The GetAttributes function is overridden to instruct the Object Inspector that this property has a dialog box. This is done by returning the paDialog flag, which instructs the Object Inspector to display an ellipsis (...) button when the property is selected, as well as the paMultiSelect flag, which permits the property editor to be used on multiple objects simultaneously.

```
function TTextFileProperty.GetAttributes: TPropertyAttributes;
begin
  Result := [paDialog, paMultiSelect];
end;
```

In addition to setting the paDialog attribute flag, you must also override the Edit method when you want to display a dialog box. The Object Inspector calls the property editor's Edit method when the ellipsis (...) button is clicked or when the user double-clicks the property value field.

The following is the code from the overridden Edit method:

```
procedure TTextFileProperty.Edit;
var
  FileOpen: TOpenDialog;
begin
  FileOpen := TOpenDialog.Create(Application);
  FileOpen.Filename := GetValue;
  FileOpen.Filter := 'Text files (*.txt)|*.TXT|'+
                     'INI Files (*.ini)|*.INI|'+
                     'Doc files (*.doc)|*.DOC|'+
                     'All files (*.*)|*.*';
  FileOpen.Options := FileOpen.Options + [ofPathMustExist,
                                          ofFileMustExist];
```

```
    try
      if FileOpen.Execute then SetValue(FileOpen.Filename);
    finally
      FileOpen.Free;
    end;
  end;
```

This method declares a variable named FileOpen of the type TOpenDialog, which is a class that encapsulates the Windows OpenFile common dialog box. Windows defines a number of common dialogs in order to provide standard behaviors (such as loading or saving a file, or picking a font) so that all applications can have a consistent look. Within the body of this method, the dialog box is created by calling the TOpenDialog constructor to instantiate an OpenDialog component. Next, properties of this component are set to customize the OpenDialog. In this example, only the Filter and the Options properties are set.

Once the dialog box is ready for use, its Execute method is called. This method returns a value of True if the user selects a valid filename, or False if the user closes the dialog box without selecting a file. The code then tests this return value, and if the user selected a file, calls the inherited SetValue method, thereby storing the selected filename into the property being edited.

***NOTE:** The property editor uses a try-finally protection block to ensure that the OpenDialog component is freed. If this were not done and an exception occurred, the resources allocated to the OpenFile variable would not be released.*

The property editor's registration procedure defines that this property editor will be used for any property named TextFile belonging to any component in the component palette (nil is equivalent to TComponent is the second parameter).

```
procedure Register;
begin
  RegisterPropertyEditor(TypeInfo(string), nil,
    'TextFile',TTextFileProperty);
end;
```

This dialog box–based property editor is demonstrated in Figure 4-5. This figure depicts what happens when the user double-clicks a TextFile property in the Object Inspector.

The component displayed in Figure 4-5 is defined in the following code, which declares yet another trivial component. This component has a property named TextFile and, therefore, will automatically use the TTextFileProperty property editor. Also, an access method is defined for the TextFile property. When this property is set, this access method loads the file if a filename was set and clears the control if the filename was erased.

```
unit TextFile;

interface

uses
  SysUtils, WinTypes, WinProcs, Messages, Classes, Graphics, Controls,
  Forms, Dialogs, StdCtrls;

type
  TTextFile = class(TMemo)
  private
    FTextFile : String;
    procedure SetTextFile(Value: String);
  protected
    { Protected declarations }
  public
    { Public declarations }
  published
    property TextFile: String read FTextFile write SetTextFile;
  end;

procedure Register;

implementation

procedure Register;
begin
  RegisterComponents('Samples', [TTextFile]);
end;

procedure TTextFile.SetTextFile(Value: String);
begin
if Value <> FTextFile then
  begin
    FTextFile := Value;
    try
      if Value = '' then
        Lines.Clear
      else
        Lines.LoadFromFile(FTextFile);
      Invalidate;
    except
      raise Exception.Create('Invalid TextFile');
    end;
  end;
end;

end.
```

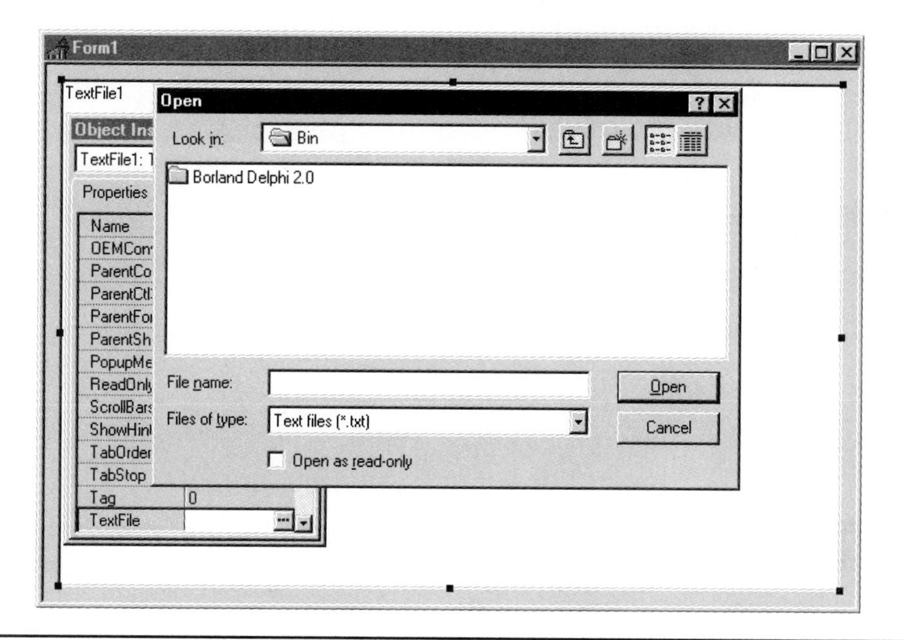

Figure 4-5. *The TextFile property editor, based on the OpenDialog component, is displayed when the component user double-clicks a TextFile property, or clicks the ellipsis (...) button in a TextFile property value field*

Building Custom Dialog Box–Based Property Editors

As you can see, it is easy to create a dialog box–based property editor if Delphi already provides an appropriate dialog box. However, this is rarely the case. Most of the time it is necessary to build your property editor's dialog box from scratch.

The remainder of this chapter focuses on a replacement property editor for the Bitmap property editor supplied by Delphi. This new property editor uses a custom dialog box. Before considering the technique used to create this dialog box, this section begins with a discussion of the shortcomings of the default Bitmap property editor.

Delphi's Graphics Property Editor

Delphi provides the rudimentary property editor that is used for all bitmap properties. It is called the Picture Editor and is shown in Figure 4-6. Although Delphi's bitmap editor works, it is far from perfect. Its use requires excessive clicking on buttons and dealing with filenames when you can't see the bitmap contained with that file.

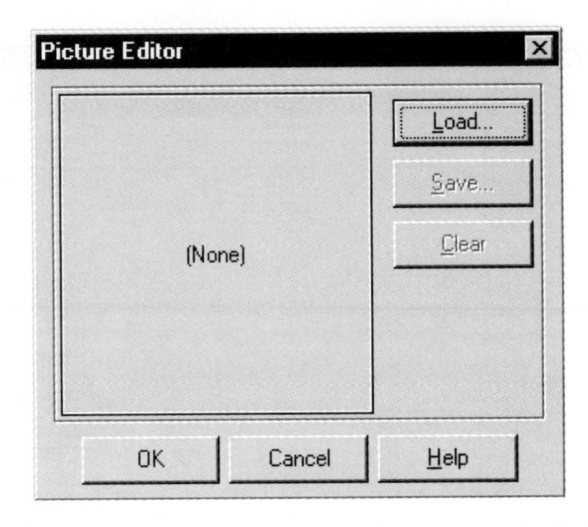

Figure 4-6. *The Picture Editor provided with Delphi*

The BmpView Property Editor

The property editor created in this chapter is an alternative to the bitmap editor that comes with Delphi. This new Bitmap/Glyph property editor allows users to look at all the bitmaps in a directory and then pick one visually rather than by filename. This editor provides a much more intuitive approach to the selection of a bitmap graphic. In addition, with a little extra effort, this editor can be a robust and fault-tolerant editor that will be a pleasure to use, rather than an annoyance. This is accomplished by maintaining a variety of user preferences so that the editor can be configured by the user/developer.

Figure 4-7 shows an example of how this property editor will appear when it is completed. Notice that it automatically displays the icons available in the current directory. This editor also has a number of additional features that will be described later in this chapter.

Design Issues

The TBitMapProperty editor will be dialog box-based. Some editors only need basic pieces of data that can be provided by the fields in the Object Inspector. However, when the data required is too complex, or is not suited for such an input method, developers typically create a "mini-application" that allows the developer to fill in that particular property's data.

Allowing Users to Pick a Bitmap

The first step in creating this Bitmap property editor is to provide the basic ability of allowing a user to pick a bitmap. Various approaches are available for accomplishing

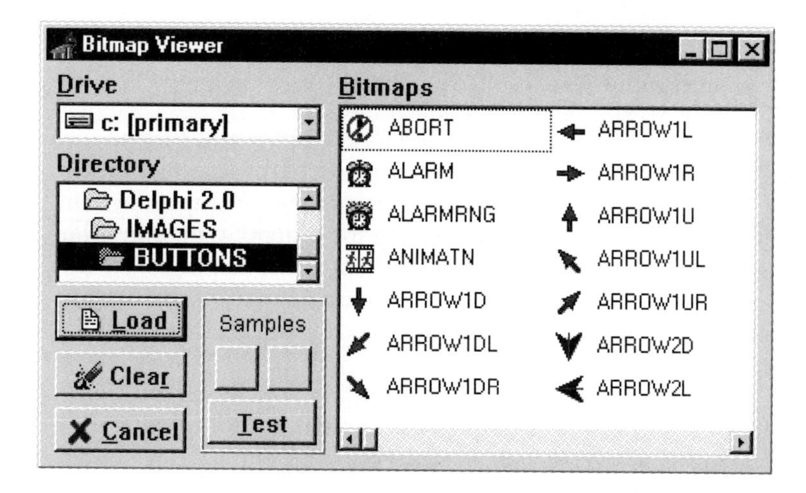

Figure 4-7. *The TBitMapProperty property editor provides extensive support for the display and selection of bitmaps*

this goal. For example, the component could simply ask for a filename, which would be typed directly into the Object Inspector. Such an approach would require the user to know where the bitmap is located (so that the full path name could be entered) and would also require the application to verify that the data entered is valid (i.e., that it points to a valid bitmap file). With this approach, however, the behavior of the component might be a bit awkward as the component would need to load the bitmap after the user finished typing in the filename.

Another solution is Delphi's Bitmap property editor (see Figure 4-6). This editor eliminates the need for developers to key in filenames for graphic images. This property editor's form is distinct and separate from the Object Inspector. When the user double-clicks on a property that is attached to this kind of editor, the form is created and displayed. When the user makes a selection, the form is put away, and the chosen bitmap is inserted into the component appropriately. But as mentioned previously, this editor has several disadvantages.

An even better solution would be to present the user with a visual list of all available bitmaps and allow him or her to select from this list. At a glance, the user would be able to see which graphic fits a particular need, rather than having to select bitmaps one at a time to see what the file looks like. This is the approach that we will demonstrate in this chapter.

Designing the Interface

One of the first things that should be done when developing a property editor is to design the user interface. The form should be designed so that the needed information is readily accessible and easy to manage. The basic elements of this Bitmap property editor are that the user will be able to move to a particular drive and/or directory (which we will implement by means of the DriveComboBox and the DirectoryListBox) and then select an appropriate bitmap file (which will be implemented by means of a multi-column list box).

The list box on the right-hand side of the form displays the bitmap files in the current directory. The Load button sets the property to the selected bitmap, and the Clear button removes the current bitmap property for the component being edited. The Cancel button aborts the selection, leaving the bitmap in the control unchanged.

To the right of these three buttons is a small area that displays how the bitmap will appear in various situations. It displays the bitmap on two speed buttons (one enabled and one disabled), as well as on a BitBtn with text. These buttons don't do anything; they just show the user how the selected bitmap will look.

As mentioned before, a number of configuration options need to be made available to the user. In this example, these options are implemented through a right-click menu that is attached to the bitmap list box. Following is the entire source code for this component:

The BmpView Property Editor Code

```
(*******************************************************************)
(* BMPVIEW Bitmap Property Editor for Delphi                       *)
(* Written by Robert Vivrette - RobertV@ix.netcom.com              *)
(* Copyright 1995 - Prime Time Programming                         *)
(*******************************************************************)

unit BmpView;

interface

uses
  WinProcs, WinTypes, Messages, Forms, SysUtils, Controls, StdCtrls,
  FileCtrl, Buttons, LibConst, Dialogs, Graphics, IniFiles,
  Menus, DsgnIntf, Classes, ExtCtrls;

type
  TBitmapEditorDialog = class(TForm)
    DriveList: TDriveComboBox;
    DirList  : TDirectoryListBox;
    BmpList  : TListBox;
    DirectoryLabel: TLabel;
    DriveLabel: TLabel;
    BitmapLabel: TLabel;
    btnLoad: TBitBtn;
    btnCancel: TBitBtn;
    btnClear: TBitBtn;
    PopupMenu1: TPopupMenu;
    pmItemHeight: TMenuItem;
    pmColumns: TMenuItem;
```

```
pmColumns1: TMenuItem;
pmColumns2: TMenuItem;
pmColumns3: TMenuItem;
pmColumns4: TMenuItem;
pm20Pixels: TMenuItem;
pm24Pixels: TMenuItem;
pm28Pixels: TMenuItem;
pm32Pixels: TMenuItem;
pm36Pixels: TMenuItem;
pm40Pixels: TMenuItem;
pmHints: TMenuItem;
pmSaveSettings: TMenuItem;
pmLowerCase: TMenuItem;
pmNoExtension: TMenuItem;
pmColumns5: TMenuItem;
pmColumns6: TMenuItem;
pmNoFilename: TMenuItem;
N1: TMenuItem;
N2: TMenuItem;
SamplesPanel: TPanel;
btnBitBtnSample: TBitBtn;
btnInactiveSample: TSpeedButton;
btnActiveSample: TSpeedButton;
Label1: TLabel;
{Form handlers}
procedure FormCreate(Sender: TObject);
procedure FormDestroy(Sender: TObject);
procedure FormKeyDown(Sender: TObject; var Key: Word;
  Shift: TShiftState);
procedure FormResize(Sender: TObject);
{BmpList Handlers}
procedure BmpListDrawItem(Control: TWinControl; Index:
  Integer; Rect: TRect; State: TOwnerDrawState);
procedure BmpListClick(Sender: TObject);
procedure BmpListDblClick(Sender: TObject);
{DirList Handlers}
procedure DirListChange(Sender: TObject);
{Button Handlers}
procedure btnLoadClick(Sender: TObject);
procedure btnClearClick(Sender: TObject);
{Popup Menu Handlers}
procedure pmColumnsClick(Sender: TObject);
procedure pmPixelsClick(Sender: TObject);
procedure pmHintsClick(Sender: TObject);
procedure pmSaveSettingsClick(Sender: TObject);
procedure pmLowerCaseClick(Sender: TObject);
procedure pmNoFilenameClick(Sender: TObject);
procedure pmNoExtensionClick(Sender: TObject);
```

```
    {Misc Procedures}
    procedure ReadBitmaps;
    procedure ReadSettings;
    procedure WriteSettings;
    procedure SelectAndQuit;
    procedure SetColumnCheck(TmpChecked: Integer);
    procedure SetPixelCheck(TmpChecked: Integer);
    procedure SetHintsCheck;
  private
    SettingsIni : TIniFile;
    TextPixels  : Integer;
    FormL,FormT : Integer;
    FormW,FormH : Integer;
    FormState   : Integer;
    ChosenBmp   : TBitmap;
    procedure WMGetMinMaxInfo(var Message :TWMGetMinMaxInfo );
      message WM_GETMINMAXINFO;
  end;

  TBitmapEditor = class(TComponent)
  private
    FBmpDlg: TBitmapEditorDialog;
    FBitmap: TBitmap;
    procedure SetBitmap(Value: TBitmap);
  public
    constructor Create(AOwner: TComponent); override;
    destructor Destroy; override;
    function Execute: Boolean;
    property Bitmap: TBitmap read FBitmap write SetBitmap;
  end;

  TBitmapProperty = class(TClassProperty)
  public
    procedure Edit; override;
    function GetAttributes: TPropertyAttributes; override;
    function GetValue: string; override;
    procedure SetValue(const Value: string); override;
  end;

const
  VK_1 = $31;

  procedure Register;

implementation

{$R *.DFM}

procedure Register;
```

```
begin
  RegisterPropertyEditor(TypeInfo(TBitmap),TComponent,
    'Glyph',TBitmapProperty);
end;

(************************)
(*  TBitmapEditorDialog  *)
(************************)

procedure TBitmapEditorDialog.FormCreate(Sender: TObject);
begin
  {Create the bitmap that holds the one we have picked}
  ChosenBmp := TBitmap.Create;
  {Load configuration settings from BMPVIEW.INI}
  ReadSettings;
  TextPixels := Canvas.TextHeight('X');
end;

procedure TBitmapEditorDialog.FormDestroy(Sender: TObject);
begin
  WriteSettings;
  ChosenBmp.Free;
end;

procedure TBitmapEditorDialog.FormKeyDown(Sender: TObject;
           var Key: Word; Shift: TShiftState);
begin
  if (Shift = [ssCtrl]) and (Key = VK_1) then
    PopUpMenu1.PopUp(Left+BmpList.Left+(BmpList.Width div 2),
      Top+BmpList.Top+Height-ClientHeight+(BmpList.Height div 2));
end;

procedure TBitmapEditorDialog.FormResize(Sender: TObject);
begin
  {The Cancel button will sit 6 pixels above the bottom of the form}
  btnCancel.Top := ClientHeight-btnCancel.Height-6;
  {The Clear button will be 6 pixels above the Cancel button}
  btnClear.Top := btnCancel.Top-btnClear.Height-6;
  {And the Top button will be 6 pixels above the Clear button}
  btnLoad.Top := btnClear.Top-btnLoad.Height-6;
  {Now align the Samples panel to the right of the 3 buttons}
  with SamplesPanel do
    SetBounds(Left,btnLoad.Top,Width,Self.ClientHeight-btnLoad.Top-6);
  {The DirList should take up all the space remaining above the buttons}
  DirList.Height := btnLoad.Top-DirList.Top-6;
  {Do an update here to make sure all controls paint before the BmpList}

Update;
```

```
  {The BmpList should take up all remaining space on the form}
  with BmpList do
    SetBounds(Left,Top,Self.ClientWidth-Left-6,Self.ClientHeight-Top-6);
end;


procedure TBitmapEditorDialog.WMGetMinMaxInfo(var Message
                                              :TWMGetMinMaxInfo);
begin
  with Message.MinMaxInfo^ do
  begin
    ptMinTrackSize.X := 300; {Minimum width}
    ptMinTrackSize.Y := 250; {Minimum height}
  end;
  Message.Result := 0;
  inherited;
end;

procedure TBitmapEditorDialog.ReadBitmaps;
var
  Bitmap    : TBitmap;
  SearchRec : TSearchRec;
  Result    : Integer;
begin
  {Set the hourglass cursor}
  Screen.Cursor := crHourglass;
  {Clear the previous items from the BmpList}
  BmpList.Clear;
  {Move to the directory pointed to in the DirList}
  ChDir(DirList.Directory);
  {Now start looking for the bitmaps names}
  Result := FindFirst('*.bmp',faAnyFile,SearchRec);
  While Result = 0 do
    begin
      {Only load bitmaps less than 4001 bytes in size}
      if SearchRec.Size <= 4000 then BmpList.Items.Add(SearchRec.Name);
      {Find the next one}
      Result := FindNext(SearchRec);
    end;
  FindClose(SearchRec);
  {Restore the standard cursor}
  Screen.Cursor := crDefault;
end;

procedure TBitmapEditorDialog.ReadSettings;
begin
  {Read all configuration and window settings from the INI file}
  SettingsIni := TIniFile.Create('BMPVIEW.INI');
  {Configuration Settings}
```

```
  DirList.Directory      :=
    SettingsIni.ReadString( 'Options', 'Directory','C:\');
  BmpList.Columns        :=
    SettingsIni.ReadInteger('Options', 'Columns',2);
  BmpList.ItemHeight     :=
    SettingsIni.ReadInteger('Options', 'ItemHeight',24);
  pmHints.Checked        :=
    SettingsIni.ReadBool('Options','Hints',True);
  pmSaveSettings.Checked :=
    SettingsIni.ReadBool('Options','SaveSettings',True);
  pmLowerCase.Checked    :=
    SettingsIni.ReadBool('Options','LowerCase',False);
  pmNoFilename.Checked   :=
    SettingsIni.ReadBool('Options','NoFilename',False);
  pmNoExtension.Checked  :=
    SettingsIni.ReadBool('Options','NoExtension',True);
  {Window position settings}
  FormL           := SettingsIni.ReadInteger('Window','Left',-99);
  FormT           := SettingsIni.ReadInteger('Window','Top',-99);
  FormW           := SettingsIni.ReadInteger('Window','Width',-99);
  FormH           := SettingsIni.ReadInteger('Window','Height',-99);
  FormState        := SettingsIni.ReadInteger('Window','State',0);
  {Only do a setbounds if all parameters have been specified}
  If (FormL >= 0) and (FormT >= 0) and
    (FormW > 0) and (FormH > 0) then
    SetBounds(FormL,FormT,FormW,FormH);
  {Set the previous window state}
  Case FormState of
    0 : WindowState := wsNormal;
    1 : WindowState := wsMaximized;
    2 : WindowState := wsMinimized;
  end;
  {Set initial menu check states}
  SetColumnCheck(BmpList.Columns);
  SetPixelCheck(BmpList.ItemHeight);
  SetHintsCheck;
  {Free the TIniFile object}
  SettingsIni.Free;
end;

procedure TBitmapEditorDialog.WriteSettings;
begin
  {Write out configuration & Window settings to INI file}
  SettingsIni := TIniFile.Create('BMPVIEW.INI');
  SettingsIni.WriteBool('Options','SaveSettings',
    pmSaveSettings.Checked);
  {Only save remaining items if SaveSettings is checked}
  if pmSaveSettings.Checked then
    begin
```

```
      SettingsIni.WriteString( 'Options',
        'Directory',DirList.Directory);
      SettingsIni.WriteInteger('Options', 'Columns',BmpList.Columns);
      SettingsIni.WriteInteger('Options', 'ItemHeight',
        BmpList.ItemHeight);
      SettingsIni.WriteBool('Options','Hints',pmHints.Checked);
      SettingsIni.WriteBool('Options','LowerCase',
        pmLowerCase.Checked);
      SettingsIni.WriteBool('Options','NoFilename',
        pmNoFilename.Checked);
      SettingsIni.WriteBool('Options','NoExtension',
        pmNoExtension.Checked);
      SettingsIni.WriteInteger('Window', 'Left',Left);
      SettingsIni.WriteInteger('Window', 'Top',Top);
      SettingsIni.WriteInteger('Window', 'Width',Width);
      SettingsIni.WriteInteger('Window', 'Height',Height);
      Case WindowState of
        wsNormal    : SettingsIni.WriteInteger('Window', 'State',0);
        wsMaximized : SettingsIni.WriteInteger('Window', 'State',1);
        wsMinimized : SettingsIni.WriteInteger('Window', 'State',2);
      end;
    end;
  SettingsIni.Free;
end;

procedure TBitmapEditorDialog.DirListChange(Sender: TObject);
begin
  {Whenever we move into a new directory,
   we need to re-read the bitmap names}
  ReadBitmaps;
end;

procedure TBitmapEditorDialog.BmpListDrawItem(Control: TWinControl;
  Index: Integer; Rect: TRect; State: TOwnerDrawState);
var
  Bmp      : TBitmap;
  BmpH     : Integer;
  OffsetT : Integer;
  OffsetL : Integer;
  DstRect : TRect;
  SrcRect : TRect;
  TheText : String[12];
  DotLoc  : Integer;
  bkColor : TColor;
begin
  with Control as TListBox,Canvas do
    begin
      {Create a temporary bitmap}
```

```
Bmp := TBitmap.Create;
try
  {Load the image from the file}
  Bmp.LoadFromFile(Items[Index]);
  {and draw it}
  BmpH := Bmp.Height;
  If BmpH > ItemHeight then BmpH := ItemHeight;
  OffsetL := 3;
  OffsetT := (ItemHeight-BmpH) div 2;
  if OffsetT <= 0 then
    begin
      OffsetT := 0;
      OffsetL := 0;
    end;
  FillRect(Rect);
  {The SrcRect is the area we will paint of the bitmap}
  SrcRect := Bounds(0,0,BmpH,BmpH);
  {The DstRect is the rectangle defining where the bitmap will go}
  DstRect := Bounds(Rect.Left+OffsetL,Rect.Top+OffsetT,BmpH,BmpH);
  if not pmNoFilename.Checked then
    begin
      {Determine the horizontal and vertical
       offsets for painting the text}
      OffsetT := (ItemHeight-TextPixels) div 2;
      if OffsetT < 0 then OffsetT := 0;
      {Get the text from the list box}
      TheText := (Control as TListBox).Items[Index];
      {Shift label into lower case if required}
      if pmLowerCase.Checked then TheText := LowerCase(TheText);
      {Does the user want no extensions?}
      if pmNoExtension.Checked then
        begin
          {Find where the period is in the filename}
          DotLoc := Pos('.',TheText);
          {If found, chop off the extension}
          if DotLoc > 0 then TheText :=  Copy(TheText,1,DotLoc-1);
        end;
      {Write out the text}
      TextRect(Rect,Rect.Left+ItemHeight+3,
        Rect.Top+OffsetT,TheText);
    end;
  {Background color is the bottom left pixel in the bitmap}
  with Bmp do bkColor := Canvas.Pixels[0,Height-1];
  {Paint the bitmap, replace all pixels
   of bkColor with form color}
  if Bmp <> nil then BrushCopy(DstRect, Bmp, SrcRect, bkColor);
finally
  {Release the temporary bitmap}
```

```
        Bmp.Free;
      end;
    end;
end;

procedure TBitmapEditorDialog.BmpListClick(Sender: TObject);
begin
  with BmpList do
    {Is there an item selected?}
    if ItemIndex >= 0 then
      begin
        {If there is a bitmap selected, load it into the BitBtn}
        btnBitBtnSample.Glyph.LoadFromFile(Items[ItemIndex]);
        {Copy that bitmap into the Active button as well}
        btnActiveSample.Glyph.Assign(btnBitBtnSample.Glyph);
        {Set the number of glyphs the same as BitBtn}
        btnActiveSample.NumGlyphs := btnBitBtnSample.NumGlyphs;
        {Copy the bitmap also into the Inactive button}
        btnInactiveSample.Glyph.Assign(btnBitBtnSample.Glyph);
        {And set its number of glyphs also}
        btnInactiveSample.NumGlyphs := btnBitBtnSample.NumGlyphs;
      end;
end;

procedure TBitmapEditorDialog.BmpListDblClick(Sender: TObject);
begin
  {If the user double-clicks an item in the
   list box, select it and close the form}
  SelectAndQuit;
end;

procedure TBitmapEditorDialog.SelectAndQuit;
begin
  with BmpList do
    {Is there an item selected in the list box?}
    if ItemIndex >= 0 then
      {Load it into the ChosenBmp}
      ChosenBmp.LoadFromFile(Items[ItemIndex]);
  {Close the form}
  ModalResult := mrOK;
end;

procedure TBitmapEditorDialog.btnLoadClick(Sender: TObject);
begin
  SelectAndQuit;
end;

procedure TBitmapEditorDialog.btnClearClick(Sender: TObject);
```

```
begin
  {Clear the ChosenBmp}
  ChosenBmp := Nil;
  {And close the form}
  ModalResult := mrOK;
end;

procedure TBitmapEditorDialog.pmColumnsClick(Sender: TObject);
begin
  SetColumnCheck((Sender as TMenuItem).Tag);
end;

procedure TBitmapEditorDialog.pmPixelsClick(Sender: TObject);
begin
  SetPixelCheck((Sender as TMenuItem).Tag);
end;

procedure TBitmapEditorDialog.pmHintsClick(Sender: TObject);
begin
  pmHints.Checked := Not pmHints.Checked;
  SetHintsCheck;
end;

procedure TBitmapEditorDialog.pmSaveSettingsClick(Sender: TObject);
begin
  pmSaveSettings.Checked := Not pmSaveSettings.Checked;
end;

procedure TBitmapEditorDialog.pmLowerCaseClick(Sender: TObject);
begin
  pmLowerCase.Checked := not pmLowerCase.Checked;
  BmpList.Refresh;
end;

procedure TBitmapEditorDialog.pmNoFilenameClick(Sender: TObject);
begin
  pmNoFilename.Checked := not pmNoFilename.Checked;
  BmpList.Refresh;
end;

procedure TBitmapEditorDialog.pmNoExtensionClick(Sender: TObject);
begin
  pmNoExtension.Checked := not pmNoExtension.Checked;
  BmpList.Refresh;
end;

procedure TBitmapEditorDialog.SetColumnCheck(TmpChecked: Integer);
begin
```

```
  {Set check states}
  pmColumns1.Checked := (TmpChecked = 1);
  pmColumns2.Checked := (TmpChecked = 2);
  pmColumns3.Checked := (TmpChecked = 3);
  pmColumns4.Checked := (TmpChecked = 4);
  pmColumns5.Checked := (TmpChecked = 5);
  pmColumns6.Checked := (TmpChecked = 6);
  {Set the columns appropriately}
  BmpList.Columns := TmpChecked;
end;

procedure TBitmapEditorDialog.SetPixelCheck(TmpChecked: Integer);
begin
  {Set the check states}
  pm20Pixels.Checked := (TmpChecked = 20);
  pm24Pixels.Checked := (TmpChecked = 24);
  pm28Pixels.Checked := (TmpChecked = 28);
  pm32Pixels.Checked := (TmpChecked = 32);
  pm36Pixels.Checked := (TmpChecked = 36);
  pm40Pixels.Checked := (TmpChecked = 40);
  {Set the item height appropriately}
  BmpList.ItemHeight := TmpChecked;
end;

procedure TBitmapEditorDialog.SetHintsCheck;
begin
  btnLoad.ShowHint := pmHints.Checked;
  btnClear.ShowHint := pmHints.Checked;
  BmpList.ShowHint := pmHints.Checked;
end;

(************************)
(*    TBitmapEditor     *)
(************************)

constructor TBitmapEditor.Create(AOwner: TComponent);
begin
  inherited Create(AOwner);
  FBitmap := TBitmap.Create;
  FBmpDlg := TBitmapEditorDialog.Create(Self);
end;

destructor TBitmapEditor.Destroy;
begin
  FBitmap.Free;
  FBmpDlg.Free;
  inherited Destroy;
```

```
end;

function TBitmapEditor.Execute: Boolean;
begin
  FBmpDlg.ChosenBmp.Assign(FBitmap);
  Result := (FBmpDlg.ShowModal = mrOK);
  if Result then FBitmap.Assign(FBmpDlg.ChosenBmp);
end;

procedure TBitmapEditor.SetBitmap(Value: TBitmap);
begin
  FBitmap.Assign(Value);
end;

(************************)
(*   TBitmapProperty    *)
(************************)

procedure TBitmapProperty.Edit;
var
  BitmapEditor : TBitmapEditor;
  SavedDir     : String;
begin
  {Save the current directory}
  GetDir(0,SavedDir);
  BitmapEditor := TBitmapEditor.Create(nil);
  try
    BitmapEditor.Bitmap := TBitmap(Pointer(GetOrdValue));
    if BitmapEditor.Execute then
      SetOrdValue(Longint(BitmapEditor.Bitmap));
  finally
    BitmapEditor.Free;
  end;
  {Restore the saved directory}
  ChDir(SavedDir);
end;

function TBitmapProperty.GetAttributes: TPropertyAttributes;
begin
  Result := [paDialog];
end;

{This function returns a string representation of
 how the property is set. If no bitmap is loaded,
 it will be set to 'None'. Otherwise it will show
 the bitmaps class name (should be TBitmap).}
function TBitmapProperty.GetValue: string;
var
```

```
  Bmp : TBitmap;
begin
  Bmp := TBitmap(GetOrdValue);
  if (Bmp = nil) or Bmp.Empty then
    Result := LoadStr(srNone)
  else
    Result := '(' + Bmp.ClassName + ')';
end;

procedure TBitmapProperty.SetValue(const Value: string);
begin
  if Value = '' then SetOrdValue(0);
end;

end.
```

NOTE: *If you want to create this component by typing in this code, recall that this unit is associated with a form. Typing this code in by hand requires that you also create a form, named BMPVIEW. This form must have on it the object specified in the TBitmapEditorDialog class definition. Both this unit and its associated form are also located on the CD-ROM for this book.*

One useful technique when creating a property editor is to first create it as a stand-alone program, if possible. For example, the bitmap viewer in the current example lends itself well to simply being a bitmap viewer. You can first create the viewer so that it behaves as you want, and then add the new functionality to make it a property editor. Granted, not all projects would lend themselves to this approach, but it is a useful development technique when you can use it.

NOTE: *In Chapter 18, you learn of an additional advantage of property editors. Not only can they be used to permit the developer to set properties at design time, they can sometimes be incorporated into the application as a feature. Using this BMPVIEW as both a bitmap viewer and as a Glyph property editor is an example of this approach.*

Defining the BmpView Property Editor

Notice the way the property editor is defined. First is the definition of the form itself, which is called TBitmapEditorDialog. It holds all the components mentioned previously (the list box, buttons, drive and directory lists, and so on) and is the visual portion of this project.

Next, a component is defined that is a wrapper around this form. This component is called TBitmapEditor and has two private variables. The first variable, FBmpDlg, is an instance of the TBitmapEditorDialog form, and the second variable, FBitmap, is of the type TBitmap. This second variable will hold the chosen graphic and make it available to the Object Inspector even after the TBitmapEditorDialog form has been closed.

The last item defined is the TBitmapProperty object, which is provided to define the interface that the Object Inspector will use to communicate with the TBitmapEditor component. Visually, this relationship is as follows:

TBitmapProperty

TBitmapEditor

TBitmapEditorDialog

As mentioned earlier, the TBitmapProperty provides an interface to the Object Inspector. When the user double-clicks on the Glyph property (or selects the ellipsis (…) button in the property's field), the Object inspector communicates with TBitmapProperty and says, in effect, "Go get a TBitmap."

Registering the Property Editor

This first requirement for a property editor is that it be registered with the Delphi IDE. Once this has been accomplished, Delphi will know when it needs to call up this editor. This is accomplished by means of the RegisterPropertyEditor procedure:

```
procedure Register;
begin
  RegisterPropertyEditor(TypeInfo(TBitmap),TComponent,
   'Glyph',TBitmapProperty);
end;
```

As described earlier in this chapter, the parameters here register the scope and behavior of the property editor with the Delphi Object Inspector. The first parameter is the Property Type and is used to provide runtime information about a particular object type, in this case a TBitmap. The next parameter is the ComponentClass which restricts which components are allowed access to this particular property editor. TComponent is specified here which means that the property editor is only available to the TComponent object or any of its descendants. The third parameter defines the actual name of the property that this editor will be attached to, in this case, "Glyph". This means the property must actually be named "Glyph" for the property editor to be associated with it.

Taking these parameters together, this registration procedure, in effect, says, *"Use this property editor on any property of type TBitmap that is named "Glyph" that occurs in any component that is of type TComponent or one of its descendants."*

This gives developers a great deal of control over how "exposed" a property editor is. In the present example, the bitmap property editor is restricted to a fairly small subset of the VCL Object Hierarchy. In fact, for an unmodified component library, this would mean only the Glyph properties of TBitBtn and TSpeedButton.

The TBitmapProperty Editor

```
TBitmapProperty = class(TClassProperty)
  public
    procedure Edit; override;
    function GetAttributes: TPropertyAttributes; override;
    function GetValue: string; override;
    procedure SetValue(const Value: string); override;
  end;
```

The TBitmapProperty descends from a TClassProperty component defined within Delphi. The TClassProperty is the default property editor for all properties that are themselves objects. In this case, the TBitmap is an object.

Now let's look into TBitmapProperty a bit more. Note that the property object basically only has four public methods: Edit, GetAttributes, GetValue, and SetValue.

```
procedure TBitmapProperty.Edit;
var
  BitmapEditor : TBitmapEditor;
  SavedDir     : String;
begin
  {Save the current directory}
  GetDir(0,SavedDir);
  BitmapEditor := TBitmapEditor.Create(nil);
  try
    BitmapEditor.Bitmap := TBitmap(Pointer(GetOrdValue));
    if BitmapEditor.Execute then
      SetOrdValue(Longint(BitmapEditor.Bitmap));
  finally
    BitmapEditor.Free;
  end;
  {Restore the saved directory}
  ChDir(SavedDir);
end;
```

The Edit method of TBitmapProperty is what is called when the user double-clicks on the property's field or clicks on the ellipsis (...) button in the Object Inspector. The Delphi IDE knows that this action represents a request to edit or change the property's value. The first thing that is done here is to save the current directory. Since the dialog box can switch the currently logged directory (to go find bitmap files), it is important to make sure that the old directory can be restored when the user is done with the dialog.

Next, an instance of the TBitmapEditor component is created. TBitmapEditor, in turn, knows how to create and destroy the dialog used to select the bitmap. Once TBitmapEditor is created, its Bitmap property is set with the bitmap that has already been selected into the component (if there is one).

Next, the BitmapEditor is executed, which displays the TBitmapEditorDialog form. This Execute method returns True (the user selected a bitmap) or False (no bitmap was selected). If the return value is True, the BitmapEditor knows to insert the newly chosen bitmap into the component's Glyph property. Finally, the BitmapEditor is released from memory, and the original directory is restored.

The BitmapEditor reads and writes the property's value from the Object Inspector by means of the GetOrdValue and SetOrdValue methods, which are being overridden in the present example. These two methods originate in the base TPropertyEditor class and pass a LongInt value to and from the component's property. In this case, the LongInt returned by GetOrd contains a pointer to the area of memory that is storing the Bitmap.

```
function TBitmapProperty.GetValue: string;
var
  Bmp : TBitmap;
begin
  Bmp := TBitmap(GetOrdValue);
  if (Bmp = nil) or Bmp.Empty then
    Result := LoadStr(srNone)
  else
    Result := '(' + Bmp.ClassName + ')';
end;
```

Within the Object Inspector, you obviously would not be able to display the bitmap in the value field of the Glyph property. However, the user needs to know whether this property has a value, hence, the need for the GetValue and SetValue methods. GetValue determines the value the property is currently assigned to. If it is a TBitmap, it returns to the Object Inspector an appropriate string (in this case "TBitmap"), and if it is empty, it returns the string "None." The Object Inspector then displays this string so that the user can see whether a bitmap has been assigned to this property or not.

The TBitmapEditor Component

```
TBitmapEditor = class(TComponent)
  private
    FBmpDlg: TBitmapEditorDialog;
    FBitmap: TBitmap;
    procedure SetBitmap(Value: TBitmap);
  public
    constructor Create(AOwner: TComponent); override;
    destructor Destroy; override;
    function Execute: Boolean;
    property Bitmap: TBitmap read FBitmap write SetBitmap;
  end;
```

The TBitmapEditor, as mentioned earlier, is a wrapper around the previously designed form. This component provides a means by which you can pass the chosen value back and forth between the Form and the component's property. Without this intermediate level, the selected bitmap would be lost because the form would already have been destroyed. Before the form is released from memory, the selected bitmap can be extracted and passed back to the TBitmapProperty editor:

```
constructor TBitmapEditor.Create(AOwner: TComponent);
begin
  inherited Create(AOwner);
  FBitmap := TBitmap.Create;
  FBmpDlg := TBitmapEditorDialog.Create(Self);
end;
```

When the TBitmapEditor component is created, it in turn creates the following:

1. The temporary bitmap used to hold the selected glyph.
2. An instance of the TBitmapEditorDialog form previously designed.

```
function TBitmapEditor.Execute: Boolean;
begin
  FBmpDlg.ChosenBmp.Assign(FBitmap);
  Result := (FBmpDlg.ShowModal = mrOK);
  if Result then FBitmap.Assign(FBmpDlg.ChosenBmp);
end;
```

The Execute function of the TBitmapEditor component assigns the default bitmap into the ChosenBmp variable within the form. It then tells the form to show itself modally and returns the modal result code in Result. If the modal result is mrOK (meaning the user selected a bitmap), the Result of the Execute function is set to True, and the new bitmap is assigned to the temporary bitmap. Now, even if the form is destroyed, you still have access to the bitmap by means of this temporary variable.

We're done with the property editor aspect of this project. The basic methods have been established to allow the Object Inspector to communicate with the property editor, which in turn communicates with the form. The next section describes enhancements made to the bitmap property editor.

Improvements the TBitmapPropertyEditor

This section describes improvements to the property editor that allow the user to customize and save various settings. Following are some of the methods and procedures used in the actual operation of the property editor so that you can see the thought processes behind its creation.

FormKeyDown

The FormKeyDown event handler allows a keyboard equivalent of a right-click on the bitmap list box. Such a right-click is used to access the pop-up menu so that the user can configure the appearance and operation of the program. The program should not require the user to have a mouse; therefore, this code allows the user to use CTRL-1 to access the pop-up menu. When the user depresses CTRL-1, the pop-up menu associated with the list box is activated at the listed coordinates.

```
procedure TBitmapEditorDialog.FormKeyDown(Sender: TObject;
           var Key: Word; Shift: TShiftState);
begin
  if (Shift = [ssCtrl]) and (Key = VK_1) then
    PopUpMenu1.PopUp(Left+BmpList.Left+(BmpList.Width div 2),
      Top+BmpList.Top+Height-ClientHeight+(BmpList.Height div 2));
end;
```

FormResize

With the wide range of display resolutions and monitor sizes available these days, it is increasingly important to allow an application to take advantage of extra (or restricted) screen size. By carefully inserting a few lines of code when the form resizes, the form can automatically move and resize other controls as needed in an intelligent way. In the FormResize event handler, the Cancel, Clear, and Load buttons are all placed a fixed distance from the bottom left-hand corner of the form, while the directory list box is enlarged to fill up spare room. The bitmap list box does not move its upper left-hand corner, but it does resize to fill the remainder of the form to the bottom right-hand corner.

```
procedure TBitmapEditorDialog.FormResize(Sender: TObject);
begin
  {The Cancel button will sit 6 pixels above the bottom of the form}
  btnCancel.Top := ClientHeight-btnCancel.Height-6;
  {The Clear button will be 6 pixels above the Cancel button}
  btnClear.Top := btnCancel.Top-btnClear.Height-6;
  {And the Top button will be 6 pixels above the Clear button}
  btnLoad.Top := btnClear.Top-btnLoad.Height-6;
  {Now align the Samples panel to the right of the 3 buttons}
  with SamplesPanel do
    SetBounds(Left,btnLoad.Top,Width,Self.ClientHeight-btnLoad.Top-6);
  {The DirList should take up all the space remaining above the buttons}
  DirList.Height := btnLoad.Top-DirList.Top-6;
  {Do an update here to make sure all controls paint before the BmpList}
```

```
Update;

  {The BmpList should take up all remaining space on the form}
  with BmpList do
    SetBounds(Left,Top,Self.ClientWidth-Left-6,Self.ClientHeight-Top-6);
end;
```

BmpListDrawItem

The bitmap list box is an owner-drawn control. By specifying its Style property as *lbOwnerDrawFixed* and providing a method for its OnDrawItem event, you can control how each item in the list box is drawn. The BmpListDrawItem method pays attention to many of the user's configuration settings, such as the ability to show or hide filenames and/or file extensions.

```
procedure TBitmapEditorDialog.BmpListDrawItem(Control: TWinControl;
  Index: Integer; Rect: TRect; State: TOwnerDrawState);
var
  Bmp     : TBitmap;
  BmpH    : Integer;
  OffsetT : Integer;
  OffsetL : Integer;
  DstRect : TRect;
  SrcRect : TRect;
  TheText : String[12];
  DotLoc  : Integer;
  bkColor : TColor;
begin
  with Control as TListBox,Canvas do
    begin
      {Create a temporary bitmap}
      Bmp := TBitmap.Create;
      try
        {Load the image from the file}
        Bmp.LoadFromFile(Items[Index]);
        {and draw it}
        BmpH := Bmp.Height;
        If BmpH > ItemHeight then BmpH := ItemHeight;
        OffsetL := 3;
        OffsetT := (ItemHeight-BmpH) div 2;
        if OffsetT <= 0 then
          begin
            OffsetT := 0;
            OffsetL := 0;
          end;
        FillRect(Rect);
        {The SrcRect is the area we will paint of the bitmap}
```

```
        SrcRect := Bounds(0,0,BmpH,BmpH);
        {The DstRect is the rectangle defining where the bitmap will go}
        DstRect := Bounds(Rect.Left+OffsetL,Rect.Top+OffsetT,BmpH,BmpH);
        if not pmNoFilename.Checked then
          begin
            {Determine the horizontal and vertical
             offsets for painting the text}
            OffsetT := (ItemHeight-TextPixels) div 2;
            if OffsetT < 0 then OffsetT := 0;
            {Get the text from the list box}
            TheText := (Control as TListBox).Items[Index];
            {Shift label into lower case if required}
            if pmLowerCase.Checked then TheText := LowerCase(TheText);
            {Does the user want no extensions?}
            if pmNoExtension.Checked then
              begin
                {Find where the period is in the filename}
                DotLoc := Pos('.',TheText);
                {If found, chop off the extension}
                if DotLoc > 0 then TheText :=  Copy(TheText,1,DotLoc-1);
              end;
            {Write out the text}
            TextRect(Rect,Rect.Left+ItemHeight+3,
              Rect.Top+OffsetT,TheText);
          end;
        {Background color is the bottom left pixel in the bitmap}
        with Bmp do bkColor := Canvas.Pixels[0,Height-1];
        {Paint the bitmap, replace all pixels
         of bkColor with form color}
        if Bmp <> nil then BrushCopy(DstRect, Bmp, SrcRect, bkColor);
      finally
        {Release the temporary bitmap}
        Bmp.Free;
      end;
    end;
end;
```

Note that the bitmap image is loaded when the item is drawn. This may seem inefficient, but it is actually very efficient. If you were to read all bitmaps in a directory into some kind of TList structure, you would quickly burn up what little resources Windows has available (particularly if the directory had a large number of bitmap files). Instead, the ReadBitmap procedure loads just the names of the bitmap files into a TList, and the bitmaps themselves are loaded individually as the control is painted. The performance is only slightly slower (because of the way that Windows caches disk reads), but you are then able to load and display a great number of bitmaps in a single directory while never using more than a single TBitmap to do it.

BmpListClick

When the user single-clicks on an item in the bitmap list box, that bitmap is then loaded into the various test buttons in the Samples panel. This feature allows the user to get a feel for how the bitmaps will appear on a button.

```
procedure TBitmapEditorDialog.BmpListClick(Sender: TObject);
begin
  with BmpList do
    {Is there an item selected?}
    if ItemIndex >= 0 then
      begin
        {If there is a bitmap selected, load it into the BitBtn}
        btnBitBtnSample.Glyph.LoadFromFile(Items[ItemIndex]);
        {Copy that bitmap into the Active button as well}
        btnActiveSample.Glyph.Assign(btnBitBtnSample.Glyph);
        {Set the number of glyphs the same as BitBtn}
        btnActiveSample.NumGlyphs := btnBitBtnSample.NumGlyphs;
        {Copy the bitmap also into the Inactive button}
        btnInactiveSample.Glyph.Assign(btnBitBtnSample.Glyph);
        {And set its number of glyphs also}
        btnInactiveSample.NumGlyphs := btnBitBtnSample.NumGlyphs;
      end;
end;
```

BmpListDblClick

The BmpListDblClick event handler selects and loads the bitmap, puts away the property editor, and fills the component's Glyph property with the selected image. This step obviates the need to force the user to click on the Load button. Users will appreciate every little shortcut that you can provide.

```
procedure TBitmapEditorDialog.BmpListDblClick(Sender: TObject);
begin
  {If the user double-clicks an item in the
   list box, select it and close the form}
  SelectAndQuit;
end;
```

ReadBitmaps

The ReadBitmaps procedure is used to fill the bitmap list box with string values representing the filenames that were found in the current directory. An artificial restriction was implemented to only pay attention to bitmap files that were 4000 bytes or smaller. Any image larger than this would typically be unsuitable for a button glyph anyway.

```
procedure TBitmapEditorDialog.ReadBitmaps;
var
  Bitmap    : TBitmap;
  SearchRec : TSearchRec;
  Result    : Integer;
begin
  {Set the hourglass cursor}
  Screen.Cursor := crHourglass;
  {Clear the previous items from the BmpList}
  BmpList.Clear;
  {Move to the directory pointed to in the DirList}
  ChDir(DirList.Directory);
  {Now start looking for the bitmaps names}
  Result := FindFirst('*.bmp',faAnyFile,SearchRec);
  While Result = 0 do
    begin
      {Only load bitmaps less than 4001 bytes in size}
      if SearchRec.Size <= 4000 then BmpList.Items.Add(SearchRec.Name);
      {Find the next one}
      Result := FindNext(SearchRec);
    end;
  FindClose(SearchRec);
  {Restore the standard cursor}
  Screen.Cursor := crDefault;
end;
```

DirListChange

When the user moves to a new directory, you need to re-read the bitmaps from the new directory. This step is accomplished by calling the ReadBitmaps.

```
procedure TBitmapEditorDialog.DirListChange(Sender: TObject);
begin
  {Whenever we move into a new directory,
   we need to re-read the bitmap names}
  ReadBitmaps;
end;
```

WriteSettings and ReadSettings

The WriteSettings and ReadSettings methods are used to save and restore the configuration information to an INI file. Items saved include the last directory viewed, the number of columns, the height of each item, the display settings for the filenames themselves, and the size and state of the window.

```
procedure TBitmapEditorDialog.ReadSettings;
begin
  {Read all configuration and window settings from the INI file}
  SettingsIni := TIniFile.Create('BMPVIEW.INI');
  {Configuration Settings}
  DirList.Directory       :=
    SettingsIni.ReadString( 'Options', 'Directory','C:\');
  BmpList.Columns         :=
    SettingsIni.ReadInteger('Options', 'Columns',2);
  BmpList.ItemHeight      :=
    SettingsIni.ReadInteger('Options', 'ItemHeight',24);
  pmHints.Checked         :=
    SettingsIni.ReadBool('Options','Hints',True);
  pmSaveSettings.Checked :=
    SettingsIni.ReadBool('Options','SaveSettings',True);
  pmLowerCase.Checked     :=
    SettingsIni.ReadBool('Options','LowerCase',False);
  pmNoFilename.Checked    :=
    SettingsIni.ReadBool('Options','NoFilename',False);
  pmNoExtension.Checked   :=
    SettingsIni.ReadBool('Options','NoExtension',True);
  {Window position settings}
  FormL           := SettingsIni.ReadInteger('Window','Left',-99);
  FormT           := SettingsIni.ReadInteger('Window','Top',-99);
  FormW           := SettingsIni.ReadInteger('Window','Width',-99);
  FormH           := SettingsIni.ReadInteger('Window','Height',-99);
  FormState        := SettingsIni.ReadInteger('Window','State',0);
  {Only do a setbounds if all parameters have been specified}
  If (FormL >= 0) and (FormT >= 0) and
    (FormW > 0) and (FormH > 0) then
    SetBounds(FormL,FormT,FormW,FormH);
  {Set the previous window state}
  Case FormState of
    0 : WindowState := wsNormal;
    1 : WindowState := wsMaximized;
    2 : WindowState := wsMinimized;
  end;
  {Set initial menu check states}
  SetColumnCheck(BmpList.Columns);
  SetPixelCheck(BmpList.ItemHeight);
  SetHintsCheck;
  {Free the TIniFile object}
  SettingsIni.Free;
end;

procedure TBitmapEditorDialog.WriteSettings;
begin
  {Write out configuration & Window settings to INI file}
  SettingsIni := TIniFile.Create('BMPVIEW.INI');
```

```
    SettingsIni.WriteBool('Options','SaveSettings',
      pmSaveSettings.Checked);
    {Only save remaining items if SaveSettings is checked}
    if pmSaveSettings.Checked then
      begin
        SettingsIni.WriteString( 'Options',
          'Directory',DirList.Directory);
        SettingsIni.WriteInteger('Options', 'Columns',BmpList.Columns);
        SettingsIni.WriteInteger('Options', 'ItemHeight',
          BmpList.ItemHeight);
        SettingsIni.WriteBool('Options','Hints',pmHints.Checked);
        SettingsIni.WriteBool('Options','LowerCase',
          pmLowerCase.Checked);
        SettingsIni.WriteBool('Options','NoFilename',
          pmNoFilename.Checked);
        SettingsIni.WriteBool('Options','NoExtension',
          pmNoExtension.Checked);
        SettingsIni.WriteInteger('Window', 'Left',Left);
        SettingsIni.WriteInteger('Window', 'Top',Top);
        SettingsIni.WriteInteger('Window', 'Width',Width);
        SettingsIni.WriteInteger('Window', 'Height',Height);
        Case WindowState of
          wsNormal    : SettingsIni.WriteInteger('Window', 'State',0);
          wsMaximized : SettingsIni.WriteInteger('Window', 'State',1);
          wsMinimized : SettingsIni.WriteInteger('Window', 'State',2);
        end;
      end;
    SettingsIni.Free;
end;
```

Making changes to an INI file is quite simple. To write or read an entry is a simple three-step procedure. First, the INI file must be opened by using the Create method of the TIniFile object:

```
SettingsIni := TIniFil.Create('BMPVIEW.INI');
```

This line will open the BMPVIEW.INI file (or create it if it doesn't exist) and assign access to that file through the variable provided, in this case, the variable SettingsIni. Next, you can read an entry using any of the Read options defined by the TIniFile class. For example, to read a string you could do the following:

```
DirList.Directory := SettingsIni.ReadString('Options', 'Directory', 'C:\');
```

This line will read a string from the Directory entry of the Options section. If this entry does not exist, the default value of 'C:\' will be returned. This portion of the INI file might look something like this:

```
[Options]
Directory=C:\DELPHI
```

GetMinMaxInfo

Whenever a user begins to resize a form, a message is sent to the application to enquire about the maximum and minimum limits that will restrict the movement of the window. The response from this message limits how the form can be resized. In this example, the minimum size of the form is restricted to a minimum width of 300 pixels and a minimum height of 250 pixels. These restrictions ensure that the user cannot resize the form to a condition that makes it unusable.

```
procedure TBitmapEditorDialog.WMGetMinMaxInfo(var Message
                                                     :TWMGetMinMaxInfo);
begin
  with Message.MinMaxInfo^ do
  begin
    ptMinTrackSize.X := 300; {Minimum width}
    ptMinTrackSize.Y := 250; {Minimum height}
  end;
  Message.Result := 0;
  inherited;
end;
```

The Final Result

The final product of these improvements is illustrated in the next few figures. Figure 4-8 shows the standard property editor after activation.

Because of the customization features built into this editor, if the user doesn't like the appearance of the editor, he or she can change it. In Figure 4-9, for example, the form was dragged to the lower right corner, and then sized a bit differently. In addition, the right-click menu on the bitmap list was used to turn off the filenames and to increase the number of columns to four.

The key to creating a useful property editor (or any other programming project for that matter) is to make the tools available to the programmer (or user) in such a way that they are never in the way. If you had a hammer whose head fell off every third time you hit a nail, you would soon discover that you spent more time fiddling with the hammer than you did driving nails. The same holds true for programming tools. The tools should be useful and functional, and they should adapt to the way the user intends to implement them. They should not cause additional problems that the user normally wouldn't (or shouldn't) have to deal with. That way, the user can concentrate on more important things, rather than having to deal with quirks or difficulties in the tools.

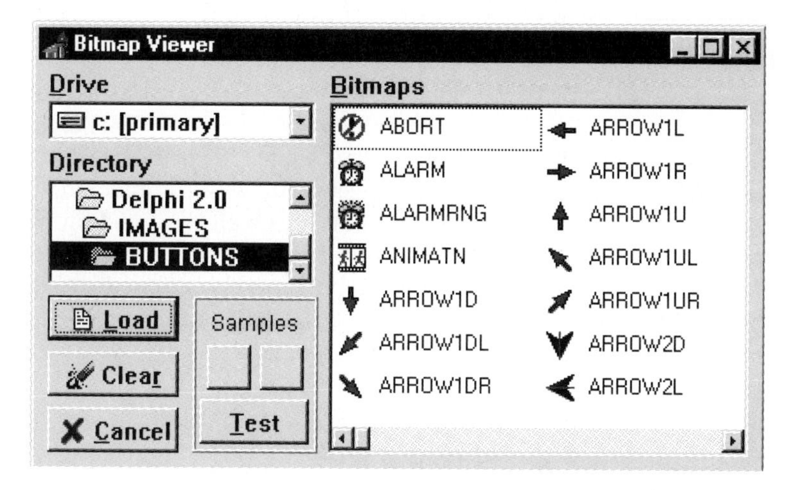

Figure 4-8. *Form shown when you first view the custom property editor*

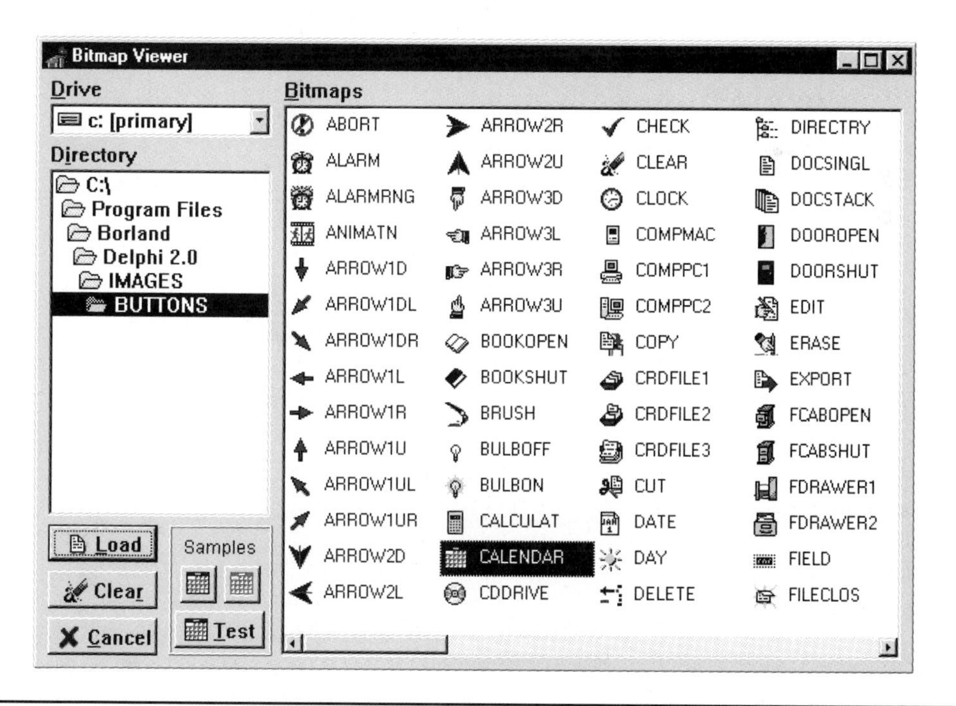

Figure 4-9. *Form after you customize the property editor*

Conclusion

This chapter has covered some of the essential techniques used to create property editors. The best resource for moving on from here is the DSGNINTF.PAS (or DSGNINTF.INC) file that comes with Delphi. This source file is the heart of how property editors function, and fortunately, it is generally well commented.

Property editors are in a field by themselves. With a well-designed property editor, a developer can create sophisticated front-ends to specialized properties in their components. Once again, Borland has shown us how modern application development was really meant to be done!

Chapter Five

Databases and Database Components

The code for the examples presented in this chapter can be found in the \CODE\CH05 subdirectory on the CD-ROM that accompanies this book. Please refer to Appendix A for information on using the code files for this chapter.

Database connectivity and functionality is a major part of Delphi's feature set. Delphi includes components that connect to data files and data-aware components to display the data in a form. These components provide built-in features to create single-user and multi-user applications, providing access to data residing on local workstations, file servers, or database servers running one of the multiple SQL database servers available in the marketplace.

This chapter provides an introduction to the database-related components in Delphi and a general overview of how these components are used, beginning with an overview of Delphi's data connectivity. The basics of using visual and non-visual components and their properties are discussed. Also discussed is the BDE (Borland Database Engine) and how you can use it to provide access to data independent of the VCL (Visual Component Library) or to enhance the access of data-aware controls.

Data Connectivity Overview

Delphi provides connectivity to a variety of data file formats. You can connect to virtually any type of data if a driver is available for the data format. The BDE (Borland Database Engine) is the nucleus for providing access to local tables in Paradox, dBASE, and ASCII formats. SQL (Structured Query Language) database server connectivity is provided using either SQL Links or ODBC (Open Database Connectivity) drivers. Borland provides SQL Links that are native drivers for a number of the more popular SQL databases, including InterBase, Informix, Oracle, Microsoft SQL Server, and SYBASE servers. Using ODBC, you can connect to databases such as MS Access, AS/400, DB2, and many others. Figure 5-1 shows a diagram of the database connectivity overview in Delphi.

The heart of any data connection is the BDE. All Borland products use the API (Application Programming Interface) found in the BDE to provide data access (this API is formally referred to as IDAPI—Independent Database Application Programming Interface). These calls are transparent to Delphi users and, if you are using data-aware components, also to the Delphi developer. The methods of the data-aware components use the BDE to open, close, modify, and navigate through any data set. The BDE is covered in greater detail later in this chapter.

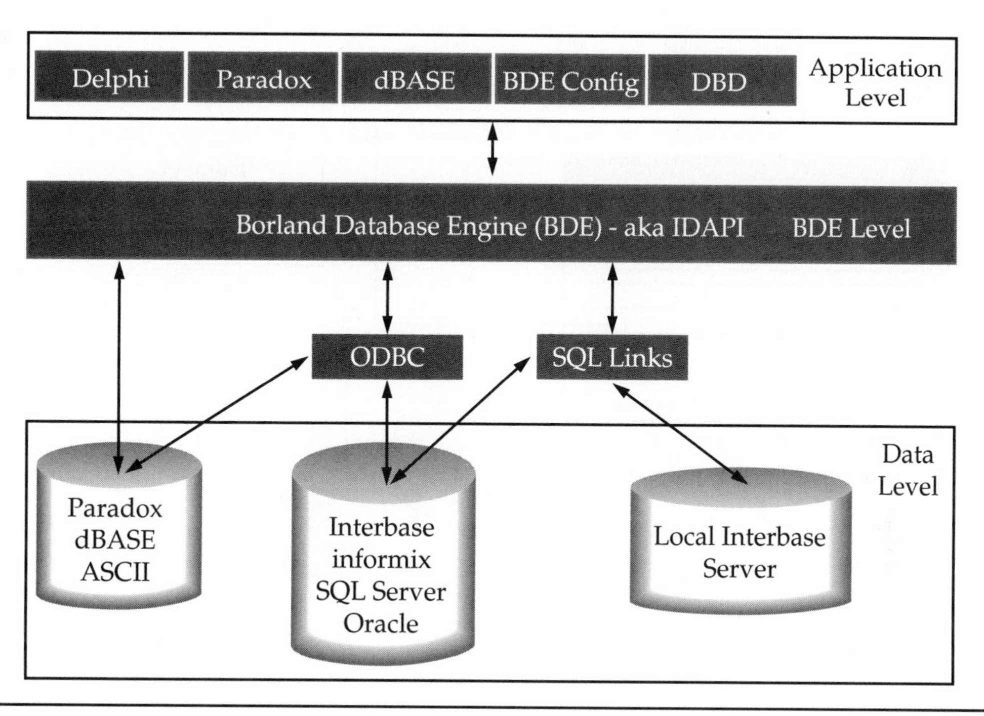

Figure 5-1. *Database connectivity overview in Delphi*

Basics for Connecting to Data

A basic understanding of the foundational concepts of data connectivity is essential before examining the many database features Delphi supports. These areas include the definition of terminology and the basics steps to display data in Delphi forms. To view and modify data using Delphi, you need to define the source of the data you intend to use, how to display the data at runtime, and how to connect the two. These steps are done using DataSets, DataSources, and data-aware controls.

Figure 5-2 shows the dependencies between a Delphi form and data displayed in the form. The data files are defined using a DataSet component. The form contains the data-aware components that display the data. A DataSource component is used to connect the data-aware components to the DataSet components. The next section looks at the components used to provide data connectivity.

DataSet Components

DataSet components are required to define the properties of the data. These components are available on the Data Access page of the component palette. There are three types of DataSet components: TTable, TQuery, and TStoredProc. Each component

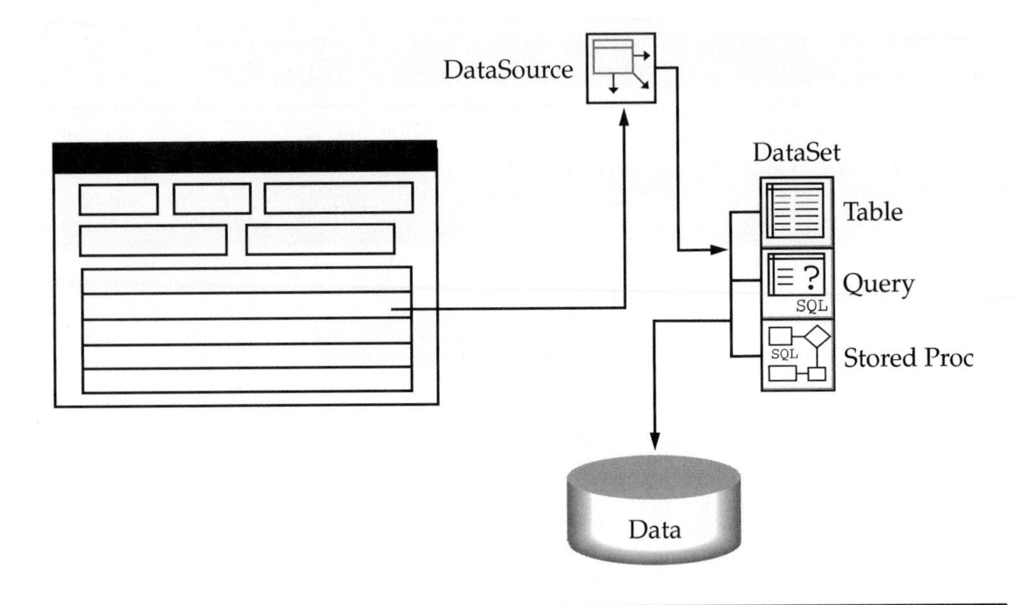

Figure 5-2. *Basic requirements to display data in a form*

provides a different set of features and functionality. These components appear as the second through fourth components on the Data Access page shown here:

The Table Component

The Table component provides access to a table in a database. You must set at least three properties in the Object Inspector to open a table: the DatabaseName, TableName, and Active. The DatabaseName property defines where the data resides. This location could be a drive and directory name or an alias. (Aliases are discussed later in this chapter.) The name of the table to access is set in the TableName property. To open the table, the Active property must be set to True. Once these three properties have been set (the Active property cannot be changed from False to True without the DatabaseName and TableName set), you have an open table.

NOTE: Setting the Active property to True at design time permits you to view the contents of the table while you are designing your forms. This is also necessary in order to instantiate Field components (TField class descendants) at design time. However, it is not always necessary, practical, or even possible to activate a Table object at design time. In those instances, you can set the Active property to True at runtime (usually in the form's OnCreate event handler), or by calling the table's Open method.

The Query Component

A Query component permits you to define and execute SQL statements. Certain SQL statements, such as SELECT, return a cursor (pointer) to one or more records, called a *dataset*. For these types of SQL statements, the Query component is very similar to a Table component in that it permits your code, as well as the user, to navigate the returned records.

There are three essential properties of a Query component. In addition to the DatabaseName and Active properties of a Query, the SQL property is a StringList property that holds the SQL statements that the Query executes.

The StoredProc Component

A StoredProc component, like a Query component, can return a cursor to a dataset. A StoredProc component is used to execute a stored procedure on an SQL database. When the stored procedure returns a dataset, the StoredProc component can be used to access the data similar to Query and Table components.

There are three important properties of StoredProc components. You assign DatabaseName to the alias defined for the database server. StoredProcName is used to hold the name of the stored procedure, and Params is a StringList that you use to define any parameters that need to be passed to the stored procedure.

Data-Aware Components

The Data Controls page of the component palette shown here contains the data-aware components. These components provide users with the ability to view, edit, and navigate the data pointed to by DataSet components.

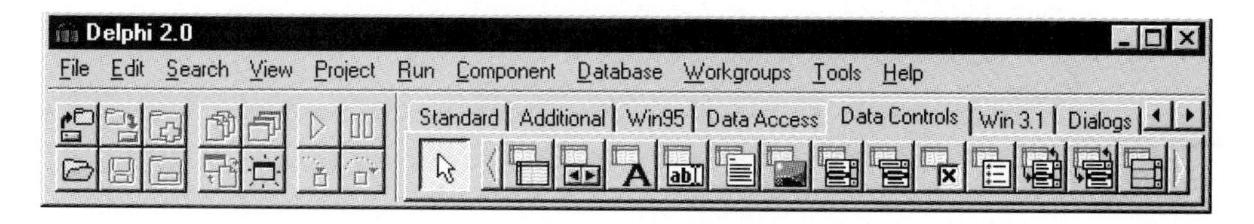

The thirteen data-aware components from which you can select are listed in Table 5-1. These components give you the choice of showing data from multiple rows or a single row, including a navigation bar to move between rows in your table, showing memo and image data, using list and combo boxes, check boxes, and radio buttons.

Component Class	Description
TDBGrid	A fixed row and column tabular display of data.
TDBNavigator	Navigation bar providing record movement and datainsertion, deletion, and saving.
TDBText	Displays the values from a field but does not allow modification to the data.
TDBEdit	An edit box allowing the data in a field to be modified.
TDBMemo	A memo box displaying variable length text and allowing the data to be edited.
TDBImage	An image box for BLOB data.
TDBListBox	A list box showing multiple values from a dataset.
TDBComboBox	A multi-column drop-down edit box.
TDBCheckBox	A check box display for a field in a dataset.
TDBRadioBox	A radio button display for a field in a dataset.
TDBLookupList (in Delphi 1.0) TDBLookupListBox (in Delphi 2)	Values from another dataset providing a list of possible values for a field using a list box display.
TDBLookupCombo (in Delphi 1.0) TDBLookupComboBox (in Delphi 2)	Values from another dataset providing a list of possible values for a field using a combo box display.
TDBCtrlGrid (Delphi 2 only)	A free-form multi-record grid display.

Table 5-1. *Data-Aware Components*

NOTE: In Delphi 2 the DBLookupListBox and DBLookupComboBox replaced the DBLookupList and DBLookupCombo components. These Delphi 1.0 components are still available in Delphi 2, but they are on the Win 3.1 page of the component palette.

In addition to data-aware controls, you also need to include a DataSource component. The DataSource component can be found on the Data Access page of the component palette.

NOTE: Data-aware controls are necessary only if you want to permit the user to interact with the data. If your code only needs to access the data, for example, to look up a particular value, data-aware controls are not necessary.

Other Data-Related Components

In addition to DataSet and data-aware components, several additional components provide data-related services. These components, like the DataSet components, are found on the Data Access page of the component palette: DataSource, Database, Session (Delphi 2 only), BatchMove, UpdateSQL (Delphi 2 only), and Report. These components are described in the following sections.

The DataSource Component

The DataSource component provides the link on your form between the DataSet component and the data-aware controls. You need a single DataSource component for each DataSet component that data-aware controls need to access. The DataSource component is the first component on the Data Access page of the Component palette.

Each visual component has a DataSource property. This property needs to be set to the name of the correct DataSource component for the data to be shown on the form.

NOTE: If you are not using data-aware controls on a form, you usually do not need to use a DataSource component. The exception to this rule is when you want to link two datasets. Linked datasets, even those that are not designed for user access, require a DataSource to provide for the linking. Linking DataSets is described in Chapter 6.

The Database Component

The Database component provides options for connecting to databases, including both local tables and remote databases. The drive and directory for local or file server tables can be defined for an application using the file location or an alias (a label for a data location). For remote databases, this component can be used to set user names, passwords, and other remote connection parameters. If you do not explicitly use a Database component, Delphi creates a temporary one for you and uses it dynamically for connection purposes. Defining properties for local table access is discussed further in the "Using the Database Component with Local Tables" section in this chapter. Dynamic settings for remote databases are discussed in Chapter 8.

TIP: You can use a Database component to define an alias that is local to an application. This alias can then be used by any DataSet components in the application, even those that appear on forms other than the one on which the Database component appears. This cross-form alias availability does not require the inclusion of the Database form's unit in other unit's uses clauses. Aliases are discussed in greater detail later in this chapter.

The Session Component

New on the Data Access page in Delphi 2 is the Session component. This object existed in Delphi 1.0, but it was not part of the component palette. The Session component provides global control in an application for databases. Some of its properties include the names and count of the active Database components, the names of the Netfile and Private directories used by Paradox tables, and the language driver used for the session.

The BatchMove Component

You can move data between tables using the BatchMove component. You specify the source DataSet and destination Table using properties. You can also designate if the operation is to abort when there are problems moving the data or when a record duplicates the value in a primary key. Chapter 6 describes this component in more detail.

The Update SQL Component

Also new on the Delphi 2 Data Access page is the UpdateSQL component. This component provides a way to use Delphi's cached updates support with datasets. You define SQL statements to perform inserts, deletes, and modifications to a dataset. Chapter 7 contains more information on how to use the UpdateSQL component.

The Report Component

The last component on the Data Access page is the Report component. You use it to provide runtime access to a ReportSmith report. ReportSmith is an SQL-based report generator that ships with Delphi. See Chapter 9 for more information on creating and using ReportSmith reports.

The next section looks at the steps to providing data connectivity in a form.

Using Data in a Delphi Form

There are four basic steps to providing access to data on a Delphi form:

1. Place a DataSet, a DataSource, and appropriate data-aware controls on the form.
2. Define the DataSet.
3. Link the components.
4. Compile and run the program.

These four steps are demonstrated in the following example. This demonstration will create a form that permits users to edit the data in a Paradox table named CUSTOMER.DB. This table is located in a directory that is associated with an alias named DBDEMOS, which is created when you install Delphi.

Placing the Components

Begin by creating a new project in Delphi. Once you have the new form displayed in the Delphi designer, place one Table (a DataSet) and one DataSource component from the Data Access page onto the form. Next, add one DBGrid component from the Data Controls page. The DBGrid provides your users with a tabular display. Your form should look something like the one shown in Figure 5-3.

Defining the DataSet

To define the dataset, select the Table component and then display the Object Inspector. Click the drop-down arrow in the DatabaseName property to display the alias list. Select DBDEMOS. Next, select CUSTOMER.DB from the TableName drop-down list. Finally, switch the Active property from False to True. The Customer table is now open.

Linking the Components

In this step you set the properties of your components to make them aware of one another. Begin by selecting the DataSource. Set its DataSet property to Table1 (the name of the DataSet component).

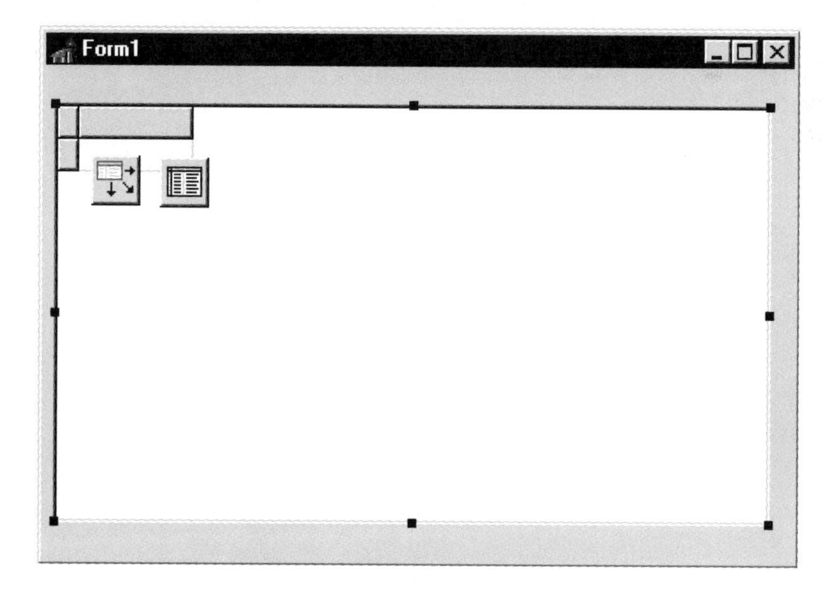

Figure 5-3. *Initial form design for data connectivity*

Now, select the DBGrid and set its DataSource property to point to the DataSource. Because the DBGrid points to the DataSource, and the DataSource points to an active DataSet, the DBGrid will now display live data from the defined DataSet, as shown in Figure 5-4.

Compiling and Running the Form

You are now ready to compile and run the form. To run the form from within the Delphi IDE, select Run | Run, or press F9. Your form will immediately compile and then run. Your running form will now look something like that shown in Figure 5-5.

Notice that two objects that you placed on the form are not displayed when the form is run—the DataSource and Table components. These are non-visual components. Therefore, you will see them only when the form is in design mode; they are not visible when the form is run.

Although it is relatively easy to display table data on a form, it is easier still if you use the Database Form Expert to create your form. You access the Database Expert in Delphi 1.0 by selecting Help | Database Expert. In Delphi 2, you access this expert from the Experts page of the Repository.

Regardless of which technique you use to create a form, you need to expand upon these basic steps to fully utilize the multitude of Delphi features available for database application development. Chapter 6 contains a discussion of many different basic database tasks, along with demonstrations of how they can be accomplished in Delphi.

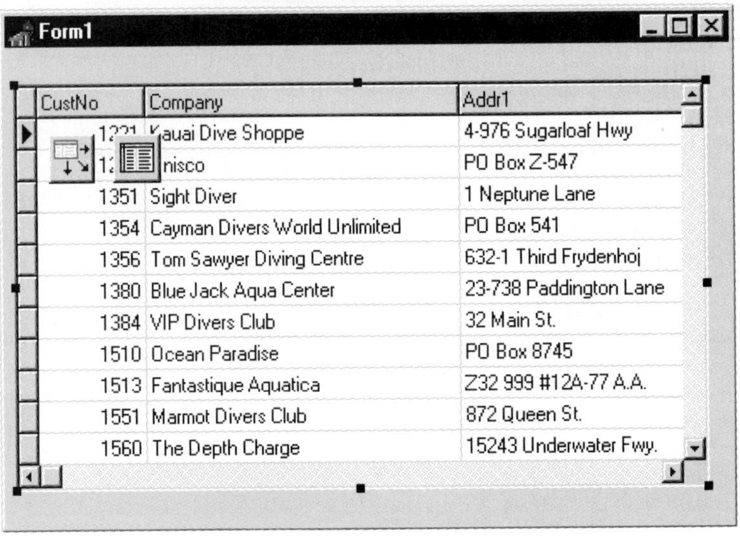

Figure 5-4. *When a DBGrid points to a DataSource for an active Table component, the data can be viewed while you are designing the form*

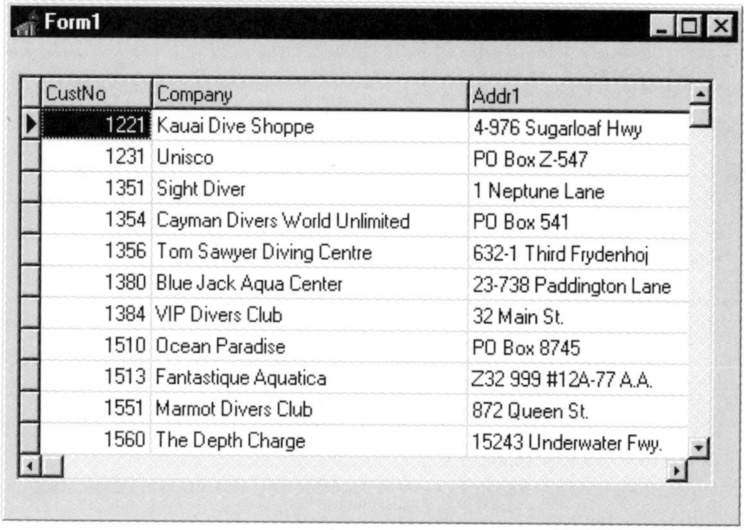

Form1

CustNo	Company	Addr1
1221	Kauai Dive Shoppe	4-976 Sugarloaf Hwy
1231	Unisco	PO Box Z-547
1351	Sight Diver	1 Neptune Lane
1354	Cayman Divers World Unlimited	PO Box 541
1356	Tom Sawyer Diving Centre	632-1 Third Frydenhoj
1380	Blue Jack Aqua Center	23-738 Paddington Lane
1384	VIP Divers Club	32 Main St.
1510	Ocean Paradise	PO Box 8745
1513	Fantastique Aquatica	Z32 999 #12A-77 A.A.
1551	Marmot Divers Club	872 Queen St.
1560	The Depth Charge	15243 Underwater Fwy.

Figure 5-5. *A running Delphi application displaying data from the CUSTOMER.DB table*

Additional Database Topics

The remainder of this chapter focuses on several additional database topics, including aliases, basic event handlers for data access, and a more in-depth look at the BDE.

Database Aliases

An alias is a name you assign as a shortcut to the location of your data. This will be a directory on your local machine or a network server when you are using Paradox or dBASE tables. The files in a directory can be considered a database for local tables. If your data resides in an SQL database, the alias points to the server and contains basic connection parameters to the remote database. This chapter covers establishing an alias for local tables. Using aliases for remote databases is covered in Chapter 7.

Using the BDE Configuration Utility

Included with all Delphi versions is the BDE Configuration Utility. This utility is used to create aliases before you use them in your Delphi applications. The BDE Configuration Utility is also used to configure database server drivers and ODBC connectivity. In Delphi 1.0, you load the utility by selecting either the Database Engine Configuration program item in the Delphi program group or the BDE Config option from the Tools menu when Delphi is running. In Delphi 2, you select the BDE Configuration program item from the Borland Delphi 2.0 Folder.

TIP: Unlike in Delphi 1.0, the Tools menu in Delphi 2 does not contain a BDE Config option by default. You can add this option by selecting Tools | Tools from the Delphi main menu to display the Tools Options dialog box, through which you can add entries for any executable file.

The initial form displayed for the BDE Configuration Utility is similar in both versions of Delphi. Figure 5-6 shows the initial Delphi 2 BDE Configuration Utility screen with the PARADOX driver selected. The Options menu choice is not available in the Delphi 1.0 BDE Configuration Utility.

The BDE Configuration Utility uses a visual notebook format, with tabbed pages containing the parameters for the system configuration options. The first page, Drivers, is where the currently available drivers are listed. Drivers are copied to your machine when Delphi is installed. The STANDARD driver is used for Paradox, dBASE, and ASCII file formats. Drivers for SQL servers are installed if you have the Client/Server version of Delphi or you add Borland SQL Links to your system. These drivers include INTRBASE (InterBase servers), MSSQL (Microsoft SQL Server), ORACLE (Oracle servers), and SYBASE (Sybase servers).

Default parameters are set for each driver type on the Drivers page. Parameters specify how the BDE is to handle connections to the data. Which parameters appear here depend on the driver, since different drivers need different parameters to handle the specifics of connecting to a given server type. The Help system for the BDE Config

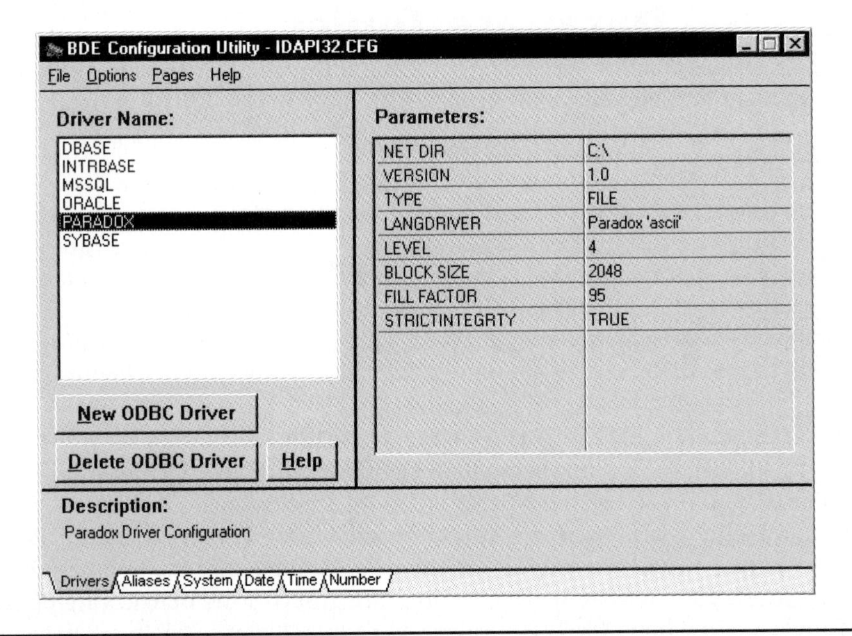

Figure 5-6. *Delphi 2 BDE Configuration Utility showing parameters for the PARADOX driver*

lists the descriptions for each of the drivers. As an example, Table 5-2 lists the parameters and description for the PARADOX driver contained in the help system.

Parameter	Description
VERSION	Internal version number of the Paradox driver.
TYPE	Type of server to which this driver helps you connect. Can be SERVER (SQL server) or FILE (standard, file-based server).
NET DIR	The directory location of the Paradox network control file PDOXUSRS.NET. The active NET DIR parameter is stored in the Paradox section of the BDE configuration file and has precedence over any other NET DIR parameters that may be stored in older 16-bit configuration files, or in the System Init section of the current configuration file, or in the Registry. These other NET DIR entries will have no effect. To access a Paradox table on a network drive, the active NETDIR parameter in the Paradox section of the BDE configuration file must point to a network drive.
LANGDRIVER	Language driver used to determine table sort order and character set. US default: ASCII.
LEVEL	Type of table format used to create temporary Paradox tables: Level 7: Paradox for Windows 32-bit tables (Delphi 2 only) Level 5: Paradox 5.0 tables Level 4: STANDARD table format for Paradox 4.0 Level 3: Compatible table format used by Paradox 3.5 and earlier versions. Default: Level 4 To use Blob fields, secondary indexes, and strict referential integrity, specify either Paradox Level 4 or Paradox Level 5 tables. You will probably want to use the lowest level possible in order to maximize backward compatibility. Choose Level 7 only if you need the advanced indexing features supported by that table format.

Table 5-2. *Configuration Parameters for the PARADOX Driver*

Parameter	Description
BLOCK SIZE	Size of disk blocks used to store Paradox table records, in multiples of 1024 bytes. Can be any multiple of 1024 (e.g., 2048, 3072, 4096) up to 32 kilobytes. Default: 2048
FILL FACTOR	Percentage of current disk block which must be filled before Paradox will allocate another disk block for index files. Can be any integer ranging from 1 to 100. Default: 95 Note: Smaller values offer better performance but increase the size of indexes. Larger values give smaller index files but increase the time needed to create an index.
STRICTINTEGRTY	Specifies whether Paradox tables can be modified using applications that do not support referential integrity (e.g., Paradox 4.0). For example, if this parameter is set to TRUE you will be unable to change a table with referential integrity using Paradox 4.0; if it is FALSE, you can change the table, but you risk the integrity of your data. Default: TRUE

Table 5-2. *Configuration Parameters for the PARADOX Driver* (continued)

The default settings are assigned when the driver is installed. These values can be changed for any of the drivers. To make a change, highlight the driver to display its parameters. Highlight the parameter you want to change and then enter a new value. These parameters are used when you create an alias based on a driver.

Creating a New Alias

The Aliases page, shown in Figure 5-7, is where you add, delete, and modify an alias. To create a new alias, click the New Alias button, which displays the Add New Alias dialog box. In the New Alias Name text box, enter the name of the alias you want to add. The Alias type is a drop-down list of the drivers that are installed. STANDARD is the default type. To change to a different driver, drop down the list, select the driver for the alias, and click the OK button to accept the new alias.

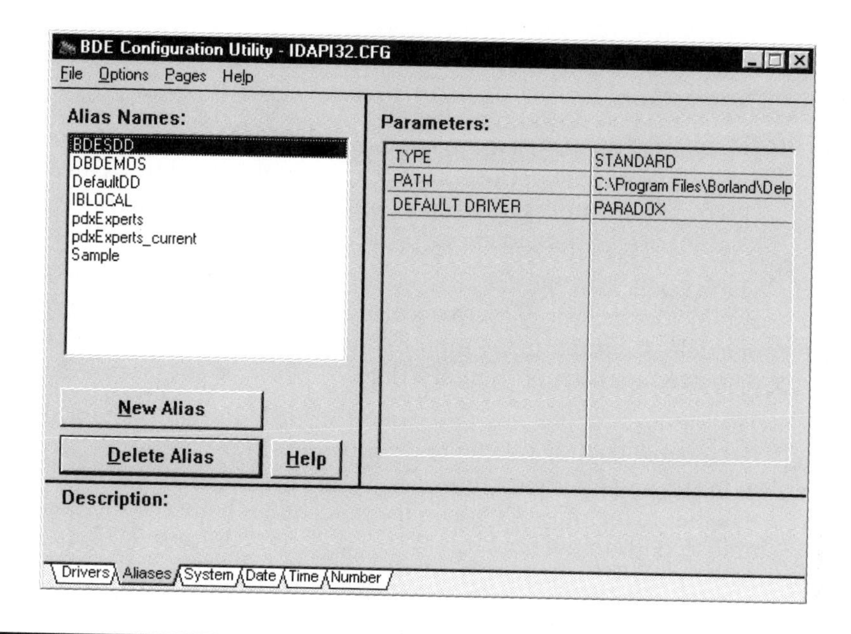

Figure 5-7. *Alias page in the BDE Configuration Utility*

The alias name you entered is now in the Alias Names list. Depending on the driver type selected, you now need to enter the parameters for the alias. If you selected a STANDARD alias, you need to enter the value for the PATH parameter. In this parameter you specify the drive and directory where the tables reside with which the alias is associated.

To delete an alias, highlight the alias you want to remove and click the Delete Alias button. This displays the Delete Alias dialog box, which asks you to confirm the deletion. Click Yes to remove the alias or No to cancel the delete action.

Modifications to existing parameters are also made using the Aliases page. To change a parameter, highlight the alias to display its parameters, and then highlight the parameter and enter in the new value. Table 5-3 lists the additional pages in the BDE Configuration Utility.

Other BDE Configuration Pages

There are four additional pages in the BDE Configuration Utility: System, Date, Time, and Number. They provide additional options for configuring the BDE environment but are not used when you add or modify an alias. Table 5-3 gives a brief description of each page. The BDE help system provides greater details on these pages and the parameter options in each.

Modifying the parameters on any of the pages is basically the same as for the Drivers or Aliases page: you highlight the parameter and enter a new value. Some of

Page	Description
System	The settings the BDE uses to start an application. The parameters track the system and network settings that are maintained by BDE. Parameters include BDE version, buffer sizes, maximum file handles, local sharing of files, memory usage, and others.
Date	The settings the BDE uses to convert string values into date values. Parameters include character to separate the month/day/year portions of a date, the order of the month/day/year, and how the digits are displayed for each portion of a date.
Time	The settings the BDE uses to convert string values into time values. Parameters include twelve-hour or twenty-four-hour clock, strings for morning and afternoon time when a twelve-hour clock is used, whether to include seconds in the time, and whether to include milliseconds in the time.
Number	The settings the BDE uses to convert string values into numeric values. Parameters include decimal separator character, thousand separator character, maximum number of decimals, and whether to include a leading zero for numbers between 1 and –1.

Table 5-3. *Additional Pages in the BDE Configuration Utility*

the parameters provide a drop-down menu containing valid entries for the parameter. Some of the parameters that you are able to change should not be modified (for example, Version on the System page). The help system for the BDE Configuration Utility identifies which parameters should not be modified.

Saving BDE Configuration Information

Once you have entered new aliases and set their parameters, you need to save the information entered into the BDE Configuration Utility. If you are using Delphi 2, you can save the configuration information either in two different places or in both. Delphi 1.0 has only a single location to store the information.

In Delphi 1.0, the Save option from the File menu is used to save changes to the current configuration (.CFG) file. By default, IDAPI.CFG is the name of the configuration file. Alternatively, you can use a different name for the file. If you create or modify a configuration file that is not the default, you will be asked if you want to make the file you are saving the default configuration file. If you click Yes, the WIN.INI file is updated to reflect the name and location of the configuration file.

The BDE Configuration Utility in Delphi 2 stores the information in the Windows Registry or in the default.CFG file. The Registry includes all driver information, the size of the Swap Buffer, and other system information. The .CFG file contains the database aliases and the NET DIR entry for Paradox. If saved in the Windows 3.1–compatible format (composite 16-/32-bit), it may duplicate some of the System and Driver entries.

The Configure WIN3.1 option in the Options menu is used to specify where to store the configuration information. If you check the Configure Win3.1 option, the configuration information is saved in a composite 16-/32-bit format to provide backward compatibility with BDE applications for Windows 3.1. The System and Driver settings existing in the .CFG file are written to the new configuration file along with the database and NET DIR settings. All of the remaining System and Driver settings are written to the Registry.

If the Configure WIN3.1 option is not checked, the System and Driver settings are saved to the Registry, and the database settings and the NET DIR are saved to the new configuration file.

Once the configuration file is saved, the new aliases will be included in the DatabaseName drop-down list the next time you load Delphi.

NOTE: Most BDE applications read the configuration information only when they first load. Consequently, changes you make to the BDE configuration will not affect a running BDE-based application. Such an application must be exited and restarted for it to use the new BDE configuration.

Creating Local Aliases

In addition to using aliases defined in the BDE Configuration Utility, you can use the Database component to create *local aliases* in Delphi projects. The Database component provides a single object to establish all information to connect to a set of data. For local tables, using a Database component is not as critical as when the data resides in an SQL server.

Each of the TDataSet components has a DatabaseName property that you use to specify the database that contains the data. This value can based on an alias defined in the BDE configuration, or on one defined by a Database component.

NOTE: Delphi creates a temporary Database component automatically if an explicit Database component does not exist in the application.

A Database component is not required to access data, but it does provide the ability to change the data location in a single component instead of changing it for each DataSet component. For local tables, this means that the directory in which the data is located can be set at runtime. Since the alias is available only to the application that contains the Database object and is not stored in the BDE configuration, an alias defined by a Database component is referred to as a local alias.

Using the Database Component with Local Tables

The following properties need to be set for the Database component using local tables:

- the name of the database
- where the data resides
- the type of driver for the data

The DatabaseName is the name of the database connection that is used by DataSet components. The name assigned to this property is included in the DatabaseName drop-down list of Table, Query, and StoreProc components.

You can specify where the data resides either by using a predefined alias or by specifying the parameters at runtime. The AliasName property is set when an existing BDE alias is used. This alias is defined with the BDE Configuration Utility. The parameters set in the Configuration Utility are copied for the connection. The path name is the only parameter set when an alias points to local tables. The Params property contains the connection parameters for the alias.

Defining the Alias at Runtime

Alternatively, the data location can be set at runtime. This requires both the AliasName property to be blank and the DriverName property to be set. The DriverName property is the name of a BDE driver for the type of data being accessed. For local tables (e.g., Paradox, dBASE, and ASCII files), STANDARD is the name of the driver to use. The names for SQL databases are ORACLE, SYBASE, INFORMIX, and INTRBASE.

NOTE: *When the AliasName property is set, the DriverName property is cleared. If the DriverName property is set, the AliasName property is cleared.*

The drive and directory where the local data resides is set in design mode using either the Database Editor or the Params property, or by setting the Params property at runtime. The first selection of the Database component pop-up menu is Database Editor. Selecting this menu choice displays the dialog box shown in Figure 5-8.

The values set in the dialog box are assigned to the Database component properties. The Name edit box is the value assigned to the DatabaseName property. The Alias name and Driver name drop-down lists contain the BDE aliases and driver types. Only one of the two values (Alias name or Driver name) can be defined. In the Parameter overrides list, the path name is specified. The values entered here are placed in the Params property.

Before using the Database component, the database needs to be opened by setting the Connected property to True or by using the Open method. The PATHTST project shows an example of using the Database component and setting the properties for local tables at runtime. Figure 5-9 shows the form in design mode.

Figure 5-10 shows the Object Inspector for the Database component. The AliasName property is left blank. The DatabaseName property is assigned _TEMPDB. Using an underscore as the first character of the name puts the value at the top of the list when setting the DatabaseName property for DataSet components. If you only have a single entry with an underscore, you don't have to display the Alias name list.

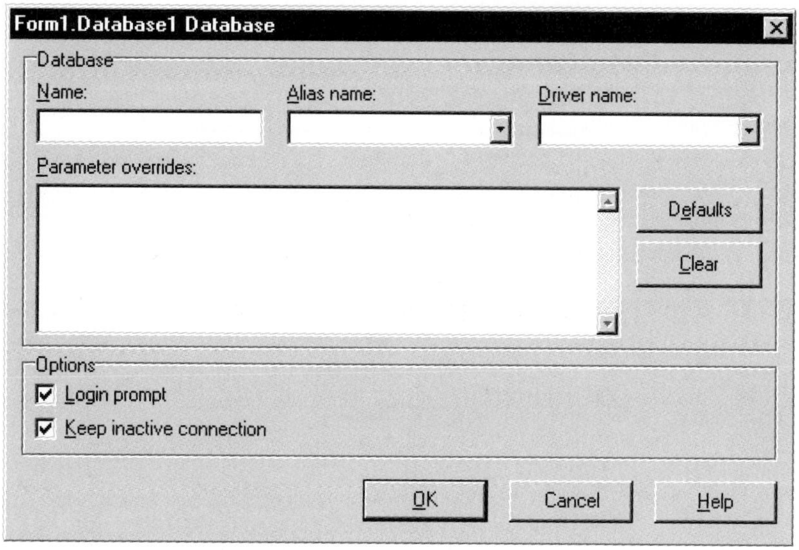

Figure 5-8. *Database Editor dialog box*

You just double-click to set the DatabaseName property in a Query or Table component. In the PATHTST project, the DatabaseName property of the Table component is assigned _TEMPDB.

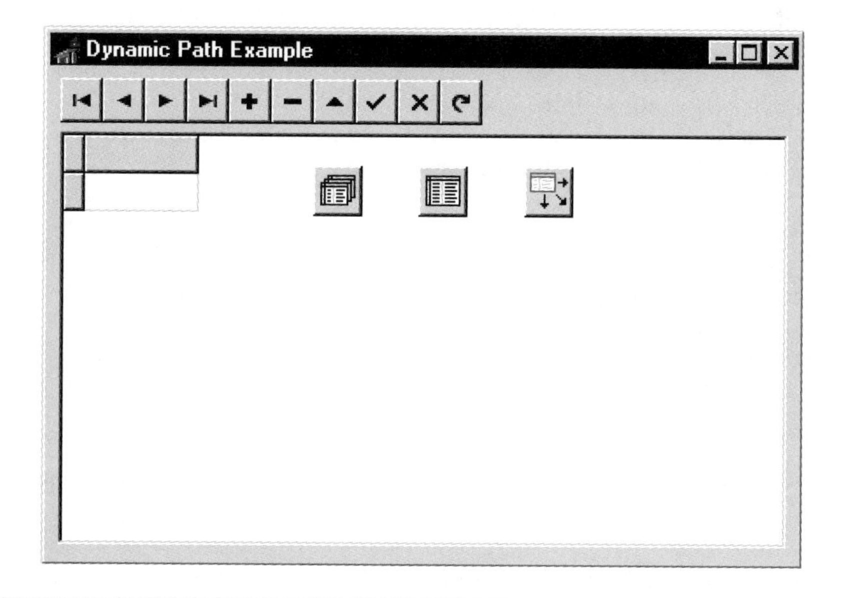

Figure 5-9. *PATHTST project Form1 in design mode*

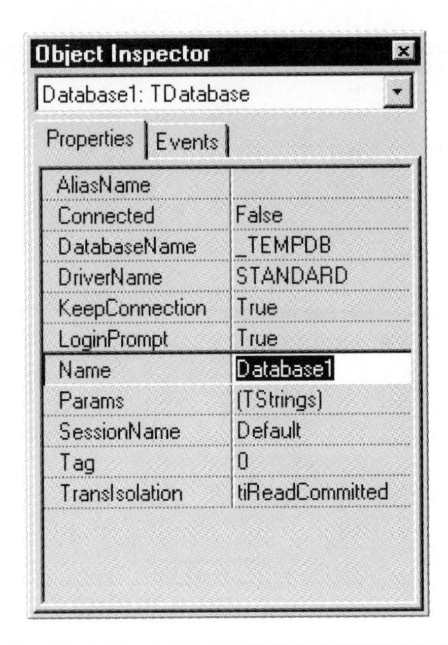

Figure 5-10. *Properties for the Database component*

The directory where the data resides is set when the application is run. For this example, the CUSTOMER.DB table is used and assumed to be in the same directory as the EXE file. (To use this demonstration, you must copy the compiled project .EXE file, PATHTST.EXE, to the directory where the CUSTOMER.DB table is stored. For Delphi 1.0, the location of this file is C:\DELPHI\DEMOS\DATA. For Delphi 2, the path is c:\Program Files\Borland\Delphi 2.0\Demos\Data.)

The OnCreate event handler of the form is used to define the remaining Database properties. Following is the code for this procedure:

```
procedure TForm1.FormCreate(Sender: TObject);
begin
 with Database1 do
 begin
  Close; { Ensure the database is closed }
  Params.Clear; { Remove any parameters accidently set is design mode}
  { Set the path to be the same directory as EXE. This works
   only when the EXE and data reside in the same directory }
  Params.Add('PATH='+ExtractFilePath(Application.ExeName));
  Open; { Open the database }
 end;
 Table1.Open;
end;
```

The Database's Connected property is set to False using the Close method. This ensures that the database is not open and allows properties to be changed for the component. The Params property is cleared before setting the path. This is done to prevent an error from occurring if the Params property is accidentally set in design mode.

A function and an Application component property are used to define the database path. The ExeName property of the Application component contains the name of the path information and name of the executable file. To assign the correct path for the Database component, the ExtractFilePath function is used. This function returns only the drive and directories contained in the parameter. This value is appended to PATH= statement and assigned to the Params parameter. After the Database component is opened, the table is opened and the data is displayed, as shown in Figure 5-11.

TIP: *Although ExeName and ExtractFilePath were used here to define the location of the data, it is not necessarily the case that your local alias will point to the application's execution directory. You could just as easily store the location of the data files in an INI file, or the Windows Registry. In the form's OnCreate event handler you would assign the PATH parameter of the Database component to this stored value.*

Defining the location of the data at runtime eliminates the need for predefined aliases. It also allows development to be done on a different drive and directory structure than where it will reside in production.

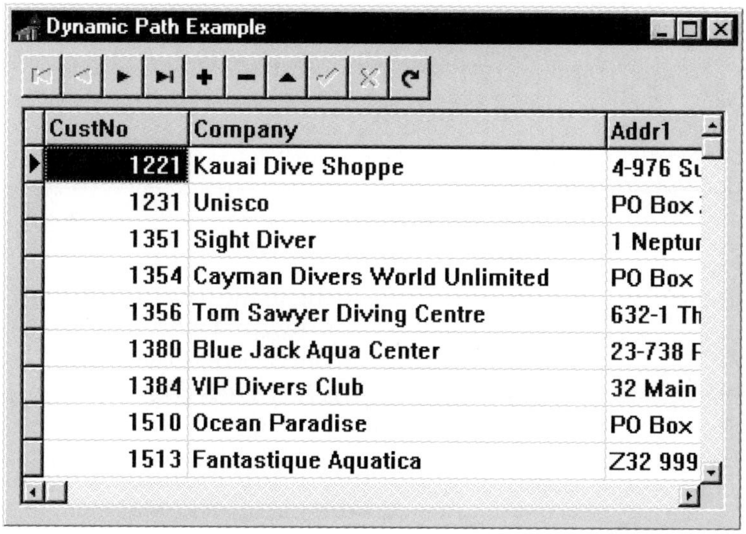

Dynamic Path Example

CustNo	Company	Addr1
1221	Kauai Dive Shoppe	4-976 Su
1231	Unisco	PO Box :
1351	Sight Diver	1 Neptur
1354	Cayman Divers World Unlimited	PO Box
1356	Tom Sawyer Diving Centre	632-1 Th
1380	Blue Jack Aqua Center	23-738 F
1384	VIP Divers Club	32 Main
1510	Ocean Paradise	PO Box
1513	Fantastique Aquatica	Z32 999

Figure 5-11. *PATHTST project with the open table. This project assumes that the table is stored in the same directory as the project EXE*

The Event Model for Table and DataSource Components

Understanding the different Table and DataSource events and when they occur provides valuable information on where to place your code. In this section, the events for these two components are discussed along with the order in which they are triggered relative to other common events.

The DataSource component has three events, which are listed in Table 5-4. The DataSet components have a separate set of events from those of a DataSource component. These events are executed based on the methods used on the component. Table 5-5 contains a list of the events, a brief description, and the minimum list of events in a sequence where the event occurs.

Understanding the event cycle for both the DataSource and Table components provides insight into the insert, delete, and save actions for a dataset. It also indicates where code should be place to trap for possible errors.

Events whose names begin with the word *Before* are used to prevent an action from occurring. For example, to prevent an insert or delete action from inserting or removing a record, you can raise an exception. Project NOINSDEL demonstrates this technique. Figure 5-12 shows the form for the project. It contains a single DataSource, Table, DBNavigator, and DBGrid component. The CUSTOMER.DB table from the DBDEMOS alias is used. The Table component has code attached to the BeforeInsert and BeforeDelete event handlers.

The following is the code for the BeforeInsert event handler:

```
procedure TForm1.Table1BeforeInsert(DataSet: TDataSet);
begin
 MessageDlg('Inserts not permitted',mtError,[mbOK],0);
 Abort;
end;
```

Event	Description
OnDataChange	Executed when something in the dataset changes. The OnDataChange event is triggered when the dataset changes data. This includes moving to a new row in the table, making a change to a column in a row, inserting a new row, and deleting a row.
OnStateChange	Executed when the State property of the dataset changes.
OnUpdateData	Executed when the Post or UpdateRecord method of a dataset is triggered.

Table 5-4. *DataSource Component Events*

Event	Description	Event Sequence
AfterCancel	Executed when the dataset finishes a call to the Cancel method.	BeforeCancel OnStateChange OnDataChange **AfterCancel**
AfterClose	Executed after a dataset is closed.	BeforeClose OnStateChange **AfterClose**
AfterDelete	Executed when the dataset finishes a call to the Delete method. This event occurs after the record is physically removed from the dataset. The cursor for the dataset is positioned on a new record.	BeforeDelete OnStateChange **AfterDelete**
AfterEdit	Executed when the dataset finishes a call to the Edit method.	BeforeEdit OnStateChange OnDataChange **AfterEdit**
AfterInsert	Executed before the dataset begins an insert, which is done using either the Insert or Append method.	BeforeInsert OnStateChange OnNewRecord OnDataChange **AfterInsert**
AfterOpen	Executed after a dataset is opened. This can be done either by using the Open method or by setting the Active property to True.	BeforeOpen OnStateChange OnDataChange **AfterOpen**
AfterPost	Executed after a call to the Post method.	OnUpdateChange BeforePost OnStateChange OnDataChange **AfterPost**
BeforeCancel	Executed when a call to the Cancel method is initiated. This event is the first action taken by Cancel. If the state of the dataset is not Edit, or there are no unposted changes to the record, the BeforeCancel is not executed.	**BeforeCancel** OnStateChange OnDataChange AfterCancel
BeforeClose	Executed before the dataset is closed. Setting Active to False or calling the Close method triggers this event.	**BeforeClose** OnStateChange AfterClose

Table 5-5. *DataSet Component Events*

Event	Description	Event Sequence
BeforeDelete	Executed before the dataset begins a call to Delete. This event is the first action taken by the Delete method.	**BeforeDelete** OnStateChange AfterDelete
BeforeEdit	Executed before the dataset begins a call to the Edit method.	**BeforeEdit** OnStateChange OnDataChange AfterEdit
BeforeInsert	Executed before the dataset begins an insert, which is done using either the Insert or Append methods.	**BeforeInsert** OnStateChange OnNewRecord OnDataChange AfterInsert
BeforeOpen	Executed before the dataset is opened. This can be done either by using the Open method or by setting the Active property to True.	**BeforeOpen** OnStateChange OnDataChange AfterOpen
BeforePost	Executed when a call is made to the Post method. This event is typically used to validate data before the record is saved.	OnUpdateChange **BeforePost** OnStateChange OnDataChange AfterPost
OnCalcFields	Expressions defined for calculated fields are placed in the OnCalcFields event. Executed for each record read from a dataset that is displayed in a form. If a single record is displayed, then OnCalcFields is executed only once. In a DBGrid, OnCalcFields is executed for each row in the grid containing a record from the dataset.	BeforeOpen **OnCalcFields** **OnCalcFields** **OnCalcFields** **OnCalcFields** OnStateChange OnStateChange AfterOpen
OnDeleteError (Delphi 2 only)	Executed when a call is made to the Delete method and the record cannot be deleted. For Paradox tables, this occurs when the record is the parent in a referential integrity rule and child records exist.	BeforeDelete **OnDeleteError**
OnEditError	Executed when a call is made to the Edit method for a dataset and the state cannot change to Edit. This occurs when another user has the record locked.	BeforeEdit **OnEditError**

Table 5-5. *DataSet Components Events* (continued)

Event	Description	Event Sequence
OnFilterRecord (Delphi 2 only)	Executed when the Filter property is changed to True or when specific methods, such as FindNext, are used with filtering.	OnFilterRecord OnDataChange
OnNewRecord	Occurs whenever a new record is added to the dataset. The event occurs after the BeforeInsert event and before the AfterInsert event. OnNewRecord enables you to initialize any fields of the record without marking the record as Modified. Any changes to the record after this event will cause Modified to be set.	BeforeInsert OnStateChange **OnNewRecord** OnDataChange AfterInsert
OnPostError (Delphi 2 only)	Executed in the posting process after a call is made to the Post method. If a record cannot be saved, the OnPostError event is triggered.	BeforePost **OnPostError**
OnUpdateError (Delphi 2 only)	Used with the cached update feature of Delphi 2. Executed when errors occur in applying the updates to the dataset.	**OnUpdateError**
OnUpdateRecord (Delphi 2 only)	Used with the cached update feature of Delphi 2. Executed for each record updated.	**OnUpdateRecord** OnDataChange

Table 5-5. *DataSet Components Events* (continued)

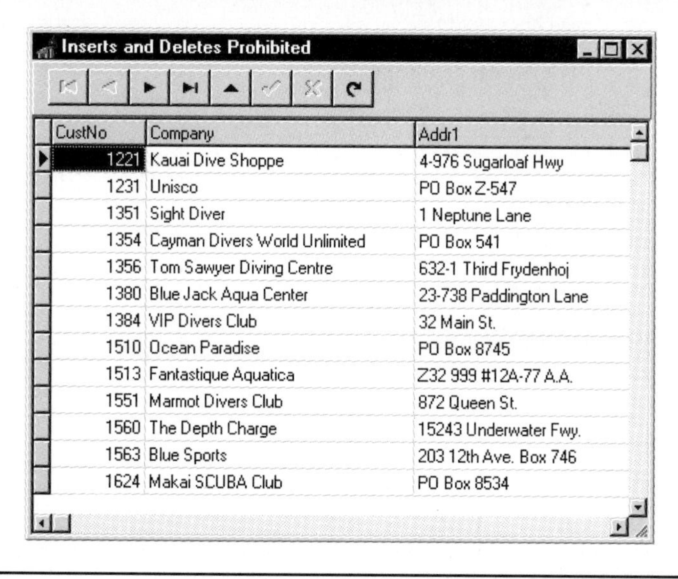

Figure 5-12. *Form for project NOINSDEL*

A message is displayed indicating that an insert is not permitted. Next, the Abort procedure is called, which raises what is called a *silent exception.* Silent exceptions are like other exceptions in that processing in the current procedure is stopped, but Abort does not display an error message. A similar segment of code is used in the BeforeDelete but with a different message.

When a navigator and grid are used, additional properties need to be set in order to present a reasonable interface to the user. You can use the VisibleButtons property of a DBNavigator to suppress the display of some of the buttons. When prohibiting insertions and deletions, it make sense to remove the Insert and Delete buttons from the DBNavigator.

The DBGrid property Options is a set property that includes a dgConfirmDelete flag. Set this flag to False. Otherwise, the user will first see the DBGrid's request to confirm a record deletion, and then, if the user selects Yes to delete the record, your code will display an error message indicating that deletions are prohibited. While such behavior will not damage data, it is inconsistent. Additional uses of the Table events are discussed in Chapter 6.

A Basic Event Monitor

The project EVENTS2 contains a single form shown in Figure 5-13. It is a basic event monitor for a DataSource component and a Table component for Delphi 2. A similar project, EVENTS1, is for Delphi 1.0. Two different projects are necessary because of the new events and features in Delphi 2. In the Delphi 2 version, a ListView component is used to display the event sequence. A ListBox component is used for the Delphi 1.0

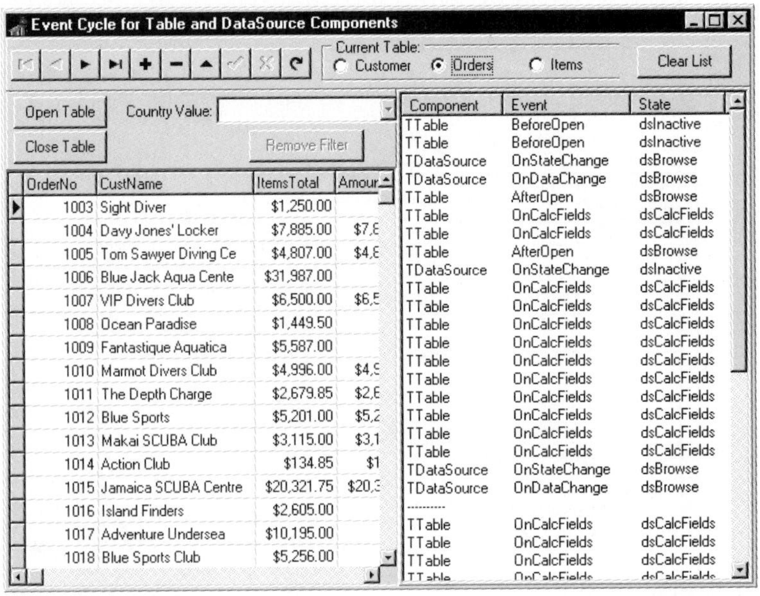

Figure 5-13. *Simple event monitor for Table and DataSource components*

version. When an event occurs, the component name generating the event, the event name, and the state of the Table/DataSource component are listed.

Three tables from the DBDEMOS alias are available in the form: CUSTOMER.DB, ORDERS.DB, and ITEMS.DB. Both the Orders and Items tables have calculated fields. In the Delphi 2 version, lookups are used to display data from other tables. The Orders table includes the name of the Customer instead of the CustNo field. The PartDesc field from the Parts table is displayed in the grid for the Items table in addition to the PartNo field. The Customer table has the option to set a filter when it is current. Using the three tables provides a set of data and features to demonstrate the different event cycles.

The current table displayed is specified using the radio button group at the top of the form. When the Customer table is current in the Delphi 2 version, the drop-down list titled Country Value and the push button Remove Filter are enabled. Changing the value of the drop-down list filters the data in the Customer table to the selected country. When the form is opened, the following query is run:

```
SELECT DISTINCT Country
FROM Customer
ORDER BY Country
```

This generates a unique list of all the current Country values. This list is placed into the Items property of the ComboBox component using the AfterOpen of the Query component as follows:

```
procedure TForm1.Query1AfterOpen(DataSet: TDataSet);
begin
 with Query1 do
 begin
  ComboBox1.Items.Clear; { Empty the item list }
  First;
  while not EOF do { Add each Country in the result set }
  begin      { as an entry in the combo box }
   ComboBox1.Items.Add(FieldByName('Country').AsString);
   Next;
  end;
  Close; { Close the query result set since it is no }
 end;    { longer needed }
end;
```

The current items, if any, are removed from the Items property of the ComboBox by calling the Clear method. All the values from the query are placed into the ComboBox by scanning the entire dataset and placing each value in the drop-down list. Using a SELECT DISTINCT in the SQL statement ensures only unique values are returned, thus there is a single entry for each country in the combo box. After entering all the values, the Query component is closed because the result set is no longer needed.

The form also provides the ability to adjust the form's height and width so that you can see more of the data and event list. Panels are used in the form to provide the correct resizing. The Align property of the Panel components are used along with the Align property of the ListView, ListBox, and DBGrid to indicate how they align with their containers or parent components.

A Panel component with the Align property of alTop is used to contain the DBNavigator and RadioButtonGroup. It also contains another Panel component with the Align property set to alRight. Inside this panel is the Clear List push button. The intent here is to keep the Clear List button always on the left side of the form. This Panel component has its BevelOuter property set to bvNone to hide the component.

Another Panel component is used to keep the ListView/ListBox component on the right side of the form. Its Align property is set to alRight. Its width does not increase as the form is maximized; only the height of the Panel increases. The Align property of the ListView/ListBox is set to alClient. This setting keeps the size of the ListView/ListBox component as large as its container panel.

The remaining free space on the form is occupied by another Panel component. It contains an additional panel for the Open Table, Close Table, Remove Filter, and ComboBox components. The DBGrid component has its Align property set to alClient so that its height and width adjust as the form expands and contracts.

The Table components are named tblCustomer, tblOrders, and tblItems for the Customer, Orders, and Items tables. Each of the events for the tblCustomer component has code attached to them. The events for the Orders and Items tables point to the procedures for the same event on the Customer Table. Figure 5-14 shows the Object Inspector for tblCustomer component. Following is a sample set of code that is typical for each of the events:

```
procedure TForm1.tblCustomerBeforeInsert(DataSet: TDataSet);
begin
 DisplayEvent('TTable','BeforeInsert',DataSet.State);
end;
```

A custom procedure, DisplayEvent, is called, sending to it the name of the component, the type of event, and the value of the State property for the dataset that called the event procedure. In this example, DataSet.State is used because any of the three tables could call the event. For example, each of the Table component's BeforeInsert events points to the tblCustomerBeforeInsert procedure. This allows one event handler to be used for all of the three tables. The only exception is the OnCalcFields events for the Orders and Items tables. A separate procedure is required to include the correct expressions for the calculated fields in each of the tables. Following is the DisplayEvent procedure code for the Delphi 2 version:

```
procedure TForm1.DisplayEvent(ObjectName,EventName: String;
 ObjectState: TDataSetState);
var
 StrState: String;
```

```
begin
 case ObjectState of
  dsInactive  : StrState := 'dsInactive';
  dsBrowse   : StrState := 'dsBrowse';
  dsEdit    : StrState := 'dsEdit';
  dsInsert   : StrState := 'dsInsert';
  dsSetKey   : StrState := 'dsSetKey';
  dsCalcFields : StrState := 'dsCalcFields';
 end;
with ListView.Items.Add do
 begin
   Caption := ObjectName;
   SubItems.Add(EventName);
   SubItems.Add(StrState);
 end;
 IsTimerActive := False;
end;
```

The State property is first converted to a String value using a case statement. The component type and event type are passed as String arguments, which allows all three values to be inserted into the ListView component.

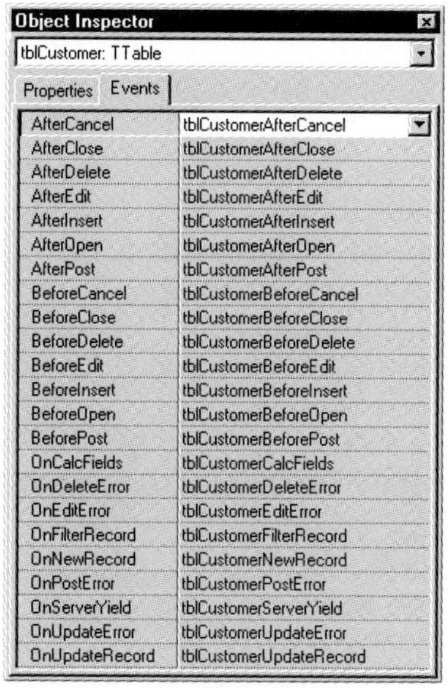

Figure 5-14. *Object Inspector showing events for Customer table*

The last line of the procedure sets a global variable IsTimerActive to False. A Timer component is used to place a dashed line in the Component column when there is inactivity in a cycle. The timer checks every second to see if an event has occurred. If it has occurred, the dashed line is entered. This dashed line provides a visual separation between the event cycles in the display.

The Delphi 1.0 version uses the same code for the DisplayEvent code, with the exception of ListView code. The ListBox component used to display the events does not have the ability to place the three separate pieces of text in three columns. The format function is used to create a single text value at the time of the insert into the Items property of the ListBox. The following is the portion of the DisplayEvent procedure that places the event information into the ListBox:

```
ListBox.Items.Add(Format('%-13s%-15s%-12s',
    [ObjectName,EventName,StrState]));
```

NOTE: *The Font property of the ListBox is changed to Courier New. This monospaced font is used so that the three pieces of text in the ListBox will appear in column format.*

A single DataSource component is used in the form. It is assigned to the selected dataset when the RadioButtonGroup is changed. The three events of a DataSource component have the same type of code attached. Following is the code:

```
procedure TForm1.DataSource1DataChange(Sender: TObject; Field:
          TField);
begin
 DisplayEvent('TDataSource','OnDataChange',DataSource1.State);
end;
```

The main difference here, besides the text of the first two parameters, is that the State property of the DataSource is used as the third parameter. This code always displays the State of the dataset attached to the DataSource.

One other component can be displayed in the Componet column of the ListView/ListBox component—the DBNavigator. The following code appears in the OnClick event:

```
procedure TForm1.DBNavigator1Click(Sender: TObject; Button:
          TNavigateBtn);
begin
 DisplayEvent('TDBNavigator','OnClick',DataSource1.State);
end;
```

The DataSource State property is used here because the navigator is attached to the dataset using the DataSource component. When one of the buttons is clicked, it is always the last event in the cycle. The Table and DataSource components execute before the OnClick event is triggered.

This event monitor is intended to provide a basic set of features to explore the event cycle. It includes a display of each event for both the Table and DataSource components as actions are taken on a table. It can be used to see how the State of the dataset changes during the cycle of events. In addition, it shows how the OnCalcFields and OnFilterRecord events are affected based on the number of records in the dataset and how many records are being displayed in the grid.

By inspecting the event listings provided by the event monitor, you can gain valuable insight into the order and types of events that the Delphi database components generate. Through an understanding of these events, and the order in which they are triggered, you can make intelligent decisions concerning which event handlers are best suited for your custom code for a particular situation.

The Borland Database Engine

The Borland Database Engine (BDE) is the core of all data access for Delphi. It is the API that Borland uses for connecting to multiple data sources in all their data-driven products. The BDE is used for connecting to local tables and text files, as well as SQL databases. BDE provides direct support for Paradox, dBASE, InterBase, Oracle, Sybase, Informix, and any ODBC dataset.

BDE does not provide features based on the least common denominator among all data source types. The unique features of Paradox and dBASE tables are supported as well as transparent access to SQL data sources, including transaction support for SQL database servers. This allows database developers to take advantage of each data repository type and provide the option to switch database sources in an application.

The following is a list of the basic categories that BDE supports:

- Opening and closing of databases and tables
- Creating tables and indexes
- Deleting tables and indexes
- Copying and renaming tables
- Viewing, modifying, and querying data
- Creating, deleting, and modifying aliases

That the BDE is even present is typically not obvious to the Delphi database developer until an application is delivered (at which time the BDE must also be delivered if it is not already present on the target computer). This is because calls to the BDE are, for the most part, encapsulated by components on the Data Access and Data Controls pages of the component palette, or their ancestors.

NOTE: An interesting exception is the Report component on the Data Access page. This component initiates a DDE link with ReportSmith. While Delphi does not invoke the BDE in order to use ReportSmith, ReportSmith can use the BDE for access to local tables (Paradox, dBASE, and ASCII).

The primary advantage of this encapsulation is that you can add data access capabilities to your Delphi applications simply by adding one or more data-aware objects onto your form. These objects, in turn, contain methods and properties that provide you with indirect, yet greatly simplified, access to the procedures and functions of the BDE. For example, the open method of a Table component is a very simple method call, requiring no arguments. This method, however, ultimately results in a call to the BDE function DbiOpenTables, which requires twelve parameters, in addition to several prerequisite calls (specifically, DbiInit and DbiOpenDatabase).

There are times, however, when you need to get information from and control features of the BDE not surfaced by these controls. Fortunately, most of the BDE methods and procedures are directly available to your applications with a minimum of effort.

BDE Programming Support

If you want to program calls to the BDE directly you will need information about the functions and procedures of the BDE. If you have the Delphi Developer or Client/Server versions of Delphi 2, extensive help is available in the form of a Windows help file. This help file, BDE.HLP, includes documentation for all the BDE calls, as well as examples of their use. (The BDE help system includes both Delphi and C++ examples.) Delphi 1.0 did not ship with a BDE help file in any version; however, at the time of this writing, a copy of the 16-bit BDE help file was available for download from Borland's Delphi forum on CompuServe.

In addition to the help files, all versions of Delphi include a file that that can be found in Delphi's DOC subdirectory (c:\Delphi\Doc for Delphi 1.0, and c:\Program Files\Borland\Delphi 2.0\Doc for Delphi 2). This file is named BDE.INT in Delphi 2, and there are three files for Delphi 1.0 (DBIPROCS.INT, DBITYPES.INT, and DBIERRS.INT). These files contain the Interface definition for the BDE import units (the unit source code is not shipped with Delphi, only the compiled version). Figure 5-15 shows a portion of the BDE.INT file appearing in the Delphi editor window.

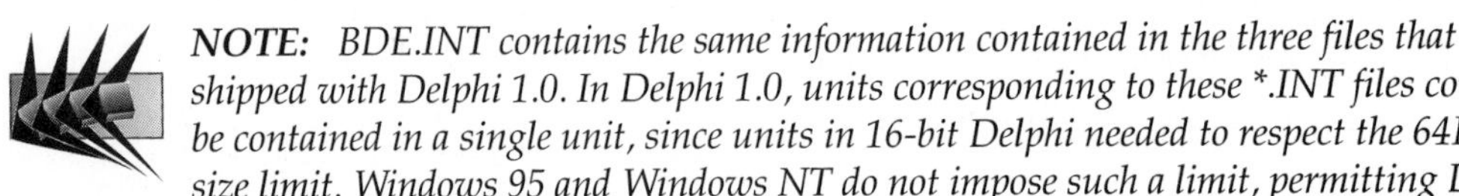

*NOTE: BDE.INT contains the same information contained in the three files that shipped with Delphi 1.0. In Delphi 1.0, units corresponding to these *.INT files could not be contained in a single unit, since units in 16-bit Delphi needed to respect the 64K file size limit. Windows 95 and Windows NT do not impose such a limit, permitting Delphi 2 to place more code within a given unit.*

Making BDE Calls From Delphi Applications

There are two general approaches for working with the BDE. The first is to make all BDE calls directly, without the intervention of data-aware controls. Accessing BDE functions and procedures this way is a lot of work. To do this, you must take responsibility for initializing the BDE, as well as establishing database handles, cursor handles, and record handles. The following section demonstrates how to do this.

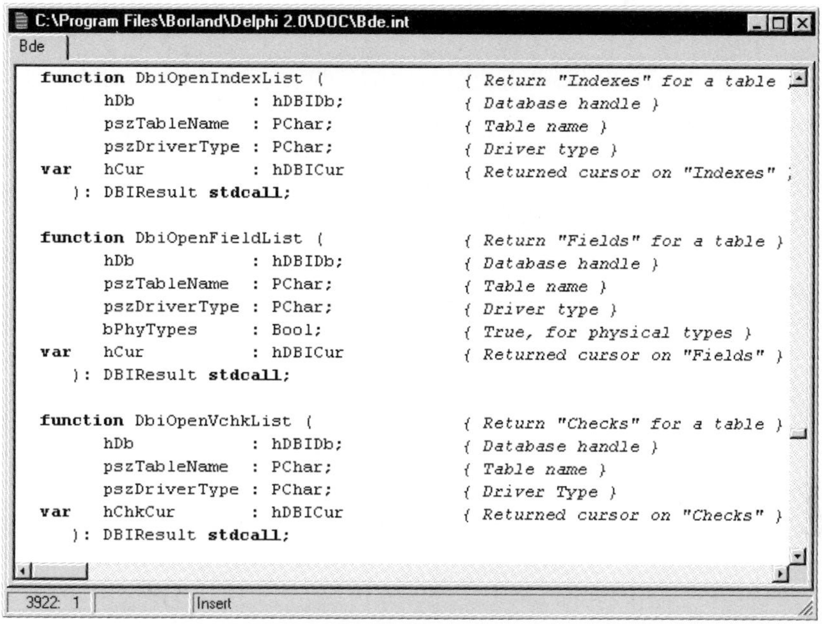

```
C:\Program Files\Borland\Delphi 2.0\DOC\Bde.int
Bde
  function DbiOpenIndexList (                 { Return "Indexes" for a table
        hDb             : hDBIDb;             { Database handle }
        pszTableName    : PChar;              { Table name }
        pszDriverType   : PChar;              { Driver type }
  var   hCur            : hDBICur             { Returned cursor on "Indexes" ;
     ): DBIResult stdcall;

  function DbiOpenFieldList (                 { Return "Fields" for a table }
        hDb             : hDBIDb;             { Database handle }
        pszTableName    : PChar;              { Table name }
        pszDriverType   : PChar;              { Driver type }
        bPhyTypes       : Bool;               { True, for physical types }
  var   hCur            : hDBICur             { Returned cursor on "Fields" }
     ): DBIResult stdcall;

  function DbiOpenVchkList (                  { Return "Checks" for a table }
        hDb             : hDBIDb;             { Database handle }
        pszTableName    : PChar;              { Table name }
        pszDriverType   : PChar;              { Driver Type }
  var   hChkCur         : hDBICur             { Returned cursor on "Checks" }
     ): DBIResult stdcall;
3922: 1        Insert
```

Figure 5-15. *The file BDE.INT contains the interface section of the BDE unit*

Packing Tables

Figure 5-16 shows the main form of a project named PACKTAB.DPR. This form permits you to pack Paradox or dBASE tables. (Packing releases space from Paradox tables occupied by deleted records, and removes records marked for deletion from dBASE tables.)

The following is the code for this form's unit:

```
unit Packtabu;

interface

uses
  SysUtils, WinTypes, WinProcs, Messages, Classes, Graphics, Controls,
  Forms, Dialogs, StdCtrls, DbiProcs, DbiTypes, DbiErrs, FileCtrl,
  ExtCtrls;

type
  TForm1 = class(TForm)
    Button1: TButton;
    FilterComboBox1: TFilterComboBox;
    DriveComboBox1: TDriveComboBox;
    FileListBox1: TFileListBox;
```

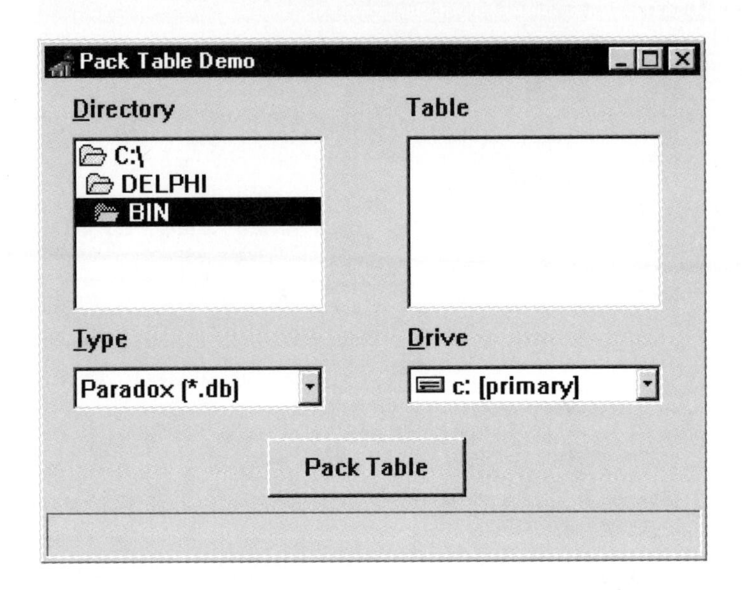

Figure 5-16. *The PACKTAB main form*

```
    DirectoryListBox1: TDirectoryListBox;
    Label1: TLabel;
    Label2: TLabel;
    Label3: TLabel;
    Label4: TLabel;
    Panel1: TPanel;
    procedure PackTable(Sender: TObject;TabName: PChar);
    procedure Button1Click(Sender: TObject);
  private
    { Private declarations }
  public
    { Public declarations }
  end;

var
  Form1: TForm1;

implementation

{$R *.DFM}

procedure TForm1.Button1Click(Sender: TObject);
var
  Tab: PChar;
```

```
begin
if FileListbox1.FileName = '' then
  begin
    MessageDlg('No table select',mtError,[mbOK],0);
    Exit;
  end;
  GetMem(Tab,144);
  try
  StrPCopy(Tab,FileListBox1.FileName);
  PackTable(Sender,Tab);
  finally
    Dispose(tab);
  end;
end;

procedure TForm1.PackTable(Sender: TObject; TabName: PChar);
var
  hDb       :hDBIDb;
  hCursor   :hDBICur;
  dbResult  :DBIResult;
  PdxStruct :CRTblDesc;
begin
{Initialize the BDE.}
dbResult := DbiInit(nil);
if dbResult <> DBIERR_NONE then
  begin
    case dbResult of
      DBIERR_MULTIPLEINIT: ShowMessage('DBIERR_MULTIPLEINIT');
    else
     ShowMessage('Some other error');
    end;
    DbiExit;
    Exit;
  end;

{Open a Database.}
dbResult := DbiOpenDatabase('','STANDARD',dbiREADONLY,dbiOPENSHARED,'',
                0,nil,nil,hDB);
if dbResult <> DBIERR_NONE then
  begin
    case dbResult of
      DBIERR_UNKNOWNDB: ShowMessage('DBIERR_UNKNOWNDB');
      DBIERR_NOCONFIGFILE: ShowMessage('DBIERR_NOCONFIGFILE');
      DBIERR_INVALIDDBSPEC: ShowMessage('DBIERR_INVALIDDBSPEC');
      DBIERR_DBLIMIT: ShowMessage('DBIERR_DBLIMIT');
    else
      ShowMessage('DbiOpenDatabase failure');
    end;
    DbiExit;
```

```
    Exit;
  end;

{Open a table. This returns a handle to the table's
cursor, which is required by many of the BDE calls.}
dbResult := DbiOpenTable(hDB, TabName, '','','',0,dbiREADWRITE,
             dbiOPENEXCL,xltNONE,False,nil,hCursor);
if dbResult <> DBIERR_NONE then
  begin
    case dbResult of
      DBIERR_INVALIDFILENAME     :
        ShowMessage('DBIERR_INVALIDFILENAME');
      DBIERR_NOSUCHFILE          :
        ShowMessage('DBIERR_NOSUCHFILE');
      DBIERR_TABLEREADONLY       :
        ShowMessage('DBIERR_TABLEREADONLY');
      DBIERR_NOTSUFFTABLERIGHTS :
        ShowMessage('DBIERR_NOTSUFFTABLERIGHTS');
      DBIERR_INVALIDINDEXNAME    :
        ShowMessage('DBIERR_INVALIDINDEXNAME');
      DBIERR_INVALIDHNDL         :
        ShowMessage('DBIERR_INVALIDHNDL');
      DBIERR_INVALIDPARAM        :
        ShowMessage('DBIERR_INVALIDPARAM');
      DBIERR_UNKNOWNTBLTYPE      :
        ShowMessage('DBIERR_UNKNOWNTBLTYPE');
      DBIERR_NOSUCHTABLE         :
        ShowMessage('DBIERR_NOSUCHTABLE');
      DBIERR_NOSUCHINDEX         :
        ShowMessage('DBIERR_NOSUCHINDEX');
      DBIERR_LOCKED              :
        ShowMessage('DBIERR_LOCKED');
      DBIERR_DIRBUSY             :
        ShowMessage('DBIERR_DIRBUSY');
      DBIERR_OPENTBLLIMIT        :
        ShowMessage('DBIERR_OPENTBLLIMIT');
    else
      ShowMessage('DbiOpenTable failure');
    end;
    DbiCloseDatabase(hDB);
    DbiExit;
    Exit;
  end;

{The BDE is initialized, a database is open, and a cursor
is open for a table. We can now work with the table.
The following segment shows how to pack a dBASE or
Paradox table. Note that before we can pack the Paradox
table, the table's cursor handle must be closed, otherwise
```

```
we would get a 'Table in use' error.}

try
  Panel1.Caption := 'Packing '+ FileListBox1.FileName;
  Application.ProcessMessages;
  if AnsiUpperCase(ExtractFileExt(FileListBox1.FileName)) = '.DB' then
    begin
    {Close the Paradox table cursor handle.}
    DbiCloseCursor(hCursor);
    {The method DoRestructure requires a pointer to a record
    object of the type CRTblDesc. Initialize this record.}
    FillChar(PdxStruct, SizeOf(CRTblDesc),0);
    StrPCopy( PdxStruct.szTblName,FileListBox1.Filename);
    PdxStruct.bPack := True;
    dbResult := DbiDoRestructure(hDB,1,@PdxStruct,nil,nil,nil,False);
    if dbResult = DBIERR_NONE then
      Panel1.Caption := 'Table successfully packed'
    else
      Panel1.Caption := 'Failure: error '+IntTostr(dbResult);
    end
  else
    begin
    {Packing a dBASE table is much easier.}
    dbResult := DbiPackTable(hDB, hCursor,'','',True);
    if dbResult = DBIERR_NONE then
      Panel1.Caption := 'Table successfully packed'
    else
      Panel1.Caption := 'Failure: error '+IntTostr(dbResult);
    end;
finally
  DbiCloseCursor(hCursor);
  DbiCloseDatabase(hDB);
  DbiExit;
end;
end;

end.
```

Before any calls to the BDE can be made, you must give your unit access to the BDE unit(s). This is achieved by adding BDE to the uses clause for the unit from within which the BDE calls will be made (DbiProcs, DbiTypes, and DbiErrs with Delphi 1.0). In this example, these units are listed in the Interface uses clause.

Since this form contains no data-aware components, all access to the BDE must be performed through code. This is achieved through the use of three basic BDE calls: DbiInit, DbiOpenDatabase, and DbiOpenTable. Each of these three calls are demonstrated in the procedure PackTable. In this case, the table that is selected from the main form is opened for exclusive use, which means that no other user can access this table while this procedure has the table opened. It is also possible, and usually desirable, to open a table for shared use.

The PackTable procedure then demonstrates how to pack a table. For a Paradox table, you use the function DbiDoRestructure, while a dBASE table requires the use of DbiPackTable. The use of DbiDoRestructure in this example is as simple as this function can get. To change the structure of a Paradox table with this function would require a much more complex argument list.

Once your work with the BDE is done, it is necessary to clean up after the application. In this case, both the table cursor handle and the database handle need to be released (using DbiCloseCursor and DbiCloseDatabase), and then the BDE must be deactivated (using DbiExit).

Displaying Table Information

As you can see from the preceding example, managing all of the access to the BDE is a lot of work. It is much easier if you permit data-aware components to do some of this work for you. For example, if you place a Table component onto a form, and then open that table, the BDE will already be initialized, a database handle will be established, and a cursor handle will also exist. (The database handle can be obtained from the DBHandle property of the table, and the cursor handle can be obtained from the Handle property.) Furthermore, when the application no longer needs the BDE, the data-aware components release the handles and deactivate the BDE.

This combination of using data-aware controls and BDE calls is demonstrated in the project named RECINFO, whose main form is shown in Figure 5-17.

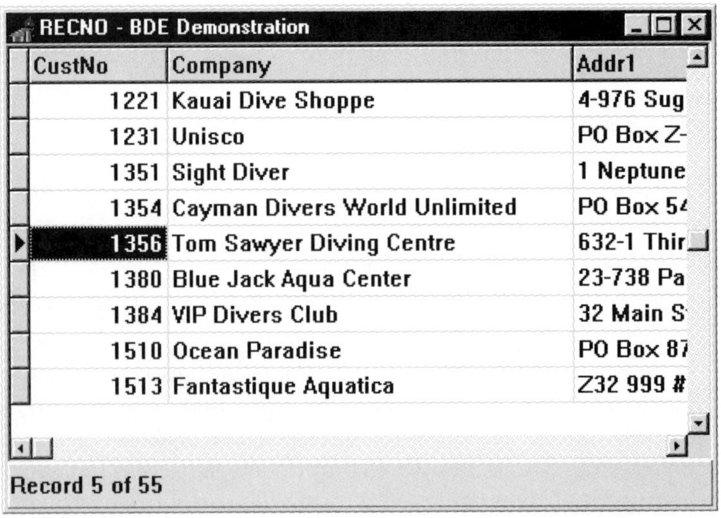

Figure 5-17. *The main form of RECINFO. Notice the record information displayed in the panel at the bottom of the form.*

The following is the source code for the form's unit:

```
unit Recnou;

interface

uses
  SysUtils, WinTypes, WinProcs, Messages, Classes, Graphics, Controls,
  Forms, Dialogs, Grids, DBGrids, ExtCtrls, DbiProcs, DbiTypes, DbiErrs,
  DB, DBTables;

type
 TForm1 = class(TForm)
  DataSource1: TDataSource;
  Table1: TTable;
  Panel1: TPanel;
  DBGrid1: TDBGrid;
  procedure DataSource1DataChange(Sender: TObject; Field: TField);
 private
  { Private declarations }
 public
  { Public declarations }
 end;

var
 Form1: TForm1;

implementation

{$R *.DFM}

procedure TForm1.DataSource1DataChange(Sender: TObject;
                    Field: TField);
var
 i,j: LongInt;
begin
 Table1.UpdateCursorPos;
 DbiGetSeqNo(Table1.Handle,i);
 DbiGetRecordCount(Table1.Handle,j);
 Panel1.Caption := 'Record '+ IntToStr(i) + ' of ' + IntToStr(j);
end;

end.
```

You may immediately recognize two characteristics in this code sample. First, it is short, requiring far less code than that contained within PACKTABU.PAS. This is because the internal code for the Table and DataSource components placed on this form take responsibility for the initialization of the BDE. The second important feature to observe is that the BDE unit (or DbiProcs, DbiTypes, and DbiErrs units) still needs to appear in the uses clause, even when data-aware components are present.

The calls to the BDE in this example are found in the event handler assigned to the OnDataChange event property of a DataSource component. This event handler is called any time there is a change to the current record. Within this event handler, the BDE procedures DbiGetSeqNo and DbiGetRecordCount are used to get the current record number and total number of records, respectively. These values are then used to update a message displayed in a Panel component. Notice that both of these BDE calls require the cursor handle. As mentioned previously, these handles can be obtained from the Handle property of the table.

NOTE: *DbiGetSeqNo only works with the Paradox driver. Therefore, you cannot use it with dBASE tables or SQL files.*

Creating New Aliases

The BDE provides multiple functions to manage aliases in the configuration file. In Delphi 1.0, the options are limited to just creating new aliases and getting the list of current aliases. In Delphi 2, you can create, list, delete, and modify aliases. Delphi 2 supports both direct calls to the BDE and built-in methods to perform the same tasks. The TSession object provides these new methods.

The limiting factor in Delphi 1.0 is the DBIPROCS unit. It only contains the options to add a new alias using DbiAddAlias. To get a list of aliases, you use DbiOpenDatabaseList. By using DbiAddAlias and DbiOpenDatabaseList you can completely control the initialization of the BDE from within your Delphi application.

The project BDEALS1.DPR demonstrates how to create and list aliases in Delphi 1.0. STANDARD aliases are used in this example. Following is the main form for the project:

Alias Creation Using BDE

New Alias Name:

New Alias Path:

Add New Alias

Get Alias List

Two separate buttons contain the different code for each task. The Add New Alias button uses the two Edit components at the top of the form to specify a new alias name and the path for the alias. The Get Alias List button retrieves the names of the defined aliases and places them in the ListBox on the right side of the push buttons. The following is the code for this form's unit:

```
unit Bdeals1u;

interface

uses
  WinProcs, WinTypes, Messages, SysUtils, Classes, Graphics, Controls,
  Forms, DbiProcs, DbiTypes, DbiErrs, Dialogs, StdCtrls, DB;

type
  TForm1 = class(TForm)
    pbAddAlias: TButton;
    pbGetAliasList: TButton;
    ListBox1: TListBox;
    Label1: TLabel;
    Edit1: TEdit;
    Label2: TLabel;
    Edit2: TEdit;
    procedure pbAddAliasClick(Sender: TObject);
    procedure pbGetAliasListClick(Sender: TObject);
    procedure GetAliasList(DatabaseList: TStringList);
  private
    { Private declarations }
  public
    { Public declarations }
  end;

var
  Form1: TForm1;

implementation

{$R *.DFM}

var
  AliasName,AliasPath: Array[0..79] of Char;

procedure TForm1.pbAddAliasClick(Sender: TObject);
begin
  { Verify the alias name is entered }
  if Edit1.Text = '' then
    begin
      ShowMessage('Alias Name must be entered');
      Edit1.SetFocus;
```

```
      Exit;
    end
  else
    StrPCopy(AliasName,Edit1.Text);
  { Verify the alias path is entered }
  if Edit2.Text = '' then
    begin
      ShowMessage('Alias Path must be entered');
      Edit2.SetFocus;
      Exit;
    end
  else
    StrPCopy(AliasPath,Edit2.Text);
  { Initialize the BDE }
  case DbiInit(nil) of
    DBIERR_NONE :  { No errors occurred in initialization }
      { Attempt to add the alias name and path }
      case DbiAddAlias (nil,AliasName,nil,AliasPath,True) of
        DBIERR_NONE          :
          ShowMessage('Alias added');
        DBIERR_NAMENOTUNIQUE :
          ShowMessage('Alias already exists');
        DBIERR_INVALIDPARAM  :
          ShowMessage('Null alias not allowed');
        DBIERR_OBJNOTFOUND   :
          ShowMessage('One of the optional parameters not found');
        DBIERR_UNKNOWNDRIVER :
          ShowMessage('Driver name not found');
      else
        ShowMessage('An untrapped error occurred in DbiAddAlias');
      end;
    DBIERR_MULTIPLEINIT :
      ShowMessage('Multiple initialize of Database Engine');
  else
    ShowMessage('An untrapped error occurred in DbiInit');
  end;
  DbiExit;

end;

procedure TForm1.pbGetAliasListClick(Sender: TObject);
var
  dbResult :DBIResult;
  AliasList: TStringList;
  I: Integer;
begin
  { Initialize the BDE }
  case DbiInit(nil) of
    DBIERR_NONE :  { No errors occurred in initialization }
```

```
        { Attempt to add the alias name and path }
        try
          AliasList := TStringList.Create;
          GetAliasList(AliasList);
          ListBox1.Items.Clear;
          for I:= 0 to AliasList.Count - 1 do
            ListBox1.Items.Add(AliasList.Strings[I]);
        finally
          AliasList.Free;
        end;
      DBIERR_MULTIPLEINIT :
        ShowMessage('Multiple initialize of Database Engine');
    else
      ShowMessage('An untrapped error occurred in DbiInit');
    end;
    DbiExit;
  end;

  procedure TForm1.GetAliasList(DatabaseList: TStringList);
  var
    TmpCursor: hDbiCur;
    Database: DBDesc;
    rslt: DbiResult;
  begin
    DatabaseList.Clear;
    Check(DbiOpenDatabaseList(TmpCursor));
    repeat
      rslt:= DbiGetNextRecord(TmpCursor, dbiNOLOCK, @Database, nil);
      if (rslt <> DBIERR_EOF) then
        DatabaseList.Add(StrPas(Database.szName))
    until rslt <> DBIERR_NONE;

    Check(DbiCloseCursor(TmpCursor));
  end;

  end.
```

Like the previous two BDE examples, you need to include the DbiProcs, DbiTypes, and DbiErrs units to support the BDE functions. In this example, the BDE is initialized each time an alias is added. The Delphi project is disconnected from the BDE when a task is complete. The same connect and disconnect process is used to retrieve the list of currently defined aliases.

Using DbiAddAlias

The procedure pbAddAliasClick is called when the Add New Alias button is clicked. This adds a new alias to the configuration file using the DbiAddAlias function. The first two checks in the procedure ensure that the Edit components are not blank. In this example, there is no checking for valid alias and directory values. An assumption is made that valid values are entered. If a value exists in each, the BDE is initialized using DbiInit. The syntax for DbiAddAlias is as follows:

```
DbiAddAlias (hCfg: hDBICfg; pszAliasName: PChar; pszDriverType: PChar;
    pszParams: PChar; bPersist: Bool): DBIResult
```

Table 5-6 lists the parameters for DbiAddAlias and gives a brief description for each.

Three of the parameters need to be a value other than nil. The alias name, the alias path, and True are used to make the alias permanent.

A case statement is used with DbiAddAlias to check the return value from the function. The possible values returned from the call are used as the expressions to match. DbiAddAlias has five documented return values. If an alias is added, the return value is DBIERR_NONE. In this example, if one of the other results are returned, ShowMessage is used to display a brief message for the error.

The last BDE call is to DbiExit. Like in the previous examples, this call is required to disconnect the Delphi project from the BDE. This allows the next BDE call to initialize and use the BDE.

GETTING A LIST OF DEFINED ALIASES A list of the currently defined alias can be retrieved using DbiOpenDatabaseList. This function returns a cursor pointing to the list of aliases in the configuration file. The DbiGetNextRecord is used to retrieve

Parameter	Description
hCfg	Specifies the configuration file to be used. When it is NULL, the current configuration file is used.
pszAliasName	Name of the alias to be added.
pszDriverType	The type of driver for the alias. If the value is NULL, STANDARD is used. If a driver other than STANDARD is used, the driver must be installed and currently in the configuration file as one of the installed drivers.
pszParams	List of the parameters that define the alias. The PATH is the only parameter used when defining an alias for the STANDARD driver.
bPersist	Indicator for the scope of the alias. True is used to make the alias permanent; False is used to indicate the alias is for the session only.

Table 5-6. *DbiAddAlias Parameters*

each record from the list. In this example, only the name of the alias is retrieved from the record.

A separate procedure, GetAliasList, is used to fill a StringList object with the alias information. A click on the Get Alias List button calls the pbGetAliasListClick procedure. After initializing the BDE and creating a StringList object, the StringList object is passed to GetAliasList.

The Check procedure in Delphi is used to call DbiOpenDatabaseList. Check is a procedure used in conjunction with calls to the BDE. If the return value from a BDE function is non-zero, a call is made to DbiError procedure. This procedure creates a text error message based on the error code returned from DbiOpenDatabaseList. From here, the DatabaseError procedure is called, which raises an exception using the text message retrieved by DbiError.

The pointer returned by DbiOpenDatabaseList is used to cycle through all the records in the list with a repeat…until control structure. The function DbiGetNextRecord is used to get the record from the list. In this example, only the name of the alias (szName) is used. Once the entire set is read, control is returned to pbGetAliasListClick, where the contents of the TStringList object are placed in the ListBox to display the aliases.

Alias Management Using BDE in Delphi 2

Creating aliases and listing the currently defined aliases in Delphi 2 is essentially the same as in Delphi 1.0. Delphi 2 provides additional support for removing aliases, however. The BDE unit contains support for the DbiDeleteAlias function. Its syntax is as follows:

```
DbiDeleteAlias (hCfg: hDBICfg; pszAliasName: PChar): DBIResult
```

There are only two parameters for DbiDeleteAlias: hCfg, which is NULL to point to the current configuration file, and pszAliasName, which is the name of the alias to delete. The project BDEALS2.DPR demonstrates how to add and delete aliases in Delphi 2. Following is the main form for the BDEALS2 project:

BDEALS2 contains push buttons similar to the previous example for adding and list aliases and a push button for removing an alias. The majority of the code is the same for the unit as in BDEALS1, with the addition of the following code to delete an alias:

```
procedure TForm1.pbDeleteAliasClick(Sender: TObject);
begin
  { Make sure an alias is selected in the ListBox }
  if ListBox1.ItemIndex = -1 then
  begin
    MessageDlg('Need to select an alias first',mtError,[mbOK],0);
    Exit;
  end;
  { Confirm the alias deletion }
  if MessageDlg('Are you sure you want to delete the alias "' +
    ListBox1.Items[ListBox1.ItemIndex] + '"?',mtConfirmation,
    [mbNo,mbYes],0) <> mrYes then
      Exit;

  { Initialize the BDE }
  case DbiInit(nil) of
    DBIERR_NONE :  { No errors occurred in initialization }
      { Attempt to add the alias name and path }
      case DbiDeleteAlias(nil,
          PChar(ListBox1.Items[ListBox1.ItemIndex])) of
        DBIERR_NONE :
          ShowMessage('Alias Deleted');
        DBIERR_OBJNOTFOUND :
          ShowMessage('Alias name does not exist');
        DBIERR_INVALIDPARAM :
          ShowMessage('Null alias not allowed');
      else
        ShowMessage('Untrapped error for DbiDeleteAlias');
      end;
    DBIERR_MULTIPLEINIT :
      ShowMessage('Multiple initialize of Database Engine');
  else
    ShowMessage('An untrapped error occurred in DbiInit');
  end;
  DbiExit;
end;
```

Minor validation is done before the alias is deleted. First, an alias needs to be selected from the ListBox. When the form is opened, there are no entries in the ListBox. You need to click the Get Alias List button to create the alias list and place it into the ListBox. After selecting from the list, a dialog is displayed to confirm the alias deletion. If Yes is clicked, the remaining code is executed to delete the alias.

After the BDE is initialized, DbiDeleteAlias is called using the selected alias. If the alias is removed, the return result is DBIERR_NONE. ShowMessage is used to display the result of the delete—either the alias is removed or the reason for the delete failure is displayed.

You don't need to use the BDE to manage aliases when you have choices like the Database component, which allows you to create local aliases at runtime. Because you cannot delete an alias in Delphi 1.0, you do not have complete control over the configuration file form within that version of Delphi.

Delphi 2 also allows you to use methods to add, delete, modify, and save alias settings using the Session component. These new features are covered in Chapter 7.

Conclusion

This chapter has provided you with an introduction to the basic principles of data use in Delphi. In essence, all data access requires the use of DataSet components. Furthermore, if you want to provide users with access to this data by way of onscreen controls, you must use data-aware controls in combination with one or more DataSource components. The DataSource component provides the interface between data-aware controls and DataSets.

This chapter has not provided any details concerning the use of data-aware controls. Using data-aware controls, as well as working with DataSet and DataSource components, is discussed in detail in Chapter 6. Also, you will find a discussion of the Delphi 2 specific data-aware controls and related components for data access in Chapter 7.

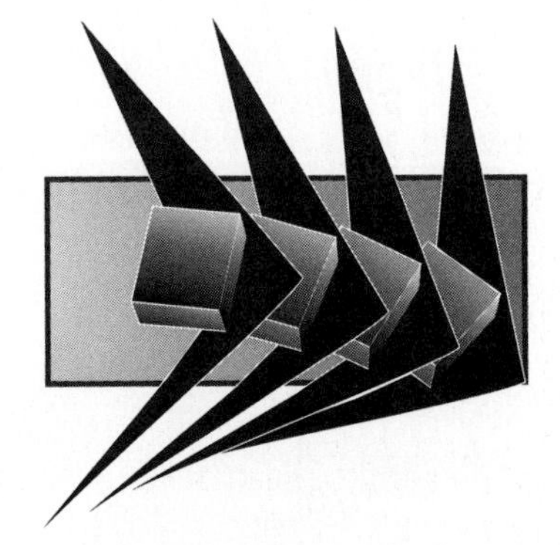

Chapter Six

Using Database Components

The code for the examples presented in this chapter can be found in the \CODE\CH06 subdirectory on the CD-ROM that accompanies this book. Please refer to Appendix A for information on using the code files for this chapter.

Chapter 5 provided a general introduction to creating databases in Delphi. In that chapter you learned the basics of working with data in Delphi. In this chapter the focus is on using the database components to produce specific database-related results.

One of the biggest challenges in writing this particular chapter was choosing which of the various database related topics to cover. The problem was that it would be rather easy to write an entire book detailing the use of Delphi in building databases. Consequently, it was necessary to be selective, covering only a sample of database-related topics.

The topics chosen for inclusion in this chapter are varied, covering a wide range of problems and their solutions. Furthermore, these issues relate to both Delphi 1.0 and Delphi 2. In addition, these techniques can be applied to local applications (those running on a stand-alone machine or on a local area network) as well as client/server applications. For details concerning the new database features added to Delphi 2, see Chapter 7. For a discussion of issues that apply to client/server applications, refer to Chapter 8.

Because the topics included in this chapter are so varied, they do not necessarily build upon one another. In other words, you do not need to read this chapter from start to finish. If you want, you can go directly to the topics that interest you most. The following topics are covered in this chapter:

- Creating tables and indexes at runtime
- Changing grid display at runtime
- Single DataSource and DataSet components for multitable forms
- Using multiple Table components with a single DataSource
- Locating records
- Using ranges
- Using queries
- Creating master/detail forms
- Comparing table structures at runtime

NOTE: Most of the examples used in this chapter make use of the Paradox table structure. This table type is considered the default table type for Delphi applications. However, these techniques also apply to other types of tables. If you are interested specifically in techniques that are used in client/server applications, refer to Chapter 8.

Creating Tables and Indexes at Runtime

All tables used in an application do not have to exist before starting the application. You can build them at runtime using a Table component and the CreateTable method.

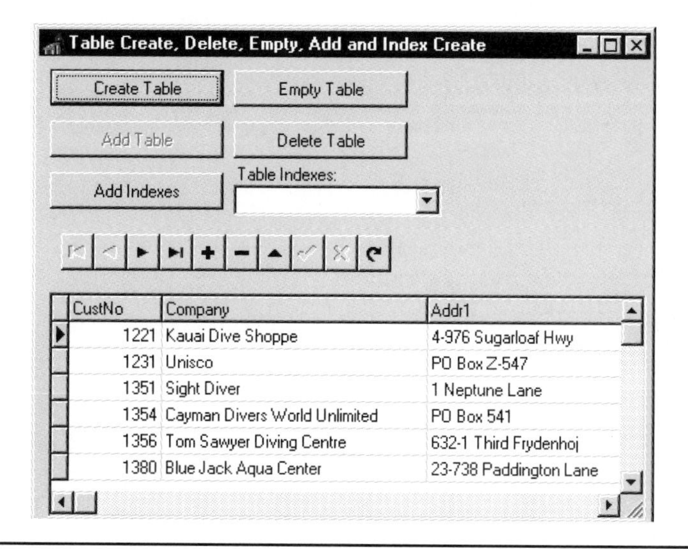

Figure 6-1. *Main form for the TBLMTHD project*

You can also delete tables, create indexes, and remove indexes. The TTable class provides methods for all these activities.

Figure 6-1 shows the main form in the TBLMTHD.DPR project. This project demonstrates how to use Table methods for table and index management. The table name TEST_TBL.DB is created by this project. TEST_TBL.DB has the same structure as the CUSTOMER.DB table in the DBDEMOS alias, which is used in the Add Table demonstration used in this project.

The main form of TBLMTHD contains a set of buttons and a DBGrid to display data. The event handlers for the buttons contain code that demonstrates how to create a table, delete a table, empty a table, add data using a TBatchMove component, and add indexes at runtime. Each of these operations is discussed in turn.

Creating Tables

You can use the Table method CreateTable to create a new table at runtime. The Table object that you use to execute this method can be placed at design time or can be instantiated at runtime. In the example contained in this form, the Table component, named pbTblDelete, was placed at design time. Following is the OnClick event handler for the Create Table button:

```
procedure TForm1.pbTblCreateClick(Sender: TObject);
begin
  if FileExists('TEST_TBL.DB') then
   begin
    pbTblDelete.Enabled := True;
```

```
    MessageDlg('Table TEST_TBL already exists.  Use the ' +
      'Delete button to remove the existing table',
      mtError,[mbOK],0);
   end
 else
   with Test_Tbl do
     begin
     Screen.Cursor := crHourGlass;
     Active := False;
     IndexName := '';
     { Set the DatabaseName, TableName and TableType }
     DatabaseName := ExtractFilePath(Application.ExeName);
     TableName := 'TEST_TBL';
     TableType := ttParadox;
     { Define the fields in the table }
     with FieldDefs do
     begin
       Clear;
       Add('CustNo', ftFloat, 0, True);
       Add('Company', ftString, 30, True);
       Add('Addr1', ftString, 30, False);
       Add('Addr2', ftString, 30, False);
       Add('City', ftString, 15, False);
       Add('State', ftString, 20, False);
       Add('Zip', ftString, 10, False);
       Add('Country', ftString, 20, False);
       Add('Phone', ftString, 15, False);
       Add('FAX', ftString, 15, False);
       Add('TaxRate', ftFloat, 0, False);
       Add('Contact', ftString, 20, False);
       Add('LastInvoiceDate', ftDateTime, 0, False);
     { Valid field types: ftUnknown, ftString, ftSmallint,
         ftInteger, ftWord, ftBoolean, ftFloat, ftCurrency, ftBCD,
         ftDate, ftTime, ftDateTime, ftBytes, ftVarBytes, ftBlob,
         ftMemo or ftGraphic  }
     end;
     { Define the primary key for the table }
     with IndexDefs do
     begin
       Clear;
       Add('', 'CustNo', [ixPrimary, ixUnique]);
     end;
     { Create and open the table }
     CreateTable;
     Open;

     pbTblAddData.Enabled := True;
     pbTblAddIndex.Enabled := True;
```

```
        Screen.Cursor := crDefault;
      end;
  end;
```

As demonstrated in this code, a number of steps need to be completed before a table can be created using CreateTable. Specifically, the DatabaseName and TableName properties of the Table component need to be set. In this example, DatabaseName property is set to the directory in which the project .EXE file is located. Identifying the application directory is performed using the ExeName property of the Application variable that Delphi creates automatically for an application. ExeName returns the entire path and filename of the executable. Then, the ExtractFileName function is used to identify just the drive and subdirectory. It is this value that is assigned to the DataBaseName property. TableName is set to TEST_TBL.DB, the name of the table being created.

In the preceding event handler, the TableType property was set to ttParadox. This setting specifies that a Paradox table will be created. If the table type can be determined from the extension used in the TableName property, the TableType property is optional.

Defining Fields for the Table

Before you can create a table, you must also define the fields that will constitute the table's structure. In the current example, this is done using the FieldDefs property. The FieldDefs property defines a list of FieldDef objects, each of which defines a field in the Table. When you open an existing table, the Table component automatically loads the FieldDef objects based on information supplied by the BDE (Borland Database Engine). However, when you create a table, you must create the FieldDef objects using code.

Although several different techniques can be used to set the FieldDefs property of a Table component, the easiest is to use the Add method of the FieldDefs object. This method, has the following syntax:

```
procedure Add(const Name: String;
              DataType: TFieldType;
              Size: Word,
              Required: Boolean)
```

The first argument, Name, defines the name of the field you are adding to the FieldDefs property. This name needs to conform to the naming conventions for the table type you are creating. The second argument, DataType, is a value of the type TFieldType. The following are the available TFieldType values: ftString, ftSmallint, ftInteger, ftWord, ftBoolean, ftFloat, ftCurrency, ftBCD, ftDate, ftTime, ftDateTime, ftBytes, ftVarBytes, ftBlob, ftMemo, and ftGraphic. Note, however, that not all table types support all of these field types. You must make sure that the field type you are defining for a table is permitted by the type of table you are creating.

The third argument, Size, applies to only some of the TFieldType types. For ftBCD, use Size to identify how many decimal places the field will support. For ftString, ftBlob, ftVarBytes, ftBytes, and ftGraphic, Size indicates how many bytes will be allocated within the primary table for storage of the value. For all other field types, any non-negative integer value can be passed.

The final argument permits you to define whether the field you are adding will be a required field. To make the field a required field, pass the value True; otherwise, pass the value False.

The following is the portion of the OnClick event handler for the Create Table button that defines the fields:

```
{ Define the fields in the table }
      with FieldDefs do
      begin
        Clear;
        Add('CustNo', ftFloat, 0, True);
        Add('Company', ftString, 30, True);
        Add('Addr1', ftString, 30, False);
        Add('Addr2', ftString, 30, False);
        Add('City', ftString, 15, False);
        Add('State', ftString, 20, False);
        Add('Zip', ftString, 10, False);
        Add('Country', ftString, 20, False);
        Add('Phone', ftString, 15, False);
        Add('FAX', ftString, 15, False);
        Add('TaxRate', ftFloat, 0, False);
        Add('Contact', ftString, 20, False);
        Add('LastInvoiceDate', ftDateTime, 0, False);
      end;
```

Defining Indexes When the Table Is Created

Like the FieldDefs property, the IndexDefs property contains a list of objects. These IndexDef objects have information about the indexes for a table. You can use the Add method of the IndexDefs object to define the index. The syntax for the method is as follows:

```
procedure Add(const Name,
              Fields: string;
              Options: TIndexOptions);
```

The first argument, Name, defines the name of the index. The second argument is the field or fields used in the index. When multiple fields are used, they are separated using semicolons (;). You can also use numbers instead of the field names. These numbers correspond to the physical field positions in the table. You should be cautious using this option. If the relative position of a field in the table changes, you will end up using a different field than you intended in your index definition. Using field names is the safest solution to ensure the correct field name defines the index.

The final argument, Options, specifies the type of index that is to be created. The options are ixPrimary, ixUnique, ixDescending, ixExpression, and ixCaseInsensitive. For Paradox tables, using the combination of ixPrimary and ixUnique is required to define the primary index.

***NOTE:** The Delphi Help system in Delphi 1.0 shows that the values for TIndexOptions Type are ixPrimary, ixUnique, ixDescending, ixNonMaintained, and ixCaseInsensitive. This is incorrect. The preceding paragraph includes the correct values.*

The following code segment is the portion of the OnClick event handler for the Create Table button that defines the index. Only the primary key is defined here. The Name argument is left blank because the primary index in a Paradox table does not have a name.

```
{ Define the primary key for the table }
      with IndexDefs do
      begin
        Clear;
        Add('', 'CustNo', [ixPrimary, ixUnique]);
      end;
```

Adding Secondary Indexes

In addition to defining indexes using the IndexDefs property at the time a table is created, you can use the AddIndex method of the Table component. This method has the same syntax as the Add method for IndexDefs. The Add Indexes button defines three secondary indexes for the table. The index creation portion of the Add Indexes OnClick event handler is shown here:

```
{ Add the indexes to the table }
    Test_Tbl.AddIndex('ByCompany','Company', [ixCaseInsensitive]);
    Test_Tbl.AddIndex('ByTaxRate','TaxRate', [ixCaseInsensitive]);
    Test_Tbl.AddIndex('ByStateCity', 'State;City', [ixCaseInsensitive]);
```

The first two uses of AddIndex add a single-field index. Both are case insensitive indexes. The third AddIndex usage creates a two-field index based on the State and City fields.

***TIP:** In Delphi 2, you can use the Level 7 Paradox tables. These tables permit unique and descending secondary indexes. To use this feature, the Level parameter for the Paradox driver needs to be set to 7 in the BDE Configuration Utility. By default, the Level is set to 4, which does not support these new secondary index options.*

Creating a List of Available Indexes

Included in the code to generate the secondary indexes is an example of how to generate a list of available indexes for a table. In the TBLMTHD project, this list is displayed using a combo box, and code added to the combo box permits the user to change the selected index at runtime. The following code is the OnClick event handler for the Add Indexes button:

```
procedure TForm1.pbTblAddIndexClick(Sender: TObject);
var
  J: Integer;
begin
  Screen.Cursor := crHourGlass;
  Test_Tbl.DisableControls;
  try
    { Need to get Exclusive access to the table.  After closing
      it, set Exclusive property to True and open the table }
    Test_Tbl.Close;
    Test_Tbl.Exclusive := True;
    Test_Tbl.Open;
    { Add the indexes to the table }
    Test_Tbl.AddIndex('ByCompany','Company', [ixCaseInsensitive]);
    Test_Tbl.AddIndex('ByStateCity', 'State;City', [ixCaseInsensitive]);
    { Update the index list and clear the item list in the ComboBox }
    Test_Tbl.IndexDefs.Update;
    ComboBox1.Items.Clear;
    { Add the entries into the ComboBox for each available index }
    ComboBox1.Items.Add('<Primary Key>');
    for J := 0 to Test_Tbl.IndexDefs.Count - 1 do
      if Test_Tbl.IndexDefs.Items[J].Name <> '' then
        { Primary Index Name = '' }
        ComboBox1.Items.Add(Test_Tbl.IndexDefs.Items[J].Name);
  finally
    Test_Tbl.EnableControls;
    if not Test_tbl.Active then
      Test_tbl.Open;
    pbTblAddIndex.Enabled := False;
    Screen.Cursor := crDefault;
  end;
end;
```

Some preliminary settings need to be checked and set before the indexes can be generated. To generate secondary indexes for a Paradox table, you need to have exclusive rights to the table. This can be accomplished using the Exclusive property for the Table component. Setting the Exclusive property to True requires that the Active property first be set to False. The Close method sets Active to False. After setting Exclusive to True, the Open method is used to set Active to True. With Exclusive set to True, other users are prevented from accessing the table.

The Update method for IndexDefs is called to ensure that the correct information is set in the property. This information is used to generate the list of available indexes. The current list of indexes is removed from the combo box using the Clear method on the Items property. Next, the text <Primary Key> is added as the initial item in the list to represent the table's primary key.

The Count property of the IndexDefs object indicates the number of indexes for a table. This value allows a for loop to be used to get the name of each index. IndexDefs has the Items property, which holds the TIndexDef objects. The Name property of the TIndexDef object provides the index name. The Name property is used to add the name of each index to the ComboBox Items property using the Add method.

When all index names have been added to the combo box list, the AddIndex button is disabled. For this project, disabling the AddIndex button prevents the user from attempting to add the two indexes a second time.

The preceding code section included a call to DisableControls, which prevents a DataSet component from informing its DataSource when data is changed. After executing DisableControls, it is essential to include a try-finally control structure. The try block should contain every statement that you want to execute while the DataSet is disabled, and the finally block should include the call to EnableControls. This step ensures that the Table will be enabled even if an exception occurs within the try block. If you fail to do this and an exception occurs before EnableControls is executed, the DataSet will appear frozen.

Changing the Data Display Order Using Indexes

The IndexName property of the Table component specifies which index to use for ordering records in a table. This property can be changed at runtime without your needing to open and close the table. This is demonstrated in the following code, which is found in the OnChange event handler for the ComboBox component:

```
procedure TForm1.ComboBox1Change(Sender: TObject);
begin
  with ComboBox1 do
    if ItemIndex = 0 then
     Test_Tbl.IndexName := ''
    else
      Test_Tbl.IndexName := Items[ItemIndex];
end;
```

This code chooses the index based on the ItemIndex property of the ComboBox component. If the ItemIndex is equal to zero, the user selected <Primary Key> from the combo box (the index of a combo box is zero-based, meaning that the first item in the list is associated with the value zero). In this case, the IndexName property of the Table component is set to blank, which causes the table to default to the primary index. If one of the other index names is selected, the IndexName property is set to the name of the selected index using the Items property of the combo box.

Deleting a Table

The Delete method of the Table component allows you to delete an existing table in a database. The DatabaseName and TableName properties of the Table component must be set before you call this method (TableType must also be set if Delphi cannot determine the type of table based on the table name). You also need to make sure that the table is closed before calling DeleteTable. The use of DeleteTable is demonstrated in the code in the Delete Table button's OnClick event handler:

```
procedure TForm1.pbTblDeleteClick(Sender: TObject);
begin
  if not FileExists('TEST_TBL.DB') then
    MessageDlg('Table TEST_TBL does not exits.  Use ' +
      'Create Table button to create the table.',
      mtError,[mbOK],0)
  else
    with Test_Tbl do
    begin
      Screen.Cursor := crHourGlass;
      Active := False;
      { Set the DatabaseName, TableName and TableType }
      DatabaseName := ExtractFilePath(Application.ExeName);
      TableName := 'TEST_TBL';
      TableType := ttParadox;
      { Delete the table }
      DeleteTable;
      { Disable the Data and Index add buttons }
      pbTblAddData.Enabled := False;
      pbTblAddIndex.Enabled := False;
      { Remove all Index Name entries in the ComboBox }
      ComboBox1.Items.Clear;
      Screen.Cursor := crDefault;
    end;
end;
```

Before attempting to delete the table, a check is performed using FileExists to see if the table actually exists. If the table is not found, MessageDlg is used to display a message indicating the table does not exist. Also included in the message is a prompt to use the Create Table button to create the table.

The first step in deleting the table is to close the dataset. This is done by setting Active to False. The Close method could have been used here instead. The DatabaseName is then set to the directory in which the current .EXE is located. The TableName property is then set to the same name used by the Create Table button (TEST_TBL). The last step is to call the DeleteTable method, which removes the table and all its related files from the disk drive.

Emptying a Table of Data

You can delete every record from a table by executing a DELETE query, or by using the Table method EmptyTable. Unlike the Delete method, EmptyTable can be performed on an open table. However, to empty an open table, you must have exclusive rights to it. If you do not set the Exclusive property to True, you can simply close the table and then empty it. This procedure is demonstrated in the following code for the Empty Table button's OnClick event handler:

```
procedure TForm1.pbTblEmptyClick(Sender: TObject);
begin
  if not FileExists('TEST_TBL.DB') then
    MessageDlg('Table TEST_TBL does not exits.  Use ' +
      'Create Table button to create the table.',
      mtError,[mbOK],0)
  else
    with Test_Tbl do
    begin
      Screen.Cursor := crHourGlass;
      DisableControls;
      try
        Active := False;
        { Set the DatabaseName, TableName and TableType }
        DatabaseName := ExtractFilePath(Application.ExeName);
        TableName := 'TEST_TBL';
        TableType := ttParadox;
        { Remove all rows from the table }
        EmptyTable;
        Test_Tbl.Open;
      finally
        EnableControls;
        pbTblAddData.Enabled := True;
        Screen.Cursor := crDefault;
      end;
    end;

end;
```

The Empty Table event handler is similar to that for the Delete Table button. First, a check is made to see if the table exists. If TEST_TBL is not found, a message is displayed and you are instructed to use the Create Table button. After the table is closed, the DatabaseName, TableName, and TableType are assigned before the call to EmptyTable is made. The table is then reopened, and the Add Table button is enabled.

Adding Data to the New Table Using BatchMove

The last example in the TBLMTHD project demonstrates the use of the BatchMove component to copy data from one table to another. The BatchMove component supports four major capabilities:

- Creating a table and placing the current records of a dataset in it.
- Deleting records from a table that correspond to those in a dataset.
- Inserting records from a dataset to a Table.
- Updating existing records in a table based on those in a dataset.

BatchMove Basics

There are three essential properties for the BatchMove component: Source, Destination, and Mode. The Source property can be assigned any DataSet component. In other words, you can assign a Table, a Query, or a StoredProc component name to this property. Although any Table component is acceptable, you should only assign one of the other dataset descendants to this property if they return a cursor to a dataset. For example, it would reasonable to assign a Query component that contains an SQL SELECT statement to the Source property, but it would not make sense to assign to this property a Query containing an ALTER TABLE statement. An SQL SELECT statement returns a cursor, but the ALTER TABLE statement does not.

The Destination property is always assigned a Table component. This table is where the records of the source dataset records are copied, deleted, inserted, or updated.

The Mode property defines the type of operation performed by the BatchMove component. Table 6-1 lists the five available modes. This table also indicates whether the table assigned to the Destination property must exist prior to calling the Execution method of BatchMove, as well as whether the destination table must be indexed.

Mode	Destination Must Exist?	Must Be Indexed?
batAppend (default)	Yes	No
batAppendUpdate	Yes	Yes
batCopy	No	No
batDelete	Yes	Yes
batUpdate	Yes	Yes

Table 6-1. *BatchMove Mode Property Options*

Adding CUSTOMER.DB to TEMP_TBL.DB

In the TBLMTHD project, the BatchMove component is used to add data from an existing table into the newly created table. The data in the CUSTOMER.DB table residing in the alias DBDEMOS is used as the source table. The Table component named Customer exists on the form and is opened before the BatchMove is executed. The following is the code for the Add Table button's OnClick event handler:

```
procedure TForm1.pbTblAddDataClick(Sender: TObject);
begin
  Screen.Cursor := crHourGlass;
  { Set the destination and source tables }
  BatchMove1.Destination := Test_Tbl;
  BatchMove1.Source := Customer;
  { Open the Customer table }
  Customer.Open;
  { Execute the batch copy }
  BatchMove1.Execute;
  { Prevent further adds to occur until the table is deleted }
  pbTblAddData.Enabled := False;
  Screen.Cursor := crDefault;
end;
```

Both the Destination and Source properties are set before executing the BatchMove. The names of the two Table components are assigned, and then the BatchMove is run. After completion, the DBGrid displays the data added.

Changing Grid Display at Runtime

One of the most important components for displaying data in Delphi is the DBGrid. This control provides the user with a tabular, or columnar, display. This component has a number of properties that provide you with flexibility on how the data is displayed and treated within the DBGrid. The following sections demonstrate how to control the appearance of a DBGrid through the use of the published set property Options, as well as through code placed in the OnDrawDataCell event handler.

Setting Grid Options

The DBGrid component provides a set property called Options that permits you to control several DBGrid display characteristics. A set property is one that can contain zero, one, or more of a fixed number of values. From within the Object Inspector, set properties can be expanded to display the individual values. These individual values appear as Boolean properties. If a particular value is associated with a Boolean True, that value is part of the set; if the value is associated with a Boolean False, it is absent from the set. Figure 6-2 shows the Object Inspector with all the Options property expanded and the individual values displayed.

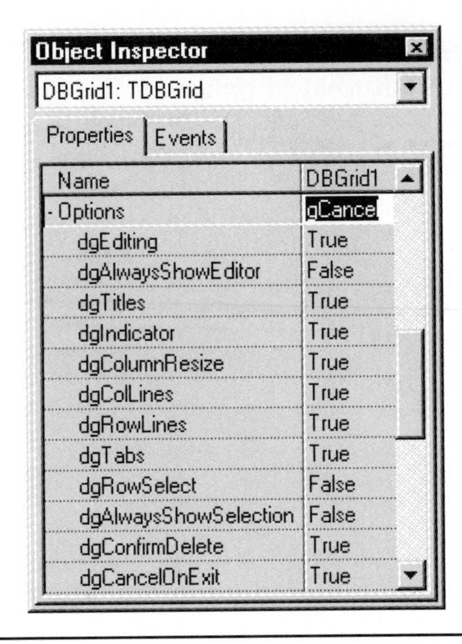

Figure 6-2. *DBGrid Options property in the Object Inspector*

Table 6-2 lists each of the possible values for the Options set, along with a brief description of the value's effect.

You control the Options property at runtime by adding one or more values to the set, or by removing one or more values from the set. For example, if you wanted to enable row highlighting at runtime, you would add the dgRowSelect value to the Options set. This is demonstrated in the following code:

```
DBGrid1.Options := DBGrid1.Options + [dgRowSelect]
```

If you wanted to add more than one value to the set, the parentheses in the preceding array would include a comma-delimited list of the values you were adding.

You can use the project RTDBGRD.DPR to see how the various Options values affect the appearance and behavior of a DBGrid. Figure 6-3 displays the main form of this project. This form contains a single DBGrid, which is associated with a DataSource that points to a dataset for the CUSTOMER.DB table from the DBDEMOS alias.

At the bottom of the form is a check box for each of the values in the TDBGridOptions set. If the Checked property of a given check box is True (checked), the corresponding DBGrid option is True. Each of the CheckBox components has code attached to the OnClick event handler similar to the following:

```
procedure TForm1.cbTitlesClick(Sender: TObject);
begin
```

```
    if cbTitles.Checked = True then
      DBGrid1.Options := DBGrid1.Options + [dgTitles]
    else
      DBGrid1.Options := DBGrid1.Options - [dgTitles];
    DBGrid1.SetFocus;
  end;
```

Within this event handler, the current value of the Checked property is evaluated to see if it is True. If Checked is True, the corresponding value, dgTitles in this case, is added to the set; otherwise, the value is removed. After changing the set defining the

Value	Meaning When Enabled (Value is True)
dgEditing	Allows editing of the data in the grid.
dgAlwaysShowEditor	Field is in edit mode when it is selected.
dgTitles	Displays the titles of the columns at the top of the grid.
dgIndicator	A column on the left side of the grid is used to display the current record pointer. The pointer changes to an I-beam when editing a record and to an asterisk when inserting a new record.
dgColumnResize	Allows the columns in the grid to be resized at runtime.
dgColLines	Displays lines between the columns.
dgRowLines	Displays lines between the rows.
dgTabs	The Tab key and the Shift-Tab keys are enabled to move between the columns in the grid.
dgRowSelect	The entire row is always displayed as the current selection. Individual fields are not accessible.
dgAlwaysShowSelection	The current cell in the grid continues to display as selected even when the grid does not have focus. If RowSelect is True, the entire row remains highlighted when another object has focus.
dgConfirmDelete	A confirmation message box is displayed when Ctrl-Del is pressed to delete a row in the grid.
dgCancelOnExit	An inserted record that has not been saved is canceled when the grid is exited.

Table 6-2. *Values for the Options Property in a DBGrid*

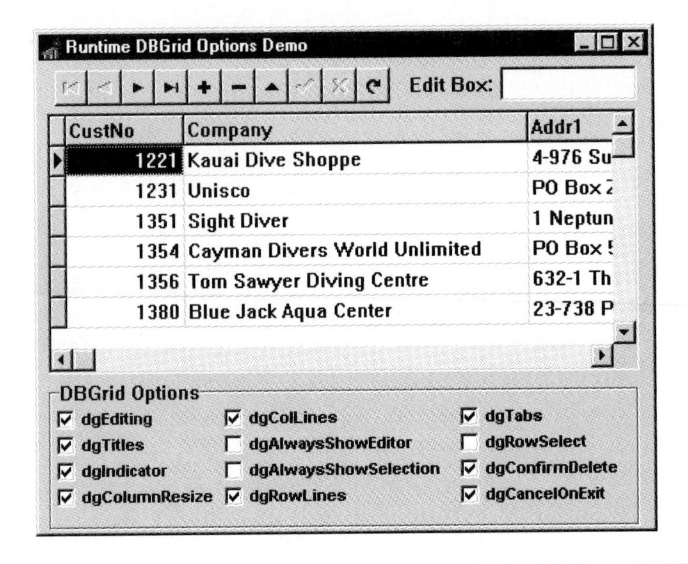

Figure 6-3. *Initial grid display for RTDBGRD project*

Options property, focus is set to the DBGrid, making it the active control (otherwise, the clicked check box would have focus). Figure 6-4 shows the form after clicking the dgTitles, dgIndicator, dgAlwaysShowSelection, and dgRowSelection check boxes.

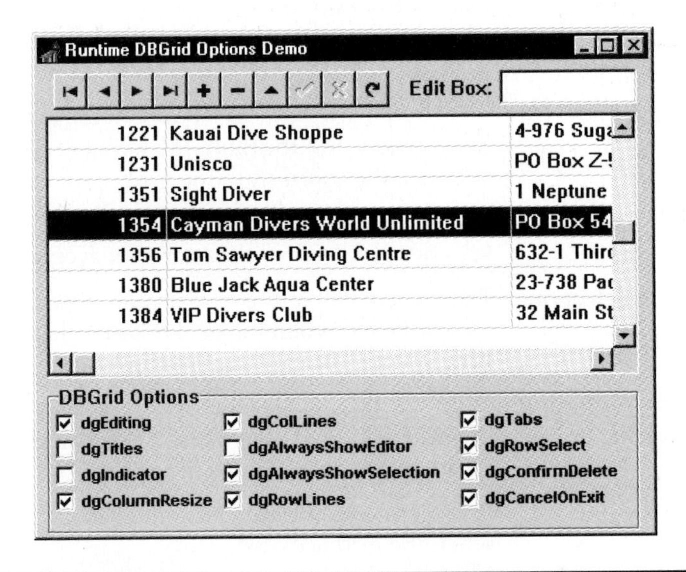

Figure 6-4. *Modifications to the grid display at runtime*

Setting the Row and Font Color in a DBGrid

Colors provide you with an effective way to highlight data and draw attention to different areas of a form. For example, you can change the color used for an entire row in a DBGrid to draw attention to that data. Using a similar technique, you can also change the font of the data, or another similar display attribute. While the dgRowSelect value of the Options property for a DBGrid permits the current row to be highlighted, it is sometimes necessary to draw attention to a row other than the current one.

The project GRDCLR1.DPR demonstrates how to color rows based on an evaluation of the underlying record data. In this example, color is used to highlight those companies located in the U.S. Furthermore, this project demonstrates how to control the row and font colors. Figure 6-5 shows an example of this project's main form after row and font colors have been changed, giving a reverse-video effect to the affected rows.

The form contains one each of the following components: Table, DataSource, DBGrid, and DBNavigator. The Table component, named Customer, is associated with CUSTOMER.DB in the DBDEMOS alias.

Two Edit controls are used to display the current color for the row and font. Since these controls will not be used for data entry, their TabStop properties have been set to False. The Color properties for the Edit controls are used to indicate the current colors selected for the row and font, and are initialized in the form's OnCreate event handler. The initial values for these controls are based on the current DBGrid colors, which can

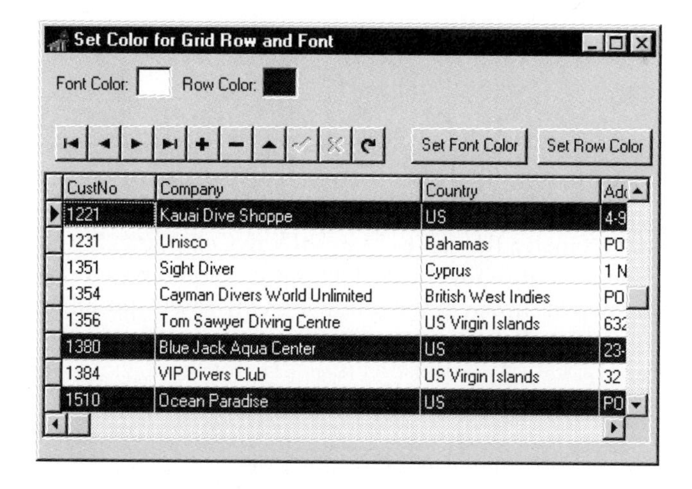

Figure 6-5. *Main form for the GRDCLR1 project*

be determined from the DBGrid's Canvas property. This step is shown in the following event handler:

```
procedure TForm1.FormCreate(Sender: TObject);
begin
  Customer.Open;
  Edit1.Color := DBGrid1.Canvas.Font.Color;    { Grid Font Color }
  Edit2.Color := DBGrid1.Canvas.Brush.Color;   { Grid Row Color }
end;
```

This form also has two buttons that allow the user to change the color for the highlighted row and font. These buttons use the ColorDialog component, which encapsulates a call to the Windows color common dialog box. If the user selects a color using this dialog box, the ColorDialog's Execute method returns True. In this case, the Color property of the ColorDialog holds the selected color, which is then assigned to the appropriate Edit control. Once this assignment has been made, the Table component's Refresh method is called, which causes the DBGrid to repaint. This step is shown in the following event handler:

```
procedure TForm1.pbSetFontColorClick(Sender: TObject);
begin
  if ColorDialog1.Execute then
  begin
    Edit1.Color := ColorDialog1.Color;
    Customer.Refresh;
  end;
  DBGrid1.SetFocus;
end;
```

As part of the DBGrid's repaint, the OnDrawDataCell event handler is executed. From within this event handler, the data from the current record is evaluated, and the current Color property of the Font and Brush properties of the DBGrid's canvas is modified, if necessary. Finally, the call to DefaultDrawCell paints the current cell of the row. The result is that the entire row of the DBGrid is colored based on data in the current record. This step is shown in the following OnDrawDataCell event handler:

```
procedure TForm1.DBGrid1DrawDataCell(Sender: TObject;
  const Rect: TRect; Field: TField; State: TGridDrawState);
begin
  if Customer.FieldByName('Country').AsString = 'US' then
  begin
    DBGrid1.Canvas.Font.Color := Edit1.Color;   { Set row font color }
    DBGrid1.Canvas.Brush.Color := Edit2.Color;  { Set row color }
  end;
  DBGrid1.DefaultDrawDataCell(Rect,Field,State);
end;
```

Setting the Color in a Field for Specific Values

While the preceding example demonstrated how to color an entire row of a DBGrid, sometimes it is desirable to color only an individual cell. This technique uses essentially the same technique as coloring rows. The main difference is that your code tests both the value of a field, as well as which field is being painted. This technique is demonstrated in the GRDCLR2.DPR project, shown in Figure 6-6.

The project uses the ORDERS.DB table from the DBDEMOS alias. In this case, only the OrderNo, CustNo, SalesDate, ItemsTotal, and AmountPaid fields are displayed. The Fields Editor was used to select these fields. (Double-click a Table component to displays its Fields Editor dialog box.) In addition, a calculated field, named Balance, was added. Balance is assigned using the following code in the OnCalcFields event handler for the Orders Table component:

```
procedure TForm1.OrdersCalcFields(DataSet: TDataset);
begin
  OrdersBalance.Value := OrdersItemsTotal.Value -
    OrdersAmountPaid.Value;
  OrdersBalance.Value = Trunc(OrdersBalance.Value * 100)/100
end;
```

Two things happen in the OnCalcFields event handler. First, the value of the Balance field (named OrdersBalance) is calculated as the difference between the ItemsTotal field and the AmountPaid field. Second, the value of the Balance field is rounded to two decimal places, first by multiplying it by 100, rounding it to the nearest integer, and then dividing it by 100. This calculation eliminates the minute, yet

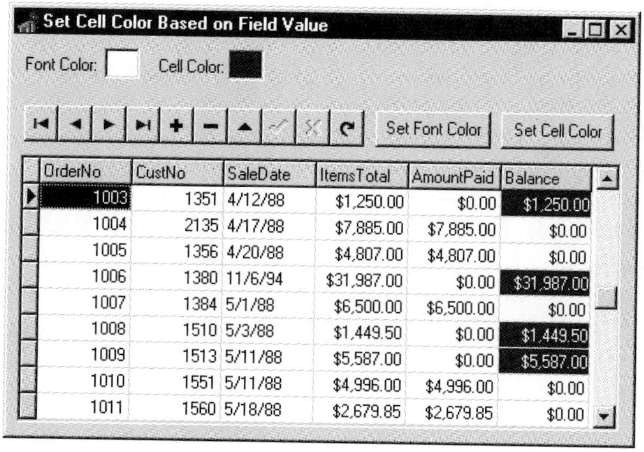

Set Cell Color Based on Field Value

Font Color: Cell Color:

Set Font Color Set Cell Color

OrderNo	CustNo	SaleDate	ItemsTotal	AmountPaid	Balance
1003	1351	4/12/88	$1,250.00	$0.00	$1,250.00
1004	2135	4/17/88	$7,885.00	$7,885.00	$0.00
1005	1356	4/20/88	$4,807.00	$4,807.00	$0.00
1006	1380	11/6/94	$31,987.00	$0.00	$31,987.00
1007	1384	5/1/88	$6,500.00	$6,500.00	$0.00
1008	1510	5/3/88	$1,449.50	$0.00	$1,449.50
1009	1513	5/11/88	$5,587.00	$0.00	$5,587.00
1010	1551	5/11/88	$4,996.00	$4,996.00	$0.00
1011	1560	5/18/88	$2,679.85	$2,679.85	$0.00

Figure 6-6. *Form for the GRDCLR2 project showing how to color individual cells in a DBGrid*

detectable, errors that occur in floating point arithmetic. Without doing this, some values that appear as 0.00 would actually be non-zero values, such as 0.000000001.

Like in the row highlighting example, the painting of the cell is produced in the OnDrawDataCell event handler for the DBGrid. The following is the code in this event handler:

```
procedure TForm1.DBGrid1DrawDataCell(Sender: TObject;
  const Rect: TRect; Field: TField; State: TGridDrawState);
begin
  if Field.FieldName = 'Balance' then
    begin
    if OrdersBalance.Value > 0.005 then
      begin
        DBGrid1.Canvas.Font.Color := Edit1.Color;  { Font color }
        DBGrid1.Canvas.Brush.Color := Edit2.Color; { Cell color }
      end;
      DBGrid1.DefaultDrawDataCell(Rect,Field,State);
    end;
end;
```

The OnDrawDataCell event handler includes a TField parameter that corresponds to the field of the DBGrid being painted. The preceding code compares the FieldName property of this Field object to determine when the Balance field is being painted. When the field is being painted, the colors of the Canvas' Brush and Font Properties are set to the corresponding Edit components' Color properties any time the value of the Balance field is a positive number.

NOTE: *In the preceding event handler the code could have tested the Name property of the Field parameter, instead of the FieldName property. In that case, the code would have had to compare the Name property against OrdersBalance, which is the instantiated field name, as opposed to Balance, which is the name of the field in the table.*

Single DataSource and DataSet Components for a Multi-Table Form

Providing access to two or more tables on a single form does not require a separate DataSource and DataSet component for each table you need to access. Instead, you can use a single DataSource component linked to a single Table component, and merely change which table the Table component points to at runtime.

NOTE: *The CD-ROM includes two example projects, TTBL1V1.DPR and TTBL1V2.DPR, which apply to Delphi 1.0 and Delphi 2, respectively. This section uses the Delphi 2 version of this project, which uses a TabControl component. The Delphi 1.0 version of this project, which can also be used in Delphi 2, uses a TabSet component. There is no TabControl component in Delphi 1.0.*

This technique is demonstrated in the TTBL1V2.DPR project shown in Figure 6-7. This form contains a TabControl component along with a single DataSource and Table component pair. The TabControl component is used to display the names of the tables that the user will be permitted to view, as well as to provide the visual appearance of a multi-page form. When the user selects a tab of the TabControl, the OnChange event handler for the TabControl changes the TableName in the Table component to the selected tab.

The following is the TabControl OnChange event handler:

```
procedure TForm1.TabControl1Change(Sender: TObject);
begin
  Table1.DisableControls;
  try
    Table1.Close;
    { Set the TableName to the text shown on the current tab }
    Table1.TableName := TabControl1.Tabs[TabControl1.TabIndex];
    Table1.Open;

 Finally
    Table1.EnableControls;
  end;
end;
```

In this example, the names of the Paradox tables match the names on each tab of the TabControl. From within the TabControl's OnChange event handler, the TabIndex property points to the current tab. Using this property to index the Tabs property provides your code with the text of the selected tab. This text is then assigned to the TableName property for Table1. Notice, however, that to change the table that the Table component points to, you must first close the component. After assigning the

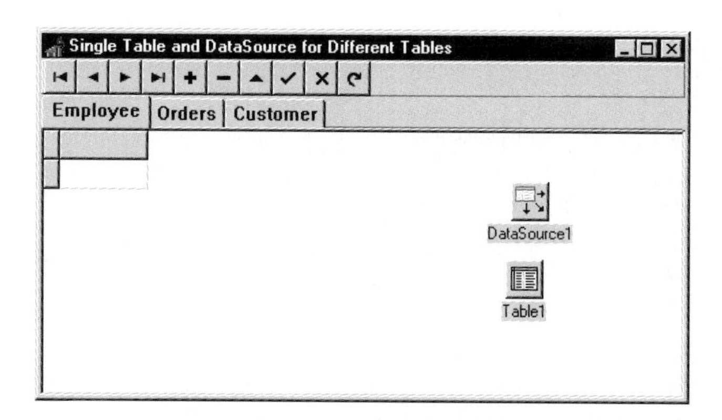

Figure 6-7. *Form in design mode for the TTBL1V2 project showing single Table and DataSource components for multiple tables*

new table name, the Table component is again opened. As demonstrated earlier in this chapter, the DisableControls and EnableControls methods are used to suppress the flicker that would otherwise occur when the Table component closed and opened.

Figure 6-8 shows how this running project looks when the Orders tab is selected.

NOTE: In the Delphi 1.0 version of this project, the OnChange event handler of the TabSet is used to switch the tables. Unlike a TabControl's OnChange event handler, the TabSet's OnChange event handler is executed before the new tab is selected. This means that the TabIndex property of a TabSet does not point to the tab being moved to, but instead points to the old tab. However, the TabSet's OnChange event handler is passed an integer, named NewTab, in its parameter list. NewTab indicates which tab has been selected. Consequently, when using a TabSet, NewTab is used to index the Tabs property instead of the TabIndex property.

Using Multiple TTable Components and a Single DataSource

One drawback to the preceding example is that each time the user changes tables, the cursor for the displayed table always points to the first record. This is because the cursor of a Table component always points to the first record when that table is opened. This can be avoided if more than one Table component is used. Specifically, instead of using a single Table component, your project can include one Table component for each table. Such a project can still use a single DataSource, however. When the user clicks on a TabControl, or a TabSet (Delphi 1.0), the DataSet property of the DataSource can be modified, pointing it to the open Table component corresponding to the selected Tab. The primary advantage of this technique is that each table retains its record pointer, and the additional overhead of opening and closing tables is avoided.

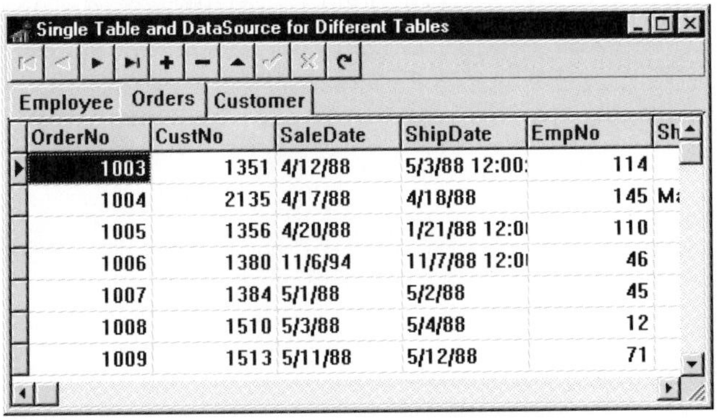

Figure 6-8. *Orders table displayed as the current table in TTBL1V2 project*

This technique is demonstrated in the project TTBL3V2.DPR shown in Figure 6-9. This project includes three Table components on the form—one for each of the tables listed in the TabControl. In this case, the Table components' names have been set to match the names of the tables to which they point. The OnCreate event handler for the form is used to ensure the form and components are initialized correctly.

These tables are opened, and the TabControl is initialized in the OnCreate event handler of the form, as shown here:

```
procedure TForm1.FormCreate(Sender: TObject);
begin
  TabControl1.TabIndex := 0;
  DataSource1.DataSet := Employee;
  Employee.Open;
  Orders.Open;
  Customer.Open;
end;
```

As you can see from Figure 6-9, the Employee table is associated with the first tab. Consequently, the DataSet property of the single DataSource component is set initially to the Table component corresponding to the Employee table. Next, each of the three tables is opened.

Switching the displayed table in the DBGrid is performed in the OnChange event for the TabControl, as shown in the following code:

```
procedure TForm1.TabControl1Change(Sender: TObject);
begin
```

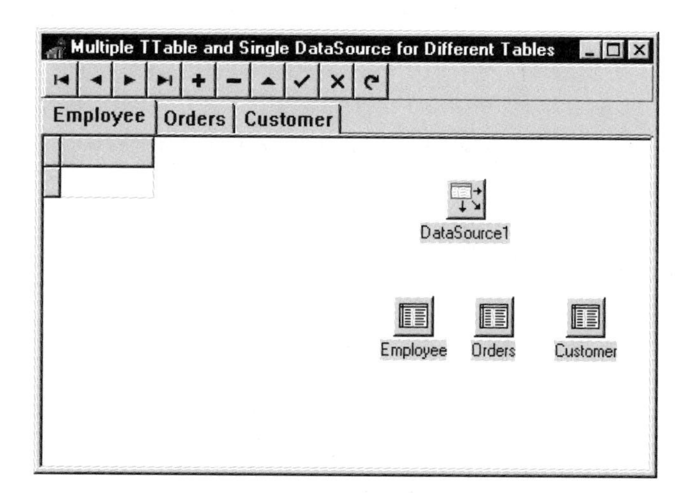

Figure 6-9. *Main form for the TTBL3V2 project in design mode*

```
  case TabControl1.TabIndex of
    0 : DataSource1.DataSet := Employee;
    1 : DataSource1.DataSet := Orders;
    2 : DataSource1.DataSet := Customer;
  end;
end;
```

A case statement is used to determine which of the three tabs is current. Depending on which tab is current, the DataSource.DataSet property is set to the appropriate Table component name.

There are several additional notable characteristics of this example. First, because a DBNavigator points to a DataSource and not a DataSet, changing the DataSet property of the DataSource effectively changes which table the DBNavigator will navigate. Second, since the Table components are not being closed and opened, it is not necessary to use DisableControls on any of them.

NOTE: As in the preceding example, if you used a TabSet instead of a TabControl, you would use the NewTab integer passed to the TabSet's OnChange event handler to determine which tab is selected. You would then use this information to set the DataSet property of the DataSource.

Locating Records in a Table

Delphi provides a variety of ways for you to locate a specific row in a table. One way is to search by moving through the table sequentially. For example, you can use the First method to move to the first record in the dataset and then use the Next method to move to each subsequent record. At each record, the data in one or more fields can be evaluated. When a match is found, the search can be terminated. The following is a code example of how you would move through the Customer table (pointed to by the Table1 component), searching for the record in which the CustNo field contains the value 2163:

```
Table1.First;
while not Table1.EOF do
    if Table1.FieldByName('CustNo').Value = '2163 then
      begin
        {Found the record}
        {Perform some task with the record and then exit}
        exit;
      end
    else
      Table1.Next;
```

This technique employs brute force, in that it makes no use of a table's indexes to locate the record. Furthermore, a sequential search can be time consuming. The more records there are in a table, and the closer the target record is to the end of the table, the longer this search will take. Typically, this type of search is only performed if the Table methods that support index-based searches cannot be employed.

As an alternative to sequential searches, the TTable class provides a number of search methods: FindKey, GotoKey, and GotoNearest. These methods require that an index exists for the field or fields used in the search.

Finding a Specific Row in a Table Using GotoKey and GotoNearest

The GotoKey method is used to move to a specific record in a table. GotoKey is a function that returns True if the search finds the record and False if it cannot. If the record is found, the cursor moves to the first row in the table that matches the search values. The current row does not change when False is returned.

The field or fields to be searched are based on the current table index. If the current index does not contain the fields necessary to perform the locate, you can switch the index, even if the table is open. You switch the index by changing the IndexName property of the Table component to one of the existing indexes for the table, or to a blank value to use the table's primary index (a primary index is the default index of a Paradox table).

Defining the Search Values Using SetKey

To define the values used in the search, the Table component's state must be changed to dsSetKey. This change creates a search key buffer containing the same number and type of fields as there are in the current index. To change the state to dsSetKey, use either the SetKey or EditKey method. The SetKey method clears all values in the search key buffer. By comparison, the EditKey method allows existing values in the search key buffer to be changed without clearing the existing values. Once this search buffer is defined, the GotoKey method initiates the search.

The SETKEY Project

The SETKEY.DPR project demonstrates how to use the SetKey, GotoKey, and GotoNearest methods. The Customer table from DBDEMOS is used as the table for searching. The primary key, based on the CustNo field, is used for the index. An Edit component permits the user to enter the customer number for the record being searched for. Figure 6-10 shows the form after searching for customer number 2163.

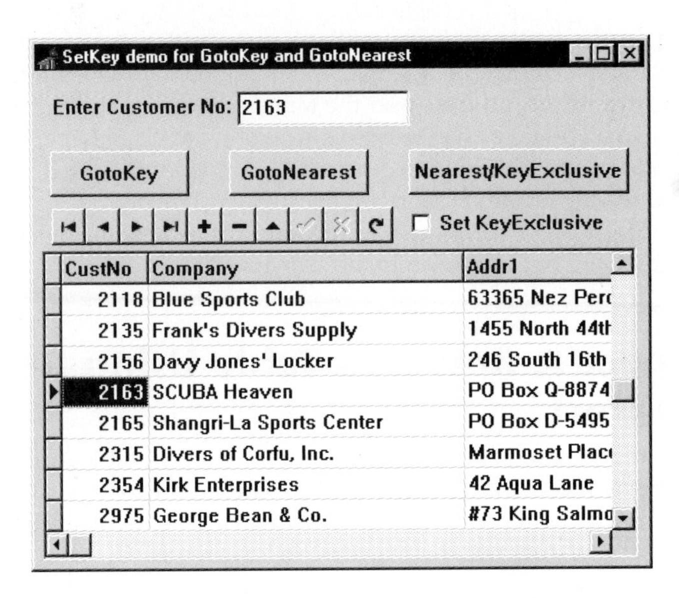

Figure 6-10. *Form for the SETKEY project after finding the specified customer number*

The GotoKey button uses the SetKey and GotoKey methods to find the record. The following is the code for this button's OnClick event handler:

```
procedure TForm1.pbGotoKeyClick(Sender: TObject);
begin
  if Edit1.Text <> '' then begin
    Table1.SetKey;
    Table1.FieldByName('CustNo').AsString := Edit1.Text;
    if not Table1.GotoKey then
      ShowMessage('Value not found');
  end;
  DBGrid1.SetFocus;
end;
```

If a value is entered into the Edit component, the search is performed. The table state is changed using SetKey, and the search value is placed in the search buffer using the FieldByName method. The return value of GotoKey is evaluated, and if a record is not found for the specified customer number, ShowMessage displays the message "Value not found." If the record is found, the cursor is automatically placed on that record, making it the current record in the DBGrid.

Using the GotoNearest Method

The GotoNearest method provides the ability to find the records in which the index field is equal to or greater than the search value. Unlike GotoKey, GotoNearest does not return a value, since it is always successful.

The GotoNearest button on the form demonstrates this method. The following is the code for the button's OnClick event handler:

```
procedure TForm1.pbGotoNearestClick(Sender: TObject);
begin
  if Edit1.Text <> '' then begin
    Table1.SetKey;
    Table1.FieldByName('CustNo').AsString := Edit1.Text;
    Table1.GotoNearest;
  end;
  DBGrid1.SetFocus;
end;
```

The only difference from the code shown for GotoKey and the code for GotoNearest is that no dialog box is displayed when a record is not found. The current record in the grid is always changed unless only a single record exists in the table. Figure 6-11 shows the SETKEY form after finding the nearest record for customer number 2456.

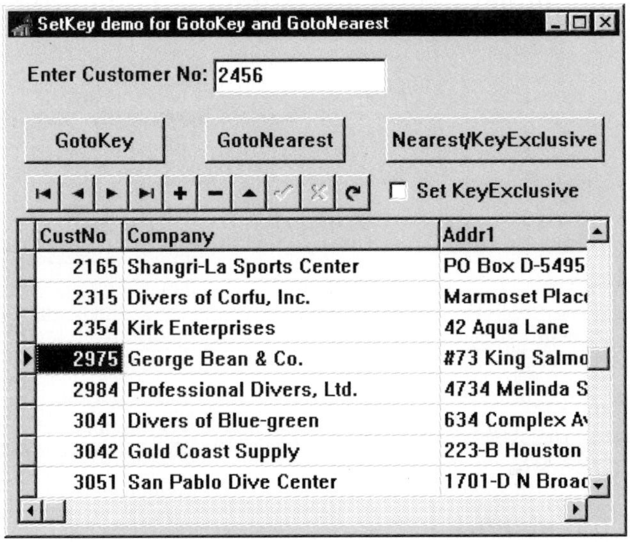

Figure 6-11. *Form for the SETKEY project after finding the nearest customer number*

Using the KeyExclusive Property

Table components have a KeyExclusive property that can be used in conjunction with the GotoNearest method. This property indicates whether a search will position the cursor on the record that is found or on the next record after the record matching the search value. The default value of KeyExclusive is False, which means the cursor stays on the record found. If KeyExclusive is True, the cursor is positioned on the record following the match.

In the SETKEY project, the Set KeyExclusive check box and Nearest/KeyExclusive button are used to show how KeyExclusive works. The code attached to the button is identical to the GotoNearest button with the addition of a single line of code. The following code is the complete event handler:

```
procedure TForm1.pbKeyExclusiveClick(Sender: TObject);
begin
  if Edit1.Text <> '' then begin
    Table1.SetKey;
    Table1.KeyExclusive := CheckBox1.Checked;
    Table1.FieldByName('CustNo').AsString := Edit1.Text;
    Table1.GotoNearest;
  end;
  DBGrid1.SetFocus;
end;
```

If a check is shown in the check box, KeyExclusive is set to True; otherwise, KeyExclusive is False. Figure 6-12 shows the form in the SETKEY project after

Figure 6-12. *Cursor position after using GotoNearest and KeyExclusive set to True*

performing the search for the nearest value with KeyExclusive set to True. This form shows that customer number 2163 does exist in the table, but customer number 2165 is the current record because KeyExclusive is True.

Using Multiple Fields in an Index

Searching on multi-field indexes is only slightly more involved than searching on single-field indexes. Using GotoKey and GotoNearest, you may assign values in the search buffer corresponding to one or more fields of the index. However, if you assign values to fewer than all of the index fields in the search key buffer, you must follow one rule: A field that appears in a later position in the index cannot be assigned a value unless all earlier position index fields are also assigned values. For example, if you are working with a four-field index, you can assign a value to the third field of the index only if the first two fields also have been assigned values. Likewise, if you assign a value to only one field of the index, it must be the first field of the index. The assignment can be made in any order, but the necessary assignments must be made prior to calling GotoKey or GotoNearest.

EditKey Versus SetKey

The EditKey method is closely related to the SetKey method. When you call SetKey, the search key buffer is cleared of the previous search contents. Calling EditKey, by comparison, leaves the search key buffer intact. This permits you to change some, but not all, search values. In other words, if you need to perform a second search, and some of the index field values for this second search are identical to those used in the first search, you can call EditKey to enter the dsSetKey state, and then assign search values only to those search key buffer fields that have changed. If you were to call SetKey prior to a second search, all search key buffer fields would need to be assigned a value.

As you can imagine, the difference between SetKey and EditKey is only important when working with multi-field indexes. One additional comment is in order concerning multi-field indexes. You do not have to assign a value for each field in the index key. By default, if you do not place any value in the search buffer for a field, a NULL value is used. If you need to search on a subset of the fields in the index and do not want to search for a NULL value in the remaining fields, use the Table's KeyFieldCount property to limit the number of key fields used in the search.

Finding a Specific Row in a Table Using FindKey

The method FindKey, and its corresponding method FindNearest, provide essentially the same capabilities as GotoKey and GotoNearest, respectively. There are two major differences, however. First, it is not necessary to place a table into the dsSetKey state before calling FindKey or FindNearest. Second, you do not explicitly assign values to the search key buffer (this is done for you by FindKey and FindNearest).

Both the FindKey and FindNearest methods require a single argument, which consists of a comma-delimited array of values to search for. The first element of this array is associated with the search value for the first field of the index, the second array element with the second field, and so on.

The FINDKEY Project

The FINDKEY.DPR project, shown in Figure 6-13, demonstrates both the FindKey and FindNearest Table methods. The form is nearly identical to the SETKEY project.

The FINDKEY project differs from the SETKEY project in that each have different captions on the push buttons and FINDKEY uses the FindKey and FindNearest methods instead of GotoKey and GotoNearest. The following is the OnClick event handler for the FindKey button:

```
procedure TForm1.pbFindKeyClick(Sender: TObject);
begin
  if Edit1.Text <> '' then begin
    if not Table1.FindKey([Edit1.Text]) then
      ShowMessage('Value not found');
  end;
  DBGrid1.SetFocus;
end;
```

The Text property of the Edit component is used as the parameter for the FindKey method. If the customer number exists, FindKey returns True and the cursor position in the grid changes. If the customer number is not found, the message "Value not found" is displayed.

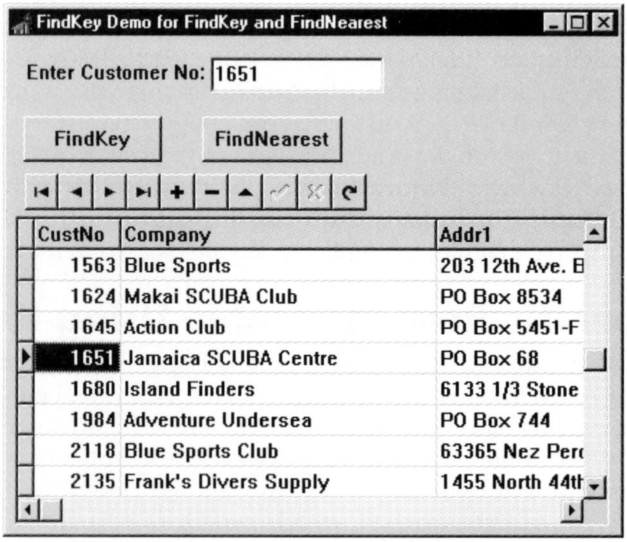

Figure 6-13. *Form for the FINDKEY project main form*

The OnClick event handler for the FindNearest button is nearly identical. It is shown here:

```
procedure TForm1.pbFindNearestClick(Sender: TObject);
begin
  if Edit1.Text <> '' then begin
    Table1.FindNearest([Edit1.Text]);
  end;
  DBGrid1.SetFocus;
end;
```

The FindNearest button also uses the value of the Text property for the Edit component. Like GotoNearest, FindNearest does not return a value, and will move to the nearest value equal to, or greater than, the search value.

Using Ranges

The Table component contains methods to restrict the available rows based on the current table index. Using these methods, you can limit the display of records in a table to only those you want the user to work with.

NOTE: *In addition to the range-related table methods, Delphi provides several alternative ways to view a subset of a table's records. One technique is to use a SELECT query. Queries are discussed later in this chapter. Another alternative is to use a filter. Filters apply only to Delphi 2 and are covered in Chapter 7.*

There are two options for defining a range: ApplyRange and SetRange. ApplyRange uses the SetKey buffer to define the starting and ending values for the range. This is similar to the GotoKey method in which SetKey or EditKey is used to change the state of the table. By comparison, SetRange defines the starting and ending search values using the parameters for this method. SetRange is comparable to FindKey. The SETRNG.DPR project shows how to use both methods to set ranges. Figure 6-14 shows the form for the project.

Using the ApplyRange Method

The ApplyRange method requires that the starting and ending values for the range be defined before the range is applied. The starting values are defined by calling SetRangeStart, and the ending values are defined by calling SetRangeEnd. This is demonstrated in the following code, which defines the OnClick event handler for the Apply Range button:

```
procedure TForm1.pbApplyRangeClick(Sender: TObject);
begin
  if (Edit1.Text <> '') and (Edit2.Text <> '') then
  begin
```

```
      Table1.SetRangeStart;
      Table1.FieldByName('CustNo').AsString := Edit1.Text;
      Table1.SetRangeEnd;
      Table1.FieldByName('CustNo').AsString := Edit2.Text;
      Table1.ApplyRange;
    end;
  end;
```

SetRangeStart is called to indicate the field assignments that follow are setting the starting range values for the fields in the current index. Once these values are set, SetRangeEnd begins the definition process of the fields specifying the ending range values. Finally, ApplyRange is executed to restrict the rows based on the defined range. Figure 6-15 shows the change to the grid after applying the customer number range of 1200 to 1400.

Using the SetRange Method

The SetRange method combines the steps required for SetRangeStart, SetRangeEnd, and ApplyRange into a single method. SetRange has two parameters: an array for the starting values and an array for the ending values. The following is the OnClick event

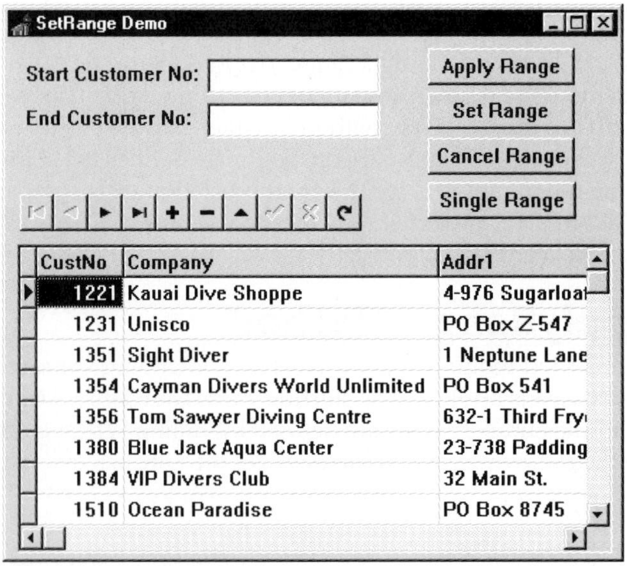

Figure 6-14. *Main form for the SETRNG project*

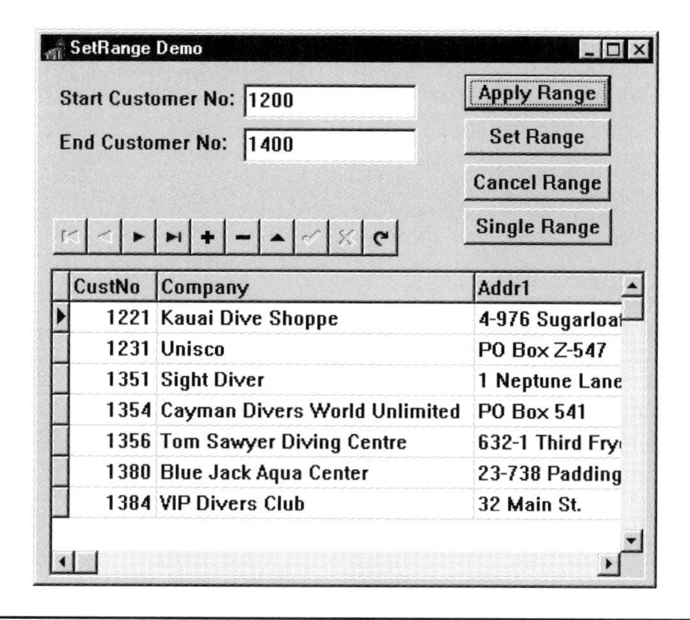

Figure 6-15. *Restricted data set using ApplyRange for customer numbers 1200 to 1400 in SETRNG*

handler for the Set Range button. This code performs the same action as the Apply Range button.

```
procedure TForm1.pbSetRangeClick(Sender: TObject);
begin
  if (Edit1.Text <> '') and (Edit2.Text <> '') then
    Table1.SetRange([Edit1.Text],[Edit2.Text]);
end;
```

The Text properties of Edit1 and Edit2 are used as the two parameters for SetRange. Edit1.Text contains the starting index value, and Edit2.Text contains the ending value.

It is perfectly acceptable to use the same value for both the start and the end of the range. You can do this to limit the display to a single record (for example, the record for a particular customer), or to a subset of records that contain the same value in an indexed field (such as all records for customers who live in California, if a state-based index is current). The OnClick event handler for the Single Range button demonstrates how to display a single customer record in the DBGrid:

```
procedure TForm1.pbSingleRangeClick(Sender: TObject);
begin
  if (Edit1.Text <> '') then
    Table1.SetRange([Edit1.Text],[Edit1.Text]);
end;
```

The value in Edit1.Text is used for both the start and the end values. In this example, only a single customer is displayed if the customer exists. Figure 6-16 shows the form after using the same value for the start and the end range. Supplying the same value for the start and the end range is similar in some respects to using FindKey or GotoKey to locate a record. It is different, however, in that both the FindKey and GotoKey methods do not limit the display to only the located record. Setting a range not only finds the record or records that match, but it also limits access only to those records. This technique is useful when only a subset of data is required to view, to fill-in drop-down lists, and as a good substitute for querying tables.

Canceling Ranges

You use CancelRange to return a table to displaying all records. The use of CancelRange is demonstrated in the OnClick event handler for the Cancel Range button, as shown in the following code segment:

```
procedure TForm1.pbCancelRangeClick(Sender: TObject);
begin
  Table1.CancelRange;
end;
```

The CancelRange method removes a range that is set using either ApplyRange or SetRange. The cursor position in the data sets remains the same after the range is canceled.

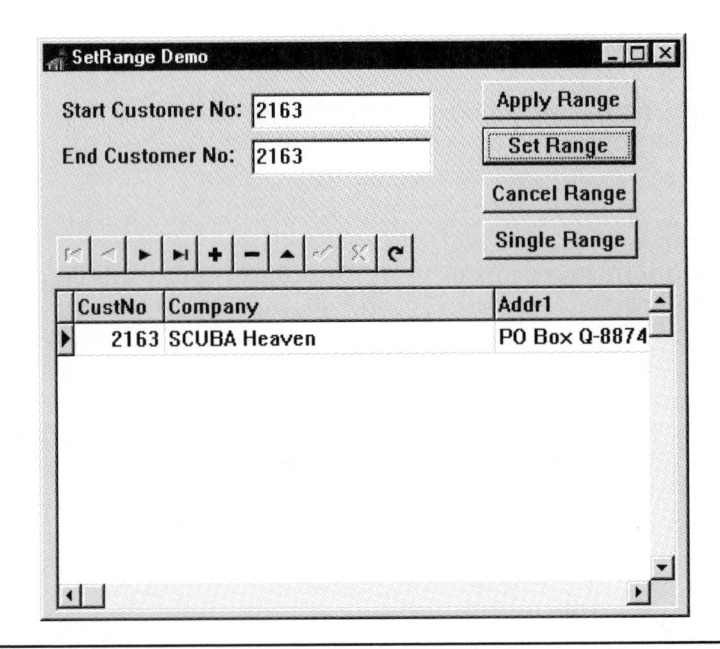

Figure 6-16. *Setting a range with the same start and end value in SETRNG*

TIP: If you set a range where the result set is empty, CancelRange does not remove the current range setting. You need to set another range that includes at least one record and then cancel the range to get all records available in the dataset.

The CD-ROM associated with this book contains several additional demonstrations of the use of ranges. The projects TINDXV1.DPR (Delphi 1.0 and 2) and TINDXV2.DPR (Delphi 2 only) demonstrate how to use a TabSet (or TabControl) to set ranges. The project RNGQRY.DPR demonstrates how to use a range in a task that would otherwise require a query.

Using Queries

The Query component permits you to define SQL statements to perform operations on tables. There are two basic categories of SQL statements: DML (Data Manipulation Language) statements and DDL (Data Definition Language) statements. Most of the examples in this section demonstrate DML statements; however, at the end of this section is an example of the CREATE TABLE DDL statement.

The basic properties of a Query component differ somewhat from a Table component. Both require that the DatabaseName property be set, but the TableName property does not exist for a Query component. Instead, the table is identified in the SQL property using a SQL statement.

Using Queries to Select Records

You select a subset of records using the SELECT SQL statement. This statement has two required parts: SELECT and FROM. In the SELECT statement you specify which fields you want to include in the answer set that is returned. You use the FROM statement to specify the tables from which the fields are to be selected. Selecting subsets of records requires one additional clause, WHERE, which you use to identify the records to select.

Let's start by considering the SELECT and FROM statements. SELECT is followed by a comma-separated list of field names that you want to include in the answer set. The FROM statement includes a comma-separated list of the tables in which these fields are found. For example, the following SQL statement will select the CustNo and Company fields from the CUSTOMER.DB table:

```
SELECT 'CUSTOMER.DB'.'CustNo','CUSTOMER.DB'.'Company'
  FROM 'CUSTOMER.DB'
```

This example assumes that the DatabaseName property has been set to DBDEMOS, an alias that points to where the CUSTOMER.DB table is stored. Alternatively, you can include the alias in the table name. For example, the following SQL statement does not require the DatabaseName property to be assigned a value:

```
SELECT ':DBDEMOS:CUSTOMER.DB'.'CustNo',
       ':DBDEMOS:CUSTOMER.DB'.'Company'
  FROM ':DBDEMOS:CUSTOMER.DB'
```

The quotation marks can be omitted, and the table name qualifiers can be dropped from the field names if the following four conditions exist:

1. Aliases are not used in the SQL statements.
2. The table extension is not specified.
3. The query includes only one table.
4. The field names do not include spaces.

For example, if the DatabaseName property has been set to DBDEMOS, the following SQL statement has the same effect as the preceding one:

```
SELECT CustNo,Company FROM CUSTOMER
```

If you want to select all fields from the specified table, you can replace the individual field names with an asterisk (*). For example, the following statement selects all fields from the CUSTOMER.DB table (again, assuming the DatabaseName property has been set to DBDEMOS):

```
SELECT * FROM CUSTOMER
```

While the SELECT clause specifies which fields will be included in the answer set, the WHERE clause specifies which records will be included. For example, the following statement will select all fields from each record in which the CustNo field is equal to 1221:

```
SELECT * FROM ':DBDEMOS:CUSTOMER.DB'
  WHERE ':DBDEMOS:CUSTOMER.DB'.'CustNo' = 1221
```

Of course, the quotation marks, aliases, and filename extensions can be omitted from these queries under the conditions described previously. (However, non-numeric comparison values must be enclosed in quotation marks.) Also, any comparison operators, including >, <, >=, and so forth, can be used in the conditions. Furthermore, the WHERE clause can include multiple conditions, using the AND and OR operators. For example, assuming that the DatabaseName property has been set to DBDEMOS, the following query will select all fields from the Orders table where CustNo is 1221 and the SaleDate is greater than 1/1/94:

```
SELECT * FROM ORDERS
  WHERE CustNo = 1221 AND SaleDate > '1/1/94'
```

Flexible Queries

You can think of queries as being divided into two categories: static queries and flexible queries. Static queries are those that are defined at design time and that always produce the same result. Flexible queries, by comparison, do not always produce the same effect. For example, during one execution of a flexible query the records for one customer may be selected, but during another execution the records for a different customer are selected. Of course, your program determines which records are being selected. Consequently, flexible queries are a powerful tool for working with data.

The following sections demonstrate three ways to create flexible queries using the basic rules for constructing SELECT queries:

- Linked queries
- Parameterized queries
- Changing the SQL property at runtime

Linked Queries

The easiest, though least flexible, way to create queries is to use a linked query. A linked query is one in which the result set of a query is defined by values in another DataSource, such as a table. The WHERE condition(s) uses one or more fields in the DataSource's dataset to select which records to display. To do this, you set the Query component's DataSource property to the name of the DataSource that contains the field(s) used in the query's WHERE clause. Then, within the WHERE clause, you include the field name(s) from the DataSource's dataset in comparisons. The only trick to this is that the field names must be preceded by colons (:), so that the query can distinguish them from static conditions.

This technique is demonstrated in the LINKQRY.DPR project. This project displays data from the Customer table in a series of DBEdits, and data from the Orders table in a DBGrid. The DBEdits are linked to Table1 through DataSource1, and the DBGrid is linked to Query1 through DataSource2. The SQL statement for the query is as follows:

```
SELECT * FROM ORDERS WHERE CustNo = :CustNo
```

The key to this SQL statement is that the WHERE clause includes a colon followed by the name of a field from the Table. What makes this work is that the DataSource property of Query1 contains the name of DataSource1, which is linked to Table1. Since Table1 contains a field named CustNo, each time Table1 is modified (the user moves to a new record), the query executes, updating the display in the DBGrid.

The LINKQRY project is shown in Figure 6-17. Notice that the Edit controls display data for customer number 1510. The linked query results, displayed in the DBGrid, contain only records for this same customer.

Parameterized Queries

Parameterized queries are similar to linked queries. The SQL property is typically defined at runtime, and the WHERE clause includes values that change. In linked queries, these values are based on values in a dataset pointed to by the query's DataSource property. In parameterized queries, you control these values through code.

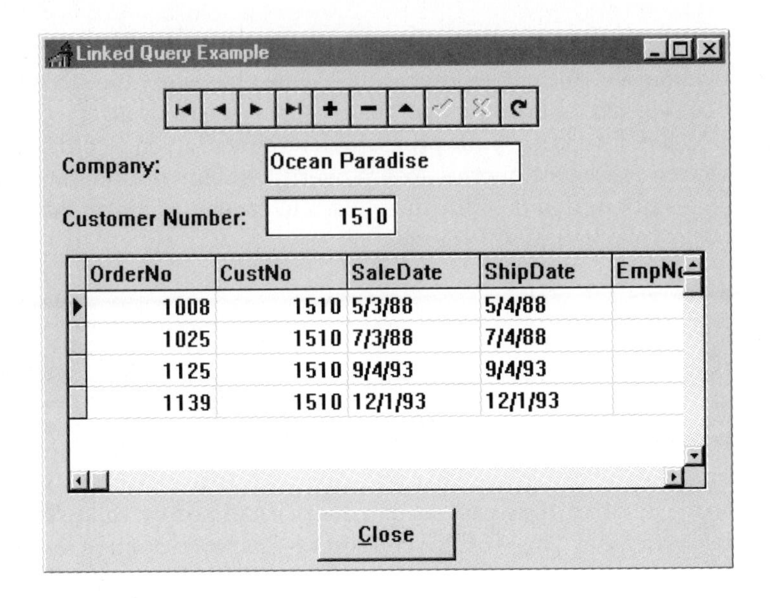

Figure 6-17. *Main form for the LINKQRY project*

The following is an example of a parameterized SQL statement. Notice that in the WHERE clause the word CustNumber is preceded by colons. In a parameterized query, these colons define a parameter.

```
SELECT * FROM ORDERS

 WHERE CustNo = :CustNumber
```

A parameterized query can have any number of parameters. The only restriction is that you must define the value for a parameter before making the query active. This can be done at design time using the property editor for the Params property of the Query component. However, the only reason for defining a parameter at design time is to make the query active at design time. In most cases, the parameters are defined and the query is activated (by setting the Active property to True or by calling the Open method) at runtime.

Defining a parameter at runtime requires the use of either the Params property or the ParamByName method. The Params property is a zero-based array. The elements of this array correspond to the Query parameters based on order of inclusion in the SQL statement. In the case of the preceding parameterized SQL statement, CustNumber is the only parameter, so it will correspond with the first element, element 0, of the Params array. The following is a sample statement that assigns the value 1221 to the CustNumber parameter using the Params property:

```
Query1.Params[0].AsInteger := 1221;
```

If the query includes more than one parameter, the first one to appear in the SQL statement is associated with element 0 of the Params property, the second is associated with element 1, and so on.

The ParamByName method permits you to set the value of a parameter based on the name of the parameter. For example, the following statement uses the ParamByName method, and it is equivalent to the preceding one that uses the Params property:

```
Query1.ParamByName('CustNumber').AsInteger := 1221;
```

The PARAM.DPR project demonstrates the use of a parameterized query, as shown in Figure 6-18. This project has two forms. Form1 displays the contents of the Customer table in a DBGrid. Form2 displays records from a query on the Orders table in a DBGrid. The following is the code associated with a button on Form1. This code assigns a value to a parameter of Query1 on Form2 based on the current record on Form1.

```
procedure TForm1.Button2Click(Sender: TObject);
begin
Form2.Query1.Close;
Form2.Query1.ParamByName('CustNumber').AsInteger :=
        Table1.FieldByName('CustNo').AsInteger;
Form2.Query1.Open;
Form2.Caption := 'Orders for '+
        Table1.FieldByName('Company').AsString;
Form2.ShowModal;
end;
```

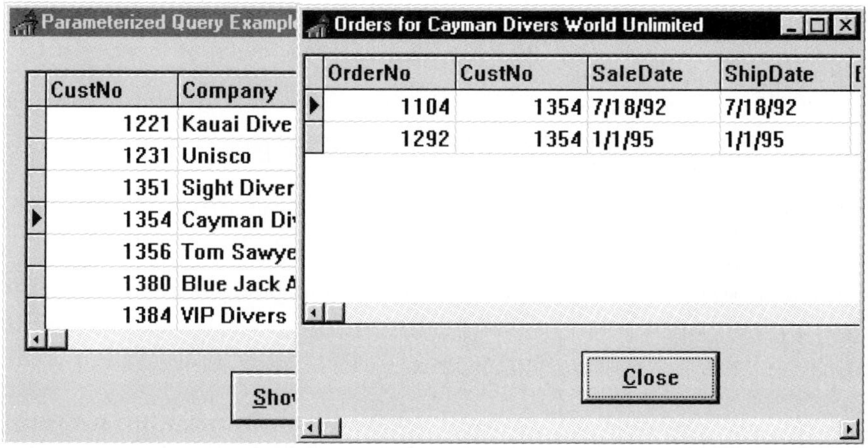

Figure 6-18. *The PARAM project showing the results of a parameterized query on a second form*

Changing the SQL Property at Runtime

Parameterized queries are great when you know beforehand which fields you want to use to select a subset of records. However, if you want to create a query in which you sometimes select all records (no WHERE clause) and sometimes select a subset based on one or more parameters, a parameterized query is not an option. Likewise, if the table being queried is not known until runtime, a parameterized query cannot be used, since a parameter cannot appear in the FROM clause. Instead, you must modify the contents of the SQL property at runtime. This permits you to create completely flexible queries.

Since the SQL property is a StringList property, it can be modified using the methods of the TStringList class. Among the most useful of these methods are Add and Clear. Add inserts a new line into a StringList in the last position, whereas Clear empties a StringList. The following code segment demonstrates how these two statements can be used to define a new SQL statement at runtime:

```
Query1.Close;      {Close the query, if it is open}
Query1.SQL.Clear; {Remove old SQL statements}
Query1.SQL.Add('SELECT * FROM ORDERS');
Query1.SQL.Add('  WHERE CustNo = 1211');
Query1.SQL.Open;   {Open the new query}
```

This technique is demonstrated in the project SQL.DPR, whose main form, Form1, is shown in Figure 6-19. This form contains three Label components, three Edit components, and three buttons.

When either the Show SQL button or the Show Records button is clicked, a StringList is constructed based on the values entered into the three Edit components (this is done with a custom procedure named BuildQueryString). If the Edit components are empty, the StringList contains no WHERE clause. Otherwise, the

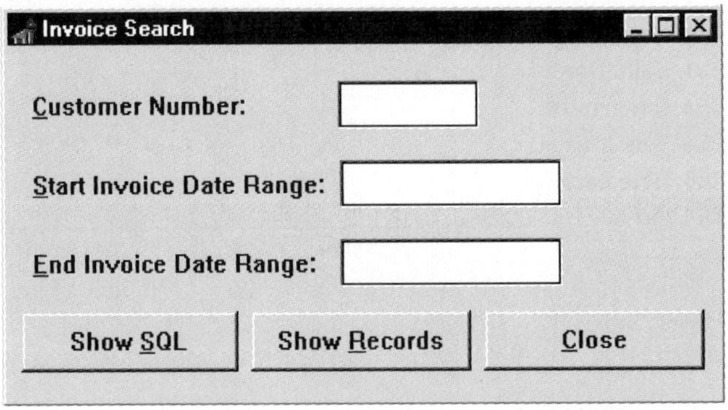

Figure 6-19. *Form1 of the project SQL*

StringList contains selection conditions based on the entered data. The following procedures are used to construct this string list:

```
procedure AddCondition(var TheQuery: TStringList;
                       const field, comparison, value: String);
begin
if TheQuery.Count > 2 then
{When Count > 2, there is already at least one condition}
  TheQuery.Add('and '+field+comparison+value)
else
  TheQuery.Add(field+comparison+value)
end;

function IsDate(Source: TEdit) :Boolean;
{This function returns True if a TEdit contains a date}
begin
try
  StrToDate(TEdit(Source).Text);
  result := True
except
  result := False;
end;
end;

Procedure TForm1.BuildSQLString(var TheQuery: TStringList);
begin
if BeginDate.Text <> '' then
  if not IsDate(BeginDate) then
    begin
     BeginDate.SetFocus;
     raise Exception.Create('Date value expected');
    end;

if EndDate.Text <> '' then
  if not IsDate(EndDate) then
    begin
     EndDate.SetFocus;
     raise Exception.Create('Date value expected');
    end;

TheQuery.Add('SELECT * FROM ORDERS') ;
if not ((CustomerNumber.Text = '') and
       (BeginDate.Text = '') and
       (EndDate.Text = '')) then
  begin
    TheQuery.Add('WHERE');
    if CustomerNumber.Text <> '' then
      AddCondition(TheQuery,'CustNo','=',CustomerNumber.Text);
    if BeginDate.Text <> '' then
```

```
        AddCondition(TheQuery,'SaleDate','>=',#39+BeginDate.Text+#39);
      if EndDate.Text <> '' then
        AddCondition(TheQuery,'SaleDate','<=',#39+EndDate.Text+#39);
    end;
  end;
```

Using a Query to Modify Data

Three additional SQL DML statements provide you with data-modification capabilities on tables: INSERT, UPDATE, and DELETE. The INSERT statement is used to insert new data into a table. The UPDATE statement is used to change existing data in a table. The DELETE statement is used to remove rows from a table. Let's look at examples for each of these statements.

The INSERT statement supports adding a single row or multiple rows into a table. The following code adds a new row to the CUSTOMER.DB table:

```
INSERT

INTO "Customer.db" ("Customer.db"."Customer No", Name,
  Street, City, "Customer.db"."State/Prov",
  "Customer.db"."Zip/Postal Code", Country, Phone,
  "Customer.db"."First Contact", TaxRate)
VALUES (1000, 'Any Diver, Inc.', '123 Main St.',
  'Anytown', 'CA', '90872', 'U.S.A.', '213-555-0422',
  '07/02/1992', 0)
```

The INTO clause identifies the table name and fields. Any field with spaces in its names is preceded by the table name and enclosed in double quotation marks. This is not required for the fields without spaces in their names.

Multiple rows can be inserted into a table when the data being inserted exists in another table. A SELECT statement is used to retrieve the data from the other table. The resulting dataset defines the fields and values that are inserted into the table. In the following example, customers from the CUSTOMER.DB table that are from the U.S.A. are inserted into the CUST_US.DB table.

```
INSERT INTO CUST_US
  SELECT * FROM CUSTOMER
    WHERE Country = 'U.S.A.'
```

In this example, the .DB and quotation marks are removed from the table names. If both tables are in the same directory specified by the DatabaseName property (either by an alias or explicit directory path), the file extension and quotation marks are not necessary.

The UPDATE SQL statement is used to modify fields in existing rows of a table. The following is an example:

```
UPDATE Parts
SET Cost = (Cost * 1.02),
    ListPrice = (ListPrice * 1.1)
WHERE(VendorNo = 3511)
```

The Parts table is used from the DBDEMOS directory. The DatabaseName property specifies the directory; it is not included in the SQL statement. Two fields are changed in this statement: ListPrice and Cost. The Cost field in increased by two percent, and a ten percent increase is applied to ListPrice. The WHERE clause specifies that only the parts with a VendorNo of 3511 are changed.

The DELETE statement can remove a single record, multiple records, or all records from a table. The number of records removed from the table depends on the presence and contents of the optional WHERE clause. The following example removes all rows from the Parts table for VendorNo 4652.

```
DELETE
FROM Parts
WHERE
(VendorNo = 4652)
```

The number of rows removed from the table depends on how many rows match the condition in the WHERE clause. Furthermore, a DELETE statement without a WHERE clause removes all the rows from a table.

To execute the INSERT, UPDATE, and DELETE query types of SQL statements when defined in a Query component, you do not use the Open method as was done with SELECT statements. Instead, you use the ExecSQL method. The Open method is used for any SQL statement for which a result set is returned from the query. ExecSQL is used when there is no result set, as in the case of INSERT, UPDATE, and DELETE queries.

The project EXECSQL.DPR, shown in Figure 6-20, includes the preceding SQL examples. Each of the examples uses a separate Query component, and the SQL properties of these Query components were defined at design time, meaning that they define static queries. The names of each component is displayed on the form in Figure 6-20. A separate push button corresponds to each of the examples.

The following is the code for the OnClick event handler for the Update button. The code for the other buttons is similar:

```
procedure TForm1.pbUpdateClick(Sender: TObject);
begin
  qryUpdate.ExecSQL;
end;
```

The name of the Query component is qryUpdate. Using the ExecSQL method the query executes and updates the rows specified in the WHERE clause.

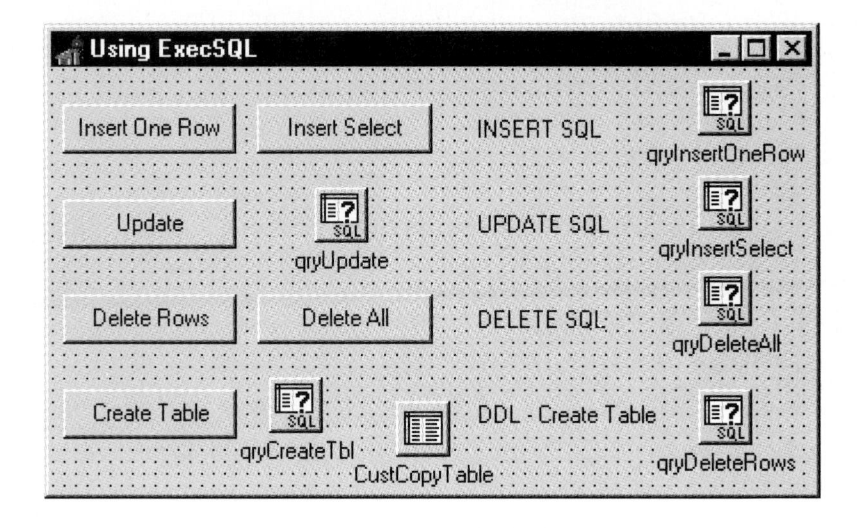

Figure 6-20. *Main form for EXECSQL in design mode*

In addition to the three SQL statement described here, ExecSQL is used for all SQL DDL statements. DDL statements are used to define tables, indexes, and views; add or remove fields from a table; create or delete indexes; and delete tables.

TIP: The component names were shown in Figure 6-20 by enabling the Show component caption check box on the Preferences page of the Environment Options dialog box. This feature is not available in Delphi 1.0.

Creating a Table Using a Query

The ExecSQL project also includes an example of a DDL statement. This statement is CREATE TABLE, and it provides you with an alternative to the Table method CreateTable. The following is an example of a CREATE TABLE SQL statement that will create a table with the same structure as the Customer table in the DBDEMOS alias:

```
CREATE TABLE CustCopy      (
  CustNo NUMERIC,
  Company CHAR(30),
  Addr1 CHAR(30),
  Addr2 CHAR(30),
  City CHAR(15),
  State CHAR(20),
  Zip CHAR(10),
  Country CHAR(20),
  Phone CHAR(15),
```

```
FAX CHAR(15),
TaxRate NUMERIC,
Contact CHAR(20),
LastInvoiceDate TIMESTAMP,
PRIMARY KEY(CustNo) )
```

This CREATE TABLE statement is assigned to the SQL property of the qryCreateTbl Query component. The Create Table button contains the following code in its OnClick event handler:

```
procedure TForm1.pbCreateTblClick(Sender: TObject);
var
  CurDir: String;
begin
  { Get the path where EXE resides to use as DatabaseName }
  CurDir := ExtractFilePath(Application.ExeName);
  { If the CUSTCOPY table exists, delete it }
  if FileExists(CurDir + 'CUSTCOPY.DB') then
    with CustCopyTable do
    begin
      DatabaseName := CurDir;
      TableName := 'CUSTCOPY';
      TableType := ttParadox;
      DeleteTable;
    end;
  { Create the table CUSTCOPY in the directory where the EXE resides }
  with qryCreateTbl do
  begin
    DatabaseName := CurDir;
    ExecSQL;
  end;
end;
```

This code first checks to see if the CustCopy table exists in the same directory in which the project resides. If so, the Table component CustCopyTable is used to delete the table. The DatabaseName property of the qryCreateTbl Query component is assigned the directory of the EXE before ExecSQL is used to create the CustCopy table.

Using the CREATE TABLE SQL statement to create Paradox and dBASE tables requires you to use the SQL data type syntax. Table 6-3 lists the data types used in both Paradox and dBASE tables and how they map to the corresponding SQL data types.

For information on other DDL statements, such as CREATE INDEX, DROP INDEX, or ALTER TABLE, use Delphi's online help.

Creating Master/Detail Forms

Delphi provides two options for creating master/detail forms. A master/detail form is one where the current record in one dataset (referred to as the *master* or *parent*)

SQL Data Type	Paradox Data Type	dBASE Data Type
SMALLINT	Short	Number (6,10)
INTEGER	Long integer	Number (20,4)
DECIMAL(x,y)	BCD	N/A
NUMERIC(x,y)	Number	Number (x,y)
FLOAT(x,y)	Number	Float (x,y)
CHARACTER(n)	Alpha	Character
VARCHAR(n)	Alpha	Character
DATE	Date	Date
BOOLEAN	Logical	Logical
BLOB(n,1)	Memo	Memo
BLOB(n,2)	Binary	Binary
BLOB(n,3)	Formatted memo	N/A
BLOB(n,4)	OLE	OLE
BLOB(n,5)	Graphic	N/A
TIME	Time	N/A
TIMESTAMP	Timestamp	N/A
MONEY	Money	Number (20,4)
AUTOINC	Autoincrement	N/A
BYTES(n)	Bytes	N/A

x = precision (default: specific to driver)
y = scale (default: 0)
n = length in bytes (default: 0)
1-5 = BLOB subtype (default: 1)

Table 6-3. *Data Types Used in Paradox and dBASE Tables and How They Map to the SQL Data Types*

determines which record, or set of records, is displayed in the other dataset (often called a *detail* or *child*). The first option is to use Table components for both the master and detail tables. The second option is to use a Table component as the master, and a Query component as the detail. The technique you use depends on the type of dataset you are using.

The following section demonstrates how to create a master/detail form using two Table components. The use of a Query component for the detail records has already been demonstrated earlier in this chapter, in the section "Linked Queries."

Using Table Components for Both Master and Detail Tables

The project TBL2.DPR shows how to use two Table components to define a master/detail form. Figure 6-21 shows the form in design mode, and Figure 6-22 shows what this form looks like when it is running. In this example, the CUSTOMER.DB and ORDERS.DB tables are used from the DBDEMOS alias. The top DBGrid displays the records from the Customer table, and the bottom DBGrid displays only those Orders records that correspond to the currently selected customer.

The link between the Customer and Orders tables is set using the MasterSource and MasterFields properties of the Table component for the Orders table. The MasterSource property defines the DataSource component to use for the linking values. In this example, the DataSource component for the Customer table is named dsCustomer. Therefore, the MasterSource property of tblOrders (the Orders table component) is set to dsCustomer.

Once the MasterSource is set, the fields that establish a relationship between the two tables are defined using the MasterFields property. Double-clicking in the edit box for this property or clicking the button displays the Field Link Designer dialog box

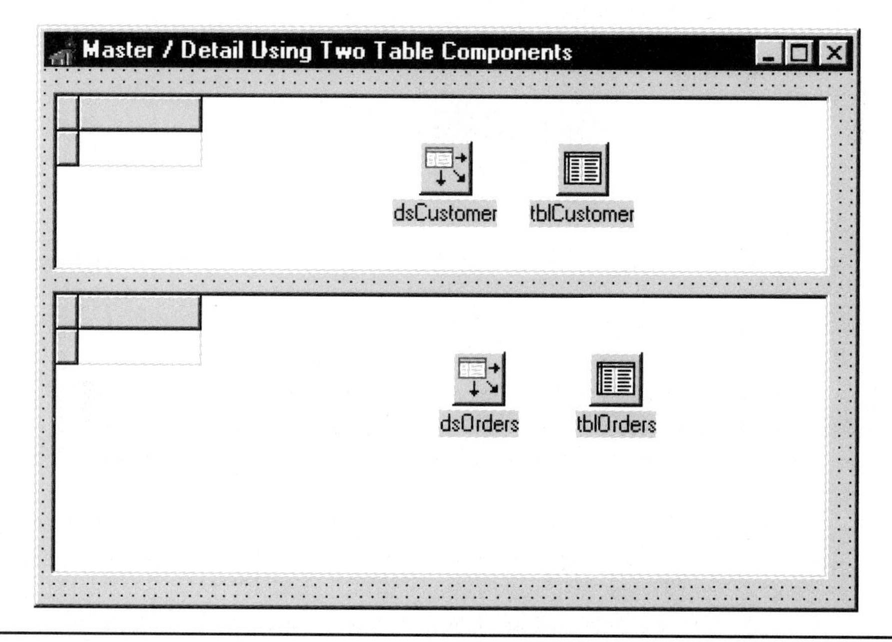

Figure 6-21. *Main form for the TBL2 project in design mode*

Master / Detail Using Two Table Components

CustNo	Company	Addr1
1221	Kauai Dive Shoppe	4-976 Sugarloaf Hwy
1231	Unisco	PO Box Z-547
1351	Sight Diver	1 Neptune Lane

OrderNo	CustNo	SaleDate	ShipDate	EmpNo	ShipToCor
1003	1351	4/12/88	5/3/88 12:0(	114	
1052	1351	1/6/89	1/7/89	144	
1055	1351	2/4/89	2/5/89	29	
1067	1351	4/1/89	4/2/89	34	
1075	1351	4/21/89	4/22/89	11	
1087	1351	5/20/89	5/21/89	127	

Figure 6-22. *Main form for the TBL2 project during runtime*

shown in Figure 6-23. This dialog box is where the index and field name(s) are set for linking the two tables.

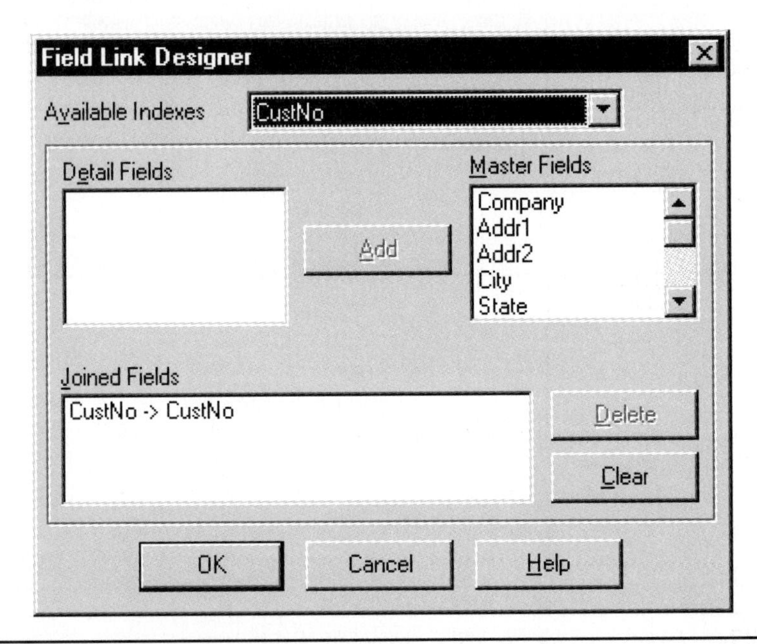

Figure 6-23. *Field Link Designer dialog box*

The first step in using the Field Link Designer dialog box is to choose the index on which the link will be based using the Available Indexes combo box. By default this combo box displays the Table component's currently selected index, as defined by the Table's IndexName property. If a secondary index is not defined, the initial value of Available Indexes is Primary, indicating that the primary key index is used.

If the link cannot be performed on the current index, select one of the alternative indexes. In this case, since the Customer and Orders tables must be linked based on customer number, it is necessary to instruct the tblOrders component to use the index named CustNo, which is a secondary index for the CustNo field.

After selecting the index, you use the Detail Fields list and the Master Fields list to define the field pairs on which to base the link. If the link is based only on a single field pair, as it is in this case, select the corresponding field from each list and then click Add. If the link is based on more than one field pair, select each pair in turn and click Add. After you have selected the field pair(s) for the link, click the OK button to complete the linking of the tables.

Linking More Than Two Tables

Delphi does not limit the number of linked tables. You can link more than one table to a single Table or Query component, or have multiple levels in a multi-table form. Project TBL3.DRP, shown in Figure 6-24, includes three linked tables.

This project includes two additional features that can be useful in many database applications. First, it contains a single DBNavigator that can be used for all three

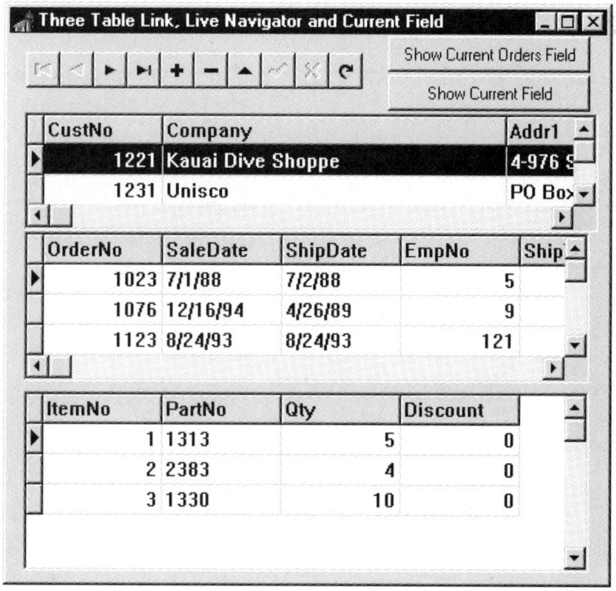

Figure 6-24. *Project TBL3 using three linked tables*

tables. The DataSet that a DBNavigator navigates is defined by its DataSource property. In the project TBL3.DPR, each DBGrid assigns its own DataSource to the DataSource property of the DBNavigator when the user enters that DBGrid. This technique is demonstrated in the following code, which is associated with the OnEnter event handler for the DBGrid associated with the Customer table:

```
procedure TForm1.gridCustomerEnter(Sender: TObject);
begin
  DBNavigator.DataSource := gridCustomer.DataSource;
end;
```

The second technique demonstrated by this project is how to identify the current field of a specific DBGrid. A similar technique was shown earlier in this chapter in the section "Setting the Color in a Field for Specific Values." That technique, however, made use of a TField parameter of the OnDrawDataCell event handler and is, therefore, quite limited. A more general approach is to use the SelectedField property of a DBGrid. This property is of the type TField, and it corresponds to the field that is active for a given DBGrid. To get the name of this field, you can use the FieldName property of this Field object. The Show Current Orders Field button in the TBL3 project contains the following code to show the current field in the Orders grid using the ShowMessage procedure:

```
procedure TForm1.sbCurOrdersFieldClick(Sender: TObject);
begin
  ShowMessage(gridOrders.SelectedField.FieldName);
end;
```

Prefacing the SelectedField property with the grid name does not work as a generic solution. In other words, it only works if you already know which DBGrid the cursor is in. If more than one component can have focus on the form, you can use the ActiveControl property of the form in order to identify the current field. For example, the following code will display the current DBGrid, as well as the current field of that DBGrid, but only if the active control is of the TDBGrid class. This code is associated with the OnClick event handler for the Show Current Field button:

```
procedure TForm1.sbCurFieldClick(Sender: TObject);
begin
if ActiveControl is TDBGrid then
  ShowMessage(TDBGrid(ActiveControl).Name +
    ' : ' + TDBGrid(ActiveControl).SelectedField.FieldName)
else
  ShowMessage('The active control is not a DBGrid');
end;
```

ActiveControl is a property of both TForm and TScreen components. In the preceding event handler, the form's ActiveControl property is being used because the event handler is a procedure of the form. Consequently, the default object, Self, is the form. Any time you reference a property of an object and do not specify the object, Delphi defaults to Self.

Data Validation and Exception Handling

A database application is only as good as the validity of the data in the database. Integral to every good database application is a means of ensuring the correctness of the data it contains. In Delphi applications, you can put code in several different event handlers to ensure data integrity. Which event handlers you use depends on the type of validation you want to apply.

Before covering where to place the code, it is best to understand some of the types of errors that can occur and the events generated by those errors. Table 6-4 lists some of the basic types of validation, the default error messages displayed in Delphi, the exception type, and the event cycle for each error. The event cycle provides an indication of where code should be placed.

The project VLIDATE.DPR demonstrates how to code data validation at various levels in an application. Figure 6-25 shows the main form for the project. The VENDORS.DB table from the DBDEMOS alias is used. A single menu selection is available to close the form. There is also a prompt to confirm the form's closure and to post any unsaved record.

Data Validation

File

VendorNo	VendorName	Address1	Addr
2014	Cacor Corporation	161 Southfield Rd	
2641	Underwater	50 N 3rd Street	
2674	J.W. Luscher Mfg.	65 Addams Street	
3511	Scuba Professionals	3105 East Brace	
3819	Divers' Supply Shop	5208 University Dr	
3820	Techniques	52 Dolphin Drive	
4521	Perry Scuba	3443 James Ave	
4642	Beauchat, Inc.	45900 SW 2nd Ave	
4651	Amor Aqua	42 West 29th Street	
4652	Aqua Research Corp.	P.O. Box 998	
4655	B&K Undersea Photo	116 W 7th Street	

Figure 6-25. *Main form for the VLIDATE project*

Validation Type	Error Message	Exception	Event to Place Code
Deleting the parent record in a referential integrity relationship	Master has detail records. Cannot delete or modify	EDBEngineError	OnDeleteError (Delphi 2 only)
Leaving a required field blank	Field <field name> must have a value	EDatabaseError	None (but, an OnUpdateChange occurs for the DataSource)
Attempting to edit a record locked by another user	Record locked by another user. Table: <table name> User <user name>	EDBEngineError	BeforeEdit OnEditError (Delphi 2 only)
Entering a duplicate primary key value	Key violation	EDBEngineError	OnUpdateChange BeforePost OnPostError (Delphi 2 only)
Entering a value below minimum or above maximum validity check	Minimum validity check failed. Field: <field name>. Maximum validity check failed. Field: <field name>	EDBEngineError	OnDataChange OnUpdateChange BeforePost OnPostError (Delphi 2 only)
Entering a value not in the lookup table	Field value out of lookup table range	EDBEngineError	OnUpdateChange BeforePost OnPostError (Delphi 2 only)
Entering a value in a child record that does not exist in the parent record where a referential integrity rule exists between the child and parent	Master record missing	EDBEngineError	OnUpdateChange BeforePost OnPostError (Delphi 2 only)

Table 6-4. *Data Validation Tasks and Default Error Messages Displayed in Delphi*

Validation in this form is done at the field level, record level, and form level. Field-level validation is performed when the newly entered contents of a field are being posted. Record-level validation normally occurs when the record as a whole is being posted. Finally, form-level validation refers to validation that is performed prior to closing or accepting a form.

Field-Level Validation

Field-level validation requires that the fields of a Table component be instantiated (created). The Fields Editor is used to create a separate TField object for each field in the table. Once a field is instantiated, you can use two published properties for record-level validation: MinValue and MaxValue. These properties permit you to specify the range of acceptable values for numeric fields. An instantiated field also has a Required property, which you use to ensure that the user enters a value. The Required property only affects a field when the current record is being posted. Consequently, it applies to record-level validation.

With the exception of the MinValue and MaxValue properties, field-level validation is provided by adding code to the OnValidate event handler for an instantiated field. This is demonstrated in the VLIDATE project, which contains code attached to the OnValidate event handler for the Table1VendorNo field. This code tests whether the value entered into this field is less than 1. When the field contains a value less than 1, the code raises an exception. This exception prevents the value from being posted to the field and also prevents the field from being exited. The following is the event handler that produces this effect:

```
procedure TForm1.Table1VendorNoValidate(Sender: TField);
begin
if Table1VendorNo.Value < 1 then
  raise Exception.Create('Positive Vendor number required');
end;
```

NOTE: You could use the MinValue maximum property to force values for the VendorNo field to be 1 or greater, but the MaxValue would also have to be set. By default both of these properties have a value of zero. If you change one of the properties, the value for the other property is enforced. Therefore, you would not want to leave the MaxValue property value of zero. When a value is entered outside the range, a message is displayed indicating the required range for the value.

Record-Level Validation

There are two ways to place record-level validation. If you instantiate a field, you can use the published Required property to require that a particular field contains a non-nil value before the record can be posted. If a user attempts to post a record without supplying values to all required fields in the record, an exception is raised automatically.

In the VLIDATE project, the Table1VendorName component (a TStringField, which is a TField descendant) has its Required property set to True. If an attempt is made to post a record with the VendorName field blank, an exception is raised automatically by Delphi and the record is not posted.

The second way to create record-level validation is to place code in the BeforePost event handler for the Table component with which the record is associated. If the code in this event handler determines that the record is invalid, it can prevent the record from being accepted by raising an exception, as demonstrated in the following code:

```
procedure TForm1.Table1BeforePost(DataSet: TDataset);
begin
  if (Table1Address1.Value = '') and
     (Table1Address2.Value <> '') then
    raise Exception.Create('Address1 is blank');
end;
```

Form-Level Validation

Form-level validation is produced by placing code in a form's OnCloseQuery event handler. If this code determines that at least one value on the form is not valid, it can set the CanClose variable (a formal parameter of the OnCloseQuery event handler) to False. When CanClose is set to False, the form will not close. In the VLIDATE project, the form-level validation first asks the user to confirm that the form should be closed, and if so, asks if the current record should be posted, if changes were made but not yet posted. The following code performs these tasks:

```
procedure TForm1.FormCloseQuery(Sender: TObject; var CanClose: Boolean);
begin
if MessageDlg('Close this form',mtConfirmation,
   [mbYes,mbCancel],0) <> mrYes then
   CanClose := False
else
  if Table1.State in [dsEdit,dsInsert] then
    if MessageDlg('Post changes',mtConfirmation,
      [mbYes,mbNo],0) = mrYes then
      Table1.Post;
end;
```

If you want to perform form-level validation but not necessarily when a form is closing, you can create a function that performs all necessary tests of the form's acceptability and returns from this function a value of True if the form passes validation, and False if it does not. You can then call this function from any event signaling that the user wants to accept this form (a button click, for example). You can even call this function from the OnCloseQuery event handler, assigning the function's return value to the formal variable CanClose.

Application-Level Exception Handling

A final note of interest in this project is the Application object's OnException event property. By assigning an event handler to this property, it is possible to handle all exceptions that are not trapped within a try block. Because you cannot display the Application object in the Object Inspector, you must assign an event handler to this property using code. The following code example demonstrates the assignment of this property in the form's OnCreate event handler, as well as the code that constitutes the OnException event handler. In this event handler, the ShowException method is used to display this exception to the user. In practice, the code in the OnException event handler would most likely do something with the exception, such as write a record of this error to a file (an error log).

```
procedure TForm1.FormCreate(Sender: TObject);
begin
  Application.OnException := AppException;
end;

procedure TForm1.AppException(Sender: TObject; E: Exception);
begin
  Application.ShowException(E);
end;
```

NOTE: Delphi 2 provides additional event handlers in which data validation code can be placed. Chapter 7 covers how to use these events and create data validation routines.

Comparing Table Structures at Runtime

Some applications need to permit the user to maintain multiple tables for their data. The project CARDS.DPR is one such example. Figure 6-26 shows the main form for the project. The application defined in CARDS permits the user to maintain multiple phone lists. The user can switch easily from one phone list to another by selecting File | Open from within the application.

There is a potential problem with providing the capability to open different files. Although it is an easy matter to open a table using a Table component, if the form contains data-aware controls that are associated with the table (through an intervening DataSource component), these components may expect the table to have a particular structure. For example, imagine that you have a DBEdit component on a form, and that this DBEdit has its DataSource property set to DataSource1 and its DataField property set to Company. If you subsequently change the dataset that is associated with DataSource1, and the new dataset does not have a Company field, an exception is raised.

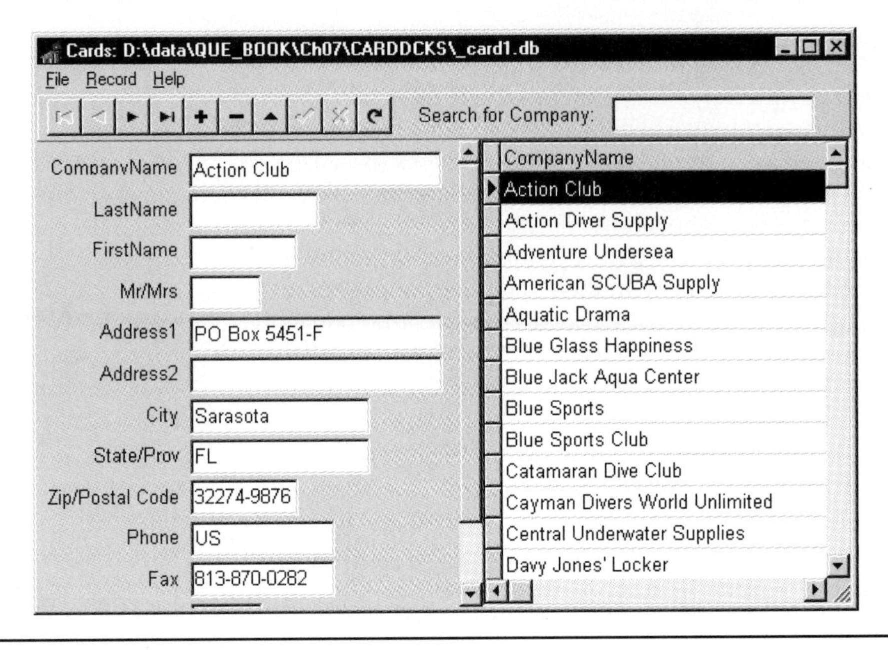

Figure 6-26. *Main form for the CARDS project*

The following ValidateTable procedure demonstrates the type of approach you can take to verifying table structures. This procedure is part of the CARDS project, and it compares a new table, defined by the Table1 component, to a standard table structure:

```
procedure TForm1.ValidateTable(const TabName: String);
var
  TempTable,
  ValTable   : TTable;
  i          : Integer;
begin
ValTable := TTable.Create(Form1);
ValTable.TableName := TabName;
ValTable.Open;
TempTable := TTable.Create(Form1);
CreateCardTable(TempTable,'__temp.db');
try
  {ValTable points to the table needing validation}
  if ValTable.FieldDefs.Count <> TempTable.FieldDefs.Count then
    begin
      raise EBadTable.Create('Invalid number of fields');
    end;
  for i := 0 to TempTable.FieldDefs.Count-1 do
    begin
    if (TempTable.FieldDefs.Items[i].Size <>
```

```
          ValTable.FieldDefs.Items[i].Size) OR
          (TempTable.FieldDefs.Items[i].FieldClass <>
          ValTable.FieldDefs.Items[i].FieldClass) OR
          (TempTable.FieldDefs.Items[i].Name <>
          ValTable.FieldDefs.Items[i].Name) then
          begin
            tempTable.Free;
            raise EBadTable.Create('Invalid table structure');
          end;
      end;
finally
  tempTable.DeleteTable;
  tempTable.Free;
  ValTable.Close;
  ValTable.Free;
end;
end;
```

When the ValidateTable procedure is called, it is passed the name of a table whose structure needs to be validated. This procedure begins by creating a Table object for this table, pointing the object to the physical table that requires validation, and then opening it. ValidateTable then calls the CreateCardsTable procedure, which creates a new table using the required structure. The code for the CreateCardTable procedure is as follows:

```
procedure TForm1.CreateCardTable(Tab: TTable;const tabName: String);
begin
  with Tab do
    begin
    Active := False;
    TableName := tabName;
    with FieldDefs do
      begin
      Clear;
      Add('CompanyName', ftString, 35,True);
      Add('LastName', ftString, 18,False);
      Add('FirstName', ftString, 15,False);
      Add('Mr/Mrs', ftString, 10,False);
      Add('Address1', ftString, 35,False);
      Add('Address2', ftString, 35,False);
      Add('City', ftString, 25,False);
      Add('State/Prov', ftString, 25,False);
      Add('Zip/Postal Code', ftString, 15,False);
      Add('Phone', ftString, 20,False);
      Add('Fax', ftString, 20,False);
      Add('LastContact', ftDate, 0,False);
      Add('Comments', ftMemo, 10,False);
```

```
      end;
    CreateTable;
    AddIndex('CompanyIndex', 'CompanyName', [ixPrimary, ixUnique]);
    end;
end;
```

The CreateCardTable procedure is passed two parameters: a pointer (Tab) to an existing Table component on the form and a string that holds the name of the table to create. In this case, that Tab parameter points to the Table component that was instantiated in the ValidateTable procedure prior to calling CreateCardTable. A with statement is used to create the table with the appropriate structure and primary index. The name of the table is the second parameter passed to CreateCardTable. This parameter is assigned to the TableName property of the Table component. Next, the FieldDefs property is cleared, the field names and data types are defined, and the table is created. The last step is to define the index for CompanyName.

The heart of this technique to compare table structures follows the call to CreateCardTable in ValidateTable. The first step is to compare the Count property of the FieldDefs property of the table that is to be opened (specifically, the one that ValTable points to) to that of the standard structure (tempTable). FieldDefs.Count identifies how many fields are in the table structure. If the two tables do not have the same number of fields, the table structures are different, and an exception is raised.

If the field counts match, the next step is to cycle through the fields of both tables, comparing the Size, FieldClass, and Name properties of each of the fields. If any one of the field pairs does not produce a perfect match, the table structures are different, and an exception is raised. If the ValidateTable procedure is able to complete its execution without raising an exception, the two tables are identical in structure.

The following code is the OnClick event handler for the Open1 MenuItem object, which is the event handler that will be executed when the user selects File | Open from the CARDS project main menu:

```
procedure TForm1.Open1Click(Sender: TObject);
var
  oldTable: String;
begin
  {Permit selection of existing tables only}
  OpenDialog1.Options := [ofFileMustExist];
  if OpenDialog1.Execute then
    begin
      CheckState;
      ValidateTable(OpenDialog1.Filename);
      with Table1 do
        begin
          FieldDefs.Clear;
          if Active then Active:= False;
          Tablename := OpenDialog1.FileName;
```

```
            ActivateTables(OpenDialog1.FileName);
            ShiftMRU(OpenDialog1.Filename);
            Self.Caption := 'Cards: '+ OpenDialog1.Filename;
          end;
        end;
end;
```

This event handler begins by adding the ofFileMustExist value to the OpenDialog object Options property. By adding this value to this property, the OpenDialog component will require the user to select the name of an existing file. Next, the OpenDialog component's Execute method is called. This method will return True if the user selects a table, and False otherwise. If the user selects a table, the name of the selected table is passed to the ValidateTable procedure.

The ValidateTable procedure raises an exception if the table is invalid. If this happens, for whatever reason, no more statements in this event handler will be executed, meaning that the invalid table will not be opened. If ValidateTable does not raise an exception, the select table is valid, and the remainder of the event handler makes this the current table for the application.

NOTE: The CARDS project includes a number of additional interesting features that you may want to look at. For example, it shows you how to provide a list of the last three files opened by using an INI file for a most recently used file list. It also shows you how to use the Table method GotoCurrent to synchronize the display of two tables to the same record.

Conclusion

This chapter has shown you several important techniques that apply to databases created with Delphi. These techniques were selected in order to expose you to the widest possible variety of database-related tasks. These examples, however, represent only a fraction of the possible tasks that you might have to perform in your applications.

For additional techniques that you can use in your own database applications, you should examine fully the projects available on the code disk. The DEMOS subdirectory of Delphi is another excellent source of database techniques. This subdirectory contains a number of database-related projects that demonstrate additional solutions to common database tasks.

Chapter Seven

Database Features in Delphi 2

The code for the examples presented in this chapter can be found in the \CODE\CH07 subdirectory on the CD-ROM that accompanies this book. Please refer to Appendix A for information on using the code files for this chapter.

Delphi 2 contains many new and enhanced features for database developers. These features include new components, enhancements to existing components, and additional tools that ship with Delphi 2. This chapter provides an introduction to these new features and enhancements. The information in this chapter is presented in two predominant styles.

1. Tables listing the new and enhanced properties, methods, and events of components. These tables allow you to look quickly at a single source so that you can be aware of the new and changed database capabilities.
2. Descriptions and examples of new database features in Delphi 2. Most of the descriptions and code examples provided are not covered in the manuals or code demos that ship with Delphi 2. Some of the example projects demonstrate a specific topic. Other projects incorporate several new features into a single application.

Before looking at the details of the new features, the next section provides an overview of the new features and identifies the major new database-related tools in Delphi 2.

Overview of Major New Options

The new database features range from new properties, methods, and events to new database tools. These tools and the enhanced areas include the following:

- The Object Repository
- Data modules
- Visual form inheritance
- SQL Monitor
- SQL/Database Explorer
- A scaleable data dictionary
- The Data Migration Expert (Data Pump)
- 32-bit BDE (Borland Database Engine) version 3.0
- Cached updates
- Filters
- Updated and enhanced VCL (Visual Component Library) components

The Object Repository replaces the Delphi 1.0 Gallery. In Delphi 2 the Object Repository provides a tool to share and reuse forms, data modules, experts, DLLs (Dynamic Link Libraries), and entire projects. You can share objects between projects, objects within a project, or even share an entire project.

Data module objects are one of Delphi's most important new features. You place non-visual components that define a data model, along with the business rules for the data, in a data module. The ability to centralize the data model and code to ensure the integrity of the data reduces maintenance and improves the reliability of data modifications.

Visual form inheritance allows you to derive new forms from an ancestor that you created as a form. The new forms inherit the ancestor form's components, properties, and code. Furthermore, changes made to the ancestor form at a later time are updated automatically in the descendant forms when you recompile. Inheritance permits you to apply standards in applications and permits easy subsequent changes with minimal effort for all descendant forms. An ancestor form can be any form already in your project or in the Object Repository.

Depending on the edition of Delphi 2 you purchased, you will find either the Database Explorer tool (Desktop and Developer editions) or the SQL Explorer tool (Client/Server edition). The Database Explorer supports database examination. You can look at table structures and at the data in the tables, and you can execute SQL (Structured Query Language) statements. The SQL Explorer supports local databases as well as remote databases on SQL servers. You can also view alias definitions and add new aliases to the BDE configuration file.

A scaleable data dictionary is part of the Database and SQL Explorers. It supports the definition of field attributes for the defined databases. These attributes, which include formatting and display settings, are used to initialize TField properties for DataSet components. The dictionary can reside in any database format, such as local Paradox tables or a remote SQL database.

Migrating data between databases is made easier using the Data Migration Expert, also called the Data Pump. It allows you to take data in one database format and move the tables, indexes, referential integrity, and data to another database format. The Data Migration Expert is available only in the Client/Server edition of Delphi 2.

The Borland Database Engine (BDE) has been improved greatly. It is the nucleus for all data access using Paradox, dBASE, SQL Links, and OBDC (Open Database Connectivity) data. Many of the new features available in Delphi 2 are based on these updates to the BDE.

Cached updates offer another technique for transaction processing (SQL-based transaction processing is discussed in detail in Chapter 8). This feature allows you to retrieve data from a database, store it locally in a cache, make modifications, and then commit all the changes at the same time. Cached updates reduce lock contentions and network traffic, as well as improve database performance.

In Delphi 1.0, restricting records in a dataset requires either an SQL SELECT statement, use of an index with a range on a Table component, or direct calls to the filter functions of the BDE (see Chapter 5). In Delphi 2, however, restrictions (filters) can be defined for any field in a DataSet component, independent of indexes. The BDE filter support is now directly available for all DataSet components. These filters support multi-field selection using AND, OR, and NOT operators.

Many of the other updates and enhancements in Delphi 2 have been made to components themselves. The following sections list the new and enhanced components on the Data Access and Data Control pages of the component palette.

New Data Access Components

The Data Access page in Delphi 2 contains two new components: Session and UpdateSQL. Both of these are non-visual components.

Session Component

The Session component on the Data Access page was not introduced in Delphi 2. It is the same as the TSession component created for you automatically in Delphi 1.0, with some modifications. In Delphi 2 you can place this non-visual component in a form and set its properties using the Object Inspector. Table 7-1 lists the published TSession component properties. The TSession class also declares two published properties: ConfigMode and TraceFlags. These properties are listed in Table 7-2.

There are also a number of new methods for the TSession class. Many of the new methods are used to create, delete, and maintain aliases, both for the current session

Property	Description
Active	Specifies whether the session is active.
KeepConnection	Specifies whether the temporary Database components automatically created by Delphi will maintain the connection to the database when all associated datasets are closed. These temporary Database components are created for DataSet objects not explicitly tied to a Database component.
Name	Name of the Session component.
NetFileDir	Location of the PDOXUSRS.NET file. This file is the network control file necessary for multiple users to share the same Paradox tables.
PrivateDir	Directory path for temporary files generated by BDE when performing data querying and manipulation tasks.
SessionName	Name used to uniquely identify a session.

Table 7-1. *Published TSession Component Properties*

Property	Description
ConfigMode	Used to determine if new aliases created with AddAlias or AddStandardAlias are available to all applications (global) or for the session only (local). Call the SaveConfigFile method to save global aliases permanently in the BDE configuration file.
TraceFlags	Controls the events that are tracked by the SQL Monitor. All Database objects owned by the session will use the same set of TraceFlags set for the Session. The SQL Monitor is described in the "SQL Monitor" section in this chapter.

Table 7-2. *New Published Properties for the TSession Component*

and for permanent storage in the BDE configuration file. Table 7-3 lists the new TSession methods, the syntax for each method, along with a brief description.

Creating and Managing Multiple Sessions

In addition to the Sessions variable that is created automatically by Delphi (if no Session object has been defined), Delphi 2 includes two system variable names associated with sessions: ActiveSession and Sessions. These variables are instantiated

Method	Syntax	Description
AddAlias	`procedure AddAlias(const Name, Driver: string; List: Tstrings);`	Adds the alias specified by Name to the session for a non-local database. Driver is the name of the database driver the alias will use. List is a StringList containing the parameters for the alias.
AddStandardAlias	`procedure AddStandardAlias (const Name, Path, DefaultDriver: string);`	Adds the alias specified by Name as an alias with STANDARD as the database. The Path parameter specifies the directory where the database is located. DefaultDriver specifies the table type to use ('PARADOX', 'DBASE', or 'ASCIIDRV') when using tables with no extension in TableName and a TableType of ttDefault.

Table 7-3. *New Methods for the TSession Component*

Method	Syntax	Description
Close	`procedure Close;`	Closes the session, producing the same effect as setting the Active property to False.
DeleteAlias	`procedure DeleteAlias(const Name: string);`	Removes the alias with the specified name from the session.
GetAliasDriverName	`function GetAliasDriverName (const AliasName: string): string;`	Returns the database driver name associated with the given alias.
GetConfigParams	`procedure GetConfigParams (const Path, Section: string; List: Tstrings);`	Returns settings from the BDE configuration file. The Path and Section names you supply depend on the type of information you're interested in.
IsAlias	`function IsAlias(const Name: string): Boolean;`	Checks to see if the alias specified in Name is an entry in the BDE configuration file.
ModifyAlias	`procedure ModifyAlias(Name: string; List: Tstrings);`	Modifies parameters for the specified alias in Name.
Open	`procedure Open;`	Opens the session and makes it the active one, producing the same effect as setting the Active property to True.
SaveConfigFile	`procedure SaveConfigFile;`	Saves all persistent aliases in the BDE configuration file.

Table 7-3. *New Methods for the TSession Component* (continued)

for you automatically by Delphi 2. Because Delphi 2 allows you to create multiple sessions using the TSession class, you need the ability to check which session is the current session. ActiveSession is of the type TSession and points automatically to the active session. This allows you to generically get the properties for the current session and use the current session's methods.

The Sessions variable is of the type TSessionList. It provides separate properties and methods to track of multiple sessions in a multithreaded database application. (See Chapters 15 and 16 for information on multithreading.) Table 7-4 lists the properties of the TSessionList class; the Table 7-5 lists its methods.

TSession Alias Methods Example

Adding and managing aliases in Delphi 2 is much easier than in Delphi 1.0. Now you can use built-in TSession methods without having to make direct calls to the BDE. Project ALIAS20.DPR demonstrates how to use many of the new TSession methods that manage aliases. Figure 7-1 shows the main form.

The form for the ALIAS20 project contains buttons separated into four groups. The left-most buttons are used to add, modify, and delete aliases. In this project, only aliases for Paradox and dBASE tables are supported. The two Edit components at the top of the form are used to enter the alias name and the directory path. The middle buttons are used to update the two ListBox components, which contain the currently defined aliases and drivers in the configuration file. The two buttons on the right side of the form are used to get detailed information about the highlighted alias or driver. The Memo component at the bottom of the form is used to display the results. The last button, Save Config File, is used to write the alias changes to the BDE configuration file.

Using GetAliasNames and GetDriverNames

When the form is opened, both ListBox components are initialized to the current alias and driver lists. This is done in the OnCreate event handler for the form, as follows:

```
procedure TForm1.FormCreate(Sender: TObject);
begin
  Session.GetAliasNames(ListBoxAliasNames.Items);
  Session.GetDriverNames(ListBoxDriverNames.Items);
  Session.ConfigMode := cmPersistent;
end;
```

Property	Description
Count	Counts the number of active and inactive sessions in the session list. Useful when you use the Session array property.
List	An array of available sessions indexed by their SessionName property.
Sessions[n]	Allows you to use sessions referenced by an ordinal value, for example Sessions[1].

Table 7-4. *Properties of the TSessionList Class*

Method	Syntax	Description
FindSession	`function FindSession(const SessionName: string): Tsession;`	Returns the TSession component that matches the SessionName supplied as the parameter. If an empty string is passed, the default global Session variable is returned. If a string that doesn't match the SessionName of any session is passed, FindSession returns nil.
GetSessionNames	`procedure GetSessionNames(List: Tstrings);`	Fills a string list object with the names of available sessions.
OpenSession	`function OpenSession(const SessionName: string): Tsession;`	Returns a TSession object. Attempts to match SessionName to an existing session. If found, the session is opened. If it is not found, a new session is created.

Table 7-5. *Methods of the TSessionList Class*

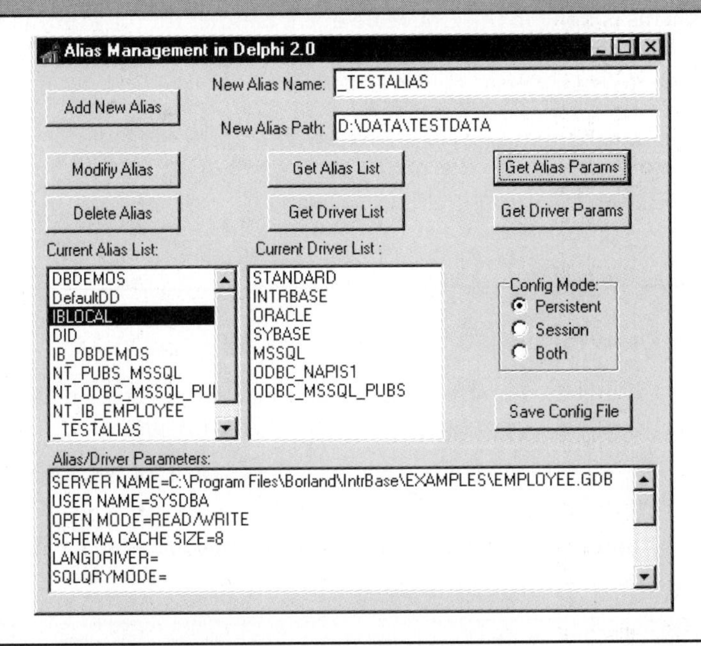

Figure 7-1. *Main form for ALIAS20 project after adding a new alias and retrieving information on IBLOCAL*

Two Session methods are used to fill the ListBox values. GetAliasNames returns a list of all currently defined aliases. This list is placed directly into the ListBoxAliasNames ListBox Items property. Likewise, GetDriverNames returns a list of currently defined drivers. This list is placed in the ListBoxDriverNames ListBox Items property. The last statement in the procedure ensures that the setting for ConfigMode is persistent. This means that only the persistent aliases are shown and, by default, any new aliases defined are persistent unless the Config Mode radio button on the form is changed to one of the other two settings.

Adding a New Alias

To add an alias for the STANDARD driver, the AddStandardAlias method is used. Three parameters are passed in this method: the alias name, the alias path, and the default driver type of PARADOX (although you can change the code to default to one of the other driver types). The two Edit components at the top of the form must be entered before a new STANDARD alias is added. The following code is from the Add New Alias button OnClick event handler:

NOTE: *Two variables, AliasName and AliasPath, are defined as String variables in the implementation of this unit section. They are used in many of the procedures in the ALIAS20 project.*

```
procedure TForm1.pbAddAliasClick(Sender: TObject);
begin
  { Verify the alias name is entered }
  if Edit1.Text = '' then
    begin
      MessageDlg('Alias Name must be entered.',mtError,[mbOK],0);
      Edit1.SetFocus;
      Exit;
    end
  else
    AliasName := Edit1.Text;
  { Verify the alias path is entered }
  if Edit2.Text = '' then
    begin
      MessageDlg('Alias Path must be entered.',mtError,[mbOK],0);
      Edit2.SetFocus;
      Exit;
    end
  else
    AliasPath := Edit2.Text;
  Session.AddStandardAlias(AliasName,AliasPath,' PARADOX ');
  MessageDlg('Alias ' + AliasName + ' added, click Get Alias List ' +
    'to update Current Alias List.',mtInformation,[mbOK],0);
end;
```

The first two tests performed in this procedure ensure there is an entry in both Edit components. If either of them is empty, an error dialog box is displayed and the addition of the new alias fails. Note that in this example there is no verification that an existing directory has been entered, or that the format of the directory entry is correct. (You might add this verification to your own code.)

Next, the call to AddStandardAlias adds the new alias to the configuration file. The list box for the defined aliases is not updated by this event handler. To see the updated list, you click the Get Alias List button, which uses GetAliasNames to update the list box.

Modifying an Existing Alias

The Modify Alias button allows an existing alias to be changed, provided it is a STANDARD alias. It uses the ModifyAlias method to change the alias parameters. The following is the code for the OnClick event handler for this button:

```
procedure TForm1.pbModifyAliasClick(Sender: TObject);
var
  ParamList: TStringList;
  AliasName,PathName: String;
begin
  { Need to select an alias before it can be modified }
  if ListBoxAliasNames.ItemIndex = -1 then
    MessageDlg('Need to select Alias to modify in the Current Alias ' +
      'List',mtError,[mbOK],0)
  else
    { Only allow STANDARD aliases to be modified }
    if Session.GetAliasDriverName(
      ListBoxAliasNames.Items[ListBoxAliasNames.ItemIndex]) =
      'STANDARD' then
      begin
        with ListBoxAliasNames do
          AliasName := Items[ItemIndex];
        try
          ParamList := TStringList.Create;
          Session.GetAliasParams(AliasName,ParamList);
          { Get alias path for the selected alias }
          PathName := ParamList.Values['PATH'];
          ModifyAliasDlg.Edit1.Text := AliasName;
          ModifyAliasDlg.Edit2.Text := PathName;
          ModifyAliasDlg.Edit2.Modified := False;
          { If changes made to path, update alias information }
          if ModifyAliasDlg.ShowModal = mrOK then
            begin
              if ModifyAliasDlg.Edit2.Modified = True then
                begin
                 ParamList.Values['PATH'] := ModifyAliasDlg.Edit2.Text;
                 Session.ModifyAlias(AliasName,ParamList);
                 MessageDlg('Alias ' + AliasName +
```

```
                    ' modified. Click Get ' +
                    'Alias Params to see updated parameters.',
                    mtInformation,[mbOK],0);
              end
            else
              MessageDlg('No changes made to alias, modify canceled',
                mtInformation,[mbOK],0);
            end;
        finally
          ParamList.Free;
        end;
      end
    else
      MessageDlg('Cannot change aliases other than STANDARD driver ' +
        'aliases.',mtError,[mbOK],0);
end;
```

An alias in the Current Alias List must be highlighted before a modify can occur. If the selected alias does not use the STANDARD driver, an error message is displayed. A second form is used as a dialog box to set the update to the alias path. Its name is ModifyAliasDlg, and it is displayed by the preceding event handler as a modal dialog box. ModifyAliasDlg is shown in Figure 7-2, where the _TESTALIAS alias is being changed.

The path for the alias in the configuration file is updated only if the dialog box OK button is clicked and the path value is changed. If both of these conditions are true, the ModifyAlias method is called to change the alias parameters.

Deleting an Alias

An alias is removed from the configuration file using the DeleteAlias method. The Delete Alias button on the ALIAS20 main form provides this option. The following is the code for the OnClick event handler for this button:

```
procedure TForm1.pbDeleteAliasClick(Sender: TObject);
begin
  if ListBoxAliasNames.ItemIndex = -1 then
    MessageDlg('Need to select Alias to delete in the Current Alias ' +
      'List',mtError,[mbOK],0)
  else
    with ListBoxAliasnames do
      if MessageDlg('Are you sure you want to delete alias "' +
        Items[ItemIndex] + '"?',
        mtConfirmation,[mbNo,mbYes],0) = mrYes then
        begin
         Session.DeleteAlias(Items[ItemIndex]);
         MessageDlg('Alias ' + Items[ItemIndex] + ' deleted. Click ' +
           'Get Alias List to update the Current Alias List.',
           mtInformation,[mbOK],0);
        end;
end;
```

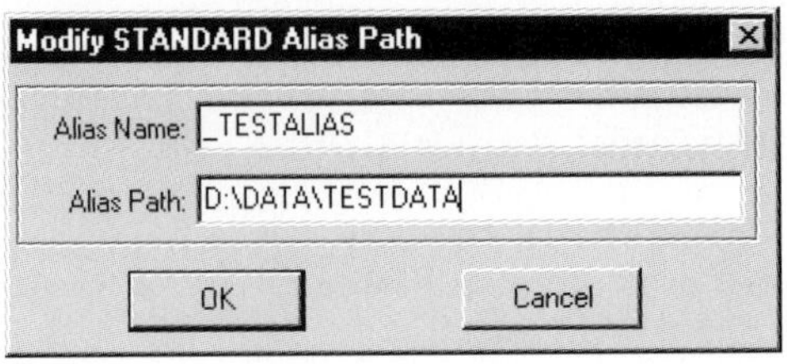

Figure 7-2. *Dialog box in ALIAS20 project used to modify the path of a STANDARD alias*

Similar to the Modify Alias code, this code first ensures that an alias is selected in the Current Alias List. If one is selected, a confirmation dialog box is displayed to confirm the deletion of the selected alias. If Yes is selected from this dialog box, the DeleteAlias method is called and the alias is removed. Again, the Get Alias List button needs to be clicked in order to update the Current Alias List without the deleted alias.

Getting Parameters for an Alias

Parameters defined for an alias are retrieved using the GetAliasParams method. This method is available in both Delphi 1.0 and 2. The use of the method is demonstrated in the OnClick event handler for the Get Alias Params button, as follows:

```
procedure TForm1.pbGetAliasParamsClick(Sender: TObject);
begin
  if ListBoxAliasNames.ItemIndex = -1 then
    begin
      MessageDlg('Need to select one of the available aliases',
        mtError,[mbOK],0);
      ListBoxAliasNames.SetFocus;
    end
  else
    with ListBoxAliasNames do
      Session.GetAliasParams(Items[ItemIndex],Memo1.Lines);
end;
```

For the selected alias name in the Current Alias List, GetAliasParams is called, returning the alias' parameters. These parameters are assigned directly to the Lines property of the Memo component at the bottom of the form. Figure 7-1 shows the form after getting the parameters for the IBLOCAL alias.

Getting Parameters for a Driver

The parameters for the installed drivers are displayed using the same technique as was employed for getting alias parameters. The OnClick event handler for the Get Driver Params button retrieves the list of parameters for the selected driver. The following is the code for this event handler:

```
procedure TForm1.pbGetDriverParamsClick(Sender: TObject);
begin
  if ListBoxDriverNames.ItemIndex = -1 then
    begin
      MessageDlg('Need to select one of the available drivers',
       mtError,[mbOK],0);
      ListBoxDriverNames.SetFocus;
    end
  else
    begin
      Memo1.Lines.Clear;
      with ListBoxDriverNames do
        Session.GetDriverParams(Items[ItemIndex],Memo1.Lines);
    end;
end;
```

A driver in the Current Driver List must be selected before the parameters are retrieved. If one is selected, the contents of the Memo components are cleared and GetDriverParams is called. The first parameter is the name of the alias, and the second parameter defines where to place the driver parameters defined in the configuration file.

Setting and Using the ConfigMode Property

Aliases can be defined to be permanent (global) or for the current session only (local). The ConfigMode property of TSession specifies if the aliases added are global or local. In the ALIAS20 project, permanent aliases are used by default. The Config Mode radio buttons allow you to change the setting of the ConfigMode property. The following is the code for the OnClick event handler for this radio button group:

```
procedure TForm1.RadioGroup1Click(Sender: TObject);
begin
  { Set the ConfigMode property for the Session. ItemIndex corresponds
    to the three TConfigMode options:
    0 : cmPersistent  Aliases you add are global. (Call SaveConfigFile
                      to make permanent.) GetAliasNames returns only
                      global aliases.
    1 : cmSession     Aliases you add are local and can't be saved.
                      (Local aliases are lost when the session ends.)
                      GetAliasNames returns only local aliases.
    2 : cmAll         Aliases you add are global. (Call SaveConfigFile
                      to make permanent.) GetAliasNames returns both
                      global and local aliases.  }
  case RadioGroup1.ItemIndex of
    0 : Session.ConfigMode := cmPersistent;
    1 : Session.ConfigMode := cmSession;
    2 : Session.ConfigMode := cmAll;
  end;
end;
```

Each time the selected radio button is clicked, the ConfigMode setting for the session changes. When the setting is Persistent, each of the aliases defined in the configuration file as well as the added aliases are listed in the Current Alias List. When the radio button is changed to Session, any new alias added is for the session only. Clicking on the Get Alias List returns only the session-level aliases. Figure 7-3 shows the ALIAS20 form after adding a session alias and listing the defined aliases.

The third radio button, Both, changes the ConfigMode setting for both adding aliases and listing them. The Both radio button sets ConfigMode to cmAll. This setting makes new aliases global, the same as cmPersistent. Displaying the alias list gets both the persistent- and session-level aliases.

Updating the Configuration File

Unless you explicitly save any aliases added, they are available only during the current session. This is true regardless of the alias' ConfigMode property. That is, even if you define a new alias with the ConfigMode property set to cmPersistent, the alias will not be available to future sessions unless it is saved to the BDE. Saving these aliases is demonstrated in the following code, which defines the OnClick event handler for the Save Config File button:

```
procedure TForm1.pbSaveConfigClick(Sender: TObject);
begin
  Session.SaveConfigFile;
end;
```

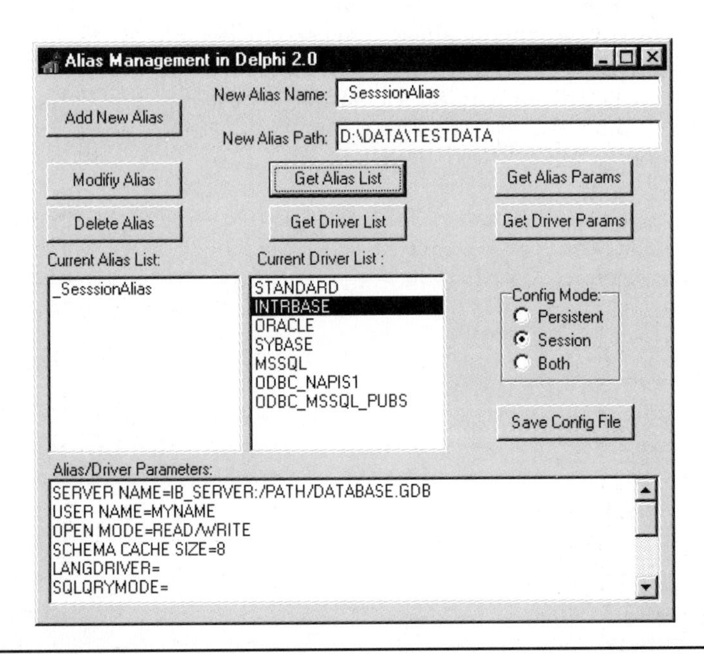

Figure 7-3. *ALIAS20 project main form after adding a session alias and alias listing*

The SaveConfigFile method saves all aliases that were added with a ConfigMode setting of cmPersistent to the configuration file. These changes are then available to any BDE application.

Since Delphi 2 provides the capabilities for maintaining both session and permanent aliases, alias management is much easier, as demonstrated in the use of Session methods in the ALIAS20 project. For information on adding aliases in Delphi 1.0, see the project BDEALS1.DPR on the CD-ROM in the subdirectory for Chapter 5.

UpdateSQL Component

The UpdateSQL component provides the ability to use Delphi 2's new cached updates feature to change data. This component encapsulates three Query components to support INSERT, UPDATE, and DELETE SQL statements. The Query components are created at runtime—you do not see them in the form. The published properties for the UpdateSQL component are listed in Table 7-6.

You associate an UpdateSQL component with a DataSet component by setting the DataSet's UpdateObject property. The dataset then automatically uses the UpdateSQL component when cached updates are applied. The ModifySQL property is an SQL

Property	**Description**
DeleteSQL	Contains the SQL statement used when applying the cached deletion of a record.
InsertSQL	Contains the SQL statement used when applying the cached insertion of a record.
ModifySQL	Contains the SQL statement used when applying the cached modification of a record.
Name	UpdateSQL component name.
DataSet	Identifies the dataset to which a TUpdateSQL component belongs. You should only assign a value to this property if you are creating an UpdateSQL component programmatically.
Query	Returns a Query component for the SQL statement corresponding to the UpdateKind index.
SQL	Returns the StringList containing the SQL statement corresponding to the UpdateKind index.
UpdateKind	Specifies what type of query to perform. The options are ukModify (UPDATE), ukInsert (INSERT), and ukDelete (DELETE).

Table 7-6. *UpdateSQL Component Properties*

statement that is executed when the cached update is a modification of an existing record. The InsertSQL property is an SQL statement that is executed when the cached update is the insertion of a new record. DeleteSQL is an SQL statement that is executed when the cached update is the deletion of a record. All three properties support an extension to normal parameter binding for cached updates. Specifically, you can prefix any field name in the SQL queries with "OLD_" to retrieve the value of the field as it was before cached updates were enabled. This extension permits you access the old field values, and is generally for use in creating the WHERE clause of the SQL statement. For example, the following SQL statement, including the OLD_ extension, updates the Name, Capital, and Continents fields of the COUNTRY.DB table based on the old (original) Name field values:

```
update "COUNTRY.DB"
set Name = :Name, Capital = :Capital, Continent = :Continent
where Name = :OLD_Name
```

You can write the DeleteSQL, InsertSQL, and ModifySQL property SQL statements by hand. Alternatively, you can use the Update SQL Editor dialog box, shown in Figure 7-4. To display this dialog box, either double-click the UpdateSQL component, or right-click the UpdateSQL component and select UpdateSQL Editor from the displayed speed menu.

The Update SQL Editor dialog box is two-page, tabbed dialog box. The first page, Options, contains objects to define SQL statements for data insertion, deletion, and

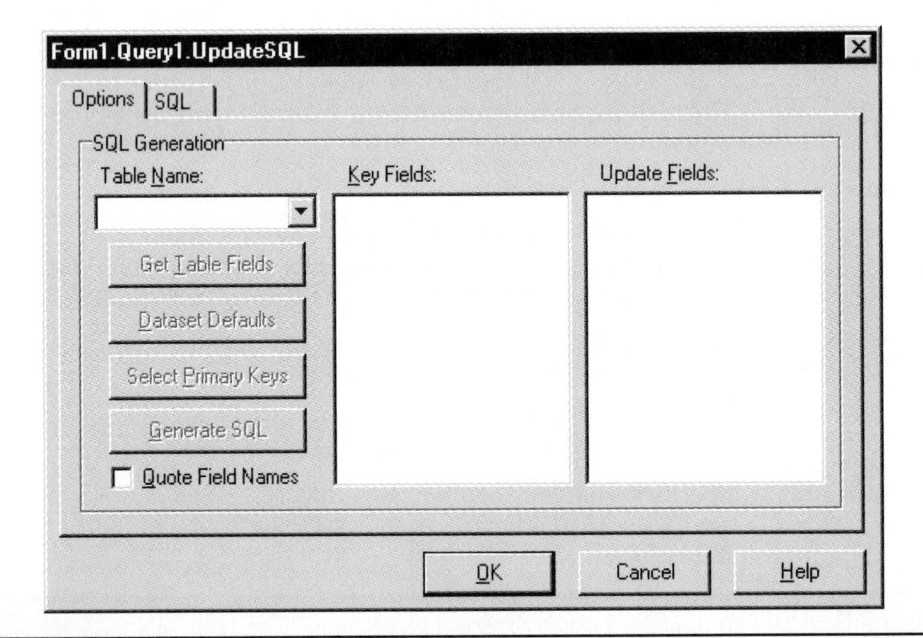

Figure 7-4. *The Update SQL Editor showing the Options page*

modification. The second page, SQL, contains the text for the UDPATE, INSERT, and DELETE SQL statements.

UpdateSQL Methods

The UpdateSQL component does not have any events associated with it. The UpdateSQL component's three methods are described in Table 7-7.

TIP: *To see a demonstration of the UpdateSQL component, refer to the demonstration program CACHE.DPR that shipped with Delphi 2. It is located in the DELPHI 2.0\DEMOS\DB\CACHEDUP directory.*

Enhanced Data Access Components

All of the Data Access components have been enhanced in Delphi 2. Most of the changes are to the TDataSet classes: TTable, TQuery, and TStoredProc. The TDataSet

Method	Syntax	Description
Apply	`procedure Apply(UpdateKind: TUpdateKind);`	Executes the SQL statement associated with the UpdateKind parameter. Apply performs the same action as calling ExecSQL and SetParams separately.
ExecSQL	`procedure ExecSQL(UpdateKind: TUpdateKind);`	Executes the SQL statement associated with the UpdateKind parameter. ExecSQL does not do any parameter binding. You need to call SetParams before calling ExecSQL.
SetParams	`procedure SetParams(UpdateKind: TUpdateKind);`	Replaces parameters in the SQL statement associated with the UpdateKind parameter with the value of the field with the same name as the parameter. Parameters are prefixed by a colon. For more information on parameterized queries, see the section "Using Queries" in Chapter 6.

Table 7-7. *UpdateSQL Component Methods*

changes are described next. Then the changes to the other Data Access components are described in following sections.

Enhancements to All TDataSet Components

All three DataSet classes include a similar set of enhancements. These are described in the following sections.

New TDataSet Properties

There are many new properties for the TDataSet components. Table 7-8 lists the new properties along with the data type and a description for each property.

Property	Data Type and Description
CachedUpdates	A Boolean value that enables cached updates when set to True. When enabled, updates you make to the dataset are cached instead of being written to the dataset. ApplyUpdates is used to apply the changes.
DBSession	Returns the TSession variable associated with the dataset.
DefaultFields	A Boolean value that returns True if the dataset is using the default TField objects, and False if it is using persistent fields instantiated with the Fields Editor.
ExpIndex	A Boolean value used with dBASE tables. Returns True if the current index is a dBASE expression index, and False if it is not.
FieldValues	An array property that returns the value of the field with the specified name as a Variant data type. With FieldValues, you do not have to specify the type (using AsString). FieldValues is the default array property for all DataSet components.
Filter	A String value used to specify which records you want to see in the dataset. The filter is applied only when the Filtered property is set to True. Filters are covered in more detail in the section "Using the New TDataSet Filter Feature."
Filtered	A Boolean value that activates or deactivates filtering specified in the Filter property or the OnFilterRecord event. True enables filtering, and False disables filtering.

Table 7-8. *New Properties for TTable, TQuery, and TStoredProc*

Property	Data Type and Description
FilterOptions	A set property that defines two Boolean values to fine-tune the filtering specified in the Filter property. Use foCaseInsensitive to filter the data without regard to case in the data. Use foNoPartialCompare to filter for exact matches only
Found	A Boolean value used with filtered data and the Find methods. The value is True when the FindFirst, FindLast, FindNext, or FindPrior method finds a record that matches the filter criteria.
KeySize	A Word data type that specifies, in bytes, the length of a key in the current index. KeySize is primarily used to make direct calls to the BDE.
RecNo	Returns a LongInt that reports the current record number in the dataset. This property applies only to Paradox and dBASE tables. The value –1 is returned for tables in a SQL database.
RecordSize	A Word data type that specifies, in bytes, the size of the physical record buffer.
UpdateObject	Points to an UpdateSQL object used by the dataset to perform cached updates.
UpdateRecordType	Allows you determine how a record's status affects its visibility in a dataset when cached updates are enabled.
UpdatePending	A Boolean value that is True if updates are pending and False if not.

Table 7-8. *New Properties for TTable, TQuery, and TStoredProc* (continued)

New TDataSet Methods

Table 7-9 lists the new TDataSet methods, the syntax for each method, and a brief description.

New TDataSet Events

There are seven new events for TDataSet components. These events, their syntax, and descriptions are shown in Table 7-10.

New State Property Values

There are three new State values for a dataset: dsUpdateNew, dsUpdateOld, and dsFilter. The first two (although they are listed in the Delphi 2 documentation) are for internal use when accessing a field's NewValue and OldValue properties using cached

Method	Syntax	Description
ActiveBuffer	`function ActiveBuffer: Pchar;`	Returns a pointer to the internal record buffer corresponding to the dataset's current record.
ApplyUpdates	`procedure ApplyUpdates;`	Applies the pending cached updates. Following a call to ApplyUpdates, CommitUpdates needs to be called to reflect that cached updates were written.
CancelUpdates	`procedure CancelUpdates;`	Discards all pending cached updates. The dataset returns to the state it was in before cached updates were enabled.
ClearFields	`procedure ClearFields;`	Clears all fields of the current record to their default values.
CheckOpen	`function CheckOpen(Status: DBIResult): Boolean;`	Used when making low-level calls to the BDE. If a table open fails due to a missing password, a dialog box is automatically opened to get a password from the user.
CommitUpdates	`procedure CommitUpdates;`	Updates the cache to reflect that pending cached updates were applied successfully.
ControlsDisabled	`function ControlsDisabled: Boolean;`	Returns True if the dataset has its controls still disabled by a call to DisableControls and an EnableControls has not been called.
FetchAll	`procedure FetchAll;`	Forces the server to release all intermediate locks and reads the entire result set.
FindFirst, FindLast, FindNext, and FindPrior	`function Findxxx: Boolean;`	Provides a way to find the first, Last, Next, and Prior records that match the filter criteria. Returns True if there is a match, and False otherwise.

Table 7-9. *New DataSet Methods*

Method	Syntax	Description
GetCurrentRecord	`function GetCurrentRecord (Buffer: PChar): Boolean;`	Fetches the current record from the dataset into a memory buffer. Buffer must point to a buffer at least as big as the value of the RecordSize property.
GetFieldList	`procedure GetFieldList(List: TList; const FieldNames: string);`	Fills a list object with the field objects representing the dataset's fields listed in FieldNames.
IsLinkedTo	`function IsLinkedTo(DataSource: TDataSource): Boolean;`	Returns True if the dataset is linked to the specified DataSource, and False otherwise.
Locate	`function Locate(const KeyFields: string; const KeyValues: Variant; Options: TLocateOptions): Boolean;`	Moves to the first record matching the supplied search criteria. KeyFields lists the field or fields you want to search. To search more than one field, separate field names with semicolons. KeyValues is a variant specifying the field value to match, or an array of field values if KeyFields lists more than one field. Use the Options property to specify case-insensitive or partial-key matching.
Lookup	`function Lookup(const KeyFields: string; const KeyValues: Variant; const ResultFields: string): Variant;`	Finds and returns lookup values. KeyFields lists the field or fields to search. To search more than one field, separate field names with semicolons. KeyValues is a variant specifying the field value to match, or an array of field values if KeyFields lists more than one field. An index is used if it exists; otherwise, a filter is used. Null is returned if a match is not found.

Table 7-9. *New DataSet Methods* (continued)

Method	Syntax	Description
RevertRecord	`procedure RevertRecord;`	Discards any changes you posted to the current record when cached updates are enabled.
SetFields	`procedure SetFields(const Values: array of const);`	Assigns the values specified in the Values array parameter to the fields in the dataset that is in Edit mode.
UpdateStatus	`function UpdateStatus: TUpdateStatus;`	Returns the TUpdateStatus value corresponding to the most recent cached update. The values are usUnmodified, usModified, usInserted, or usDeleted.

Table 7-9. *New DataSet Methods* (continued)

Event	Syntax	Description
OnDeleteError	`procedure OnDeleteError(DataSet: TDataSet; E: EDatabaseError; var Action: TDataAction)`	Triggered when there is an error deleting a record from a dataset. The DataSet parameter is the dataset that has the problem. For example, this is the type of error that occurs with Paradox tables when you attempt to delete a parent table record when a related child table record exists and there is a referential integrity rule between the tables.
OnEditError	`procedure OnEditError(DataSet: TDataSet; E: EDatabaseError; var Action: TDataAction);`	Triggered when there is an error editing the current record, for example, when a lock cannot be obtained on the record. The DataSet parameter is the dataset that has the problem.

Table 7-10. *New DataSet Events*

Event	Syntax	Description
OnFilterRecord	`procedure(DataSet: TDataSet; var Accept: Boolean) of object;`	Triggered when the Filtered property is set to True. Code you add to this event handler evaluates whether the current record should be displayed and sets the Accept parameter to False to suppress the display (Accept is True by default).
OnPostError	`procedure(DataSet: TDataSet; E: EDatabaseError; var Action: TDataAction)`	Triggered when there is an error posting the current record, such as an integrity violation if a key field is changed.
OnServerYield	`procedure(DataSet: TDataSet; var AbortQuery: Boolean)`	Called when control is being passed to a query against a database server. Set the AbortQuery parameter to True to cancel the query.
OnUpdateError	`procedure(DataSet: TDataSet; E: EDatabaseError; UpdateKind: TUpdateKind; var UpdateAction: TUpdateAction`	Triggered when errors occur using the cached updates feature.
OnUpdateRecord	`procedure(DataSet: TDataSet; UpdateKind: TUpdateKind; var UpdateAction: TUpdateAction)`	Occurs for each record being updated using cached updates.

Table 7-10. *New DataSet Events (continued)*

updates. The third new State value, dsFilter, is used by the DataSet component to signal that it is processing an OnFilterRecord event. You cannot modify a dataset while it is in the dsFilter state. This ensures the integrity of the dataset while the filtering is being done.

New TField Type

One new TField type, TAutoIncField, supports auto-incrementing fields. The TAutoIncField component represents a binary value with a range from –2,147,483,648 to 2,147,483,647. Set the DisplayFormat property to control the formatting of the field for display purposes, and set the EditFormat property for editing purposes. Use the Value property to access and/or change the current field value. Set the MinValue and MaxValue properties to limit the smallest and largest values permitted in a field, respectively.

NOTE: This field type can be used only with table types that support auto-incrementing fields, such as Paradox tables version 5.0 and later.

Using the New TDataSet Filter Feature

The new TDataSet filtering feature allows you to restrict the rows available in a dataset based on the values in a field or a combination of fields. These filters are similar to queries in that you can define conditions similar to the WHERE clause. Furthermore, the resulting records in the dataset can be modified, an advantage over some queries that do not result in a live query.

Filters can be turned on and off by changing the Filtered property to True and False, respectively. You can even use filters on Query object result sets or on datasets upon which a range has been applied. For instance, you can quickly limit which records are displayed in a dataset by using a range (which is fast because an index is used), and then further restrict the result set using a filter.

You can use three different techniques to filter data. First, you can use the new Locate method (described in the next section). Second, the OnFilterRecord event handler permits you to use code to either accept a record to the filtered view, or reject the record. This is the most flexible technique. The third option is to use the Filter property of the dataset.

Setting the value of the Filter property is like setting conditions in a WHERE clause. The operators you can use include: <, >, >=, <=, =, <>, AND, OR, and NOT. Any field can be included in the filter condition. If the field name includes spaces, use square brackets ([ ]) to enclose the field name. The following three examples can be used to set filtering conditions:

```
CustNo > 3000
```

```
ItemsTotal > 10000 and ItemsTotal < 50000
```

```
State = 'FL' or State = 'WA'
```

You can evaluate two or more fields within the Filter property; however, to do so, you must enclose the field names within brackets. For example, to filter the Customer table in the DBDEMOS alias to include only those records where the customer number is 1231 and the SaleDate field contains a date later than or equal to 1/1/91, set Filtered to True and set the Filter property to the following:

```
[CustNo] = 1231 and [SaleDate] >= '1/1/1991'
```

Two projects, GENFLTR.DPR and FLTERS, demonstrate some of the different options used with filtering. The main form of the first project, GENFLTR.DPR, is shown in Figure 7-5. (The FLTERS project is presented in the following section.) The GENFLTR project uses the CUSTOMER.DB and ORDERS.DB tables from the DBDEMOS alias. The form contains a DataSource and a Table component. The radio buttons provide the option to switch between the two tables.

The Edit component at the top of the screen in Figure 7-5 is used to enter any text for the filter. Once text is entered, the Set Filter Condition button is used to place the entered text into the Filter property of the table as shown in the following code:

```
procedure TForm1.pbSetFilterCondClick(Sender: TObject);
begin
  Table1.Filter := Edit1.Text;
end;
```

This code only sets the value of the Filter property. It does not enable the filtering process. Changing the filter processing requires the Filtered property to be set to True. You use the check box labeled Filtered to set the Filtered property to be the same value

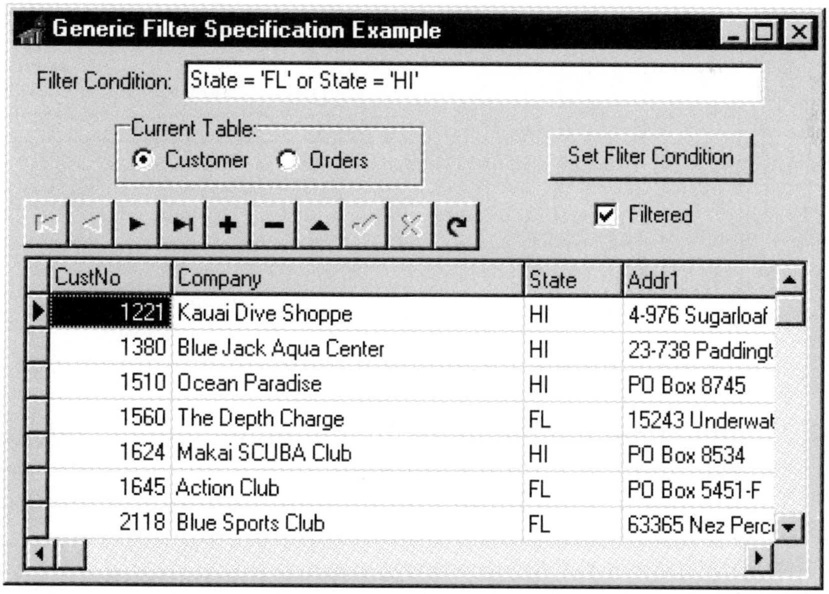

Generic Filter Specification Example

Filter Condition: State = 'FL' or State = 'HI'

Current Table: Customer / Orders

Set Fliter Condition

Filtered

CustNo	Company	State	Addr1
1221	Kauai Dive Shoppe	HI	4-976 Sugarloaf
1380	Blue Jack Aqua Center	HI	23-738 Paddingt
1510	Ocean Paradise	HI	PO Box 8745
1560	The Depth Charge	FL	15243 Underwat
1624	Makai SCUBA Club	HI	PO Box 8534
1645	Action Club	FL	PO Box 5451-F
2118	Blue Sports Club	FL	63365 Nez Perc

Figure 7-5. *Main form for GENFLTR project used to enter any filter for either the Customer or Orders table*

as the Checked property of the CheckBox component. In other words, placing a check in the check box sets the Filtered property to True.

With the table filtered, you can change the Filter Condition value and click the Set Filter Condition button to change the resulting dataset. With small datasets under 5000 records, the performance is acceptable. However, for larger tables, the filter takes longer to be applied.

Using the Find Methods with Filters

Delphi 2 provides four new Find methods that enable you to go the first, last, next, and previous records based on filter criteria, even when the dataset is not currently filtered. The methods are FindFirst, FindLast, FindNext, and FindLast. All four methods return True if a match is found.

When filtering is not enabled, these four Find methods temporarily set the Filtered property to True, and then use either the code in the OnFilterRecord, or the condition in the Filter property, to find the appropriate record. The project FLTERS.DPR, shown in Figure 7-6, demonstrates how to use these filter methods.

The ORDERS.DB table from the DBDEMOS alias is used as the dataset for the FLTERS project. The filtering is applied based on the contents of the Terms field in this table, and controlled through a radio group. The options for this field are to show all

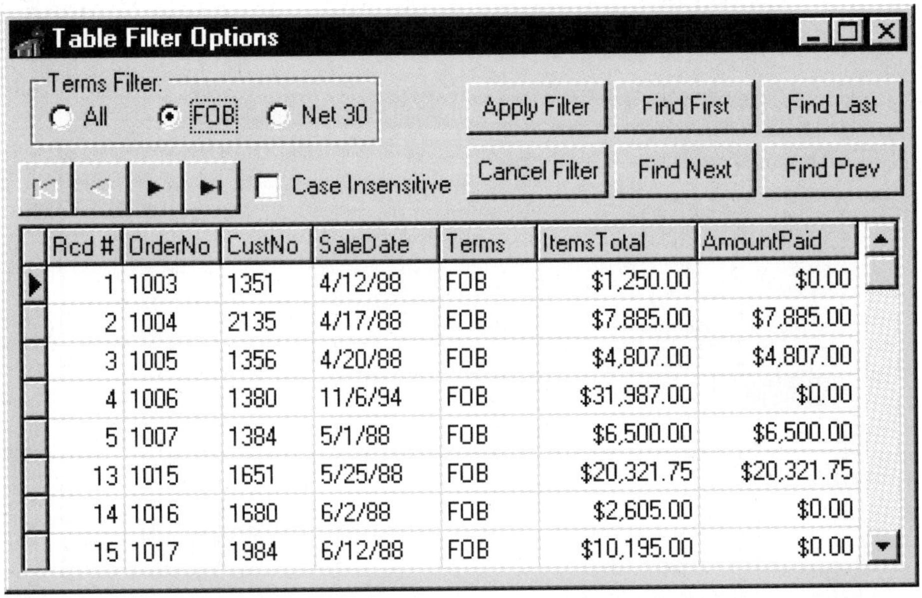

Table Filter Options

Terms Filter: All FOB Net 30

Apply Filter | Find First | Find Last | Cancel Filter | Find Next | Find Prev

Case Insensitive

Rcd #	OrderNo	CustNo	SaleDate	Terms	ItemsTotal	AmountPaid
1	1003	1351	4/12/88	FOB	$1,250.00	$0.00
2	1004	2135	4/17/88	FOB	$7,885.00	$7,885.00
3	1005	1356	4/20/88	FOB	$4,807.00	$4,807.00
4	1006	1380	11/6/94	FOB	$31,987.00	$0.00
5	1007	1384	5/1/88	FOB	$6,500.00	$6,500.00
13	1015	1651	5/25/88	FOB	$20,321.75	$20,321.75
14	1016	1680	6/2/88	FOB	$2,605.00	$0.00
15	1017	1984	6/12/88	FOB	$10,195.00	$0.00

Figure 7-6. *Main form for project FLTERS, which uses the Find methods for filters*

the records, the FOB records only, or the Net 30 records only. The following is the OnClick event handler for the RadioGroup:

```
procedure TForm1.Ra1dioGroup1Click(Sender: TObject);
begin
  with RadioGroup1 do
    begin
      if Items[ItemIndex] = 'All' then
        begin
          pbFindFirst.Enabled := False;
          pbFindLast.Enabled  := False;
          pbFindNext.Enabled  := False;
          pbFindPrev.Enabled  := False;
        end
      else
        begin
          Orders.Filter := 'Terms = ''' + Items[ItemIndex] + '''';
          pbFindFirst.Enabled := True;
          pbFindLast.Enabled  := True;
          pbFindNext.Enabled  := True;
          pbFindPrev.Enabled  := True;
        end;
    end;
end;
```

Four buttons are used for the different Find methods. These buttons are disabled when the All radio button is selected, meaning that no filter condition will be used. When either the FOB or Net 30 radio button is selected, there is a filter condition. The Apply Filter button sets both the Filter and Filtered properties based on the radio button selected. The following is the OnClick event handler for the Apply Filter button:

```
procedure TForm1.pbApplyFilterClick(Sender: TObject);
begin
  if RadioGroup1.ItemIndex = 0 then
    Orders.Filtered := False
  else
    with RadioGroup1 do
    begin
      Orders.Filter := 'Terms = ''' +
        Items[ItemIndex] + '''';
      Orders.Filtered := True;
    end;
end;
```

If the All radio button is selected, the Filtered property is set to False. This removes filtering, and all the records in the Orders table are displayed. If the FOB or Net 30 radio button is selected, the Filter property is set to the appropriate filter, and the Filtered property is set to True. For example, if FOB is selected, the Filter property is set to the following:

```
Terms = 'FOB'.
```

Filtering can be canceled at any time using the Cancel Filter button. Clicking this button sets the Filtered property for the table to False. This removes the filtering processing and all records are displayed. The value for the Filter property remains based on the selected radio button. If either FOB or Net 30 is selected, the Find buttons are still enabled and they can be used to find the first, last, next, or previous record matching the filter condition.

The FilterOptions property has two options: foCaseInsensitive, which ignores case when checking the filter condition, and foNoPartialCompare, which provides exact matching for string comparisons. In the FLTERS project, the Case Insensitive check box is used to toggle between case-sensitive and case-insensitive matches. The code for the check box is as follows:

```
procedure TForm1.CheckBox1Click(Sender: TObject);
begin
  with Orders do
    if CheckBox1.Checked then
      FilterOptions := FilterOptions + [foCaseInsensitive]
    else
      FilterOptions := FilterOptions - [foCaseInsensitive];
end;
```

If Case Insensitive is checked, the foCaseInsensitive option is added; otherwise, it is removed from the FilterOptions property. This only makes a change to the dataset results for the Net 30 filter condition. The Orders table has both the value Net 30 and net 30 in the Terms field. Checking the Case Insensitive check box displays both values.

All of the Find buttons have essentially the same code for their OnClick event handler procedures. The only difference is the particular method used. The following is the code for the FindFirst button:

```
procedure TForm1.pbFindFirstClick(Sender: TObject);
begin
  Orders.FindFirst;
end;
```

The FindFirst method uses the value in the Filter property or the OnFilterRecord event code to locate the first record matching the filter condition. This is independent of the Filtered setting. This means that you can display all the records in the dataset but set a filter condition and move through the data using the FindFirst, FindLast, FindNext, and FindPrior methods.

Enhanced Fields Editor

The Fields Editor is a tool that you use to instantiate TField components for the fields of a DataSet component. The Fields Editor in Delphi 2 is similar to that found in Delphi 1.0. However, it sports a slimmed-down interface, as well as a number of powerful new features. The most important new features are the ability to create calculated fields and lookup fields, as well as the ability to place fields on a form using the drag-and-drop technique. To access the Fields Editor, either double-click a DataSet component, or right-click the DataSet component and select Fields Editor from the displayed speed menu.

You use a speed menu to control many of the features of the new Fields Editor. For example, to instantiate one or more fields for a dataset, you right-click the Fields Editor and select Add. Figure 7-7 shows the Fields Editor speed menu displayed. The Fields Editor, empty since no fields have been instantiated, can be seen in the background.

To instantiate one or more of the existing fields from the current dataset, you select Add fields from this speed menu. To create a new calculated field or a lookup field, select New field. Each of these selections results in the display of an appropriate dialog box that you use to select or define the fields you are creating. Once you accept this

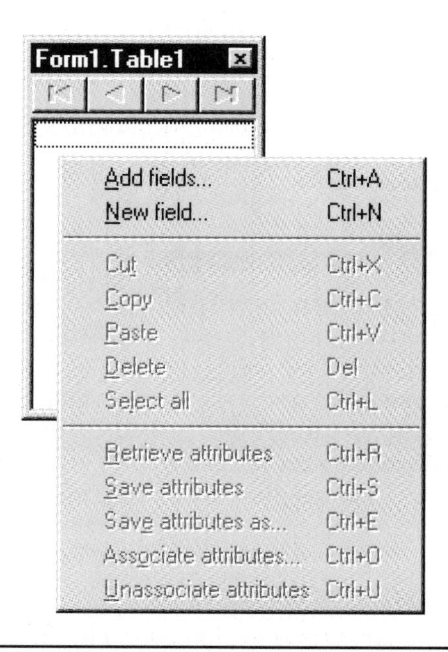

Figure 7-7. *Many of the features of the Fields Editor are accessed using its speed menu*

dialog box, control returns to the Fields Editor, and the created fields appear listed in the Fields Editor list box (just as they did in Delphi 1.0).

Placing Fields from the Fields Editor

One of the major new features of the Fields Editor is that it permits you to place fields onto a form using drag-and-drop. For example, if you want to place the CustNo field of the CUSTOMER.DB table onto a form, simply select the CustNo field in the Fields Editor, and then drag it onto the form at the desired location and release.

This drag-and-drop technique can greatly increase your productivity when designing forms. You no longer have to place a DBEdit and Label separately for each field, and then assign the appropriate properties to make them active. While you could use the Form Expert, called the Database Form Expert in Delphi 1.0, to avoid this tedious task, the drag-and-drop technique gives you greater flexibility. For example, in addition to being able to drag-and-drop onto a form, you can also drop your new fields into a DBCtrlGrid.

The Field Editor also allows you to drag-and-drop multiple fields simultaneously. To select more than one field, hold down the SHIFT key (to select sequential fields), or the CTRL key (to select any combination of fields) while you select fields in the Fields Editor. The selected fields will be highlighted. You can then drag them as a group by grabbing any part of the highlighted selection. When you perform the drop, all of the selected fields are placed on the form.

Creating Lookup Fields

In addition to instantiating the fields of a dataset, the Fields Editor permits you to define two types of new fields: calculated and lookup. Delphi 1.0 also permits you to define a calculated field. The only difference is that in Delphi 2 you click the Calculated button in the New Field dialog box. The lookup field is new to Delphi 2. This feature is described in the "Using the DBLookup Components" section in this chapter.

TTable Specific Enhancements

In addition to the new TDataSet enhancements, there are other new features for Table components. The new methods that apply to only the TTable class are listed in Table 7-11. In addition to these methods, the TTable class defines a new property named IndexFiles. It is a TStrings type and lists the filenames containing non-production indexes for dBASE tables. The Add, Insert, Delete, and Clear methods of TStrings can be used on the property. The indexes are opened as they are added. You can make an index active by setting the IndexName property to the name of the index. Indexes are closed automatically as they are cleared or deleted from the list.

TQuery Specific Enhancements

The TQuery class has additional enhancements beyond the new features covered for TDataSets. Table 7-12 lists the new properties for Query components.

Method	Syntax	Description
CloseIndexFile	`procedure CloseIndexFile(const IndexFileName: string);`	Closes the specified dBASE non-production index file. Once closed, non-production index files are not maintained.
LockTable	`procedure LockTable(LockType: TLockType);`	Locks Paradox and dBASE tables to prevent other users from being able to place other locks on the tables. The LockType parameter specifies the type of lock. You can apply more than one lock to a single table. The types of locks are ltReadLock and ltWriteLock. The ltReadLock prevents write locks from being placed on the table by other processes. The ltWriteLock prevents any other type of lock from being placed on the table.
OpenIndexFile	`procedure OpenIndexFile(const IndexName: string);`	Opens the specified dBASE non-production index file.
RenameTable	`procedure RenameTable(const NewTableName: string);`	Renames Paradox and dBASE tables to a different name.
UnlockTable	`procedure UnlockTable(LockType: TLockType);`	Removes a lock that was applied with the LockTable method.

Table 7-11. *New TTable Specific Methods*

TDatabase Enhancements

The TDatabase class includes three new properties: SessionName (a published property), and TraceFlags and InTransaction (public properties). The SessionName identifies a Session component you want the database to use. The initial value is Default. If you change this value, it must match the name of an existing Session component. The TraceFlags property controls which events are tracked in the SQL Monitor. Its data type is TTraceFlags, the same as the TraceFlags property for TSession.

Property	Type and Description
Constrained	Boolean value that, when set to True, prevents updates and insertions that don't comply with the WHERE clause of the SELECT statement that produced the result set.
ParamCheck	Boolean value that specifies whether parameters are to be rechecked when changing the query.

Table 7-12. *New TQuery Specific Properties*

The initial values for the Database component are the values from its session. The third property, InTransaction, is public and read-only. It is a Boolean type that indicates whether a transaction is active or not. If it is True, a StartTransaction has been issued for the database without a corresponding Commit or Rollback.

One new method is directly available for Database components. It is ApplyUpdates and applies to cached updates. It applies and commits all pending cached updates for all DataSets that use the Database component, as defined in the DataSet open array property of the Database. Specifically, ApplyUpdates calls the ApplyUpdates and CommitUpdates methods for each DataSet using the Database component. A transaction is started automatically prior to this operation, if one is not active, to ensure that either all cached updates are applied or that none are.

New Data Control Components

There are three new Data Control components. The DBLookupListBox and DBLookupComboBox in Delphi 2 replace the DBLookupList and DBLookupCombo components in Delphi 1.0. (The Delphi 1.0 components still exist in Delphi 2, but appear on the Win 3.1 page on the component palette instead of the Data Controls page.) The third new component is DBCtrlGrid, which provides for flexible, multi-record layouts.

Using the DBLookup Components

The DBLookupListBox and DBLookupComboBox components have similar properties and methods for creating table lookups (displaying data from another dataset to be used as possible valid entries for a field). The major difference between the two methods is the appearance of the data—in a list or in a combo box. (A combo box is a field that displays a button that, when pressed, displays a drop-down menu of values from which to select.) The combo box has additional features when used with a DBGrid. For this reason, the DBLookupComboBox is described in detail here. (This section also demonstrates use of the Fields Editor described earlier in this chapter.)

The project LOOKUPS.DPR contains two examples of how to use a lookup field: one from within a DBGrid and the other without a DBGrid. The project's main form contains two Table components, one for the Orders table and one for the Customer table. Both tables are from the DBDEMOS alias. A single DataSource is required for the Orders table.

Once the two Table components are defined, the next step is to use the Fields Editor for the Orders table. Only the following fields are instantiated for this project: OrderNo, CustNo, SaleDate, ItemsTotal, and AmountPaid. The lookup field is created using the New field menu selection from the speed menu in the Fields Editor. This displays the New Field dialog box. Figure 7-8 shows the dialog box being used to define a lookup field.

All of the information necessary to define a lookup field is contained in this dialog box. In Name, CustName is entered to indicate the name used for the lookup field. The name of the TField component that will be created is entered for you in the Component box as you enter the Name value.

In the Type field you enter the data type of the lookup field. In this case, String is selected, since Company field, which holds the customer's company name, is a string field. The size is set to 30, which matches the size of the Company field in the CUSTOMER.DB table.

TIP: *The default size of the field is 20. You will want to set the Size property to the appropriate size so that it is large enough to display all of the field.*

Figure 7-8. *Use the New Field dialog box to create Calculated and Lookup fields*

The Lookup Definition group is used to define the relationship between the current table (in this case, ORDERS.DB) and the lookup table (CUSTOMER.DB). The options in this group are enabled by selecting Lookup in the Field type radio buttons. The two tables used in the current example are linked on CustNo. This value is selected for the Key Fields and the Lookup Keys. Before you can set the Lookup Keys value, the lookup table (CUSTOMER.DB) must be selected in the Dataset field. Finally, set the Result field to the name of the field to display in the lookup field. This field name is Company in this example. When you are done defining the lookup field. click the OK button to return to the Fields Editor dialog box. The newly defined lookup field will now appear in the Fields Editor.

NOTE: While the Key Fields drop-down menu only includes single fields, it is possible to define a lookup based on more than one field. To do so you must manually enter the fields that associate the two datasets. These field names must be separated with semicolons. If you have entered two or more fields into Key Fields, you must also enter the corresponding fields in Lookup Keys.

When you run the form, all instantiated fields, including the lookup field, are displayed in the DBGrid. As you scroll through the data, you can see the associated Company for each record in the Orders table, even though this information is not part of this table. You can even change which customer an order is for using the lookup field. To do this, move to the CustName column and double-click it to display a drop-down menu button. When you click this button, the list of all company names from the Customer table is displayed. Select a new company name, and press ENTER. The CustNo value for the current record is then updated to the CustNo value for the selected company.

TIP: If you want to use a lookup field to display associated values from another table without permitting the user to modify the record based on the lookup field, set the instantiated lookup field's ReadOnly property to True.

Dragging Lookup Fields

You can use the Fields Editor to place lookup fields on a form. When you drag a lookup field from the Fields Editor, Delphi does not just place a DBEdit and Label—it places a DBLookupComboBox and a Label. The contents of the tab page shown in Figure 7-9 were created by dragging all the fields from the Fields Editor onto the form, with the exception of the SaleDate field.

A DBLookupComboBox permits the user to drop down a menu of all possible lookup values in the lookup table. Unlike the lookup in a DBGrid, when you click on the DBLookupComboBox, the list automatically drops down and displays company names.

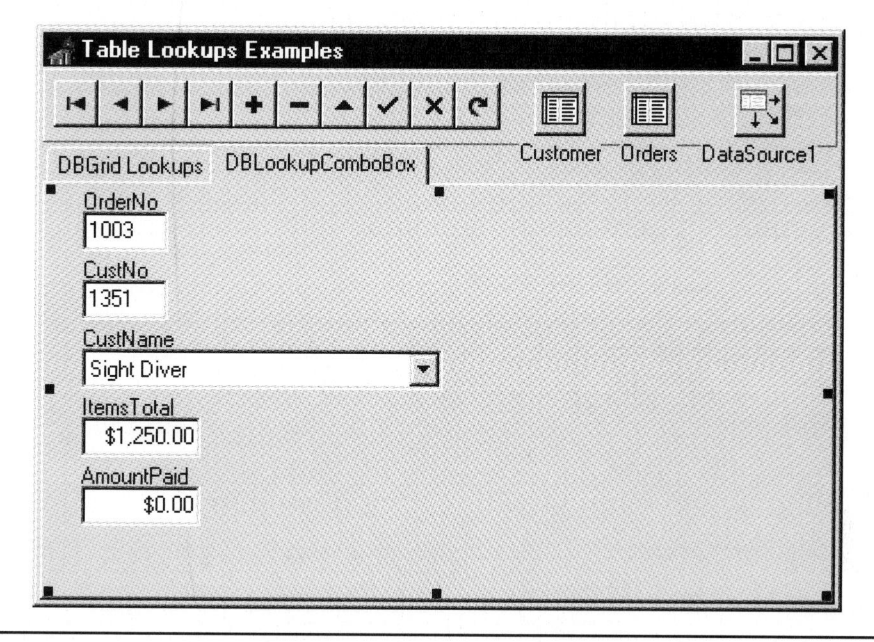

Figure 7-9. *Dropping a lookup field onto a form produces a DBLookupComboBox*

Using the TDBCtrlGrid Component

The DBCtrlGrid is the last option on the Data Control component palette. It enables multiple records to be displayed in a single component—but without restricting the display to a single row per record. Rather, each record is displayed in a single panel. Multiple rows of data-aware components can be placed in each panel.

The CTRLGRD.DPR project demonstrates three techniques for using the DBCtrlGrid option. Figure 7-10 shows the main form for the project. A TabControl is used to place each of the three examples on a different page. Figure 7-10 shows the basic use of the DBCtrlGrid on the first tab page. The RowCount property controls the number of rows displayed in the DBCtrlGrid, which is three by default. Likewise, the ColCount property controls the number of columns, which is one by default.

The height of each panel in the grid is set in one of two ways. Since the number of rows and the overall height of the grid specify each panel's height, you increase the height of the grid or reduce the number of rows in the grid to produce a corresponding change in the size of each panel. You also can change the size of each panel by changing the PanelHeight and PanelWidth properties. Increasing these two properties changes the size of the overall grid based on the number of rows.

Data-aware components are placed only in the top-most panel of the grid. This panel contains the layout of how each row in the grid is going to look at runtime. In

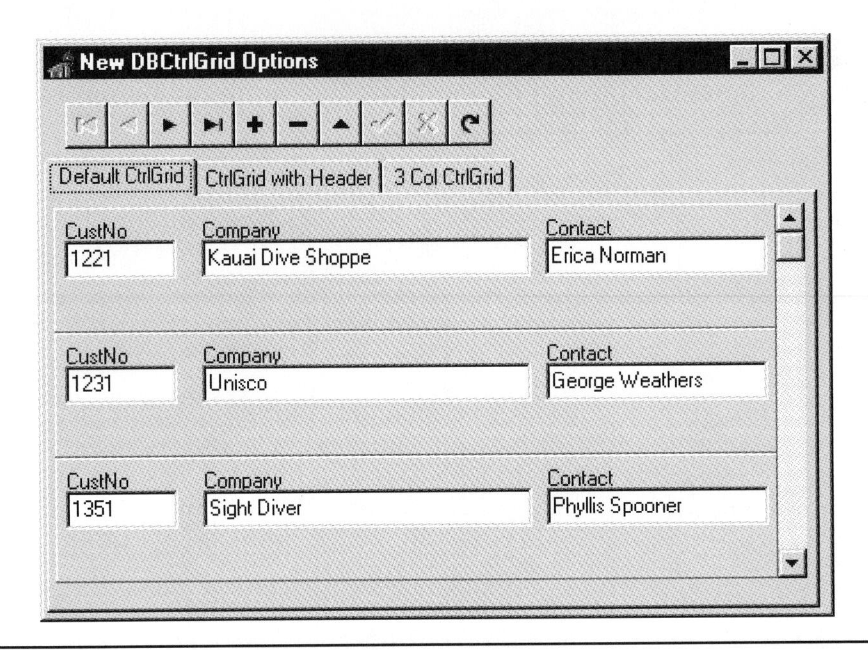

Figure 7-10. *Main form for the DTRLGRD project showing different techniques for using the DBCtrlGrid option*

the Default CtrlGrid tab page, each field was placed using the Fields Editor. The default automatically places both a label and DBEdit component for each field placed. When the form is run, the titles for each field are replicated in each row of the grid.

Using a HeaderControl for Column Headings

You can remove the duplicate label display using the HeaderControl object from the Win95 page of the component palette. The CtrlGrid with Header tab page shows how the display changes using this component. Figure 7-11 shows how this page looks at runtime.

The HeaderControl's Align property is set to alTop, causing it to be automatically aligned to the top of the TabSheet for the second tab page. The Sections property of the HeaderControl is used to define the text that appears in each portion of the header. Double-clicking on this property in the Object Inspector displays the HeaderControl Sections Editor dialog box. Use this dialog box to define the number of sections to be displayed and the attributes of each section. Attributes include the text, font, width, and justification for each section element.

Displaying Multiple Columns in a DBCtrlGrid

The orientation of the data can be changed from rows to columns by setting the ColCount to a value greater than 1 and the RowCount to 1. Figure 7-12 shows the third tab page in the CTRLGRD project, which demonstrates this technique. Not all of the data-aware components can be placed in the DBCtrlGrid. Those that can be placed into

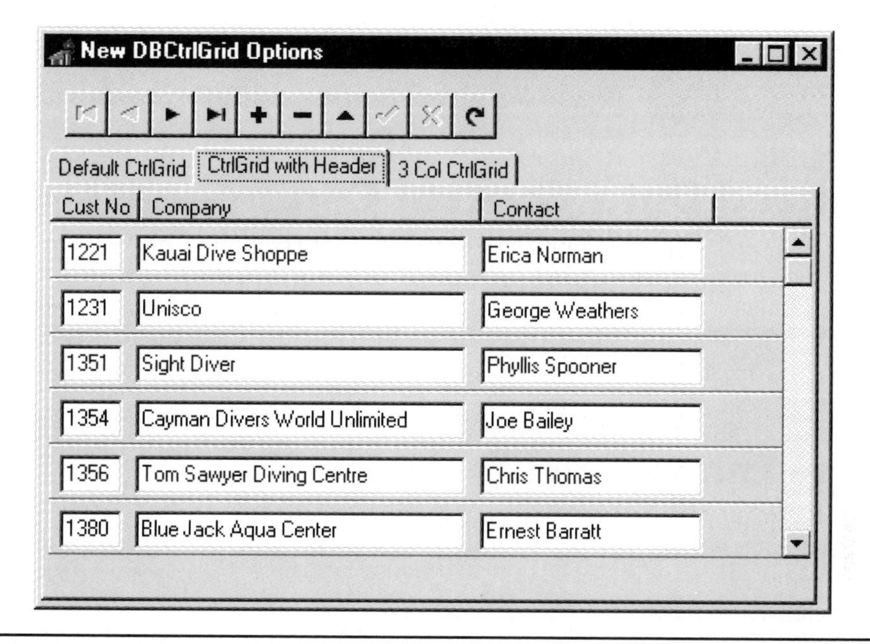

Figure 7-11. *Using a HeaderControl object to provide column headings for the DBEdit components in a DBCtrlGrid*

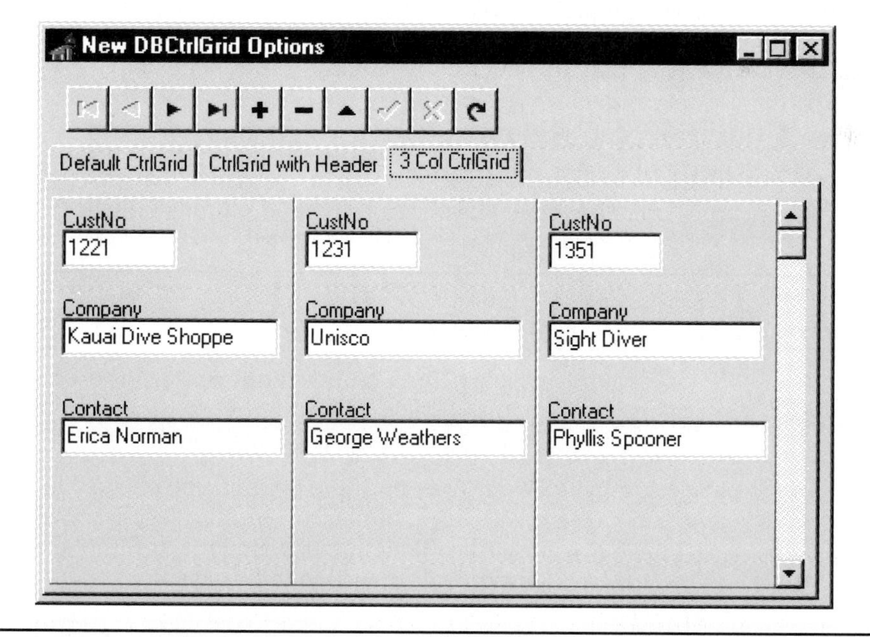

Figure 7-12. *Using multiple columns and a single row in the DBCtrlGrid*

the grid are DBText, DBEdit, DBComboBox, DBCheckBox, and the DBLookupComboBox. The remaining data-aware components cannot be used, primarily for performance reasons.

Enhanced Data Control Components

All of the Data Control components have one addition in common—the OnStartDrag event. OnStartDrag is invoked when a user begins a drag operation on the object. Two other enhancements to the Data Control components are covered in the next two sections. First the new QuickDraw property for the DBImage component is described. Then the following section describes the added properties, events, and methods to the DBGrid component.

TDBImage Enhancements

The QuickDraw property for the DBImage component is a Boolean value. This property indicates if the image is displayed using its own palette. If QuickDraw is False, the image's own palette is used. This provides the best possible image quality, but at the expense of additional processing time. If QuickDraw is True, the current palette is used. This is faster but results in poorer picture quality, especially with 256-color images on a 256-color video driver.

TDBGrid Enhancements

The DBGrid in Delphi 2 has substantial changes that are a welcome addition for database developers. Table 7-13 lists the properties, Table 7-14 lists the events, and Table 7-15 lists the methods that are new for the DBGrid component.

Using the Columns Editor

The Columns Editor shown in Figure 7-13 allows you to customize the appearance of the grid at design time. There are three ways to display the Columns Editor:

Property	Description
Columns	Displays the Columns Editor, which is used to manipulate the attributes of one or more columns, or to add or delete columns from the grid.
Options | dgMultiSelect	When True, multiple rows can be selected in the grid. This is similar to a multi-select list box described later in the "Using the dgMultiSelect Option Value" section in this chapter.

Table 7-13. *DBGrid Properties*

Event	Description
OnColumnMoved	Occurs when the user moves a column using the mouse. The user can move a column only if the Options property set includes the value goColMoving.
OnDrawColumnCell	Occurs whenever the contents of a data grid cell need to be repainted.
OnEditButonClick	Occurs whenever the user presses the ellipsis button in a grid column. Use the Columns Editor to enable an ellipsis (. . .) button for a column.

Table 7-14. *New Events for the DBGrid Component*

double-click on the grid's Columns property in the Object Inspector, select Columns Editor from the grid's speed menu, or double-click on the grid itself.

The first time the Columns Editor is invoked for a grid, the Columns list box is empty. (This is true whether or not the Fields Editor has been used to instantiate fields.) The buttons located below the list box are used to create a single column entry, delete an entry in the list box, create a column for all fields in the dataset, or delete all the dataset fields. The Add All Fields button is disabled if the grid's DataSource property is not assigned, or if the dataset assigned to the grid is not open.

The properties for each defined column can be set using the two tab pages on the right side of the dialog box. The properties on the two tab pages are column specific,

Method	Syntax	Description
DefaultDrawColumnCell	`procedure DefaultDrawColumn-Cell(const Rect: TRect; DataCol: Integer; Column: TColumn; State: TGridDrawState);`	Provides default drawing of the data in a cell. This method is called from the code in the new OnDrawColumnCell event handler when the default behavior is sufficient.
ValidFieldIndex	`function ValidFieldIndex-(FieldIndex: Integer): Boolean;`	Returns True if FieldIndex is a valid index for a field in the dataset pointed to by the grid's DataSource.

Table 7-15. *New Methods for the DBGrid Component*

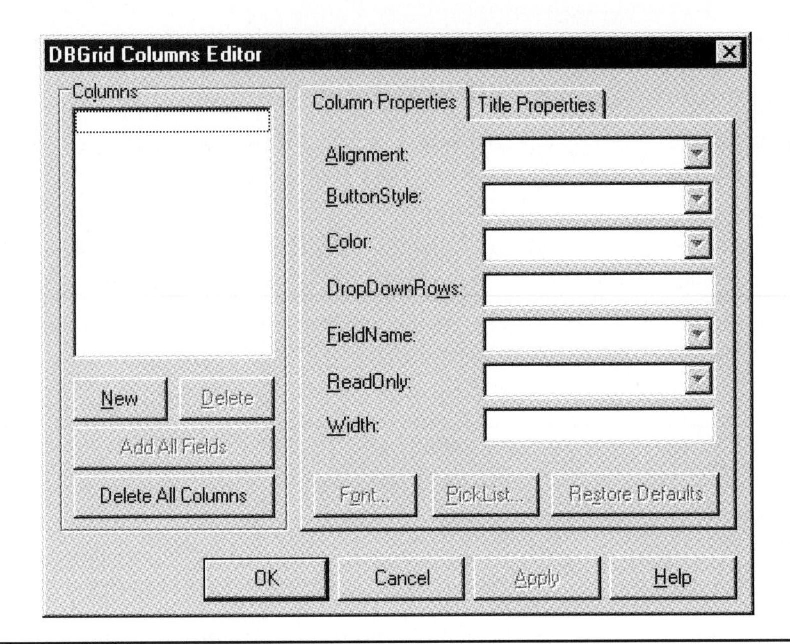

Figure 7-13. *Columns Editor for the DBGrid*

applying to the currently selected column in the Columns list. The first tab, Column Properties, contains options to set the appearance of the selected column in the grid. The second page, Title Properties, allows you to set the alignment, caption, and font for the columns title. Table 7-16 lists the properties on the Column Properties page, and Table 7-17 lists the properties on the Title page.

Using the dgMultiSelect Option Value

The new dgMultiSelect value of the Option property supports two ways to select multiple rows in a DBGrid: SHIFT + arrow keys or CTRL + mouse click. Both techniques add to the selected multiple rows, which appear highlighted in the DBGrid. The selected rows are maintained in the SelectedRows property, which is a TBookmarkList object. A TBookmarkList is a list of bookmark strings, and each string is a TBookmarkStr object for a selected row.

Table 7-18 lists the properties and Table 7-19 lists the methods of the DBGrid's SelectedRows property.

Using the dgMultiSelect value of the Option property of a DBGrid gives you the option of displaying data in a grid along with the benefits of a multiple-selection list box. The project MLTIRCD.DPR demonstrates how to use this new DBGrid feature. Figure 7-14 shows the main form after selecting multiple records and listing the Company for each selected record in a list box.

Property	Description
Alignment	Alignment for data in the column. Options are left, right, or center justification.
ButtonStyle	Use when the field associated with the column is defined as a lookup field. Options are cbsAuto (the default), which displays a drop-down list; cbsEllipsis, which displays an ellipsis button; and dbsNone, which uses the normal edit controls for a column.
Color	The background color for the column cells.
DropDownRows	Number of items displayed in the drop-down list. The default is seven.
FieldName	Name of the field associated with the column.
ReadOnly	Set to True if the column data cannot be edited, or False if the data can be changed.
Width	Width of the column.
Font button	Sets the font type, size, and color for the data in the column.
PickList button	Sets the list values in the drop-down list.

Table 7-16. *Properties for the Column Properties Page of the Columns Editor*

The first requirement to use the multiple-row selection is to set the dgMultiSelect Option property to True. This setting enables the keystroke and mouse click

Property	Description
Alignment	Alignment for caption text of the column. Options are left, right, or center justification.
Caption	Text for the column title.
Color	Background color for the column title.
Font button	Sets the font type, size, and color for the column title text.

Table 7-17. *Properties for the Title Properties Page of the Columns Editor*

Property	Description
Count	Integer value that returns the number of selected rows.
CurrentRowSelected	Boolean value that returns True if the current row is selected, and returns False otherwise.

Table 7-18. *Properties for the SelectedRows DBGrid Property*

combinations to select multiple rows. The MLTIRCD project uses the CUSTOMER.DB table from the DBDEMOS alias. The form contains a ListBox object that displays the names of the selected rows when the List Selected button is clicked. The remaining buttons show how to use many of the methods and properties of the SelectedRows TBookMarkList object.

Method	Syntax	Description
Refresh	`function Refresh: Boolean`	Loops through the bookmark list and determines if the record for each bookmark is still in the dataset. If it is not, the bookmark is removed from the list. Refresh returns True if a bookmark is removed from the list. False is returned if no bookmarks are removed.
Clear	`procedure Clear;`	Removes all bookmarks from the list.
Delete	`procedure Delete;`	Removes all selected rows from the dataset.
Find	`function Find(const Item: TBookmarkStr; var Index: Integer) : Boolean`	Finds a specific bookmark and sets the Index var to the index in the bookmark list.
IndexOf	`function IndexOf(const Item: TBookmarkStr) : Integer`	Returns the index of the Item in the bookmark list.

Table 7-19. *Methods for the SelectedRows DBGrid Property*

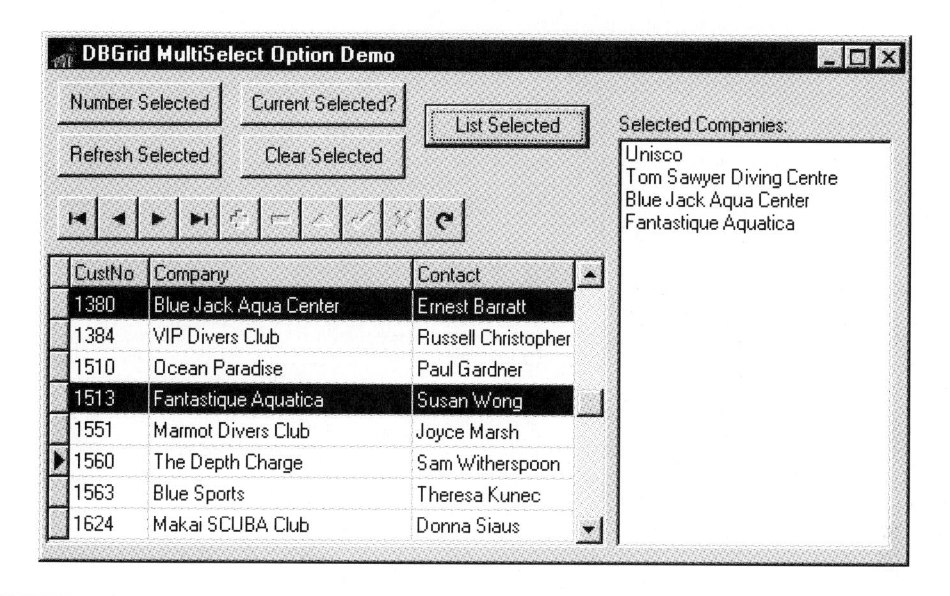

Figure 7-14. *Project MLTIRCD uses the MultiSelect option of the DBGrid component to select multiple records*

The Count property is used to count the number of rows selected. The Number Selected button displays the value of this property in a dialog box. The following is the code for the OnClick event handler of the Number Selected button:

```
procedure TForm1.pbNumberSelectedClick(Sender: TObject);
begin
  ShowMessage(IntToStr(DBGrid1.SelectedRows.Count));
end;
```

To determine if the current row in the grid is one of the selected rows, the CurrentRowSelected property is checked. The Current Selected? button contains the following code in its OnClick event handler:

```
procedure TForm1.pbCurSelectedClick(Sender: TObject);
begin
  if DBGrid1.SelectedRows.CurrentRowSelected = True then
    MessageDlg('Current row is selected',mtInformation,[mbOK],0)
  else
    MessageDlg('Current row is NOT selected',mtInformation,[mbOK],0);
end;
```

In a multi-user environment, it is possible for the currently selected records to be removed from the dataset by another user. Therefore, before you make use of the selected records, you should verify that the records still exist. This can be accomplished using the Refresh method. The Refresh Selected button demonstrates this method call in the following OnClick event handler:

```
procedure TForm1.pbRefreshSelectedClick(Sender: TObject);
begin
  if DBGrid1.SelectedRows.Refresh = True then
    MessageDlg('One or more bookmarks deleted',mtInformation,[mbOK],0)
  else
    MessageDlg('No bookmards were deleted',mtInformation,[mbOK],0);

end;
```

Refresh cycles through each bookmark in the list and verifies that the record still exists for the bookmark. If the record is not found, the bookmark is removed from the list. Refresh returns True if one or more bookmarks are deleted. False is returned if all the records in the list still exist.

To removes all records from the selected list, the Clear method is called. This method cancels the currently selected records by removing the entries in the SelectedRows list. Clear also repaints the dialog box to remove the highlighting in each row that indicated selected rows. The following is the OnClick event handler for the Clear Selected button. This code also removes any items displayed in the Selected Companies list box:

```
procedure TForm1.pbClearSelectedClick(Sender: TObject);
begin
  DBGrid1.SelectedRows.Clear;
  ListBox1.Items.Clear;
end;
```

Once the rows are highlighted, what you do with the selected records depends on your application requirements. In the MLTIRCD project, the List Selected button is used to cycle through all the selected records and place their names into the ListBox object on the right side of the form. The following is the OnClick event handler for the List Selected button:

```
procedure TForm1.pbListSelectedClick(Sender: TObject);
var
 CurRow: TBookmarkStr;
 I: Integer;
begin
  if DBGrid1.SelectedRows.Count > 0 then
    with DBGrid1.DataSource.DataSet do
    begin
      DisableControls;
      try
```

```
        ListBox1.Items.Clear;
        CurRow := Bookmark;
        for I := 0 to DBGrid1.SelectedRows.Count - 1 do
        begin
          Bookmark := DBGrid1.SelectedRows.Items[I];
          ListBox1.Items.Add(FieldByName('Company').AsString);
        end;
        BookMark := CurRow;
        finally
          EnableControls;
        end;
    end
  else
    MessageDlg('No rows are currently selected',mtError,[mbOK],0);
end;
```

This code first verifies that at least one record is selected in the DBGrid. If the Count property is greater than zero, one or more records are selected. The grid's DataSet component is used to get the values for the Company field. Using the DBGrid.DataSource.DataSet value, the code cycles through each entry in the Items array. Items contains an entry for each record selected as a bookmark.

Before getting to the first selected record, the current position in the dataset is saved. Using the new Bookmark property of a dataset, the variable CurRow, which is defined the same as the dataset's Bookmark property (TBookmarkStr), saves the current record. The controls for the dataset are also disabled so that the form's display does not change as the code moves through the dataset. Also, the current contents of the list box are cleared before entering the currently selected companies.

A for loop is used to cycle through the Items array. The Bookmark property for the dataset is set to each entry in Items. The value of the Company field is added to the list box until all records are read. Finally, the record that was current before processing the selected rows is reset along with the controls for the dataset.

The same technique described here can be used to copy records, move the selected records from one dataset to another, or to perform any other requirement where multiple row selection in a DBGrid improves the user interface.

The Object Repository for Database Developers

Delphi 2 provides the Object Repository as a means for sharing and reusing forms and projects. The Object Repository replaces the Gallery in Delphi 1.0. The Repository itself is a text file that contains references to forms, projects, and experts. Details of the file format are available in the online help. The Object Repository stores a variety of objects, forms, dialog boxes, DLLs, entire projects, and a new object type called *data modules*. This object type is described in the next section.

Data Module Objects

A data module is an object used as a central location to define data access and business rules for an application. Data Access components are placed into the data module and the unit is then used by other units accessing the defined datasets. The data module can also be used to place other standard non-visual components, dialogs boxes, and timers used by multiple units in a project.

Common data access is provided by placing components from the Data Access component palette page on a data module. Then, the properties and event handlers for these objects can be made available to one or more forms in the project.

Data modules are not visible at runtime. They act like a hidden form in that the objects in the unit are available, but end users never see them. Other units have access to the objects in the data module if the data module is included in a uses clause in each form's unit.

Creating a New Data Module

You create a new data module by selecting File | New Data Module. This creates a new object in the project of type TDataModule and opens an empty data module container, which is a blank window titled DataModule2, for example.

Placing components into the data module is the same as placing them on a form. You select a component from the component palette, and then click in the data module. If your data module is the active window, you can double-click a component in the component palette to automatically place it on the data module. Within the data module, the component names are always displayed below the component, independent of the setting of the Show component captions check box on the Preferences page of the Environment Options dialog box.

Figure 7-15 shows a completed data module used in the DATAMDL.DPR project. Three tables from the DBDEMOS alias are used in this project: CUSTOMER.DB, ORDERS.DB, and ITEMS.DB. The Items table is linked to Orders based on the OrderNo field. The Customer table is used as a lookup for CustNo in Orders.

Once the data module contains the DataSource and DataSet components, the data sources and datasets can be linked, and code can be assigned to any of their event handlers. This is demonstrated in the DATAMDL project, in which inserts and deletes are prevented in the Customer table. This is done by executing the Abort procedure in the BeforeInsert and BeforeDelete event handlers for the Customer Table component.

The main form for the DATAMDL project contains two grids. The DBGrid at the top of the form uses the Orders table. Data from the Items table is displayed in the lower grid. After placing the two DBGrid components on the form, set the DataSource properties of the DBGrids to the corresponding DataSource components on the data module. However, it you try this on a new form and data module that you have created, the drop-down menu for the DBGrid's DataSource properties is likely to be empty, since there are no DataSources in the current form. Before you can link the DBGrids to the DataSources, you have to tell the form on which the DBGrids appear where to find the DataSources.

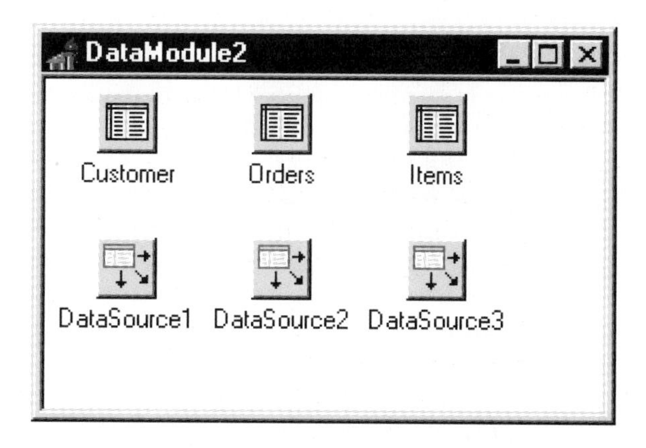

Figure 7-15. *Data module object used in the DATAMDL project*

To give a form access to the components placed on a data module, add the unit for the data module to one of the form's uses clauses. Instead of adding this reference manually, you can select File | Use Unit from the main menu to display the Use Unit dialog box. This dialog box contains a list of units in the project that are not currently in a uses clause for the form's unit. Select the unit associated with the data module you want to use. After doing this, the DataSource property drop-down menu for the DBGrids will include the names of any data sources appearing on the data module. In fact, any property that displays a drop-down menu of components in the Object Inspector will include the added data module's components in its drop-down menu, if the components are of the appropriate type.

Events for the TDataModule Object

There are two events for the data module object: OnCreate and OnDestroy. The purpose of these events is the same for the corresponding form events. For example, an OnCreate event handler is called when the data module is first created. Likewise, OnDestroy is called when the application is closed or when the data module is about to be destroyed. In the DATAMDL project, the OnCreate event of the data module object is used to ensure that three tables are opened. The following is the code for the OnCreate event:

```
procedure TDataModule2.DataModule2Create(Sender: TObject);
begin
  Customer.Open;
  Orders.Open;
  Items.Open;
end;
```

Using the Fields Editor in the Data Module

In the DATAMDL project, there is a separate form to look at the complete information for the Company of the current Orders record. The fields for this form were created using the new drag-and-drop feature in the Fields Editor.

After using the Fields Editor to instantiate fields for a dataset located in a data module, you can drag those fields and drop them onto any form in your project. If you do this to a form that is not already using the data module's unit, a dialog box is displayed that asks you if you want to add this data module's unit to the form's uses clause. If you select the Yes button from this dialog box, the data module's unit name is added to the form's uses clause, and then the fields are dropped onto that form.

NOTE: If there is no DataSource component defined for the dataset in the data module from which you are dropping fields, Delphi automatically adds a DataSource component to the form on which you are dropping the fields. Delphi also links the DBEdit objects to this new DataSource. If a DataSource does exist on the data module, the DataSource property of the new DBEdits points to that existing DataSource.

Saving and Using Data Modules in the Object Repository

Data modules can be placed in the Object Repository for later use in any project, by any user who has access to the same Object Repository. You can use the same data module in multiple applications and, when any modification is necessary, those changes made to the data module are available for all projects that inherited the data module from the Object Repository (changes are apparent only after each project is recompiled). Using this new feature will save you time and reduce maintenance if you incorporate the use of an Object Repository into your application development.

Adding a New Data Module

A data module can be added to the existing set of data modules in the Object Repository once you have saved the data module's unit. After saving the unit, right-click the data module to display its speed menu. Select Add to Repository from this menu to display the Add To Repository dialog box shown in Figure 7-16. Use this dialog box to insert any new object from the current project into the Object Repository. The Forms list contains the list of forms and data modules that have been opened in the Delphi IDE (Integrated Development Environment) for the current project. If a form or data module is not open, it does not appear in the list. From this list you select the form or data module to place into the Object Repository.

Four additional fields are available to enter information for the new object. Title is used to specify the form's title. Description contains additional details about the object you are adding. This description is displayed when the New Items dialog box is opened and the View Details item is selected from the speed menu. The Page drop-down menu allows you to specify the page of the Repository on which you want to place the form or data module. The last field, Author, is where you can enter the

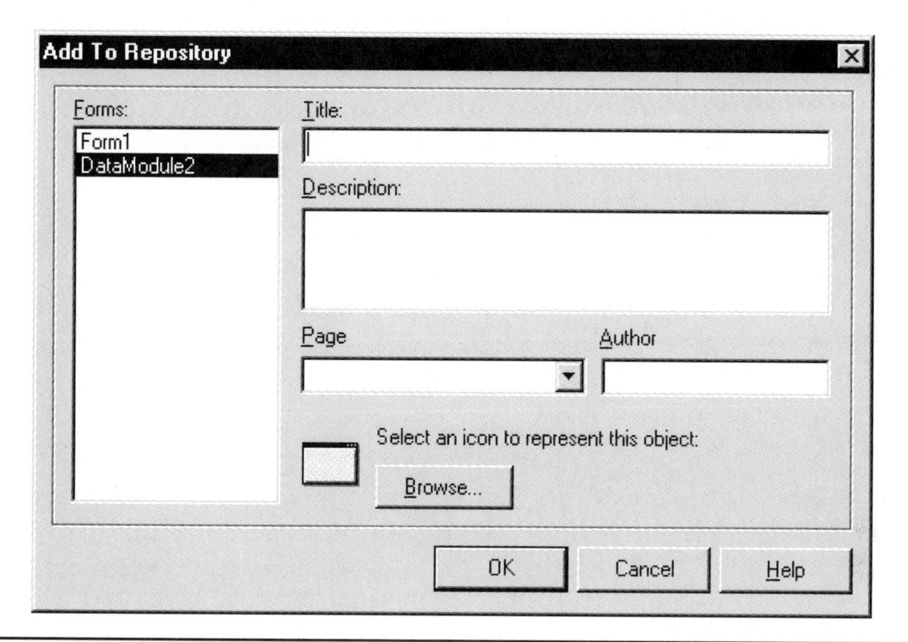

Figure 7-16. *Add To Repository dialog box used to add a data module to the Object Repository*

name or identifier to indicate who created the object. You can also assign an icon for the form or data module, which is used in both the New Items and Repository dialog boxes. If you want to define an icon different from the default icon, click the Browse button to open the Select Icon dialog box.

NOTE: The bitmap size is limited to 60 x 40 pixels. If you select a bitmap with larger dimensions it will be cropped to the maximum size.

Using a Data Module in the Object Repository

To use an existing data module in an application, select New from the File menu. This displays the New Items dialog box. Click on the Data Modules page to list the data modules in the Object Repository. Figure 7-17 shows the Data Module page after adding the data module from the DATAMDL project. This data module was saved using the name Orders & Items.

The three radio buttons at the bottom of the Object Repository dialog box specify how you intend to use the data module. The Copy button indicates you want to make a copy of the data module. The copy, which is an exact duplicate of the data module at the time you copy it, does not have any additional relationship with the Object Repository. This means that any subsequent changes to the Object Repository data module will have no effect on the copy. The Inherit button is used if you want to

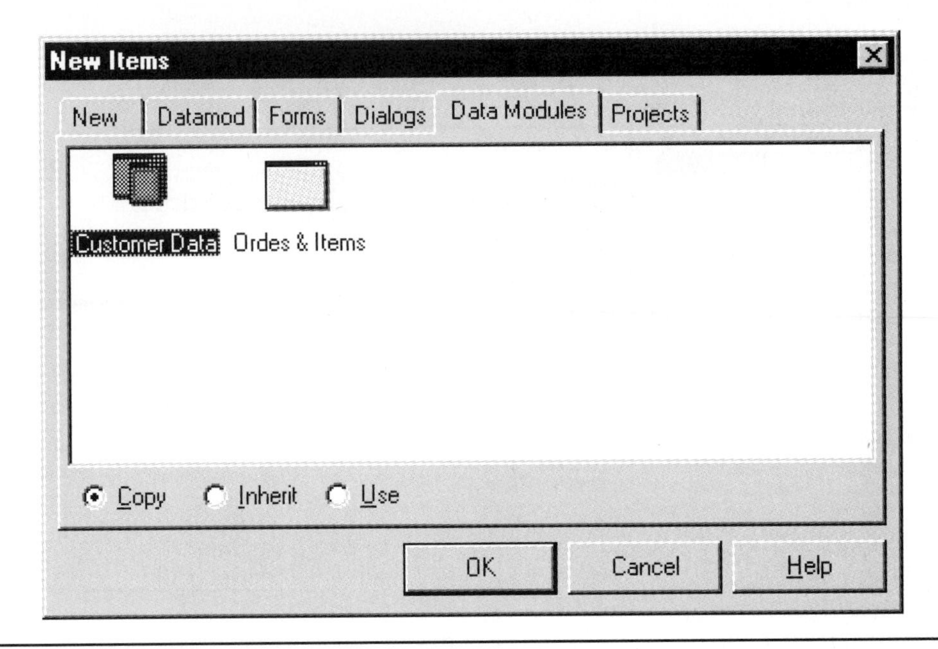

Figure 7-17. *Data Module page in the New Items dialog box after adding the data module from the DATAMDL project*

maintain a relationship with the data module you select. This ensures that any changes to the data module in the Object Repository are automatically incorporated into your inherited data model when your project is recompiled. The last option, Use, puts a copy of the data module into your application. You can make changes to the data module, which has the effect of updating the data module in the Object Repository.

Once you have selected the type of use for the data module, click the OK button to add a new unit to the application. Finally, add the data module's unit to the uses clause of any form from which you want to use the data module's components. The command File | Use Unit, as described earlier in this chapter, can be used here for this purpose.

Database Explorer and SQL Explorer

The Database or SQL Explorer is a browser for viewing database information. The features in the Explorer differ depending on the edition of Delphi 2 you purchased (Desktop, Developer, or Client/Server). The Database Explorer is included in the Desktop and Developer editions. The SQL Explorer is included in the Client/Server edition.

The Database Explorer in the Desktop edition provides the base feature set. It supports local table browsing only; that is, only Paradox and dBASE tables can be used. The Database Explorer in the Developer edition includes the features just described plus the ability to use Local InterBase, ODBC (Open Database Connectively) databases, and the data dictionary.

The SQL Explorer has the most robust feature set. In addition to the options provided in the Database Explorer, the SQL Explorer is SQL enabled, accesses remote database servers, and the scaleable data dictionary is enabled.

Following are features of the Database Explorer:

- Browse database server-specific schema objects, including tables, fields, stored procedure definitions, triggers, and indexes.
- View, insert, and modify data in existing tables.
- Create and maintain aliases.
- Enter SQL statements to query a database.

The Developer and Client/Server Suite also supports the ability to create and maintain data dictionaries and attribute sets.

You can access the Database or SQL Explorer from either the main menu by selecting Database | Explore, or from a speed menu by selecting the Explore option. The Database, Table, Query, and StoredProc components all have the option Explore on their speed menus. Figure 7-18 shows the SQL Explorer with the DBDEMOS and IBLOCAL databases open.

There are two panels in the Explorer. The left side of the window contains a two-page pane. The Databases page of this pane contains the aliases defined in the BDE configuration file. The Dictionary page of this pane contains the items placed in the data dictionary. For each of the aliases on the Databases page, you can open the

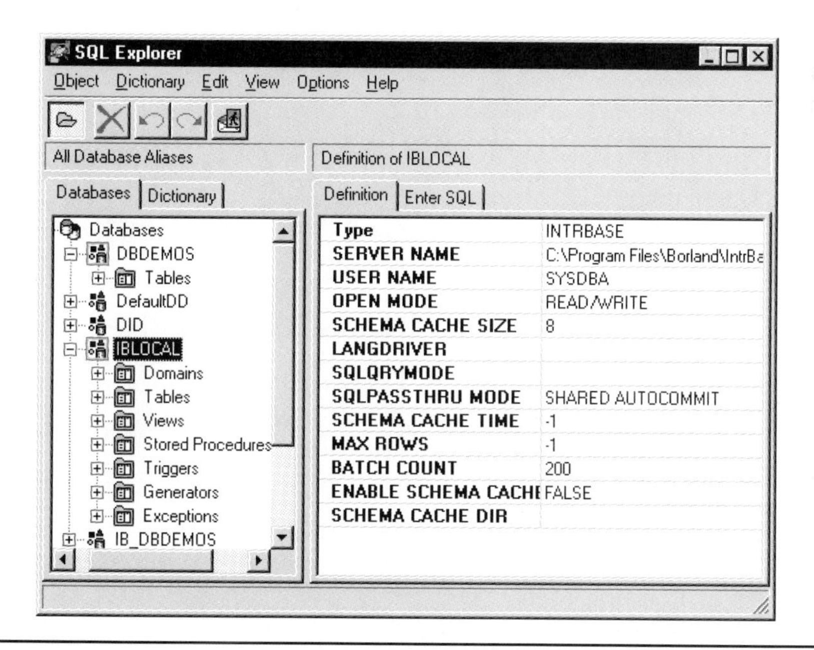

Figure 7-18. *SQL Explorer with two open databases*

database and select an item defined in the database. Tables, fields, indexes, validation constraints, triggers, stored procedures, and alias configuration parameters can be displayed. The right side of the window changes based on the current selection in the left panel. Details are available for highlighted items. In addition, you can enter SQL statements for an open database and display data from a table. If you have update privileges, you can even modify the data.

Scaleable Data Dictionary

The Dictionary page contains the aliases that have been added to the data dictionary. The dictionary stores information for databases, tables, and field attributes. Any existing database can be added to the dictionary using the import feature (accessed by selecting Dictionary | Import from Database from the Explorer main menu). The attributes can also be added to the dictionary using the Fields Editor. Figure 7-19 shows the Dictionary page of the SQL Explorer with the DBDEMOS database open.

The field attributes in the dictionary describe the data type, properties, and the type of visual control to create when the field is dragged onto a form. This allows you to have the Explorer open and use the same drag-and-drop features of the Fields Editor to place fields onto a form. If you drag a table entry onto a form, a Table, DataSource, and DBGrid are created with the components linked and the DatabaseName and TableName properties assigned. Defining these attributes in a single location and using the definitions in applications ensures consistency in validation enforcement and display format.

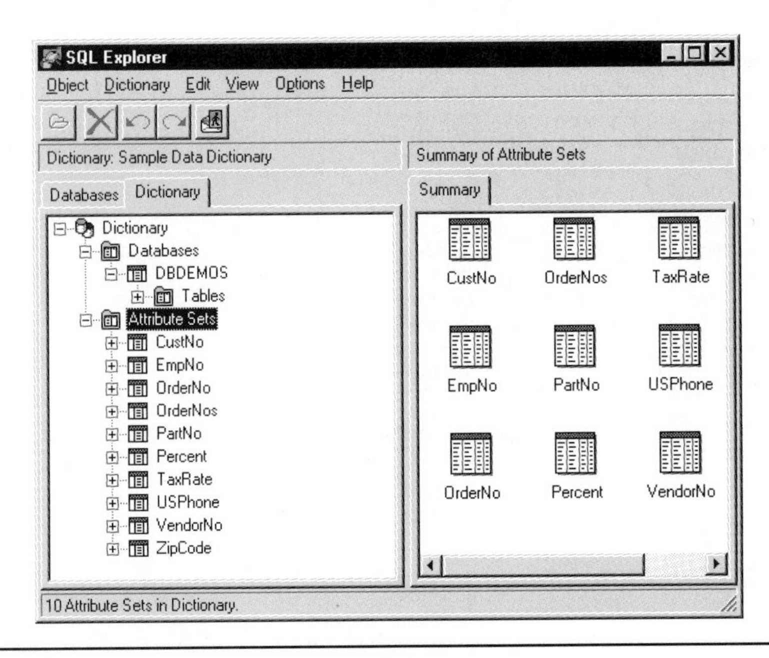

Figure 7-19. *Data Dictionary page in the SQL Explorer*

When Delphi 2 is installed, the initial data dictionary is stored in a Paradox table. You are not required to use Paradox as the only repository for the dictionary information. Any database format can be used. Before you create a new dictionary, you need to have an alias defined for the database. The alias determines the database format in which the dictionary stores its information.

SQL Monitor

The SQL Monitor is a tool to assist in client/server development and is available only in the Client/Server edition of Delphi. The SQL Monitor enables you to trace calls made through SQL Links to a remote server, or through the ODBC socket to an ODBC data source. You can use SQL Monitor to test, debug, and tune your calls to SQL databases. Using the information reported, you can optimize the SQL and improve performance. Figure 7-20 shows the SQL Monitor after opening the Customer table in the Local InterBase database assigned to the IBLOCAL alias.

Using the Data Migration Expert

A new tool for Delphi 2 is the Data Migration Expert, also known as the Data Pump. Like the SQL Monitor, the Data Migration Expert is available only in the Client/Server edition of Delphi. You use the Data Migration Expert to move tables and their data between databases. The source can be either local tables or SQL databases; likewise for the target database. Figure 7-21 shows the initial window with the source selection based on a directory.

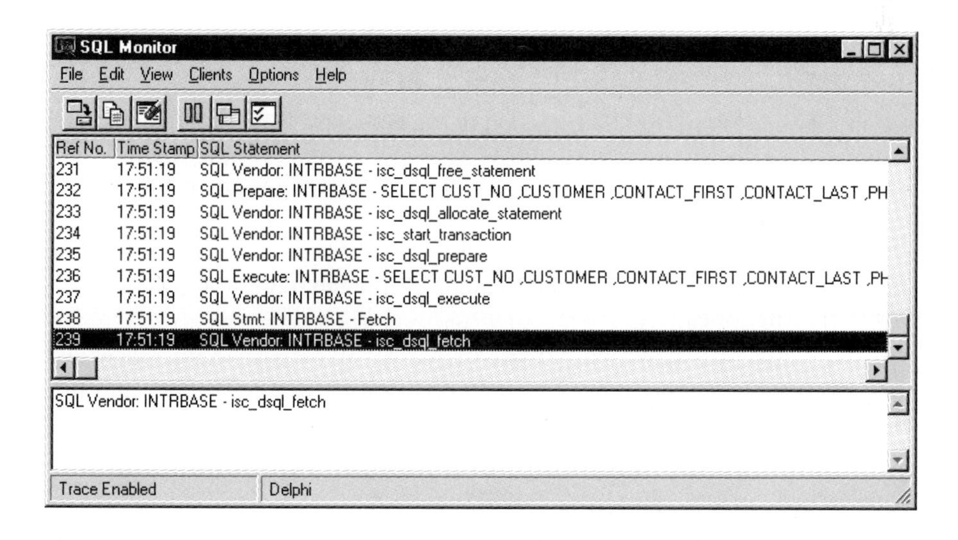

Figure 7-20. *SQL Monitor after opening the Customer table for the IBLOCAL alias*

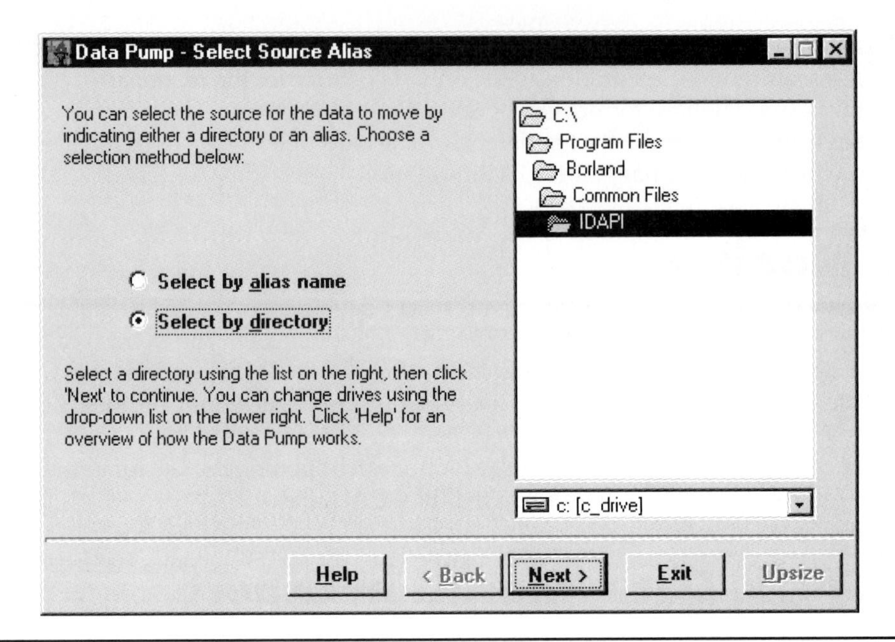

Figure 7-21. *Data Pump initial screen showing selection of the source data location*

NOTE: The Data Migration Expert is not an installed option to be started from within Delphi. You start the Expert using the Data Migration Expert icon in the Borland Delphi 2.0 folder.

Updated Database Desktop

The Database Desktop is an updated version of the Database Desktop that ships with Delphi 1.0. The basic features are the same as in Delphi 1.0, with some changes to the menu locations, menu options, and new BDE. The major changes are as follows:

- Movable toolbars that can be docked or left floating.
- Use of tabbed dialog boxes that contain multiple tab pages for different property categories.
- Menu organization that includes Save, Save As, and Close on the File menu; Utilities, Password, and Alias Manager on the Tools menu; and updates to Table and Query menus.
- SQL Query properties that specify where to run the query, how to handle auxiliary tables, and support for constrained queries.
- Creation of calculated fields in live queries.

- Enhanced SQL Editor.
- Both vertical and horizontal window tiling.
- Use of Windows common dialog boxes for file handling.

Borland Database Engine

Version 3.0 of the Borland Database Engine is a new, 32-bit implementation of the Borland Database Engine, the standard for data connectivity used across all Borland products. This version has improved features and performance for local and remote SQL databases. It includes a new query engine, optimization for 32-bit native SQL Links drivers, ANSI SQL-92 DML compliance, improved ODBC 2.1 configuration drivers, and support for all the new features mentioned in this chapter.

BDE 3.0 supports full 32-bit functionality, including multithreading, preemptive multi-tasking, the universal naming convention (UNC), and long filenames (up to 260 characters). The following sections expand on some of these new features. A more in-depth description of these features can be found in the Borland Database Engine Online Reference Help file (BDE32) that is located in the Common Files\IDAPI directory.

New Paradox and dBASE Support

Borland has recently released 32-bit versions of Paradox and Visual dBASE. The file formats associated with these products now support features that cannot be accessed using the earlier version of the BDE. BDE 3.0, however, is the same BDE used by these new releases and, consequently, permits your Delphi applications to support all of the features of these file formats.

Level 7 Paradox tables (a new file format introduced with Paradox 7 for Windows 95 and Windows NT) have the following changes:

- Filenames for tables and lookup tables can be up to 79 characters in length.
- There can be up to 255 simultaneous record locks and 255 validity checks per table.
- The time and timestamp field defaults are identified by the keyword NOW.
- Secondary indexes can be unique and/or descending.

BDE 3.0 also supports the enhancements to Visual dBASE files. These include features for security and encryption, Clipper indexes, and a maximum of 100 record locks per table.

Limited transaction processing is available for Paradox and dBASE tables. This means that you can commit and rollback transactions using local tables. A log is maintained of the updates performed on the table. Records that are modified are locked until the transaction is either committed or rolled back. A commit releases all the locks that were placed while the transaction was active. If a rollback is issued, the updates are applied to the underlying table to place the table back into its original state and the locks are released. As mentioned earlier in this chapter, there are limits to the transaction-processing features that can be applied to local tables. These limits include the following:

- There is no automatic crash recovery to table and index creates and drops.
- A valid index must exist for Paradox tables.
- Soft deletes are used when inserts are rolled back on dBASE tables.
- Local transactions do not work for temporary tables and ASCII files used with the Text driver.

Universal Naming Convention (UNC)

You can use the universal naming convention to access database servers by using their path names rather than mapped drive letters. Path names using the UNC start with a double backslash (\\). Support for UNC eliminates the issue of how a client machine has mapped the servers.

New SQL Query Engine

The SQL Query Engine is brand new in BDE 3.0. The following is a list of many of its features:

- There is full SQL 92 entry-level support for INSERT, DELETE, and UPDATE queries.
- Low-level cursor query capabilities are expanded to filter SQL tables.
- The UNION set operator is supported.
- Subqueries are supported in both WHERE and HAVING clauses.
- Expressions are allowed in GROUP BY and ORDER BY.
- The BDE attempts to create updateable queries by default.
- Single and multi-table updateable queries are available. (The linking field cannot be updated and indexes cannot be switched.)
- Constrained queries are available. (Updates are limited to the constraints specified in the WHERE clause.)
- Calculated fields can be included in updateable queries.

Conclusion

Delphi 1.0 provided developers with a wealth of features for building databases. Delphi 2 includes many new database-related features that offer additional functionality and that also simplify the development process.

Chapter 8 continues the discussion of Delphi's database features with a look at its tools for creating client/server applications.

Chapter Eight

Building Client/Server Applications

The code for the examples presented in this chapter can be found in the \CODE\CH08 subdirectory on the CD-ROM that accompanies this book. Please refer to Appendix A for information on using the code files for this chapter.

One of Delphi's many strengths is its ability to build client/server applications. Delphi provides you with several options for connecting to remote, server-based data. The two primary options are Borland SQL Links and ODBC (Open Database Connectivity) drivers.

Using remote database servers based on SQL (Structured Query Language) provides a structured approach to accessing data in locations other than local tables. Local tables are those residing on a stand-alone machine or on a LAN (Local Area Network). Tapping the power of SQL database servers gives you features that are not available using local tables, such as greater security, access to transaction processing, and improved data integrity. In some cases, improved performance is also gained, although this is often a hardware issue.

This chapter provides you with an introduction to using Delphi in a client/server environment. The basic concepts of client/server methodology are discussed, as well as the differences between file server and database server technology. Understanding the strengths and weaknesses of both architectures can help you select the best solution for your applications. Also discussed in this chapter are Delphi features that support client/server applications and how to set up an ODBC driver to connect to data from within Delphi.

What Is Client/Server Architecture?

Before looking at the features Delphi provides in a client/server environment, it is important to understand the basics of client/server technology. Client/server architecture has two major components: a client side and a server side. A *client* is a workstation or microcomputer that has access over a network to data stored on the server. A *server* is a computer that provides processing and services and typically runs an SQL-based database management system such as Oracle, Sybase, or Borland's Interbase. The physical server hardware comes in a variety of sizes; servers can be mainframes, minicomputers, or even personal computers running Windows NT or network operating software such as Novell NetWare.

The server's main tasks are to provide access to the data and to control the database. These tasks include data storage, security, and integrity; data dictionary and catalog maintenance; query optimization, logging, and recovery; and locking management.

The client provides the interface to the data. The GUI (Graphical User Interface) design tools available today are used to create forms for viewing and modifying data, defining and executing queries, and formatting the data returned from the server into reports and graphs. The client/server model places the user interaction, which is time-intensive for input tasks, on the client. The server, in contrast, is charged with processing data.

Client/server architecture attempts to utilize the strengths of each side of the client/server relationship. Servers tend to be high powered, have large storage capacities, and be centrally controlled (by a database administrator). They have a higher degree of security than do individual desktop machines. On the flip side, today's PCs provide excellent graphical tools to provide easy-to-use interfaces to view and manipulate data. A key to successful utilization of the client/server concept is to allocate the various tasks to the client and the server appropriately.

SQL is the cornerstone upon which client/server architecture is built. It is important to understand that the SQL language is not strictly a query language; you can also use it to create and delete tables and to insert, delete, and modify data.

Most database management systems are based on the SQL standard. These systems usually also add their own extensions to the standard SQL to support the own special capabilities. As a result, there are a number of different SQL dialects, which can prevent you from easily migrating from one database server solution to another. The most common SQL statements—SELECT, INSERT, UPDATE, and DELETE, and some of the CREATE statements—work easily between different servers. However, the data integrity constraints—domain integrity, business rules, and referential integrity—vary greatly between products. Once you have selected a SQL database server, this language difference is not an issue; however, it is a problem if you need to write applications for more than one database management system.

File Server Technology Versus Database Server Technology

Data that resides in Paradox or dBASE tables on a local machine or on a network server provides a limited set of data management capabilities. *File servers* are server products that permit the use of these file types in a multi-user environment, that is, permitting two or more users to edit a given table simultaneously. The feature set of file servers differs greatly from the feature set of an SQL database server. But one is not always better than the other. It is crucial to understand the differences between the two so that you can use the appropriate technology to satisfy the requirements of an application.

The basic difference between a file server and a database server is in where the processing is done. In a file server environment, the network server is little more than a large hard disk that you can use as an extension to the hard disk in your local workstation. All requests for data from machines connected to the file server go into the same queue; however, the data is not processed on the file server. It is only requested from, and then returned to, the local machine to be processed.

A bottleneck can arise quickly in the queue and create a larger amount of network traffic as more and more users request the information from the server. For example, if you have a 50,000-record table on the file server, and you need to create a summary of the data for a specific subset of the data, it is possible that all 50,000 records will be returned to the local machine. This taxes the network and, in a dial-up (remote) environment, can be very expensive.

When a database server is used, the data is processed on the server itself, and only the results of the processing are sent back to the client. This processing does not simply supply query results; it also leverages the power of the server hardware to add intelligence to the retrieval and manipulation of the data. Many database server vendors say that they provide programmable servers. This means that the database management system not only does file I/O (input/output), but also provides programming features. These features provide for centralized integrity constraints, the definition of business rules, and server-based programs (stored procedures and triggers) that are not available in the file server arena.

Migrating from a file server environment to a client/server environment requires some investigation of how the local file formats differ from the SQL database systems. If you intend to move a Paradox- or dBASE-based system to a server database, you need to be aware of the naming convention differences along with the data type differences. Table 8-1 lists the restrictions for naming fields, and Table 8-2 lists the data types of the products and how they map to each other.

These two tables can help you identify differences that you need to be aware of when moving data in one format to another (for Paradox and dBASE file server systems). They also show that there are some significant differences between the products, especially in the naming conventions for fields. The differences in the number of characters for field names will cause you some additional work, depending

Data Format	**Max. Length**	**Valid Characters**	**First Character**
Paradox	25	All except ", [,], {, }, (,)	Any valid character
dBASE	10	All alphanumeric except punctuation marks, blank spaces, and other special characters	Letter
InterBase	31	Letters (A-Z, a-z), digits, $, or _	Letter
SQL Server	30	All except spaces and hyphens (-)	Letter
ORACLE	30	A-Z, 0-9, _, #, $	Letter
Informix	18	Letters (A-Z, a-z), digits, or _	Letter

Table 8-1. *Comparison of Field Naming Requirements*

Paradox	InterBase	SQL Server	ORACLE	Informix
A1..A255	VARYING(n)	VarChar(n)	CHAR(n)	Char
Number	DOUBLE	Float	NUMBER	Float
Money	DOUBLE	Money	NUMBER	Money {16.2}
Date	DATE	DateTime	DATE	Date
Short	SHORT	SmallInt	NUMBER	SmallInt
Memo	BLOB (Text)	Text	LONG	Text
Formatted memo	BLOB (Binary)	Image	LONG RAW	Byte
Binary	BLOB (Binary)	Image	LONG RAW	Byte
Graphic	BLOB (Binary)	Image	LONG RAW	Byte
OLE	BLOB (Binary)	Image	LONG RAW	Byte
Long Integer	Long	Int	NUMBER	Integer
Time	Character {>8}	Character {>8}	CHARACTER {>8}	Character{>8}
Timestamp	Date	DateTime	DATE	DateTime
Logical	Character {1}	Bit	CHARACTER{1}	Character
Autoincrement	Long	Int	NUMBER	Integer
Bytes	BLOB	Image	LONG RAW	Byte
BCD	N/A	N/A	N/A	N/A

Table 8-2. *Field Data Type Conversions Between Paradox and Servers*

on which way you move the data. One very important difference between naming restrictions in Paradox and in the other products is the use of spaces in field names. Paradox supports this capability, but the other formats shown in Table 8-1 do not. Fortunately, the mapping of the data types is not as restrictive as is the field-naming conventions.

Client/Server Architecture Strengths

The client/server architecture allows you to harness the horsepower of bigger machines, thus supporting faster performance and an increase in the number of concurrent users. The following is a list of some other advantages the client/server architecture has over file server technology:

- Provides a cost-effective solution for many companies as an alternative to larger mainframe solutions.
- Improves network performance by reducing the amount of network traffic between the server and the client.
- Provides scaleability and portability as the application grows (when using the same database server).
- Enables direct connectivity to the current source of the data in the mainframe or minicomputer, thus eliminating the export/import requirements of file server technology.
- Eliminates redundant data in the original source (on the server) and local tables.
- Provides centralized control for defining and ensuring data integrity. This single location reduces the risk of invalid data by having a single source for validation rules. In the file server environment, each application has to ensure the integrity of the data, most often through the use of program code.
- Most SQL servers have an active data dictionary. A data dictionary provides a single definition for field-naming conventions and allows for strict adherence for all uses of the same type of field.
- Supports a logical unit of work to be used in transaction processing with complete commit and rollback functionality.

NOTE: The 32-bit BDE (Borland Database Engine) now supports limited transaction processing for Paradox and dBASE tables. However, it is not the full support that is provided in SQL database servers.

- Offers backup and recovery capabilities, even while the database server is still running. This supports the need to have the data available 24 hours a day, 7 days a week.
- Allows larger machines to be utilized to provide increased storage capacity and improved performance. This is especially true when multiple separate physical locations need connectivity to the data. Having the database server process the data and return the results is much quicker than shipping the contents of an entire table across a modem line to be processed on the client machine.

Disadvantages of Client/Server Architecture

Although it may sound like client/server technology provides the best of all worlds, it is not the correct solution for every application. The client/server architecture also has some disadvantages. The following is a list of some additional points to consider when choosing between client/server and file server environments:

- Administering an SQL database server typically requires more time and effort than does a file server database. A database administrator is required for SQL servers. The administrator grants access privileges and performs system maintenance, among other duties.

- Database servers require a hardware investment beyond what is required for a file server system. The additional expense of adding a database server to a system can be very high.
- The technology investment required to implement a database server is greater than that for a file server. For example, developers trained in delivering client/server systems often command higher salaries than do those building file server systems.
- When you move between SQL servers, the different dialects can create migration problems.
- Changing table structures, validation rules, and indexes can be a substantial undertaking in a client/server environment. Similar changes in a file server-based system are often less complex.
- Data refreshing on client screens is not automatic in a client/server environment. In some file server-based systems, this refresh can be set up to occur automatically.
- Table and record locking differs between the various servers. Some applications need record-level locking whereas high transaction-oriented applications do not. If record-level locking is necessary, programmatic schemes have to be implemented in some servers.

What does all this mean? It means that client/server and SQL is not the appropriate solution for all applications. File servers work well in an environment in which there is a small number of users and they are directly connected to the server. You typically cannot have more than 500 or 1000 users in a file server environment. Client/server is better geared toward large datasets, transaction-oriented applications, and a large number of users. Client/server development requires a mind shift from file server development in how you think about applications and how you develop them.

Delphi Client/Server Feature Overview

Delphi includes all the capabilities developers need to create client/server applications. Table 8-3 lists the major features examined in this chapter.

Database Server Connection Basics for Table and Query Components

Connecting directly to a table in an SQL database is almost identical to using local tables in Delphi. The major difference is that for SQL databases, the Database Login dialog box is displayed. This is where you enter your user ID and password to connect to the database. Let's look at a simple example of connecting to the CUSTOMER table

Task	How to Achieve This Task in Delphi
Connecting to data	Use Table, Query, and StoredProc components to connect directly to a remote database, or use the Database component to connect for all TDataSet components.
SQL statements	The BDE can translate your DataSet method calls into the appropriate dialect of SQL for the server to which you are attached.
SQL passthrough	You can write explicit SQL statements that are passed directly to the SQL database without any interpretation by the BDE.
Transaction processing	Delphi provides both implicit transaction processing (Delphi does the transaction processing automatically) and explicit transaction processing (the developer defines transactions).
Using stored procedures	Stored procedures are "precompiled" code modules that reside on the SQL database server. You can pass parameters to stored procedure and, in some cases, receive values in return. Stored procedures provide a higher degree of maintainability and improved performance.
Bulk data moves	You can use Delphi to move large amounts of data between databases. This could be between local and remote tables or between two different tables in the same remote database.

Table 8-3. *Basic Client/Server Features Supported in Delphi*

in a Local InterBase EMPLOYEE database that ships with the Delphi product. Figure 8-1 shows the form for the DATATBL.DPR project in design mode.

The form contains the minimum set of components needed to view and navigate through a table. A DataSource component and a Table component provide the dataset connectivity. A DBGrid will display the data once the connection is made. A DBNavigator component is used to navigate through the data and to insert and delete records.

In this project, the DatabaseName property of the Table component is set to the alias IBLOCAL and the TableName is set to CUSTOMER. IBLOCAL is one of the aliases defined when Delphi is installed. IBLOCAL points to the InterBase database EMPLOYEE.

NOTE: *For more information on aliases, refer to the "Database Aliases" section in Chapter 5.*

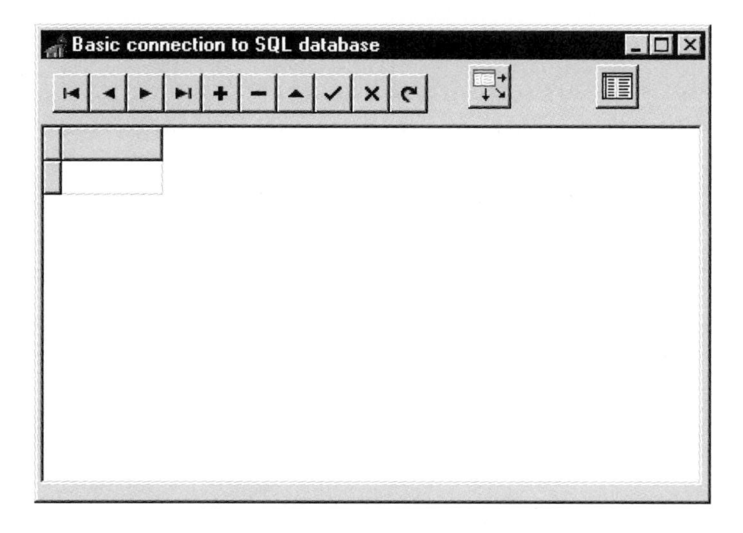

Figure 8-1. *DATATBL main form in design mode with connection to IBLOCAL*

SQL databases require both a user name and password before data access is granted. This is true whether you are opening a table in the designer or from a running application. Therefore, if you attempt to open the DATATBL project, Delphi will begin by asking you to log into the server and displaying a dialog box like the one shown in Figure 8-2.

Local InterBase databases have SYSDBA as the system administrator user name. The default password is masterkey, all in lowercase letters. This user name (SYSDBA) and password (masterkey) are used for all of the examples in this chapter. After entering the values in the Database Login dialog box, the form is displayed and any table in the EMPLOYEE.GDB database can be accessed. If your access occurs in the

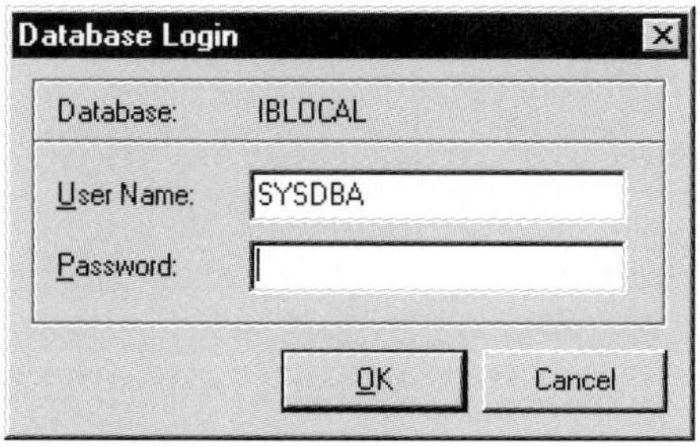

Figure 8-2. *The Database Login dialog box*

designer, your connection to the database will last until you exit Delphi. If you connect by running an application, the connection will be dropped when the application closes, although there are methods available that permit you to drop a connection even before the application closes.

NOTE: You can follow along with these examples if you have installed the Local InterBase Server (LIBS) that ships with Delphi 1.0 and the Developer and Client/Server editions of Delphi 2.

By using a predefined alias, such as IBLOCAL, the login is automatic. However, there may be times when you want to control aspects of the login from your application. For example, you might want to create an application that issues the login password, rather than asking the user to enter it. You do this using the Database component.

WARNING: It is generally a good idea to force the user to enter the password directly. If you set up an application that issues the password for the user, you may also be providing database access to unauthorized users.

Using the Database Component with Remote Data

The Database component provides you with the ability to control the access to a database. Table 8-4 shows the published properties for a Database component. This table contains a brief description of the commonly used properties and identifies the properties that are only available in Delphi 2.

In most cases you will use three properties before you can connect to the database using a Database component:

- Alias
- DatabaseName
- Connected

The standard technique for connecting to the database is to use a predefined alias created using the BDE Configuration Utility. For the samples in this book, IBLOCAL is used. You can use a Database component without an existing alias, but this requires you to define the type of Driver to use with the DriverName property and to provide connection information with the Params property of a Database component. This procedure is described later in the section "Setting Login Parameters."

The DatabaseName property defines the name of the alias that this component will create (this type of alias is referred to as a *local alias*). This alias will appear in the DatabaseName drop-down menu for all Table, Query, and StoredProc components in

Property	Description
Alias	An existing Alias defined in the BDE configuration. This property is used to define a new alias by overriding one or more parameters of an existing alias. If the DriverName property is defined, this property must be blank.
Connected	True/False setting to indicate if the database connection is open. It is similar to the Active property of a Table component.
DatabaseName	Database name that DataSet components use to connect to this Database component.
DriverName	Driver name based on the file type being used.
KeepConnection	True/False setting to indicate if the connection is to be kept open when all DataSets components are closed. Setting this property to True increases efficiency when an application is opening and closing remote tables by limiting the overhead of connecting to the database each time a dataset is opened.
LoginPrompt	True/False setting to indicate that the Database Login dialog box is to be displayed.
Name	Component name.
SessionName (Delphi 2 only)	Name for the associated Session object.
Params	Parameters used to open the database.
TransIsolation	The transaction isolation level used with the remote database. (You can find more information on this method in the section "Transaction Processing.")

Table 8-4. *Properties of the Database Component*

your project, even those that appear on forms other than the one in which the Database component is stored.

The last step to defining a Database component is to open the database connection. This is done either by setting the Connected property to True in the Object Inspector or by using the Open method in code. When either technique is used, the Database Login dialog box is displayed, and your user name and password must be entered. Note that the user name and password have to be valid before the connection is open. If it is not, the open fails and datasets that use the database cannot be activated.

Any DataSet component in your application can now use the database connection. This is demonstrated in the project DATADB.DPR, shown in Figure 8-3. This project is

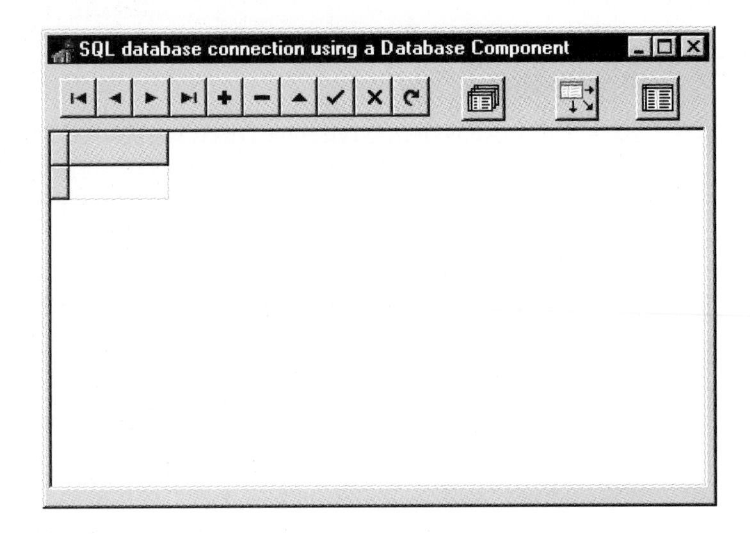

Figure 8-3. *Main form for DATADB in design mode*

almost identical to DATATBL, except that DATADB includes a Database component. Furthermore, the Table component uses this database, instead of the IBLOCAL alias.

TIP: If you assign the DatabaseName property of a database using an initial underscore, this DatabaseName will be the first name listed in the DatabaseName property of datasets. From a given dataset, you can easily select the database with this special name by double-clicking the DatabaseName property.

The Database component can be used by all Table components in an application, provided that each Table component uses a table from the same database. If multiple forms rely on the same Database component, it is best to place the Database component on the main form. This form is generally open for the duration of the application. In Delphi 2, however, you may want to place the Database component on a data module. Data modules are discussed in Chapter 7.

Setting Login Parameters

The login parameters can be provided at design time or at runtime using a Database component. The Params property allows you to specify any of the parameters used by the database connection. By default, the parameter values are initialized to those set in the BDE Configuration Utility for the selected alias. Opening the Params property displays the String list editor dialog box. Figure 8-4 shows the String list editor dialog box with values entered for the user name and password.

In this dialog box, you can place any of the connection parameters that you want to define, or you can override the default. In this example, only the user name and password are entered.

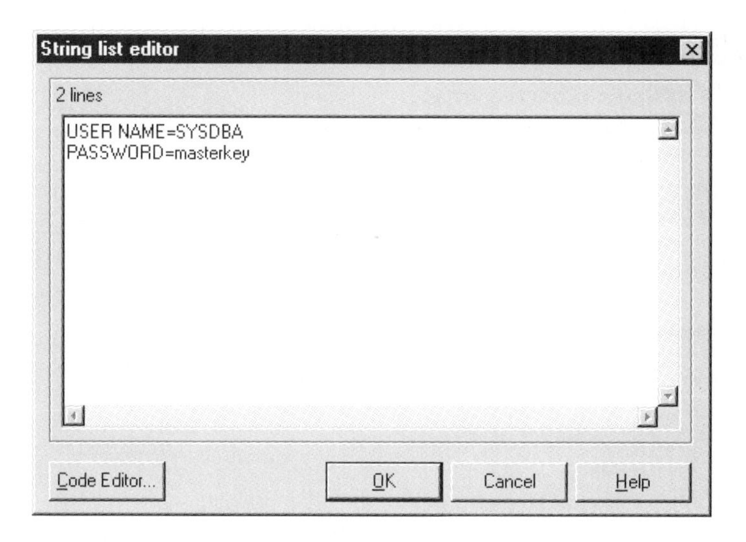

Figure 8-4. *Params settings for user name and password*

WARNING: In typical application development you would not define a single user name and password for anyone using the application. This is done here strictly to demonstrate how to use this feature. Also, as mentioned earlier, storing the password with the application usually compromises the security of the SQL database.

The Database component LoginPrompt property also needs to be set to False. This prevents the Database Login dialog box from being displayed. Delphi then looks for the values in the Params property to define the login values. The PARAMDB.DPR project contains the same components as the DATADB.DPR project. The Params property contains both the user name and password values. When you run PARAMDB, you will be given access to the database even though you are never asked for a user name or password.

Using the Database Editor Dialog Box

You can also use the Database Editor to set connection parameters. You can display this dialog box either by double-clicking a Database component, or by right-clicking a Database component and then selecting Database editor. The Database Editor dialog box is shown in Figure 8-5.

The current parameters for the Database component are always displayed on the Database Editor dialog box. If you want to look at the default parameters, the ones specified in the BDE Configuration Utility, click on the Defaults push button. For example, from Delphi 2, the Database Editor dialog box loads the following values

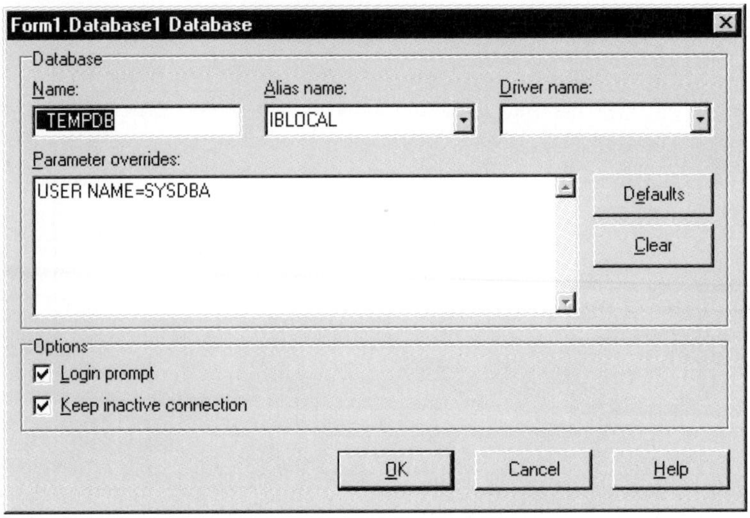

Figure 8-5. *Database Editor dialog box*

into the Parameter overrides list for the IBLOCAL alias (in Delphi 1.0, you get comparable values):

```
SERVER NAME=C:\Program Files\Borland\IntrBase\EXAMPLES\EMPLOYEE.GDB
USER NAME=SYSDBA
OPEN MODE=READ/WRITE
SCHEMA CACHE SIZE=8
LANGDRIVER=
SQLQRYMODE=
SQLPASSTHRU MODE=SHARED AUTOCOMMIT
SCHEMA CACHE TIME=-1
PASSWORD=
```

Any of these default values may be changed. Any values that you do not change may be removed from this list. This will cause the Database component to use the default values for the alias specified in the Alias field. Refer to the help files in the BDE Configuration Utility for a detailed explanation of the effects of each of these parameters.

Using a Custom Login Dialog Box

As pointed out earlier in this chapter, it is rarely acceptable to provide users with access to a database server without requiring them to enter a password or otherwise provide proof that they have the right to access the data. As you have learned, if you do not assign a user name and password at design time, the Database component will automatically display a dialog box, requiring users to enter their user name and password, before the connection can be made to the database server. But sometimes this is not enough. You may want to create a custom dialog box in which users enter their user name, a password, or any other type of information you require before granting access.

The primary reason for using a custom login dialog box is that it permits you to separate the database server login information from the application's login information. Specifically, although you may want to provide users with access to the database server through your application, you may not want to provide direct access to the server. You can limit access by using a custom login dialog box to permit users to input the password that your application requires. If a user enters valid login information in this dialog box, your application issues the database server's password programmatically. Since the application password information can be completely independent from the database server information, this technique provides you with additional tools for restricting access to server data.

There are two basic ways to employ a custom login dialog box from within Delphi applications. You can use the Database component's OnLogin event handler, or you can display the custom login dialog box from the project file itself (as opposed to displaying it from the main form). These techniques are demonstrated in the following sections.

Using the OnLogin Event Handler

When your Database component is assigned to a remote database server, there is an event handler that you can use to display a custom login dialog box. This is the OnLogin event handler. The following is an example of this event handler from the LOGIN.DPR project. This event handler is implemented from the LOGIN1U.PAS unit:

```
procedure TForm1.Database1Login(Database: TDatabase;
  LoginParams: TStrings);
begin
  dlgDBlogin := TdlgDBlogin.Create(Application);
  try
    if dlgDbLogin.ShowModal = mrOK then
      begin
        LoginParams.Values['USER NAME'] := 'SYSDBA';
        LoginParams.Values['PASSWORD'] := 'masterkey';
      end
    else
      Application.Terminate;
  finally
    dlgDBlogin.Free;
  end;
end;
```

Two parameters are passed to this event handler:

- A pointer to the Database component calling this event handler
- The current alias parameter values

In the OnLogin event handler, you set any desired login parameters before the SQL database is open. In this example, only the user name and password are added to the parameter list.

The code for this example begins by creating the custom dialog box dlgDBlogin (defined in the LOGIN2U.PAS unit, which must appear in a uses clause for this form's unit). This dialog box is displayed in a modal mode using ShowModal. (A user must close a modal dialog box before being permitted to return to the form that opened it.) In this case, the evaluation of the user name and password occurs entirely within this dialog box. It is designed to return a value of mrOK if a valid user name and password are entered, and mrCancel if not. Therefore, the value returned by ShowModal is compared against mrOK. If mrOK is returned, a valid user name and password are assigned to the LoginParams StringList. Delphi then uses these parameters to attempt to open the database. If ShowModal does not return mrOK, the application is terminated.

NOTE: *You must have the LoginPrompt Database property set to True. If this property is False, the OnLogin event handler is not called, no user name and password are placed in the Params list when Delphi opens the database, and the Database component fails to achieve a connection. This raises an exception, and the application is terminated.*

In this case, the custom login dialog box is completely self contained. That is, it performs all validation of the data entered by the user. The code logic within this dialog box verifies that a user name and password were entered and also determines if the user name/password combination is valid. This logic can also test for repeated failures to enter a valid user name/password combination, or any other test that you like. In the custom login dialog box used here, users are denied access to the database if they enter three consecutive invalid user name/password combinations. This dialog box is shown in Figure 8-6.

Figure 8-6. *The dlgDBLogin dialog box*

The following is the code for the LOGIN2U.PAS unit for this dialog box:

```
unit Log22u;

interface

uses WinTypes, WinProcs, Classes, Graphics, Forms, Controls, StdCtrls,
  Buttons, Dialogs, SysUtils;

type
  TdlgDBlogin = class(TForm)
    Label1: TLabel;
    editPassword: TEdit;
    OKBtn: TBitBtn;
    CancelBtn: TBitBtn;
    Label2: TLabel;
    editUserName: TEdit;
    procedure OKBtnClick(Sender: TObject);
    procedure FormCreate(Sender: TObject);
  private
    { Private declarations }
  public
    { Public declarations }
  end;

var
  dlgDBlogin: TdlgDBlogin;
  Tries:      Integer;

implementation

{$R *.DFM}

procedure TdlgDBlogin.OKBtnClick(Sender: TObject);
begin
  { Ensure user name is entered }
  if editUserName.Text = '' then
  begin
    MessageDlg('User Name must be entered',mtError,[mbOK],0);
    editUserName.SetFocus;
    Abort;
  end;

  { Ensure password is entered }
  if editPassword.Text = '' then
  begin
    MessageDlg('Password must be entered',mtError,[mbOK],0);
    editPassword.SetFocus;
    Abort;
```

```
  end;

  if Tries = 0 then
    Tries := 1
  else
    Tries := Tries + 1;

  {The following uses string literals to hold the user name and
   password. A more flexible, and practical, solution would be to
   store the names and passwords in an encrypted table, and to
   use a FindKey to locate the name and password the user enters.
   If the name and password cannot be located, the user has
   entered invalid data.}
  if (editUserName.Text = 'NAME') and
     (editPassword.Text = 'PASSWORD') then
    ModalResult := mrOK
  else
    if Tries = 3 then
      begin
        MessageDlg('Login failed',mtError,[mbOK],0);
        ModalResult := mrCancel;
      end
    else
      begin
        MessageDlg('Invalid name and/or password',mtError,[mbOK],0);
        editUserName.SetFocus;
      end;
end;

procedure TdlgDBlogin.FormCreate(Sender: TObject);
begin
Tries := 0;
end;

end.
```

The dialog box contains two Edit components, one for the user name and the other for the password. It also contains two buttons. The ModalResult of the Cancel button is set to mrCancel, which will close the dialog box if clicked, returning mrCancel to the ShowModal method in unit LOGIN1U.PAS and terminating the application. The primary procedure in the unit is the OnClick event handler for the OK button. It is within this procedure that the validation occurs. If the user enters a valid user name/password combination, the button sets this dialog box's ModalResult property to mrOK, signaling to the OnLogin event handler that the user has been validated.

WARNING: Storing an application's valid user names and passwords in a unit, as was done in the LOGIN2U.PAS file, constitutes a security risk. Anyone who can view the .EXE file with a file viewer, or who can gain access to the source code, can violate the security of the application. The same is true of the LOGIN1U.PAS unit, which holds the database server user name and password as literals. An alternative to storing these values as literals is to store them in an encrypted file, which can be read from at runtime. Another solution is to always accept the user name and password entered by the user, and assign these values to the LoginParams parameter of the OnLogin event handler, or to the Params property of the Database. The problem with this approach is that if the user enters invalid data, the application opens, but the database connection fails without terminating the application. You can solve this problem by creating an OnException event handler for your Application object. From within this event handler, you can test for the exception raised when the Database open failure occurs, and respond by terminating the application. This technique, however, means that the user must know the server username and password.

The OnClick event handler for the OK button also verifies that the user name and password Edits have been entered. If not, an error message is displayed, SetFocus is called to move focus to the blank Edit, and Abort is called to exit the event handler. This procedure also keeps track of how many times a user has entered an invalid user name/password combination. This is done with the Tries variable, which is initialized to zero in the form's OnCreate event handler and incremented in the OnClick event handler. If Tries reaches the value 3 without a valid user name/password combination being entered, the dialog box's ModalResult property is set to mrCancel, closing the dialog box and terminating the application.

Note that the OnClick event handler for the OK button will only operate properly if this button's ModalResult property is set to mrNone, the default. If the ModalResult property is a value other than mrNone, the Abort causes the OnClick event handler to terminate, but not before the ModalResult property of the button is assigned to the form. Whenever a modal form's ModalResult property is set to a value other than mrNone, it returns control to the ShowModal method that called it (the form's ModalResult is also used as the return value of the ShowModal method function). Consequently, if you set the button's ModalResult property to mrOK, for instance, the Abort procedure would terminate the OnClick event handler, but the form would also close, and the user would gain access to the database server.

Using a Project-Based Login

Although the OnLogin event handler for a Database component provides you with a convenient place to display a custom login dialog box, this technique is appropriate only when you are connecting to a database server. If the Database component is assigned to an alias for local data (that is, with dBASE or Paradox tables), the OnLogin event handler is not called, regardless of the properties of the Database component.

Even if you are accessing a remote database server, the OnLogin event handler is not sufficient if the Database component is on a form that is not necessarily opened when the application starts. This event handler is executed only when the form on which the Database component appears is created. If the Database component appears on a form that is created at a time other than application launch, you might be in the awkward position of terminating an application that the user has been using for some time.

Delphi provides you with a very general solution to application login that is appropriate for any application, not just client/server applications. This technique is to display the custom login dialog box before the main form is created. This is performed in the main body of the project file (*.DPR) and is demonstrated in the LOG2.DPR project.

The following is the source for the LOG2 project:

```
program Log2;

uses
  Forms, Controls,
  Log21u in 'Log21u.pas' {Form1},
  Log22u in 'Log22u.pas' {dlgDBlogin};

{$R *.RES}

begin
  dlgDBlogin := TdlgDBlogin.Create(Application);
  if dlgDBlogin.ShowModal = mrCancel then
    Application.Terminate
  else
    Application.CreateForm(TForm1, Form1);
    Application.Run;
end.
```

This project uses the same dlgDBLogin dialog box shown in the preceding section. As discussed earlier, this dialog box performs all validation on the user name and password, returning a value of mrOK if the user is validated, and mrCancel if the user either clicks the Cancel button on the dialog box or fails to enter a valid user name/password combination within three tries. Before this project launches the main form (Form1, in this case), it creates the dlgDBLogin dialog box and waits for it, using ShowModal. If ShowModal returns mrCancel, the application is terminated—before the main form is created. If any other value is entered, which is this case can be only mrOK, the application launches normally.

Because the validation occurs before the main form opens, it is not necessary to perform any additional validation from the main form. Therefore, the Database component on the main form of the LOG2 project includes the user name and password to the database server in its Params property, and no OnLogin event handler is defined.

One final note is in order. The uses clause of this project file includes the Controls unit. This is the unit in which the mrCancel constant is defined. If you fail to include this unit in this project, you will have no value against which to compare the return value of ShowModal.

TIP: This technique can be used by any application (not just database applications) to restrict access to only those users who pass the validation provided by the custom login dialog box.

Transaction Processing

Transaction processing is one of the definitive features of SQL databases. Transactions ensure consistency of the data in those applications that include two or more data modifications that must be performed in an all-or-nothing fashion.

NOTE: Until BDE version 3.0 (available in Delphi 2), transactions were only available using SQL servers. Now you can perform limited transaction processing using Paradox and dBASE tables. This section covers transactions for SQL databases. Chapter 7 describes how to use the limited transaction capabilities for local tables.

Delphi provides transaction processing on remote tables in one of two ways: implicitly or explicitly. Implicit transaction processing is the default. Transactions are automatically started and committed when the Post method is called. This means that a change to a single record is a complete transaction.

If you want to control when a transaction is started and committed (explicit transaction processing), you need to program the transaction processing as described in the next section. This can be done using methods for a Database component or with SQL passthrough.

Database Methods for Explicit Transaction Control

The Database component has three methods for controlling the transactions of your DataSet components:

- StartTransaction
- Commit
- Rollback

StartTransaction is used to start a new transaction on the database server. The Commit method is used to commit an existing transaction. Rollback is used to cancel a pending transaction.

The EDatabaseError exception class is raised if an error occurs for any of these three methods. If a transaction is already active, calling StartTransaction raises an exception. When no transaction is active, calling either Commit or Rollback also raises an exception. In Delphi 2, the Database component has a property, InTransaction, that can be used to indicate whether there is an active transaction.

Transactions Using Passthrough SQL

Passthrough SQL refers those explicit SQL statements that you include in the SQL property of a Query. These statements are called passthrough SQL because they are sent directly to the server without modification. By comparison, calls to DataSet object methods will also result in SQL statements. These statements, however, are generated automatically by the BDE. For example, calling a Query object's DeleteRecord method will automatically generate an SQL DELETE statement. However, this statement is generated by the BDE, using the correct syntax for the server. By comparison, when you use passthrough SQL, you are responsible for the syntax of the SQL statements that you use.

In addition to the DataSet methods mentioned in the preceding section, passthrough SQL also can be used to control transactions in an application. A Query component is used to send server-specific transaction control statements for each stage of the process. You must know the exact syntax to start, commit, and rollback a transaction for each server type. Using the Database component and its methods removes the need to know the exact syntax; consequently, it is the recommended solution.

If you are going to use SQL passthrough, you need to understand the available options for the BDE Configuration Utility parameter SQLPASSTHROUGHMODE. Table 8-5 lists the three passthrough mode settings.

Passthrough Mode	**Description**
SHARED AUTOCOMMIT	Each operation on a row is automatically committed. Non-passthrough and passthrough SQL operations share the same connection to the database. This setting is the BDE configuration default.
SHARED NOAUTOCOMMIT	The same connection is shared for both non-passthrough and passthrough SQL operations. The application must use the Database transaction processing methods to start and commit transactions.
NOT SHARED	The same connection is not shared between non-passthrough and passthrough SQL operations, and server-specific transaction processing statements must be used.

Table 8-5. *SQLPASSTHROUGHMODE Settings*

Isolation Levels

In a multi-user environment (two or more users accessing the same tables at the same time), multiple transactions can occur simultaneously. The isolation level of a transaction determines how it will interact with other transactions for the same table. The TransIsolation property of the Database component provides three options to set this value. Table 8-6 lists these options.

These isolation levels are not supported exactly the same way in every SQL databases. If an isolation level that is requested is not supported by the database, the next highest level is used. When an ODBC driver is used, the driver must support the isolation level you define for it in the BDE Configuration Utility. For information on how the different Borland SQL Links support these three isolation levels, refer to the Delphi online help.

The next section looks at how to use transaction processing in a Delphi application.

Basic Transaction Processing Example

Project TRAN1.DPR demonstrates basic transaction processing. Figure 8-7 shows the form for this project in design mode. The same table, EMPLOYEE, from the IBLOCAL alias is shown twice. Separate Database, Table, and DataSource components are used for each instance. The three push buttons at the top of this form execute StartTransaction, Commit, and Rollback methods on the Database component for the upper table.

When a change is made to a record in either of the grids without first starting a transaction, the record in the database is updated when the Post method is executed. This occurs when the cursor moves to a new record or when the Post button on the navigator is clicked. The display in the other grid is not updated until one of two things happens: you either explicitly issue a refresh to force a retrieval of data, or you

Isolation Level	Description
ttDirtyRead	Uncommitted transactions from other users can be read by the pending transaction. This is the lowest isolation level.
ttReadCommitted	The pending transaction can only read committed transactions by other users. This is the default.
ttRepeatableRead	The pending transaction cannot read any changes made by other transactions. This ensures a record read by a transaction will continue to get the same values for the record if it is re-read during the same transaction.

Table 8-6. *Database Component TransIsolation Property Values*

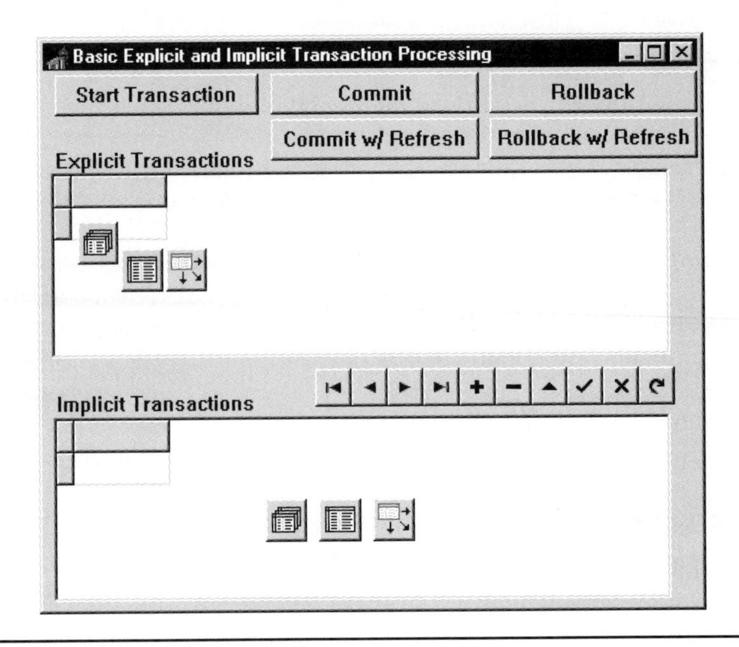

Figure 8-7. *Basic transaction processing form in the TRAN1 project*

navigate the data to such an extent that the BDE must fetch a new set of records that includes the updated row.

A click on the Start Transaction button begins a transaction for the upper table. It executes the following code:

```
procedure TForm1.pbStartTranClick(Sender: TObject);
begin
  Database1.StartTransaction;
end;
```

All subsequent changes to the data in the upper table are now part of an active transaction. A click on the Commit push button saves the changes (commits the transaction) by issuing the following statement:

```
procedure TForm1.pbCommitClick(Sender: TObject);
begin
  Database1.Commit;
end;
```

This code commits all the changes in the transaction and updates the database table. As with the implicit transactions, the lower grid does not display the committed changes. A refresh needs to be executed to update the data displayed in the lower grid.

A click on the Rollback button cancels the changes in an active transaction. The Rollback button's OnClick event contains the following code:

```
procedure TForm1.pbRollbackClick(Sender: TObject);
begin
  Database1.Rollback;
end;
```

The pending changes to the data are rolled back on the server, but the grid is not updated. Again, a refresh is required.

You also need to be aware of the State of the table when a commit or rollback is issued. If a record is still in the process of being changed and the State is either dsEdit or dsInsert, the record is not part of the transaction until the Post method is executed. Therefore, one change to the code that might be important, using the Commit button, is contained in the Commit w/ Refresh button OnClick event as follows:

```
procedure TForm1.pbCommitRefreshClick(Sender: TObject);
begin
if Table1.State in [dsInsert,dsEdit] then
  Table1.Post;
Database1.Commit;
end;
```

This code ensures that the current record becomes part of the transaction log on the server and part of the transaction commit process.

The same type of changes are needed for the Rollback button. The Rollback w/ Refresh button has the following code in its OnClick event:

```
procedure TForm1.pbRollbackRefreshClick(Sender: TObject);
begin
if Table1.State in [dsInsert,dsEdit] then
    Table1.Cancel;
Database1.Rollback;
Table1.Refresh;
end;
```

For a Rollback, if the State is dsInsert or dsEdit, the Cancel method cancels the current modifications. A Refresh is also issued to automatically update the display in the grid to show the current values at the time the rows are last retrieved from the server.

NOTE: *The Employee table from the EMPLOYEE.GDB database contains a number of server-based integrity checks. If you run the TRAN1 project you may have difficulty inserting a new record that does not violate these constraints. To avoid this problem, try modifying the values in existing records, instead of inserting or deleting entire records.*

Server Locking Issues

Locking mechanisms vary greatly among the different SQL servers. Some servers provide record-level locking; others do not. In an SQL database you often want to maintain the highest possible level of data availability to increase the number of transactions that can be processed in a given time period. If a given record is locked for all but the shortest period of time, concurrency suffers. SQL database servers use two types of locking mechanisms:

- Optimistic locking
- Pessimistic locking

Optimistic Locking

The primary locking technique used by servers is called *optimistic locking*. The term optimistic is used because there is an assumption that no more than one user will attempt to edit a given record at a given time. A copy of the server record is modified on the client side, removing the need to lock the record on the database server while changes are made to the data. This eliminates the performance and concurrency penalty that comes with making a record lock.

When you attempt to save the modified record, the record on the server is read again, to see whether it has been changed in the meantime by another user. If it has not, the client updates the database server data with the modified copy of the record. If the record on the server has been changed since it was originally read, the client displays a message that the record as originally read has changed. A decision now has to be made to either read the new record and start to change the data again, replace the changes made by the other user with the edited data, or to cancel the edits that could not be posted. The action taken depends on the type of application and the features of the server.

Pessimistic Locking

Pessimistic locking is a more restrictive type of lock that is typically done using a lock on the record. Servers such as Microsoft SQL Server and Sybase do not provide record-level locking. They use what is called a page-level lock. A page of data may contain a single record or it may contain multiple records, all depending on the size of the record size and the page. Both InterBase and Oracle provide a row-level (record-level) lock feature. Although row-level locking and the potentially more restrictive page-level locking may be appropriate in a decision support-type application where few transactions are occurring, pessimistic locking can have a negative impact on performance for those applications in which a large number of transactions occur simultaneously.

The Borland Database Engine uses optimistic locking for SQL databases. SQL Links is also based on this type of locking, as are most of the ODBC drivers. Inside an application, you can use the UpdateMode property of Table and Query components to specify the level to which BDE determines if a record has been changed, as described in the next section.

The UpdateMode Property for Table and Query Components

Control of the type of optimistic locking used in a Delphi application is established using the Update mode for Table and Query components. If a Table component, or a Query component with its RequestLive property set to True, is used to modify data, the UpdateMode property determines how Delphi locates the record to be updated.

The UpdateMode property dictates which fields in the table are used to find the record. Specifically, this property indicates the fields that are used in the WHERE clause of the BDE UPDATE statement. If the record does not contain the same values it did when it was originally read, the update fails and an exception is raised. Table 8-7 lists the three settings for UpdateMode.

Careful consideration should be given to the setting selected for the UpdateMode. Each setting has its advantages and drawbacks. The default setting, upWhereAll, uses all fields in the WHERE clause. It is the most restrictive and creates the greatest performance decrement. However, using all the fields in the WHERE clause to locate the original record ensures that the record has not been changed since it was originally read.

NOTE: If you set UpdateMode to upWhereAll, and then get an error message stating the query is too complex when you attempt an update, the SQL database is indicating it cannot handle a WHERE clause that includes all the fields in the table.

The upWhereKeyOnly setting is the least restrictive. This setting allows anyone to change any field (except the primary key) without consideration of what the original values were. This setting provides the best performance, but if two users are editing the same record simultaneously, the last user to post those changes replaces the edits of the first one to post, as long as neither user modifies the key fields.

UpdateMode Setting	Description
upWhereAll	Every column in the record is used to find the record. This is the Delphi default.
upWhereChanged	Both the key fields, as well as the columns that were edited in the record, are used to find the record.
upWhereKeyOnly	Only the columns that define the key are used to find the record.

Table 8-7. *UpdateMode Property Settings*

The upWhereChanged setting provides intermediate performance, as well as an intermediate level of assurance that one user's edits will not overwrite another user's edits.

Having a good database design and a well thought out set of business rules will help you to determine the correct UpdateMode setting.

Cached Updates

Delphi 2 provides a new option for transactions—cached updates. This feature allows you to select data from a table and make changes to it locally. The updates are cached at the client workstation and then applied to the database. This feature, and how to use cached updates, is discussed in Chapter 7.

Stored Procedures

Server-based subroutines can be run from within your applications using stored procedures. These subroutines are written using the server's specific programming language. Stored procedure code is not directly transferable between servers because of the proprietary languages.

Input parameters can be sent to a stored procedure, and stored procedures can return values to an application. There are three main advantages of using stored procedures instead of static or dynamic SQL:

- Modular design
- Maintenance
- Performance

Using a stored procedure ensures that all clients are using the exact same code to retrieve or update tables. For example, the database server may define a stored procedure that generates a new, unique account number for a customer. Even if more than one client application needs to add new customers, each can use the same stored procedure to "ask" for a new account number.

Stored procedures also improve application maintenance by only having to update a single location (the database server) when the code needs to be changed. For example, if a new policy dictates that the rules for assigning account numbers change, only the stored procedure needs to be changed, even if multiple client applications need to request new account numbers. Provided that the input and output parameters do not change, the client applications can remain unchanged.

Finally, stored procedures improve performance. Because stored procedures are executed on the server, they reduce network traffic. When multiple tables are used in a stored procedure, the number of SQL statements can be reduced to a single call—to the stored procedure.

The StoredProc component is used in a Delphi application to execute a stored procedure. The DatabaseName property is the same as it is for Table and Query components. Once this property is defined and the database is open, a list of stored procedure names is available in the drop-down list for the StoredProcName property.

The Params property of the StoredProc component identifies the input and output parameters. (A given stored procedure may not have any parameters, however.) Based on the stored procedure selected, Delphi automatically defines the parameter names. You can assign values to be passed to each of these parameter names either at design time or at runtime.

Project SPRCONE.DPR demonstrates the use of a stored procedure from the EMPLOYEE Local InterBase database. Figure 8-8 shows the form after retrieving data from the stored procedure.

In this project, the DEPARTMENT table is displayed in the grid. The DEPT_BUDGET stored procedure is used to return the entire budget for each department lower in the organization. On the form in Figure 8-8, the highlighted Department is number 120. The total budget for this department is calculated from the budget summaries for DEPT_NO 120, 121, 123, and 125. The Budget Amount is the value returned from the stored procedure—2,000,000—which is the sum of the BUDGET column for the four departments.

In this project, a Database component is used for both the Table and StoredProc components. The Table component is associated with the DEPARTMENT table. The Fields Editor of this table was used to limit the fields displayed in the DBGrid.

The Params property of the StoredProc component contains two parameters: DNO and TOT, as shown in Figure 8-9, which displays the property editor for the StoredProc Params property. The DNO parameter is an input parameter for the department number. The TOT parameter is the output parameter—the value of this parameter is displayed below the DBGrid in a Label component, shown in Figure 8-8.

Basic Stored Procedure Example

Total Budget

DEPT_NO	DEPARTMENT	BUDGET	HEAD_DEPT
900	Finance	400000	000
600	Engineering	1100000	000
100	Sales and Marketing	2000000	000
120	European Headquarters	700000	100
110	Pacific Rim Headquarters	600000	100
140	Field Office: Canada	500000	100
130	Field Office: East Coast	500000	100

Budget Amount: 2000000

Figure 8-8. *Basic stored procedure form*

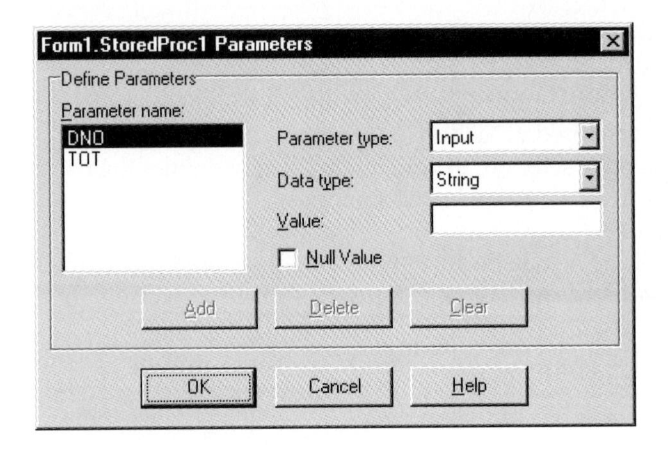

Figure 8-9. *Parameters for the StoredProc1 component*

The Total Budget push button is used to execute the stored procedure. The following is the code in the OnClick event:

```
procedure TForm1.Button1Click(Sender: TObject);
begin
  with StoredProc1 do
  begin
    Params.ParamByName('DNO').AsString :=
      tblDeptDEPT_NO.Value;
    ExecProc;
    Label1.Caption := ParamByName('TOT').AsString;
  end
end;
```

You assign the DNO parameter value the same way that you assign query parameter values. Line 5 of the preceding listing assigns the value of the DEPT_NO for the current record to the DNO parameter. The stored procedure is executed using the ExecProc method. Once the database server has completed execution and the return value is sent back to the application, the value from the TOT parameter is assigned to the Caption property of the label.

The code for the stored procedure is contained in the InterBase server and, therefore, is not written in Object Pascal. The following is the code behind the DEPT_BUDGET stored procedure:

```
ALTER PROCEDURE DEPT_BUDGET (DNO CHAR(3))
RETURNS (TOT NUMERIC(15, 2))
AS

 DECLARE VARIABLE sumb DECIMAL(12, 2);
 DECLARE VARIABLE rdno CHAR(3);
 DECLARE VARIABLE cnt INTEGER;
BEGIN
 tot = 0;

 SELECT budget FROM department WHERE dept_no = :dno INTO :tot;

 SELECT count(budget) FROM department WHERE head_dept = :dno INTO :cnt;

 IF (cnt = 0) THEN
  SUSPEND;

 FOR SELECT dept_no
  FROM department
  WHERE head_dept = :dno
  INTO :rdno
 DO
  BEGIN
   EXECUTE PROCEDURE dept_budget :rdno RETURNING_VALUES :sumb;
   tot = tot + sumb;
  END
 SUSPEND;
END
```

Stored procedures provide a variety of offerings to reduce the amount of code passed between the client and the server. For example, InterBase supports two types of stored procedures: Executable procedures (as shown in project SPRCONE) and Select procedures. The Select type of stored procedures uses a Query component and SELECT statement. The stored procedure returns one or more values for a single output parameter. The next section shows an example of the Select type of procedure.

Using Stored Procedures that Return Multiple Rows

Stored procedures that return multiple rows cannot use the StoredProc component; they use a Query component instead. To use a stored procedure that returns multiple rows, the name of the stored procedure is included in a SELECT statement in the same position where a SQL table name would appear. This use of stored procedures in Query SQL properties is demonstrated in the SPRCMNY.DPR project.

NOTE: The Params property of the Database component in SPRCMNY includes both the user name and password. This prevents the login dialog box from being displayed.

This project uses the IBLOCAL alias. The Query component gets its data from the ORG_CHART stored procedure from the EMPLOYEE database. The following code demonstrates how this stored procedure is placed in the Query's SQL property:

```
SELECT * FROM ORG_CHART
```

The ORG_CHART stored procedure steps through the department table and creates an organizational chart. It displays the head department, the department, manager, title, and number of employees in the department. The InterBase code for the stored procedures is as follows:

```
CREATE PROCEDURE ORG_CHART
RETURNS (HEAD_DEPT CHAR(25), DEPARTMENT CHAR(25),
      MNGR_NAME CHAR(20), TITLE CHAR(5), EMP_CNT INTEGER)
AS
 DECLARE VARIABLE mngr_no INTEGER;
 DECLARE VARIABLE dno CHAR(3);
BEGIN
 FOR SELECT h.department, d.department, d.mngr_no, d.dept_no
  FROM department d
  LEFT OUTER JOIN department h ON d.head_dept = h.dept_no
  ORDER BY d.dept_no
  INTO :head_dept, :department, :mngr_no, :dno
 DO
 BEGIN
  IF (:mngr_no IS NULL) THEN
  BEGIN
   mngr_name = "--TBH--";
   title = "";
  END

  ELSE
   SELECT full_name, job_code
   FROM employee
   WHERE emp_no = :mngr_no
   INTO :mngr_name, :title;

  SELECT COUNT(emp_no)
  FROM employee
  WHERE dept_no = :dno
```

```
    INTO :emp_cnt;

    SUSPEND;
  END
END
```

The SPRCMNY project provides for either all of the columns or a subset of the columns to be used in the result set. At the bottom of the form are check boxes to indicate the number of columns used. By default, the All check box is checked. This sets the SQL statement to:

```
SELECT * FROM ORG_CHART
```

The Run Query button at the top of the form is used to reissue the SQL statement to the server. After changing the fields to return, you click this button to return the new result set. You can see the current SQL statement that produced the return set by clicking the Show SQL button. This displays the contents of the SQL property in a custom dialog box that uses a Memo component to show the SQL statement, as shown in Figure 8-10.

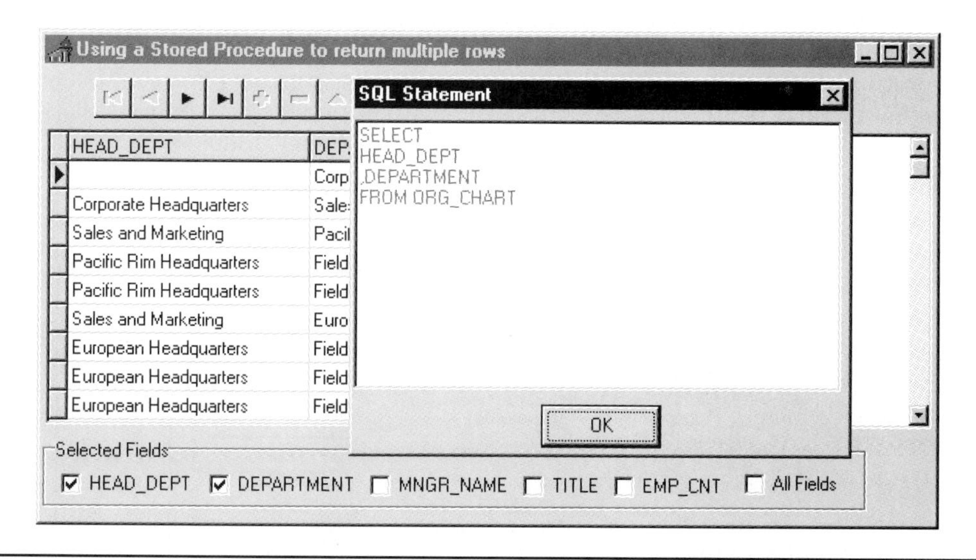

Figure 8-10. *A SQL SELECT statement references selected fields of a stored procedure*

Using ODBC Drivers

The Borland Database Engine supports data connections using the Microsoft ODBC standard in addition to Borland's SQL Links. ODBC drivers allow you to query, view, and update data in SQL servers, as well as any other format supported by an ODBC driver, such as MS Access. Although ODBC is the Microsoft database connectivity standard, ODBC drivers are available from many other software vendors. The database that you need to connect to determines which driver you use.

To use an ODBC driver with Delphi, you must do the following:

1. Install the driver on your machine.
2. Define an ODBC Data Source using the driver.
3. Create an entry in the IDAPI (independent database application programming interface) ODBC connection driver list.
4. Create an alias to connect to the data.

The next section walks you through each of these steps and describes how to use the newly defined alias in a Delphi application. The InterBase ODBC driver is shipped with the Delphi 1.0 Client/Server edition.

Setting Up a New ODBC Data Source

The first step is to make sure that the ODBC driver is installed. If you installed Delphi 1.0 and included the full ReportSmith installation, the Borland InterBase ODBC driver is also installed. To verify that the driver is available, open the Control Panel. In Windows 3.x and Windows NT 3.51 or earlier, this is done from the Program Manager. In Windows 95 and Windows NT 4.x, this is done by clicking the Start button, selecting Settings, and then selecting Control Panel. In the Control Panel, double-click the ODBC icon to open the Data Sources dialog box shown in Figure 8-11.

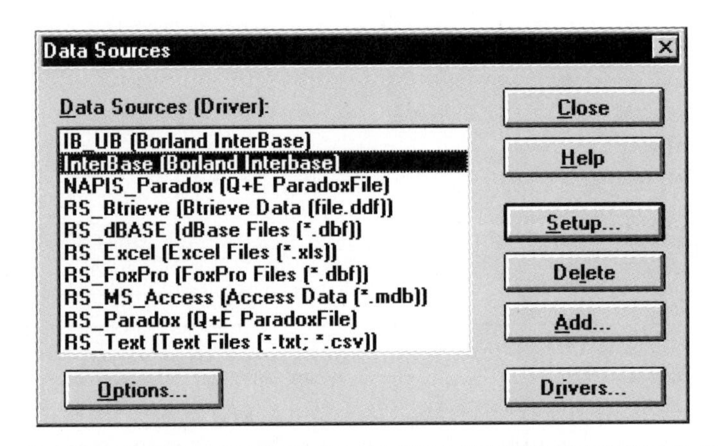

Figure 8-11. *Data Sources dialog box*

You use the Data Sources dialog box to configure data sources that use ODBC drivers. You also use this dialog box to install new ODBC drivers. To create a data source to InterBase, click the Add button to display the Add Data Source dialog box, shown in Figure 8-12.

NOTE: *In Windows 95, if you have 32-bit ODBC drivers, you will have an icon with the title 32bit ODBC. This icon is only used for 32-bit drivers. All 16-bit drivers use the ODBC icon.*

The Add Data Source dialog box lists the currently installed ODBC drivers. Select the type of driver you want to use from this list. In this example, you need to select Borland InterBase and then click OK to display the ODBC InterBase Driver Setup dialog box shown in Figure 8-13.

At a minimum, you need to enter the Data Source Name, to identify this connection, and Database Name, which includes the name and path of the server database that you are creating the ODBC driver for. The Logon ID, which defines the default user name for the connection, is optional, as is the Description field. Figure 8-13 shows the dialog box with all options entered. When you are done defining the ODBC driver setup, click OK to return to the Data Source dialog box. Your newly defined driver will now appear in the list box of this dialog box.

Defining the New Driver in BDE

You use the BDE Configuration Utility to create a driver and alias for an ODBC driver. After loading the BDE Configuration Utility, click the New Driver button on the Drivers page to display the Add ODBC Driver dialog box, shown in Figure 8-14.

NOTE: *In this example, the IDAPI file name used is named IDAPIDID.CFG. This is not a requirement, it is only done here in order to keep a separate set of IDAPI settings.*

Add Data Source
Select which ODBC driver you want to use from the list, then choose OK.
OK
Cancel
Help
Installed ODBC Drivers:
Access Data (*.mdb)
Access Files (*.mdb)
Borland InterBase
Btrieve Data (file.ddf)
Btrieve Files (file.ddf)
dBase Files (*.dbf)
Excel Files (*.xls)

Figure 8-12. *Add Data Source dialog box*

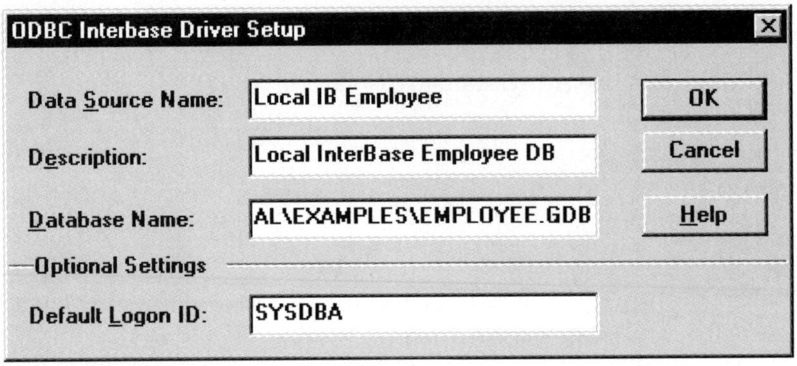

ODBC Interbase Driver Setup

Data Source Name: Local IB Employee

Description: Local InterBase Employee DB

Database Name: AL\EXAMPLES\EMPLOYEE.GDB

Optional Settings

Default Logon ID: SYSDBA

OK Cancel Help

Figure 8-13. *ODBC InterBase Driver Setup dialog box*

Three values are required in the Add ODBC Driver dialog box. In the SQL Driver edit box you enter the name for the driver. In this example, the name used is ODBC_IB_EMPLOYEE (the name must begin with ODBC_, therefore you only need to actually enter the IB_EMPLOYEE part). The drop-down list for the Default ODBC Driver contains the name of the installed ODBC drivers. In this example, you select Borland InterBase. This value limits the options in the Default Data Source Name drop-down list to the Data Sources defined for the Borland InterBase driver. Choose the Local IB Employee option. After clicking the OK button, the Driver Name list on the Drivers page contains ODBC_IB_EMPLOYEE as a new entry, as shown in Figure 8-15.

Add ODBC Driver

SQL Link Driver: ODBC_ IB_EMPLOYEE

Default ODBC Driver: Borland InterBase

Default Data Source Name: Local IB Employee

OK Cancel Help

Figure 8-14. *Add ODBC Driver dialog box*

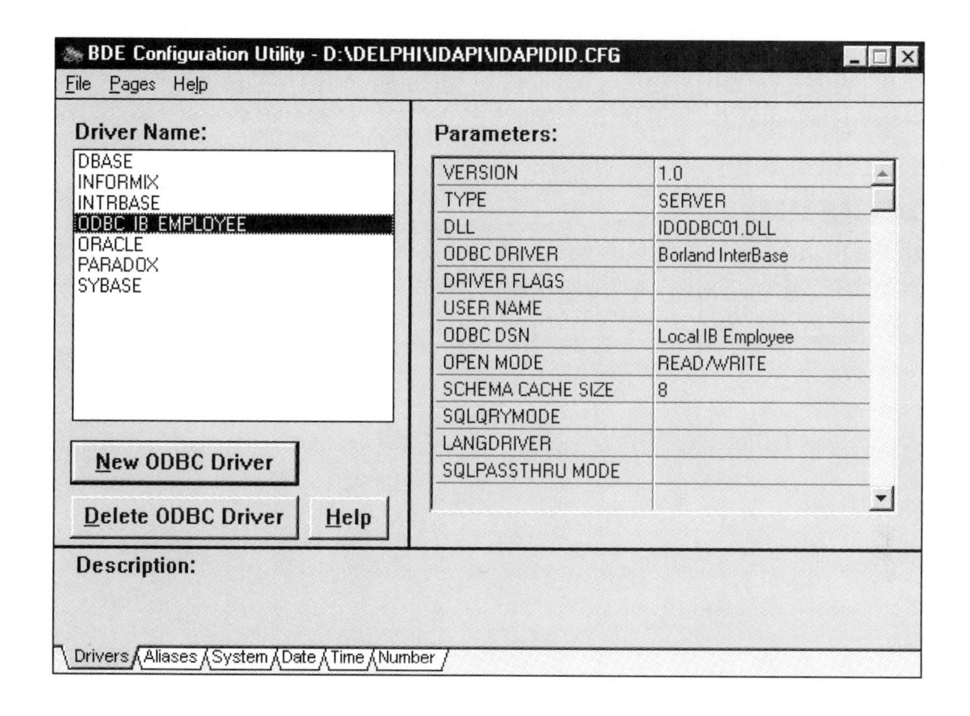

Figure 8-15. *Updated driver list in the BDE Configuration Utility*

Defining an Alias Using an ODBC Driver

Defining an alias using an ODBC driver is no different than it is for any other driver listed in the Driver Name list. From the Alias page of the BDE Configuration Utility, click the New Alias button. This action displays the Add New Alias dialog box. In this dialog box, you enter the alias name and select the driver name. For this example, enter the value Employee_IB_ODBC for the alias name. In the Alias type drop-down menu, select ODBC_IB_EMPLOYEE, the name of the ODBC entry just added.

After saving the configuration file with the new alias, you can start Delphi and use the alias to connect to InterBase. For example, create a new form, and then add to it a DataSource, a Table, and a DBGrid. Set the DataSet property of the DBGrid to DataSource1. Set the DataSet property of DataSource1 to Table1. With Table1, set its DatabaseName property to Employee_IB_ODBC. Next, attempt to display the drop-down menu of the TableName property. This will require Delphi to connect to the server using the ODBC driver. Once you supply the masterkey password and SYSDBA user name if you did not define a default using the Logon ID field of the ODBC InterBase Driver Setup dialog box, the connection is made and the list of tables is displayed. You are now connected using the ODBC driver.

To demonstrate the connection at runtime, set the TableName property of Table1 to CUSTOMER and the Active property to True. Now you can run the project. Before the main form becomes visible, you will again be asked to supply the password for the server. After entering the password masterkey, the main form will become visible, and the data from the database will be displayed.

Conclusion

Through the BDE, Delphi provides you with the ability to connect to data on remote database servers. This chapter has described some of the many ways in which you can work with this remote SQL data from your Delphi applications.

Chapter Nine

Using ReportSmith

The code for the examples presented in this chapter can be found in the \CODE\CH09 subdirectory on the CD-ROM that accompanies this book. Please refer to Appendix A for information on using the code files for this chapter.

This chapter covers the basic concepts you'll need to understand to create reports with ReportSmith. It also demonstrates how to integrate those reports into your Delphi applications. You'll learn how to create a variety of reports, as well as some advanced reporting techniques. This chapter also covers the new 32-bit Delphi Connection that ReportSmith 3.0 supports. It finishes with some performance tuning tips for ReportSmith, along with a list of sample reports that are included on the CD-ROM for further study.

Delphi's Advanced Reporting Facilities

Delphi now provides two ways to report on information displayed by your programs: a VCL-based report writer named QuickReport and a WYSIWYG (What You See Is What You Get) report designer called ReportSmith. It might seem redundant to have more than one report designer, but this is not the case. Each designer has its own strengths and limitations. Consequently, these two reporting tools complement one another. The challenge is knowing which one to use for a particular report.

QuickReport: Simple, Fast Reporting

QuickReport is designed for applications where simple reporting is needed, and the reporting facility needs to be a part of the application's executable (.EXE) file. QuickReport follows the Delphi development model very closely. It is, however, a design-time, developer-only solution. As such, QuickReport is best suited for applications where all reporting needs to be controlled from within the application.

This internal reporting model provides for easier distribution. It also supplies a faster report start-up. QuickReport's smaller overhead results in reports that generally run faster as well.

When deciding whether to use QuickReport, ask yourself these questions: Are load-time performance and distribution size the overriding decision factors? Do I want a totally closed solution, where users cannot change or create reports? Are all the report users also going to be users of my Delphi application? A "yes" answer to all of these questions indicates that QuickReport is probably the best choice.

ReportSmith: Robust, Full-Featured Reporting

ReportSmith is the best choice if power and flexibility are your key concerns. It is well suited for creating complex reports that require the inclusion of multiple crosstabs (spreadsheet-style layouts), live data pivoting (dynamically changing which data is used for the columns and rows), or other ad hoc analysis capabilities. ReportSmith can also be used to build intelligent reports that can be run either within the context of a

Delphi program or as a separate report. Thus, ReportSmith is the better choice when your application needs to support both data-entry/reporting users and report-only users with the same reports.

ReportSmith also offers a flexible method whereby end users can design their own reports. The ability of end users to perform their own reporting frees you for other, more important tasks. ReportSmith's WYSIWYG design mode, along with its live data display, also makes report design much simpler than with QuickReport. In fact, even though both QuickReport and ReportSmith can build mailing label reports, ReportSmith is a much better choice for creating them easily.

The following questions apply when you are considering ReportSmith: Are flexibility and power the most important reporting features for my application? Are crosstabs an essential analysis tool? Do my reports need to include data graphs as well? Do I need to build an open-ended solution where end users can create their own reports? Do I have two communities of report users, one that just runs reports (a "read-only" group) and another that also runs my Delphi application (a "read/write" group)? If you answered "yes" to all of these questions, then ReportSmith is the way to go.

Using ReportSmith—An Overview

The design concept behind creating reports in ReportSmith is similar to creating data-aware forms with an active DataSet in Delphi. There is no design mode versus preview mode split. All design is performed in a live data WYSIWYG display.

Delphi 2.0 ships with a new 32-bit version of ReportSmith. Table 9-1 lists the new features of this version.

ReportSmith 3.0 also preserves important features from the 16-bit edition. These are listed in Table 9-2.

Feature	Description
The Delphi Connection type	Allows reports to use the data already buffered in the application's Borland Database Engine (BDE) connection.
32-bit performance	Record processing is visibly faster because of 32-bit-wide data processing.
Included macros	Sample macros add customization to report functionality.
The ReportSmith API	A programmable API now exists for interfacing other tools with ReportSmith. (The API can be purchased separately from Borland.)

Table 9-1. *The New Features in ReportSmith 3.0*

Feature	Description
Royalty-free Runtime Viewer	Reports can be run on client machines without having to give users the ability to modify the reports.
Adaptive Data Access	ReportSmith can tune itself to cache data in a variety of locations on either the client or server machine.
Visual Criteria Selection	Users can limit the records included in a report by simply dragging data values from the report into a selection criteria box.
Report Variables	Variables that reside inside the report itself is the basis for much of the flexible reporting capabilities of ReportSmith.
Master-Detail Reports	Heterogeneous data sources and multiple groupings can be used to build complex multi-table reports easily.
Macro Language	Programmable reporting is possible even when reports are run outside of a Delphi-controlled environment.
The Formula Editor	End users can design complex reports without having to know details of the macro language by using this editor.
The SQL Editor	Reports can take advantage of specific back-end functionality by directly entering SQL code.

Table 9-2. *Features Found in Both ReportSmith 2.5 and ReportSmith 3.0*

Unfortunately, a few version 2.5 features are not supported in the 32-bit version of ReportSmith. These features are listed in Table 9-3.

The ReportSmith Toolbars

Many of the features in ReportSmith are accessed using the ReportSmith toolbars. The buttons and controls on these toolbars are roughly divided into clusters that provide complementary features. These clusters are shown and described in Table 9-4.

In addition to the toolbars, ReportSmith supports drag-and-drop, as well as speed menus, much like Delphi itself does. Also, ReportSmith provides access to many of its advanced features through the use of dialog boxes. One of the most important ReportSmith dialog boxes is the Report Query dialog box, shown in Figure 9-1. You use this dialog box to define many of the essential details of your reports.

Feature	Description
ReportSmith Data Dictionary	ReportSmith 2.5 has a data dictionary that allows a developer to predefine table and column aliases, field visibility rights, and so on. This feature is not provided in the 32-bit version.
Identical Menu Structures	Some of the menu selection items have changed from version 2.5 to version 3.0 to better reflect the Win32 standards. For example, version 2.5 uses "Character" whereas version 3.0 uses "Font" in the speed menus. This difference may affect program code that relies on specific text in a menu selection when migrating from 16-bit to 32-bit.
Broader Picture Support	Both versions support the use of .BMP, .PCX, and .DIB file formats. The 16-bit version also supports the .GIF and .TIF file formats.

Table 9-3. *ReportSmith 2.5 Features Not Supported in ReportSmith 3.0*

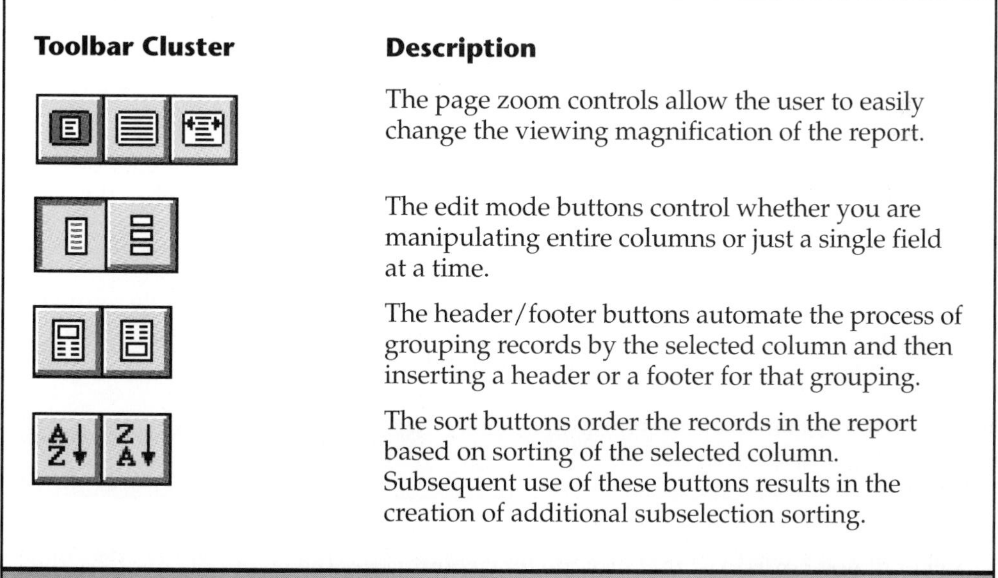

Toolbar Cluster	Description
	The page zoom controls allow the user to easily change the viewing magnification of the report.
	The edit mode buttons control whether you are manipulating entire columns or just a single field at a time.
	The header/footer buttons automate the process of grouping records by the selected column and then inserting a header or a footer for that grouping.
	The sort buttons order the records in the report based on sorting of the selected column. Subsequent use of these buttons results in the creation of additional subselection sorting.

Table 9-4. *Related ReportSmith Toolbar Clusters*

Toolbar Cluster	Description
Σ n̄ Min Max 123	The summary buttons automate the creation of fields that display the sum, average, minimum, and maximum values, or the count of records in the selected column. If the selected column is one that defines a group, the summary field will display the summary value for the group instead of for the report as a whole.
SQL	The report control buttons provide easy access to the merge report, direct SQL entry, and best-fit capabilities of ReportSmith.
Arial 9 B I U	The font controls allow the user to specify common text settings, such as font type, font size, boldface, italics, and underlining. (Other font settings are available via right-mouse click speed menus.)
	These buttons control the alignment of text within a field. (A separate alignment tool is available for lining up fields.)
$, %	The numeric format buttons provide a quick way of setting common numeric formats (e.g., currency, comma, and percent).
	These buttons provide access to some of the power functions in ReportSmith. From left to right, these buttons allow the user to insert text, pictures, graphs, and crosstabs.
	The style buttons let the user copy the style settings of one field and use them in another. Global style settings also can be applied.

Table 9-4. *Related ReportSmith Toolbar Clusters* (continued)

Other dialog boxes exist that provide total control over the layout of crosstabs, the creation of master-detail reports, the definition of selection criteria, and the control of report groupings and summary fields.

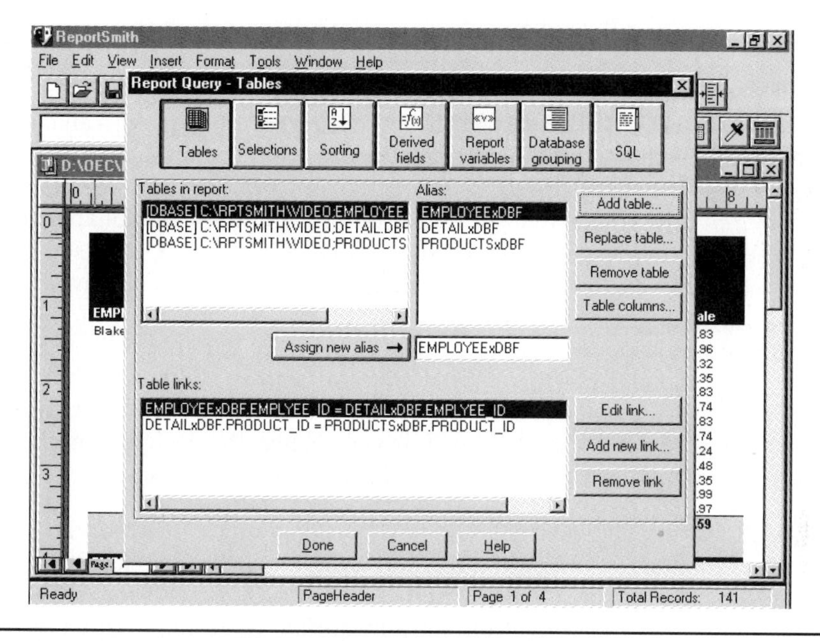

Figure 9-1. *The Tables page of the Report Query Dialog Box*

Preparing to Create a ReportSmith Report

In most cases, you must perform some setup operations before you create your first ReportSmith report. ReportSmith connects to data through a data type, which must be created or selected. You can also define a data connection, which is similar to a BDE alias in that it encapsulates the data type and connection location information.

Data Types

All data access is made through a data type. ReportSmith supports four classes of data type:

- Native ReportSmith data drivers
- BDE aliases (limited support)
- ODBC drivers
- The Delphi Connection (in version 3.0 only)

NATIVE REPORTSMITH DATA DRIVERS The Client/Server editions of ReportSmith ship with a set of native API drivers for a variety of SQL data sources. These drivers are separate from the IDAPI drivers that are part of the BDE. They are performance tuned for read-only operations and supersede the BDE SQL Link drivers for that reason. Connections that are supported with these drivers are DB2 via the MDI and Gupta gateways, Oracle, SQL Base, MS SQL Server, and Sybase Server. A native driver for Unify 2000 is also available for download from Borland's Web site (http://www.borland.com).

BORLAND DATABASE ENGINE ALIASES All ReportSmith versions can use BDE aliases that have been defined previously via the BDE Configuration Utility. However, only aliases that connect to dBASE, Paradox, InterBase, and Informix will be available for use in ReportSmith. Aliases that connect to other data types will not appear in the list of available types. For example, if you have a BDE alias for an Oracle server, that alias will not appear in this list. Instead, you must use ReportSmith's native API drivers.

When you launch ReportSmith, supported BDE aliases automatically show up in the list of available data types shown in the lower left corner of the Add Table dialog box. These data types are noted with the alias name, followed by an "(IDAPI)" designation. (The BDE makes use of IDAPI drivers, hence, the designation. IDAPI stands for Independent Database Application Programming Interface.)

ODBC DRIVERS Any ODBC driver you have installed in your system can be used for making data connections. ReportSmith ships with ODBC drivers for Btrieve, dBASE, Excel, FoxPro, Paradox, and ASCII text files. (ODBC drivers for Access and other data formats can be obtained from the appropriate vendors.) Chapter 8 covers installation of ODBC drivers.

TIP: ODBC drivers that deal with PC databases (e.g., dBASE, Paradox, FoxPro, and Access) can be set up in either a generic fashion or in a way to target a specific file directory. You should configure such ODBC drivers to use the current report directory for maximum flexibility. Make sure the "Use current directory" check box is turned on in the ODBC driver setup dialog box. Define the table location in a ReportSmith connection name you create later for the ODBC driver.

DELPHI CONNECTION ReportSmith 3.0 adds a new connection type that obtains its data from the current data context of the Delphi application that launched the report. When you use this connection type, the selected Delphi DataSet component controls the sorting, grouping, record selection, and SQL generation for the report.

Managing Data Connections

A connection is similar to a BDE alias, in that it predefines the type and location of the data you want to include in your report. Although you can hook up data to a report at any time, setting up predefined connections will be useful in the long run, especially if you work with the same data location repeatedly.

CREATING REPORTSMITH CONNECTIONS You can predefine names for data connections that are not related to a BDE alias. To create a connection name, select File | Connections from the ReportSmith menus. A dialog box similar to the one shown in Figure 9-2 will appear.

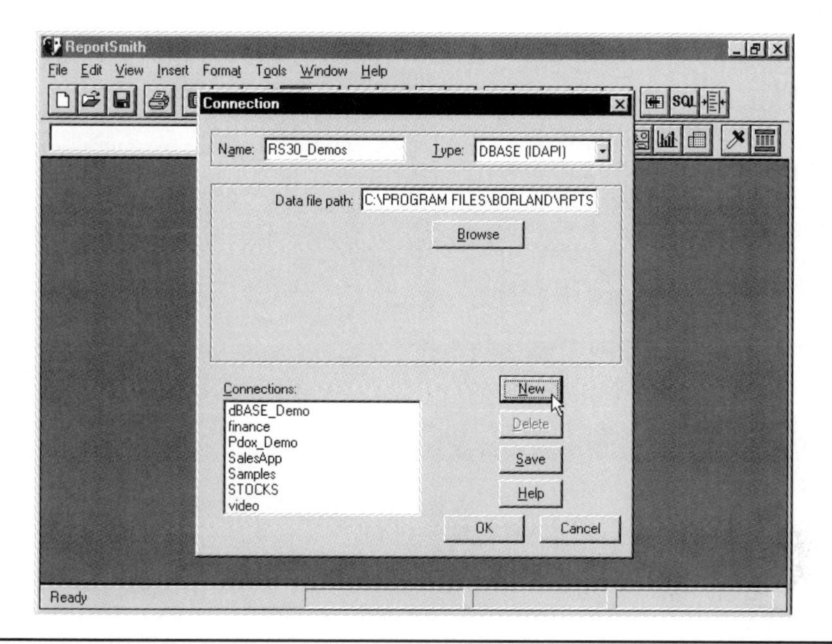

Figure 9-2. *Creating a ReportSmith connection name*

Note that connection names can be based on any data type supported by ReportSmith. The connection type you select will determine the options presented to you in the Connection dialog box. For example, an SQL Server connection using the ReportSmith native API driver will prompt you to supply information for a Server and User ID.

Once you have created these connection names, they will appear in the list of available connections displayed in the lower right corner of the Add Table dialog box. Figure 9-3 shows a sample list of connection names that includes the one defined in Figure 9-2.

Setting Defaults

ReportSmith provides a variety of report options that control how ReportSmith will operate. These can be configured from the Options dialog box. To display this dialog box, select Tools | Options (or File | Options from the Runtime Viewer). For information on these option settings, click the Help button on the Options dialog box, or refer to the "Customizing Reports" chapter in the ReportSmith manual that comes with Delphi.

Creating Report Examples

In this section you will learn how to create two of the more common types of reports, mailing labels and columnar reports. These examples demonstrate some of the basic techniques that you will use with every report, including selecting a table, placing fields, and formatting those fields. These examples also demonstrate how to use some

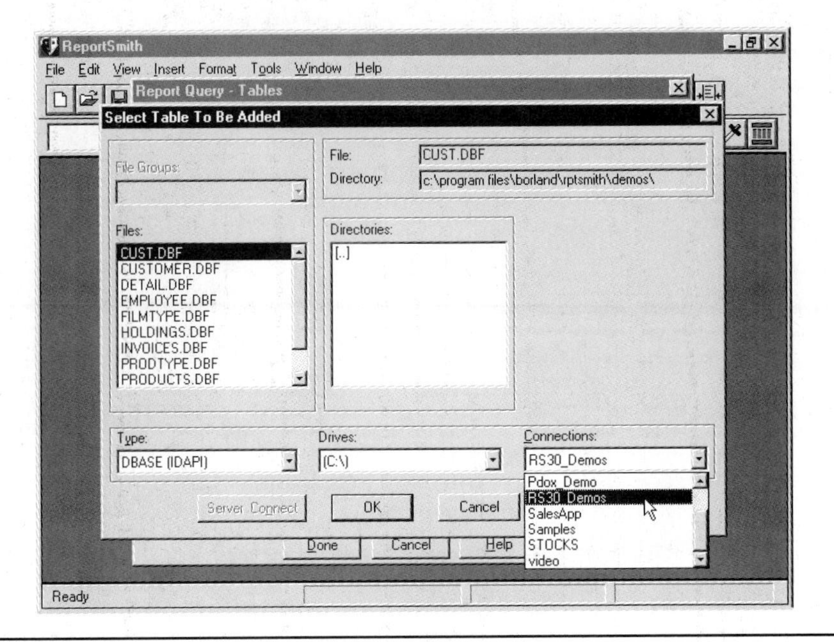

Figure 9-3. *Selecting a ReportSmith connection name*

of ReportSmith's more advanced features, such as placing calculated fields, using grouping bands, and sorting records.

Mailing Labels

Besides creating standard columnar reports, the single task probably performed most often with a database is the creation of mailing labels. ReportSmith makes this process very simple. It includes templates for a variety of mailing labels, and you can choose these templates by name.

The creation of a label report uses most of the elementary features of ReportSmith without adding a lot of complexity. Therefore, this example will begin this type of report. You will also use many of the techniques demonstrated here to build other types of reports.

Starting a Mailing Label Report

The following steps demonstrate the initial creation of a label-type report:

1. Begin creating the report by selecting File | New from the ReportSmith main menu to display the Create New Report dialog box.
2. From the Create New Report dialog box, select Label Report.
3. At this time, you might also want to select a label style. Click the Style button to display the New Report Style dialog. Select the desired style and click the OK button.

4. Once back at the Create New Report dialog box, click the OK button. ReportSmith then displays the Report Query - Tables dialog box shown in Figure 9-1.
5. Select the table to use for the mailing labels by clicking on the Add table button to display the Select Table To Be Added dialog box. Select the table you want and then click the OK button to return to the Report Query - Tables dialog box.
6. Click the Sorting button at the top of the Report Query dialog box to sort the records in a particular order. Use point-and-click to add fields to the sorting order list. If you place a field in the wrong spot, simply drag it to its proper place in the list.
7. If you want to create any calculated fields, click the Derived Fields button at the top of the Report Query dialog box. (Derived fields are discussed in detail later in this chapter.)
8. Click the Done button. ReportSmith now presents you with a blank set of labels and a list of fields. Just select each field you want in your label, and drag it into place on the label. If you have defined derived fields that you want to include on the label, select Derived Fields from the available drop-down menu. When you are finished placing all the fields, click the Done button.

Don't be concerned if you later need to add another field to the labels. Just select Insert | Field from the ReportSmith menus to bring back the Insert Fields dialog box. Once all the fields are placed on the label, you can proceed with any cosmetic changes you want.

Adjusting the Layout

ReportSmith supports a variety of formatting options and tools for finalizing the look of your reports. Some of the common tools and techniques available are listed here:

- An alignment tool can be accessed by selecting Tools | Alignment.
- The toolbar icons can be used to change font characteristics.
- Right-click on a field to invoke its speed menu. The speed menu provides detailed control over font color and background, borders, numeric formatting, and more.
- Select Tools | Drawing to bring up a set of drawing tools. Use these tools to add lines, boxes, and shapes to your report. The drawing tools also let you control whether items are in front of or behind others.

ALIGNING THE FIELDS To use the alignment tool, first make sure that the Snap-To grid is turned off. (If the Snap-To grid is active, it takes precedence over the alignment tool. You control the grid by selecting View | Grid.) The alignment process consists of the following steps:

1. CTRL-click on all the fields you want to align together.
2. Click on the appropriate alignment tool in the palette.

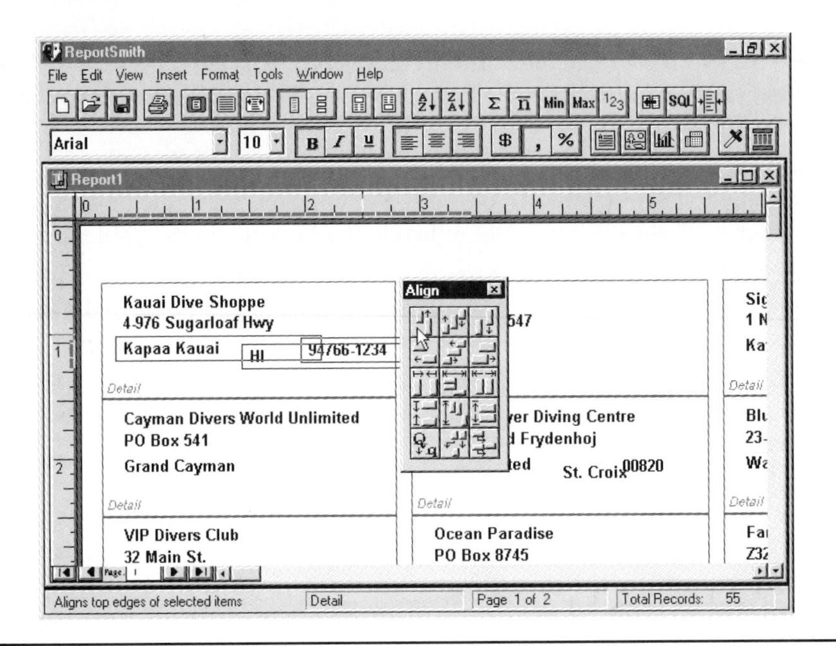

Figure 9-4. *Aligning fields*

In Figure 9-4, the upper-left-most tool is being used to align the tops of the City, State, and Zip Code fields so that they display as a single line of data.

Some textual information contains letters that have *descenders.* Descenders are the "tails" that fall below the main baseline in the letters g, j, p, q, and y. To align items that have descenders, use the button with the uppercase and lowercase Q that appears in the lower left corner of the alignment tool. This button will align the baselines of the text of the selected items rather than just aligning the boundaries of the items themselves.

CHANGING FONT CHARACTERISTICS If the change you want to perform is not represented by the toolbar icons, use the right mouse button to bring up the field's speed menu. The speed menus provide access to all the formatting options. Selecting Font from the speed menu (Character in version 2.5) brings up the Font dialog, from which you can set all the font attributes including text color.

REVERSED TEXT DISPLAY You will need to use this capability to set font color if you want to create a "reversed image" textual display (light text on a dark background). Reversed image displays are created in the following steps:

1. Use the field's right-click speed menu to select the Font dialog.
2. Set the font color to something light such as White or Silver.
3. Use either the field's or the region's speed menu to select the Border dialog.
4. Change the background to something dark such as Navy or Black by selecting Custom in the Patterns area of the Border dialog box. Select a pattern (for

example, solid) and a dark color. The sample display on the right will change to reflect your selections. When you click the OK button, you will have finished creating a reversed display.

OTHER SPEED MENU OPTIONS Other options appear in a field's speed menu when you are creating a columnar report. These options allow you to control the column width and field height of the selected items. (Note that the Display as Picture option is discussed in the "Creating Photo ID Labels" section in this chapter.)

THE DRAWING TOOLS The drawing palette lets you draw squares, circles, lines, and polygons anywhere on your report. If you place them in a repeating region such as the detail band, they will appear everywhere that region is repeated. The drawing palette also provides tools for grouping and ungrouping elements and for controlling which overlapping items appear on top and which appear in the background. If you don't like the way borders work, you can use a square that is set behind a field to highlight it.

Selecting the Label Format

The label style selection defaults to a standard label format. This default setting usually will not be exactly what you want. Use the File | Page Setup menu option to invoke the Page Setup dialog box. This dialog box allows you to control the page margins, size, and orientation of your reports, and to select specific label formats.

INCLUDED LABEL TYPES From the Page Setup dialog box, click the Labels radio button at the top of the dialog box. Then display the drop-down menu under "Label type and dimensions", and select the format of the labels on which you will be printing.

The numbers at the top of the list refer to the standard Avery label numbering system. The list includes formats for name badges, rotary index cards, video and audio cassette labels, and many other uses. Other label types are supported farther down in the list.

USER-DEFINED LABEL TYPES If none of the built-in selections match your labels, you can define a custom label definition from within the same dialog box. Simply navigate to the very bottom of the Label type list, select Custom, and enter the dimensions you need.

Creating Photo ID Labels

ReportSmith lets you create "embedded picture" reports by using the Display as Picture option. For example, you could use this option to create a set of name badges that include each person's photograph. Follow these steps to use this option:

1. Use a digital camera or scanner to save photos in either .BMP, .PCX, or .DIB file format.
2. Add a field in your data table for storing the filename for each person's picture.

3. Tell ReportSmith where the pictures can be found. Bring up the Options dialog box by selecting Tools | Options from the main menu. In the lower right corner is an edit box for specifying the location of picture files.
4. Create a label as you normally would. Include the field that calls out the name of the specific picture file for each record.
5. Tell ReportSmith to use the picture the data is pointing to instead of the textual data in the field. Right-click the picture field and select Display as Picture. A dialog box will appear that allows you to select various options such as file format (if not specified in the field's data) and the initial magnification to use. Select the options you want, press the OK button, and you will see results similar to those shown in Figure 9-5.

Creating Multiple Copies of Each Label

Once a label report is laid out, you might decide that you need more than one copy of each label. Simply select Format | Repeat Item from the main ReportSmith menu. A dialog box will appear that lets you define how many copies of each label you want in your report.

Parts of a Non-Label Report

ReportSmith organizes its other report types into a series of *report bands*. Each type of band supports specific functionality. Since most of your reports will be columnar, this discussion focuses on the bands supported by that type of report. The other report types (form and crosstab) use some of the same band types.

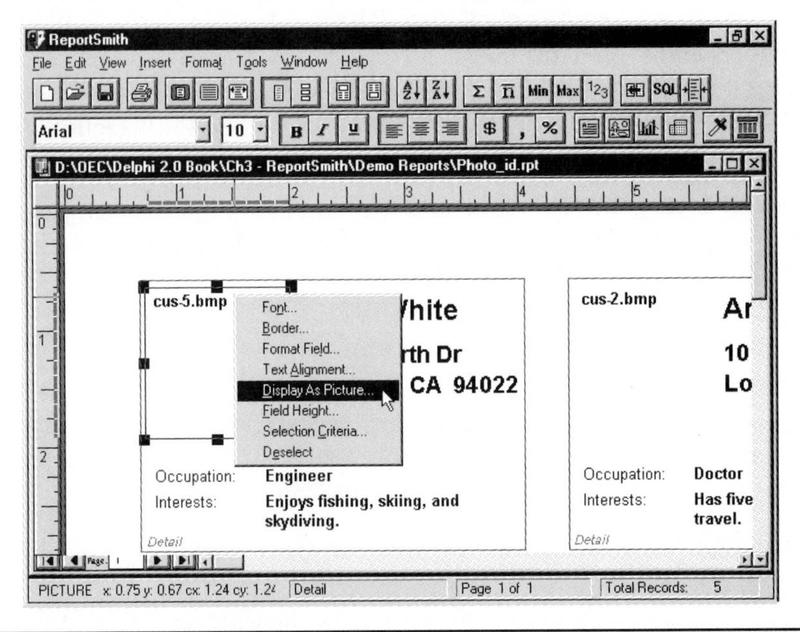

Figure 9-5. *Displaying a field as a picture*

Header and Footer Bands

All report types except labels can have *header and footer bands*. In columnar reports, headers and footers can be set at several levels:

- Page level
- Report level
- Group level

PAGE LEVEL These headers and footers appear at the extreme top and bottom of every page of the report. Page-level headers and footers are the only kind that can be used in a form or crosstab report.

REPORT LEVEL This type of header and footer appears only on the first page (header) or last page (footer) of the report. Report-level items always appear inside any page-level header and footer you have defined.

GROUP LEVEL Group-level headers and footers appear for each group defined. They are repeated each time the field value (or defined group record count) for the group changes.

Detail Band

The main body of every report is called the *detail band*. When you have defined a group-level header or footer, the detail band will hold the individual records that belong to the group. By default, the detail band also holds the labels for the fields contained in the report. You can drag these labels into another band if you wish.

Columnar Reports

Most of the reports you build will be columnar in design. The basic sequence for creating a simple, single-table columnar report is as follows:

1. Select a report type and style.
2. Select the table to use.
3. Select the fields to include.
4. Determine any stylistic elements.
5. Sort the records.
6. Group the records.
7. Select the specific records to include.

Selecting a Report Type and Style

This process is identical to starting the creation of a label report. You can also select a report style in the opening dialog box. Notice that the styles that appear for a columnar report differ from those shown for a label report. Each report type has its own set of predefined styles.

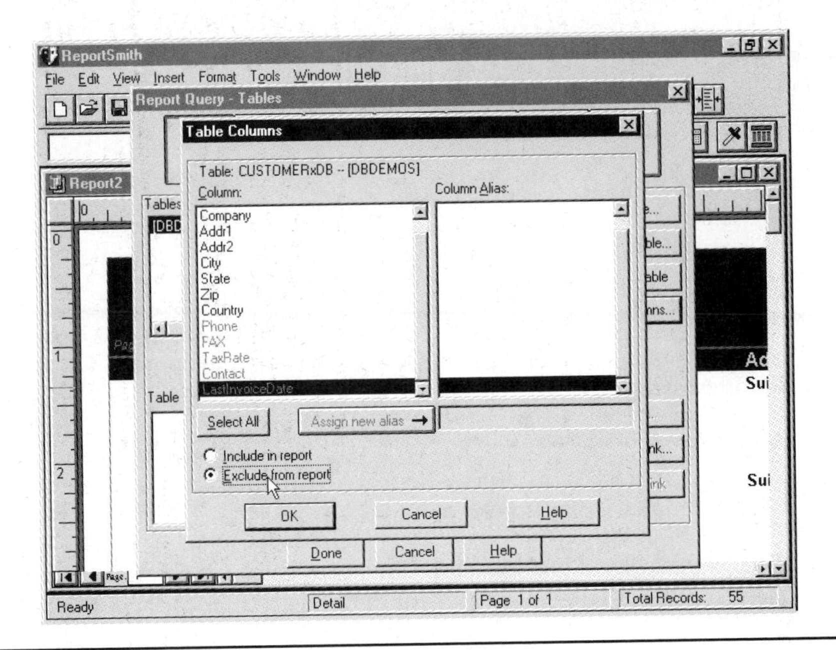

Figure 9-6. *The Table Columns dialog box*

Selecting a Table

The process for selecting a table is identical for all reports. The same Report Query - Tables dialog box shown in Figure 9-1 will appear once you have selected a report type.

Selecting Fields

Field selection in a columnar report is different from a label report. In a label report, you control which fields get placed where. Because ReportSmith automatically places all the selected fields for a columnar report, it is crucial that you limit the fields included in the report.

ReportSmith will default to include all the fields from the table selected for the report. To change this setting, click the Table columns button in the Report Query - Tables dialog box. The dialog box in Figure 9-6 will be displayed.

There are three ways to select the fields to include in your report:

- If you want to include most of the fields in your report, simply double-click the fields you do not want included. You will see the text of the field name turn from black to gray to denote that field has been deselected. (You will also see the selection of the radio buttons below the field list switch from "Include in report" to "Exclude from report.")
- If you want to exclude a large number of fields, hold the CTRL key down while you click on each of the fields you want excluded from the report. Then click the "Exclude from report" radio button in the lower left of the dialog box. You

can also use the SHIFT key while you click to select a contiguous range of fields to exclude.

- If you want to exclude most of the fields, ReportSmith provides an even faster way to remove fields:

  1. Click the Select All button. ReportSmith will highlight all the fields.
  2. Click the "Exclude from report" radio button below the field list. All the fields will be deselected (the text will turn gray).
  3. Double-click the fields you want included in the report.

If you make a mistake in selecting fields, remember that you can always hit the Select All button and then the "Include in report" radio button to return to the original state of having all fields included in the report.

Derived Fields

Sometimes you want to use a field that doesn't exist in the raw data. These *derived fields* can be created at report time. Derived fields can be calculated in one of two ways:

- Defined by SQL
- Defined by ReportBasic macro

DEFINED BY SQL This method provides the most functionality for the *use* of the derived field. Only derived fields defined by SQL can be used for record selection, grouping, and sorting.

DEFINED BY REPORTBASIC MACRO This method provides the most power for *defining* the derived field. This power comes at a cost, however. Derived fields defined by ReportBasic macro can only be displayed. They will not even appear in the list of fields available for record selection, grouping, and sorting.

BUILDING A DERIVED FIELD The following steps are used to create any derived field:

1. Select Tools | Derived Fields from the ReportSmith main menu. The Report Query - Derived Fields dialog box will be displayed.
2. Click in the edit box labeled Derived Field Name and enter the name of your new field.
3. Select how you want to create the derived field: by SQL or by ReportBasic macro.
4. Click the Add button. This will bring up the Edit Derived Field formula editor. The format of the formula editor is determined by the method you selected for defining the derived field.

THE FORMULA EDITOR Figure 9-7 shows the result of selecting the Derived by SQL option. The formula editor is divided into three panels on top, and an editor window is displayed in the bottom half. The left panel displays fields, the middle panel shows legal operators, and the right panel displays available functions. Each panel is restricted to showing only one type of item in the related class. The type currently displayed is controlled by the drop-down menu that sits on the top of each panel.

Just point and click in the panels, and the formula editor will add the selected item to the edit window. You can add items from the panels in three ways: point-and-click, drag-and-drop, or by clicking the Insert button shown between the panels and the edit window. To make sure your formula is built correctly, click the Test button.

TIP: When you are concatenating field data and text as in Figure 9-7, make sure to enclose the text in double quotes ("). Some data drivers do not support the use of single quotes ('), but all of them support double quotes.

Summary Fields

ReportSmith lets you create summary values based on any field in your report. Non-numeric fields can be counted. Numeric fields can also be summed, averaged, and have their minimum or maximum value displayed. All summary fields are based on a specific group-level, page-level, or report-level grouping. The summary field itself must be placed in either a header or footer band. Following are the steps to create a summary field.

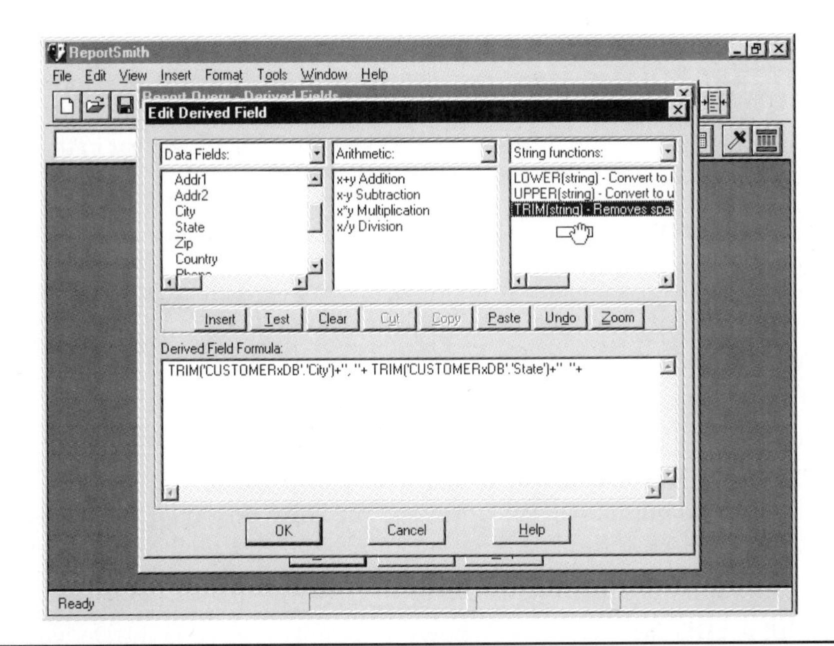

Figure 9-7. *The Edit Derived Field formula editor*

1. Click on the data column you wish to summarize.
2. Click the appropriate summary button in the toolbar. The summary field will appear automatically in the group footer band if one exists.
3. If no group footer band has been defined, you will get an error message dialog box. You can either create a group footer or decide to place the summary field in a page- or report-level header or footer.

CREATING A REPORT-LEVEL HEADER OR FOOTER FOR A SUMMARY FIELD
Place a summary field in a report header or footer with the following steps:

1. Select Insert | Header/Footer from the ReportSmith menu system to add a report level header or footer.
2. Select Entire Report Group and turn on the header and/or footer check box.
3. You can now place the summary field. Select Insert | Fields from the main menu to display the Insert Fields dialog box. Select Summary Fields from the drop-down menu at the top of this dialog box.
4. Click on the appropriate summary field, and drag it into the proper header or footer band as desired.

System Fields

The Insert Fields dialog box can also be used to place system variables onto your report. Here's how:

1. Select Insert | Fields from the main menu.
2. Select System Fields from the drop-down menu in the Insert Fields dialog box. Place the desired system field onto your report.

You can place the date and time of the report's printing, the report's name and title, the page number, and any general text you may want to add to the report.

Customizing Your Reports

Once you have set up the basic layout, you may want to refine the look of your report. You have already seen how you can change the font characteristics and add borders and drawing elements to your reports. Columnar reports also involve several other common tasks.

CENTERING THE REPORT TITLE Although the alignment tools do not offer a "center this on the page" option, you can still center text. For example, to center the report title on the page, follow these steps:

1. Stretch the sides of the title box so that it touches both the left and right margins.
2. Click the center align button in the toolbar.

FITTING YOUR DATA Often your columns will be wider than they need to be when you first create a report.

1. Select one or more columns by SHIFT-clicking on them.
2. Click the SpeedFit button in the toolbar. ReportSmith will fit each column width to match the length of the longest data element in that column.

COPYING EXISTING STYLISTIC SETTINGS The eyedropper tool allows you to copy all the style settings in a given column and then apply them onto any other columns that you want to have the same style settings.

GRAPHICS Use the picture button to drop a graphic such as a logo onto your report. Graphic files in .BMP, .PCX, and .DIB file formats are supported.

Data Graphs

ReportSmith makes use of MS Graph to provide data graphing capabilities for your reports. You should already have MS Graph on your system if you have installed any member of the MS Office suite of products. If not, the graphing capabilities of ReportSmith will be disabled.

To graph columnar data, follow these steps:

1. CTRL-click on the fields that you want for the X- and Y-axis labels.
2. CTRL-click on the data field you want to graph.
3. Click the toolbar's graph button and place your graph in either a header or footer region on your report.

To modify the graph, double-click on it. MS Graph is an OLE local server application that allows you to perform in-place editing of the graph.

Sorting Data

Most reports will need to have the records sorted in a particular order. ReportSmith provides two methods for sorting data. You've already seen the Sorting dialog box method in the section discussing label reports. You can also use the toolbar's sorting buttons, the ones with the A-to-Z and Z-to-A designations. To sort data:

1. Click on a column of data to select it.
2. Click on the appropriate toolbar button to apply an ascending or descending sort order to that column.

You can create secondary sort orders by repeating the process on another column of data. Multiple record sorts performed using the toolbar buttons are cumulative. For example, if you sort the state field and then sort the city field, your data will be sorted by state and, within each state, by city.

Grouping Data

Another common task in reporting is the grouping of related records. You may, for example, want all the records from a particular city to appear together. Once again, ReportSmith provides both a visual method and a dialog box-based method for accomplishing this task.

VISUAL TECHNIQUES Grouping can be accomplished easily by creating a group header or footer. The group header and footer buttons are the ones with the boxed area at the top or bottom. To create a group using the toolbars:

1. Select the column that determines how the data is to be grouped.
2. Click on the group header or footer toolbar button. ReportSmith will automatically sort the data by the selected field and then group together all the records with the same value in that field.

Figure 9-8 shows how the grouping-by-city example might look. You might want to create both a header and a footer for the same group. To do this, simply make sure you have the same field selected, and then click the other grouping button.

THE GROUPING DIALOG BOXES There are two ways to group reports:

- Database grouping
- Report grouping

Each method has its advantages. You can use both types of grouping in a single report if the data source supports database grouping. Just remember that database grouping (as the name suggests) applies to data-oriented options such as record order and selection. Report grouping involves actions that affect the appearance of the report.

DATABASE GROUPING ReportSmith is a client/server reporting tool in the true sense of the word. The database grouping option lets you perform record grouping on the server before the records are loaded into the report. You are actually building a GROUP BY clause in the SQL text used by ReportSmith to fetch the records for the report. You can also use this option to limit the records included in the report to those that match specific grouping criteria. When you create a group selection criteria, you are building a HAVING clause for the GROUP BY statement.

Database grouping relies on the power of the back-end RDBMS (Relational Database Management System) to provide the record grouping. This server-based grouping can significantly increase report performance when you are reporting on data stored in an SQL RDBMS such as InterBase, Oracle, SQL Server, Informix, and so forth. However, you may not be able to use this feature at all if the back-end or the driver that talks to that back-end does not support the GROUP BY or the HAVING syntax. Use the Test button to make sure the capability is supported for your selected data source.

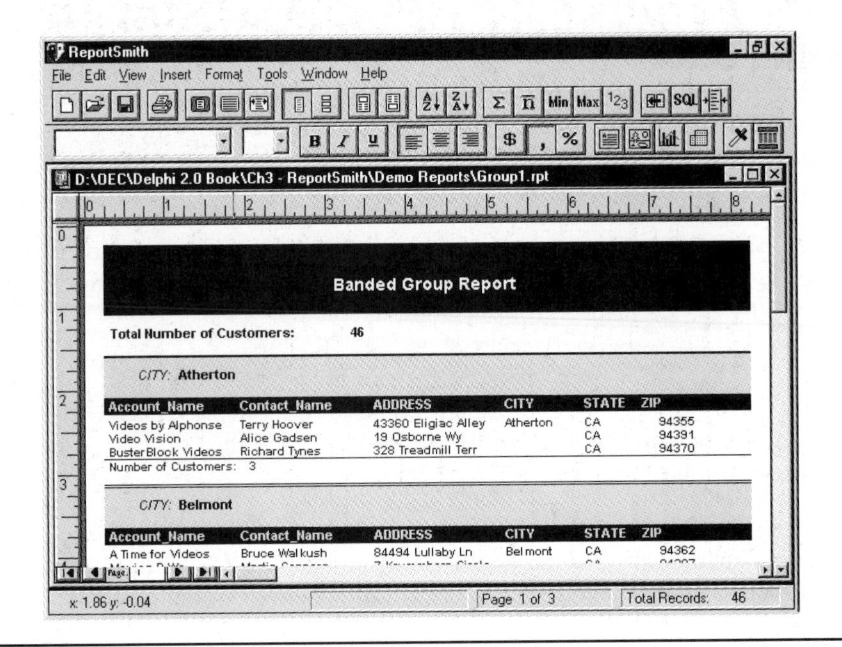

Figure 9-8. *A report grouped by city*

To use database grouping, perform these actions:

1. Select Tools | Database Grouping from the ReportSmith menus. The Database Grouping dialog box, shown in Figure 9-9, will appear.
2. Turn on the "Group data" check box near the top of this dialog box. This step activates database grouping.
3. You can either drag fields to reflect the proper order, or use the button on the right to move fields into the proper order.
4. At the bottom of the dialog box is an area for creating group selection criteria. All options are built with drop-down menus, so you never have to remember what syntax to use.

REPORT GROUPING This type of grouping is performed by ReportSmith itself after the data has been loaded into the report. Although it may slow report performance, this type of grouping is always supported regardless of data source. To use report grouping, follow these steps:

1. Select Tools | Report Grouping from the menu to display the Define Groups dialog box shown in Figure 9-10. All of the currently existing report groups will be displayed.
2. Select a field on which to group.
3. Click the New Group button.
4. Click the Group Properties button to set the specific options of the group.

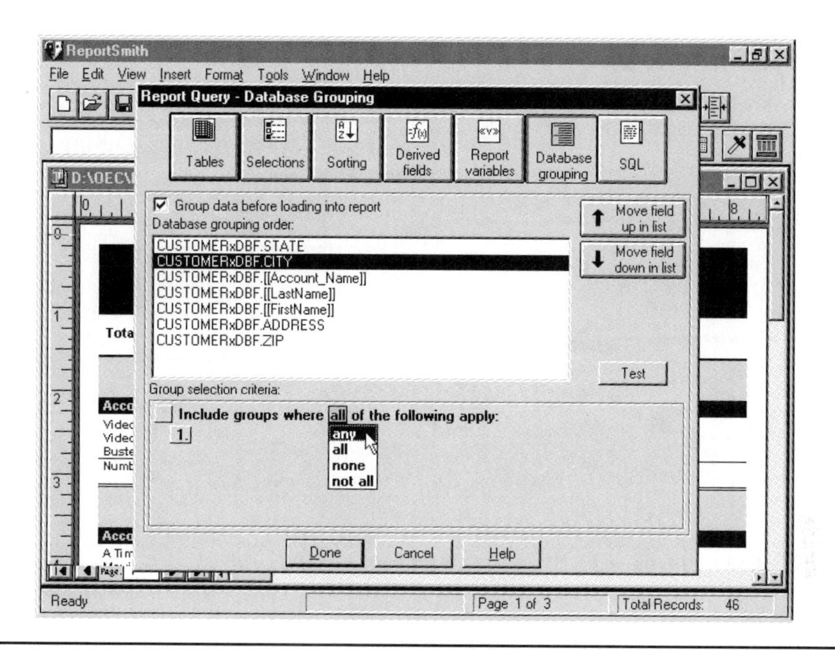

Figure 9-9. *The Database Grouping dialog box*

The Group Properties dialog box lets you define how groups are controlled. You can either group records based on which ones have the same value in a field, or you can simply specify that you want a certain number of records in each group, regardless of the field values. This dialog box also allows you to control the suppression of duplicate values within a group.

ACTIVATING REPEATING GROUP COLUMN LABELS By default, ReportSmith places column labels at the top of each page. For regular columnar reports, this default works fine. However, when you create groups in your reports, the default behavior for column labels means that only the first group on each page gets column labels. ReportSmith provides a simple way to fix this. Just select Insert | Field Labels from the menu and turn on the Group Header/Footer option.

Selecting Records

Like sorting and grouping, record selection can be performed either in a visual fashion or through a dialog box.

VISUAL DRAG-AND-DROP SELECTION You can perform "selection by example" directly from the data in your report using the following steps:

1. Right-click on the field containing the data you want to select and pick the Selection Criteria option from the ReportSmith speed menu. ReportSmith displays the Field Selection Criteria dialog box.
2. Click in the left margin of the report to select the record area.

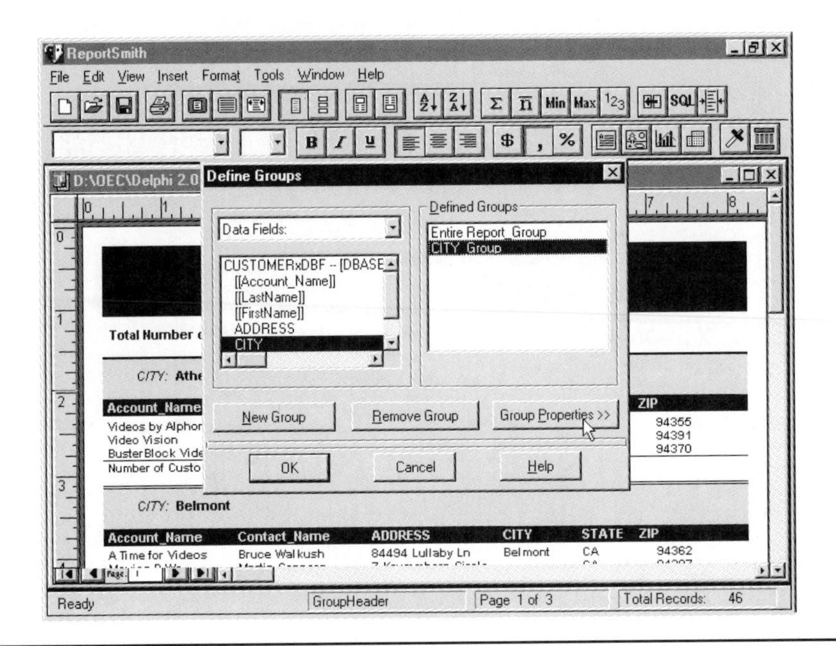

Figure 9-10. *The Define Groups dialog box*

3. Click on an example of the exact value you want included in your report and drag it into the Field Selection Criteria dialog box.
4. If you want more than one selection item, click in the yellow box to the left of the first selection item. Select "Insert new selection criteria after this item".
5. At the top of the selections, change the "All of the following must apply" by clicking on the word "All" and selecting "At least one".
6. Continue to drag new examples into the selection criteria area.
7. Click the Apply or Done button when you have finished with the selections you want included. Your selection criteria will now be applied to your report, and only records that meet those criteria will appear.

Figure 9-11 shows this process being used to define the selection criteria for a report.

EXPLICIT SELECTION You can build even more complex selection criteria by using the Selections dialog box shown in Figure 9-12. To display this dialog box, select Tools | Selections from the main menu.

The example shown in Figure 9-12 will display only those records from the Bahamas or the U.S. that are in the state of California or that have no state specified. Notice that this selection criteria builds upon the drag-and-drop selections shown in Figure 9-11.

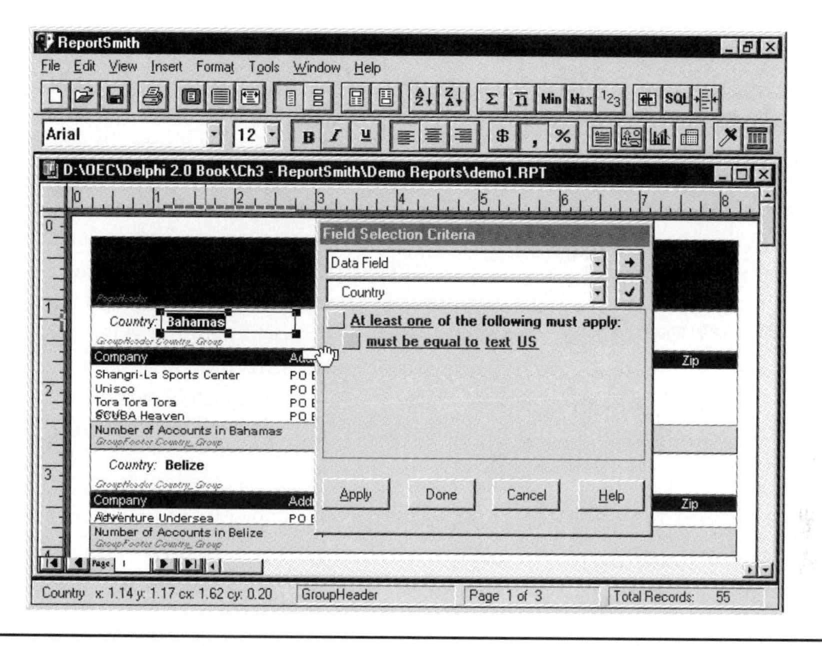

Figure 9-11. *Using drag-and-drop to specify record selections*

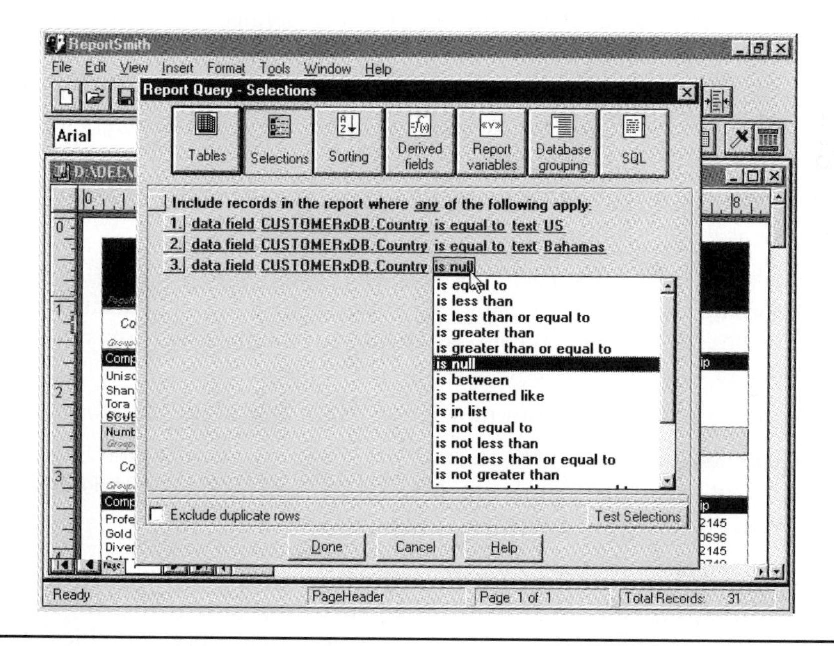

Figure 9-12. *The Selections dialog box*

Report Variables

ReportSmith allows you to create variables that are not tied to the data at all. Instead, these report variables have values that are supplied by the user and then become available within the report for tasks such as record selection.

SMART REPORTS Many applications have far more report users than data-entry users. Report variables become the mechanism whereby you can create "smart" reports. The values for report variables can be supplied directly by the end user or indirectly by passing them from a Delphi application. When the report is run from the Delphi application, ReportSmith checks to see if all report variables have already been supplied values. If they have, the report proceeds and automatically uses the values supplied by Delphi. If any of the report variables have not been assigned a value, or if the report is run as a stand-alone (that is, outside of any Delphi application), then ReportSmith prompts the user to supply values.

DEFINING A REPORT VARIABLE Like variables in Delphi's Object Pascal, report variables must first be defined and assigned a variable type. Follow these steps to set up each report variable:

1. Use the Tools | Report Variables menu selection to display the Report Variables dialog box shown in Figure 9-13.
2. Enter a name for your report variable in the Name field.
3. Select the type for the report variable. It can be defined as String, Number, Date, Time, or Date and Time.
4. Enter a value for the title. ReportSmith automatically creates a dialog box to prompt the user for a report variable's value. The Title value refers to the title ReportSmith will display on that dialog box.
5. Enter a value for the prompt. The Prompt value refers to the string that will appear as the message within the prompting dialog box.
6. Select an entry method. The report variable's value can be entered by typing it in, choosing from a list, choosing the value from a table, or choosing between two values (yes/no, true/false). Various option settings will appear based on the type of the report variable and the entry option chosen.
7. To save the definition of your new report variable, click the Add button.
8. To create another report variable, you must click the New button first. Editing the current data on the right side of the dialog will change the existing report variable; it will not create a new one.

When you are finished creating report variables, ReportSmith will prompt you to supply initial values for each variable. You won't see any effect on your report, though, because you haven't told ReportSmith how to use your new report variables.

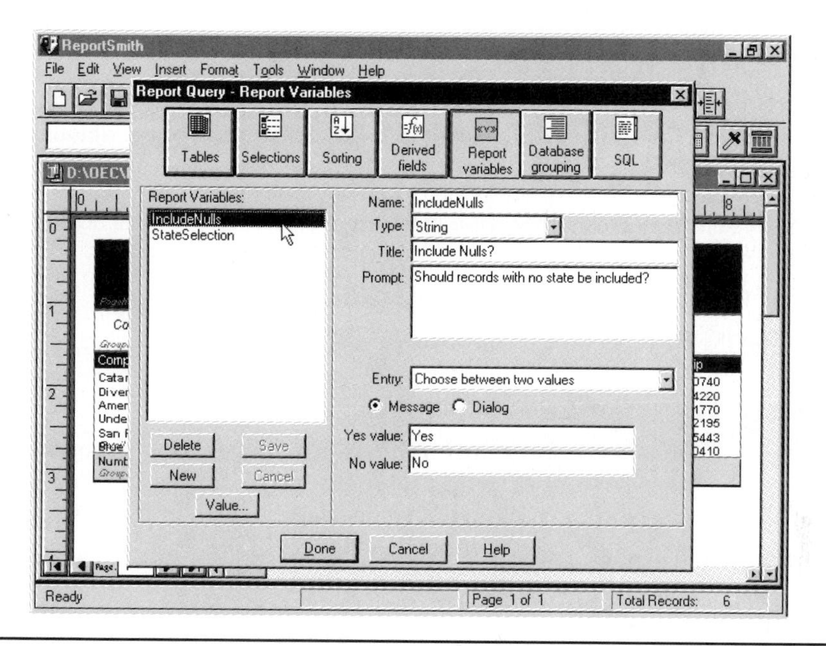

Figure 9-13. *The Report Variable dialog box*

USING A REPORT VARIABLE Report variables are most often used to provide runtime record selection. Just use the drop-down menus in the Selections dialog box to switch from a hard-coded text value to the use of your report variable. You can also use selection lists in conjunction with report variables to create complex criteria. Say, for example, that you want to include records from a specific state along with records with no state specified. However, you only want these null-state records included if the user wants to include them.

The sample report DEMO1.RPT uses two report variables named StateSelection and IncludeNulls to accomplish this task. Figure 9-14 shows how the report uses these variables. Note that a list is used as a logical "AND" to determine whether to include records with a blank state field.

CHANGING THE VALUE OF A REPORT VARIABLE You may want to test multiple parts of a report controlled by a report variable. Likewise, you may want to print a different set of records without having to reload the report. In either case, you want to alter the value initially assigned to a report variable. Here's how:

1. Select Tools | Report Variables from the main menu to display the Report Variables dialog box shown in Figure 9-13.
2. Click on the name of the report variable whose value you want to change.
3. Click the Value button that appears near the bottom of the dialog box. ReportSmith will prompt you for a different value in the same manner that it prompted for the initial value.

Summary-Only Reports

Sometimes you only want to display the summary information contained in the group headers and footers. Follow these steps to suppress the printing of the detail band to create a summary-only report.

1. Start by selecting Format | Section from the menu to display the Section dialog box.
2. Select the detail band in the Apply to Section area.
3. Turn on the Hide Section check box.

Controlling Group Settings

You can control which bands appear in your report from the Section dialog box. You can also determine the page control settings used by each band. To prevent the splitting of a group between the bottom of one page and the top of the next, select the group header and turn on the Keep Section Together check box.

Multitable Reports

Some reports require information that is stored in more than one table. When you create a multitable report, you need to tell ReportSmith not only which tables to use but also how to link the tables together.

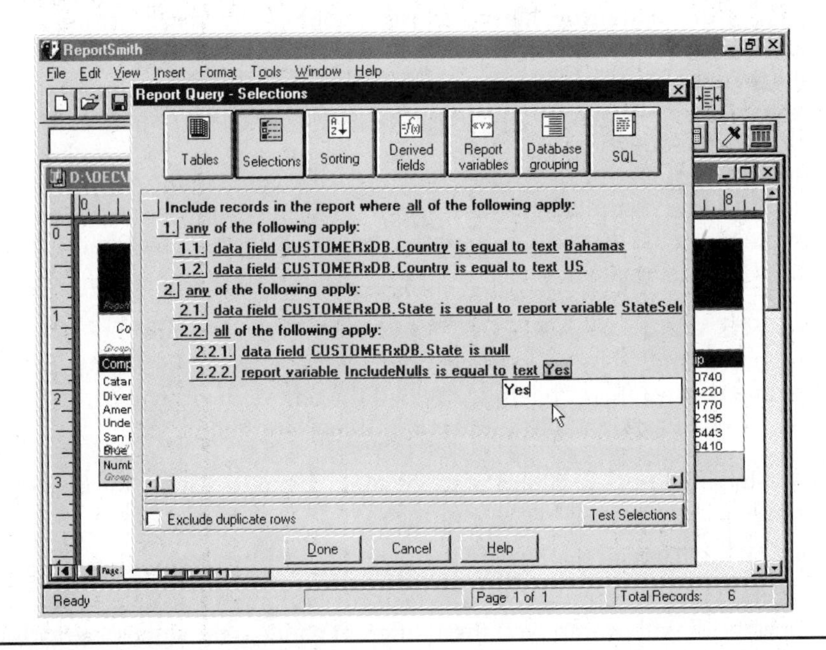

Figure 9-14. *Using report variables in the selection criteria*

Selecting the Tables

Creating multitable reports is similar to creating single-table reports. You just need to select more than one table, and then link the tables together. The following steps involved are involved:

1. Select the master table. This process is identical to that for the single-table report.
2. Select a child table by clicking on the Add table button again. Select any related child table the same way you did the master table. Repeat this step until you've selected all the tables you want.

Linking the Tables

Once you have selected the tables you want to include in your report, you need to tell ReportSmith how to relate them:

1. From the Report Query - Tables dialog box, click the Add new link button in the lower right-hand area. ReportSmith will bring up the Create New Table Link dialog box.
2. Select the tables to link together. When you only have two tables in the report, ReportSmith will automatically select both tables properly. If you have more than two tables in your report, simply click on the master table in the left-hand list of tables, and click on the child table in the right-hand list.
3. Select the fields to link. The field names don't have to match; however, the data type of the fields must match exactly.
4. Click the OK button to return to the Report Query - Tables dialog box. Repeat the process for each table link you need to define.

Selecting Fields

Now that the tables have been selected and linked, the final step in creating your report is to select which fields you want in your report. Once again, ReportSmith will default to include all the fields from all the tables selected for the report. Follow the same steps outlined for selecting fields in the single-table report (see the "Columnar Reports" section).

Running the Report

Once you have selected the fields, return to the Report Query - Tables dialog box and click the Done button. ReportSmith will then generate an initial report based on your selections. You can then customize the appearance of your report using the variety of standard ReportSmith formatting features.

MISSING ANY DATA? If you do not see any rows of data displayed, it probably means that you had no related data in your detail table. This occurs because, by default, ReportSmith only displays master records that have corresponding detail records. To display all records in the master table regardless of the presence or absence of associated detail records, you must perform what is known as an *outer join*. Here's how:

1. Click on the current link in the Report Query - Tables dialog box and select the Edit link button. The Edit Table Link dialog box will appear, as shown in Figure 9-15.
2. Select the appropriate "Include unmatched records" check box that appears under the list of fields for each table.

Visually Joining Tables

ReportSmith also provides an easier way of creating multitable reports more suited for end users who are less familiar with SQL join semantics. You can visually merge two single-table reports. To perform a visual merge, do the following:

1. Create or open two single-table reports that contain the data you want to join.
2. Click to select the common field in each report.
3. Click the merge reports button in the toolbar (this button shows two reports connected by an arrow). You can also select Tools | Merge Reports from the menu.

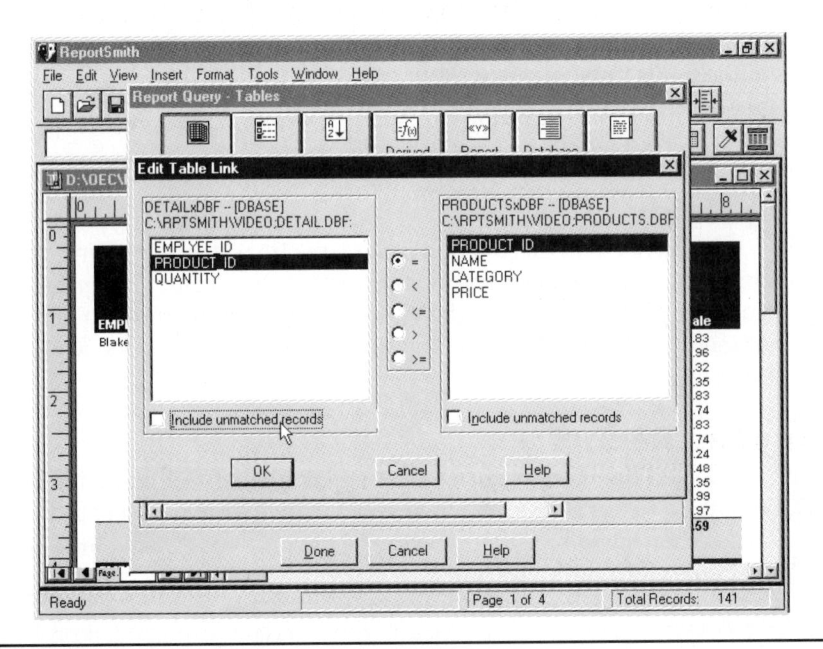

Figure 9-15. *The Edit Table Link dialog box*

ReportSmith will perform the table join on the selected columns and add all the fields from one report into the other. You can then proceed to create report groups, format the report, and so on.

Crosstab Reports

A crosstab report can be thought of as a kind of baseball box score for your data. Just as a box score summarizes a baseball game's important highlights, a crosstab can provide an excellent summary analysis of pertinent aspects about your data. ReportSmith lets you create multi-layered crosstabs and supports live data pivoting (the dynamic switching between the fields used for the columns and rows) within these multi-level crosstabs. You can also place multiple crosstabs on a single page.

Say, for example, you want to analyze sales in a video store. You want to know how much each employee has sold, broken down by category of video. This type of analysis is perfect for a crosstab. The employee names become the "teams" of the box score, the video categories become the "innings," and the sum of the total sales for each employee become the "runs scored" in each cell of the box score.

Creating a Crosstab Report

As in many aspects of ReportSmith, two ways exist for creating crosstabs: a visual, end-user-oriented method, and a more powerful dialog-based way. The visual method is designed for easily creating summaries of existing report data and placing the crosstab within the same report. The power method is for creating a crosstab from scratch or modifying an existing crosstab.

BUILDING CROSSTABS VISUALLY FROM A COLUMNAR REPORT These are the steps to create a crosstab visually:

1. Build or open a columnar report that contains the data you want to summarize. You will need to have two columns of non-numeric data to provide the row and column groupings for the crosstab, plus a column of numeric data to summarize.
2. The crosstab must be placed in either a header or a footer band. If you want the crosstab to appear on every page of the report, place it in the page header band that is created automatically for every report. (You can also decide to create a page footer and place it there.) Create a report group header or footer if you want the crosstab to appear only once at either the beginning or end of the report.
3. CTRL-click on the "rows" field, the "columns" field, and the data field to select all three.
4. Click the crosstab button in the toolbar. The cursor will change to a barred circle (the international "No" sign) until you are pointing to an area where the crosstab can be placed. The cursor will change to a mini-crosstab once you are over a legal area.

5. Click where you want to place the crosstab. ReportSmith will format and place the crosstab at that location in your report, as shown in Figure 9-16. Use the right-mouse speed menu to reach the various options available for further enhancing your crosstab. (The details about these options are covered in the next section.)

STARTING A NEW CROSSTAB REPORT You can generate a crosstab-only report by selecting the Crosstab Report button from the Create New Report dialog box when you start a new report. You will be prompted, as you are for all new reports, for the tables to include in your report and how they are to be linked. At this point, you should also define any needed derived fields and report variables. ReportSmith will display the Crosstab Report dialog box, shown in Figure 9-17, when you click the Done button in the Report Query dialog box.

You use the Crosstab Report dialog box to specify how to lay out the crosstab, what summary operations to perform, how to format the information displayed, how to aggregate the data groupings, plus a variety of other options. The right-hand side of the dialog box provides the basic layout information. Notice in Figure 9-17 that you can place multiple items in the Rows, Columns, and Values areas. In fact, you can place the same item in the Values area and then set the options to provide a different kind of data display (percent of total, for example). The Type drop-down menu in the upper left corner provides access to data fields, derived fields, and calculated fields.

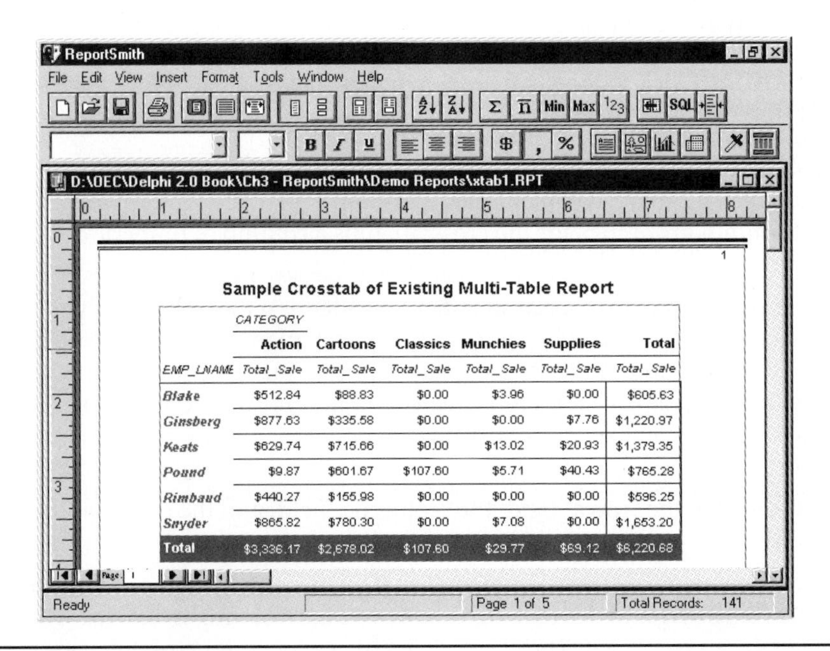

Figure 9-16. *A simple crosstab*

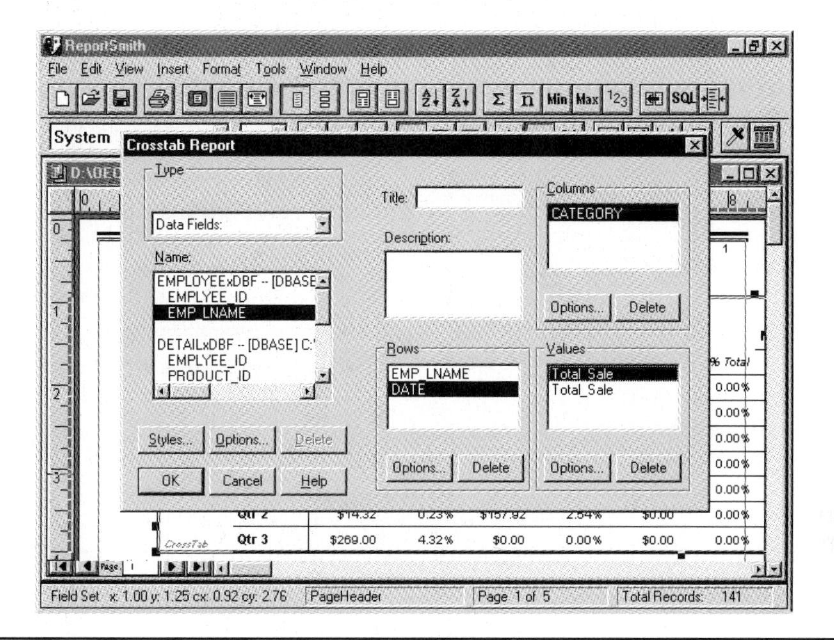

Figure 9-17. *The Crosstab Report dialog box*

To add a field to a crosstab area, simply drag-and-drop it into the appropriate region in the dialog. ReportSmith usually expects numerical data of some kind to be placed in the Values area. You can, however, place textual information there as long as you select an appropriate summary operation such as a count of values. Textual data usually gets placed in the row and column areas. Date information can be placed in the row or column area as well.

Data will be grouped in the order in which fields appear in the row and column lists. The top-most field is the master group, and each subsequent entry in the row or column list represents a subgrouping of the item immediately above it in the list. Placing multiple items in the Values area results in the creation of multiple summary columns.

Crosstab Options

Each area in the crosstab definition has an Options button for setting the various data related options for the selected item of that area.

DATE AGGREGATION Figure 9-18 shows the option settings for creating a date-oriented grouping that gets aggregated by quarter.

PERCENT OF TOTAL You can create a crosstab that contains both summary data as well as a percent of total display of the same data. To do so, follow these steps:

1. Place the data field in the Values area twice.
2. Format the first copy of the data field normally.

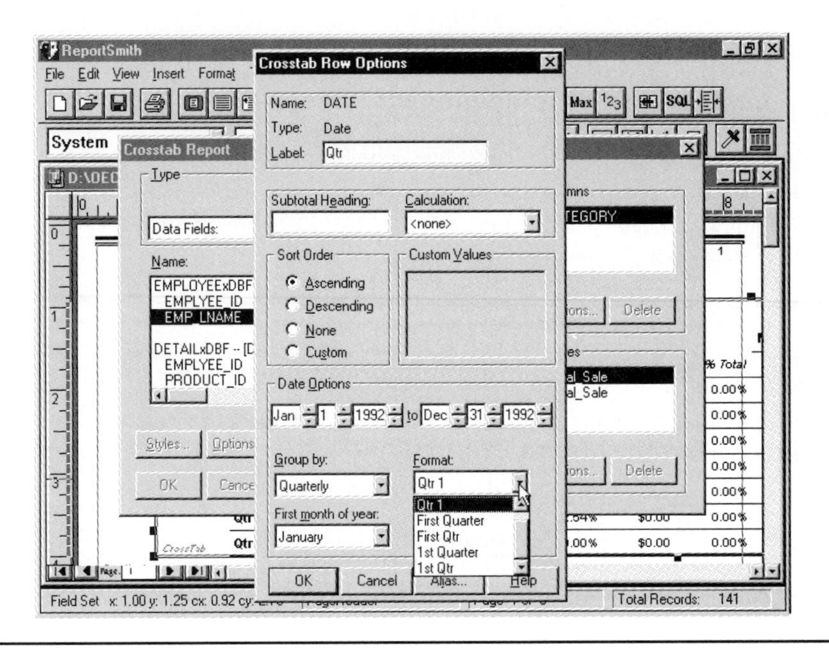

Figure 9-18. *Setting date options*

3. Select the second copy of the data field and click the Options button in the Values area.
4. Select the appropriate radio button in the Shown Value area to produce the percent of total column that is desired.

Ad Hoc Analysis with Crosstabs

ReportSmith lets you perform data pivoting with any crosstab that has multiple levels being analyzed. For example, say you have data analyzed by employee by quarter. If you want to reverse that analysis so that the data is analyzed by quarter by employee, simply drag the employee name column to the right of the quarters column. Even more interesting would be an analysis by employee by category across the four quarters of the year. To perform this kind of analysis from the same crosstab, just drag the quarters column and drop it on the top of the crosstab columns. Then drag the categories and drop them to the right of the employees column.

Graphing a Crosstab

ReportSmith's link to MS Graph can also be used to graph a crosstab:

1. Double-click in the crosstab to select it.
2. Click the toolbar's graph button. ReportSmith will automatically create a graph of the entire data set of the crosstab.
3. Place graphs in either a header or a footer region in the report.

4. Double-click on the graph to modify its settings.

Form Reports

ReportSmith supports creation of form-type reports, in which each record of the report appears on a separate page. Form reports are well suited for customer invoices and for form letters where you want to automate a process that needs to appear as if each letter were created on its own.

Creating Form-Based Reports

Form reports are created in much the same manner as are columnar reports. Select the New Report button from the Create New Report dialog box, then select a table and format the report. To create a form letter that embeds field data within standard text, you will need to build a derived field that concatenates the text and the field data.

Report Styles

Every report type has its own set of predefined styles. You can apply a style either when you first create a report or later by using the style button in the toolbar.

Creating New Styles

ReportSmith also lets you define new styles. Every new style you create is based on an existing report you have built. Follow these steps to create new styles:

1. Open the report that is styled the way you like.
2. Click the style button in the toolbar.
3. Click the New button in the Report Style dialog and name your new style.

This style will now be available wherever that kind of style can be applied.

Using ReportSmith with Delphi

There are two techniques for integrating ReportSmith reports into your Delphi applications. The first method applies to both 16-bit and 32-bit versions. The second method, using the direct Delphi Connection, is new with ReportSmith 3.0 and is only available for 32-bit applications.

Using Delphi-Supplied Parameters

Delphi's Report component provides a mechanism whereby you can pass values from your Delphi application into report variables contained within your report.

The Report Component

The Report component resides in the Data Access page of Delphi's component palette.

REPORT PROPERTIES Table 9-5 lists the key Report properties on which most of your development attention will be focused.

REPORT METHODS The Report component also supplies several methods for dealing with ReportSmith from within your Delphi application. All Report methods return a Boolean value. This return value gives you feedback on the success or failure of your Report's action. If the method's action gets a "command received" confirmation from ReportSmith, the return value will be True. A return value of False indicates some kind of problem. Table 9-6 lists the key Report methods.

Property	Function
AutoUnload	Determines whether ReportSmith exits or stays in memory once the report is finished. Keeping ReportSmith resident can significantly increase the performance of applications that print multiple reports at the same time. Use the CloseApplication method to shut down ReportSmith if AutoUnload is set to False.
InitialValues	Use this array of TStrings to specify initial values for any report variables included in the report. See the discussion in "Integrating RS Report Variables into your Delphi Applications" for complete details.
LaunchType	Determines whether ReportSmith or the ReportSmith Runtime will be launched. The default value of ltDefault will launch the ReportSmith 3.0 design environment when you double-click on the TReport in Delphi's IDE, and it will execute the ReportSmith 3.0 Runtime when you launch a report from within a running Delphi application (Delphi 2 only).
Preview	Determines whether the RUN method launches a print preview or a hard-copy output run. If Preview is set to True, use the PRINT method instead of RUN to force hard-copy output.
ReportDir	The directory where the report resides. At runtime, use the function ExtractFilePath(ParamStr(0)) to set this property to the current application directory. Do not leave this property blank.
ReportName	The name of the RPT file to run. Only place the filename here. All directory information should be placed in the ReportDir property. Any directory information placed in the ReportName property will be ignored.

Table 9-5. *Key Properties of the Report Component*

Method	Function
CloseApplication	Tells ReportSmith to perform a File | Exit. Use this method when your Report's AutoUnload property is False. Make sure you call CloseApplication before exiting your Delphi 1.0 applications. In Delphi 1.0, ReportSmith will not exit even when your application shuts down. This behavior has changed with 32-bit applications. ReportSmith will automatically shut down when you exit a Delphi 2 application, even if AutoUnload is False.
Connect	Allows you to connect to a database and bypass the ReportSmith database login. The Connect method is not needed for reports that use the Delphi Connection.
Print	Forces a hard-copy output of the report, regardless of the value of the Preview property.
RecalcReport	Tells ReportSmith to refresh the report. Use this method whenever you change the value of a report variable or navigate to a new record set in a Delphi Connection report.
Run	Runs the designated report, looking at the value of the Preview property to determine whether a preview or a hard copy should be made.
RunMacro	Lets you run a ReportBasic macro.
SetVariable	Lets you set or change the value of a report variable. If you specify a report variable name that is not used in the current report, the variable will be ignored.
SetVariableLines	Similar to SetVariable, this method lets you set or change the value of a report variable by using an array of type TStrings.

Table 9-6. *Key Methods of the Report Component*

Integrating RS Report Variables into your Delphi Applications

Delphi applications can control ReportSmith by predefining the values of any report variables used. ReportSmith will still prompt the user for any report variables that do not yet have a value.

Keep in mind that Delphi deals with report variables in two separate ways, depending on whether the report is already open. If the report hasn't been opened, you need to assign values by setting up the InitialValues property of the Report object.

Once the report is running, set or change the values of report variables using the SetVariable or SetVariableLines methods.

Do not use SetVariable or SetVariableLines without an open report. These methods try to establish a DDE (Dynamic Data Exchange) conversation with ReportSmith. If ReportSmith isn't running, these methods will launch it without the proper setup. Your report variable changes will be ignored, and Delphi will not know they have been lost. Make sure you use the InitialValues property to establish report variable values prior to launching a report.

ASSIGNING INITIAL VALUES TO REPORT VARIABLES You can assign initial values to report variables either at design time in the Delphi IDE, or in your application's code. To set initial values at design time, double-click on the edit box for the InitialValues property and enter the report variable name and its value in the string editor.

The proper syntax for each entry in the InitialValues property is @ReportVarName=<ValueToAssign>. No spaces are allowed, and the @ sign and angle brackets are required. Remember that report variable names are case sensitive. You must duplicate the report variable's name exactly as it was defined in ReportSmith.

You can also attach code to an application event that sets up the initial values as well. For example, you might place the following code on a print button to initialize a report and then launch it:

```
procedure TForm1.BtnPreviewClick(Sender: TObject);
begin
  Report1.ReportDir := ExtractFilePath(ParamStr(0));
  Report1.ReportName := 'Demo1.rpt';
  Report1.InitialValues.Add('@StateSelection=<CA>');
  Report1.InitialValues.Add('@IncludeNulls=<No>');
  Report1.run;
end;
```

CHANGING THE VALUE OF A REPORT VARIABLE Once a report is opened, you have to change report variables in a way that can be recognized by an active report. To do so, use the SetVariable or SetVariableLines method. Changing a report variable does not automatically refresh the report based on the new value. This separation allows you to set multiple new values before using the RecalcReport method to force a refresh of the report. You should usually test the success of any changes before telling ReportSmith to recalculate the report. One example is given here:

```
if Report1.SetVariable('IncludeNulls', 'Yes') then
  Report1.RecalcReport;
```

It is extremely important to note that the syntax used by the SetVariable and SetVariableLines methods is very different from what you use to set the InitialValues property. Do not precede the variable name with an @ sign. Variable names must still be entered in the correct case, however.

AN EXAMPLE DELPHI APPLICATION USING REPORT VARIABLES The RS_DEMO1.DPR project on the CD demonstrates how to control a ReportSmith report from within a Delphi application with report variables. This project uses the techniques described above to control the running of the DEMO1.RPT report file.

DEMO1.RPT is an example of a "smart" report. First, start up ReportSmith and open the DEMO1.RPT report file by itself. The report automatically prompts you to supply values for two report variables. Once you answer these questions, the report proceeds.

Now try running the Delphi application RS_DEMO1.EXE and see the difference in running the same report controlled by this Delphi application. Since Delphi is supplying the values for the two report variables, the report already has all the information it needs before it starts. The user is never prompted by ReportSmith.

The main code that runs the RS_DEMO1 application is listed here. Take particular note of the SetVars procedure. It tests whether the application has run ReportSmith before deciding whether to use the InitialValues property or the SetVariable method.

Try changing the value of one or both items in RS_DEMO1 and watch the effect of pressing the Recalc Report button. The report will update behind the scene.

```
procedure TForm1.SetVars(Sender: TObject);
begin
  if BtnPreview.Visible then
    begin
    Report1.InitialValues.Add('@StateSelection=<'+cbStateList.Text+'>');
    if CbxNulls.checked then
       Report1.InitialValues.Add('@IncludeNulls=<Yes>')
    else
       Report1.InitialValues.Add('@IncludeNulls=<No>');
    end
  else
    begin
    Report1.SetVariable('StateSelection', cbStateList.Text);
    if CbxNulls.checked then
       Report1.SetVariable('IncludeNulls', 'Yes')
    else
       Report1.SetVariable('IncludeNulls', 'No');
    BtnRecalc.Enabled := true;
    end;
end;

procedure TForm1.BtnRecalcClick(Sender: TObject);
begin
  Report1.RecalcReport;
  BtnRecalc.Enabled := false;
end;
```

```
procedure TForm1.BtnPreviewClick(Sender: TObject);
begin
  Report1.ReportDir := ExtractFilePath(ParamStr(0));
  Report1.run;
  BtnRecalc.Top := 16;
  BtnPreview.Visible := false;
  BtnRecalc.Visible := true;
end;
```

Using a Generic Report Selection DLL

A generic report selection project named GETREP.DPR can also be found on the CD that accompanies this book. This project compiles to a DLL that provides an open-ended way of running reports from your Delphi applications. Using this DLL provides two main benefits:

- It supports creating "long" report descriptions.
- It supports letting end users create new reports.

Each report can have an associated text file that provides a description of what the report is supposed to do. To add a description for a new report, simply create a text file with the same name as the .RPT file but with a .TXT extension. If a description file exists for the currently highlighted report, that text will be displayed in the description area.

SETTING UP YOUR APPLICATION TO USE GETREP You first need to copy GETREP.DLL into your Windows System directory or into the application's directory. Then, add the following code at the very beginning of the implementation section of your application:

```
{ connect to external Report Browser routine in GETREP.DLL }
function GetReportFile(Buffer:pointer;BufLen:integer):integer;
                 far; external 'GETREP' name 'GetReportFile';
```

USING GETREP Now you just need to call the GetReportFile function whenever you want your application to invoke the GETREP functionality. This function returns a value of zero if the user successfully selected a report file. The code below is one example of how to use GetReportFile:

```
procedure TForm1.BtnPrintClick(Sender: TObject);
{ This routine runs an existing report using the
  RS Runtime(which MUST be in the DOS Path). The
  specific report to run is selected by calling
  the GETREP Report Browser DLL.}
const
   BufLen = 127;
var
```

```
    Repname: array[0..BufLen] of char;
begin
  if GetReportFile(@RepName,BufLen) = 0 then
  begin
    Report1.ReportDir := ExtractFilePath(strpas(RepName));
    Report1.ReportName := ExtractFileName(strpas(RepName));
    Report1.Run;
  end;
end;
```

Using the New Delphi Connection

So far, nearly everything covered in this chapter has discussed features available to all versions of Delphi and ReportSmith. The Delphi Connection capability is new to ReportSmith 3.0. The Delphi Connection consists of a new data type that gets its data from a Delphi 2.0 Dataset object. The Delphi Connection provides ReportSmith with a shared connection to the BDE data buffer in use by the chosen DataSet component. To use the Delphi Connection, follow these steps:

1. Invoke ReportSmith from within the Delphi 2 IDE by double-clicking on a TReport component.
2. Select Delphi as the data type.
3. Click the Server Connect button. ReportSmith will display the names of all the DataSet components.
4. Select the desired DataSet.

Even if you have more than one DataSet in your Delphi application, you will only be able to select one of them. As a result, you will probably use a Query with the Delphi Connection. The single DataSet restriction usually proves too limiting to make Tables a useful DataSet for these kinds of reports.

Where Do You Control Each Option?

ReportSmith relinquishes all control of the DataSet to Delphi. Thus, all table joins and all data selections, groupings, and sortings are performed by the Delphi DataSet object. Using the Delphi Connection requires a little forethought when setting up the DataSet. You may have to adjust the way you set up the SQL of your Query to accommodate the results you want in your report. You may also have to adjust some of the ways you work with ReportSmith to gain the desired report result. Table 9-7 indicates whether particular ReportSmith tools are controlled by the Delphi DataSet or by ReportSmith.

Why Use the Delphi Connection?

Report variables can still be used, just like in 16-bit reporting. However, the primary use of report variables in a Delphi/ReportSmith application is to limit the record selection to a user-supplied value. The techniques described in this section provide an alternative way of limiting the records reported on. Although they are still available, report variables are much less necessary in reports that use the Delphi Connection.

The Delphi Connection also largely eliminates the need for any kind of computations on the ReportSmith side. Calculated fields, for example, are now all created on the Delphi side of your application. Consequently, you can usually focus on developing your entire application in a single language, Delphi's Object Pascal. You may still need ReportBasic for some reporting tasks, but those occasions will now be fairly rare.

When deciding whether to use the Delphi Connection, remember that it is a shared data buffer between ReportSmith and Delphi. You can not use the Delphi Connection to create "smart" reports that need to be run in a stand-alone fashion.

Limiting the Record Scope

By default, a Delphi Connection provides all the records in the DataSet to your report. Even if you can't see the records on-screen in your Delphi application, they will be

ReportSmith Tool	Option Control
Tables	Controlled mostly by ReportSmith, but limited to selecting a single DataSet.
Selections	Determined by the DataSet only.
Sorting	Determined by the DataSet only.
Derived Fields	Still controlled in part by ReportSmith; however, only derived fields created by ReportBasic macro can be created. Any derived field that needs to be part of the record selection criteria or data grouping should be built as a calculated field in the DataSet.
Report Variables	Still controlled by ReportSmith.
Database Grouping	Determined by the DataSet only.
SQL Text	Determined by the DataSet only.
Report Grouping	Still controlled by ReportSmith. In fact, this is the only way to provide grouping in the report beyond what was created in the DataSet.
Summary Fields	Still controlled by ReportSmith.
Field Selection Criteria	Determined by the DataSet only.
Merge Reports	This option is disabled, since the Delphi Connection only allows a single data source.

Table 9-7. *ReportSmith Options*

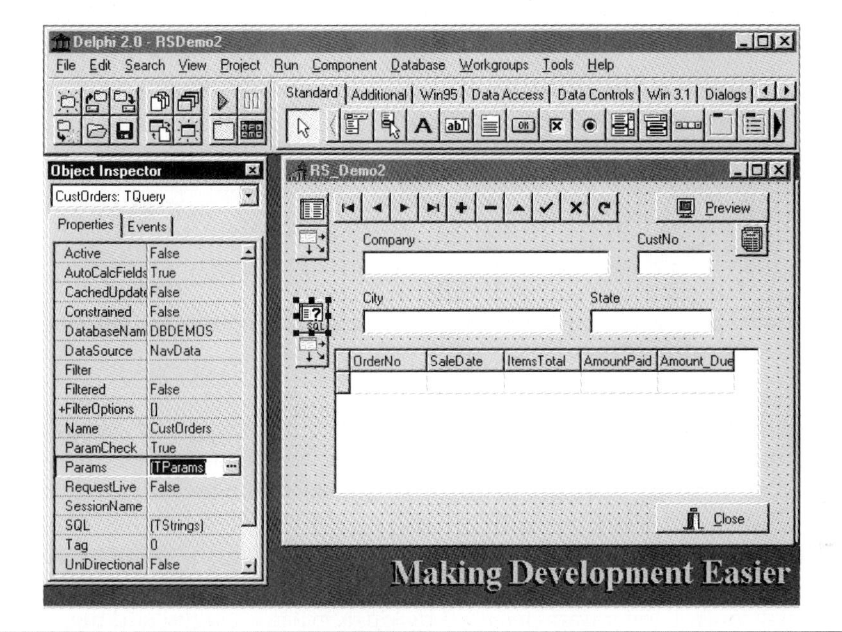

Figure 9-19. *The RS_Demo2.DPR Project*

included in your Delphi Connection report. This can present a bit of a challenge if you want to limit which records are included in a report yet provide access to a broader range of records in your Delphi application.

The solution is to make use of a parameterized query as the DataSet used by the report. This Query object will be controlled by another DataSet object within your Delphi application. The controlling DataSet object will limit the records displayed at any one time in the report's Query. By navigating through the controlling DataSet, you will be able to navigate through the report's Query data as well.

The RS_Demo2.DPR project, shown in Figure 9-19, illustrates this technique. It uses a DBNavigator that is hooked to a table named CustControl. A Query named CustOrders is the data source for the DEMO2.RPT report. It is also used in the DBEdit components and the DBGrid that provide the data display. The records selected by the CustOrders Query are controlled by the CustNo field in the CustControl table. To provide the coordination between CustOrders and CustControl, the DataSource property of CustOrders is set to NavData, the DataSource connected to the CustControl DataSet.

The SQL for the CustOrders DataSet is shown here:

```
SELECT CUSTOMER."CustNo" , CUSTOMER."Company" ,
 CUSTOMER."City" , CUSTOMER."State" ,
 ORDERS."OrderNo" , ORDERS."SaleDate" ,
 ORDERS."ItemsTotal" ,
```

```
 ORDERS."AmountPaid" ,
 ( ORDERS.ItemsTotal - ORDERS.AmountPaid ) as Amount_Due ,
 ( CUSTOMER.Company + "     " + CUSTOMER.City + ", " + CUSTOMER.State )
   as Account
FROM "CUSTOMER.DB" CUSTOMER , "ORDERS.DB" ORDERS
WHERE ( CUSTOMER.CustNo = ORDERS.CustNo )
  AND
 (
 ( CUSTOMER."CustNo" = :CustNo )
 )
ORDER BY
 CUSTOMER."Company" , ORDERS."OrderNo"
```

The WHERE clause that states CUSTOMER."CustNo" = :CustNo is the key. The colon designates the name of a parameter to use in determining which records get selected and displayed. When the name of a parameter matches the name of a data field in a DataSet pointed to by a query's DataSource property, the value of that field in the current record is used in the WHERE clause. Thus, as you navigate through the records in CustControl, the parameter used by CustOrders changes, and the query is rerun automatically. The result is that you can scroll through all the customer accounts, yet only display and report on one account at a time. The data display results of this kind of set up are shown in Figure 9-20.

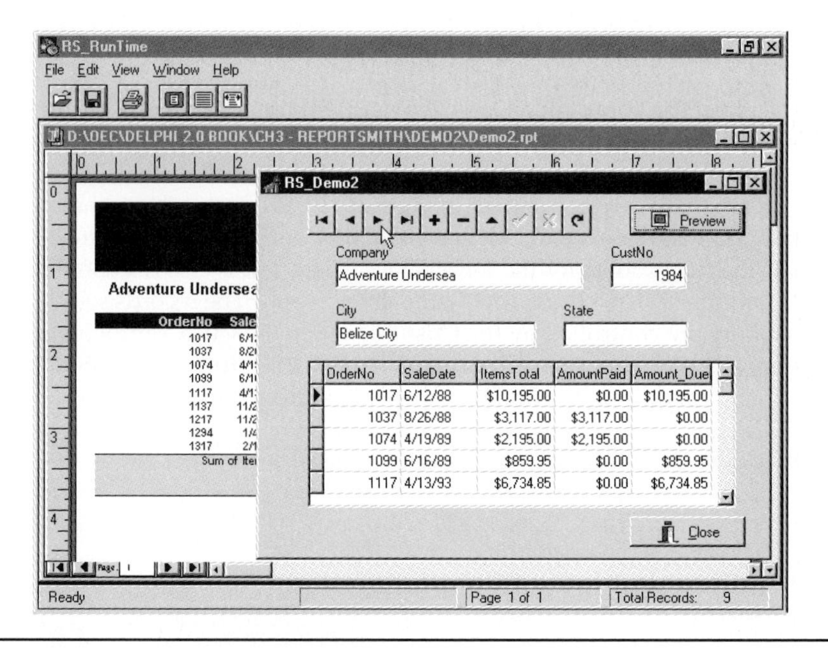

Figure 9-20. *Running RS_Demo2*

Side Effects of Using the Delphi Connection

Your Delphi DataSet is in control of the SQL text being used to build this type of report. Since most of the toolbar buttons affect the SQL code being built, the Delphi Connection will disable many of them. Many of the items in the Tools menu are also disabled. As a result, you will need to use alternate reporting techniques.

DERIVED FIELDS If you need to create derived fields or record selections within your SQL, you will need to do that in the Delphi DataSet. That is why the SQL text of the CustOrders query includes SQL code to create two calculated fields, the Amount_Due field and the Account field (a concatenation of the company's name, city, and state). You will also have to remove the DataSet and then add it back to your report if you make any changes to the Dataset once you begin designing your report. Otherwise, any newly created calculated fields will not show up in the list of available fields in ReportSmith.

GROUP HEADERS AND FOOTERS Included in the collection of disabled buttons are the ones that create group headers and footers. Fortunately, ReportSmith also provides a dialog box-based method for creating these report constructs. Creating group headers and footers thus becomes a multi-step process. Since even calculated fields are coming from the Delphi DataSet, ReportSmith considers all fields supplied by the Delphi Connection as data fields. You will need to create a data field-based group and then insert a header and/or footer for that group. To do this, follow these steps:

1. Use the Tools | Report Grouping menu selection to call up the grouping dialog.
2. Select from the list on the left the field upon which you want to group the data.
3. Click the New Group button. You can also click the Group Properties button to further define the group's options.
4. Click the OK button to complete creation of the group.
5. Select Insert | Header/Footer from the ReportSmith menu.
6. Select the group name you just created from the list on the left.
7. Activate the header, footer, or both check boxes on the right.
8. Click the OK button to finish the process.

You can, of course, repeat this process with multiple report groups. Once you have created a header or footer region, the summary buttons in the toolbar will become activated.

DESIGN TIME VERSUS RUNTIME CONSIDERATIONS Because you want to create a new report at design time, you usually don't want to fill in values for the report name or report directory properties of your Report component. This means that you will have to supply them at runtime when you try to activate the report. An example of typical code is shown here:

```
procedure TRS_Demo2.BtnPreviewClick(Sender: TObject);
begin
  Report1.ReportName := 'Demo2.rpt';
  Report1.ReportDir := ExtractFilePath(ParamStr(0));
  Report1.Run;
  CustOrders.Active := true;
end;
```

MAINTAINING AN ACTIVE CONNECTION You can also see that the CustOrders DataSet is activated by this code after the report is run. Why? You'll notice that the CustOrders DataSet is active when you first open the RS_Demo2 project. Now double-click on the Report component and open the DEMO2.RPT report. When you close down ReportSmith, you will see that the CustOrders DataSet is no longer active.

To preserve the safety of data concurrency, the Delphi Connection automatically deactivates the data connection in your Delphi application as it passes control of the DataSet to ReportSmith. This is actually a good idea. Unfortunately, Delphi has no real way to determine when control can be safely returned back from ReportSmith. So your code has to reactivate the data connection on its own.

NAVIGATING BETWEEN RECORDS You naturally want the report to reflect the current set of records displayed in your application. This coordination happens automatically when you first activate the report. After that point, however, you have two separate applications running in a semi-independent fashion. If you want to maintain the coordination between the two, you will have to code for that yourself in your Delphi application.

You should recalculate the report whenever you navigate to a new record in the controlling DataSet. Unfortunately, recalculating the report will also deactivate the data connection in your Delphi application. So your code needs to handle a couple of side effects: the reactivation of the data connection in your application and the elimination of the resulting screen flicker. The following code represents one way this can be done:

```
procedure TRS_Demo2.DBNavigator1Click(Sender: TObject;
  Button: TNavigateBtn);
begin
  if Report1.ReportName <> '' then
    begin
     Screen.cursor := crHourGlass;
     LockWindowUpdate(RS_Demo2.handle);  {Eliminate screen flicker}
     try
     Report1.RecalcReport;      {Refresh the report with the new data}
     CustOrders.Active := true;{Reactivate Deplhi's connection to data}
     finally
     LockWindowUpdate(0);       {Restore form updating}
     Screen.cursor := crDefault;
```

```
      end;
    end;
end;
```

The above code uses the Windows API function LockWindowUpdate() to eliminate any screen updates throughout the process of recalculating the report, the resulting deactivation of the data connection in Delphi, and the coded reactivation of that same DataSet. The value this function expects to receive is the window handle of the form to be locked. Only one window at a time can have its updates locked, and no window will have a handle of zero. Thus, telling LockWindowUpdate to lock window handle zero turns off the screen lock and automatically refreshes your form—with the currently selected data.

Advanced ReportSmith Techniques

Many power user and developer techniques are available for getting the most out of ReportSmith. This section covers a few of these techniques.

Controlling ReportSmith via DDE

All versions of ReportSmith support DDE as both a client and a server. You can take advantage of this ability to control the runtime reporting environment from within your Delphi application.

The RS_PANEL.DPR project, shown in Figure 9-21, builds a Delphi application that uses DDE to control the zoom factor, window state, and toolbar status of the running version of ReportSmith. Several aspects of the RS_PANEL code should be noted.

This code uses a manual DDE connection. Opening and closing the DDE connection will only let you change ReportSmith once per execution. To provide repeatable control of ReportSmith, you need to leave each DDE connection open until the Delphi form is closed.

The form's OnActivate procedure uses conditional compiler directives to change RS_PANEL's behavior in a 16-bit versus 32-bit environment. This action is needed because the text of some of the menu selections is different in version 2.5 and version 3.0 of ReportSmith.

```
1.procedure TRSCtrlPanel.FormActivate(Sender: TObject);
begin
{$IFNDEF WIN32}
{ 16-bit ReportSmith v2.5's View menu selection uses the
  word "Ruler", not the "Rulers" of the 32-bit RS version }
  CbxRuler.Caption := 'Ruler';
{$ENDIF}
end;
```

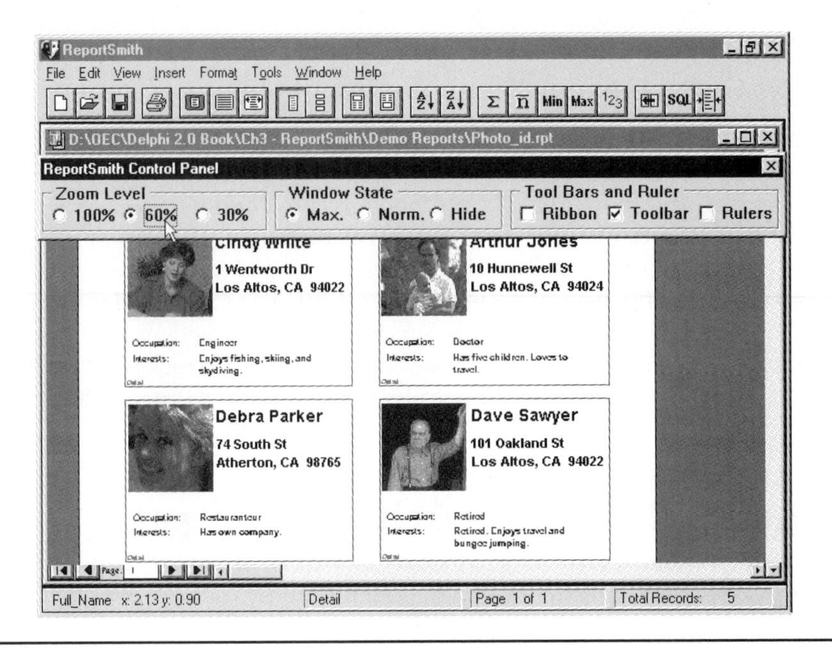

Figure 9-21. *RS_PANEL controlling ReportSmith's IDE*

For more details on using Delphi DDE to control ReportSmith, check out the complete code of RS_PANEL. Also, the ReportSmith manual contains an in-depth discussion of DDE usage.

ReportBasic—The Report Macro Language

Sometimes you need to control ReportSmith in a more direct fashion from within the ReportSmith environment itself. For example, you may wish to conditionally suppress the printing of a field if it contains a certain value. You might also want to transform a code or abbreviation into a more meaningful piece of data when you run the report. This is where ReportBasic, the ReportSmith macro language, comes into play.

Types of Macros

ReportBasic macros can be classified as either global macros or report macros. Global macros are linked to ReportSmith itself, whereas report macros are linked to a particular report. Report macros can be linked to a variety of report events, much like Delphi procedures can be linked to application events such as OnClick. ReportSmith events fall into five categories, which are listed in Table 9-8.

ReportSmith macros also can be used to create derived fields. These macro-derived fields cannot be used in grouping or record selection. However, the power of the ReportBasic language makes it much more flexible than SQL when it comes to creating derived fields.

Event Category	Description
Application	These events are recognized and controlled at the global ReportSmith level. Thus, global macros can be linked only to application events. Application events include trapping keystrokes, before and after operations on a report, and the opening and closing of ReportSmith.
Report	These events are trapped by the report itself. Macros attached to these events will be executed when the report recognizes them, so they will run after any global macros have executed. Many of the same events that are considered application events can also be used as report events.
Data Field	Only one type of data field event exists—the display event. Use this event to process information before it gets sent to the report. For example, a display event macro can be used for conditional formatting, data clean-up, and the transformation of internal codes into more meaningful representations.
Group Header	The only group header event that exists is the creation event. Macros tied to this event will execute every time a new header is being formatted. This event is particularly useful when you want to perform some logic at the start of every new group.
Group Footer	The group footer creation event is identical to the group header event but is triggered by the creation of a new footer.

Table 9-8. *ReportSmith Event Categories*

Creating a Macro

The Macro Commands dialog box is the central control area for creating new macros, saving macros to a file for reuse, loading existing saved macros, and assigning macros to one or more ReportSmith events. Follow these steps to create a macro:

1. Use the Tools | Macro menu selection to display the Macro Commands dialog box.
2. Type in a new macro name in the edit box at the top, and click the New button.
3. ReportSmith displays the Edit Macro dialog box. This dialog box is very similar in operation to the Formula Editor discussed previously.
4. Click on OK in the macro editor. ReportSmith will return you to the Macro Commands dialog box.

Assigning a Macro to a Report Event

You now need to assign your macro to an event. To do so, follow these steps:

1. Click the Links button to invoke the Macro Links dialog box shown in Figure 9-22.
2. Select an object type and event from the lists on the left.
3. Select a specific item from the list on the right.
4. Click the Link button.

You must assign the macro to at least one event for it to be run. ReportSmith gives you the ability to link a single macro to multiple events.

Sample Macros

ReportSmith ships with a collection of useful sample macros. You will find them in the MACROS subdirectory under the directory that ReportSmith is installed in. Table 9-9 lists these macros and their descriptions.

The ReportSmith manual also includes some very useful sample macro code. These macros show you how to:

- Connect to a database (eliminating the connection dialog)
- Determine a percent of total (without creating a crosstab)
- Summarize a macro-derived field
- Create and refresh a temporary table (which is useful for report variables defined with the "Choose from a table" option)

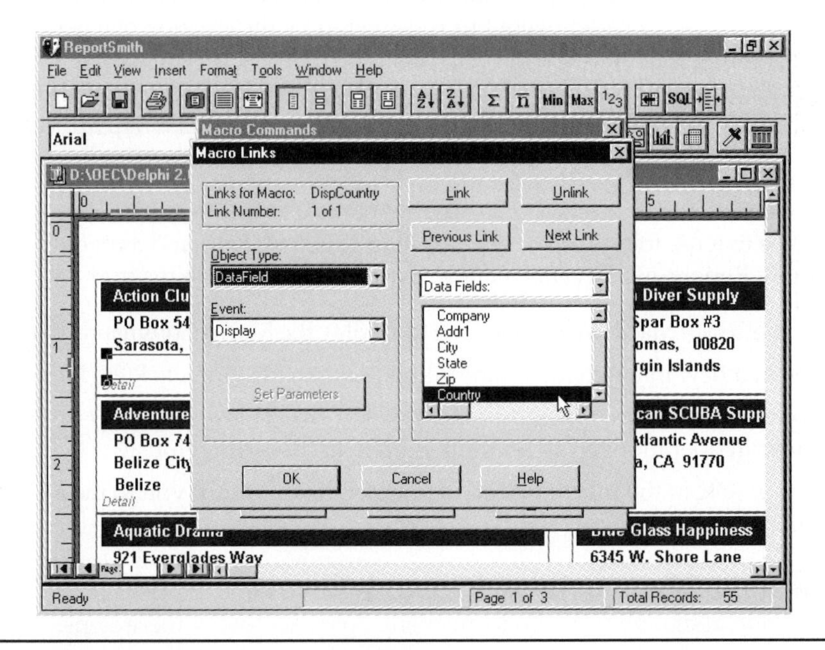

Figure 9-22. *The Macro Links dialog box*

Macro File Name	Function Demonstrated
B4RPT.MAC	Prompts the user to specify the film types to be included in the video store report.
CONDFMT.MAC	Changes the color of the data fields to which it is linked, depending on the film type.
CUSTOM.MAC	Provides a dialog box for customizing which toolbar buttons will be enabled and disabled. (ReportSmith 3.0 only)
DATE.MAC	Gets the value of a date field in Julian date format.
DISABLE.MAC	Demonstrates how to disable a submenu (specifically the Tools | Tables submenu).
ENABLE.MAC	Demonstrates how to enable a menu item (specifically, the Tools | Tables submenu).
GREETING.MAC	Fetches the user's name and offers a greeting.
ID2NAME.MAC	Searches for a record based on a particular Employee ID number.
LOADREP.MAC	Loads a single specific report.
LOADREPS.MAC	Prompts the user for a list of multiple reports to load.
RECNO.MAC	Defines a derived field called Record_Number.
THETIME.MAC	Displays the current system time.

Table 9-9. *Macros in the ReportSmith Directory*

Performing a Line Squeeze

You may need to suppress a null data field without leaving any blank space. This situation often arises with address information. For example, some addresses may include a second line of data for an apartment or suite number, while others don't. The following procedure uses a macro-derived field to prepare address information for the report:

1. Create a label report based on the Customer table.
2. Use Tools | Derived Fields to create a derived field defined by ReportBasic. Enter the following sample code:

```
Sub TheAddress()
If Field$("ADDR1") > "" Then Address$ = Field$("ADDR1") + Chr(10)
If Field$("ADDR2") > "" Then Address$ = Address$ +
   Field$("ADDR2") + Chr(10)
Address$ = Address$ + Field$("CITY") + ", " +
```

```
   Field$("STATE") + "  " + Field$("ZIP")
DerivedField Address$
End Sub
```

3. Choose Insert | Field from the menus and add the macro-derived field in one of the labels.
4. Select the new macro-derived field, click the right-mouse button, select Field Height, and check Can Grow.

Conditional Data Display

You may want to suppress the display of a particular field, but only when the record contains a specific value in that field. For example, most domestic U.S. mail omits the country from the mailing address. However, international mail requires that the country be included. The following procedure can be used, tied to the Data Field Display Event:

1. Use the same label report as before, using the Customer table from the DBDEMOS alias created when you installed Delphi.
2. Select Tools | Macro, and create a new macro named DispCountry.
3. Click the New button and enter the macro code shown below. Note that assigning a null value won't work. At least one space must exist for the field to display the new value:

```
Sub DispCountry()
  if RTrim$(Field$("Country")) = "US" then
    FieldText " "
  end if
End Sub
```

4. Click the OK button to save the macro.
5. Click the Links button. Select DataField as the Object Type, Display as the Event, and Country as the Data Field. Click the OK button to return to the Macro Commands dialog box.
6. Click the OK button. ReportSmith will now update the report based on this new macro.

Controlling Field Layout

Other formatting tasks can be accomplished through a combination of derived fields and creative use of report bands.

Performing a Field Squeeze

Squeezing out space from between two fields is a common reporting task. ReportSmith supports this task through the creation of a derived field. For example, the following code creates a derived field based on SQL code:

```
TRIM('CUSTOMERxDBF'.[[FirstName_Contact]]) +" "+
  TRIM('CUSTOMERxDBF'.[[LastName_Contact]])
```

Some SQL drivers do not support the TRIM function, in which case, you can create the same derived field using the following ReportBasic macro code:

```
Sub FullName()
  FName$ = RTrim$(Field("FIRST_NAME"))+" "+
  RTrim$(Field("LAST_NAME"))
  DerivedField FName$
End Sub
```

Creating Column Reports with Multiple Lines per Record

You will often find it necessary to place more data in a record than can fit in a single row. Many times, landscape printing just isn't enough. You need to create a report that prints the data in multiple rows per record. To accomplish this task, follow these steps:

1. When you create the report, include the table columns that will end up on the second row of the record's display.
2. Delete columns that will appear on the second row from the report for now. (You'll add them back later in a different fashion. Including them at the outset ensures that they'll be available later when you need them.)
3. Move the cursor into the left-hand side of the blank border area. The cursor will turn into a right-pointing arrow. Click the mouse to select a row.
4. Use drag-and-drop or the right-mouse speed menu to adjust the row height.
5. Switch to field editing mode by clicking on the field mode button in the toolbar (the fourth group of buttons from the left).
6. Select Insert | Field from the main menu.
7. Turn off the "Include field name" option and place the fields you want on the second line of the row. Your results should look something like Figure 9-23.

Direct SQL Entry

ReportSmith is an SQL-based report tool. Almost all of the design work you do with the visual tools in ReportSmith is building some part of a massive SQL statement that

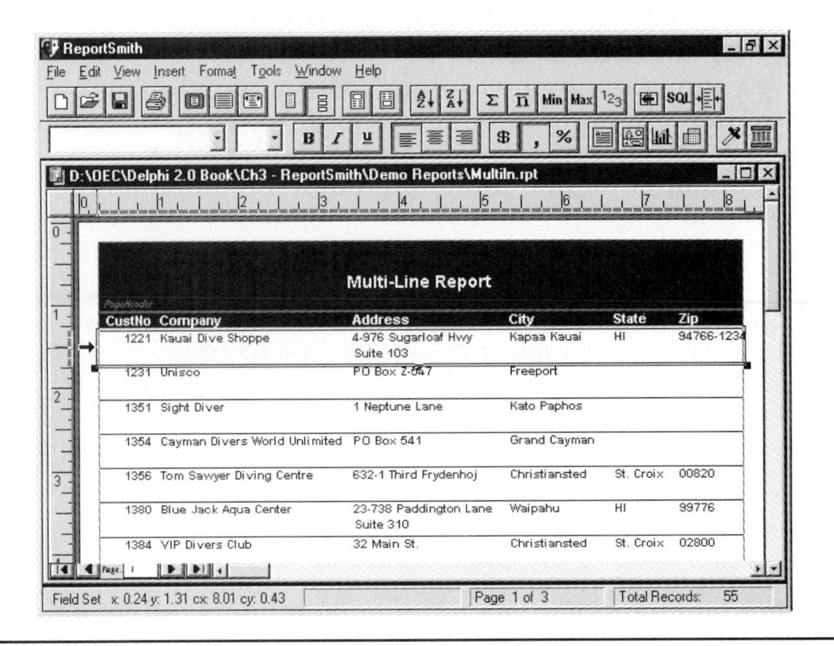

Figure 9-23. *A report with multiple lines per record*

sits behind the scenes. You can directly edit the SQL code being used by the report by following these steps:

1. Select Tools | SQL Text or click the SQL button in the toolbar.
2. The Report Query - SQL dialog will appear, showing you the current text of the SQL command.
3. Click the Edit SQL button. When you do, ReportSmith will warn you that the report cannot be changed back to the regular mode.

The effect of editing the SQL code is the same as if you had selected the Delphi Connection. All of the visual SQL generation tools will be disabled. Only the derived fields, report variables, report groupings, and summary fields tools will still be available. You will need to add groups, headers, and footers in the same way described in the section "Using the New Delphi Connection." You will also be responsible for making sure that the SQL code you enter is syntactically correct.

Passing Derived SQL Statements

Whenever you use a report variable in a selection criteria, it places the report variable into the report's SQL text as a parameter. The code fragment below is taken from the DEMO1.RPT report included on the code disk:

```
WHERE
(( (('CUSTOMERxDB'.'Country' = 'Bahamas') OR
  ('CUSTOMERxDB'.'Country' = 'US')) AND
  (('CUSTOMERxDB'.'State' = '<<StateSelection>>') OR
    (('<<IncludeNulls>>' = 'Yes') AND
    ('CUSTOMERxDB'.'State' IS NULL)))))
```

ReportSmith allows any legal SQL construct to appear in the value of a report variable. Thus, you can edit any portion of the SQL text of your report to simply be '<<SQLReportVarName>>'. As long as either your Delphi application or the end user supplies a complete SQL phrase that makes sense in the context of the report's SQL code, ReportSmith can use that phrase to determine the contents of the report.

Master-Detail Reports

All other reports discussed so far have all revolved around a single DataSet. A master-detail report is a columnar report based on multiple SQL queries. A bank statement is one example of this report type. For each bank customer, there will be a series of deposits and another series of withdrawals for each account they own. The standard report format of a bank statement separates the deposits from the withdrawals even though they come from the same account. Without using multiple queries, this report would be impossible to generate.

Each query in a master-detail report is designed as though it were a separate report. This concept provides several big benefits.

Separate Formatting

Each section of the master-detail report is treated as a separate entity. Thus, you can apply different styles to each report. For example, you might want to highlight deposits one way and withdrawals a different way.

Separate Data Sources

When you use the merge reports button to join tables, both reports must be using the same data-connection type. Master-detail reports are more flexible. They provide a way to perform a heterogeneous joining of information, that is, the data types can be totally different.

Planning Ahead

As the name implies, a master-detail report has one report query that is the master. You can link in more than one report to this master, but all linked reports must be detail reports of that master. Thus, you can have multiple detail sections to a single master, but you cannot directly create a master-child-grandchild type of report. You can fake a master-child-grandchild report by envisioning the links in a sideways fashion. In other words, make the child table the master and link in the parent table and the grandchild table as details.

Setting up the Reports

Each report in a master-detail report is designed separately as its own report. Once you have designed the individual reports, ReportSmith will link them together to build the final report. For complete details on setting up master-detail reports, refer to the "Advanced Techniques" section in your ReportSmith manual.

Dual 16/32-bit Reports

ReportSmith 3.0 saves 32-bit reports in a newer format than the ones created by the 16-bit ReportSmith 2.5 that ships with Delphi 1.0. This new format results in a couple of important migration issues.

Moving 32-bit Reports to ReportSmith 2.5

The newer .RPT format is not supported in the 16-bit version, so reports saved in the 32-bit version cannot be accessed by ReportSmith 2.5. If you need dual-platform reporting, you must create the reports in the 16-bit version. This means, of course, that you cannot use the new Delphi Connection type. Use report parameters that feed values to ReportSmith report variables instead.

Moving 16-bit Reports to ReportSmith 3.0

Migrating reports from version 2.5 to version 3.0 usually involves just opening the report in the 32-bit version. However, a few issues need to be considered.

16-BIT VERSUS 32-BIT ODBC DRIVERS If you use ODBC drivers in your reports, the 16-bit and 32-bit versions of ReportSmith may use different connection naming conventions. For example, the ODBC connection for dBASE in version 2.5 appears as RS_dBASE. If you installed MS Office, then ReportSmith 3.0 will display the same connection type as dBASE Files (ODBC). As a result, version 3.0 will bring up a Replace Connection dialog box. Just pick the default replacement selection. It is usually the correct one.

DELPHI AND REPORTBASIC CODE THAT ACCESS REPORTSMITH MENUS The specific text of some of the ReportSmith menu items is different between the two versions. You will need to check any code that uses ReportSmith menu text carefully to see if these differences affect your code. Examine the RS_PANEL project again for an example.

PICTURE FORMAT SUPPORT Remember that the .TIF and .GIF graphic formats are only supported in the 16-bit version of ReportSmith. To avoid problems with logos and other graphical elements, stick with either .BMP or .PCX files.

MODIFYING 16-BIT REPORTS ReportSmith 3.0 can read the version 2.5 format. However, do not use ReportSmith 3.0 to save any changes to a version 2.5 report that still needs to be run by the 16-bit version. ReportSmith 3.0 will automatically upgrade the report's file format without any warning. Once converted, the report will not run in the 16-bit version. The only way to recover 16-bit use of a converted report is to recreate the report from scratch in ReportSmith 2.5.

Threads and Reporting

Delphi 2.0 adds the ability to create and use execution threads. You can, in effect, create your own background processing, much like MS Word for Windows 95 automatically prints in the background.

You might think that creating a separate report thread for your Delphi applications is a good idea. Under certain circumstances, this is true. For example, when you fire off a QuickReport-based report, you are normally sharing the same execution thread with the rest of your Delphi application. Creating a separate thread to run the report would be a good idea in that case.

When you use ReportSmith reports, however, you are already creating a separate execution thread (process) by invoking ReportSmith. Thus, you can control how reports affect your Delphi application simply by always previewing the report. This technique transfers control of the hard-copy printing to ReportSmith itself. Once the preview is formatted, control of your Delphi application proceeds independently of the printing of the report.

Effects of Spawning a Separate Reporting Thread

You may not want to force users to always preview the report, or you might have some reports that can take quite a while to format. In those cases, you may want to create a separate thread and just run the report from that thread within your Delphi application. You won't gain as much benefit as with threading of QuickReport, but there can be advantages for ReportSmith reports that deal with large amounts of data.

What Threads Will and Will Not Do

Creating a report thread will not make either your reports or your Delphi application run faster. In fact, you are splitting the processor between more execution threads so that overall processing time will be a bit longer. What you are reducing is the amount of time your user has to wait before they can proceed with other work.

Optimizing Performance

Two areas of performance tuning should be considered. You can make certain adjustments to enhance the performance of the design process, and you can also set various options that will affect runtime performance.

Tuning Design-Time Performance

The areas that affect design performance have to do with how many records you load into the report designer at design time.

DRAFT MODE If your report will select a large number of records, certain operations (like performing a best-fit column sizing) could take quite a while. ReportSmith lets you design a report in draft mode. In ReportSmith, draft mode refers primarily to limiting the number of records that get loaded into the report. All the formatting of a regular report is available. You are simply working with a sample dataset.

To open a report in draft mode, just click on the draft mode check box in the Open Report dialog box. You can also create a new report in draft mode. The Draft Mode Options dialog box will appear when you select draft mode. Whenever you are running a report in draft mode, the word Draft will appear repeatedly as a background to your report. This reminder will show up both on-screen and in printed output.

DYNAMIC DATA ACCESS SETTINGS Most of these setting have more of an effect on runtime performance. However, you can speed the apparent design-time performance by turning on the Pre-load Records option. This option will load buffered records into the report prior to accessing the rest of the dataset.

Tuning Runtime Performance

A variety of developer-controlled options can create noticeable improvements in the runtime performance of your reports.

CHECK THE ODBC DRIVER VERSION As mentioned in Chapter 1, ODBC drivers can adhere to a number of version standards and one of three levels of functionality. Most 32-bit ODBC drivers support the most modern and feature-rich standard. ODBC drivers in the 16-bit world, however, come in all levels within all standards' versions. As a result, they vary widely in their performance. If you are seeing poor performance when using a particular ODBC driver, make sure that it is one of the more recent versions.

SETTING THE DYNAMIC DATA ACCESS PARAMETERS Usually, the default setting of automatic provides the best balance of local and remote record caching. Special cases may require you to change these settings, based on your most common reporting needs. These options are listed in Table 9-10.

CREATING LOCAL LOOKUP TABLES If you have one or more report variables that use the "Choose from table" option, you might increase runtime performance substantially by creating a copy of the lookup table on your local hard drive. This strategy can greatly reduce the network traffic involved in running these kinds of reports.

DDA Option	When to Use
Client Memory	Some reports perform a great deal of local processing. Crosstab reports are a prime example. This option minimizes the network traffic needed to formulate this kind of report.
On Server	Reports that deal with large amounts of data perform better when this option is selected. Set the "Buffer ___ records" option to a number that reflects about two to three pages worth of data. Your printer will most likely have its buffer full by then. Any delay in fetching the next set of records from the server will be more than compensated for by the time it takes your printer to output the pages.

Table 9-10. *Dynamic Data Access Options*

Reports Included on the Code Disk

Several example reports are included on the CD that comes with this book. These reports, along with some associated Delphi applications, are broken out into two groups: sample reports and demo reports.

Sample Reports

The first group is found in the \CH09\SAMPLES directory. These reports demonstrate a variety of ReportSmith techniques, and they may be run from both the 16-bit and the 32-bit versions of ReportSmith. You will need to install these reports onto your hard drive to use them, since they use data tables that are installed along with them (and these tables cannot be accessed directly from the CD-ROM). Simply copy the entire contents of the CH09\SAMPLES subdirectory from the CD-ROM to your hard disk. Alternatively, run the SETUP.BAT file located in this subdirectory to automatically copy these files to the directory C:\RPTSMITH\SAMPLES on your hard disk. These files also include the necessary text files for use with GETREP. Table 9-11 lists the reports from this subdirectory.

The SAMPLES directory also includes a couple of powerful ReportSmith macros. These are listed in Table 9-12.

Demo Reports

These reports are the ones used in the figures in this chapter. Some of the reports use the tables found in the DBDEMOS alias created when you installed Delphi. The crosstab reports use the video store files installed in the SAMPLES directory.

These reports are listed in Table 9-13. All of them except DEMO2.RPT can be run in both the 16-bit and the 32-bit ReportSmith. (DEMO2.RPT illustrates the use of the Delphi Connection, which is supported only in the 32-bit version.)

Report File	Capability Demonstrated
ACCOUNT.RPT	Contains a report for demonstrating the use of running a report with report variables. Contains three report variables. Try various combinations of supplying one or more values but not others.
ANALYSIS.RPT	Demonstrates using macros to create menu items. Creates two menu items: What if Analysis under Tools, and Report Help under Help.
CUSTCARD.RPT	Demonstrates ReportSmith's labels capability.
PMV.RPT	Shows how you can use ReportSmith's macro language to create complex derived fields. Creates a derived field named Projected Market based on the Rating field and uses the conditional formatting command, FieldFont, to highlight results.
HOLDINGS.RPT	Uses a report variable to prompt for selection criteria.
MASTER.RPT	Shows how you can combine macros to create sophisticated reporting applications. Uses a macro-defined dialog box to prompt for several report parameters and uses conditional formatting macros to highlight results. This report includes a graph.
SUMM.RPT	Displays a crosstab report that has multiple row and column labels. Displays market values by rating within each industry and analyst recommendation within each risk level.
MULTITAB.RPT	Contains two crosstabs: one for 1993 and one for 1992. Shows how you can use ReportSmith crosstab's date-selection capability to select data for a crosstab report.
PROFIT.RPT	Uses ReportSmith's crosstab to calculate Profit based on Market Value and Cost. Also demonstrates the ability to create crosstabs displaying multiple numeric values.
STATEMENT.RPT	Shows how you can combine several of ReportSmith's capabilities to produce sophisticated and professional reports. This report includes a graph.
STOCKANL.RPT	Demonstrates ReportSmith's crosstab and selection capabilities in a simple columnar report.

Table 9-11. *Reports from the ReportSmith SAMPLES Directory*

File Name	Macro Use
INTBOX.MAC	This stand-alone macro prompts for interest calculation parameters and runs the INTEREST.MAC macro with arguments. You can simply load and run this macro to see it in action. You can also use ReportSmith's AddMenu macro command to add this macro to one of ReportSmith's menus.
INTEREST.MAC	INTBOX.MAC uses this macro to calculate interest earned and display interest calculation results.

Table 9-12. *Macros from the ReportSmith SAMPLES Directory*

Report File	Capability Demonstrated
DEMO1.RPT	Shows how to create and use report variables. This is the report run by the RS_DEMO1 program.
DEMO2.RPT	Shows how to use and work with the Delphi Connection. This is a 32-bit-only report that is run by the RS_DEMO2 program.
GROUP1.RPT	Shows how to create a grouped report. It also illustrates using a derived field to perform a field squeeze.
LABEL1.RPT	Illustrates how to create a label report. Various formatting options are shown, and a display macro is used to suppress the printing of the country field if it equals "US".
MULTILN.RPT	Demonstrates a columnar report with multiple rows per record.
MULTITBL.RPT	Demonstrates a multi-table report. This report uses three tables from the ReportSmith 2.5 VIDEO subdirectory.
PHOTO_ID.RPT	Shows how to display field data as pictures.
XTAB1.RPT	Provides an example of how to visually create a crosstab from an existing report. Included in the crosstab are two presentations of the same data, once as a sum and once as a percent of total. (This report uses the data tables from the CH09\SAMPLES directory.)

Table 9-13. *ReportSmith Report Examples from the CD*

Report File	Capability Demonstrated
XTAB2.RPT	This report is an extension of XTAB1. In this case, another summary grouping (by quarter) has been added to the crosstab. Try various combinations of pivoting the various groupings around within the crosstab. (This report uses the data tables from the CH09\SAMPLES directory.)
XTAB3.RPT	This report is a crosstab report created from scratch. Its data analysis is similar to XTAB2. (This report uses the data tables from the CH09\SAMPLES directory.)
XTAB4.RPT	Shows a crosstab and a graph of the crosstab on the same page. (This report uses the data tables from the CH09\SAMPLES directory.)

Table 9-13. *ReportSmith Report Examples from the CD* (continued)

Conclusion

ReportSmith is a powerful and flexible report tool that can be used not only to generate reports from a Delphi application, but also as a stand-alone report generator. Chapter 10 continues the discussion of adding reports to your Delphi applications by looking at QuickReport.

Chapter Ten

Reporting with QuickReport in Delphi 2

The code for the examples presented in this chapter can be found in the \CODE\CH10 subdirectory on the CD-ROM that accompanies this book. Please refer to Appendix A for information on using the code files for this chapter.

Although ReportSmith reports are extremely flexible and powerful, not every application requires all of ReportSmith's features. In addition, not every application needs the overhead that including ReportSmith reports requires. For example, in order to include ReportSmith reports in your Delphi application, you must also ship ReportSmith Runtime with your applications. Not only does this mean that your application's installation disk set must include the three ReportSmith Runtime installation disks, but also your application will occupy an additional 6 MB of hard disk space (this is a one-time concern, however, as only one copy of ReportSmith Runtime is required per machine).

To provide Delphi developers with the ability to include reports in applications without the overhead of ReportSmith, a number of third-party developers have made available, often through shareware, component-based reporting tools. These tools permit Delphi developers to define reports that can be printed and previewed from an application without the need for additional files. Specifically, these tools permit all code necessary for the production of the reports to be included in the executable (.EXE) file of your application.

One of these component-based report tools, QuickReport, is included with Delphi 2. This chapter provides you with an introduction to building reports using QuickReport, as well as how to use the reports in your applications. Among the topics discussed here are how to leverage report bands, create groups, define master/detail reports, and use graphics and memos. You will also learn how to create a custom report previewer for your QuickReport reports. This chapter concludes with a list of frequently asked questions about QuickReport, along with their answers.

NOTE: *QuickReport is also available as shareware for Delphi 1.0. You can find a copy of the 16-bit shareware version of QuickReport on the CD that accompanies this book. Consequently, most of the techniques that are described in this chapter can be applied equally to Delphi 1.0, although this requires that you install and register the 16-bit version of QuickReport.*

Overview of QuickReport

Using the components found on the QReport page of the component palette, you can create reports that range from very simple lists, including data from a single dataset, to highly sophisticated reports, including related data drawn from multiple datasets. These reports are compiled into your applications and can be easily previewed and/or printed at runtime.

Six essential components are used to create a report in QuickReport:

- a Form
- a QuickReport
- a DataSource
- one of the DataSet descendants (a Table, a Query, or a StoredProc)
- a QRBand
- one or more of the QuickReport-printable components. (The most basic of the QuickReport-printable components are QRLabel, which is used for printing a static text label, and QRDBLabel, which is used for printing data fields from a dataset.)

The Form component provides the container in which the QuickReport is built. In most cases, you will use one Form for each QuickReport report in your application.

The QuickReport component, found on the QReport page of the component palette, is the central component in a QuickReport report. Conceptually, you can think of a QuickReport component as changing a Form into a report. The QuickReport component links, by way of its DataSource property, to the required DataSource component. This DataSource, in turn, must point to the required DataSet. The data in this DataSet is the main source of data for the report.

Most QuickReport reports contain more than one QRBand component. The QRBand is a container in which you place the printable elements of the report. As mentioned previously, these include the QRLabel and QRDBLabel components.

How the printable elements you place in a QRBand are displayed depends primarily on the BandType property of the QRBand. If individual records from the QuickReport's DataSource are being printed, at least one QRBand component in the report will have a BandType of rbDetail. The printable elements within this QRBand are printed for every record in a DataSet. The BandType property of the TQRBand class is discussed in detail later in this chapter.

Creating a Simple Report Example

To create a simple report example, use the following steps:

1. Create a new project.
2. On the main form of the project place a DataSource, a Table, a QuickReport, and a QRBand. The default Align property for the QRBand is alTop, so the QRBand will automatically move to the top of the form.
3. Set the DataSet property of the DataSource to Table1. For the Table component, set its DatabaseName property to DBDEMOS, its TableName property to CUSTOMER.DB, and its Active property to True.
4. Set the QuickReport's DataSource property to DataSource1. Set the QRBand's BandType property to rbDetail.
5. Place one QRLabel and one QRDBLabel in the QRBand. Set the QRLabel's Caption property to Company Name. For the QRDBLabel, set its DataSource

property to DataSource1 and its DataField property to Company. Since Table1 is active, as soon as you have set the DataField property of the QRDBLabel component to Company, the company name associated with the first record in the CUSTOMER.DB table will appear in this component. The form should now look like the following:

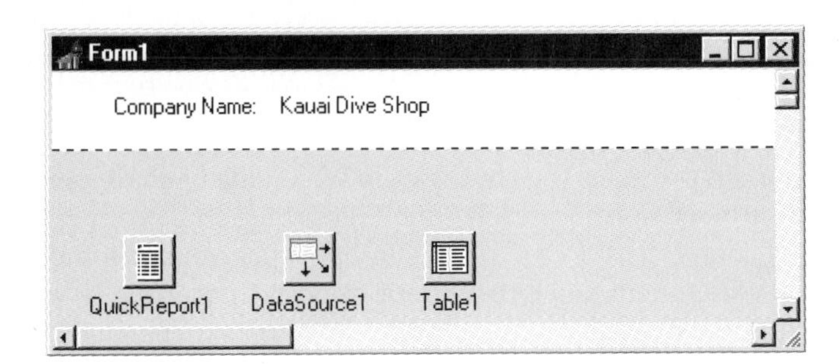

Previewing a QuickReport Report at Design Time

It is not necessary to run a project to preview a QuickReport report. As long as the datasets being used for the report are active, you can view the report at design time. To do this, double-click the QuickReport component, or right-click the QuickReport component and select Preview report from the displayed speed menu. The QuickReport component will format your report and display it in the default QuickReport previewer, as shown in Figure 10-1.

NOTE: If you have assigned an event handler to any of the QuickReport components, those event handlers are not executed when you preview a report at design time. Consequently, if the event handlers have any effect on the content, format, or page control of the report, a design time-previewed report will be different from the same report when previewed or printed at runtime.

Using a QuickReport Report at Runtime

To permit a user to preview or print a QuickReport report, at a minimum you must explicitly call the QuickReport Preview or Print method. Using a QuickReport report from a Delphi application should include several additional steps to set it up properly. For example, you will generally never display to the user the form on which the QuickReport component appears. Instead, you will call the QuickReport's Preview or Print methods from another form. Furthermore, although Delphi will automatically call the constructor of the form on which the QuickReport is placed, you may decide to explicitly call the form's constructor at runtime and then release the form when it is no longer needed. Doing so reduces the resources required by your application.

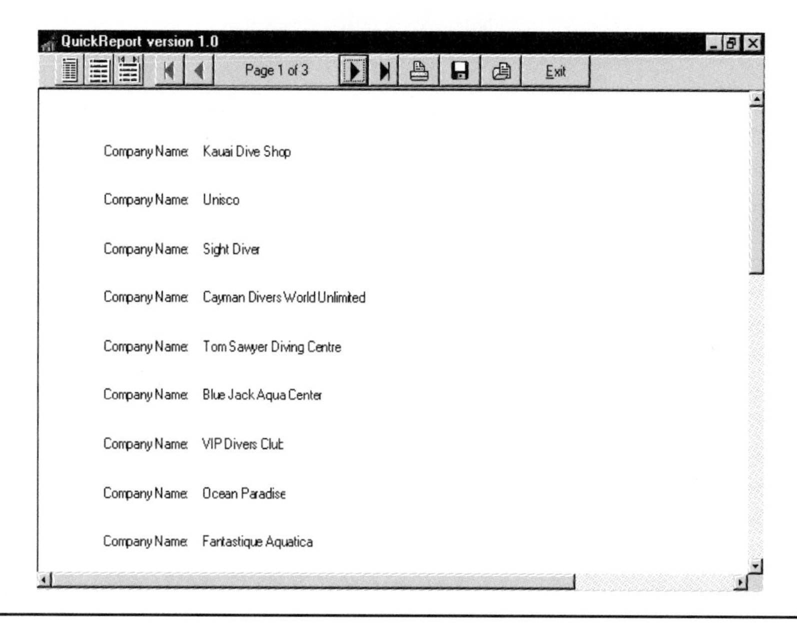

Figure 10-1. *A QuickReport report in the default previewer*

Both of these techniques can be performed easily with the QuickReport report created in the preceding section. The following two sections describe how to set up this QuickReport report for runtime use.

Previewing and Printing an Auto-Created QuickReport

Use the following steps to demonstrate printing or previewing at runtime with the report created in the preceding section:

1. From the Delphi main menu, select File | New Form.
2. On this new form, place two buttons. Change the Caption property of Button1 to Preview Report, and change the Caption property of Button2 to Print Report.
3. Double-click the Preview Report button to create an OnClick event handler for it. In this event handler enter the following code:

```
procedure TForm2.Button1Click(Sender: TObject);
begin
  Form1.QuickReport1.Preview;
end;
```

4. Double-click the Print Report button, and enter the following code into the automatically created OnClick event handler:

```
procedure TForm2.Button2Click(Sender: TObject);
begin
  Form1.QuickReport1.Print;
end;
```

5. While in unit2, add the following uses clause to the implementation section:

```
uses Unit1;
```

6. Make this new form, Form2, the Main form. Do this by selecting Project | Options (Delphi 2) or Options | Project Options (Delphi 1.0) to display the Project Options dialog box. From the Forms page of this dialog box, select Form2 from the Main Form drop-down menu.
7. Run the form. Now, when you click the Preview Report button, the default QuickReport previewer dialog box will appear. When you click the Print Report button, the QuickReport will be sent to the printer.

Creating a QuickReport Form at Runtime for Preview or Printing

The preceding example demonstrated how to access a QuickReport component on another form at runtime. This was accomplished simply by adding the unit that the QuickReport is associated with to a uses clause in the unit for the form that needs to print or preview the QuickReport report. Once that is done, any event handler can call the QuickReport's Preview or Print methods.

The preceding technique required that the form on which the QuickReport appears be auto-created, that is, created by the project when the application is first loaded. This is not required, however. Instead, you can tell the project not to automatically create the QuickReport form at runtime and instead create it from within the event handler that prints or previews the form. In addition to the steps for printing or previewing an auto-created form, you need to perform two more steps to create the form within the event handler:

1. From the Forms page of the Project Options dialog box, remove the form on which the QuickReport component is placed from the Auto-create forms list box.
2. From within your event handlers that print or preview the report, call the QuickReport form's constructor, then print or preview the report, and finally, release that form. For example, doing this from the Preview Report button created in the preceding section may use the following event handler:

```
procedure TForm2.Button1Click(Sender: TObject);
begin
  Form1 := TForm1.Create(Self);
  Form1.QuickReport1.Preview;
```

```
    Form1.Release;
  end;
```

This code can be found in the project DEMO1.DPR on the code disk.

Using Data Modules with QuickReport Reports

While the preceding report example included both the DataSource and DataSet components on the same form as the QuickReport components, Delphi 2 provides you with a more attractive option—data modules. Using a data module to hold all datasets used by your QuickReport components simplifies the creation and maintenance of the reporting side of your applications.

In most cases, however, the data module that you use for reporting should be separate from the one you use for the interactive elements of your user interface, such as data entry. Consequently, a Delphi 2 application will often include at least two data modules, one for the user interface and another for reporting.

The reason for using separate data modules for data entry and printing is fairly simple. When a QuickReport report is either previewing or printing the data in a dataset, it must navigate that dataset. Although this behavior is harmless if the QuickReport report is not using a dataset accessible to the user, it can pose problems if the QuickReport report and the user are sharing the same dataset.

For example, if a user is editing a record and then, before posting changes to the record, attempts to preview the report, QuickReport will cause the changes to be explicitly posted. Furthermore, once the user is through previewing the report, the user will be returned to the last record in the report as determined by QuickReport. In other words, they will probably not be on the same record they were editing. By comparison, if the user interface and QuickReport report use different datasets, even if they point to the same table, previewing a QuickReport report will have no effect on a record's state.

Components Used in QuickReport

The report created earlier in this chapter represents the simplest report that you can create with QuickReport. Consequently, it used only a few of the available QuickReport components. The QReport page of the component palette lists eleven components that you can use in your QuickReport reports. In addition, there are two other components from the component palette that you can include in your reports. Table 10-1 lists these thirteen components.

In addition to these components, two additional QuickReport components are used with QuickReport reports. These components, however, do not appear on the component palette. The QRPrinter component is a non-visual component that is created automatically for every QuickReport report. This component provides you with low-level access to the printer's features. The second component, QRCustomControl, is the base class for the QuickReport components. Normally you will not use this component in your applications.

Component	Description
QuickReport	Required component that makes a form a QuickReport report.
QRBand	Panel-type object on which you place printable components. The BandType property defines what feature a particular QRBand provides.
QRLabel	Static, single line of text.
QRDBText	Used to display a field or memo from a DataSource.
QRDetailLink	Defines the link between a master and detail QRBand, as well as between a detail and a subdetail QRBand.
QRMemo	Used to define multiple lines of static text.
QRShape	Shape component for a QuickReport report.
QRDBCalc	Component for displaying simple summary statistics. Can also be used for single fields inside of the detail and subdetail bands for the purpose of applying picture (display) formats.
QRPreview	Panel-like object used to display the image of a report preview. Used to create a custom report previewer.
QRGroup	Used to identify which QRBands are the detail, header, and footer bands for groups of records.
QRSysData	Field used to display system and report data, such as the date, time, page number, and record number.
DBImage	Field used to display bitmaps from a DataSet component.
Image	Use to display bitmaps.

Table 10-1. *Components for Use with QuickReport Reports*

QuickReport Demonstrations

This section demonstrates how to use many of QuickReport's powerful features. All techniques shown here can be found in the QREP.DPR project. The main form for this project is shown in Figure 10-2. In addition to the main form, the QREP project contains one data module that holds the datasets that are used for each report. This data module contains the CUSTOMER.DB, ORDERS.DB, and BIOFLIFE.DB tables from the DBDEMOS alias. In addition, this data module contains three DataSource components, one of each type of Table component.

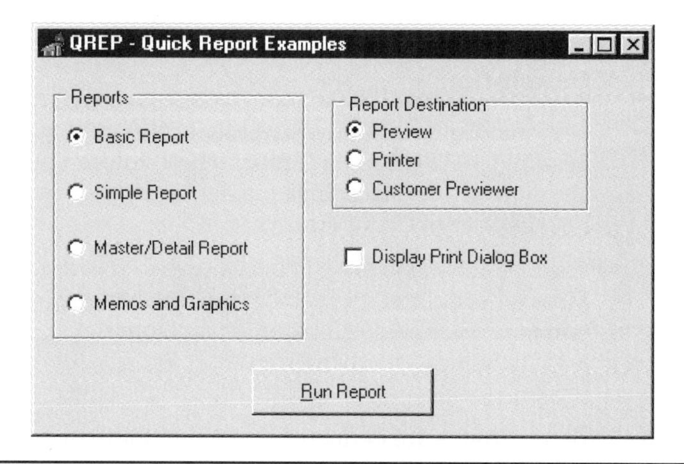

Figure 10-2. *The main form of the QREP project*

The QREP project also contains a number of additional forms. Specifically, there is one form for each of the QuickReport reports the project includes. These forms' units include the data module's unit in their uses clause, providing these forms with access to the DataSource and DataSet components on the data module. There is one additional form that demonstrates how to create a custom report previewer. The code behind this form is discussed later in this chapter. Each of the topics discussed in the remaining sections of this chapter make reference to one or more of these QREP project forms.

Using QRBands

All QuickReport reports use at least one QRBand, and most use at least three. As pointed out earlier in this chapter, the most important property of a QRBand is BandType. This property defines the role that the band will play. Table 10-2 displays a list of the various BandType values and how they affect the QRBand.

Most reports use at least three QRBands, one acting as the page header, one acting as the detail, and one acting as the page footer. The page header and page footer provide the top and bottom margin for the page, whereas the detail band displays the data from each individual record.

After the BandType property, the second most important property of a QRBand is its Height. The Height of a QRBand determines how much space the band will occupy on the report. For example, the Height property of a band designated at a PageHeader will determine the top margin of each page of your report. Likewise, the Height of a Detail band determines how much vertical space is used for each record in the master table and, consequently, influences the maximum number of records that can appear on any given page.

BandType	Description
rbColumnHeader	Optional ColumnHeader band that contains column headings for a columnar report. These column headings can alternatively be placed in a header band, such as a PageHeader of GroupHeader.
rbDetail	The Detail band is printed once for each record in a dataset. Most reports have one detail band. In a master/detail report, you may use one detail band for each dataset (an alternative is to use a SubDetailBand for detail records). Only summary reports do not include at least one detail band.
rbGroupFooter	When groups are defined using either QRGroup or QRDetailLink components, an optional GroupFooter band can be used to print elements at the end of a group.
rbGroupHeader	When groups are defined using either QRGroup or QRDetaiLink components, an optional GroupHeader can be used to print elements before each group.
rbOverlay	The optional Overlay band contains printable elements that will be printed over all other bands in a report. For example, an overlay can contain a logo on top of which elements from other bands will print.
rbPageFooter	The optional PageFooter band contains elements that will be printed at the bottom of each page of the report.
rbPageHeader	The optional PageHeader band contains elements that will be printed at the top of each page of the report.
rbSubDetail	The SubDetail band is essentially the same as a Detail band but is designed to be used for a detail table in a master/detail report. While you always use a Detail band for the master table in a report, you can use either a Detail or a SubDetail band for the detail records. You use a QRDetailLink component to identify a SubDetail band.
rbSummary	The optional Summary band is printed once at the end of a report, after the last master record in a single table report, or after the last detail record in a master/detail report.
rbTitle	The optional Title band is printed once at the beginning of the report. The QuickReport property TitleBeforeHeader defines whether the Title band is printed prior to the page header on the first page of the report.

Table 10-2. *QRBand BandType Property Values*

TIP: You can set the Ruler property of a QRBand to a value other than qrrNone to display a vertical, horizontal, or both vertical and horizontal ruler in either inches or centimeters. These rules can provide invaluable assistance in the accurate placement of objects in your QRBands.

Creating a MultiBand Report

As soon as your QuickReport reports contain more than one band, the reports can become much more difficult to create and maintain. This is because there is nothing that distinguishes one type of band from another, other than the published properties of the band in the Object Inspector. These properties, however, are only displayed for one band at a time, and only for the selected band.

If you use the following guidelines, you will find your multiband reports much easier to create and modify:

- Design your report on paper first. This will allow you to identify ahead of time how many and what types of bands you will place onto your form.
- Place your bands onto the form in the logical order in which they will be printed. For example, if you are going to have a title band on your report, place it first, and then place your page header, detail band, page footer, and summary band. The QRBand components are top-aligned. The first band placed will always appear at the top of the form, and the second will appear in the second position. Although the order of the bands has no influence on their behavior, a multiband report is much easier to use if the order of the bands on the form duplicates the role they will play in the report.

TIP: If you accidentally place a band in the wrong order, you can drag the band to a new position. For example, if you want to add a Title band after the fact, and it appears as the last band on the form, you can drag it to the top position.

- Always give your bands meaningful names that indicate their role in the report. For example, set the Name property of your Title band to Title, or some other name that identifies the band's role. This is especially important when creating master/detail reports, or reports that contain groups that include headers and/or footers.

The form named SimpleReport in the QREP project, shown in Figure 10-3, contains a simple report that includes three bands. The BandType of the Top band is set to rbPageHeader, so it will appear at the top of every page. Here the report title is displayed using a QRLabel component.

The second band is a Detail band. It contains the values that will be displayed for every record in the master table. In this case, the DataSource for the QuickReport component is set to DataModule2.DataSource1, which is the DataSource associated with the CUSTOMER.DB table. The Detail band includes four QRLabel and four QRDBLabel components. These components are included to display a label and data for four fields in the CUSTOMER.DB table.

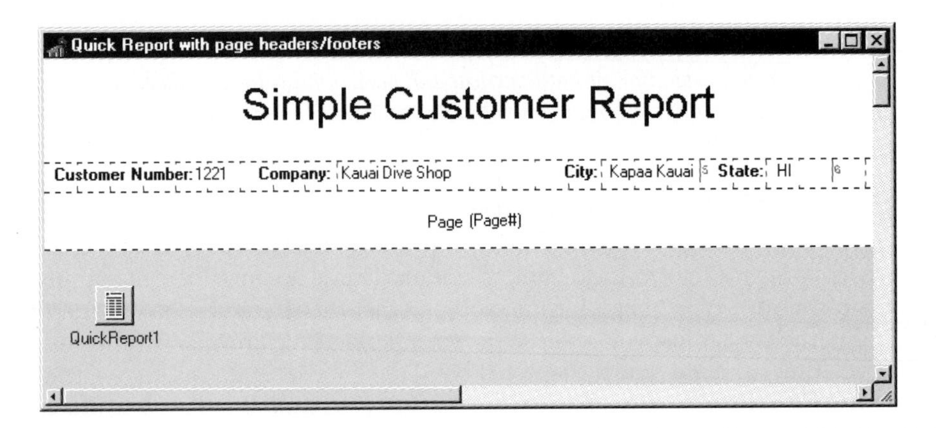

Figure 10-3. *The SimpleReport form from the QREP project*

Printing System Information

The final band is a PageFooter band that will appear at the bottom of every page. This band includes two components, a QRLabel, with its Caption property set to Page, and a QRSysData component, with its Data property set to qrsPageNumber (to display the current page number). You use the QRSysData component to display data relevant to the QuickReport, including Date, DataTime, DetailCount, DetailNumber, PageNumber, ReportTitle (which refers to the ReportTitle property of the QuickReport component), and Time. Figure 10-4 shows how this report looks in the default report previewer.

Using Groups and Linked Detail Bands

Although groups and linked detail bands are two separate subjects, they are often used together to create master/detail reports, as demonstrated in the QREP project form MasterDetailReport, shown in Figure 10-5.

Using Groups

A group organizes the records in a Detail or SubDetail band based on data in one or more fields of the associated dataset. For example, you can create a group that sorts the records displayed in a Detail band by the values in a State field.

There are two steps to creating a group in QuickReport:

1. Ensure that the dataset uses an index that corresponds to the group. For example, if you want to display reports sorted by state, the corresponding dataset must use an index where the state field is the first field in the index. This index can be a Table's primary index, or one of its secondary indexes. Alternatively, you can use a Query DataSet with an ORDER BY *StateFieldName* clause.

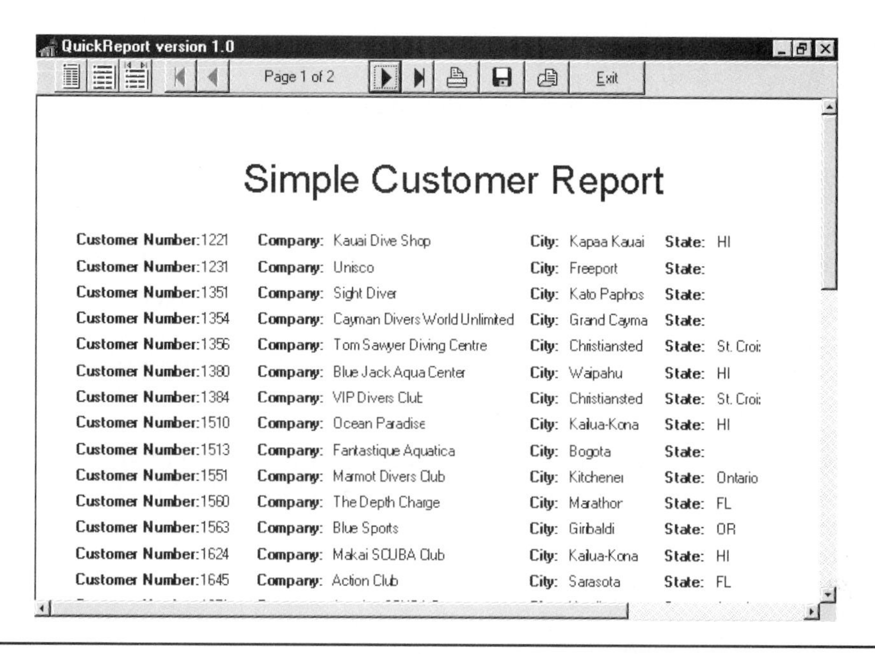

Figure 10-4. *The SimpleReport displayed in the default report previewer*

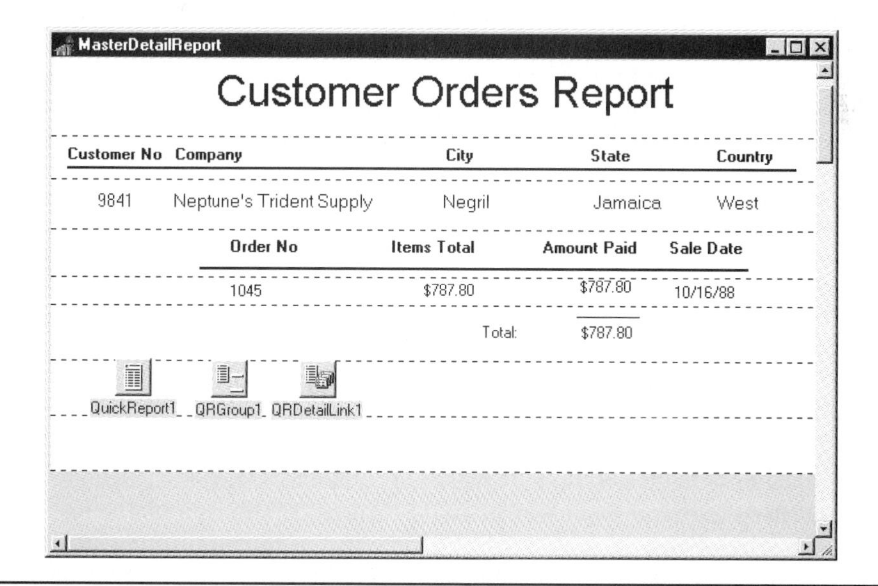

Figure 10-5. *The MasterDetailReport form of the QREP project*

2. Place a QRGroup component on the form. You must set three of the properties for this component. Use the DataSource and DataField properties of the QRGroup to identify the field on which the group is based. The third essential property is the DetailBand property, which you use to point to the QRBand that displays the records you want to group.

One of the primary benefits of grouping is that it permits you to provide a separate header and footer for each group. The header is used to print information at the beginning of each group, such as data column headings, and the footer is used to print information at the end of each group, such as group column totals. Bands used for this purpose should be positioned above (header) and below (footer) the detail band that is being grouped. Furthermore, these bands require their BandType properties to be set to rbGroupHeader and rbGroupFooter, respectively.

When group headers and/or footers are used, you must consider two additional QRGroup properties. If you have defined a group header band, set the QRGroup's HeaderBand property to this band. If you have defined a group footer band, assign the name of this band to the QRGroup's FooterBand property.

The QRBand shown in Figure 10-5 provides the grouping for the SubDetail Band, used to display the ORDERS records for each customer. This SubDetail band is surrounded by a header and a footer band. The header band contains column headings for the ORDERS records, and the footer contains group summary values.

Performing Calculations

The summary value appearing in the footer band for the ORDERS records contains a QRLabel with its Caption property set to Total. The value also contains a QRDBCalc component, which is used to calculate the total of the amount paid field. This QRDBCalc component has four critical properties: Operation, DataSource, DataField, and PrintMask. The Operation property is set to qrcSum. Other available operations include qrcAverage, qrcCount, qrcMin, and qrcMax. The DataSource and DataField properties identify the Amount Paid field of the ORDERS.DB table as the field to summarize. The PrintMask formats the field.

TIP: A QRDBCalc is used to calculate descriptive statistics across records. However, despite its name, you do not use it to create calculated fields within a record. To include a calculated field, such as the sum of Quantity and Price, create a calculated TField component using the Fields Editor, and then include a QRDBLabel in the report for this instantiated field.

The QRDBCalc component will continue to perform its calculation as it processes records. Use the ResetBand field to tell QRDBCalc when to restart the calculation by setting this field to the band that identifies where the calculation should be restarted. In this case, the ResetBand field is set to SubFoot, which is the name of the detail table's footer. After the detail table's footer is printed, the summary field is reset to zero, making it ready to perform the summary calculation for the next group of detail records.

The fourth QRDBCalc property of interest is the PrintMask property. You assign to this property the same type of expression that you use in the FormatFloat RTL (Run-Time Library) function to format a number. In this case, the value ######,##0.00 is used, which instructs this component to always display two decimal places and to include thousands separators.

TIP: *You can also use QRDBCalc components in a detail band to format numerical data. The QRDBLabel component does not have a PrintMask property. If you want to print formatted numbers in a detail band, use a QRDBCalc component with its Operation property set to qrcSummary and its ResetBand set to the band within which the component appears. You can then use the PrintMask property to format the number. This was done in the MasterDetailReport form, permitting the numeric fields appearing in the SubDetail band of the report to be formatted.*

Creating Linked Detail Bands

A master/detail report permits you to display records from one table that are associated with the records of another table. The primary table is referred to as the master table. For each record in the master table, the detail table will contain zero, one, or more records that are associated with the current master table record. For example, in the MasterDetailReport form in the QREP application, the master table is CUSTOMER.DB and the detail table is ORDERS.DB. For each customer in the CUSTOMER table, the orders executed for that customer appear in the detail table.

Two steps are required for creating a master/detail report. First, you must link the DataSet for the detail table to the DataSource for the master table. In this project, this linking was performed at design time with the components in the data module. The Index property of Table2 is set to CustNo (a secondary index), the MasterSource property is set to DataSource1 (the DataSource for the CUSTOMER.DB table), and the MasterFields property is set to CustNo (which is why the secondary index CustNo needed to be selected). For more information on linking DataSets, see the section "Creating Master/Detail Forms" in Chapter 6.

The second step to creating a master/detail report is to use a QRDetailLink component to link the Detail band associated with the master table to the Detail or SubDetail band associated with the detail table. There are three key properties for using a QRDetailLink. You use the Master property to point to the QuickReport component for the report (if this is a detail link of a master/detail report) or a QRDetailLink component (if this is a subdetail of a master/detail/detail report). In this case, the Master property is set to QuickReport1.

The DataSource property of the QRDetailLink is set to the DataSource for the detail table, which, in this case, is DataModule2.DataSource2. Finally, the DetailBand property must be set to the QRBand that holds the detail table's individual records (SubDetBand, in this example).

You can also use the HeaderBand and FooterBand properties to point to the detail table's header and footer bands, respectively.

Figure 10-6 shows the report MasterDetailReport from the QREP project displayed in the default report previewer. Note that the lines used in this report to underline column headings and separate sections were created using QRShape components.

Displaying Graphics and Memos

QuickReport makes it very easy to display graphics and memos stored in your tables. Figure 10-7 shows an example of a report that makes use of graphics and memos. This form is named MemoGraphicReport and is part of the QREP project.

All techniques for creating reports already demonstrated in this chapter apply to displaying graphics, with one exception. To display a graphic from a table, you use a DBImage component. In other words, instead of using a control from the QReport page of the component palette, you use a DBImage component from the Data Controls page.

In addition to the DBImage component, there is only one other component that you can place on a QuickReport report that does not reside on the QReport page of the component palette. This second component is the Image component from the Additional page, and it is used to display static graphics on your QuickReport report.

To place memos from a table, you use the QRDBLabel component. During design time, this component will appear as a single line; however, at runtime it will expand and word-wrap to accommodate your entire memo field.

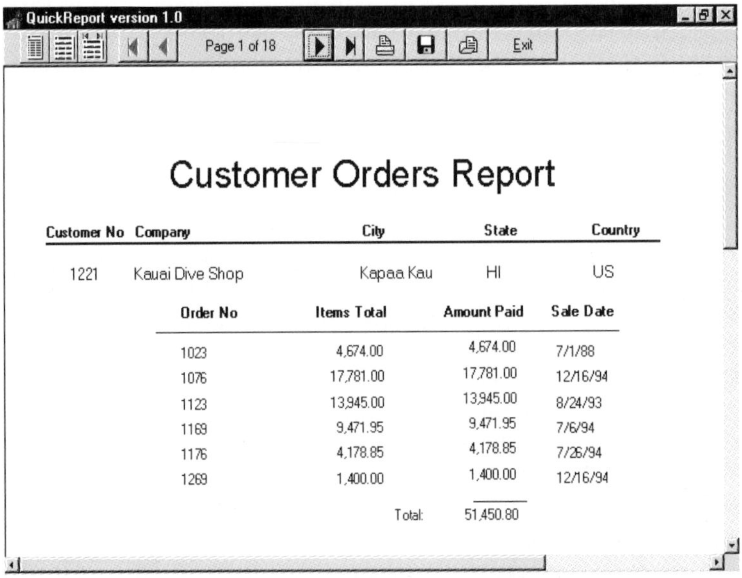

QuickReport version 1.0

Page 1 of 18 Exit

Customer Orders Report

Customer No	Company	City	State	Country
1221	Kauai Dive Shop	Kapaa Kau	HI	US

Order No	Items Total	Amount Paid	Sale Date
1023	4,674.00	4,674.00	7/1/88
1076	17,781.00	17,781.00	12/16/94
1123	13,945.00	13,945.00	8/24/93
1169	9,471.95	9,471.95	7/6/94
1176	4,178.85	4,178.85	7/26/94
1269	1,400.00	1,400.00	12/16/94
	Total:	51,450.80	

Figure 10-6. *The MasterDetailReport from the QREP project*

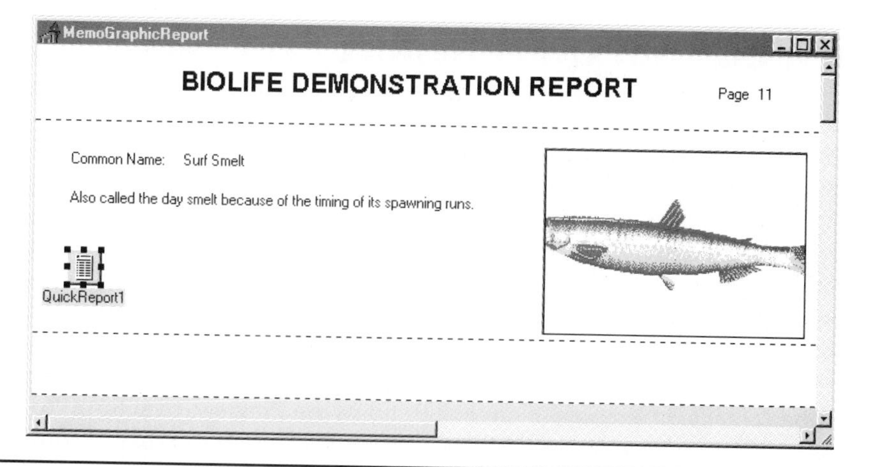

Figure 10-7. *The MemoGraphicReport from the QREP project*

The MemoGraphicReport displays data from the BIOLIFE.DB table, which is associated with Table3 on the data module of the QREP project. Figure 10-8 shows this report displayed in the default report previewer.

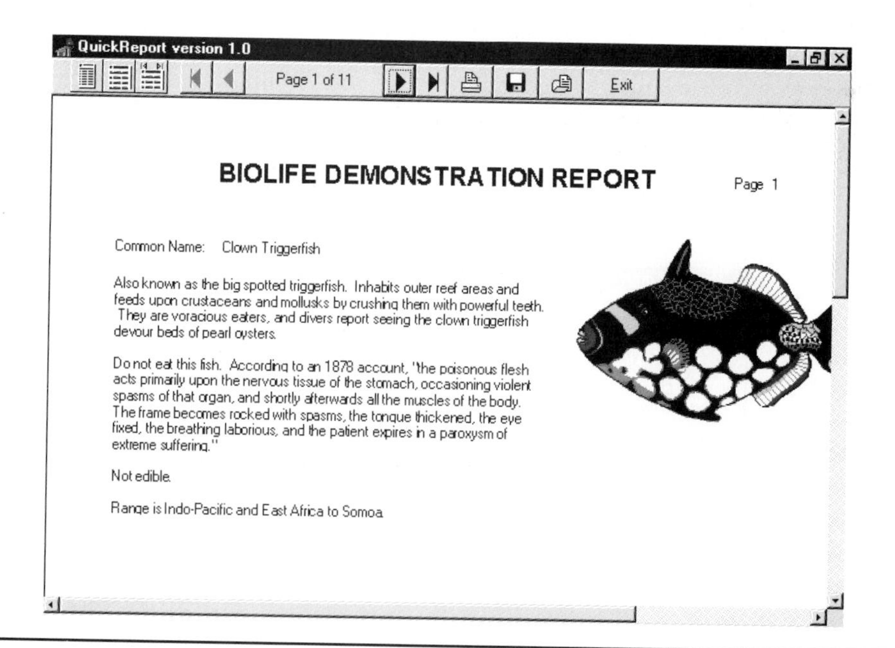

Figure 10-8. *The MemoGraphicReport displayed in the default report previewer*

Creating a Custom QuickReport Previewer

The default report previewer that is available to all QuickReport reports provides your users with the ability to easily view and navigate a report. There may be times, however, when you want to have complete control over the look and behavior of the report previewer. In those cases, you will create a custom previewer and instruct the QuickReport component to use that previewer when its Preview method is called.

There are two steps to creating a custom report previewer. The first step is to place a QRPreview component onto the form that will be used as the previewer. The second step is to instruct the QuickReport to use this previewer instead of its default previewer.

The QRPreview component is a TScrollBox descendant that QuickReport can use to display the contents of a report. Figure 10-9 shows the PreviewForm form from the QREP project. This form contains a QRPreview with its Align property set to alClient. If the QRPreview is the only object on the form, the user can preview the first page of the report, but no more. Therefore, it is also desirable to permit the user to navigate the report, as well as zoom in and out, save the report (in a QuickReport format), load a previously saved report, and select Printer options. The form shown in Figure 10-9 also contains the following four components that provide these features: MainMenu, OpenDialog, CloseDialog, and PrintDialog.

To control the previewing of a QuickReport form within a custom previewer, you use the properties and methods of two objects: QRPreview and QRPrinter. The QRPreview component provides properties that permit you to set the zoom proportion of the display, as well as to set the page number. It also provides you with methods to fit the display to the width or height of the report.

The following code example demonstrates how you would display the second page of a multipage report in the previewer named QRPreview1:

```
QRPreview1.PageNumber := 2;
```

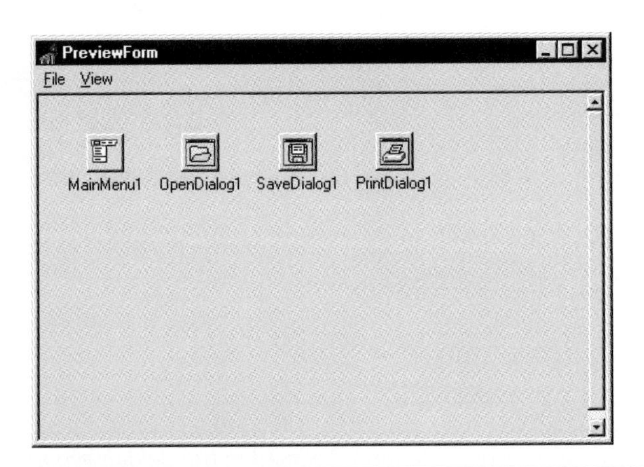

Figure 10-9. *Creating a custom QuickReport previewer*

QRPrinter is a printer-level object that is automatically created by a QuickReport report—you cannot place a QRPrinter onto a form at design time. This object permits you to issue a form feed, load a previously saved QuickReport report, save a QuickReport report, as well as print the current report, among many other tasks. For example, you can execute the following statement to print the report currently being displayed in the custom previewer:

```
QRPrinter.Print;
```

For many more examples of calling the methods of the QRPreview and QRPrinter, inspect the QREPU6.PAS unit of the QREP project.

After you have created a form to be used as the custom previewer, you must then instruct the QuickReport to use this previewer instead of its default previewer. To do this, assign an event handler to the OnPreview event property of the QRPrinter object. From within this event handler, you display the form on which the QRPreview appears. After assigning this event handler to the OnPreview event property, a subsequent call to the Preview method of the QuickReport will result in the display of this form, and the report will appear in the QRPreview component.

The OnPreview event handler is unusual, in that it takes no parameters. The use of this event handler to display a custom report previewer is shown in the following segment. This code assumes that the unit QREP6U.PAS defines a form named PreviewForm, and that this form includes a QRPreview component. Furthermore, this code segment assumes that a QuickReport component named QuickReport1 exists, and that this object appears on a form named SimpleReport defined in unit QREP4.PAS. The SimpleReport report displayed in the custom previewer is shown in Figure 10-10.

```
implementation

{$R *.DFM}

uses qrep6u, qrep4u;

procedure TForm1.ShowPreview;
begin
  PreviewForm.ShowModal;
end;

procedure TForm1.Button1Click(Sender: TObject);
begin
  QRPrinter.OnPreview := ShowPreview;
  SimpleReport.QuickReport1.Preview;
end;
```

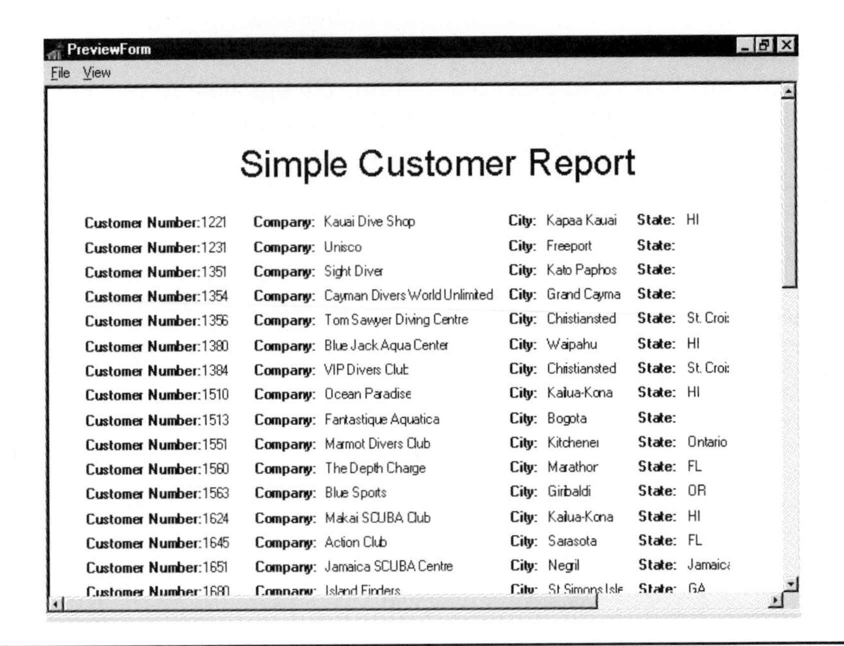

Figure 10-10. *The SimpleReport report displayed in the custom report previewer*

The QREP Project Main Form

Up to this point, the focus of the QREP project has been on the individual reports and the custom report previewer. This section considers the issue of accessing multiple QuickReport reports from within a project.

The main form of the QREP project, shown back in Figure 10-2, contains two RadioGroup components, a check box and a button. The Reports RadioGroup is used to permit the user to select which report to display, while the Report Destination RadioGroup is used to determine where to send the report. The check box permits the user to control whether a Print dialog box will be displayed when a report is being sent to the printer. The button is used to initiate the process of sending the selected report to the selected destination.

The code for this form is very simple in that it contains only one event handler and two procedures. This following is the complete code for this form:

```
unit qrepu1;

interface

uses
  Windows, Messages, SysUtils, Classes, Graphics, Controls,
  Forms, Dialogs, Quickrep, StdCtrls, ExtCtrls;
```

```
type
  TForm1 = class(TForm)
    RadioGroup1: TRadioGroup;
    RadioGroup2: TRadioGroup;
    Button1: TButton;
    CheckBox1: TCheckBox;
    procedure Button1Click(Sender: TObject);
    procedure ShowPreview;
    procedure RunReport(Qreport: TQuickReport);
  private
    { Private declarations }
  public
    { Public declarations }
  end;

var
  Form1: TForm1;
  CurrentReport: TQuickReport;

implementation

uses qrepu3, qrepu4, qrepu5, qrepu6, qrepu7;

{$R *.DFM}

procedure TForm1.Button1Click(Sender: TObject);
begin
case RadioGroup1.ItemIndex of
  0: RunReport(BasicReport.QuickReport1);
  1: RunReport(SimpleReport.QuickReport1);
  2: RunReport(MasterDetailReport.QuickReport1);
  3: RunReport(MemoGraphicReport.QuickReport1);
  else
  MessageDlg('Invalid Report',mtError,[mbOK],0);
end;
end;

procedure TForm1.RunReport(QReport: TQuickReport);
begin
CurrentReport := QReport; //Set global variable
CurrentReport.DisplayPrintDialog := CheckBox1.Checked;
QRPrinter.OnPreview:=nil;
  case RadioGroup2.ItemIndex of
    0: QReport.Preview;
    1: QReport.Print;
    2: begin
         QRPrinter.OnPreview := ShowPreview;
         QReport.Preview;
```

```
        end;
  end;
end;

procedure TForm1.ShowPreview;
begin
  PreviewForm.ShowModal;
end;

end.
```

The event handler, Button1Click, is associated with the OnClick event property of the button. This event handler calls the procedure RunReport, to which it passes the name of the QuickReport component based on the report selected in the Reports RadioGroup. This procedure, in turn, sets the DisplayPrintDialog property of the selected QuickReport component based on the current Checked property of the check box. If this check box is checked, the QuickReport component will display a Print dialog box if the report destination is the printer. The OnClick event handler then displays the report using the destination defined in the Report Destination RadioGroup.

The final procedure, ShowPreview, is designed to act as the OnPreview event handler for the QRPrinter component. If the user sets the Report Destination RadioGroup to Custom Previewer, the QRPrinter's OnPreview event handler is assigned ShowPreview prior to the current QuickReport's Preview method being called. Notice that when Custom Previewer is not the destination, the OnPreview event property of the QRPrinter component is set to nil. While the QRPrinter's OnPreview event property does not always need to be set to nil, it is used in this example to undo any previous assignments to the OnPreview event handler.

Conclusion

Delphi provides you with two powerful techniques for including reports in your Delphi applications. When you need a powerful SQL report generator, the ability for users to design their own reports, and high-end reporting features, ReportSmith is the report generator of choice. However, when ReportSmith's specialized features are not required, or when you want to minimize the number of files that must be shipped with your finished application, QuickReport provides for most all of your reporting needs.

Chapter Eleven

Graphics

The code for the examples presented in this chapter can be found in the \CODE\CH11 subdirectory on the CD-ROM that accompanies this book. Please refer to Appendix A for information on using the code files for this chapter.

Almost every program you create with Delphi will involve a canvas at one time or another. For example, if you've created a form to display data or to accept input from the user, that form is a canvas, and the buttons that you click on have canvases as well. Just about every visual element of a Delphi program involves a canvas in one form or another.

What exactly is a *canvas*? Basically, it is a wrapper around a construct in Windows called the *device context*. In object-oriented terminology, the Delphi Canvas is an object that encapsulates the graphics device interface (GDI). Device contexts are one of the lowest level elements of Windows programming, and if you understand what a device context does for you, you will have a much greater appreciation for the power and flexibility of the Delphi canvas.

This chapter serves as an introduction to programming graphics using the Canvas object. A number of technique are described here, including displaying transparent images, displaying masked images against complex backgrounds, and rotating fonts. Before these topics can be addressed it is necessary to consider how Windows supports graphics.

The Windows Device Context

Device independence is one of the key advantages of the Windows programming environment (both 16-bit and 32-bit versions). Can you imagine the difficulties you would encounter if you, as an application developer, had to write code to handle all of the multitude of video cards and printers on the market? If you have experience in programming DOS graphics, you are already familiar with the complexities involved. Scores of video modes and resolutions are available. Many of these modes are common to a wide range of video cards, but some are card-specific. Assuring device independence was a major concern when Windows was developed. Programs that ran under the Windows environment needed to be insulated from the intricacies of the hardware involved.

With Windows you don't need to deal with the issue of hardware dependence. When you write a program under Windows, you don't have to assume the program is going to run on a particular brand of video card because Windows will handle that for you. When Brand Z decides to make a video card, they also develop software drivers that translate the high-level instructions that Windows provides into the low-level instructions the card expects to see. The application developer then issues even higher level instructions to Windows and is isolated further from the problem of hardware dependence. As a result, the programmer can write code that says, in effect, "draw a filled circle here" without worrying about how the individual pixels are getting turned on. These details are left to the Windows graphics engine, the video card's device driver software, and the video card itself.

Many of the principles of the Windows graphics engine and of device contexts relate to printing devices as well. Windows provides the same level of hardware independence in relation to printers that it does for video displays.

NOTE: Although all visual components, such as buttons, edits, forms, and so forth, have a canvas, it is not necessarily surfaced by the Delphi canvas property. All visual objects have a Handle property that descends from their TWinControl ancestor. Using this property you can access the device context for the object using the GetDC Windows API call. As mentioned earlier, this device context is the canvas for that object.

The Graphics Device Interface

The Windows graphics engine is based on a DLL (dynamic link library) called GDI.DLL. The GDI, or graphics device interface, is responsible for much of the translation of graphics commands down to the video card for display onto the screen.

The GDI is responsible for the drawing operations that most programmers are familiar with such as displaying a line of a certain width or pattern, drawing text with a specific font size and style, or drawing on the screen with a particular brush. These tasks are all accomplished by means of the device context structure, which maintains information about various graphic objects such as Pens, Brushes, Fonts, Bitmaps, and so on.

Windows maintains a finite number of device contexts for use by the system. As a result, whenever a device context is requested, it must be released when it is done. If it is not, the program will leak resources. In the worst case, the program will be unable to get a device context when it needs one and will crash on you.

Understanding the Delphi Canvas

Enter Delphi and its use of the canvas. The developers of Delphi saw the level of complexity necessary for programming graphics in Windows and decided that it needed to be much easier for a programmer to accomplish these common tasks. The TCanvas class is the result. This class encapsulates the properties and behaviors involved in displaying graphic elements on the screen as well as printing.

NOTE: A particular instance of a canvas object is typically a property of another object. For example, a Form component has a canvas property of the type TCanvas.

Consider painting a simple bitmap on a form. If you wanted to accomplish this in Borland Pascal 7.0 you would need to create the following code:

```
TheDC := CreateCompatibleDC(0);
OldBmp := SelectObject(TheDC,MyBitmap);
BitBlt(TheDC, 0, 0, 100, 100, TheBmp, 0, 0, SrcCopy);
SelectObject(TheDC,OldBmp);
DeleteDC(TheDC);
```

Delphi's Object Pascal, however, encapsulates much of the work into its canvas object, surfacing these features in methods that are much easier to use. As a result this code in Delphi boils down to a single line:

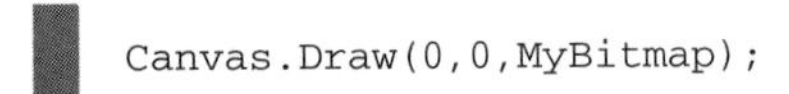

```
Canvas.Draw(0,0,MyBitmap);
```

Not only is this command easier to type, but it is also much easier to read when it appears in code. Delphi's approach is much safer programming as well. When a form is destroyed, its associated graphic elements are destroyed along with it. The lack of this kind of feature has been quite a problem for Windows programmers in the past. Programmers would discover that if they ran a particular program over and over, it would start dragging the system's resources down. This problem led to the creation of a flurry of resource management utilities so that programmers could see when Windows was about to crash. Because Delphi's Object Pascal removes the responsibility of creating and freeing many of the mundane graphics elements in a program, the resulting application is much more stable and reliable. Whenever a form is destroyed, Delphi manages the destruction of the elements that were on it, thus removing a huge burden from today's Windows developer.

As mentioned before, the TCanvas class is really just a wrapper for the various Windows elements associated with a device context. When you draw a line on a form, the canvas assumes the responsibility for obtaining a device context, selecting the width, style, color, and drawing mode of the desired pen, and then actually drawing the line. Afterwards, the canvas deselects the pen, and releases the device context it obtained to do the drawing.

AdjustableImage Component Example

The code in this example creates a component called AdjustableImage that is used in this section to illustrate several graphics concepts and capabilities. This component may look to you like an Image component. As it turns out, the TImage class was the original basis of this component, but for now, it is really just a chopped up Image. For the most part, AdjustableImage contains only the portions of the Image component that deal with the basic behavior of displaying an image on a form. Some of the other capabilities of this componenet, such as stretching and centering, were removed.

The AdjustableImage component will be extended throughout this chapter. As the component is extended, the discussion will progress from elementary concepts into more difficult areas of graphics management. If you are following along with the code examples found on the CD-ROM, add to your component library the file named

ADJIMAGE.PAS (found in the Chapter 11 directory). Then as the discussion continues, you can incrementally add new functionality to the component.

TIP: You can create a unit named ADJIMAGE.PAS, and then type the code as it appears here. Alternatively, the ADJIMAGE.PAS file is located in the Chapter 11 directory of the CD-ROM for this book, and you can simply copy it from there.

Initial AdjustableImage Component Code

```
unit AdjImage;

interface

uses
  SysUtils, WinTypes, WinProcs,
  Messages, Classes, Graphics, Controls,
  Forms, Dialogs, Consts;

type
  TAdjustableImage = class(TGraphicControl)
  private
    FPicture         : TPicture;
    function GetCanvas: TCanvas;
    procedure SetPicture(Value: TPicture);
    procedure PictureChanged(Sender: TObject);
  protected
    function GetPalette: HPALETTE; override;
    procedure Paint; override;
  public
    constructor Create(AOwner: TComponent); override;
    destructor Destroy; override;
    property Canvas: TCanvas read GetCanvas;
  published
    property Picture: TPicture read FPicture write SetPicture;
  end;

procedure Register;

implementation
procedure Register;
begin
  RegisterComponents('Samples', [TAdjustableImage]);
end;

constructor TAdjustableImage.Create(AOwner: TComponent);
```

```
begin
  inherited Create(AOwner);
  FPicture := TPicture.Create;
  FPicture.OnChange := PictureChanged;
  Width := 100;
  Height := 100;
end;

destructor TAdjustableImage.Destroy;
begin
  FPicture.Free;
  inherited Destroy;
end;

function TAdjustableImage.GetPalette: HPALETTE;
begin
  Result := 0;
  if FPicture.Graphic is TBitmap then
    Result := TBitmap(FPicture.Graphic).Palette;
end;

function TAdjustableImage.GetCanvas: TCanvas;
var
  Bitmap: TBitmap;
begin
  if Picture.Graphic = nil then
  begin
    Bitmap := TBitmap.Create;
    try
      Bitmap.Width := Width;
      Bitmap.Height := Height;
      Picture.Graphic := Bitmap;
    finally
      Bitmap.Free;
    end;
  end;
  if Picture.Graphic is TBitmap then
    Result := TBitmap(Picture.Graphic).Canvas
  else
    raise EInvalidOperation.Create(LoadStr(SImageCanvasNeedsBitmap));
end;

procedure TAdjustableImage.SetPicture(Value: TPicture);
begin
  FPicture.Assign(Value);
end;

procedure TAdjustableImage.PictureChanged(Sender: TObject);
```

```
begin
  SetBounds(Left, Top, Picture.Width, Picture.Height);
end;

procedure TAdjustableImage.Paint;
begin
  with inherited Canvas do
    begin
      if csDesigning in ComponentState then
        begin
          Pen.Style := psDash;
          Brush.Style := bsClear;
          Rectangle(0, 0, Width, Height);
        end;
      Draw(0,0,Picture.Graphic);
    end;
end;

end.
```

Examine the code of this component a little closer: The part to be concerned about at this point is the Paint method of the object. The primary function of the entire component is, for the most part, in the single call to the Draw method of a canvas:

```
Draw(0,0,Picture.Graphic);
```

There is nothing new to this procedure. It simply takes the graphic stored in the Picture property of the component and draws it in the upper left corner of the component's canvas area.

Now let's start using this component. The following illustration shows a form with a graphic placed on it:

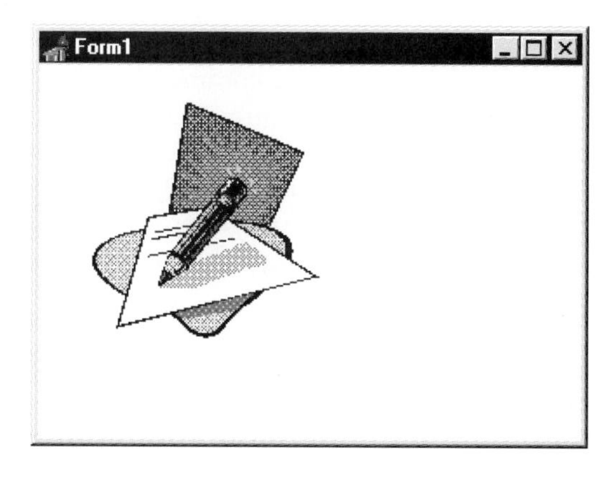

To display this graphic, a simple bitmap named PENPAPER1.BMP was loaded into the Picture property of AdjustableImage. So far so good. The graphic is a 16-color bitmap with a white background and is displayed on a standard Delphi form in which the form's color property is also set to white. However, what happens when the form does not happen to have a white background? Changing the form's color to, say, clSilver would produce the following effect:

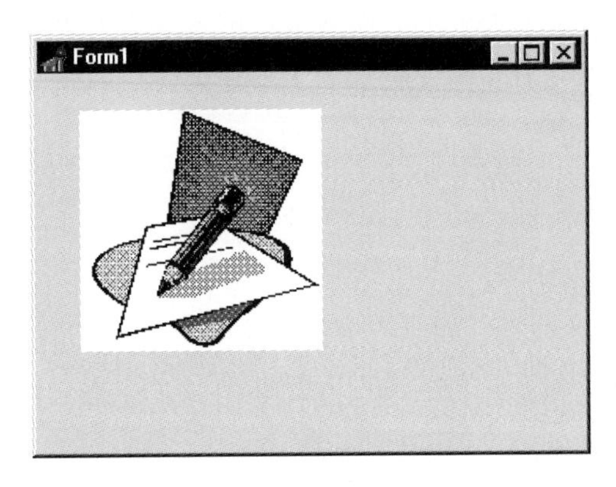

NOTE: *The PENPAPER bitmaps used in these examples were published originally in the Corel Gallery 2 Clipart Library (Corel Corporation, 1995), and appear here with permission from the publisher. They are intended for demonstration purposes only, and cannot be used for any other purpose without consent from the publisher.*

Because the bitmap encompasses a rectangular area, the background color of the bitmap (white) paints over the forms color (silver), ruining the visual effect of the graphic. In most cases, this is not a desirable effect. In the first example, the image painted correctly because the background color of the bitmap happened to be the same as the color of the form on which it was placed. A good program should not make many assumptions about the color of forms or controls.

Granted, you could force all your forms to have a white background so that a bitmap like the one used here would display correctly. However, if every application did this, the Windows system color settings would be worthless. Windows provides these settings so that all applications can have a common look. This is particularly important for users who might be visually impaired. Such a user might have chosen high contrast for their system colors. You should also keep in mind that some users may be running the program on a monochrome or LCD display, for example, on a laptop. If your application chooses a specific color in order to make your bitmaps display correctly, you may be making your program more difficult to view under these circumstances.

The key element of the problem is that the bitmap background consists of white pixels. The term *background* may be confusing in this context because there is nothing in this bitmap that indicates that there is a background. We know it is a background because our brains see the graphic and identify the space around it as something that does not belong to the graphic. However, the computer cannot make that assumption. It has to copy every pixel of the graphic to the form. This leads to a discussion of transparency.

Transparent Images

Windows, and Delphi in particular, provide the ability to simulate transparent areas of a graphic. By using the BrushCopy procedure instead of the Draw procedure, the Paint method can substitute one color for another. For example, say you want the background area of the bitmap to be substituted with the color of the canvas it is sitting on, in this case, the main form. To add this capability to the AdjustableImage component requires only a few extra lines of code. However, to make this and any future modifications to the component easier, you need to add a property that tells the component how to paint itself. The following is the component template with the changes in bold. (Note that only the code section that requires modification is shown here. For the complete code, refer to the Initial AdjustableImage Component Code section earlier in this chapter):

```
type
  TImageStyles = (isNormal,isTransparent);
  TAdjustableImage = class(TGraphicControl)
  private
    FPicture        : TPicture;
    FStyle          : TImageStyles;
    function GetCanvas: TCanvas;
    procedure SetPicture(Value: TPicture);
    procedure SetStyle(Value: TImageStyles);
    procedure PictureChanged(Sender: TObject);
  protected
    function GetPalette: HPALETTE; override;
    procedure Paint; override;
  public
    constructor Create(AOwner: TComponent); override;
    destructor Destroy; override;
    property Canvas: TCanvas read GetCanvas;
  published
    property ImageStyle: TImageStyles read FStyle write SetStyle default
isNormal;
    property Picture: TPicture read FPicture write SetPicture;
  end;
```

Here we have defined a type for the possible values of the ImageStyle property, declared the ImageStyle property using direct access for reading the property, and declared an access method for writing it. This access method now needs to be defined by adding the following code to the unit:

```
procedure TAdjustableImage.SetStyle(Value: TImageStyles);
begin
  if FStyle <> Value then
    begin
      FStyle := Value;
      Refresh;
    end;
end;
```

Within this code, any time the property is changed the component will call its refresh method, causing the component to be repainted. Finally, we need to modify the Paint method to allow the component to draw itself in one of two ways depending on the state of the ImageStyle property. Again, the changes for the component are indicated in bold in the following code:

```
procedure TAdjustableImage.Paint;
begin
  if csDesigning in ComponentState then
    with inherited Canvas do
      begin
        Pen.Style := psDash;
        Brush.Style := bsClear;
        Rectangle(0, 0, Width, Height);
      end;
  with inherited Canvas do
    case ImageStyle of
      isNormal      : Draw(0,0,Picture.Graphic);
      isTransparent : begin
                        Brush.Color := (Parent as TForm).Color;
                        BrushCopy(ClientRect,Picture.Bitmap,
                          ClientRect, Picture.Bitmap.TransparentColor);
                      end;
    end;
end;
```

Using Transparent Colors for Backgrounds

The critical section of this new code is the reference to the TransparentColor property in the BrushCopy procedure in the Paint method. TransparentColor holds the color defined as the transparent portion of the bitmap. By convention, the color of the pixel in the lower left corner of a bitmap defines its transparent color. The BrushCopy procedure then uses this value to substitute the appropriate color. In the Paint method, this is done with the following two lines:

```
Brush.Color := (Parent as TControl).Color;
BrushCopy(ClientRect,Picture.Bitmap,ClientRect,Picture.Bitmap.TransparentColor);
```

The BrushCopy method substitutes the requested color with the color of the destination canvas, that is, the canvas being painted. If you set the new ImageStyle property of the AdjustableImage to isTransparent, the graphic will look like this:

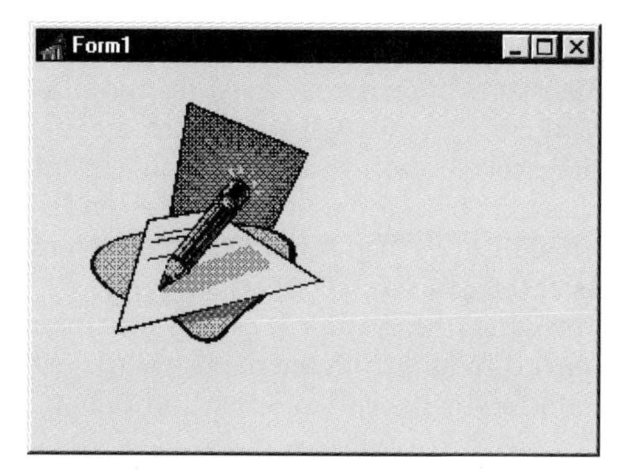

As you can see here, the BrushCopy procedure took the color supplied (white, from the lower left corner of the bitmap), and replaced all white pixels on the bitmap with the color of the form, in this case, gray. Unfortunately, the white areas essential to the graphic itself (like the white of the sheet of paper in the bitmap) were also turned gray with this code, an undesirable effect. White was too broad a color for such a substitution.

This is not a problem with our component, but rather the *.BMP file that we chose.You need to select one color for the graphic's background color, and make sure that this particular color does not occur any other place in the graphic so that the background color will not bleed through the graphic.

NOTE: *Changing the background of a bitmap is usually a simple matter of using some kind of "fill" tool from within a paint program to apply a color to the outside areas of the bitmap.*

You can see the effect of this kind of decision in the development of Delphi itself. If you look at all of the bitmaps provided with Delphi (in the C:\DELPHI\IMAGES\BUTTONS directory), you will notice that the backgrounds of these graphics are brown (specifically, the color referred to by the Delphi constant clOlive). Apparently there was some meeting at Borland and they decided that the ugliest and most unused color on the computer's palette was this olive color, hence it was chosen as the default background color for all of their graphics.

Following this logic, fill the background color of the graphic with olive. An easy way to fill the background color is to use the Paint program provided with Windows. Select the brown (olive) color on the palette and use the paint-bucket "fill" tool as shown in Figure 11-1. Save this modified graphic using the name PENPAPER2.BMP.

NOTE: The PENPAPER2.BMP file is located in the Chapter 11 directory of the CD-ROM for this book, and you can copy it from there.

Once you save the graphic, you need to assign this new graphic to the Picture property of the AdjustableImage. Even if you saved the modified bitmap using its original name (PENPAPER1.BMP), you must still reload the graphic into this Picture property. This reload is necessary because once you load a graphic into the Picture property of an Image or Button object (or any of their descendants, such as AdjustableImage), the actual bits of the graphic are stored internally to the object. There is no further connection to the file.

If you run the program again, the graphic is changed as intended. Specifically, the background color is now different from the paper color. Furthermore, since only the background color is affected by the call to BrushCopy, the paper remains the correct color.

TIP: This technique will work for any background form color, not just olive. For example, you could just as well have changed the form's background color to red. Olive was used in this example because it is less likely that a particular bitmap you want to use contains that color for one of its visual elements. If you colored the background with a more popular color, such as red, any instance of red in the image will become transparent when you use the technique just described.

Using a Bitmap as a Background

The graphics concepts covered so far have been fairly elementary. Stepping up the difficulty as bit, suppose that your form does not have a solid color background, but rather is a complex bitmap. The form shown in Figure 11-2 is associated with the project BMPFORM. You can find this project in the file BMPFORM.DPR in the Chapter 11 subdirectory on the CD-ROM.

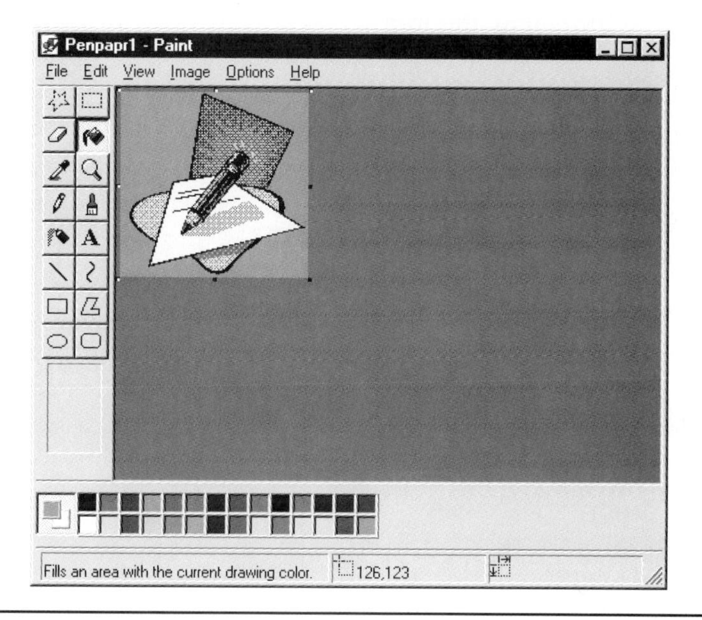

Figure 11-1. *Filling the background color with the Windows Paint program*

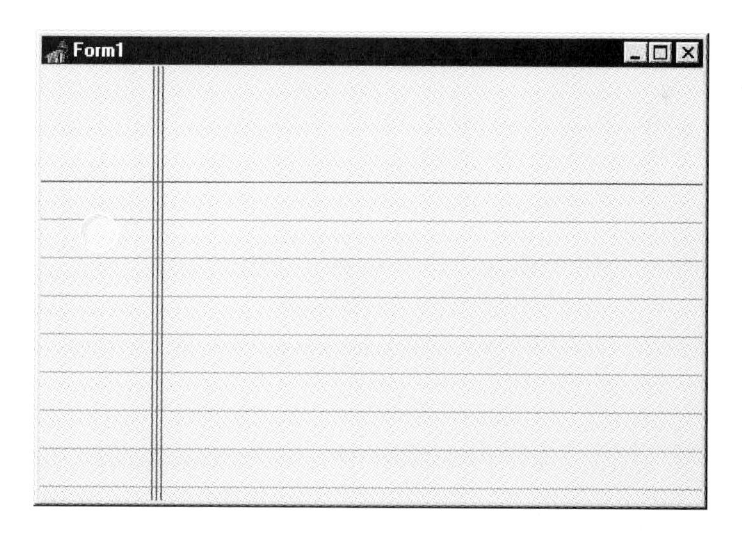

Figure 11-2. *The BMPFORM form*

The following code is the unit for this form:

```
unit BmpFormu;

interface

uses
  SysUtils, WinTypes, WinProcs,
  Messages, Classes, Graphics, Controls,
  Forms, Dialogs, Adjimage;

type
  TForm1 = class(TForm)

    procedure FormCreate(Sender: TObject);
    procedure FormDestroy(Sender: TObject);
    procedure FormPaint(Sender: TObject);
  private
    BackgroundBmp : TBitmap;
  public
    { Public declarations }
  end;

var
  Form1: TForm1;

implementation

{$R *.DFM}

procedure TForm1.FormCreate(Sender: TObject);
begin
  BackgroundBmp := TBitmap.Create;
{$IFDEF WIN32}
  BackgroundBmp.LoadFromFile('C:\Program Files\Borland\' +
      'Delphi 2.0\Images\Backgrnd\Writing.BMP');
{$ELSE}
  BackgroundBmp.LoadFromFile('C:\DELPHI\IMAGES\BACKGRND\WRITING.BMP');
{$ENDIF}
end;

procedure TForm1.FormDestroy(Sender: TObject);
begin
  BackgroundBmp.Free;
end;
procedure TForm1.FormPaint(Sender: TObject);
begin
  Canvas.Draw(0,0,BackgroundBmp);
end;

end.
```

In this code, a private variable called BackgroundBmp of type TBitmap is created. In the FormCreate method of our main form, the Bitmap object is instantiated and one of the large background images provided with Delphi is loaded (WRITING.BMP, a picture of a lined piece of paper). Next, to make sure that the bitmap is released when the form is destroyed, BackgroundBmp.Free is added to the FormDestroy method. Finally, a line of code that paints the bitmap onto the surface of the form in the FormPaint method is added.

The form's canvas has a color, but we cannot see it in this image because the bitmap (WRITING.BMP) gets painted on top of the form's canvas. The use of the bitmap introduces a new problem that becomes apparent when you add an AdjustableImage component onto it. The AdjustableImage component gets its color from the form color. However, if the form has a bitmap on it, the bitmap will obscure the background. This problem can be seen in Figure 11-3.

The AdjustableImage component creates its transparent effect by replacing a color in the bitmap with the color of the form on which it sits. Although you can see the outside of the form's background bitmap (the piece of paper), there is still a rectangle around the AdjustableImage graphic. Obviously, in order to get a transparent effect, you cannot count on a single color to be behind the graphic. You need to define an area of the bitmap in such a way as to allow all colors that sit behind that area to show through. This would permit the pencil graphic to appear on the paper without the rectangle around it. The technique that achieves this effect is called *masking*.

Figure 11-3. *Tranparency does not work when the background is a bitmap*

Masking

Masking is a cookie-cutter approach to graphics manipulation. Along with the basic image of the bitmap, you need to provide a mask that defines the region of the graphic that you want displayed. Figure 11-4 shows our original graphic and the mask that has been made for it. The mask is the right-hand side of the bitmap.

In Figure 11-4 you can see that the width of the bitmap is doubled with the mask added to the right side. Think of the mask as a kind of "keyhole." If you were to superimpose the two halves of this image over each other and then imagine that only the black areas of the mask portion allowed you to see through, then the only portion of the left graphic that you would be able to see would be the pencil graphic in the rectangle. This is the portion of the bitmap we are interested in. (Note that in the left-side graphic in Figure 11-4 black has been substituted for olive in the form's background for the purposes of contrast, since we are no longer concerned with just substituting a single color for another).

Many programs that use masking actually have one bitmap for the graphic and another bitmap for the mask. However, having them both in a single image has some advantages. First, since the two images are always together, it is easier to work with them and to utilize them in a program. Second, it is more efficient. Each bitmap used in Windows requires one resource handle from the operating system. There are a limited number of these handles, so it is best to use as few as possible. Since the two

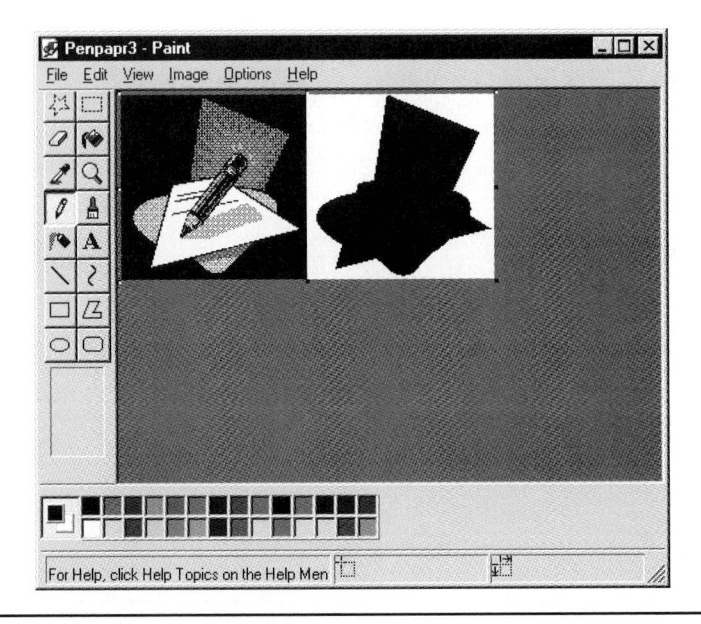

Figure 11-4. *A bitmap with a mask*

images are together in a single bitmap, the bitmap uses a single handle rather than two handles.

Using the Masking Technique

Now for the tough part—implementing this masking in code. Recall that the AdjustableImage component already has two styles with which the bitmap can be painted: isNormal and isTransparent. The first step is to add a new style, isMasked.

The AdjustableImage component needs to be modified as follows: First, the Styles property is extended to include the new painting style. Then, a new property, NumImages, is added, along with a field for this property and an access method. In the Type section of the object, make the following changes to the object definition. The new object template follows with the changes to the code shown in bold:

```
type
  TImageStyles = (isNormal,isTransparent,isMasked);
  TAdjustableImage = class(TGraphicControl)
  private
    FPicture         : TPicture;
    FStyle           : TImageStyles;
    FNumImages       : Integer;
  function GetCanvas: TCanvas;
    procedure SetPicture(Value: TPicture);
    procedure SetStyle(Value: TImageStyles);
    procedure SetNumImages(Value: Integer);
    procedure PictureChanged(Sender: TObject);
  protected
    function GetPalette: HPALETTE; override;
    procedure Paint; override;
public
    constructor Create(AOwner: TComponent); override;
    destructor Destroy; override;
    property Canvas: TCanvas read GetCanvas;
  published
    property ImageStyle: TImageStyles read FStyle
      write SetStyle default isNormal;
    property NumImages: Integer read FNumImages
      write SetNumImages default 1;
    property Picture: TPicture read FPicture write SetPicture;
  end;
```

You also need to modify a few of the methods in this object. These changes are identified in bold:

```
constructor TAdjustableImage.Create(AOwner: TComponent);
begin
  inherited Create(AOwner);
```

```
  FNumImages := 1;
  FStyle := isNormal;
  FPicture := TPicture.Create;
  FPicture.OnChange := PictureChanged;
  Width := 100;
  Height := 100;
end;

procedure TAdjustableImage.SetNumImages(Value: Integer);
begin
  if Value > 0 then
    begin
      FNumImages := Value;
      PictureChanged(Self);
    end;
end;

procedure TAdjustableImage.PictureChanged(Sender: TObject);
begin
  SetBounds(Left, Top, Picture.Width div NumImages, Picture.Height);
end;

procedure TAdjustableImage.Paint;
var
  TmpBmp           : TBitmap;
  BmpRect,MaskRect : TRect;
begin
  if csDesigning in ComponentState then
    with inherited Canvas do
      begin
        Pen.Style := psDash;
        Brush.Style := bsClear;
        Rectangle(0, 0, Width, Height);
      end;
  with inherited Canvas do
    case ImageStyle of
      isNormal      : Draw(0,0,Picture.Graphic);
      isTransparent : begin
                        Brush.Color := (Parent as TForm).Color;
                        BrushCopy(ClientRect,Picture.Bitmap,
                          ClientRect,Picture.Bitmap.TransparentColor);
                      end;
      isMasked      : begin
                        {Make a temporary bitmap to hold
                        intermediate results}
                        TmpBmp := TBitmap.Create;
                        try
                          {Set its initial size equal to
```

```
                 that of the component}
                TmpBmp.Width := Width;
                TmpBmp.Height := Height;
                {Make a rectangle of the mask area of the bitmap}
                MaskRect :=
                  Rect(Width,0,Width*NumImages,Height);
                {Copy the portion of the parents canvas
                 that is sitting under the component onto the
                 temp bitmap using SRCCOPY}
                TmpBmp.Canvas.CopyMode := cmSrcCopy;
                TmpBmp.Canvas.CopyRect(ClientRect,
                   (Parent as TForm).Canvas,BoundsRect);
                {Copy the mask onto the working
                 bitmap with SRCAND}
                TmpBmp.Canvas.CopyMode := cmSrcAnd;
                TmpBmp.Canvas.CopyRect(ClientRect,
                  Picture.Bitmap.Canvas,MaskRect);
                {Copy the bitmap image onto the
                working bmp with SRCPAINT}
                TmpBmp.Canvas.CopyMode := cmSrcPaint;
                TmpBmp.Canvas.CopyRect(ClientRect,
                  Picture.Bitmap.Canvas,ClientRect);
                {Now draw this accumulated image}
                Draw(0,0,TmpBmp);
              finally
                {Ensure that the bitmap is freed}
                TmpBmp.Free;
              end;
            end;
    end;
  end;
```

Two basic changes have been made to the component in the preceding code. Since the bitmap is wider than the graphic that it represents (remember that the mask is on the right side now), you need a way to tell the component what the boundaries of the graphic really are. This is achieved with the NumImages property. This property simply allows you to tell the component how many images are represented in the graphic. For the mask example, the value of this property is set to 2.

The real brain work of masking occurs within the component's Paint procedure. When the ImageStyle property is set to isMasked, the new segment of code becomes active. Let's look through this procedure line by line to better understand what is taking place.

First, a temporary bitmap is created as a kind of workspace for the steps involved. The graphics are manipulated in layers on this temporary bitmap, and once this manipulation is done, the bitmap is transferred to the component's canvas to be painted on the screen. After creating the bitmap, the remaining code is placed within a try-finally block. This step allows the program to recover the memory used by the temporary bitmap in the event of some error in the code. Even if an exception error occurs between the try-finally keywords, Delphi will always execute the code following the finally keyword. In this case, the line after the finally keyword is:

```
TmpBmp.Free;
```

This line releases the memory and resources consumed when the temporary bitmap was created, which ensures that the temporary bitmap will be released from memory, even if some unforeseen error occurs.

The real work is done within the try-finally block. First, the temporary bitmap's Width and Height is set to match the Width and Height of the component. Since the component's bounds are correctly representing the size of the image (and not the entire bitmap) by means of the NumImages property, the Width and Height of the component will be correct.

After the temporary bitmap size is determined, a TRect structure that will hold the rectangular region of the bitmap's mask portion is defined as shown in the following code. A TRect structure is simply a record that holds the left, top, right, and bottom coordinates of our mask. In this example, the structure will be the entire right side of the bitmap:

```
TRect = record
    left: Integer;
    top: Integer;
    right: Integer;
    bottom: Integer;
  end;
```

Raster Operation Codes

At this point, the graphics work of masking needs to be addressed. A key player in this technique is the use of *Raster Operation codes*, or *ROP codes*. These codes are bit-level flags that control how Windows combines pixels of different colors between different sources. Although learning to use ROP codes may seem daunting at first glance, they are quite simple to understand and their power in Windows graphics programming is undeniable.

Using CopyMode Properties of Canvas Objects

ROP codes are managed by means of the CopyMode property for canvas objects. Whenever you perform a Windows BitBlt operation (by means of the Delphi Draw and StretchDraw methods, for example), the Windows graphics engine utilizes the value in the CopyMode property to determine which pixels get painted on the canvas. The end result is a kind of filtering process that can be controlled depending on the selected CopyMode value.

The most common CopyMode is SrcCopy. This mode tells Windows to copy all pixels from the source canvas/bitmap to the destination canvas. The next two lines show this technique being used in the first graphic operation in the AdjustableImage component:

```
TmpBmp.Canvas.CopyMode := cmSrcCopy;
TmpBmp.Canvas.CopyRect(ClientRect,(Parent as TForm).Canvas,BoundsRect);
```

Essentially, the first step is to copy the area of the form's canvas that is sitting under the component onto the temporary bitmap. The first line of code sets the CopyMode property of the temporary bitmap's canvas to SrcCopy. Then the second line of code uses the CopyRect method to copy a portion of the form's canvas to the temporary bitmap. Since SrcCopy is being used, all pixels will transfer from the source (the parent's canvas) to the destination (the temporary bitmap). The destination region of this copy is defined in the first parameter as ClientRect. The size of the region being copied is defined by BoundsRect, which is a TRect property of the AdjustableImage component. The temporary bitmap contains a copy of the image that appears immediately beneath the component.

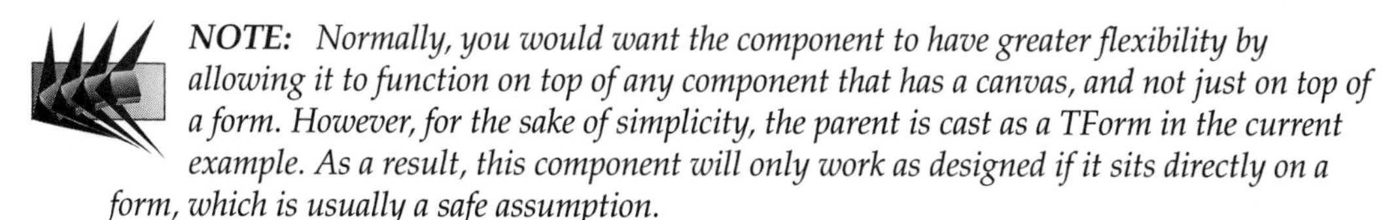

***NOTE:** Normally, you would want the component to have greater flexibility by allowing it to function on top of any component that has a canvas, and not just on top of a form. However, for the sake of simplicity, the parent is cast as a TForm in the current example. As a result, this component will only work as designed if it sits directly on a form, which is usually a safe assumption.*

The next step is to "punch out" a section of the image stored in the temporary bitmap. This is where the mask comes into play. The CopyMode SrcAnd technique is used for this purpose. This method tells Windows to combine the pixels from the source and destination using the AND bitwise operator, as shown in the next two lines of code:

```
TmpBmp.Canvas.CopyMode := cmSrcAnd;
TmpBmp.Canvas.CopyRect(ClientRect,Picture.Bitmap.Canvas,MaskRect);
```

If you refer back to Figure 11-4 and look at the mask portion of the bitmap (the right side), you will see that the mask is just white and black pixels. A white pixel has red, green, and blue (RGB) values of (255,255,255), and a black pixel has values of (0,0,0). The SrcAnd mode tells Windows to take each individual pixel from the mask bitmap and then AND it with the corresponding pixel from the destination. Because of the way the AND operator works, any color pixel combined with a black pixel using the AND operator always become black (zero AND any value is still zero). In contrast, any color pixel that is combined with a white pixel using the AND operator will always result in that pixel's original color (255 and any color from 0 to 255 will result in that color).

The source rectangle for the CopyRect procedure is using the MaskRect structure defined earlier. This rectangle defines the mask (right-hand) side of the source bitmap.

After these two lines are executed, the temporary bitmap would look something like the image on the left side of Figure 11-5. Because the border areas of the mask are white, the bitwise operation of the ROP code SrcAnd allows the colored portions of the background to come through. In other words, the area the graphic will occupy is "punched out."

The final step is to insert the new graphic onto the punched-out area. This step is accomplished with the following SrcPaint ROP code:

```
TmpBmp.Canvas.CopyMode := cmSrcPaint;
TmpBmp.Canvas.CopyRect(ClientRect,Picture.Bitmap.Canvas,ClientRect);
```

This code takes the left side of the bitmap (defined by the third parameter, ClientRect) and copies that area to the temporary bitmap using the SrcPaint CopyMode. SrcPaint performs essentially the same type of filtering as SrcAnd, but instead of using the AND bitwise operator, it uses the OR operator. The result is that the two images are merged together. Now it is just a simple matter of drawing the temporary bitmap onto the surface of the component's canvas. This is done with the last line of the paint procedure:

```
Draw(0,0,TmpBmp);
```

That's it! Masking permits a complex image to show through the AdjustableImage component. The result produces the effect shown in Figure 11-6.

Figure 11-5. *The mask is combined with a copy of the bitmap beneath the component to create a section of the background where the mask appears to be "punched out"*

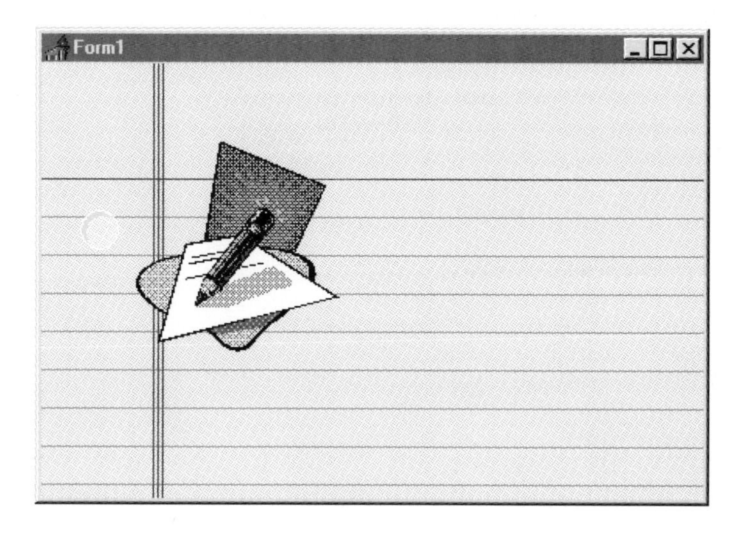

Figure 11-6. *The final result of masking*

As long as the bitmap is created correctly with the appropriate mask, the bitmap will always draw correctly regardless of the color behind it. Both the transparent and masking methods of painting have their advantages and disadvantages. The primary advantage of painting with transparent colors is that it only requires a line or two of Object Pascal code. Of course, it cannot handle the complex background situation illustrated in this second example.

The masking method takes a bit more work because you need to prepare the bitmap with a mask. It also takes more code to achieve this effect, and as a result is a bit slower since the in-memory manipulation of a temporary bitmap takes a little time. The masking method's primary advantage is that you can overcome any problems associated with using complex backgrounds.

Final AdjustableImage Component Code

Now that all changes have been made to the AdjustableImage component, here is the final code listing:

```
unit AdjImage;

interface

uses
  SysUtils,  WinTypes, WinProcs,
```

```
  Messages, Classes, Graphics, Controls,
  Forms, Dialogs, Consts;
type
  TImageStyles = (isNormal,isTransparent,isMasked);
  TAdjustableImage = class(TGraphicControl)
  private
    FPicture         : TPicture;
    FStyle           : TImageStyles;
    FNumImages       : Integer;
    function GetCanvas: TCanvas;
    procedure SetPicture(Value: TPicture);
    procedure SetStyle(Value: TImageStyles);
    procedure SetNumImages(Value: Integer);
    procedure PictureChanged(Sender: TObject);
  protected
    function GetPalette: HPALETTE; override;
    procedure Paint; override;
  public
    constructor Create(AOwner: TComponent); override;
    destructor Destroy; override;
    property Canvas: TCanvas read GetCanvas;
  published
    property ImageStyle: TImageStyles read FStyle
      write SetStyle default isNormal;
    property NumImages: Integer read FNumImages
      write SetNumImages default 1;
    property Picture: TPicture read FPicture write SetPicture;
  end;

procedure Register;

implementation

procedure Register;
begin
  RegisterComponents('Samples', [TAdjustableImage]);
end;

constructor TAdjustableImage.Create(AOwner: TComponent);
begin
  inherited Create(AOwner);
  FNumImages := 1;
  FPicture := TPicture.Create;  FPicture.OnChange := PictureChanged;
  Width := 100;
  Height := 100;
end;

procedure TAdjustableImage.SetNumImages(Value: Integer);
```

```
begin
  if Value > 0 then
    begin
      FNumImages := Value;
      PictureChanged(Self);
    end;
end;

destructor TAdjustableImage.Destroy;
begin
  FPicture.Free;
  inherited Destroy;
end;

procedure TAdjustableImage.SetStyle(Value: TImageStyles);
begin
  if FStyle <> Value then
    begin
      FStyle := Value;
      Refresh;
    end;
end;

function TAdjustableImage.GetPalette: HPALETTE;
begin
  Result := 0;
  if FPicture.Graphic is TBitmap then
    Result := TBitmap(FPicture.Graphic).Palette;
end;

function TAdjustableImage.GetCanvas: TCanvas;
var
  Bitmap: TBitmap;
begin
  if Picture.Graphic = nil then
  begin
    Bitmap := TBitmap.Create;
    try
      Bitmap.Width := Width;
      Bitmap.Height := Height;
      Picture.Graphic := Bitmap;
    finally
      Bitmap.Free;
    end;
  end;
  if Picture.Graphic is TBitmap then
    Result := TBitmap(Picture.Graphic).Canvas
  else
```

```
    raise EInvalidOperation.Create(LoadStr(SImageCanvasNeedsBitmap));
end;

procedure TAdjustableImage.SetPicture(Value: TPicture);
begin
  FPicture.Assign(Value);
end;

procedure TAdjustableImage.PictureChanged(Sender: TObject);
begin
  SetBounds(Left, Top, Picture.Width div NumImages, Picture.Height);
end;

procedure TAdjustableImage.Paint;
var
  TmpBmp            : TBitmap;
  BmpRect,MaskRect : TRect;
begin
  if csDesigning in ComponentState then
    with inherited Canvas do
      begin
        Pen.Style := psDash;
        Brush.Style := bsClear;
        Rectangle(0, 0, Width, Height);
      end;
  with inherited Canvas do
    case ImageStyle of
      isNormal      : Draw(0,0,Picture.Graphic);
      isTransparent : begin
                        Brush.Color := (Parent as TForm).Color;
                        BrushCopy(ClientRect,Picture.Bitmap,
                        ClientRect,Picture.Bitmap.TransparentColor);
                      end;
      isMasked      :begin
                     {Make a temporary bitmap to
                      hold intermediate results}
                     TmpBmp := TBitmap.Create;
                     try
                     {Set its initial size equal to
                      that of the component}
                     TmpBmp.Width := Width;
                     TmpBmp.Height := Height;
                     {Make a rectangle of the mask area of the bitmap}
                     MaskRect := Rect(Width,0,Width*NumImages,Height);
                     {Copy the portion of the parents canvas that
                      is sitting under the component onto the temp
                      bitmap using SRCCOPY}
                     TmpBmp.Canvas.CopyMode := cmSrcCopy;
```

```
                            TmpBmp.Canvas.CopyRect(ClientRect,
                            (Parent as TForm).Canvas,BoundsRect);
                            {Copy the mask onto the working bitmap with SRCAND}
                            TmpBmp.Canvas.CopyMode := cmSrcAnd;
                            TmpBmp.Canvas.CopyRect(ClientRect,
                            Picture.Bitmap.Canvas,MaskRect);
                            {Copy the bitmap image onto the
                            working bmp with SRCPAINT}
                            TmpBmp.Canvas.CopyMode := cmSrcPaint;
                            TmpBmp.Canvas.CopyRect(ClientRect,
                                Picture.Bitmap.Canvas,ClientRect);
                            {Now simply draw this accumulated image}
                            Draw(0,0,TmpBmp);
                            finally
                            {Ensure that the bitmap is freed}
                            TmpBmp.Free;
                            end;
                            end;
    end;
end;
end.
```

NOTE: The final code for this component can be found in the file named ADJIMAGE.END located in the Chapter 11 subdirectory on the CD-ROM.

Creating Rotated Text

To many developers, allowing for rotated or angled text in a Windows application may seem like a complicated task. Fortunately, this could not be further from the truth, and with Delphi, it's even easy.

Windows manages information about all the fonts it is using for a particular application. From Delphi you have access to some of this information, such as the font name, its size, style, and color (for example, Arial, 10pt, Bold and Italic, and clRed). However, Windows needs a great deal of additional information in order to display the text correctly. One of the more commonly overlooked values is a font's *Escapement value,* which the Windows API (in the help topic on TLogFont) defines as "the angle, in tenths of degrees, between the base line of a character and the x-axis."

The form shown in Figure 11-7 demonstrates the Escapement value's function. This form contains a Button, a SliderBar, a CheckBox, a PaintBox, a Label, a SpinBox, and a Timer. Whenever the SpinBox is changed, the low-level font record associated with the object assigned to the PaintBox's Font property is changed. After making the change, the SpinBox's OnChange event handler tells the PaintBox to refresh itself.

Although changes to the SpinEdit triggers the font change, the other objects on the form indirectly modify the font by also changing the SpinEdit. The SliderBar has code

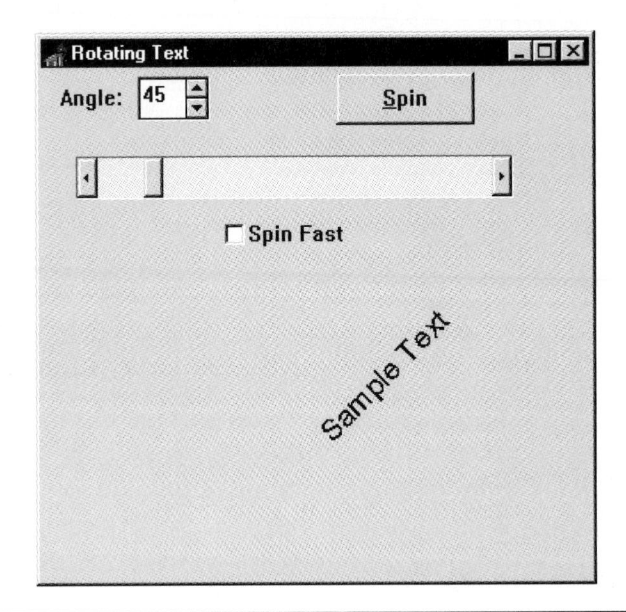

Figure 11-7. *A fun example that rotates text within a PaintBox*

associated with its OnChange event that updates the value in the SpinBox each time the SliderBar is moved. Code on the Button's OnChange event handler enables and disables the Timer. Like the SliderBar, the Timer's OnTimer event handler updates the SpinBox value. If the CheckBox is checked, the Timer updates the SpinEdit by a large amount, and a smaller amount if not. After making the font change, the timer tells the PaintBox to refresh itself.

The PaintBox's Paint method isn't doing anything special on its own. It is simply performing a TextOut to print out the words "Sample Text" in the center of the PaintBox's canvas. TextOut is one of the simplest ways to control a canvas, permitting you to print text to a specific area of a canvas using the current font.

Rotated Text Code Example

The following is the code associated with the project ROTEXT.DPR. You can find this project on the CD-ROM in the Chapter 11 directory:

```
unit Rotextu;

interface

uses
  SysUtils, WinTypes, WinProcs,
  Messages, Classes, Graphics, Controls,
```

```
  Forms, Dialogs, StdCtrls, Spin, ExtCtrls;

type
  TForm1 = class(TForm)
    SpinEdit1: TSpinEdit;
    Label1: TLabel;
    PaintBox1: TPaintBox;
    ScrollBar1: TScrollBar;
    Button1: TButton;
    Timer1: TTimer;
    CheckBox1: TCheckBox;
    procedure SpinEdit1Change(Sender: TObject);
    procedure PaintBox1Paint(Sender: TObject);
    procedure ScrollBar1Change(Sender: TObject);
    procedure Timer1Timer(Sender: TObject);
    procedure Button1Click(Sender: TObject);
  private
    FontRecord : TLogFont;
  public
    { Public declarations }
  end;

var
  Form1: TForm1;

implementation

{$R *.DFM}

procedure TForm1.SpinEdit1Change(Sender: TObject);
begin
  {First, go get the font record associated
   with the PaintBox's Font Property}
  GetObject(PaintBox1.Font.Handle,SizeOf(FontRecord),Addr(FontRecord));
  {Change the lfEscapement value to 10 times the angle in the SpinEdit}
  FontRecord.lfEscapement := (SpinEdit1.Value * 10);
  {Rebuild the font record and assign it back to the Font property}
  PaintBox1.Font.Handle := CreateFontIndirect(FontRecord);
  {Repaint the text}
  PaintBox1.Refresh;
end;
procedure TForm1.PaintBox1Paint(Sender: TObject);
begin
  {Place the text in the middle of the PaintBox}
  PaintBox1.Canvas.TextOut(PaintBox1.Width div 2,
    PaintBox1.Height div 2,'Sample Text');
end;
```

```
procedure TForm1.ScrollBar1Change(Sender: TObject);
begin
SpinEdit1.Value := ScrollBar1.Position;
end;

procedure TForm1.Timer1Timer(Sender: TObject);
var
  SpinSpeed : Integer;
begin
if CheckBox1.Checked then
  SpinSpeed := 20
else
  SpinSpeed := 5;
if SpinEdit1.Value > 360 - SpinSpeed then
  SpinEdit1.Value := 0
else
  SpinEdit1.Value := SpinEdit1.Value + SpinSpeed;
end;

procedure TForm1.Button1Click(Sender: TObject);
begin
if Timer1.Enabled then
  begin
    Button1.Caption := '&Spin';
    Timer1.Enabled := False
  end
else
  begin
    Button1.Caption := '&Stop';
    Timer1.Enabled := True
  end;
end;
end.
```

Conclusion

Delphi can be a very powerful graphics tool if you know how to tap its power. This chapter has shown you just a few of the tricks that you can use to master graphic manipulation in Delphi. The next chapter covers more advanced graphic techniques.

Chapter Twelve

Advanced Graphics: Animation and Moveable Objects

The code for the examples presented in this chapter can be found in the \CODE\CH12 subdirectory on the CD-ROM that accompanies this book. Please refer to Appendix A for information on using the code files for this chapter.

This chapter continues the discussion of using graphics that began in Chapter 11. It starts with a look at techniques for allowing users to drag components around on the screen at runtime. Next, a technique for adding animation to your applications is described. Finally, several moveable container components are introduced that you can use to easily add drag-and-drop capabilities to your forms.

Runtime Movable Components

Imagine that you want to allow the pencil image from the masking example in the last chapter (in the section "Final AdjustableImage Component Code") to be dragged around the screen with the mouse at runtime. This will be demonstrated by starting with the project BMPFORM.DPR from Chapter 11. This project is shown in Figure 12-1.

NOTE: To follow along with this demonstration, you must first create the project BMPFORM.DPR. If you worked through the examples in Chapter 11, you can use that version of the application. If you did not, copy to your computer the project named BMPFORM.DPR, which is located in the Chapter 12 subdirectory on the CD-ROM. You should also make sure that you have added the version of the AdjustableImage component created in Chapter 11 to your component palette. If you did not follow along with the examples in Chapter 11, you can copy the file ADJIMAGE.PAS from the CD-ROM to the directory on the computer where you store components, and then add this component to your component palette.

Figure 12-1. *The BMPFORM project from Chapter 11*

You can make an AdjustableImage component moveable at runtime by adding a few more lines of code to the component definition. Do this by making the following changes to the AdjustableImage component code (ADJIMAGE.PAS) as indicated in bold. For the sake of space, only the methods that require changes are shown:

```
TAdjustableImage = class(TGraphicControl)
  private
    FPicture          : TPicture;
    FStyle            : TImageStyles;
    FNumImages        : Integer;
    GrabX,GrabY       : Integer;
    function GetCanvas: TCanvas;
    procedure SetPicture(Value: TPicture);
    procedure SetStyle(Value: TImageStyles);
    procedure SetNumImages(Value: Integer);
    procedure PictureChanged(Sender: TObject);
  protected
    function GetPalette: HPALETTE; override;
    procedure Paint; override;
    procedure MouseDown(Button: TMouseButton; Shift: TShiftState; X, Y:
Integer); override;
    procedure MouseMove(Shift: TShiftState; X, Y: Integer); override;
  public
    constructor Create(AOwner: TComponent); override;
    destructor Destroy; override;
    property Canvas: TCanvas read GetCanvas;
  published
    property ImageStyle: TImageStyles read FStyle write SetStyle
                         default isNormal;
    property NumImages: Integer read FNumImages write SetNumImages
                        default 1;
    property Picture: TPicture read FPicture write SetPicture;
  end;

procedure TAdjustableImage.MouseDown(Button: TMouseButton; Shift:
TShiftState; X, Y: Integer);
begin
  GrabX := X;
  GrabY := Y;
end;

procedure TAdjustableImage.MouseMove(Shift: TShiftState; X, Y: Integer);
begin
  if ssLeft in Shift then
    {Move object to the new coordinates}
    SetBounds(Left-GrabX+X,Top-GrabY+Y,Width,Height);
end;
```

The principles involved here are quite simple. First, two variables, GrabX and GrabY, are assigned the values of the X and Y screen coordinates of the mouse pointer at the moment the mouse button is depressed. Since any drag operation must begin with the left mouse button being depressed, these variables serve as a reference point for subsequent movements of the mouse.

The runtime drag operation is performed within the overridden MouseMove procedure, which executes any time the mouse pointer changes position. Within this procedure, the code checks to see if the left mouse button is down. This is done by testing whether the Shift parameter of the MouseMove procedure contains the value ssLeft. Shift is a parameter of the type TShiftState, which is a set that consists of the following values: ssShift, ssAlt, ssCtrl, ssRight, ssLeft, ssMiddle, and ssDouble. The left mouse button is down if the ssLeft statement in Shift returns True.

Once the MouseMove procedure determines that the AdjustableImage component is being dragged, the position of this component is assigned to a new location. This repositioning is performed by the SetBounds method, which assigns new values to the Top and Left properties in a single step, rather than assigning the Left and Top properties of the AdjustableImage component separately. If instead you assigned a new value to the Left and Top properties in two separate operations, the control would repaint itself after each property change, producing an undesirable visible effect. Furthermore, the new Top and Left positions, as specified by the first two parameters of the SetBounds method, take into account the offset of the mouse with respect to the Top and Left of the AdjustableImage. Specifically, the Left-GrabX+X statement defines the new Left position to be the component's old Left position minus the distance the mouse has moved (specified by GrabX, the mouse position at the beginning of the drag operation, and X, the current mouse position). The result is that the mouse pointer appears to grab the AdjustableImage component at the position where the mouse pointer is first depressed.

Note also that this procedure does not use Delphi's inherent Drag and Drop functionality, which adds a few things that are undesirable at this point. This procedure illustrates a simple technique that you can add to any of your components to permit them to be moved at runtime.

Running the program now allows you to move the AdjustableImage component around on the form. Whenever it moves to a new location, it is repainted, and since the masking paint routine is written to be generic, the component will always paint correctly.

Image Flicker

When you try this modified component, you may notice a problem that has sprung up as a result of allowing the component to move. Its image flickers like crazy as the component is moved.

There are a number of reasons for this flicker. First, whenever the component moves, it disappears momentarily, giving the main form an opportunity to repaint the area that it occupied. Unfortunately, the main form has a bit of work to do to repaint that area. Specifically, it must repaint any objects that appear within this area, including the form's canvas. The end result is (if you look very closely) that you will see a flash of the form's canvas, followed by a flash of objects that appear on the canvas at that location, and then finally, the flash for the AdjustableImage component itself. Furthermore, the flashing is not limited to the displayed area of the image (which is less than the whole image if you have set the component's ImageStyle to isTransparent or isMasked) but includes the complete rectangular bounds of the AdjustableImage.

The problem is that the parent's Paint method is being called repeatedly as the component is moved. A much smoother animation would result if the code controls when the actual painting occurs. To reduce or eliminate flicker, it is necessary to reduce the number of images that are being placed on the screen on top of each other. Before a solution is offered, it is necessary to first discuss how Windows determines the areas to paint on a form.

Valid and Invalid Screen Regions

Whenever a visual element on the screen is modified, Windows needs to have a way of identifying that area and regenerating the appropriate pixels. Think about how a scrolling list box is displayed. When it is first displayed on a form, the entire contents of the list box must be painted. This includes the border, the individual strings in the list, the scroll box, and the highlight bar. Now, suppose the user moves the bar up or down, selecting some other item in the list. Assuming that the list itself does not scroll, the only visual effect is that the next string will now be highlighted, and the one that was highlighted before is now displayed normally. However, it doesn't seem like the rest of the control was painted at all. Was it? The control only has a single Paint method, and its job is to paint the entire control, so obviously, something is going on here to prevent the drawing of certain elements of the control.

Deep inside the Windows graphics engine is a system that manages regions on the screen that need updating, which are called *valid* and *invalid* regions. Any painting that is done on a control only reaches the screen if the painting is done in an invalid region. You may be familiar with the Invalidate method in Delphi (which is really just a wrapper around the InvalidateRect API call for Windows). This method tells the affected display surface (in this case, the form) that the area occupied by the control is now invalid and need repainting. Windows sets up a region that is associated with the form and defines that region as being invalid. When control passes to the form's Paint method, the entire control will be regenerated on the screen, since the entire area within the bounds of the control corresponds to a portion of that invalidated region. Once the Paint method is done, the region is marked as valid and no longer requires updating.

Returning again to the scrolling list box example, whenever the highlight bar is moved, the only areas that are invalidated are the line that had been selected and the line that has now become selected. The list box's Paint method still paints the entire control, but everything outside of this invalid region is ignored and doesn't make it to the screen. If the list box has to scroll itself to show lines outside of the visible portion of the control, then all of the items will be invalidated, as would be the scroll bar used to move it to a new location. If the entire list box was invalidated after every adjustment to the highlight bar, it would generate flicker.

Flicker and Invalid Screen Regions

One way to eliminate flicker involves manipulation of a control's validation region. This section describes a simple technique for controlling invalid and valid regions of the screen. A later section in this chapter describes the creation of a component that manages a complex invalid region for solving more complicated problems. The following adjustment (shown in bold) to the MouseMove method will suppress the parent's painting of the form by the use of the ValidateRect method:

```
procedure TAdjustableImage.MouseMove(Shift: TShiftState; X, Y: Integer);
begin
  if Drag and (ssLeft in Shift) then
    begin
      {Move us to the new coordinates}
      SetBounds(Left-GrabX+X,Top-GrabY+Y,Width,Height);
      ValidateRect(Parent.Handle,Nil);
      Paint;
    end;
end;
```

Before examining the effects of this code, consider what happens when the mouse moves. First, the method determines if the left mouse button is still down. Then, it sets the bounds of the AdjustableImage component to the new location to which the mouse has moved.

If you look at the VCL (Visual Component Library) source code, you will notice that one of the last things the SetBounds routine does is to invalidate the region on which the control is sitting. This indirectly tells Windows to completely regenerate this image. Because Windows is a message-based operating system, a WM_PAINT message is placed in the form's message queue that tells it to repaint itself. This message is placed at the end of the message queue, so the only thing you can count on is that it will *eventually* repaint. If Windows is busy doing other things, or there are higher priority messages in the component's message queue, then there could be a considerable amount of lag time before the Paint method is actually entered.

Note that there is already a message being handled for the AdjustableImage component, namely MouseMove. Windows is going to process the MouseMove message before it gets around to processing the message queue for the form (and, thereby, finding the WM_PAINT message there). As a result, there is still an opportunity to affect the form's invalidated region.

The effect of the ValidateRect command in this example is that the region that was just invalidated is now revalidated. When the form gets to its own Paint method, it finds that it has no area that is marked invalid, and so nothing changes on the screen. However, this also prevents the component from redrawing itself since the component also rests on the same region. As a result, it is necessary to send the control into its own Paint procedure so that it can paint itself in its new location. (If the Paint procedure was left out, nothing would happen on the screen. For example, you could click on the control and start dragging it around, but there would be no visual change on the screen. The component would be moving, but all updates to the screen would be suppressed; consequently, you would not see the movement of the object.)

Figure 12-2 shows the object, as it is moved, being painted in its new locations. The MouseMove method instructs the AdjustableImage component to repaint itself, but prohibits the form from being repainted. As you can see if you are running this program, the movement of the graphic is completely fluid—no flickering at all. However, the ValidateRect command has, in effect, suppressed all the repair work that the form has been trying to do to keep the image displayed correctly. Although the movement of AdjustableImage is now flicker-free, old images remain on the form. Obviously, this solution goes one step too far. The code prevents the form from doing any updates of its own and only allows the image to paint itself. As a result, when the image moves from an old location to a new location, the form does not try to repair the portion of itself that had previously displayed the image. This leaves the trail of image pixels behind as the control moves.

What is needed is a way to repair the area previously occupied by the image without forcing the form to do any painting, since it is also important to eliminate redundant painting on the form. The fewer image copies on the form at one time, the less flicker there will be. The next sections address this flicker problem one step at a time so that you can see what influences the flicker.

Reducing Flicker

The ideal solution is to have only a single bitmap paint on the screen as the image moves from one spot to the next. With only a single image being copied, there is no possibility of flicker. However, there is another issue that comes into play. The AdjustableImage object has definite boundaries, and you really cannot (and should not) paint outside of those boundaries. When the image is moving, however, the areas

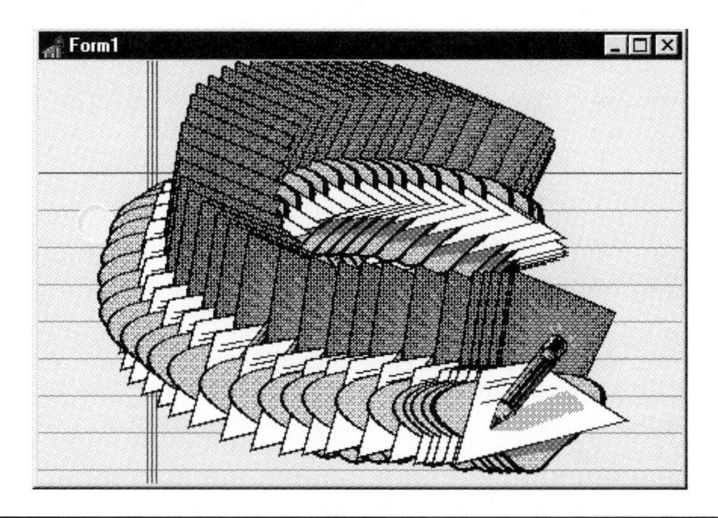

Figure 12-2. *The MouseMove method instructs the Adjustable Image component to repaint itself, but prohibits the form from being repainted*

that the component no longer resides in need to be repaired. Ultimately, multiple images will need to be painted simultaneously. But this will not completely eliminate sources of flicker from the image. The following code example improves the situation. (A more complex solution that provides a completely flicker-free painting on the screen is illustrated in the next section, "Flicker-Free Animation.")

If you run the demo program at this point, you may notice that when the image is moving, the entire rectangular shape of the image's canvas flickers, not just the image. This flicker can improved by restoring the background that was underneath the image. To have the component do this, declare a TBitmap variable private in the TAdjustableImage type declaration as shown here:

```
type
  TImageStyles = (isNormal,isTransparent,isMasked);
  TAdjustableImage = class(TGraphicControl)

  private
    FPicture          : TPicture;
    FStyle            : TImageStyles;
    FNumImages        : Integer;
    GrabX,GrabY       : Integer;
    SavedBmp          : TBitmap;
```

Next, create this bitmap when the component is created, as follows:

```
constructor TAdjustableImage.Create(AOwner: TComponent);
begin
  inherited Create(AOwner);
  FNumImages := 1;
  FPicture := TPicture.Create;
  FPicture.OnChange := PictureChanged;
  Width := 100;
  Height := 100;
  SavedBMP := TBitmap.Create;
end;
```

Each time the AdjustableImage component is painted, copy the canvas underneath the component to this saved bitmap by making the following adjustment (shown in bold) to the Paint method:

```
procedure TAdjustableImage.Paint;
var
  TmpBmp            : TBitmap;
  BmpRect,MaskRect  : TRect;
begin
  {If in design mode, provide a rectangle around}
```

```
    {the control to show where it is, particularly if it has no bitmap}
    if csDesigning in ComponentState then
      with inherited Canvas do
        begin
          Pen.Style := psDash;
          Brush.Style := bsClear;
          Rectangle(0, 0, Width, Height);
        end;
    {Save the area of the parent's canvas that is sitting under the control}
    SavedBmp.Width := Width;
    SavedBmp.Height := Height;
    SavedBmp.Canvas.CopyRect(ClientRect,(Parent as TForm).Canvas,BoundsRect);
    {Save the color of the lower-left corner pixel of the bitmap}
    with inherited Canvas do
    {... include the rest of the Paint method here... }
```

As the AdjustableImage component is moved, paint this saved bitmap by modifying the MouseMove method to include the following change (shown in bold):

```
procedure TAdjustableImage.MouseMove(Shift: TShiftState; X, Y: Integer);
var
  R : TRect;
begin
  if Drag and (ssLeft in Shift) then
    begin
      {Paint the saved bitmap}
      (Parent as TForm).Canvas.Draw(Left,Top,SavedBmp);
      SetBounds(Left-GrabX+X,Top-GrabY+Y,Width,Height);
      ValidateRect(Parent.Handle,Nil);
      Paint;
      Update;
    end;
end;
```

Finally, it is necessary to free this temporary bitmap when the AdjustableImage component is destroyed. Make the following addition (shown in bold) to the component's destructor:

```
destructor TAdjustableImage.Destroy;
begin
  FPicture.Free;
  SavedBMP.Free;
  inherited Destroy;
end;
```

Now that you have made these changes, save ADJIMAGE.PAS and then recompile the library. Then, recompile BMPFORM and run it. When you do, you will notice that the moving component causes less flicker. The situation is vastly improved because many of the sources of flickers have been supressed by the use of the off-canvas bitmap SAVEDBMP.

Unfortunately, this is about as good as can be expected from a moving component such as this. The benefits of the AdjustableImage component are its ability to draw itself in various styles in order to demonstrate techniques such as transparency and masking. However, it is really not well suited to fluid, flicker-free animation. Let's leave the AdjustableImage component and move on to a different approach.

NOTE: *The final version of the AdjustableImage component can be found in the file named ADJIMAGE.END in the Chapter 12 directory on the CD-ROM. If you want to create this component without making the manual changes outlined in this chapter, rename this file ADJIMAGE.PAS and add it to your component palette.*

Flicker-Free Animation

In the previous example, there was a fundamental restriction in what could be accomplished because a component was used. With a component, it is normally possible to affect only the areas that are within the bounds of that component. During animation, however, a graphic is typically moving on the screen rather than staying in one place. Because it is moving, you find that you need to repair areas that the component had just occupied prior to its shifting from one location to the next. However, this old position is now outside of the component's confines, and as a result, the component itself cannot really repair that damage.

Instead of creating a component that can handle the aspects of animation on its own, the next technique addresses this issue from a different angle. To be able to move an object on the screen without causing flicker, you need complete access to the canvas on which it is being drawn. This was not the case in the AdjustableImage component example presented in the preceding section. Access was available only to the AdjustableImage's canvas.

The next example demonstrates some animation techniques by drawing directly on the background of a form. Custom components are not involved in this example, just several standard components from Delphi's component palette. The behavior of these components has been modified through the use of event handlers.

Figure 12-3 shows the ANIMATE.DPR project main form. This form contains three PaintBox components, each placed within a Panel component and labeled by a Label component. The form also contains four SpeedButton components, as well as a Timer component.

Following is the code defined for this form:

```
unit AnimateU;

interface
```

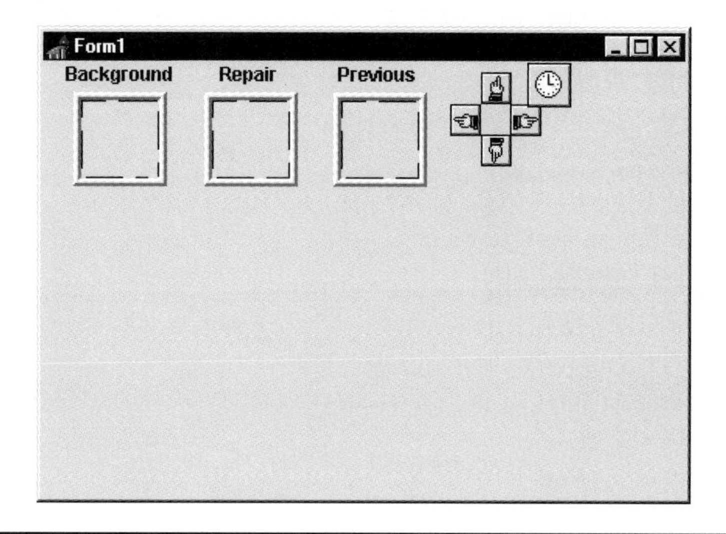

Figure 12-3. *The main form for ANIMATE.DPR*

```
uses
  SysUtils, WinTypes, WinProcs, Messages, Classes, Graphics, Controls,
  Forms, Dialogs, ExtCtrls, StdCtrls, Buttons;

type
  TForm1 = class(TForm)
    Timer1: TTimer;
    Panel1: TPanel;
    Panel2: TPanel;
    Panel3: TPanel;
    PaintBox1: TPaintBox;
    PaintBox2: TPaintBox;
    PaintBox3: TPaintBox;
    Label1: TLabel;
    Label2: TLabel;
    Label3: TLabel;
    SpeedButton1: TSpeedButton;
    SpeedButton2: TSpeedButton;
    SpeedButton3: TSpeedButton;
    SpeedButton4: TSpeedButton;
    procedure FormCreate(Sender: TObject);
    procedure FormDestroy(Sender: TObject);
    procedure FormPaint(Sender: TObject);
    procedure Timer1Timer(Sender: TObject);
```

```
    procedure SpeedButton3Click(Sender: TObject);
    procedure SpeedButton2Click(Sender: TObject);
    procedure SpeedButton1Click(Sender: TObject);
    procedure SpeedButton4Click(Sender: TObject);
  private
    X1,Y1               : Integer;
    OldX,OldY           : Integer;
    XOff,YOff           : Integer;
    ObjWidth,ObjHeight  : Integer;
    SavedBmp            : TBitmap;
    LastSavedBmp        : TBitmap;
    BackgroundBmp       : TBitmap;
    OldRect,NewRect,R1  : TRect;
    NoLastBitmap        : Boolean;
    LimitL,LimitR       : Integer;
    LimitT,LimitB       : Integer;
  end;

var
  Form1: TForm1;

implementation

{$R *.DFM}

procedure TForm1.FormCreate(Sender: TObject);
begin
  Randomize;
  {Set the width and height of the animated object}
  ObjWidth := 50;
  ObjHeight := 50;
  {Set its initial location}
  X1 := 0;
  Y1 := ObjHeight*2;
  {Set its initial movement offsets... horizontal & vertical}
  XOff := Random(4)+1;
  YOff := Random(4)+1;
  {Create a bitmap that will hold the background image}
  BackgroundBmp := TBitmap.Create;
  {Load the background image}
  BackgroundBmp.LoadFromFile('C:\DELPHI\IMAGES\BACKGRND\WRITING.BMP');
  {Create a bitmap that will hold the background under the image}
  SavedBmp := TBitmap.Create;
  with SavedBmp do
    begin
      Width := ObjWidth;
      Height := ObjHeight;
      Canvas.CopyMode := srcCopy;
```

```
    end;
  {Create a bitmap that will hold the previous background image}
  LastSavedBmp := TBitmap.Create;
  with LastSavedBmp do
    begin
      Width := ObjWidth;
      Height := ObjHeight;
      Canvas.Pen.Color := clBlack;
      Canvas.Brush.Color := clRed;
      Canvas.Brush.Style := bsSolid;
      Canvas.CopyMode := srcCopy;
    end;
  {Boolean to track that we have not yet initially saved the background}
  NoLastBitmap := True;
  {Set default properties for the form's canvas}
  Canvas.Pen.Color := clBlack;
  Canvas.Brush.Color := clRed;
  Canvas.Brush.Style := bsSolid;
  {Set limits that restrict the movement of the image}
  LimitL := Abs(XOff);
  LimitT := Abs(ObjHeight*2);
  LimitR := ClientWidth-ObjWidth-Abs(XOff);
  LimitB := ClientHeight-ObjHeight-Abs(YOff);
  {Turn on the timer}
  Timer1.Enabled := True;
end;

procedure TForm1.FormDestroy(Sender: TObject);
begin
  SavedBmp.Free;
  LastSavedBmp.Free;
  BackgroundBmp.Free;
end;

procedure TForm1.FormPaint(Sender: TObject);
begin
  {Paint the background image on the form}
  Inherited Canvas.Draw(0,ObjHeight*2,BackgroundBmp);
  NoLastBitmap := True;
end;

procedure TForm1.Timer1Timer(Sender: TObject);
begin
  {Save the location where the image currently is}
  OldRect := Rect(X1,Y1,X1+ObjWidth,Y1+ObjHeight);

  {Move the image}
  inc(X1,XOff);
```

```
inc(Y1,YOff);

{Save the images new location}
NewRect := Rect(X1,Y1,X1+ObjWidth,Y1+ObjHeight);

{Save the area of the background to be drawn on}
with SavedBmp.Canvas do CopyRect(ClipRect,Self.Canvas,NewRect);

{Paint this image in a PaintBox to see the intermediate result}
PaintBox1.Canvas.Draw(0,0,SavedBmp);

{The first time in, we need to save the starting background}
if NoLastBitmap then
  begin
    with LastSavedBmp.Canvas do
      CopyRect(ClipRect,Self.canvas,OldRect);
    NoLastBitmap := False;
  end;

{Determine the area of overlap from the last saved bitmap}
R1 := Rect(-XOff,-YOff,-XOff+SavedBmp.Width,-YOff+SavedBmp.Height);

{Repair this portion of the SavedBmp from the last saved bitmap}
SavedBmp.Canvas.CopyRect(R1,LastSavedBmp.Canvas,
  LastSavedBmp.Canvas.ClipRect);

{Paint this image in a PaintBox to see the intermediate result}
PaintBox2.Canvas.Draw(0,0,SavedBmp);

{Paint the image on the screen. This could be
 pretty much whatever you want}
Inherited Canvas.Ellipse(X1,Y1,X1+ObjWidth,Y1+ObjHeight);

{Draw the same image over the saved background
 bitmap offset by the last move}
LastSavedBmp.Canvas.Ellipse(XOff,YOff,XOff+ObjWidth,YOff+ObjHeight);

{Paint this image in a PaintBox to see the intermediate result}
PaintBox3.Canvas.Draw(0,0,LastSavedBmp);

{Clear the image from the screen using the last saved bitmap}
inherited Canvas.Draw(OldRect.Left,OldRect.Top,LastSavedBmp);

{Make the saved bitmap the last saved bitmap}
with LastSavedBmp.Canvas do
  CopyRect(ClipRect,SavedBmp.Canvas,ClipRect);

{Flip direction if it hits a wall}
```

```
  if (X1 < LimitL) or (X1 > LimitR) then XOff := -XOff;
  if (Y1 < LimitT) or (Y1 > LimitB) then YOff := -YOff;
end;

procedure TForm1.SpeedButton3Click(Sender: TObject);
begin
  if XOff < 8 then Inc(XOff);
end;

procedure TForm1.SpeedButton2Click(Sender: TObject);
begin
  if YOff > -8 then Dec(YOff);
end;

procedure TForm1.SpeedButton1Click(Sender: TObject);
begin
  if XOff > -8 then Dec(XOff);
end;

procedure TForm1.SpeedButton4Click(Sender: TObject);
begin
  if YOff < 8 then Inc(YOff);
end;

procedure TForm1.FormResize(Sender: TObject);
begin
  LimitR := ClientWidth-ObjWidth-Abs(XOff);
  LimitB := ClientHeight-ObjHeight-Abs(YOff);
  Self.Invalidate;
end;
end.
```

The principal function of this program is to draw a moving circle across a complex background. Figure 12-4 shows what the form looks like when it is running. The lower portion of the form is the area in which the circle moves around, and the upper area displays the intermediate steps that are occurring behind the scenes.

Having a graphic paint on the background of the form is quite easy. The variable BackgroundBmp is declared to hold the bitmap, which is loaded with a graphic file inside the FormCreate method. Then, the code simply paints the background bitmap onto the canvas in the desired location during the form's Paint method. Again, the WRITING.BMP bitmap that ships with Delphi is used. This technique was demonstrated in Chapter 11. You should refer back to that chapter if you want additional information.

In order to control the pacing of the animation, the code also includes a Timer component for the form. The timer is set to click off as fast as it can, which is roughly once every 55 milliseconds. (You use the Interval property to specify the number of milliseconds between each triggering of a Timer component. However, if you set the

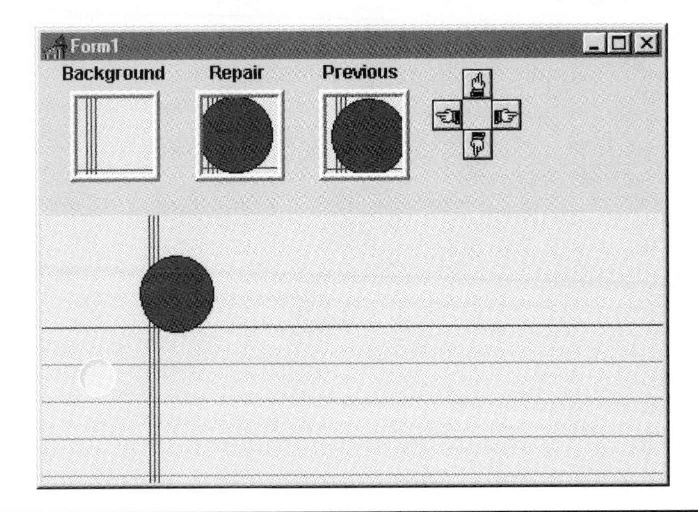

Figure 12-4. *The ANIMATE.DPR form running*

timer to an interval shorter than 55 milliseconds, it will still only trigger every 55 milliseconds. In this case, the interval is set to 1.) Every time the timer is triggered, the circle is moved to its next location. As a result, the bulk of the code is in the timer's OnTimer method.

In the following code, the timer has just gone off and control has been passed into its OnTimer event handler. The first thing that needs to be done is to save the circle's current location before it can be moved. This is done by saving its coordinates in a TRect structure called OldRect as follows:

```
{Save the location where the image currently is}
 OldRect := Rect(X1,Y1,X1+ObjWidth,Y1+ObjHeight);
```

Next, the variables being used to hold the location of the graphic are incremented as shown in the following code segment. The amount by which they are incremented is held in the variables XOff and YOff. Initially (when the form is created), these two variables are set to random values between 1 and 4. As you will see later, this form also has speed buttons that will allow the user to change the circle's direction and speed. These buttons directly change the XOff and YOff values, so the next time the timer event occurs, the code uses the new values:

```
{Move the image}
 inc(X1,XOff);
 inc(Y1,YOff);
```

Now that the variables holding the location of the circle are adjusted, the area that the circle will soon occupy is saved in a TRect structure called NewRect:

```
{Save the images new location}
 NewRect := Rect(X1,Y1,X1+ObjWidth,Y1+ObjHeight);
```

The next code section shows the real work. First, a copy of the form's canvas that the circle will be moving into needs to be saved. The program has already calculated the value for this area and stored it in the NewRect variable. Now it is a simple matter of using the CopyRect procedure to clip out the area represented by NewRect and save it in the SavedBmp variable created in the FormCreate. Keep in mind, however, that the area to clip out will likely have a piece of the circle already drawn in it. For example, if the new location is four pixels down and to the right of the old location, then a majority of the canvas being saved will have the circle that had been painted on the previous time through this routine. This problem is repaired a little later.

```
{Save the area of the background to be drawn on}
 with SavedBmp.Canvas do CopyRect(ClipRect,Self.Canvas,NewRect);
```

In order to better visualize what is going on in the inner workings of this program, the intermediate results of these bitmap operations are displayed at the top of the form in three PaintBoxes. The image just saved (in SavedBmp) is now copied into the PaintBox labeled "Previous":

```
{Paint this image in a PaintBox in order
  to see the intermediate result}
 PaintBox1.Canvas.Draw(0,0,SavedBmp);
```

To get a true representation of what the background canvas looks like in its new location (without the piece of the circle previously painted), you need to look at the background image saved from the prior pass through this procedure. However, you also need to test whether this is the first pass through the procedure, that is, whether the program just started executing and this is the first time the timer has gone off. If this is the case, you need to fill the LastSavedBmp variable with a beginning image. This image is, again, taken from the form's canvas. This is performed in the following code segment:

```
{The first time in, save the starting background}
 if NoLastBitmap then
   begin
     with LastSavedBmp.Canvas do
       CopyRect(ClipRect,Self.canvas,OldRect);
     NoLastBitmap := False;
   end;
```

In the following code, the actual repair of the saved background image (in SavedBmp) is performed. First, the amount of offset from the prior pass through is calculated with the result saved in a TRect structure called R1. This region is then copied from the LastSavedBmp to the SavedBmp. These intermediate results are copied to the PaintBox labeled "Background." This image, then, is the true background image that resides under, and is undamaged by, the graphic. As a result, you should always see the real background image in the left PaintBox.

```
{Determine the area overlapped from the last saved bitmap}
 R1 := Rect(-XOff,-YOff,-XOff+SavedBmp.Width,-YOff+SavedBmp.Height);

 {Repair this portion of the SavedBmp from the last saved bitmap}
 SavedBmp.Canvas.CopyRect(R1,LastSavedBmp.Canvas,
   LastSavedBmp.Canvas.ClipRect);

 {Paint this image in a PaintBox to see the intermediate result}
 PaintBox2.Canvas.Draw(0,0,SavedBmp);
```

Now, the code paints the circle in the new location on the form's canvas. The Ellipse method of the form's Canvas property is used to accomplish this paint. The fact that the code draws a circle is really not relevant at this point. You could draw a square, a triangle, or even use another bitmap. Once the image is placed on the form, it is treated just like any other pixels that could appear on the canvas.

```
{Paint the image on the screen. This could be
  pretty much whatever you want}
 Inherited Canvas.Ellipse(X1,Y1,X1+ObjWidth,Y1+ObjHeight);
```

This same circle now needs to be painted on the LastSavedBmp image in order to remove the elements of the circle from its old position. Again, to show the intermediate result, the graphic is placed into the PaintBox labeled "Repair."

```
{Draw the same image over the saved background
  bitmap offset by the last move}
 LastSavedBmp.Canvas.Ellipse(XOff,YOff,XOff+ObjWidth,YOff+ObjHeight);

 {Paint this image in a PaintBox so we can see the intermediate result}
 PaintBox3.Canvas.Draw(0,0,LastSavedBmp);
```

Now, the damaged area from the last painting of the graphic is repaired by copying the LastSavedBmp graphic onto the form in the old location of the circle. To set up the routine for the next timer tick, the SavedBmp graphic is copied to the LastSavedBmp.

```
{Clear the image from the screen using the last saved bitmap}
 inherited Canvas.Draw(OldRect.Left,OldRect.Top,LastSavedBmp);
```

```
{Make the saved bitmap the last saved bitmap}
with LastSavedBmp.Canvas do
  CopyRect(ClipRect,SavedBmp.Canvas,ClipRect);
```

The last step is to have the graphic bounce when it hits the edges of the form. When it hits these limits, it flips the sign (positive/negative) of the offset values being used to move the graphic. Since the offset is now the negative of what it had been, the graphic will move away from the edge and continue to bounce around the area defined for it.

```
{Flip direction if we have hit a wall}
 if (X1 < LimitL) or (X1 > LimitR) then XOff := -XOff;
 if (Y1 < LimitT) or (Y1 > LimitB) then YOff := -YOff;
```

There is one additional concern, however. If the user resizes the form, the variables LimitR and LimitB will no longer represent the left and bottom boundaries of the form. Consequently, the following code is executed in an event handler assigned to the Form's OnResize event property:

```
procedure TForm1.FormResize(Sender: TObject);
begin
  LimitR := ClientWidth-ObjWidth-Abs(XOff);
  LimitB := ClientHeight-ObjHeight-Abs(YOff);
  Self.Invalidate;
end;
```

Notice that this code also calls the Invalidate method of the form. This is done to cause the form to repaint itself.

When this program runs, the user can click on the directional buttons clustered in the upper right-hand corner of the form to affect the movement of the image. The program will let the graphic move eight pixels at most in any direction. (This is controlled by the values in each of the speed button's click events.)

The end result is that the graphic moves totally flicker-free across the form's canvas, as shown in Figure 12-4. There is no flicker because most of the graphics work is occurring on in-memory bitmaps (SavedBmp and LastSavedBmp). There are actually only two operations that paint images to the form's canvas. Both of these, however, have been prepared so that there are never any conflicting pixels that might cause flickering.

Additional Animation Concerns

To take the topic of animation one step further, consider the version of ANIMATE.DPR running in Figure 12-5. Several additional objects have been placed on this form, including a series of Label components as well as some Button components. As the

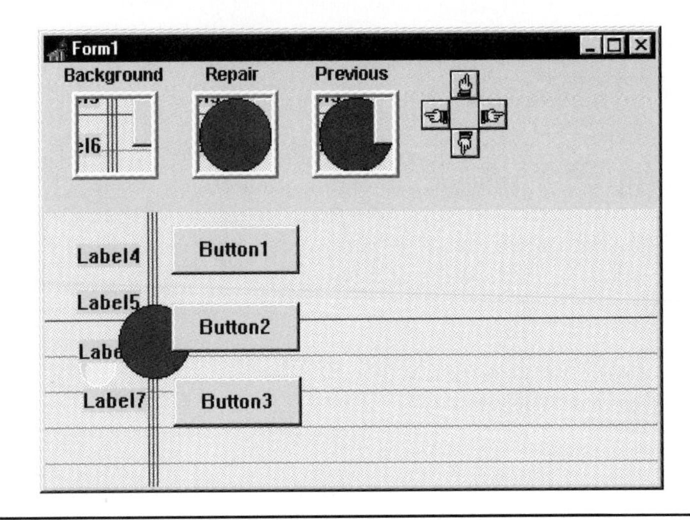

Figure 12-5. *The animated object appears beneath TWinControl descendants but appears in front of non-windowed controls*

circle continues its progress around the form, it will appear to pass underneath the Buttons, but over the Labels.

Most controls, such as Buttons, Edits, and the like, are actually their own "windows" as far as the operating system is concerned, and so painting on the form's canvas really does not affect their appearance. A notable exception to this is the Label component, which is not the same kind of component. The difference is that it does not have a handle that Windows uses to manage its visual appearance separately. Instead, the Label becomes a graphic element that is associated with the form's canvas rather than its own. Consequently, the animated object appears to move over the label, which is part of the canvas, but under the Buttons, which are separate from the canvas.

Floating Panels and Palettes

In this final section, two techniques are demonstrated. The first shows you how to create a simple floating Panel-type component using a technique demonstrated earlier for creating a moveable object. The second technique employs a more complex component, a floating palette. This floating palette is a cross between a non-modal dialog box and a floating toolbar.

A Simple Moveable Panel

Earlier in this chapter you learned how to create a component whose position can be modified by the user at runtime. While this technique is useful for creating moveable objects, what do you do if you want to take an existing Delphi component and turn it into a moveable object? One technique would be to create a new version of each of the visual Delphi components and add override to their MoveDown and MouseMove methods.

As an alternative you can create a single moveable object that can contain objects you might want to move. For example, you can create a new Panel object and make it moveable. Then, any time you want to make a moveable version of an existing object, you can place it on the moveable panel. Fortunately, this is very easy to do.

The following is the code for a type called TMoveablePanel, which is a direct descendant of TPanel. This source code appears on the CD-ROM in a file named MOVEPAL.PAS.

```
unit MovePal;

interface

uses
  SysUtils, WinTypes, WinProcs,
  Messages, Classes, Graphics, Controls,
  Forms, Dialogs, ExtCtrls;

type
  TMoveablePanel = class(TPanel)
  private
    { Private declarations }
    GrabX, GrabY    :Integer;
  protected
    { Protected declarations }
      procedure MouseDown(Button: TMouseButton; Shift: TShiftState; X, Y:
Integer); override;
      procedure MouseMove(Shift: TShiftState; X, Y: Integer); override;
public
    { Public declarations }
  published
    { Published declarations }
  end;

procedure Register;

implementation

procedure Register;
begin
  RegisterComponents('Samples', [TMoveablePanel]);
end;
procedure TMoveablePanel.MouseDown(Button: TMouseButton; Shift:
TShiftState; X, Y: Integer);
begin
  GrabX := X;
```

```
  GrabY := Y;
end;

procedure TMoveablePanel.MouseMove(Shift: TShiftState; X, Y: Integer);
begin
  if Align = alNone then
    if ssLeft in Shift then
      {Move object to the new coordinates}
      SetBounds(Left-GrabX+X,Top-GrabY+Y,Width,Height);
end;
end.
```

All that was necessary to make a moveable panel was to override the MouseDown and MouseMove methods for the TPanel class, and to declare two variables, GrabX and GrabY, for storing the coordinates of the mouse pointer at the beginning of the drag operation. In fact, with one minor exception, this code is drawn directly from the moveable object example demonstrated earlier in this chapter. The exception is that this component checks its Align property prior to attempting a movement. Only if the Align property is set to alNone is the panel position changed.

Figure 12-6 depicts a form on which the MoveablePanel object has been placed. In this case, a DBNavigator appears on this object. Although the DBNavigator is not moveable itself, placing it on the MoveablePanel permits a user to move the DBNavigator to other screen locations, if desired.

Creating a Floating Palette

While the MoveablePanel component is very easy to create, it can produce a noticeable flicker as it is moved at runtime. As described earlier, as the MoveablePanel is moved across the surface of the canvas, it causes the form underneath to repeatedly repaint its surface to repair the pixels damaged by the movement of the panel.

This is not the only limitation of the MoveablePanel component. There is nothing about the way that it looks that would necessarily lead the user to know that it can be moved. Also, it cannot be hidden or resized, at least not without adding additional code. These problems, along with the flicker mentioned earlier, are solved by the next component, Palette. Like MoveablePanel, the Palette component is a panel-like object that can be moved at runtime. However, the Palette component also has several advantages: It looks like a non-modal dialog box (or floating toolbar), provides flicker-free movement, and can be resized by the user if the appropriate property is enabled.

Valid and Invalid Complex Regions

The Palette component source code introduces many advanced graphic techniques. One of the more sophisticated of these is the use of complex regions that can be identified as either valid or invalid. Recall that the AdjustableImage component created in Chapter 11, and enhanced earlier in this chapter, managed a fairly simple

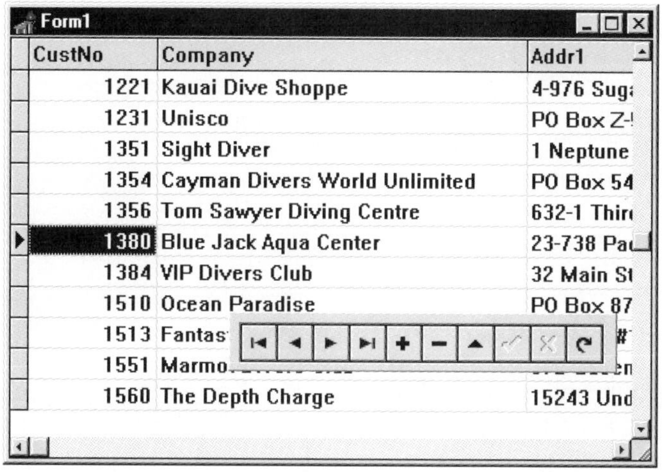

Figure 12-6. *The DBNavigator appears placed on a MoveablePanel component*

rectangular area as far as invalidation was concerned. But there is much more to this issue than meets the eye. A Windows region (HRgn) does not need to have just four sides as in a rectangle—the shape can actually have many points. What's more, regions can represent conglomerations of other regions. For example, a region could be 3 triangles widely separated (not touching), or 50 rectangles all overlapping each other. The Windows API provides a number of procedures that create, modify, and even combine regions in many different ways.

The Palette component makes use of Windows' ability to work with complex regions to alleviate the flicker caused by the form's repainting when the Palette is moved. Instead of the form repainting after every move of the Palette component, it is only allowed to repaint at the end of the entire movement of the palette. Furthermore, each time the Palette component is moved, it adds the region that it just occupied to a complex region. Only after the Palette has been dropped does the Palette component invalidate this complex region. The result is that the Palette component moves smoothly, and only one repaint takes place—after the Palette is dropped.

The Palette component is shown in Figure 12-7. This example of the Palette component has a number of speed buttons on it, although any visual component could appear on it. Notice that this figure also includes a complex image on the form (the EARTH.BMP bitmap).

In Figure 12-8, the Palette is in the middle of a drag operation. The complex graphic beneath the Palette is obliterated as the Palette is moved. Only when the Palette is dropped will the form's canvas be repainted.

The following is the source code for this component. This code is also on the CD-ROM in a file named PALETTE.PAS.

Figure 12-7. *The Palette component appearing on a form*

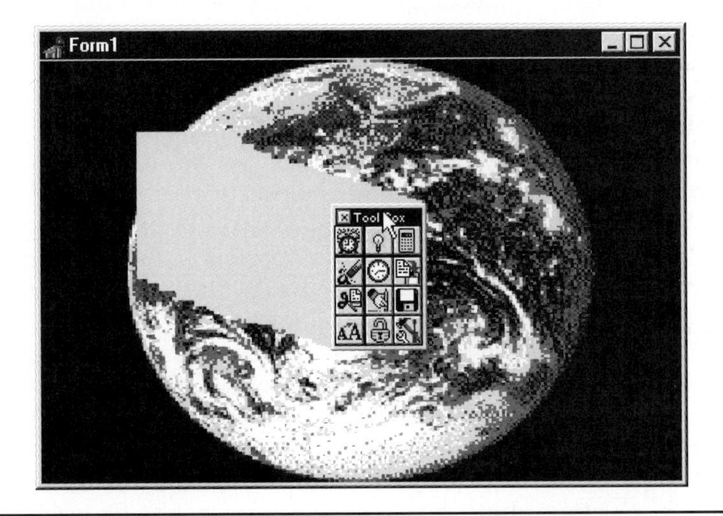

Figure 12-8. *The Palette component during a drag operation.*

```
unit Palette;

interface

uses
  SysUtils, WinTypes, WinProcs, Messages, Classes, Graphics, Controls,
  Forms, Dialogs, StdCtrls, ExtCtrls, Buttons, Menus;

type
  TBanner = class(TCustomPanel)
  private
    GrabX,GrabY   : Integer;
    CloseBtnRect : TRect;
    AllRgn       : HRgn;
  protected
    procedure Paint; override;
    procedure MouseDown(Button: TMouseButton;
      Shift: TShiftState; X, Y: ;
    procedure MouseUp(Button: TMouseButton;
      Shift: TShiftState; X, Y: Integer); override;
    procedure MouseMove(Shift: TShiftState; X, Y: Integer); override;
  public
    constructor Create(AOwner: TComponent); override;
  end;

  TPalette = class(TCustomPanel)
  private
    FBanner        : TBanner;
    FBannerCaption : String;
    FBannerHeight  : Integer;
    FSizeable      : Boolean;
    TmpPC          : Array[0..255] of Char;
    FOnHide        : TNotifyEvent;
    FOnSize        : TNotifyEvent;
    OnL,OnR,OnT,OnB: Boolean;
    OnAnEdge       : Boolean;
    GrabbedEdge    : Boolean;
    procedure SetBannerHeight(Value: Integer);
    procedure SetBannerCaption(Value: String);
    procedure WMSize(var Message: TWMSize); message WM_SIZE;
  protected
    procedure SetCursor;
    procedure SetOnEdge(X,Y: Integer);
    procedure MouseDown(Button: TMouseButton;
      Shift: TShiftState; X, Y: Integer); override;
    procedure MouseUp(Button: TMouseButton;
      Shift: TShiftState; X, Y: Integer); override;
    procedure MouseMove(Shift: TShiftState; X, Y: Integer); override;
```

```
  public
    constructor Create(AOwner: TComponent); override;
    destructor Destroy; override;
  published
    property BevelInner;
    property BevelOuter;
    property BevelWidth;
    property BorderStyle;
    property BorderWidth;
    property BannerCaption: String read FBannerCaption
      write SetBannerCaption;
    property BannerHeight: Integer read FBannerHeight
      write SetBannerHeight default 12;
    property Color;
    property Ctl3D;
    property Cursor;
    property Enabled;
    property Font;
    property ParentColor;
    property ParentCtl3D;
    property ParentFont;
    property ParentShowHint;
    property PopupMenu;
    property ShowHint;
    property Sizeable: Boolean read FSizeable
      write FSizeable default False;
    property TabOrder;
    property TabStop;
    property Visible;
    property OnHide: TNotifyEvent read FOnHide write FOnHide;
    property OnSize: TNotifyEvent read FOnSize write FOnSize;
  end;

  TPaletteClass = class of TPalette;

procedure Register;

implementation

procedure Register;


begin
  RegisterComponents('Additional', [TPalette]);
end;
{ TBanner }

constructor TBanner.Create(AOwner: TComponent);
```

```
begin
  inherited Create(AOwner);
  GrabX := -1;
  GrabY := -1;
  ControlStyle := ControlStyle - [csSetCaption];
  Align := alNone;
  Color := clActiveCaption;
  BevelInner := bvNone;
  BevelOuter := bvNone;
  BorderStyle := bsNone;
  Alignment := taCenter;
  ParentFont := True;
  Caption := '';
end;

procedure TBanner.MouseDown(Button: TMouseButton;
    Shift: TShiftState; X, Y: Integer);
var
  a : Integer;
  WndHandle : HWnd;
begin
  if Button = mbLeft then
    if PtInRect(CloseBtnRect,Point(X,Y)) then
      begin
        Parent.Visible := False;
        if Assigned((Parent as TPalette).FOnHide) then
          (Parent as TPalette).FOnHide(Self);
      end
    else
      begin
        GrabX := X;
        GrabY := Y;
        (Parent as TPalette).BringToFront;
        AllRgn := CreateRectRgnIndirect(Bounds(Parent.Left,Parent.Top,
          Parent.Width,Parent.Height));
      end;
end;

procedure TBanner.MouseUp(Button: TMouseButton;
    Shift: TShiftState; X, Y: Integer);
begin
  if Button = mbLeft then
    begin
      GrabX := -1;
      GrabY := -1;
      InvalidateRgn(Parent.Parent.Handle,AllRgn,False);
      DeleteObject(AllRgn);
    end;
```

```
end;

procedure TBanner.MouseMove(Shift: TShiftState; X, Y: Integer);
var
  L,LimitR : Integer;
  T,LimitB : Integer;
  NewRgn   : HRgn;
begin
  if (Shift = [ssLeft]) and (GrabX >= 0) and (GrabY >= 0) then
    begin
      L := Parent.Left-GrabX+X;
      T := Parent.Top-GrabY+Y;
      LimitR := Parent.Parent.ClientWidth-Parent.Width;
      LimitB := Parent.Parent.ClientHeight-Parent.Height;
      if L < 0 then L := 0;
      if T < 0 then T := 0;
      if L > LimitR then L := LimitR;
      if T > LimitB then T:= LimitB;
      {This is the rectangle of the area currently occupied}
      NewRgn := CreateRectRgnIndirect(Bounds(Parent.Left,
        Parent.Top,Parent.Width,Parent.Height));
      {Add the region into the overall invalid region}
      CombineRgn(AllRgn,AllRgn,NewRgn,RGN_OR);
      {Move to the new coordinates}
      Parent.SetBounds(L,T,Parent.Width,Parent.Height);
      {Validate the area previously occupied}
      ValidateRgn(Parent.Parent.Handle,NewRgn);
      {Erase the region captured}
      DeleteObject(NewRgn);
    end;
end;

procedure TBanner.Paint;
var
  TheRect : TRect;
begin
  inherited Paint;
  TheRect := Rect(1,1,Height-1,Height-1);
  CloseBtnRect :=
DrawButtonFace(Canvas,TheRect,0,bsAutoDetect,False,False,False);
  {Draw the Close Box}
  with Canvas do
    begin
      Pen.Color := clBlack;
      Pen.Width := 1;
      Pen.Style := psInsideFrame;
      MoveTo(CloseBtnRect.Left+3,CloseBtnRect.Top+3);
      LineTo(CloseBtnRect.Right-3,CloseBtnRect.Bottom-3);
```

```
      MoveTo(CloseBtnRect.Right-4,CloseBtnRect.Top+3);
      LineTo(CloseBtnRect.Left+2,CloseBtnRect.Bottom-3);
    end;
end;

{ TPalette }

constructor TPalette.Create(AOwner: TComponent);
begin
  inherited Create(AOwner);
  Width := 100;
  Height := 150;
  FBannerHeight := 12;
  FBannerCaption := 'Caption';
  FSizeable := False;
  ControlStyle := ControlStyle - [csSetCaption];
  Caption := '';
  {Create the panel that will serve as the banner}
  FBanner := TBanner.Create(Self);
  FBanner.Parent := Self;
  FBanner.Height := FBannerHeight-1;
  FBanner.Caption := FBannerCaption;
  {Setup font}
  Font.Name := 'Small Fonts';
  Font.Size := 7;
  Font.Color := clCaptionText;
  Font.Style := [];
end;

destructor TPalette.Destroy;
begin
  FBanner.Free;
  inherited Destroy;
end;

procedure TPalette.SetCursor;
begin
  if not Sizeable then
    begin
      Cursor := crDefault;
      exit;
    end;
  if OnL then
    if OnB then Cursor := crSizeNESW
    else if OnT then Cursor := crSizeNWSE
         else Cursor := crSizeWE
  else if OnR then
         if OnB then Cursor := crSizeNWSE
```

```
         else if OnT then Cursor := crSizeNESW
              else Cursor := crSizeWE
       else if OnB or OnT then Cursor := crSizeNS
            else Cursor := crDefault;
end;

procedure TPalette.SetOnEdge(X,Y: Integer);
begin
  OnL := X < 5;
  OnT := Y < 5;
  OnR := X > Width-5;
  OnB := Y > Height-5;
  OnAnEdge := (OnL or OnT or OnR or OnB);
end;

procedure TPalette.MouseUp(Button: TMouseButton;
    Shift: TShiftState; X, Y: Integer);
begin
  GrabbedEdge := False;
end;

procedure TPalette.MouseDown(Button: TMouseButton;
    Shift: TShiftState; X, Y: Integer);
begin
  SetOnEdge(X,Y);
  SetCursor;
  GrabbedEdge := (Button = mbLeft) and OnAnEdge;
end;

procedure TPalette.MouseMove(Shift: TShiftState; X, Y: Integer);
var
  NewL,NewT,NewW,NewH : Integer;
begin
  if Sizeable and not GrabbedEdge then
    begin
      SetOnEdge(X,Y);

      SetCursor;
    end;
  if Sizeable and GrabbedEdge and (ssLeft in Shift) then
    begin
      NewL := Left;
      NewT := Top;
      NewW := Width;
      NewH := Height;
      if OnL then begin Inc(NewL,X); Dec(NewW,X); end;
      if OnT then begin Inc(NewT,Y); Dec(NewH,Y); end;
      if OnR then Inc(NewW,X-NewW);
```

```
      if OnB then Inc(NewH,Y-NewH);
      SetBounds(NewL,NewT,NewW,NewH);
      if Assigned(FOnSize) then FOnSize(Self);
    end;
end;

procedure TPalette.SetBannerCaption(Value: String);
begin
  FBannerCaption := Value;
  if FBanner <> Nil then FBanner.Caption := FBannerCaption;
end;

procedure TPalette.SetBannerHeight(Value: Integer);
begin
  FBannerHeight := Value;
  if FBanner <> Nil then FBanner.Height := FBannerHeight;
end;

procedure TPalette.WMSize(var Message: TWMSize);
begin
  if FBanner <> Nil then
FBanner.SetBounds(2+BevelWidth,2+BevelWidth,Width-4-
BevelWidth*2,BannerHeight);
inherited;
end;

end.
```

The real work of this component (as far as the valid region manipulation is concerned) is achieved in only a few lines of code. In the Banner subcomponent is a private variable called AllRgn. It is of type HRgn, which is a handle to a region. The component uses this variable to accumulate all of the damaged areas of the main form and then uses this combined area to tell the form what to repaint.

When the mouse is clicked down on the banner (an indication to the component that dragging is likely to begin), the AllRgn is created as follows:

```
AllRgn := CreateRectRgnIndirect(Bounds(Parent.Left,Parent.Top,
                                        Parent.Width,Parent.Height));
```

Very simply, the region begins as a rectangle defining the current bounds of the palette. Then this region is added to in the MouseMove event:

```
{This is the rectangle of the area currently occupied}
NewRgn := CreateRectRgnIndirect(Bounds(Parent.Left,Parent.Top,
                     Parent.Width,Parent.Height));
{Add the region into the overall invalid region}
CombineRgn(AllRgn,AllRgn,NewRgn,RGN_OR);
```

```
{Move us to the new coordinates}
Parent.SetBounds(L,T,Parent.Width,Parent.Height);
{Validate the area we occupied}
ValidateRgn(Parent.Parent.Handle,NewRgn);
{delete the temporary region handle}
DeleteObject(NewRgn);
```

First, a temporary region called NewRgn is created, much like AllRgn, to represent the current location of the palette. Then, NewRgn is combined with AllRgn by means of the CombineRgn Windows API procedure. This procedure basically says, "Take these two regions, combine them, and return the combined area as a single region." The last option, RGN_OR, tells the procedure to combine the two regions provided using an OR operation. The Windows API help file defines additional values that can be used here that will combine the regions in different ways. These are listed in Table 12-1.

After making a union of the two regions and resaving the resulting region into AllRgn, the Palette is moved to its new location and the area on the parent that the Palette just occupied is immediately validated. This prevents the form from repainting that area. But remember, that area is saved in AllRgn, so it is possible to tell the parent how to fix the area when the dragging of the Palette is finished. This is performed in the following section of code in the MouseUp method:

```
InvalidateRgn(Parent.Parent.Handle,AllRgn,False);
DeleteObject(AllRgn);
```

The InvalidateRgn API call tells the form to repair itself. The region that is passed in InvalidateRgn is the accumulation of the rectangles from every move of the Palette.

Value	Description
RGN_AND	Uses overlapping areas of both regions (intersection)
RGN_COPY	Creates a copy of region 1 (identified by the SrcRgn1 parameter)
RGN_DIFF	Creates a region consisting of the areas of region 1 (identified by SrcRgn1) that are not part of region 2 (identified by the SrcRgn2 parameter)
RGN_OR	Combines all of both regions (union)
RGN_XOR	Combines both regions but removes overlapping areas

Table 12-1. *Values Used to Combine Regions*

When this is done, there is a single repaint of the main form, with only the areas within this invalid region (although it could be quite a complex image) being repainted. After invalidating the region, you need to delete the handle to AllRgn so that the component doesn't leak memory.

In addition to this behavior of manipulating valid and invalid regions, the Palette component has a number of additional features:

- The Palette is not allowed to leave the bounds of its parent. When it reaches the edge of the form, it will stop moving.
- When the 'X' in the upper left-hand corner of the Palette is clicked, the Palette is hidden. This will allow you to close the Palette quickly and then provide a menu option that will make it visible again.
- The Palette can be sized at runtime, if desired (if the Sizable property is also set to True). In addition, when the Palette is set to be sizable, the mouse cursor changes appropriately as the mouse moves across the edges and corners of the Palette.
- The Palette component retains all of the relevant properties of a Panel component. As a result, you can change the border, as well as the interior and exterior bevels.
- The Palette component illustrates how to move a component using a mouse.

The Palette is a fun little component that shows off a lot of handy tricks in Delphi programming. It can be used to hold buttons, edit fields, grids, slider bars, or whatever you can dream up. Basically, anything that can reside in a Panel can be placed into a Palette.

Conclusion

As you have learned in both this chapter and Chapter 11, Delphi provides a great deal of support for working with graphics. Most of this support is available through the canvas property. However, when necessary, you can employ the graphics features provided by Windows directly.

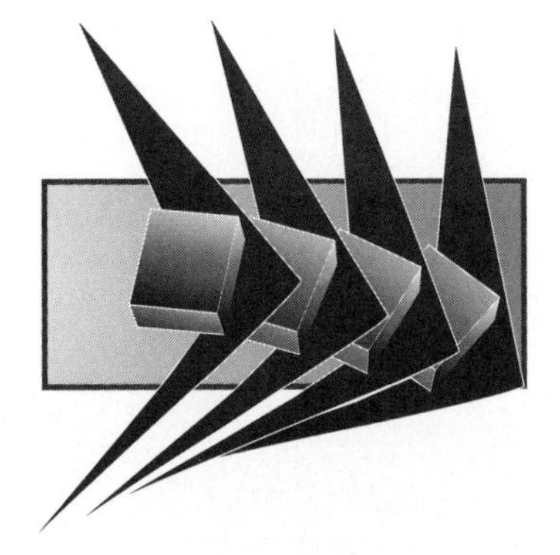

Chapter Thirteen

Resource Files

The code for the examples presented in this chapter can be found in the \CODE\CH13 subdirectory on the CD-ROM that accompanies this book. Please refer to Appendix A for information on using the code files for this chapter.

Introducing Resource Files

Resource files allow developers to store binary data within their programs as opposed to storing this data in an external file. Typical data types you will find in resource files include bitmaps, cursors, icons, strings, menus, dialog boxes, and fonts. The Windows environment has defined these types as standard resources. However, resource files are not limited to just these types. You can create and store virtually any kind of data within a resource file.

In a practical sense, resource files solve two key problems for software developers: internationalization and packaging.

The first problem, *internationalization*, refers to the processes of making an application language or culture independent. For example, imagine that you have a program that is designed in English, and you want to create a version in French. One solution (the wrong one, by the way) is to create a second copy of the application, and then to change all the text to French. The problem with this approach is that you would then have two independent applications that require separate maintenance.

The solution to the problem of internationalization is to use resource files as a way to hold all of the language dependent text of a program and none of the logic or coding. For example, you might supply an English resource file that contains all the text, alerts, and messages used in your program, and another resource file that contains the corresponding French language text. Whenever you want to create a French version of the application, you simply recompile the program using the French resource file instead of the English one. Later, if you need to ship the application in a third language, for instance, Spanish, you can simply create a Spanish language version of the resource file and then recompile the application using it.

The second problem that resource files address is *packaging*. Consider your options if your application requires ancillary files, such as bitmaps, audio files, or video files. You may be inclined to ship them along with the application as separate files. If the application relies on these files, however, what would happen if they were not present? What if the user thought the files were extraneous and deleted them? Your carefully crafted application might behave in an undesirable way if you take away files it expects to have around.

In this case, resource files help because they allow you to bind various types of data directly into the final application. Then you only need to ship the main executable (.EXE) file because all the required data files are inside the executable file.

Delphi's Resource Files

Delphi already uses resource files to a considerable extent. If you create a new project, for example, a simple SDI (Single Document Interface) application of a single blank form, and compile it, Delphi binds in quite a few resources into the resulting executable file. This is one of the reasons why simple applications like this seem to be so large. For example, consider the SDI application SDIAPP.DPR, which you can create using the SDI template in Delphi 1.0. If you take the resulting .EXE file, SDIAPP.EXE, and open it with a resource editor such as the Borland Resource Workshop, you will see something like that shown in Figure 13-1.

Because of scrolling, Figure 13-1 shows only a partial listing of the resources that appear in the Resource Workshop. (The names of the resources stored in this file are listed along the left side of this figure.) The following is a complete list of the resource names that are compiled into SDIAPP.EXE:

```
BITMAP
   BBABORT
   BBALL
   BBCANCEL
   BBCLOSE
   BBHELP
   BBIGNORE
   BBNO
   BBOK
   BBRETRY
   BBYES
STRINGTABLE
   61440
   61456
   61472
   61488
   61504
   61520
   61536
   61552
   61568
   61584
   61600
   65408
   65424
   65440
  65472
   65488
   65504
RCDATA
   TFORM1
CURSOR
   32762
   32763
   32764
   32765
   32766
   32767
ICON
   MAINICON
```

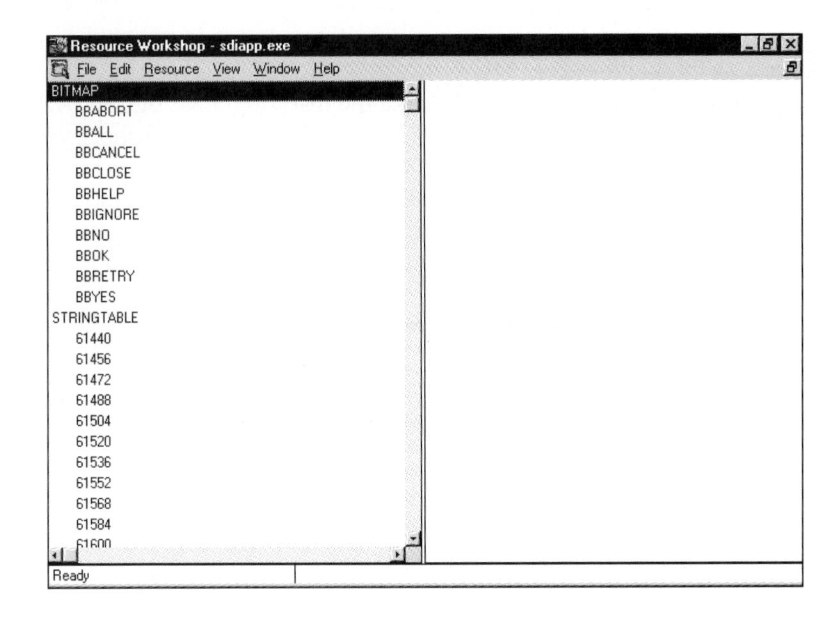

Figure 13-1. *The SDIAPP.EXE file examined using the Borland Resource Workshop version 4.5*

This list shows the resources that have been attached to the sample application. The BITMAP section holds 10 bitmaps for the BitBtn graphics used in Delphi's standard dialog boxes. The STRING section holds 17 tables of string data. Each of these tables is holding a dozen or so text strings for various error and status messages that may be needed during program execution. The RCDATA section holds details on user-defined data types, in this case, the class information on the TFORM1 object. The CURSOR section contains a few cursors not provided with Windows that Delphi applications may need (such as the SQL hourglass, drag-and-drop cursors, and so on). Finally, the ICON section holds the icon that the application will use when the form is iconized on the desktop, in this case, MAINICON.

If you were to look into the c:\Program Files\Borland\Delphi 2.0\Lib\ directory in Delphi 2 on your hard disk (in Delphi 1.0 look at C:\DELPHI\LIB\), you would note that there are roughly 20 or so .RES files. These are the resource files that are associated with their correspondingly named units. For example, the BUTTONS.RES file holds all the resource information for the BUTTONS.DCU precompiled unit. When you compile an application, and these units are used, the appropriate resource files are linked in with the application. The BUTTONS unit made it into the compiled program because it is referenced in the DIALOGS unit, and DIALOGS is in the SDIAPP's uses statement. The BUTTONS.DCU unit was compiled into the program, and the BUTTONS.RES resource file was bound into the .EXE file at link time (linking is one of the several processes that occur when you compile a project). As a result, the various bitmaps that are defined in the buttons resource file are also added to the sample application.

Creating Resource Files

Resource (.RES) files can be created in two basic ways:

- You can use a resource editor such as Borland's Resource Workshop.
- You can create a resource script and compile that script using Borland's Resource Compiler (BRCC.EXE in Delphi 1.0, BRCC32.EXE in Delphi 2).

It is probably a good time to point out that resource files are compiled specifically for the 16-bit or the 32-bit environment, and they can only be used by a project compiled within the same environment. For example, a 32-bit application compiled with Delphi 2 must use a 32-bit resource file created either using a 32-bit resource editor or compiled with BRCC32.EXE, the 32-bit Borland Resource Compiler. A Delphi 2 application cannot use a 16-bit resource file, and a Delphi 1.0 application cannot use a 32-bit resource file.

Resource Editors

One of the most common ways to create a resource file is to use a resource editor, such as the Borland Resource Workshop. The Borland Resource Workshop is a powerful and full-featured resource editor. This tool is not part of Delphi—you must purchase it separately.

NOTE: The Borland Resource Workshop is part of the Delphi 1.0 RAD Pack, an add-on product for Delphi 1.0 marketed by Borland. As of this writing, a Delphi 2 RAD Pack has not yet been released.

Another resource editor that you can use is Delphi's ImageEditor. This is a limited editor, however, in that it can be used to create graphic resource files but not other types (such as strings for internationalization). Also, at least in Delphi 1.0, the ImageEditor had some limitations that reduced its usefulness for creating bitmap resources. (It is still too early to tell if the Delphi 2 version of the ImageEditor constitutes a substantial improvement over its limited cousin.) Consequently, if you are serious about using resources in your applications, and you want to use a resource editor, you should consider using the Borland Resource Workshop.

Resource editors are applications in their own right. Furthermore, you can create resource files without using a resource editor. Consequently, this chapter does not discuss the use of resource editors. For information on using a particular resource editor, refer to the editor's online help.

Creating a Resource Script

The second way to create a resource file is to create a resource script (.RC) and compile it using Borland's Resource Compiler, which is included with all versions of Delphi (BRCC.EXE in Delphi 1.0, BRCC32.EXE in Delphi 2). Consequently, the examples in this chapter illustrate the creation of resource files by compiling resource scripts using Borland's Resource Compiler.

A resource script is a text file that describes the data types being defined. You can create the file using any text-based editor, even the Delphi editor (although this requires you to create a new unit and then remove all unit-related text). You can even use the NOTEPAD.EXE application that comes with Windows, or the EDIT.EXE that comes with DOS versions 5.0 and later. The following is an example of what a simple resource script looks like:

```
IMAGE1    BITMAP    C:\DELPHI\IMAGES\BUTTONS\ARROW1L.BMP
IMAGE2    BITMAP    C:\DELPHI\IMAGES\BUTTONS\ARROW1R.BMP
SPLASH    BITMAP    C:\DELPHI\IMAGES\BUTTONS\ARROW1U.BMP
DRAGCUR   CURSOR    C:\DELPHI\IMAGES\CURSORS\DRAGFOLD.CUR
STRINGTABLE
BEGIN
  100, "OK"
  101, "CANCEL"
END
```

NOTE: *This resource script references files that are available with Delphi 1.0. To reference the corresponding files for Delphi 2, replace the path C:\DELPHI\IMAGES\CURSORS with c:\Progra~1\Borland\Delphi~1.0\Images\Cursors (assuming you installed Delphi 2 using the default directories).*

This resource script defines three bitmaps, one cursor, and two string resources. A resource script can define binary data by means of file references, like the .BMP and .CUR file references in the preceding example, or they can include the data directly. For example, the IMAGE1 defined using a filename in the preceding resource script example could be included directly in the resource script, as demonstrated in the following example, which is functionally identical to the preceding resource script:

```
IMAGE1    BITMAP

BEGIN
 '42 4D 76 01 00 00 00 00 00 00 76 00 00 00 28 00'
 '00 00 20 00 00 00 10 00 00 00 01 00 04 00 00 00'
 '00 00 00 01 00 00 12 0B 00 00 12 0B 00 00 00 00'
 '00 00 00 00 00 00 00 00 00 00 00 00 80 00 00 80'
 '00 00 00 80 80 00 80 00 00 00 80 00 80 00 80 80'
 '00 00 7F 7F 7F 00 BF BF BF 00 00 00 FF 00 00 FF'
 '00 00 00 FF FF 00 FF 00 00 00 FF 00 FF 00 FF FF'
 '00 00 FF FF FF 00 33 33 33 33 33 33 33 33 33 33'
 '33 33 33 33 33 33 33 33 33 33 33 33 33 33 33 33'
 '33 33 33 33 33 33 33 33 33 33 33 33 33 33 33 33'
 '33 33 3F F3 33 33 33 33 33 33 00 33 33 33 33 33'
 '33 3F 77 F3 33 33 33 33 33 00 90 33 33 33 33 33'
 '3F 77 37 F3 33 33 33 33 00 99 90 33 33 33 33 3F'
 '77 33 37 FF FF FF 33 00 99 99 90 00 00 00 3F 77'
```

```
  '33 33 37 77 77 77 00 99 99 99 99 99 99 90 77 3F'
  'F3 33 33 FF FF F7 33 00 99 99 90 00 00 00 33 77'
  '3F F3 37 77 77 77 33 33 00 99 90 33 33 33 33 33'
  '77 3F F7 F3 33 33 33 33 33 00 90 33 33 33 33 33'
  '33 77 37 F3 33 33 33 33 33 33 00 33 33 33 33 33'
  '33 33 77 33 33 33 33 33 33 33 33 33 33 33 33 33'
  '33 33 33 33 33 33 33 33 33 33 33 33 33 33 33 33'
  '33 33 33 33 33 33 33 33 33 33 33 33 33 33 33 33'
  '33 33 33 33 33 33 33 33 33 33 33 33 33 33 33 33'
  '33 33 33 33 33 33'
END

IMAGE2    BITMAP   C:\DELPHI\IMAGES\BUTTONS\ARROW1R.BMP
SPLASH    BITMAP   C:\DELPHI\IMAGES\BUTTONS\ARROW1U.BMP
DRAGCUR   CURSOR   C:\DELPHI\IMAGES\CURSORS\DRAGFOLD.CUR
STRINGTABLE
BEGIN
  100, "OK"
  101, "CANCEL"
END
```

NOTE: *As you can see in the preceding resource script, strings in resource scripts are enclosed in double quotation marks, unlike string literals in Delphi, which are enclosed in single quotation marks.*

Both of these formats work equally well and will produce the same output when compiled. However, you will probably not want to enter long sequences of hexadecimal numbers manually in order to define your bitmaps (as shown in the second example). You may occasionally see these kinds of resource scripts though, as full-blown resource editors can also produce these scripts.

NOTE: *The two preceding resource scripts are appropriate for Delphi 1.0, since it references files that ship with Delphi 1.0 and that appear in the specific directory paths included in the resource file. A resource script for Delphi 2 will not look different—only the path specification will change. Since the Borland Resource Compiler is a DOS application and can make use only of eight-character filenames, you cannot use long filenames in resource files intended for Delphi 2. For example, the path for resource IMAGE2 would use the path:* `C:\PROGRA~1\BORLAND\DELPHI~1.0\IMAGES\BUTTONS\ARROW1R.BMP`.

Compiling Resource Scripts with the Borland Resource Compiler

Compiling resource scripts is very straightforward. Simply execute the BRCC program that ships with Delphi from the DOS prompt and pass the name of the resource file as a command-line parameter. For example, the following statement will compile the

IMAGES.RC resource script (assuming the BRCC.EXE is stored in the directory C:\DELPHI\BIN and IMAGES.RC is stored in the current directory):

```
C:\DELPHI\BIN\BRCC IMAGES.RC
```

NOTE: If you are using Delphi 2, the name of the resource compiler is BRCC32.EXE and is located in the c:\Program Files\Borland\Delphi 2.0\Bin directory. As mentioned earlier, because of the nature of programming in a 32-bit environment, .RES files are not generally transportable between the 16- and 32-bit versions of Delphi. Therefore, if you move your application from Delphi 1.0 to Delphi 2, you will need to recompile your resource scripts using BRCC32.EXE.

As a result of this compilation process, the resource compiler will produce a resource file called IMAGES.RES. This file contains all of the data defined in the script file but is compiled into a form that can be linked directly into a program.

WARNING: Do not give your resource script the same name as your project. The Borland Resource Compiler creates a .RES file using the same filename as the .RC file you create. Furthermore, each project has a .RES file using the same filename as the project. If your resource script has the same name as your project, the resource file created by the Borland Resource Compiler will conflict with your project's resource file, and you will encounter a compiler error when you attempt to compile your project.

Using Resource Files

Once you have a .RES file containing resource data, you must include a resource file compiler directive in your source code to instruct the linker to include the resources in the compiled program. The format of this directive is:

```
{$R filename}
```

For example, if you wanted to include the IMAGES.RES resource file created from the IMAGES.RC script, you would use the following compiler directive:

```
{$R IMAGES.RES}
```

NOTE: Compiler directives are enclosed in braces {}, just as are comments. The Delphi compiler distinguishes between a compiler directive and a comment based on the character that follows the open brace. If this character is a $, a compiler directive is assumed.

In Delphi, resource compiler directives are typically placed near the top of the section needing access to the resources. Any time you compile an application that references this unit, the linker takes the .RES file and attaches it to the .EXE file. Once resources are linked into your application, you can access these resources in Delphi using Windows API (Application Programming Interface) calls such as LoadBitmap or LoadCursor. Since linking adds these resources to the .EXE file, you do not need to deliver the resource file with your application.

If you are building applications that must be compiled in both 16 bits and 32 bits, you will need to create two resource files, a 16-bit version and a 32-bit version. You can then use the {&IFDEF WIN32} compiler directive to instruct the compiler which resource file to link in. For example, assuming that you have a 16-bit resource file named IMAGES16.RES, and a 32-bit resource file named IMAGES32.RES, you can use the following statement:

```
{$IFDEF WIN32}
  {$R IMAGES32.RES}
{$ELSE}
  {$R IMAGES16.RES}
{$ENDIF}
```

Internationalization

As described earlier in this chapter, internationalization addresses the problem of what to do when you need to create a single application in two or more languages. Programmers who are unfamiliar with Windows facilities for internationalization might opt to make a complete copy of the application (placing it in another directory) and then start sifting through the code to locate any text displayed in the application, translating the various text literals embedded in the program to the other language. Furthermore, the programmer would have to change component properties that are language specific, such as the Caption property of Button and MenuItems components. The problem with this approach is that it is very difficult to maintain two applications that are identical in every respect, with the exception of the text language. What invariably happens is that a change is made to one version without the change being made to the corresponding version. Over time, the identical applications become more and more dissimilar—in other words, a maintenance nightmare.

Fortunately, Windows provides you with the ability to separate textual information from the source code of the program. By separating the language-dependent features of the program, subsequent changes to the textual elements of the application do not affect the program logic. This permits you to maintain a single copy of the source code and not multiple, language-dependent versions.

TIP: *The techniques demonstrated in this section are presented in the context of internationalization. However, they are suited for other uses as well. For example, some developers prefer to store all strings separate from their program logic as a means of simplifying maintenance. Alternatively, these techniques can be used to create a single application that can be used by different companies. Strings that are company specific can be stored in resource files.*

The primary facility for internationalization is the LoadString function in the Windows API. This function takes several parameters, including a handle identifying the instance of the currently running program, the ID of the string you want to load, and a buffer that will hold the retrieved string (along with the maximum size of the buffer). Fortunately, Delphi has a wrapper around the LoadString function called LoadStr. The syntax for this function is:

```
LoadStr(Ident: Word): string;
```

LoadStr takes a single parameter of type Word. This parameter corresponds to the unique identifier that you assign to the resource when you create the resource file. LoadStr returns a string containing the corresponding string in the resource file. For example, in order to load the string associated with the identifier 100 defined in the IMAGES.RES resource file referred to earlier in this chapter and assign that string to the Caption property of a Button component named Button1, you use the following statement:

```
Button1.Caption := LoadStr(100);
```

Internationalization Example

The following example creates a single project that can use either English or Spanish text. You create the main form in much the same way that you design any form, with one difference. Specifically, all of the textual information on the form will be based on the contents of string tables in resource files. That includes labels, buttons, menu items, window captions, and so on—anything that contains text.

The idea is to examine the text you use in a form. If it is text, and this text is not exactly the same in all other languages, then it will replaced by text stored in a resource file at runtime. For example, Figure 13-2 shows a form from the STRING1.DPR project. This form has three panels, a RadioGroup, a few Labels, and a few Buttons. Textual information has been removed from every one of these items. This was done by clearing all of the Caption properties. As an alternative, the text could have been left in these items and replaced at runtime. It is easier to work with the form if you leave some text in these components.

In this example, the BitBtn's can have their graphics because these are not language-dependent. However, if a symbol you chose could be misinterpreted in another culture, you would also replace that symbol at runtime with one stored in a resource file. Using graphics in resource files is described later in this chapter in the section "Storing Graphics Data in Resource Files."

Creating the String Resource

The next step is to create the string resource. As mentioned earlier, you do this by creating a resource script that contains the strings, and then compiling the script into a resource file that can be linked in with your program.

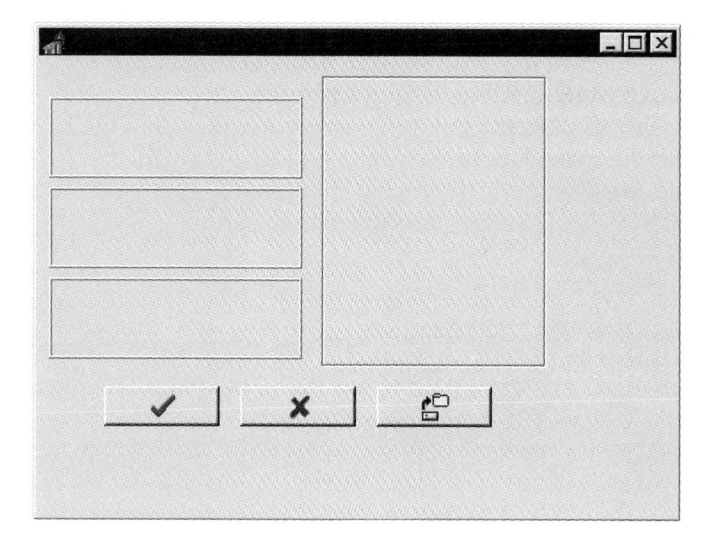

Figure 13-2. *A simple form with objects*

English Resource Script

The following is a string list created for English with the name ENGL.RC:

```
STRINGTABLE
BEGIN
  1, "Phrase:"
  2, "I hope to get through with this lesson by noon."
  3, "A politician is bound to make promises at election time."
  4, "Call in a specialist if you don't trust your doctor."
  101, "Profession:"
  102, "Cook"
  103, "Philosopher"
  104, "Minister"
  105, "Physician"
  106, "Accountant"
  107, "Painter"
  108, "Pharmacist"
  109, "Policeman"
  201, "OK"
  202, "Cancel"
  203, "Load"
  301, "Sample Program"
END
```

Each string item starts with a unique identifier. This is followed by the string itself. For example, in ENGL.RC the identifier 101 is associated with the string "Profession." The identifier can be any value that fits within a Word variable (0–65535), however, because Delphi uses some of the numbers above 61,000 to refer to basic error messages, you should avoid numbers above this value.

You now compile this resource script into a resource file using the Borland Resource Compiler. Go to the DOS prompt and change to the directory where ENGL.RC is stored. Next, enter the following command to compile the resource file. If you stored Delphi in the default directory, this will be

```
c:\delphi\bin\brcc ENGL.RC
```

using Delphi 1.0, and

```
c:\progra~1\Borland\Delphi~1.0\bin\brcc32 ENGL.RC
```

with Delphi 2.

If your compile is successful, you will have created ENGL.RES.

Multiple String Tables

Although the preceding resource script example included only a single string table, this is not a requirement. A resource script can have multiple string tables, as the following example demonstrates:

```
STRINGTABLE
BEGIN
  1, "Phrase:"
  2, "I hope to get through with this lesson by noon."
END

STRINGTABLE
BEGIN
  201, "OK"
  202, "Cancel"
  203, "Load"
  301, "Sample Program"
END
```

Good programming practice encourages the use of multiple string tables in resource scripts. The convention is to group related strings together in individual tables and then put all the tables into a single resource script file. This improves the organization of the strings as well as making it easier to find specific strings when using a resource editor such as Borland's Resource Workshop.

Using the Resource File

Following is the source code for the main form unit of the STRINGS1.DPR project:

```
unit Stringu;

interface

uses
  WinTypes, WinProcs, Messages, SysUtils, Classes, Graphics,
 Controls, Forms, Dialogs, StdCtrls, Buttons, ExtCtrls;

type
  TForm1 = class(TForm)
    Label1: TLabel;
    RadioGroup1: TRadioGroup;
    BitBtn1: TBitBtn;
    BitBtn2: TBitBtn;
    BitBtn3: TBitBtn;
    Panel1: TPanel;
    Label2: TLabel;
    Panel2: TPanel;
    Label3: TLabel;
    Panel3: TPanel;
    Label4: TLabel;
    procedure FormCreate(Sender: TObject);
    procedure BitBtn1Click(Sender: TObject);
  private
    { Private declarations }
  public
    { Public declarations }
  end;

var
  Form1: TForm1;

implementation

{$R *.DFM}

{$R ENGL.RES}

procedure TForm1.FormCreate(Sender: TObject);
begin
  Form1.Caption := LoadStr(301);
  Label1.Caption := LoadStr(1);
  Label2.Caption := LoadStr(2);
  Label3.Caption := LoadStr(3);
  Label4.Caption := LoadStr(4);
  RadioGroup1.Caption := LoadStr(101);
  RadioGroup1.Items.Clear;
  RadioGroup1.Items.Add(LoadStr(102));
  RadioGroup1.Items.Add(LoadStr(103));
  RadioGroup1.Items.Add(LoadStr(104));
  RadioGroup1.Items.Add(LoadStr(105));
```

```
    RadioGroup1.Items.Add(LoadStr(106));
    RadioGroup1.Items.Add(LoadStr(107));
    RadioGroup1.Items.Add(LoadStr(108));
    RadioGroup1.Items.Add(LoadStr(109));
    RadioGroup1.ItemIndex := 0;
    BitBtn1.Caption := LoadStr(201);
    BitBtn2.Caption := LoadStr(202);
    BitBtn3.Caption := LoadStr(203);
  end;

  procedure TForm1.BitBtn1Click(Sender: TObject);
  begin
    Close;
  end;

  end.
```

The functional part of the program is in the FormCreate procedure. Here the LoadStr function is called with the appropriate identifier for each item on the form that needs a string from the resource file. The returned values of these calls to LoadStr are then assigned to the various components on the form. Since this is all occurring within the FormCreate, the form has not shown itself yet.

When the program is compiled, the linker binds the resource file into the compiled .EXE file of the program. Consequently, these string resources will travel with the .EXE and never be unavailable. When the program is executed, you see the form shown in Figure 13-3.

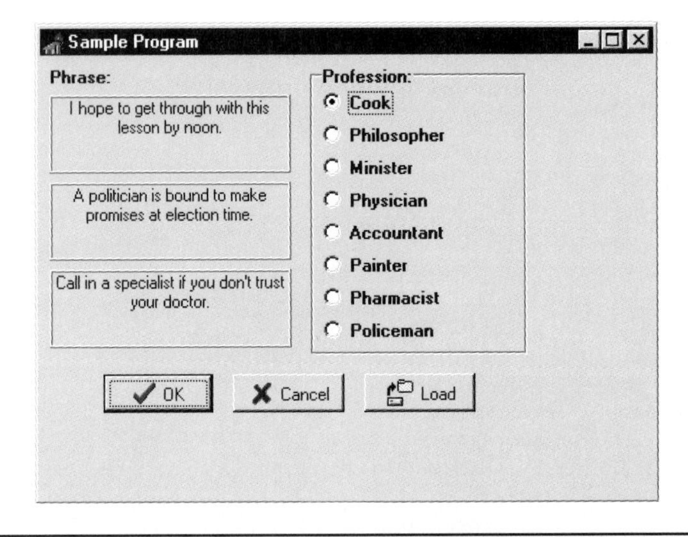

Figure 13-3. *All text displayed on this form is loaded from resources in the form's OnCreate event handler*

WARNING: If you change a resource file, always make sure to recompile every unit that uses this resource file. Delphi, however, only recompiles a unit if you have made changes to it. To ensure that all units in a project are recompiled, whether or not you have made changes to them, use Delphi's Build All feature. In Delphi 1.0, select Compile | Build All. In Delphi 2, select Project | Build All.

Converting an Application to Another Language

The advantage of using resource files for the internationalization problem becomes apparent when you want to convert your application to another language. At this stage you make a second version of your original resource script; this second resource script is in the other language you want to use. The resource script SPAN.RC on the CD-ROM with this book is a Spanish version of the ENGL.RC resource script created in the preceding section. This Spanish resource script file is a simple text file that contains the following strings:

```
STRINGTABLE
BEGIN
  1, "Expresión:"
  2, "Espero terminar esta lección al mediodía."
  3, "Un político probablemente hace promesas ín época
     de elecciones."
  4, "Consulta a un especialista si no confías en tu médico."
  101, "Profesión:"
  102, "Cocinero"
  103, "Filósofo"
  104, "Ministro"
  105, "Médico"
  106, "Contador"
  107, "Pintor"
  108, "Farmacéutico"
  109, "Policía"
  201, "Bien"
  202, "Revocar"
  203, "Cobrar"
  301, "Muestra Programa"
END
```

Once you have created this second language resource, this new script is compiled the same way the English version was compiled.

The Spanish text is applied to the project by changing a single line of text in the source code—the compiler directive that tells the compiler which resource file to link in. Specifically, the reference to {$R ENGL.RES} is changed to {$R SPAN.RES}. After making this change and recompiling, you will see the result shown in Figure 13-4.

By keeping various copies of these language resource files, the application can be converted easily from one language to another. Even better, when you need to translate the application's text to another language, only the resource script needs to be

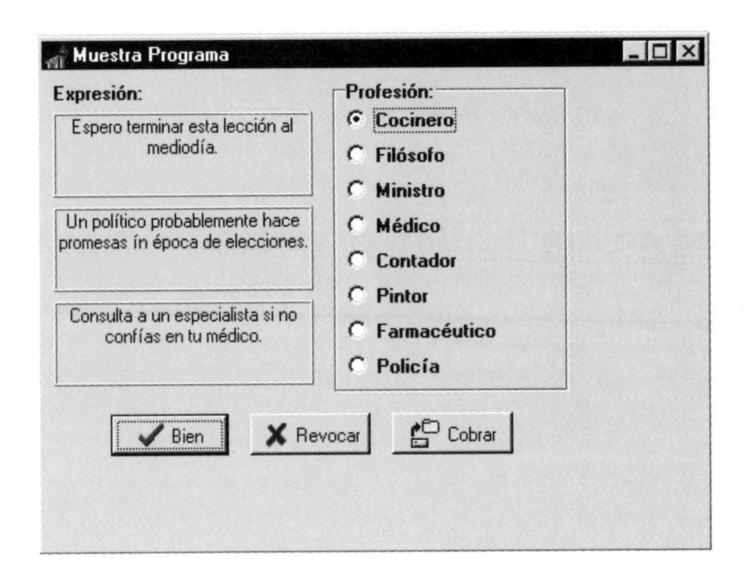

Figure 13-4. *This Spanish version of the application was created by linking in an alternative resource file*

translated. As pointed out earlier, this simplifies program maintenance because you only have the one application, that is, one version of the source code, to maintain since the source code is separate from the text displayed via resource files. This further protects the source code from unwanted changes or viewing.

One final step is involved in making an application truly language independent. Any dialog boxes, error messages, buttons, and so forth in the application also need to be displayed to the user in the correct language. Fortunately, there is a relatively easy solution for this implementation. As mentioned earlier in this chapter, Delphi compiles its own resources into your programs. Along with these resources are a wide variety of strings for dialog boxes, error messages, and so on.

With respect to Delphi 1.0, if you purchased the source code for the VCL (Visual Component Library) separately, or purchased the RAD Pack, you also received a set of VCL and RTL (Run-Time Library) resources for German, French, and English. By copying the German or French versions of these resources to the appropriate directory, and then recompiling the VCL, you will have updated the language strings for all native Delphi elements.

Although these language resources do not ship with Delphi 2.0, it can be assumed that additional language resources will be made available for the Delphi 2 version. For information on obtaining these resources, send a message to Borland through their CompuServe site (go Delphi) or their Web page (http://www.borland.com). Alternatively, contact your local Borland representative for information.

Storing Graphics Data in Resource Files

One of the more common uses of resource files is to store graphical images such as bitmaps, icons, and cursors. In this section you will learn how graphical data can be stored in resource files and used in your Delphi applications.

Loading Bitmaps from Resource Files

Why is there a need to load bitmap images out of a resource file when Delphi includes the Image and PaintBox components that hold bitmaps already? These components do not fit the need for every situation. For example, suppose you need to have images that comprise an animation sequence. It would be impractical to load every frame of the animation into separate Image components. Storing bitmap images in resource files addresses this issue.

NOTE: Delphi 2 provides you with the ImageList component. Unlike the Image and PaintBox components, the ImageList permits you to store two or more same-sized bitmaps. However, even with the availability of the ImageList component, you may still want to store bitmaps in resources.

Furthermore, bitmaps can often involve the issue of internationalization. For example, some of your images may be photos of landmarks from the country where the application is delivered. You would definitely not want to have dozens of images or paint boxes for holding bitmaps from other countries that would never be shown to a particular user. Doing so would unnecessarily bloat your .EXE file. You also would not want to keep the bitmap images on the hard disk and load them selectively, since those files may become misplaced or get deleted.

The technique of storing and retrieving images from resources is demonstrated in the BITMAP.DPR project. This application simulates animation by cycling through four single images, or frames. The program utilizes a single PaintBox component to display the current frame. In this example, the graphics are retrieved out of a resource file by means of the LoadBitmap Windows API call. The following is the code for the main form's unit for this project:

```
unit Bitmapu;

interface

uses
  SysUtils, WinTypes, WinProcs, Messages, Classes, Graphics,
 Controls, Forms, Dialogs, ExtCtrls, StdCtrls, Buttons;

type
  TForm1 = class(TForm)
    Timer1: TTimer;
    PaintBox1: TPaintBox;
```

```
    Label1: TLabel;
    procedure FormCreate(Sender: TObject);
    procedure FormDestroy(Sender: Tobject);
    procedure Timer1Timer(Sender: TObject);
    procedure FormPaint(Sender: TObject);
  private
    Images : Array[1..4] of TBitmap;
  public
    { Public declarations }
  end;

var
  Form1: TForm1;
  ImageShown : SmallInt;

implementation

{$R *.DFM}
{$R BMPS.RES}

procedure TForm1.FormCreate(Sender: TObject);
var
  TmpPC : Array[0..6] of Char;
  a     : SmallInt;
begin
  for a := 1 to 4 do
    begin
      {Create the bitmap}
      Images[a] := TBitmap.Create;
      {Build the name of the bitmap frame}
      StrPCopy(TmpPC,'FRAME'+IntToStr(a));
      {Go load the bitmap from the resource}
      Images[a].Handle := LoadBitmap(HInstance,TmpPC);
    end;
  ImageShown := 0;
end;

procedure TForm1.FormDestroy(Sender: TObject);
var
  a : SmallInt;
begin
  {Free the bitmaps}
  for a := 1 to 4 do Images[a].Free;
end;

procedure TForm1.Timer1Timer(Sender: TObject);
begin
  {When the timer goes off, display the next
```

```
    image in the array}
    Inc(ImageShown);
    {Make sure to stay in the range of 1 to 4}
    if ImageShown > 4 then ImageShown := 1;
    {Use CopyRect to stretch the image over the area of the
     Paintboxes canvas}
    PaintBox1.Canvas.CopyRect(PaintBox1.Canvas.ClipRect,
                              Images[ImageShown].Canvas,
                              Images[ImageShown].Canvas.ClipRect);
    {Force the Paintbox to paint itself immediately}
    PaintBox1.Update;
  end;

  procedure TForm1.FormPaint(Sender: TObject);
  var
    a : SmallInt;
  begin
    {Paint all of the images across the bottom of the form}
    with Inherited Canvas do
      for a := 1 to 4 do
        Draw((a-1)*(Images[a].Width+16)+8,
             ClientHeight-Images[a].Height-16,
             Images[a] as TBitmap);
  end;

  end.
```

Following is the resource script, BMPS.RC, that is used to create the resource file:

```
FRAME1  BITMAP  WORLD1.BMP
FRAME2  BITMAP  WORLD2.BMP
FRAME3  BITMAP  WORLD3.BMP
FRAME4  BITMAP  WORLD4.BMP
```

Each line in this script defines a single bitmap image that will be stored in the resource. The first column in the resource script is the identifier used for the image, for example, FRAME1. This identifier works the same way as do those in the String Resources example, except that in this case text is used to identify the resource and not a number. The identifier is simply a means by which the program can select the appropriate image. The second column defines the type of resource; in this case all are of a predefined BITMAP type. The last column is the name of the bitmap file that will be used, for example, WORLD1.BMP.

NOTE: *The bitmaps used in this example were published originally in the Corel Gallery 2 Clipart Library (Corel Corporation, 1995) and appear here with permission from the publisher. They are intended for demonstration purposes only and cannot be used for any other purpose without consent from the publisher.*

NOTE: It is not necessary to include a path with a filename in a resource script if the file is located in the same directory from which you compile the resource file. In order to compile this resource script, you will need to copy these four bitmaps from the CD to the directory where you are creating your resource. Alternatively, you can take any four bitmaps and name them WORLD1.BMP, WORLD2.BMP, and so on, and then copy them to this directory.

When the script is compiled, the resource compiler essentially collects all the bitmap data from each of these files and combines them together for the .RES file. As a result, the .RES file will be a little more than the size of the sum of all of the images. In the current example, each of the four graphics is 21,526 bytes in size. After compilation, the resulting .RES file is 86,112 bytes, almost exactly the totaled size of the four images.

TIP: Keep these calculations in mind when you are putting graphics in resource files. The final .EXE file will be inflated by this amount, since the raw bitmap data is being bound in with the program during linking.

To achieve the animation, the program uses an array of four bitmap components. Each element of this array is used to hold the graphic image for a single frame of the animation. These array elements are created and loaded in the OnCreate event handler for the form, as shown in the following code segment:

```
procedure TForm1.FormCreate(Sender: TObject);
var
  TmpPC : Array[0..6] of Char;
  a     : SmallInt;
begin
  for a := 1 to 4 do
    begin
      {Create the bitmap}
      Images[a] := TBitmap.Create;
      {Build the name of the bitmap frame}
      StrPCopy(TmpPC,'FRAME'+IntToStr(a));
      {Load the bitmap from the resource}
      Images[a].Handle := LoadBitmap(HInstance,TmpPC);
    end;
  ImageShown := 0;
end;
```

For each bitmap, this procedure first calls its Create constructor. This instantiates a copy of TBitmap class and assigns the pointer returned to the appropriate array element. Then, it is just a matter of pointing the bitmap to the graphic data from the resource file. This is done by means of the TBitmap's Handle property. This property is a pointer to the image's graphic data, which is exactly what is returned by the LoadBitmap API call. The identifier for the particular image is constructed in code and stored in a temporary variable that is used by LoadBitmap.

Once these images are in the array, they will behave just like any other Bitmap object. The images are copied onto the PaintBox component every half second, the time defined by the Timer component on the form. Finally, when the program is terminated, the Bitmap objects need to be released from memory. Figure 13-5 shows what this project looks like when it is running.

Figure 13-5 shows not only a bitmap displayed in a PaintBox component in the upper left corner of the screen, but also four bitmaps (the individual frames) that appear across the lower part of the screen. These four images are the contents of the resources and are placed on the form at runtime using the Draw method of the form's Canvas property from within the form's OnPaint event handler. For more information on working with canvases, see Chapter 11.

Loading Icons from Resource Files

Loading icon data is quite similar to loading bitmap data, and the way these two types of data are loaded from a resource is virtually identical. The procedures used to load icon and bitmap data are the Windows LoadIcon and LoadBitmap API calls, respectively. The LoadIcon procedure returns a handle to the selected icon, whereas the LoadBitmap procedure returns a handle to a bitmap.

The primary reason for changing an icon at runtime depends on which operating system you are using. With Windows 3.x, the icon is displayed when the window is minimized. You can then use this icon to convey information about the minimized application. In Windows 95, the icon is always displayed in the title bar. This makes it

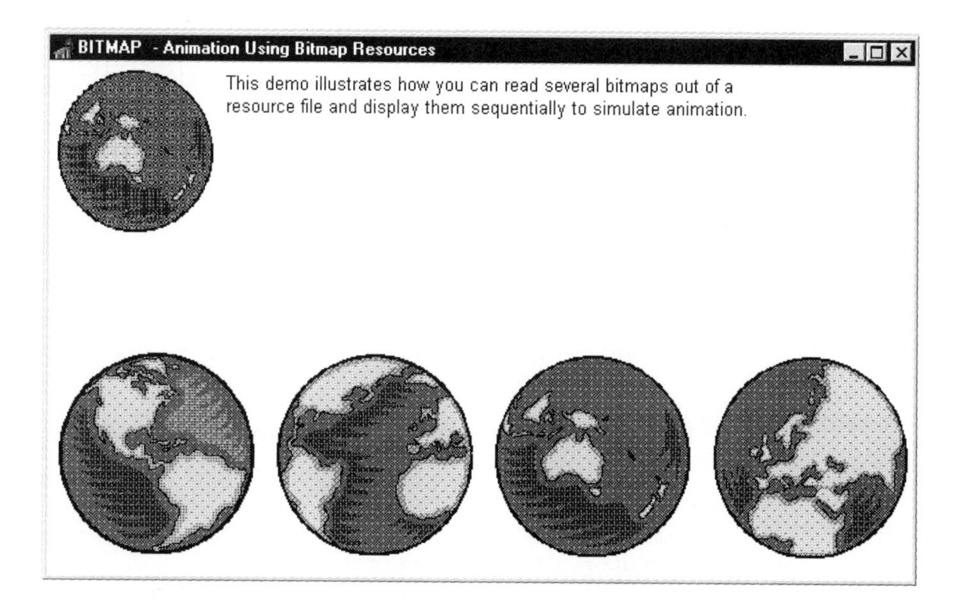

Figure 13-5. *The image in the earth displayed in the upper left corner rotates as bitmaps are loaded sequentially into a paint box*

more valuable, since it can be used to convey information to the user about the state of the application or a form (both the TApplication and TForm classes have an Icon property for holding the application and form icons, respectively). For example, you may want to display a particular icon while a user is editing a record on a form to remind the user that changes to the record have not been saved yet. When a record is not being edited, another icon is displayed.

The following technique demonstrates drawing using icons.

Drawing Using Icons from Resources

Icons have another interesting behavior, compared with bitmaps. When an icon is drawn on a canvas, it retains masking information to allow itself to be drawn transparently. (For more information on masking and transparent graphics, see Chapter 11.) As a result, once an icon has been loaded from the resource file, painting it on the form with the form's Draw method automatically masks the space around the icon image. The icon then draws just the image itself and not the unwanted white-space around its edges. This can be quite a useful feature.

This technique is demonstrated in project ICON.DPR. The following code is the main form's unit for this project. This code loads ten icons from a resource file and displays them at random on the surface of the form. As you can see from this code, the main form contains a single component, a Timer named Timer1:

```
unit Iconu;

interface

uses
  SysUtils, WinTypes, WinProcs, Messages, Classes, Graphics, Controls,
  Forms, Dialogs, ExtCtrls;

type
  TForm1 = class(TForm)
    Timer1: TTimer;
    procedure FormCreate(Sender: TObject);
    procedure FormDestroy(Sender: TObject);
    procedure Timer1Timer(Sender: TObject);
  private
    IconList  : Array[1..10] of TIcon;
  public
    { Public declarations }
  end;

var
  Form1: TForm1;

implementation

{$R *.DFM}
```

```
{$R ICON.RES}

procedure TForm1.FormCreate(Sender: TObject);
var
  a : SmallInt;
begin
  {Seed the random number generator}
  Randomize;
  {Create each of the icons in the IconList}
  for a := 1 to 10 do IconList[a] := TIcon.Create;
  {For each, read an icon from the resource and assign}
  {it to the Handle property of each array element}
  IconList[1].Handle  := LoadIcon(HInstance,'CHEMICAL');
  IconList[2].Handle  := LoadIcon(HInstance,'CHIP');
  IconList[3].Handle  := LoadIcon(HInstance,'CONSTRUC');
  IconList[4].Handle  := LoadIcon(HInstance,'EARTH');
  IconList[5].Handle  := LoadIcon(HInstance,'FACTORY');
  IconList[6].Handle  := LoadIcon(HInstance,'FINANCE');
  IconList[7].Handle  := LoadIcon(HInstance,'HANDSHAK');
  IconList[8].Handle  := LoadIcon(HInstance,'SHIPPING');
  IconList[9].Handle  := LoadIcon(HInstance,'SKYLINE');
  IconList[10].Handle := LoadIcon(HInstance,'TECHNLGY');
end;

procedure TForm1.FormDestroy(Sender: TObject);
var
  a : SmallInt;
begin
  {Make sure to free each of the icons in the IconList array}
  for a := 1 to 10 do IconList[a].Free;
end;

procedure TForm1.Timer1Timer(Sender: TObject);
var
  a,X1,Y1 : SmallInt;
begin
  {When the timer goes off, draw each icon at a random location on the
form}
  for a := 1 to 10 do
    begin
      X1 := Random(ClientWidth-32);
      Y1 := Random(ClientHeight-32);
      Inherited Canvas.Draw(X1,Y1,IconList[a]);
    end;
  Update;
end;

end.
```

The resource script looks much like the script used for the bitmap example earlier, as you can see in the following list:

```
CHEMICAL  ICON  C:\DELPHI\IMAGES\ICONS\CHEMICAL.ICO
CHIP      ICON  C:\DELPHI\IMAGES\ICONS\CHIP.ICO
CONSTRUC  ICON  C:\DELPHI\IMAGES\ICONS\CONSTRUC.ICO
EARTH     ICON  C:\DELPHI\IMAGES\ICONS\EARTH.ICO
FACTORY   ICON  C:\DELPHI\IMAGES\ICONS\FACTORY.ICO
FINANCE   ICON  C:\DELPHI\IMAGES\ICONS\FINANCE.ICO
HANDSHAK  ICON  C:\DELPHI\IMAGES\ICONS\HANDSHAK.ICO
SHIPPING  ICON  C:\DELPHI\IMAGES\ICONS\SHIPPING.ICO
SKYLINE   ICON  C:\DELPHI\IMAGES\ICONS\SKYLINE.ICO
TECHNLGY  ICON  C:\DELPHI\IMAGES\ICONS\TECHNLGY.ICO
```

NOTE: The preceding resource script uses the path for Delphi 1.0. For Delphi 2, you would use the eight-character directory names, such as C:\PROGRA~1\BORLAND\DELPHI~1.0\IMAGES\ICONS\CHEMICAL.ICO.

When you run this project, the icons are loaded in the form's OnCreate event handler. The Timer's Enabled property is set to True, and its Interval property is set to 1000. This means that the Timer's OnTimer event handler will execute every second. When it does, it draws each of the ten icons on the form's canvas. Figure 13-6 shows an example of this form running. Notice that the icons are transparent, in that you can see the form surface behind icons that are not completely square.

Loading Cursors

Many developers encounter a situation in which the set of cursors available in Delphi does not include all the cursors needed. For example, suppose you want a hand cursor

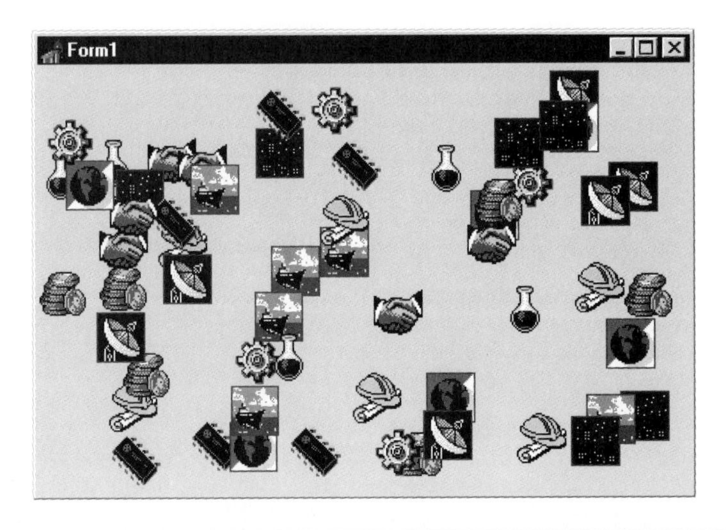

Figure 13-6. *Icons loaded from resources are drawn on the form's canvas at random*

that allows an object to be grabbed and dragged around the form. Or, perhaps a magnifying glass for indicating when the user can zoom in on a graphic.

The ability to load custom cursors at runtime is encapsulated quite nicely into Delphi. All you need to do is create the icon using the Resource Workshop, another resource editor, or even the ImageEditor included with Delphi. Then you create a resource script and compile it just like the other examples shown earlier in this chapter.

Loading a cursor resource is similar to loading a bitmap resource. However, there is no cursor object that you must create to hold the cursor graphic (unlike loading a bitmap, which requires you to provide a Bitmap object as a receptacle to hold the image). Instead, the cursor information is stored in a special structure that Delphi manages. This structure, a list called Cursors, is a part of the application's Screen object (a descendant of the TScreen class that is created automatically when the application initializes). When an application loads, the standard cursors provided with Delphi are stored in this list. This list has an index that you use to refer to loaded cursors. The standard cursors you use start with 0 (zero) and descend into negative values (0 to –17). The crHourglass cursor, for example, is in the list at position –11.

When you add a custom cursor to your program, you must also provide a constant that you can use to refer to the position the cursor occupies in this list. By convention, Borland suggests that you use positive values. It does not matter what value you choose, but it should generally be a small positive number. If you plan on having several custom cursors in your application, you may want to create a number of constants to refer to them, as shown in the following example:

```
const
  {cursor constants}
  crXHair     = 1;
  crBullsEye  = 2;
  crHandOpen  = 3;
  crHandClose = 4;
```

The project CURSORS.DPR demonstrates the use of custom cursors by loading four new cursors that are not part of the default list of cursors loaded by the Screen object. These extra cursors are found in the directory \DELPHI\IMAGES\CURSORS (Delphi 1.0) or in \Delphi 2.0\Images\Cursors (Delphi 2).

The following is the resource script POINTERS.RC for use with Delphi 1.0. For Delphi 2, supply the appropriate path.

```
XHAIR       CURSOR  C:\DELPHI\IMAGES\CURSORS\XHAIR1.CUR
BULLSEYE    CURSOR  C:\DELPHI\IMAGES\CURSORS\XHAIR2.CUR
HANDOPEN    CURSOR  C:\DELPHI\IMAGES\CURSORS\HANDFLAT.CUR
HANDCLOSE   CURSOR  C:\DELPHI\IMAGES\CURSORS\HANDGRAB.CUR
```

Create this resource script as described earlier in this chapter in the section on creating bitmap resources, and then compile it into a resource file named POINTERS.RES. After compiling the script into POINTERS.RES, you compile and run the CURSORS.DPR project to see these cursors in action. The following is the source code for this project's main form unit. Notice how this program loads the cursors into the Cursors array and assigns them to an appropriate Cursor property for a component from within the form's OnCreate event handler.

```
unit Cursoru;

interface

uses
  SysUtils, WinTypes, WinProcs, Messages, Classes, Graphics, Controls,
  Forms, Dialogs, StdCtrls, ExtCtrls;

type
  TForm1 = class(TForm)
    Label1: TLabel;
    Panel1: TPanel;
    Panel2: TPanel;
    Panel3: TPanel;
    Panel4: TPanel;
    procedure FormCreate(Sender: TObject);
  private
    { Private declarations }
  public
    { Public declarations }
  end;

const
  {cursor constants}
  crXHair     = 1;
  crBullsEye  = 2;
  crHandOpen  = 3;
  crHandClose = 4;

var
  Form1: TForm1;

implementation

{$R *.DFM}
{$R POINTERS.RES}

procedure TForm1.FormCreate(Sender: TObject);
begin
  {Insert each of the cursors from the resource
  into the Screen's Cursors array}
  Screen.Cursors[crXHair]     := LoadCursor(HInstance,'XHAIR');
  Screen.Cursors[crBullsEye]  := LoadCursor(HInstance,'BULLSEYE');
```

```
    Screen.Cursors[crHandOpen]  := LoadCursor(HInstance,'HANDOPEN');
    Screen.Cursors[crHandClose] := LoadCursor(HInstance,'HANDCLOSE');
    {Tell the Panels to use these new cursors}
    Panel1.Cursor := crXHair;
    Panel2.Cursor := crBullsEye;
    Panel3.Cursor := crHandOpen;
    Panel4.Cursor := crHandClose;
  end;

  end.
```

In this code, the constant crHandClose is defined to occupy position 4 in the Cursor list (hence, the constant declaration crHandClose = 4). The return value of the LoadCursor API call is then assigned into the appropriate array element of the Screen's Cursors array property. After that is done, the Cursor property of each of the four panels is assigned to one of the selected cursor constants. When the mouse cursor moves over one of the panels, the cursor changes to the appropriate cursor resource. For example, if you move the mouse over the panel labeled "Open Hand," the cursor changes its shape to an open hand cursor. The finished application is shown in Figure 13-7.

NOTE: It is important not to confuse the Screen's Cursors array property with a component's Cursor property. The Screen's Cursors array holds the list of constants for all currently defined cursors available to the application. A component's Cursor property is used to define which of these cursors will appear when the mouse moves over the component.

Loading Custom Data from a Resource File

One of the most powerful and, unfortunately, least exploited capabilities of resource files is that you can define and store your own data types. You don't need to stick to the predefined data types that Windows lets you use in a resource file.

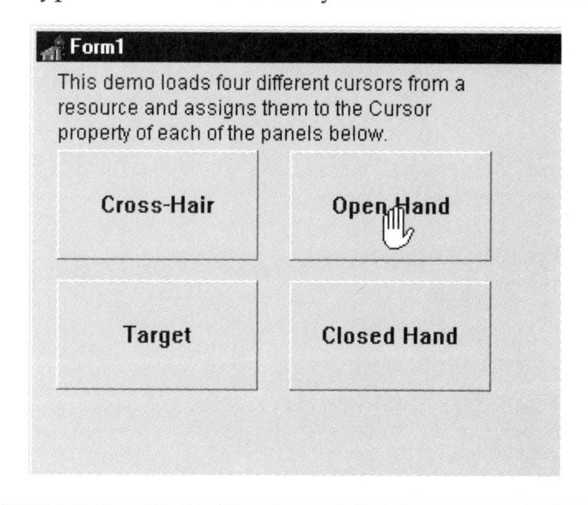

Figure 13-7. *The form for the cursor demonstration*

For example, you can store numeric data or tables of information in a resource file. This is useful if it is inappropriate or inconvenient to store such information in a database. Alternatively, the program may include some special data structures that need to be available each time the program is run. For example, suppose you are designing a system that displays subway layout information. For this system you have vector information defining the fixed layout of the underground subway system. Such data might be difficult to represent in a database but could lend itself easily to storage within a resource file. Since the application would always need to display valid subway layout information that would not typically change from day to day, the resource file would hold the information and be bound in with the executable file. This also would relieve you of having to ship the BDE (Borland Database Engine) with the application, as long as there is no other need for the program to have database access.

Loading .WAV Files as Resources

Wave or audio (.WAV) files are of a data type that is not inherently supported by Windows. Some developers may want to include custom sounds, error beeps, or audio instructions in an application. Delphi provides a MediaPlayer component that is designed to do just that. However, including the MediaPlayer component in your application adds well over 30K to your .EXE, primarily because it encapsulates other capabilities besides playing sounds, such as playing MIDI (Musical Instrument Digital Interface) files and displaying .AVI (multimedia) files.

The project WAVES.DPR takes advantage of the capabilities of resource files to hold custom data. The example of the WAVES.DPR shown here is the 32-bit version. A 16-bit version is available on the CD. These two versions differ in the makeup of the resource script, the multimedia DLL employed, and the specific Windows API statements used. These differences are pointed out in the following discussion, where appropriate.

The following is the source code for the main form's unit:

```
unit Waveu;

interface

uses
  SysUtils, WinTypes, WinProcs, Messages, Classes, Graphics, Controls,
  Forms, Dialogs, StdCtrls, Buttons;

type
  TForm1 = class(TForm)
    Label1: TLabel;
    BitBtn1: TBitBtn;
    BitBtn2: TBitBtn;
    BitBtn3: TBitBtn;
    BitBtn4: TBitBtn;
    BitBtn5: TBitBtn;
    BitBtn6: TBitBtn;
```

```
    procedure FormCreate(Sender: TObject);
    procedure FormDestroy(Sender: TObject);
    procedure BitBtn1Click(Sender: TObject);
    procedure BitBtn2Click(Sender: TObject);
    procedure BitBtn3Click(Sender: TObject);
    procedure BitBtn4Click(Sender: TObject);
    procedure BitBtn5Click(Sender: TObject);
    procedure BitBtn6Click(Sender: TObject);
  private
    procedure PlayWave(Name: PChar);
  public
    { Public declarations }
  end;

Const
  SND_SYNC      = $0000;
  SND_ASYNC     = $0001;
  SND_NODEFAULT = $0002;
  SND_MEMORY    = $0004;

var
  Form1         : TForm1;
  MMSysHandle   : THandle;
  PlaySound  : function (lpszSoundName: PAnsiChar;
    uFlags: UINT): BOOL; stdcall; {16-bit versions do not need stdcall}

implementation

{$R *.DFM}
{$R SOUNDS.RES}

procedure TForm1.PlayWave(Name: PChar);
var
  lpRes    : PChar;
  hRes     : THandle;
  hResInfo : THandle;
begin
  {Don't play the sound if LoadLibrary was unsuccessful}
  if MMSysHandle = 0 then exit;
  {Get a handle to the specified resource}
  hResInfo := FindResource(HInstance,Name,RT_RCDATA);
  if hResInfo <> 0 then
    begin
      {Load the resource into global memory}
      hRes := LoadResource(HInstance,hResInfO);
      if hRes <> 0 then
        begin
          {Lock the resource to prevent it from being discarded}
          lpRes := LockResource(hRes);
```

```
          {Call the sndPlaySoundA function in WINMM.DLL}
          PlaySound(lpRes,SND_SYNC or SND_MEMORY);
          {Unlock the resource}
          UnlockResource(hRes);
          {Release the resource}
          FreeResource(hRes);
        end;
    end;
end;

procedure TForm1.FormCreate(Sender: TObject);
begin
  {Load the WINMM.DLL and obtain a handle to it}
  MMSysHandle := LoadLibrary('WINMM.DLL');
  {Return value is <> 0 if the DLL was correctly loaded}
  if MMSysHandle <> 0 then
    {Point the PlaySound function to WINMM.DLL's sndPlaySoundA function}
    @PlaySound := GetProcAddress(MMSysHandle,'sndPlaySoundA')
  else
    {Display an error message}
    ShowMessage(SysErrorMessage(GetLastError));
end;

procedure TForm1.FormDestroy(Sender: TObject);
begin
  {If the DLL was correctly loaded, it is time to free it at this point}
  if MMSysHandle <> 0 then FreeLibrary(MMSysHandle);
end;

procedure TForm1.BitBtn1Click(Sender: TObject);
begin
  PlayWave('CHORD');
end;

procedure TForm1.BitBtn2Click(Sender: TObject);
begin
  PlayWave('CHIMES');
end;

procedure TForm1.BitBtn3Click(Sender: TObject);
begin
  PlayWave('TADA');
end;

procedure TForm1.BitBtn4Click(Sender: TObject);
begin
  PlayWave('DING');
end;
```

```
procedure TForm1.BitBtn5Click(Sender: TObject);
begin
  PlayWave('MUSIC1');
end;

procedure TForm1.BitBtn6Click(Sender: TObject);
begin
  PlayWave('MUSIC2');
end;

end.
```

The resource script for this program is as follows:

```
CHORD    RCDATA    C:\WINDOWS\MEDIA\CHORD.WAV
CHIMES   RCDATA    C:\WINDOWS\MEDIA\CHIMES.WAV
DING     RCDATA    C:\WINDOWS\MEDIA\DING.WAV
TADA     RCDATA    C:\WINDOWS\MEDIA\TADA.WAV
MUSIC1   RCDATA    C:\WINDOWS\MEDIA\MUSICAAS.WAV
MUSIC2   RCDATA    C:\WINDOWS\MEDIA\MUSICACL.WAV
```

NOTE: These files are not necessarily in the same directories as those shown in the preceding resource script. For example, on some machines the CORD.WAV, CHIMES,WAV, DING.WAV, and TADA.WAV files are stored in the Windows subdirectory and not in the MEDIA directory. Furthermore, even if you do have Windows 95, you may not have all these files on your machine. If you get an error from the Borland Resource Compiler indicating that a file is not available, search your Windows and Windows\Media directories for alternative .WAV files you can use, and replace the missing .WAV files in the resource script with those you have found.

As mentioned earlier in this chapter, the first column is the identifier used to refer to the specific .WAV file, for example, CHORD. The second column is an identifier being created that defines what to call this custom data type. In this case, the name is RCDATA, which indicates that this is a custom resource data type. The last column defines the .WAV files, for example, C:\WINDOWS\MEDIA\CHORD.WAV. These files could be any .WAV files, but in this example, they point to several audio clips that come with Windows 95.

TIP: Keep in mind that audio files can be quite large. Each audio file that you include in a resource that gets attached to your program will inflate your program's .EXE size accordingly. As a result, this technique is best for short sound clips. If you want to package larger sound clips, you might want to separate them into another resource file that gets connected to an auxiliary DLL (Dynamic Link Library) that you create. That DLL might serve no other purpose than to house these large .WAV files!

This program has two key parts. The first is a dynamic connection to Windows Multi-Media DLL. In Windows 95 this is WINMM.DLL, and in Windows 3.x it is MMSYSTEM.DLL. The second is the access to the sndPlaySoundA API call available through that DLL. (Windows 3.x uses the sndPlaySound call.)

Accessing DLLs

Before you can access routines in a DLL, the program needs to be able to connect to the DLL routines. There are two basic ways that an application can connect to a DLL. One is by defining the calling sequence of a procedure or function and declaring it as *external*. This call sequence may look something like this:

```
implementation
  function ShowInfo(const FileName: string): string;
    far; external 'FILEINFO';
```

The function resides within the DLL, but the preceding code tells the program that ShowInfo is a function that expects a string parameter and returns a string result. Furthermore, by means of the external directive, this reference indicates that the program should not look in this unit for the function, but rather to connect to FILEINFO.DLL to find the function.

There is one fundamental problem with this approach, however. If the DLL is not present or is corrupted, the program will generate an exception before you have the opportunity to execute any of your program's code. You do not want the application to crash on the user. Instead, you want the program to check the availability of the DLL and act accordingly. For example, in the WAVES.DPR project the program displays an error message and gives the user information about the problem. In other applications the solution might be to disable the features of the program that rely on that DLL.

Connecting Dynamically to a DLL

The solution to declaring DLL functions and procedures external is to connect to the DLL dynamically. This is demonstrated in the WAVESU.PAS unit, which connects dynamically to the DLL. This connection occurs within the FormCreate procedure shown here:

```
procedure TForm1.FormCreate(Sender: TObject);
begin
  {Load the WINMM.DLL and obtain a handle to it}
  MMSysHandle := LoadLibrary('WINMM.DLL');
  {Return value is <> 0 if the DLL was correctly loaded}
  if MMSysHandle <> 0 then
    {Point the PlaySound function to WINMM.DLL's sndPlaySoundA function}
    @PlaySound := GetProcAddress(MMSysHandle,'sndPlaySoundA')
  else
    {Display an error message}
    ShowMessage(SysErrorMessage(GetLastError));
end;
```

The LoadLibrary function in the Windows API performs the dynamic connection. It loads the selected DLL and returns a handle to it. In Delphi 2, if the value is other than 0 (Delphi 2) or equal to or greater than 32 (Delphi 1.0), the DLL was loaded correctly and can be accessed normally. If the return value is 0 (Delphi 2) or less than 32 (Delphi 1.0), there was a problem loading the DLL. In this application, this will display an error message. The actual problem can be determined by the GetLastError Windows API call (Delphi 2) or by the value returned by LoadLibrary (Delphi 1.0).

If the connection to the DLL was performed correctly, the GetProcAddress function is used to obtain a pointer to the desired function in the DLL—in this case the sndPlaySoundA function (sndPlaySound in Delphi 1.0). The variable PlaySound is a pointer to a function and was declared in the var statement of the Interface section to match the parameter list and return type of the sndPlaySoundA DLL function. Consequently, this PlaySound holds the address of the sndPlaySoundA function when LoadLibrary is successful. Note that this connection is not performed if the return value from LoadLibrary indicates an error.

Playing the Sound from the Resource File

The next step is to get the desired sound from the resource so that it can be played. Following is the definition of the PlayWave procedure:

```
procedure TForm1.PlayWave(Name: PChar);
var
  lpRes    : PChar;
  hRes     : THandle;
  hResInfo : THandle;
begin
  {Don't play the sound if LoadLibrary was unsuccessful}
  if MMSysHandle = 0 then exit;
  {Get a handle to the specified resource}
  hResInfo := FindResource(HInstance,Name,RT_RCDATA);
  if hResInfo <> 0 then
    begin
      {Load the resource into global memory}
      hRes := LoadResource(HInstance,hResInfO);
      if hRes <> 0 then
        begin
          {Lock the resource to prevent it from being discarded}
          lpRes := LockResource(hRes);
          {Call the sndPlaySoundA function in WINMM.DLL}
          PlaySound(lpRes,SND_SYNC or SND_MEMORY);
          {Unlock the resource}
          UnlockResource(hRes);
          {Release the resource}
          FreeResource(hRes);
        end;
    end;
end;
```

The code first checks if the connection to the DLL generated an error and, if so, exits this procedure, thus allowing the program to continue functioning normally, although the sounds will not play.

The next step is to find the desired resource. The parameter of the PlayWave procedure is the identifier of the audio clip as it is stored in the resource file. The FindResource API call retrieves a handle to this data. The first parameter of FindResource is the handle to the currently running copy of the program. The second parameter is the identifier of the desired resource. The final parameter of FindResource is the type of resource. In this case, the constant RT_RCDATA is used to refer to the custom resource type. The resource was found if the return value from this function was a non-zero value. Next, the return value from FindResource is passed to the LoadResource API call. This call returns a handle to the audio data.

The next step is to lock in memory the resource data that is being pointed to. Windows is usually given the freedom to move around, and even discard, resource data that it feels is no longer needed. This would produce a highly undesirable effect if it were to happen here. Consequently, the code uses the LockResource API call to tell Windows that it temporarily cannot move or discard the sound clip.

The program is now ready to play the sound. The locked pointer obtained for the wave file is passed to the PlaySound procedure, which in turn points to sndPlaySoundA in WINMM.DLL (sndPlaySound in MMSYSTEM.DLL for Delphi 1.0). This plays the sound. Next, the UnlockResource Windows API call is made to unlock the resource data, permitting Windows to move or discard the resource. Finally, the code executes the FreeResource Windows API call, thereby freeing the sound file from memory.

A number of flags can be passed into the sndPlaySoundA procedure to control how the sound is played and where the procedure should expect to get the data. The SND_MEMORY flag used in this example tells the procedure that the first parameter points to an in-memory copy of the audio data. If the SND_MEMORY flag is not included, the procedure assumes that the first parameter is a disk-based filename of the wave file to be loaded and played.

The SND_SYNC flag, also used in this example, tells the procedure to play the sound *synchronously,* which means that program execution will pause at this point until the sound clip is done playing. After the sound clip is played, the program resumes execution.

The alternative to SND_SYNC is to use SND_ASYNC, which tells the procedure to play the sound *asynchronously,* which means that the program will continue executing even while the sound is playing. For this particular example, including SND_ASYNC produces *very* bad behavior (be prepared to reboot your computer if you try it out!). What happens is that the PlaySound procedure starts to play the audio clip, but because SND_ASYNC was indicated, the program is allowed to continue executing. It proceeds to unlock the resource data and then to free the audio resource data from memory while it is in the process of playing, which will crash your system.

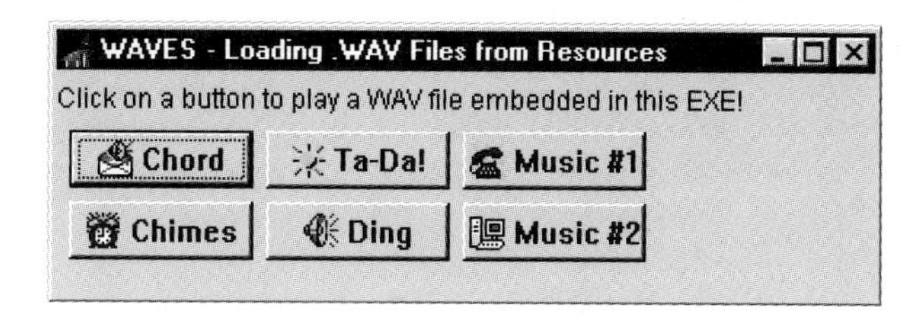

Figure 13-8. *The WAVES project plays .WAV files that are stored as resources*

This restriction is really just a side effect of how .WAV files are implemented in this example. Figure 13-8 shows the form for the WAVES.DPR application.

This program retrieves and plays the audio data from the resource files one at a time. In other words, when one of the buttons is clicked, the audio data is retrieved from the resource, it is then played and is released when the playing is done. Because of the SND_SYNC flag, you cannot click on a second button when the sound playing from a prior button selection is currently playing. If you need to play sounds asynchronously (being able to start a selected sound at any time rather than waiting until one sound is finished playing), you would need to rearrange how you access the sound clips.

For example, if you have two or three small clips that you must have access to at all times, you can retrieve those resources and lock them in memory from within the main form's OnCreate event handler, and then release them from the OnClose event handler. This is demonstrated in the WAVES2.DPR project, shown in Figure 13-9.

Figure 13-9. *The WAVES2 project demonstrates how to play sounds asynchronously*

The following source code is for the project's main form unit:

```
unit Wave2u;

interface

uses
  SysUtils, WinTypes, WinProcs, Messages, Classes, Graphics, Controls,
  Forms, Dialogs, StdCtrls, Buttons;

type
  TForm1 = class(TForm)
    Label1: TLabel;
    BitBtn1: TBitBtn;
    BitBtn2: TBitBtn;
    procedure FormCreate(Sender: TObject);
    procedure FormDestroy(Sender: TObject);
    procedure BitBtn1Click(Sender: TObject);
    procedure BitBtn2Click(Sender: TObject);
  private
    procedure PlayWave(Name: PChar);
  public
    { Public declarations }
  end;

Const
  SND_SYNC       = $0000;
  SND_ASYNC      = $0001;
  SND_NODEFAULT  = $0002;
  SND_MEMORY     = $0004;

var
  Form1          : TForm1;
  MMSysHandle    : THandle;
  PlaySound      : Function (lpszSoundName: PAnsiChar;
    uFlags: UINT): Bool; stdcall;

  ChordResInfo   : THandle;
  ChordRes       : THandle;
  ChordPtr       : PChar;
  TaDaResInfo    : THandle;
  TaDaRes        : THandle;
  TaDaPtr        : PChar;


implementation

{$R *.DFM}
{$R SOUNDS.RES}
```

```
procedure TForm1.PlayWave(Name: PChar);
begin
  if MMSysHandle = 0 then exit;
  {Call the sndPlaySound function in WINMM.DLL}
  PlaySound(Name,SND_ASYNC or SND_MEMORY);
end;

procedure TForm1.FormCreate(Sender: TObject);
begin
  {Load the WINMM.DLL and obtain a handle to it}
  MMSysHandle := LoadLibrary('WINMM.DLL');
  {Return value is non-zero if the DLL was correctly loaded}
  if MMSysHandle <> 0 then
    begin
      {Point the PlaySound function to WINMM.DLL's
      sndPlaySoundA function}
      @PlaySound := GetProcAddress(MMSysHandle,'sndPlaySoundA');
      ChordResInfo := FindResource(HInstance,'CHORD',RT_RCDATA);
      if ChordResInfo <> 0 then
        begin
          ChordRes := LoadResource(HInstance,ChordResInfo);
          if ChordRes <> 0 then ChordPtr := LockResource(ChordRes);
        end;
      TaDaResInfo := FindResource(HInstance,'TADA',RT_RCDATA);
      if TaDaResInfo <> 0 then
        begin
          TaDaRes := LoadResource(HInstance,TaDaResInfo);
          if TaDaRes <> 0 then TaDaPtr := LockResource(TaDaRes);
        end;
    end;
end;

procedure TForm1.FormDestroy(Sender: TObject);
begin
  if MMSysHandle <> 0 then
    begin
      UnlockResource(ChordRes);
      FreeResource(ChordRes);
      UnlockResource(TaDaRes);
      FreeResource(TaDaRes);
      FreeLibrary(MMSysHandle);
    end;
end;

procedure TForm1.BitBtn1Click(Sender: TObject);
begin
  PlayWave(ChordPtr);
end;
```

```
procedure TForm1.BitBtn2Click(Sender: TObject);
begin
  PlayWave(TaDaPtr);
end;


end.
```

NOTE: The version of the WAVES2 project shown here is the Delphi 2 version. A Delphi 1.0 version is available on the CD. The 16-bit version uses the sndPlaySound function from MMSYSTEM.DLL instead of sndPlaySoundA from WINMM.DLL.

The key difference with the asynchronous playing technique is that all of the setup work for accessing the audio resources is done ahead of time in the OnCreate event handler. This makes the PlaySound procedure much simpler and allows the application to play sounds asynchronously. If you test out this second sound project, you will see that you can click on the buttons as quickly as you want and the sounds will play accordingly. If you catch a sound in the middle of playing, clicking on the button again simply restarts the sound.

The disadvantage of the asynchronous playing technique is that global variables holding pointers and handles to each of the sounds are required. This creates a bit more overhead on the program, and it takes a little more work to maintain the program in the long run. Also, the audio clips accessed in this fashion are always locked in memory for the duration of the application's execution. If you are using larger sound clips in this way, you could drag down the operating system performance as it is tries to juggle memory around the large locked resources.

Conclusion

Storing data in resource files is an effective and time-saving technique that is applicable for almost any Windows programming project. In addition to simplifying distribution of your application by encapsulating needed data within the executable file, you can also take advantage of Windows's internationalization facilities in resources that allow programs to be truly language and culture independent.

You will find that after you use resource files for a time, storing information in them becomes a very straightforward, powerful, and valuable technique. Although Delphi goes a long way toward reducing the need for some of the features of resource files, you will still find many situations in which resources files provide you with just the right mix of features.

Chapter Fourteen

Controlling Applications Using OLE Automation

The code for the examples presented in this chapter can be found in the \CODE\CH14 subdirectory on the CD-ROM that accompanies this book. Please refer to Appendix A for information on using the code files for this chapter.

OLE (Object Linking and Embedding) Automation lets you expose the objects in your Delphi 2 application so that other programs and languages can manipulate them. OLE Automation also lets you control and manipulate the objects of other programs using Object Pascal code. These two capabilities allow you to create an integrated solution that combines the functionality of various programs into a single application. This chapter applies to Delphi 2 only and describes how you can use your Delphi 2 program to control the objects of other programs to add new functionality to your application.

Introducing OLE Automation

OLE Automation defines a way in which an application can programmatically control objects in another program, or in turn, expose its own objects so that they can be controlled by another application. This ability lets you tap the functionality of many applications to create a single, integrated solution. Before OLE Automation, the few ways to do this included using macro or keystroke recorders, or creating a separate macro language for an application. OLE Automation changes this by letting an application expose objects that have their own methods and properties that can be manipulated externally.

***NOTE:** DDE (Dynamic Data Exchange) provided a framework for communicating between applications. Unfortunately, DDE proved to be slow, and few, if any, standards evolved for its use. Consequently, DDE is no longer considered a viable option for inter-application cooperation.*

Applications that manipulate the objects of other programs are called OLE automation controllers. Programmable applications that expose their own objects are called OLE automation servers. An OLE automation controller can control any other OLE automation server, regardless of what language was used to create the server. Likewise, an OLE automation server can be controlled by any other OLE automation controller, such as Delphi, Visual Basic, and Paradox for Windows.

Delphi lets you create two types of automation servers: *in process servers* and *local servers.* In process servers are essentially DLLs (Dynamic Link Libraries) with an object interface that runs in the address space of the controller. Because of this, in process servers do not require the time-consuming *marshalling* associated with cross-process calls. Marshalling involves the packaging of the arguments of method calls so that they can be sent to other processes—a time-intensive operation.

Local servers, in contrast, are executable (.EXE) files that run in their own address space. Accessing methods and properties of local servers requires marshalling; consequently, operations involving local servers are inherently slower.

Delphi lets you control both types of automation servers. This is done through the objects exposed by the server. (All servers expose at least one object; otherwise, they would be useless as automation servers.) Using OLE Automation, your application creates instances of the exposed objects that exist inside an automation server. Once created, you can manipulate the objects using the standard Object Pascal notation for working with objects.

NOTE: OLE Automation should not be confused with the other parts of OLE 2.0, such as OLE Embedding and Linking (OLE Documents). OLE 2.0 has several major areas: structured storage and object persistence; persistent, intelligent names ("monikers"); uniform data transfer; and OLE Drag and Drop, OLE Automation, OLE Controls, and OLE Documents. OLE Automation is a feature that can be implemented independently of the other parts of OLE 2.0. For example, an automation server may or may not support embedding and linking of objects into OLE containers. Delphi 2, like Delphi 1.0, lets you create OLE containers using the TOLEContainer component. Delphi 2 also lets you create applications that support the entire OLE 2.0 feature set; however, it does not provide you with an automated or easy way to do so. If you want to add other OLE 2.0 features, you need to understand the underlying architecture of OLE, the Component Object Model (COM), and master the OLE 2.0 API functions.

Controlling an OLE Automation Server

Creating a simple Delphi program that can control an OLE automation server is straightforward. To begin, you instantiate an OLE object for the automation server. Once you have a reference to the OLE object, you can manipulate its methods and properties.

To use OLE Automation, you must include the OLEAUTO unit (and, optionally, the OLE2 unit) in the uses statement of your unit. This statement defines the necessary functions and procedures that you need.

Using CreateOLEObject

To access the objects inside an automation server, you use the CreateOLEObject method. CreateOLEObject creates an instance of an OLE object and returns a reference to it as a *variant*. (A variant is a data type new to Delphi 2. An instance of a variant is capable of dynamically changing data type. This is fundamentally different from all other Delphi object instances, which are statically bound to their type, meaning that they cannot change type at runtime.) You can treat this variant just like a regular object and use regular object syntax to manipulate its methods and properties. The following is the syntax of CreateOLEObject:

```
function CreateOleObject(const ProgID: string): Variant;
```

CreateOLEObject requires a single argument, which you use to specify the type of OLE object to create. Every automation server has its OLE object(s) registered in the system registry. Each OLE object is identified by a programmatic string identifier called a ProgID. You instruct CreateOLEObject which OLE object to instantiate by passing to it the ProgID for the particular server. (Internally, ProgID maps to a unique class ID, which OLE uses to identify the object.) The use of ProgID permits location independence, which means that you don't need to know or specify the location of the automation server. The automation server can exist locally on the same machine or remotely on the network. OLE takes care of masking these details.

For example, the ProgID for Microsoft's Excel 7 is Excel.Application. If you want to create an OLE object for Excel, you use a code segment similar to the following:

```
var
 ExcelObject: Variant; // declare variable to reference object
begin
 ExcelObject := CreateOleObject('Excel.Application'); // create instance
end;
```

Using Properties and Methods

Once you have instantiated an OLE object, you can use its methods and properties. Using the OLE object is similar to using a normal Delphi object, except that all the properties and method arguments must be passed as variants. This means that any value that you use must be a variant or can be implicitly or explicitly converted into a variant. Also, calls to OLE object methods are *late-bound*, which means that the validity of the method or its type or number of arguments are not checked until runtime. If you call a method that is not part of an OLE object, an exception is raised.

NOTE: Late-bound methods cannot be validated by the compiler. In other words, syntactically incorrect calls to late-bound methods will not generate a compiler error. They will, however, generate an exception when they are executed at runtime.

Methods of OLE objects can have *named* arguments or *positional* arguments. When you call a method with named arguments, the order of the arguments is irrelevant. Instead, you assign values to the names of the required arguments. When you call a method with positional arguments, you supply the arguments in the correct order. In both cases, optional arguments can be omitted.

For example, Excel 7 surfaces the Add method. This method has four arguments, all of which are optional. The syntax of Add is:

```
Worksheets.Add(Before, After, Count, Type)
```

The Before parameter specifies the sheet before which to add the new sheet. The After parameter specifies the sheet after which to add the new sheet. You use the Count parameter to indicate the number of sheets to add, and Type to control the sheet type (xlWorksheet, xlExcel4MacroSheet, or xlExcel4IntlMacroSheet). The default for Type is xlWorksheet.

The following is an example of using Add to add five worksheets of the default type to current workbook:

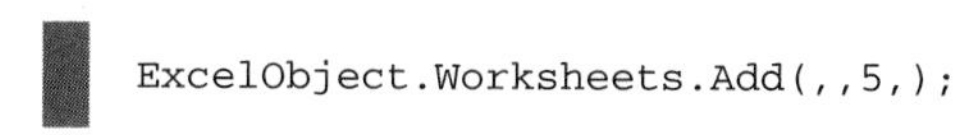

```
ExcelObject.Worksheets.Add(,,5,);
```

The preceding example used positional arguments. If you wanted to use named arguments instead, you could use the following statement, which is functionally equivalent to the preceding one:

```
ExcelObject.Worksheets.Add(Count := 5);
```

Releasing a Server

Once you have used CreateOLEObject, the variant remains assigned to the server for as long as it is in scope. An assigned variant occupies valuable resources that you will want to free when you no longer need the variant variable. This can be done by setting the variant to the variant constant UnAssigned. Although not required, it is strongly recommended that you use this setting when you no longer need to reference an automation server. The following is an example of setting a variant to UnAssigned:

```
ExcelObject := UnAssigned;
```

In addition to unassigning a variant when you are done, you may also want or need to close the server. Some servers provide a method that you can call to close it. If you are no longer using the server, you should call this method.

NOTE: Whether you must explicitly close a server depends on the server, for the most part. Most OLE automation servers keep track of how many controllers are accessing it. Assigning UnAssign to a variant for a server should signal that server that it has one less controller accessing it. In most cases, when a server sees that no controllers are accessing it, it closes itself.

The following example demonstrates how you would close Excel using its Close method. Notice that the assignment of UnAssigned to the variant occurs after the closing of the server.

```
ExcelObject.Close;
ExcelObject := UnAssigned;
```

A Simple Example

This first project, SIMPLE.DPR, shows how you can control an automation server and use its methods and properties. This example uses Excel 7 to create a new workbook,

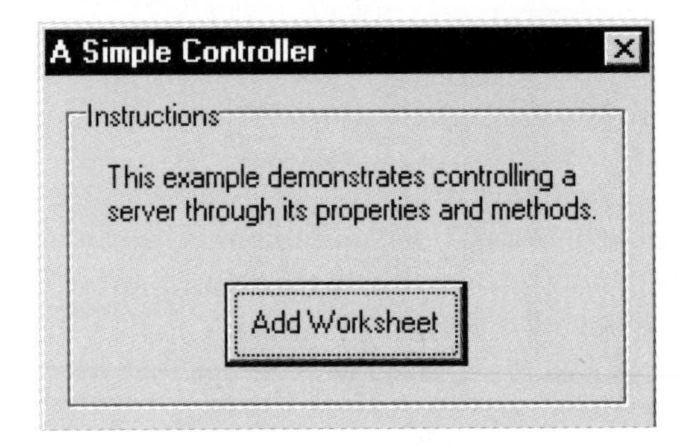

Figure 14-1. *The SIMPLE project displays a button. Clicking the button loads Excel 7 as a OLE local server*

and then adds five worksheets to the workbook. The main form for the example has a single button that performs all of the work, as you can see in Figure 14-1.

Following is the source code for SIMPLE.DPR:

```
program simple;

uses
  Forms,
  simpleu in 'simpleu.pas' {AddForm};

{$R *.RES}

begin
  Application.CreateForm(TAddForm, AddForm);
  Application.Run;
end.
```

When you press the button, AddButtonClick is executed. First, CreateOLEObject is called with a ProgID of Excel.Application. This ProgID identifies Excel's top-level object. CreateOLEObject returns the reference to this object, which is then stored in a variant, ExcelObject.

Next, a new workbook is added by calling the Add method of the Workbooks property of ExcelObject. Notice that you refer to properties and methods of the OLE server the same way that you refer to the properties and methods of Delphi components. The following is the source code for SIMPLEU.PAS:

```
unit simpleu;

interface
```

```
uses
  Windows, Messages, SysUtils, Classes, Graphics, Controls, Forms, Dialogs,
  StdCtrls;

type
  TAddForm = class(TForm)
    GroupBox1: TGroupBox;
    AddButton: TButton;
    Label1: TLabel;
    procedure AddButtonClick(Sender: TObject);
  private
    { Private declarations }
  public
    { Public declarations }
  end;

var
  AddForm: TAddForm;

implementation

uses OLEAuto;

{$R *.DFM}

procedure TAddForm.AddButtonClick(Sender: TObject);
var
  ExcelObject: Variant;
begin

  ExcelObject := CreateOLEObject('Excel.Application');
  try
    try
      ExcelObject.Workbooks.Add;

  //  Worksheets.Add(Before, After, Count, Type)
  //  Before specifies the sheet before which to add the new sheet
  //  After specifies the sheet after which to add the new sheet
  //  Count specifies the number of sheets to add
  //  Type specifies the sheet type (xlWorksheet, xlExcel4MacroSheet,
  //  or xlExcel4IntlMacroSheet). Default = xlWorksheet.
      ExcelObject.Worksheets.Add(,,5,);

  // Make Excel visible by setting its Visible property
      ExcelObject.Visible := True;
    except
      On EOLEError do
        ShowMessage('There is a problem');
```

```
    end;

  finally
    ExcelObject.Quit;
    ExcelObject := UnAssigned;
  end;

end;

end.
```

Within this code the Add method is used to add five new worksheets to the new workbook. The final line sets Excel's Visible property to True. By convention, a newly created automation server is not visible to the user. Excel provides the Visible property so that you can control this behavior.

Using Variant Arrays

You can use Delphi's variant arrays to pass an array of values to an automation server in a single assignment. Variant arrays are arrays that can be used in OLE Automation and contain elements of any of the variant base types.

TIP: *By creating an array of bytes, you can also use a variant array to pass* binary *data to an automation server.*

Being able to pass several values in a single assignment can be crucial in maintaining acceptable performance when using local automation servers. This is because each access of a property or method of a local automation server incurs the overhead of marshalling. By minimizing the number of accesses, you can keep the overhead low.

Delphi defines the VarArrayCreate and VarArrayOf functions to let you create a variant array and return it as a variant. VarArrayCreate takes Bounds, an open array of elements, and VarType, an integer indicating the variant type of each element. The list of possible types is defined in the SYSTEM unit. The following is the syntax of VarArrayCreate:

```
VarArrayCreate(const Bounds: array of Integer; VarType: Integer): Variant;
```

The following example demonstrates how to create a variant array of ten integers:

```
MyVarArray := VarArrayCreate([1, 10], varInteger);
```

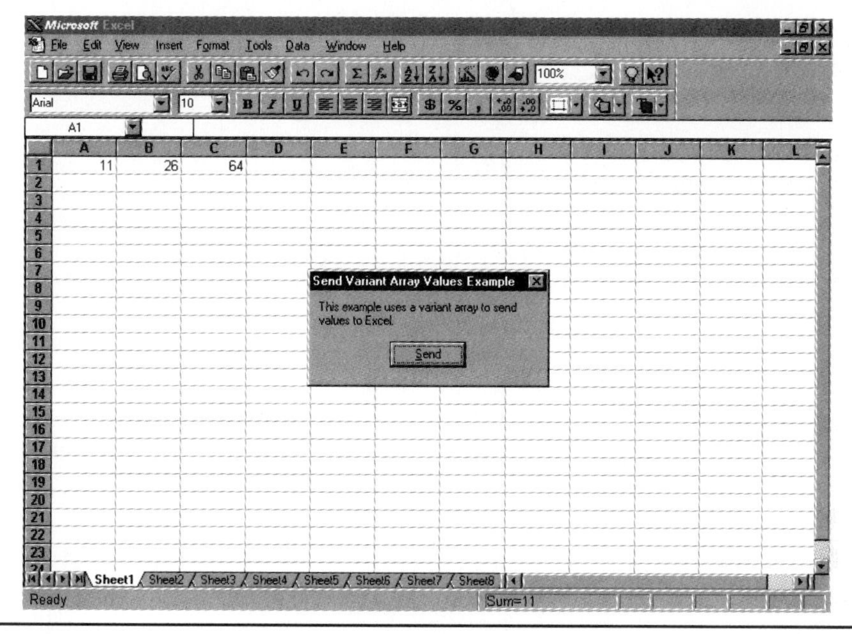

Figure 14-2. *Screen for Send Variant Array Values Example*

VarArrayOf is provided as a shortcut to let you create a one-dimensional array of variants. The following is the syntax VarArrayOf:

VarArrayOf(const Values: array of Variant): Variant;

Delphi also has functions to resize and lock/unlock a variant array, and check its boundaries at runtime. These functions are defined in the SYSTEM unit.

Sending Arrays to Excel Example

This next project, VARARRAY.DPR, uses a variant array to assign values to three cells in an Excel 7 worksheet. Instead of passing values in three separate assignments, a single assignment statement is used. The main form contains a button that performs the work when you press it. This form is shown in Figure 14-2.

Following is the source code for VARARRAY.DPR:

```
program vararray;

uses
  Forms,
  vararrau in 'vararrau.pas' {SendForm};
```

```
{$R *.RES}

begin
  Application.CreateForm(TSendForm, SendForm);
  Application.Run;
end.
```

The following is the source code for VARARRAU.PAS:

```
unit vararrau;

interface

uses
  Windows, Messages, SysUtils, Classes, Graphics, Controls, Forms, Dialogs,
  StdCtrls;

type
  TSendForm = class(TForm)
    SendButton: TButton;
    Label1: TLabel;
    procedure SendButtonClick(Sender: TObject);
  private
    { Private declarations }
  public
    { Public declarations }
  end;

var
  SendForm: TSendForm;

implementation

uses OLEAuto;

{$R *.DFM}

procedure TSendForm.SendButtonClick(Sender: TObject);
var
  ExcelObject: Variant;
  MyData: Variant;
begin
  ExcelObject := CreateOLEObject('Excel.Application');

  // add a new workbook
  ExcelObject.Workbooks.Add;
```

```
    // create a variant array of 3 numbers
    MyData := VarArrayOf([11,26,64]);

    // set the first three cells to these values
    ExcelObject.Range('A1:C1').Value := MyData;

    // make Excel visible but leave it open
    ExcelObject.Visible := True;
  end;

  end.
```

SendButtonClick, the button's OnClick event handler, creates the Excel OLE object by calling CreateOLEObject with Application.Excel as the ProgID. Then, the Workbook's Add method is called to create a new workbook. Next, a variant array of three integers is created in a call to VarArrayOf. This variant array is saved in MyData, a variant. The Range method of ExcelObject is then used to select a range of cells using Excel's A1 spreadsheet notation. The Value property of this array is then assigned the three integers stored in the variant array. Finally, after the assignment is finished, Excel is made visible by setting ExcelObject's Visible property to True.

Responding to Errors

You should be prepared to detect and trap any errors that may occur as a result of accessing an automation object. For instance, if you attempt to assign an invalid value to a property of an automation object, that object may trigger an error.

To protect your code, you can use Delphi's exception handling mechanism. To do this, place the automation code inside a try-except exception handling block. If an OLE Automation error occurs inside the block, an exception of type EOLEError will be raised. In the except part of the exception handling block, you can place code to determine the type of error and respond accordingly.

An Exception Handling Example

The next example, OLEERR.DPR, creates an Excel 7 automation object and attempts to call a non-existent method. The main form contains a single button as shown in Figure 14-3. When you push the button, an automation object for Excel is created. Next, a non-existent method, CalcNationalDebt, is called. Since OLE Automation method calls are late-bound, the compiler cannot detect this mistake. Instead, an error will surface at runtime.

Following is the source code for the OLEERR project:

```
program oleerr;

uses
```

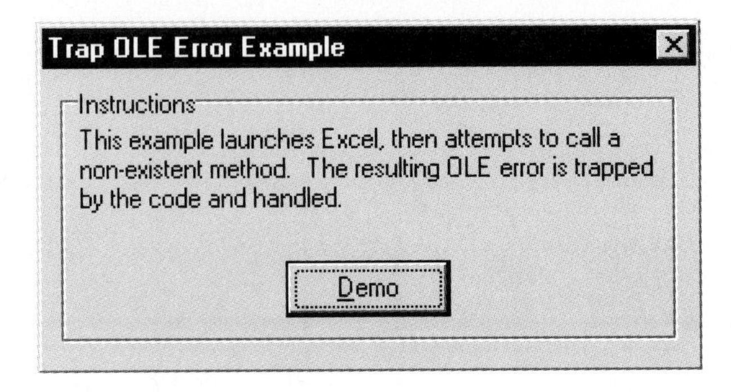

Figure 14-3. *Screen for Trap OLE Error Example*

```
  Forms,
  oleerru in 'oleerru.pas' {OLEErrorForm};

{$R *.RES}

begin
  Application.CreateForm(TOLEErrorForm, OLEErrorForm);
  Application.Run;
end.
```

The following is the source code for OLEERRU.PAS:

```
unit oleerru;

interface

uses
  Windows, Messages, SysUtils, Classes, Graphics, Controls, Forms, Dialogs,
  StdCtrls;

type
  TOLEErrorForm = class(TForm)
    GroupBox1: TGroupBox;
    ErrorButton: TButton;
    Label1: TLabel;
    procedure ErrorButtonClick(Sender: TObject);
  private
    { Private declarations }
  public
    { Public declarations }
  end;
```

```
var
  OLEErrorForm: TOLEErrorForm;

implementation

uses OLEAuto;

{$R *.DFM}

procedure TOLEErrorForm.ErrorButtonClick(Sender: TObject);
var
  ExcelObject: Variant;
begin
  ExcelObject := CreateOLEObject('Excel.Application');

  try

    try
    // call a non-existent method
      ExcelObject.CalcNationalDebt;

    except
      on E:EOLEError do
      begin
      // put your code here to handle OLE errors
        ShowMessage(E.Message);
      end;
    end;

  finally
  // Make sure to shut down Excel
    ExcelObject.Quit;
    ExcelObject := UnAssigned;
  end;

end;

end.
```

Notice that ErrorButtonClick has an exception handling block *and* a resource protection block. These blocks are protecting the code that accesses ExcelObject, the automation object. The resource protection block ensures that the automation server (Excel) is shut down and the variant ExcelObject is freed when the automation server is no longer needed. A variant variable is freed by assigning it a value of UnAssigned.

The exception handling block takes care of any OLE Automation errors that may arise. In this case, the call to CalcNationalDebt triggers an exception. The except part of the block handles all EOLEError exceptions by displaying the error message associated with the error. Your own code may augment this behavior by creating a more specific handler.

OLE Automation Examples

This section contains three examples of Delphi applications that leverage the capabilities of local automation servers. The first example demonstrates how to use Word for Windows to perform spell checking, and the other two utilize Netscape Navigator to download information from the World Wide Web.

Using Microsoft Word as a Spell Checker

Microsoft Word is a popular word processing program that has a spell-checking feature. It is also one of the earliest Windows programs to support OLE Automation. If you have Word installed, you can use the spell-checking feature from within your Delphi program to verify the correct spelling of your text and to correct any mistakes.

Word is an automation server that exposes a single automation object with a ProgID of Word.Basic. You can use this automation object to call methods that act on Word and its documents. The main form used in this application looks like the one shown in Figure 14-4.

The following project, SPELL.DPR, contains a single form that has a memo and a button. You can type any text into the memo. When you press the button, the Word automation object is launched and used to check the spelling of the text. If the text is spelled correctly, a message indicating so is displayed on the form. If any mistakes are found, Word's own dialog boxes appear, letting you correct the mistakes. This dialog box looks like the one shown in Figure 14-5.

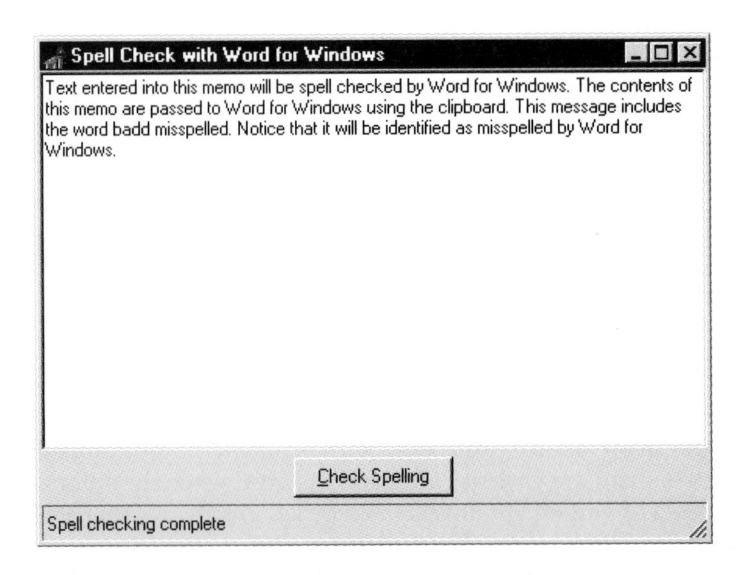

Figure 14-4. *Form for spell-checking example*

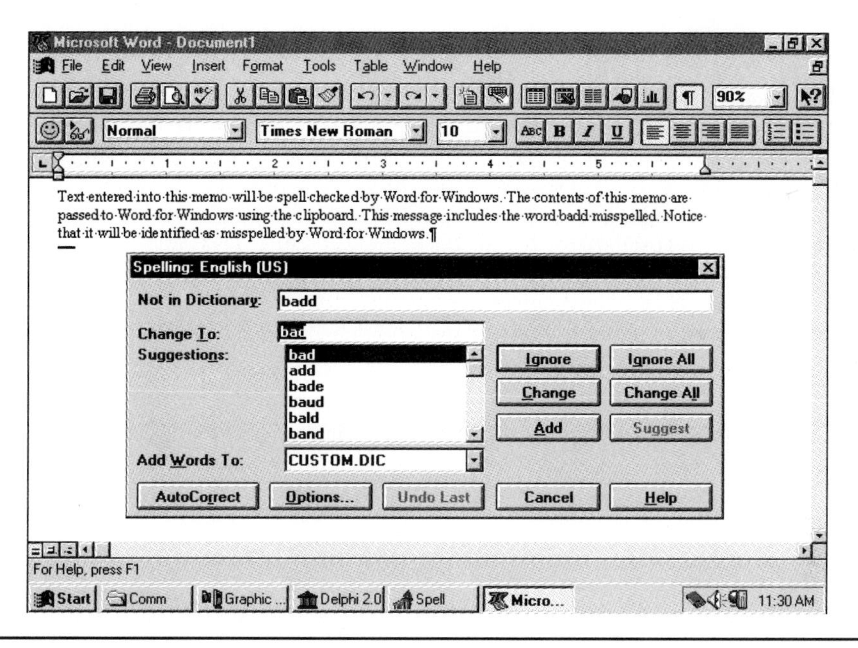

Figure 14-5. *Word's spell-checking dialog box*

Following is the source code for the SPELL project:

```
program spell;

uses
  Forms,
  spellu in 'spellu.pas' {Form1};

{$R *.RES}

begin
  Application.Initialize;
  Application.CreateForm(TForm1, Form1);
  Application.Run;
end.
```

The application's main form is associated with the SPELLU.PAS unit. The following is the source code for this unit:

```
unit spellu;

interface
```

```
uses
  Windows, Messages, SysUtils, Classes, Graphics, Controls, Forms, Dialogs,
  StdCtrls, ExtCtrls, ComCtrls;

type
  TForm1 = class(TForm)
    StatusBar1: TStatusBar;
    Panel1: TPanel;
    Button1: TButton;
    Memo1: TMemo;
    procedure Button1Click(Sender: TObject);
    procedure FormCreate(Sender: TObject);
  private
    { Private declarations }
  public
    { Public declarations }
  end;

var
  Form1: TForm1;

implementation

{$R *.DFM}
uses OLEAuto, ClipBrd;

procedure TForm1.Button1Click(Sender: TObject);
var
  WinWord: Variant;
  CB     : TClipBoard;
begin
StatusBar1.SimpleText := 'Spell checking...';
Application.ProcessMessages;
// Open the OLE link to WinWord.
WinWord := CreateOLEObject('word.basic');
// Select all of the memo text.
Memo1.SelectAll;
// Copy the selected text to the clipboard.
Memo1.CopyToClipboard;
// From WinWord, create a new file.
WinWord.FileNew;
// Paste clipboard contents into the new file.
WinWord.EditPaste;
try
  try
    try
      // Initiate spell checking
      WinWord.ToolsSpelling;
    except
```

```
      // WinWord creates a message indicating that the
      // spell check is complete. This generates an
      // exception. Ignore this exception.
    end;
    // Select the spell checked text.
    WinWord.EditSelectAll;
    // Copy it to the clipboard.
    WinWord.EditCopy;
  finally
    // Close WinWord.
    WinWord.Cancel;
    WinWord := UnAssigned;
  end; // try-finally
except
  Exit;
  StatusBar1.SimpleText := 'Could not spell check'
end; // try-except
// Bring the spell checked text back.
Memo1.PasteFromClipboard;
StatusBar1.SimpleText := 'Spell checking complete'
end;

procedure TForm1.FormCreate(Sender: TObject);
begin
// Highlight text in the memo.
Memo1.SelectAll;
end;

end.
```

When you press the button, the Word automation object is created and stored in the variant WordObject. The text of the memo is copied to the Windows clipboard by calling the TMemo's SelectAll and CopyToClipboard methods. Next, a series of methods are called that act on the automation object. These methods are wrapped in a try-except block to protect the code against any unforeseen exceptions that may occur. For instance, an exception can be raised if an automation server is busy and cannot respond to a method. The first method, FileNew, tells Word to create a new, blank document. This new document is used as a temporary area to place the text to be spell checked. The next method, EditPaste, pastes the text from the clipboard into this new document.

Next, the ToolsSpelling method tells Word to use its spell checker to check the spelling of each word in the text. If any words are spelled incorrectly, Word displays a dialog box that lets you correct each word in the text. After all words are verified, Word signals the Delphi program by raising an OLE exception. Since this is an expected outcome and you don't want Delphi's default error dialog box to appear as a result, the ToolsSpelling call is wrapped in a try-except block. This exception handling block handles the EOLEError and discards it by not performing any particular action.

Finally, the automation object's EditSelectAll and EditCopy methods are called to return the correctly spelled text to the clipboard. The TMemo's PasteFromClipboard method is then used to replace the memo's existing text with the clipboard contents.

NOTE: During testing of the preceding example, it was observed that on some machines the automation server did not close when the variant was assigned the UnAssigned constant. The server shut down only after the project terminated. No consistent pattern was observed, however. Consequently, you should use caution if you attempt to use this technique, or a variation of it, in one of your applications. Many third-party spell checkers are available for Delphi that may provide you with a more suitable solution to spell checking within your applications.

This example illustrated how you can leverage the features of a desktop application and use it as a component in your Delphi application. The next two examples expand on the possibilities created by OLE Automation.

Controlling Netscape Navigator for Internet Access

The following two sample programs show you how you can use Netscape Navigator 2.0 to connect to the Internet and download useful information. Netscape Navigator is a popular Internet client and browser for connecting to the Internet and viewing World Wide Web sites. Since Netscape Navigator is an OLE automation server, you can control it and integrate its functionality into your application. To run these examples, you'll need to establish an Internet connection and have a copy of Netscape Navigator. The Internet connection should be active before you try any of the samples. To test if this is the case, you should use your browser beforehand to connect to a World Wide Web site. If you don't have a copy of Netscape Navigator 2.0 (or later) for Windows 95, you can obtain one by purchasing the Netscape Internet Starter Kit at a store, or by downloading an evaluation copy from the Netscape home page at http://www.netscape.com.

NOTE: If you are new to the Internet, or are unfamiliar with Internet related concepts and acronyms such as a Web site, URL, HTML, and so forth, you may want to read Chapter 17 before continuing.

Netscape OLE Methods

Netscape Navigator exposes the Netscape.Network.1 object to provide you with the same Internet access and file retrieval capabilities that Navigator uses. This automation object defines many methods and properties. The following methods are used in the sample programs:

- Open
- Close

- GetStatus
- Read

THE OPEN METHOD The Open method begins retrieving from a specified URL (Uniform Resource Locator). Open has the following syntax:

```
Open(pURL: String, iMethod: Integer, pPostData: String,
   lPostDataSize: Integer, pPostHeaders: String): Boolean
```

The first argument, pURL, is a string that specifies the address of the Web site. The second argument, iMethod, indicates the type of operation to perform. When reading from a Web site, you pass a zero to indicate that you want to read. The remaining arguments pertain to posting data to the Web site. Since you are only reading, you can pass zeros as values for these arguments, even for the string type arguments. Delphi automatically converts the zeros to the correct values. In the case of the string arguments, empty values are passed. If Open fails, for example, if Navigator is busy, the method returns a False; otherwise, it returns True.

THE CLOSE METHOD The Close method disconnects any current connection and resets the automation object. You should call Close when you are finished with the automation object. Close has the following syntax:

```
Close
```

THE GETSTATUS METHOD GetStatus is a method that returns an integer indicating the status of the load. GetStatus has a non-zero value in the case of an error. The GetStatus method has the following syntax:

```
GetStatus: Integer;
```

THE READ METHOD The Read method retrieves data from the Web site and stores it into a buffer that you specify. This method has the following syntax:

```
Read(pBuffer: BSTR, iAmount: Integer): Integer
```

The first argument, pBuffer, is an OLE BSTR type and refers to the buffer that receives the data. (A BSTR is a length-prefixed string used by OLE Automation data-manipulation functions.) The second argument, iAmount, specifies the size of the buffer.

Read returns –1 if there is no more data to read, 0 if there is currently no data to read, or a positive number indicating the number of bytes actually read. Read takes two arguments, pBuffer and iAmount.

To keep things simple, you can use a string as the type for the buffer instead of a BSTR; Delphi automatically converts the types for you. When the automation server stores any returned data into your buffer, it does not update the internal byte count of the string, or BSTR for that matter. You should correct the byte count manually.

ADDITIONAL COMMENTS This is only a short description of some of the methods and properties of the server. If you are interested in learning more about the objects surfaced by Netscape Navigator, you can find the documentation for the OLE Automation interface at http://home.mcom.com/newsref/std/oleapi.html.

Each sample application loads Netscape Navigator and uses the browser to connect to a useful Web site. Specifically, the browser communicates with a CGI (Common Gateway Interface) program at the Web site and passes it some variables. In response, the CGI program returns some data. During this interaction, the Netscape Navigator does not appear visible, so that all you see is your main form. The application does the work of interfacing with the automation server and downloading any requested data.

The Web sites on the Internet are constantly changing and evolving. Sometimes a Web site address will change and be updated to a new URL. Also, many popular sites are often overloaded by users, momentarily preventing you from connecting. If you have trouble using any of the examples in this section of the chapter, you should connect to the Web site manually to determine the situation.

Downloading Stock Prices

The first project, STOCKNET.DPR, uses the Quote.Com Web site (www.quote.com) to download stock quotes. Quote.Com is a company that provides financial market data, such as stock quotes, financial commentary, and business news to Internet users. Normally, you must have a paid subscription to the service in order to use it. New users can try the service on a limited basis, but they must register online to obtain a user account and password. Users who do not register may still try the service but are limited to using the stock ticker MSFT (Microsoft) in the demonstration area. This example assumes that you are not registered and defaults to getting stock quotes for MSFT. If you register with Quote.Com, you can use other stock tickers with the sample application. The Web page used in this application looks like the one shown in Figure 14-6.

To use the example, enter a valid stock symbol and then press the Request button. This launches Netscape Navigator to connect to the Web site and download the stock information.

NOTE: Remember, your Internet connection must be established before your run the example. If you do not have access to an Internet service provider, or an Internet server, you cannot use this demonstration.

Quotes are delayed by fifteen minutes and are the responsibility of Quote.Com. The following screen shows you what the program looks like after you request a stock quote. The stock ticker, current quote, and date are shown in Figure 14-7.

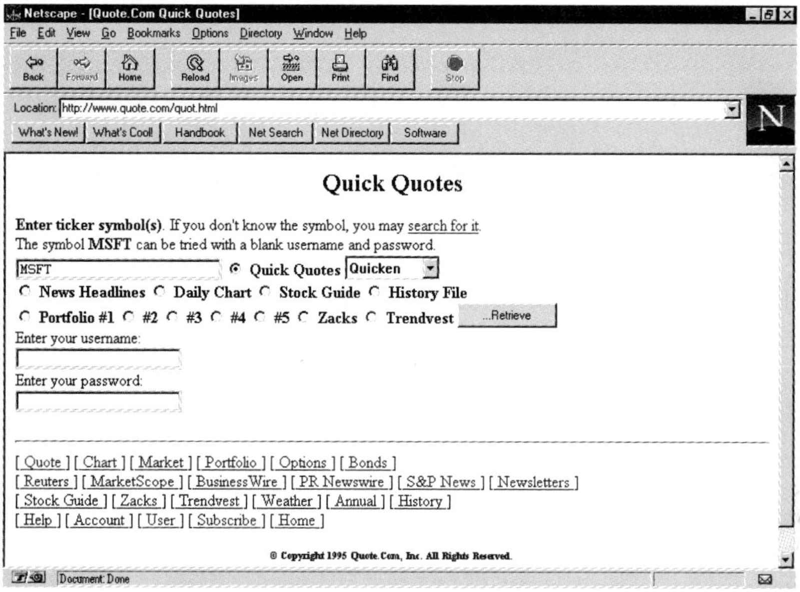

Figure 14-6. *Web page for Quick Quotes*

Following is the source code for STOCKNET.DPR:

```
program stocknet;

uses
  Forms,
```

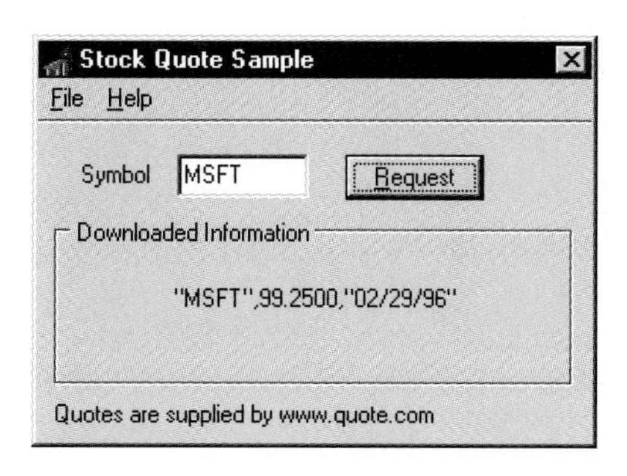

Figure 14-7. *The STOCKNET stock quote sample form*

```
  stockne1 in 'stockne1.pas' {StockForm},
  stockne2 in 'stockne2.pas' {AboutBox};

{$R *.RES}

begin
  Application.CreateForm(TStockForm, StockForm);
  Application.CreateForm(TAboutBox, AboutBox);
  Application.Run;
end.
```

The application's main form is associated with the STOCKNE1.PAS unit. The following is the source code for this unit:

```
// This sample application is provided for educational purposes only.
// All stock quotes are supplied by Quote.Com.
// For information about its Web site, email support@quote.com.
// Quote.Com is free for limited use, but you must register in
// order to use it. This sample application obtains a quote for MSFT
// which is currently free to unregistered users.  If you wish to use
// other stock symbols, you must register with Quote.Com.

unit stockne1;

interface

uses
  windows, Messages, SysUtils, Classes, Graphics, Controls, Forms,
  Dialogs, StdCtrls, ExtCtrls, Gauges, ComCtrls, Menus;

type
  TStockForm = class(TForm)
    MainMenu1: TMainMenu;
    File1: TMenuItem;
    Help1: TMenuItem;
    About1: TMenuItem;
    Exit1: TMenuItem;
    Bevel1: TBevel;
    StockButton: TButton;
    Label1: TLabel;
    StockSymbol: TEdit;
    GroupBox1: TGroupBox;
    QuoteLabel: TLabel;
    Label2: TLabel;
    procedure FormClose(Sender: TObject; var Action: TCloseAction);
    procedure Exit1Click(Sender: TObject);
    procedure About1Click(Sender: TObject);
    procedure StockButtonClick(Sender: TObject);
```

```
    procedure FormCreate(Sender: TObject);
  private
    { Private declarations }
    LoginName: String; // registered user login name
    Password:  String; // registered user password
  public
    { Public declarations }
  end;

var
  StockForm: TStockForm;
  Netscape : Variant;

implementation

uses OLEAuto, StockNe2;

{$R *.DFM}

procedure TStockForm.FormClose(Sender: TObject;
    var Action: TCloseAction);
begin

// shut down Netscape if it's open
if not VarIsEmpty(Netscape) then
  begin
    // Close Netscape.
    Netscape.Close;
    // Unassign the variant.
    Netscape := Unassigned;
  end;

end;

procedure TStockForm.Exit1Click(Sender: TObject);
begin
  Close;
end;

procedure TStockForm.About1Click(Sender: TObject);
begin
with TAboutBox.Create(Application) do
  try
    ShowModal;
  finally
    Free;
  end;
end;
```

```
procedure TStockForm.StockButtonClick(Sender: TObject);
var
  Buffer    : String;
  BytesRead: Integer;
begin

  Screen.Cursor := crHourGlass;

  // Launch Netscape Navigator
  if VarIsEmpty(Netscape) then
  begin
    QuoteLabel.Caption := 'Please wait. '+
                          'Loading Netscape for the first time';
    QuoteLabel.Refresh;
    try
      Netscape := CreateOLEObject('Netscape.Network.1');
    except
      ShowMessage('Could not start Netscape 2.0. Please exit.');
      Screen.Cursor := crDefault;
      Exit;
    end;
  end;

  try
    QuoteLabel.Caption := 'Downloading data';

    // attempt to open the URL

    if Netscape.Open('http://www.quote.com/cgi-bin/quote-form?symbols='+
       StockSymbol.Text + '&login=' + LoginName + '&passwd=' + Password+
       '&quotetype=Quicken',
       0, 0, 0, 0) then
      begin
      if Netscape.GetStatus = 0 then
        begin

        SetLength(Buffer,2048); // Set size of Buffer
        while True do
          begin
            // Read just a buffer full
            BytesRead := Netscape.Read(Buffer, 2048);
            if BytesRead = 0 then // Nothing read.  server busy?
              continue
            else
              break;
          end; // while True

        SetLength(Buffer,BytesRead); // correct the Buffer size
```

```
        if (Copy(Buffer,1,1) = '<') or (BytesRead < 1) then
          // Error at site or time-out
          QuoteLabel.Caption := 'No information downloaded.'
        else
          QuoteLabel.Caption := Buffer;
        end;//if Netscape.GetStatus = 0
      end //if Netscape.Open()
    else
    begin

      // Any one of several problems may have occurred here.
      // The DNS server may be having trouble locating the URL or
      // The connection is bad or
      // The URL has moved or is no longer there.
      QuoteLabel.Caption := 'Can not connect';
      Exit;
    end; //if Netscape.Open else...

  finally
    Screen.Cursor := crDefault;
  end; //try

end;

procedure TStockForm.FormCreate(Sender: TObject);
begin
// This sample application only works if you use MSFT as
// the stock symbol. To obtain stock quotes for other companies,
// you must register with Quote.Com and obtain a login name
// and password.  When you do, enter them here.

 LoginName := '';
 Password := '';
end;

end.
```

The main form, StockForm, contains a menu that lets you close the application or display an About dialog box. The unit defines a variant, Netscape, to reference the Netscape automation server. Two string properties, LoginName and Password, are defined as part of the form class so that you can specify an optional user name and password to access the Quote.Com server. If you register with Quote.Com, you can obtain a user name and password. This lets you use the example with different stock tickers; otherwise, you can only use MSFT.

The form contains an Edit component, StockSymbol, that lets you enter a stock ticker. After entering a valid stock ticker, you can press the Request button. This executes StockButtonClick, which retrieves the stock quote and displays it on a label, QuoteLabel, on the form.

StockButtonClick starts the Netscape Navigator automation server by calling CreateOLEObject with the ProgID Netscape.Network.1 and assigns it to the variant, Netscape. Next, the automation server's Open method is called with the correct URL for the quote server. The text for the URL is created so that all the necessary values are passed to the CGI program at the Web site to retrieve the stock quote. This includes the site address, stock ticker, quote type, and the user name/password combination (if any). Since you are only reading data, zeros can be passed as the remaining arguments to the Open call.

If the site is contacted successfully, the server's Read method is used to download the stock information into a buffer. The information is then assigned to the QuoteLabel caption to display it on the form. Before the information is displayed, the buffer is checked to see if the server returned an HTML (Hypertext Markup Language) error message instead of the stock information. To determine if the former occurred, the first character of the buffer is compared to "<" to see if the buffer contains that start of an HTML tag.

After you are finished with the program, you can close it. When the form closes, the form's OnClose handler, FormClose, uses VarIsEmpty to determine if the automation server needs to be cleared. If so, the server is closed, and then the Netscape variable is assigned a value of UnAssigned.

This project also has an About box that is displayed when the user selects Help | About. This About box is a simple modal dialog box. Since there is nothing particularly interesting about this code, it is not reprinted here.

NOTE: *When you attempt to compile the STOCKNET application, you will receive a single warning, telling you that the variable BytesRead may not have been initialized. BytesRead is initialized by the Netscape Read method. Consequently you may ignore this warning. This warning demonstrates two things. First, the Delphi compiler in version 2 is smart enough to know that your code attempts to use a variable that is not initialized using Delphi statements. Second, because of late-binding, the compiler cannot know the operations of OLE server methods.*

Checking the Weather

The second project, WEATHER.DPR, uses the NBC News Intellicast Web site (www.intellicast.com) to download a .GIF graphics image depicting the four-day weather forecast for a city. The NBC News Intellicast Web site (shown in Figure 14-8) provides weather and skiing information for major locations all over the world. This service is free to online users, and no registration is required.

The main form for the example contains a list box of major cities. When you double-click on a city, the application connects to the Intellicast site, and then downloads its weather image into a TImage on the form. The URL of the weather image for each city has the form www.intellicast.com/weather/*xxx*/4-day.gif, where *xxx* is a three-letter city abbreviation. This URL is static, but the image is updated continually by NBC News so that it displays the current weather forecast.

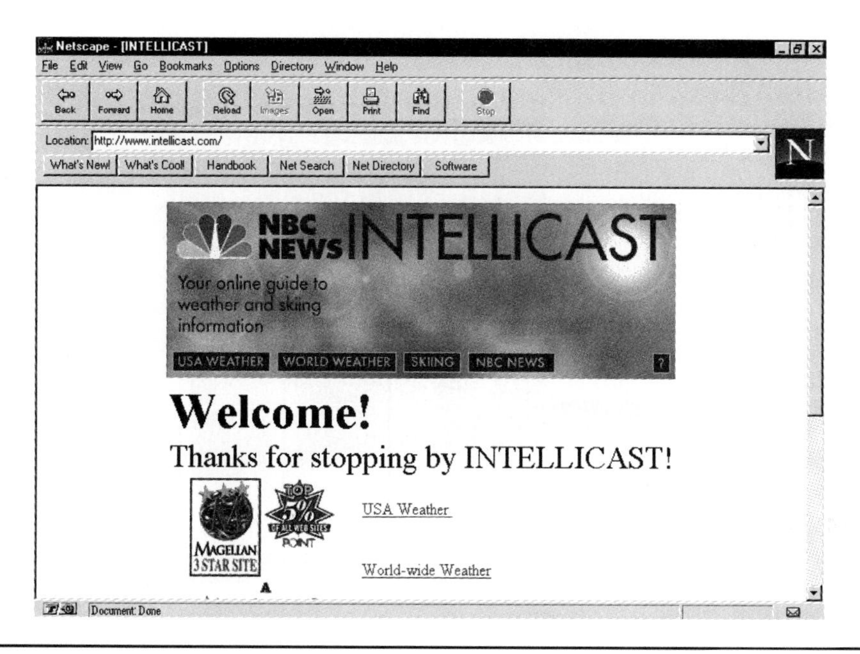

Figure 14-8. *Web page for Intellicast weather site*

Again, you must have your Internet connection established and be online before you can use this example. The screen in Figure 14-9 shows a weather forecast for the New York Metro Area.

NOTE: *This example adapts the GIF2BMP GIF-to-BMP graphics conversion routine developed originally by Sean Wenzel and updated for Delphi by Richard Dominelli. This routine is needed because TImages can not display .GIF images. The weather image is a .GIF image, so it is translated in memory into a bitmap (.BMP) file before assigning it to the TImage. The comments in the source code indicate that the code may be used freely as long as the original authors are credited. The source code, GIF2BMP.PAS, is included in the CD-ROM of this book.*

Following is the source code for WEATHER.DPR:

```
program weather;

uses
  Forms,
  weath1 in 'weath1.pas'   {WeatherForm},
  weath2 in 'weath2.pas',  {MapURL class}
  weath3 in 'weath3.pas'   {AboutBox},
  Gif2bmp in 'Gif2bmp.pas';{Gif to BMP converter}
```

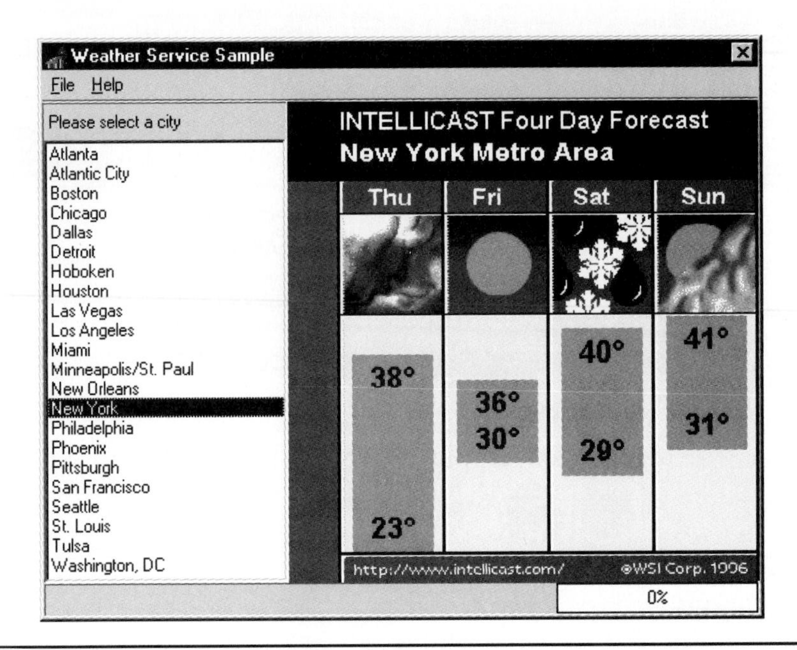

Figure 14-9. *The WEATHER project displaying a four-day weather forecast*

```
{$R *.RES}

begin
  Application.CreateForm(TWeatherForm, WeatherForm);
  Application.CreateForm(TAboutBox, AboutBox);
  Application.Run;
end.
```

The main form, WeatherForm, contains a list box, CityListBox, and a TImage, Image1, to display the weather forecast. The form's OnCreate handler, FormCreate, populates the list box with a list of cities and MapURL objects (the TMapURL class is defined in the WEATH2.PAS unit). Each city has an associated TMapURL which stores the URL for that city's weather map and retrieves the image. When you double-click on a city, a method, DisplayWeather, of its TMapURL object is executed.

The form WeatherForm is associated with the WEATH1.PAS unit. Following is the source code for this unit:

```
// This sample application is provided for educational purposes
// only. All weather forecasts are provided by Intellicast.
// For information about its Web site, email info@intellicast.com.

unit weath1;
```

```
interface

uses
  windows, Messages, SysUtils, Classes, Graphics, Controls, Forms,
  Dialogs, StdCtrls, ExtCtrls, Gauges, ComCtrls, Menus;

type
  TWeatherForm = class(TForm)
    StatusPanel: TPanel;
    Image1: TImage;
    Gauge1: TGauge;
    Label1: TLabel;
    MainMenu1: TMainMenu;
    File1: TMenuItem;
    Help1: TMenuItem;
    About1: TMenuItem;
    Exit1: TMenuItem;
    Bevel1: TBevel;
    Panel1: TPanel;
    CityListBox: TListBox;
    Panel2: TPanel;
    procedure FormCreate(Sender: TObject);
    procedure CityListBoxDblClick(Sender: TObject);
    procedure FormClose(Sender: TObject; var Action: TCloseAction);
    procedure Exit1Click(Sender: TObject);
    procedure About1Click(Sender: TObject);
  private
    { Private declarations }
  public
    { Public declarations }
  end;

var
  WeatherForm: TWeatherForm;
  Netscape : Variant;

implementation

uses gif2bmp, OLEAuto, weath2, weath3;

{$R *.DFM}

// initialize city list

procedure TWeatherForm.FormCreate(Sender: TObject);
begin
with CityListBox.Items do
  begin
    AddObject('Atlanta', TMapURL.Create('atl'));
```

```
    AddObject('Atlantic City', TMapURL.Create('acy'));
    AddObject('Boston', TMapURL.Create('bos'));
    AddObject('Chicago', TMapURL.Create('ord'));
    AddObject('Dallas', TMapURL.Create('dfw'));
    AddObject('Detroit', TMapURL.Create('dtw'));
    AddObject('Hoboken', TMapURL.Create('ewr'));
    AddObject('Houston', TMapURL.Create('iah'));
    AddObject('Las Vegas', TMapURL.Create('las'));
    AddObject('Los Angeles', TMapURL.Create('lax'));
    AddObject('Miami', TMapURL.Create('mia'));
    AddObject('Minneapolis/St. Paul', TMapURL.Create('msp'));
    AddObject('New Orleans', TMapURL.Create('msy'));
    AddObject('New York', TMapURL.Create('lga'));
    AddObject('Philadelphia', TMapURL.Create('phl'));
    AddObject('Phoenix', TMapURL.Create('phx'));
    AddObject('Pittsburgh', TMapURL.Create('pit'));
    AddObject('San Francisco', TMapURL.Create('sfo'));
    AddObject('Seattle', TMapURL.Create('sea'));
    AddObject('St. Louis', TMapURL.Create('stl'));
    AddObject('Tulsa', TMapURL.Create('tul'));
    AddObject('Washington, DC', TMapURL.Create('dca'));
  end; // with CityListBox.Items do
end;

procedure TWeatherForm.CityListBoxDblClick(Sender: TObject);
begin
with Sender as TListBox do
  (Items.Objects[ItemIndex] as TMapURL).DisplayWeather;
end;

procedure TWeatherForm.FormClose(Sender: TObject;
  var Action: TCloseAction);
begin

// shut down Netscape if it's open
if not VarIsEmpty(Netscape) then
  begin
    Netscape.Close;
    Netscape := Unassigned;
  end; // if not VarIsEmpty()
end;

procedure TWeatherForm.Exit1Click(Sender: TObject);
begin
Close;
end;

procedure TWeatherForm.About1Click(Sender: TObject);
begin
```

```
with TAboutBox.Create(Application) do
  try
    ShowModal;
  finally
    Free;
  end;
end;

end.
```

The main form also defines a variant, Netscape, to reference the Netscape Navigator automation server. When the form closes, the server is shut down by the form's OnClose handler, FormClose.

The TMapURL class is defined in the unit WEATH2.PAS. TMapURL has a constructor that accepts a three-letter city abbreviation as an argument. This abbreviation is stored in a private string, FCityAbbrev, which is used by DisplayWeather to build the correct URL for the city's weather forecast. DisplayWeather does all the work of connecting to the Web site, downloading the weather image, and then displaying it on the form.

DisplayWeather defines a TMemoryStream, GIFStream; a String, Buffer; and an Integer, BytesRead. These variables are used when downloading the weather image.

When DisplayWeather is executed, it launches the Netscape Navigator automation server by passing a ProgID of Netscape.Network.1 to CreateOLEObject, and then stores a reference to the server in the variant Netscape. Next, the server's Open method is called with the URL of the city's weather image. Zeros are passed as the remaining arguments to Open.

Once the connection is established, the process of retrieving the image begins. The image is downloaded in 2048-byte chunks into Buffer by executing the server's Read method. After each chunk is received, it is transferred into GIFStream using the TMemoryStream method WriteBuffer. These steps are repeated until the image is fully retrieved and Read returns a value of –1.

After the image is downloaded, GIFStream is assigned to Stream, a TMemoryStream variable in GIF2BMP.PAS. Next, GIFConvert is executed to convert the .GIF into a bitmap, which is then displayed on the form's TImage.

The following is the source code for WEATH2.PAS:

```
unit weath2;

interface

uses GIF2Bmp, Classes, Forms, Controls, Dialogs, SysUtils;

type TMapURL = class(TObject)
  private
  FCityAbbrev : string;
```

```
  public
  constructor Create(CityAbbrev: String);
  procedure DisplayWeather;
end;

implementation

uses Weath1, OLEAuto ;

constructor TMapURL.Create(CityAbbrev: String);
begin
  inherited Create;

  FCityAbbrev := CityAbbrev;
end;

procedure TMapURL.DisplayWeather;
const
  BaseURL : String = 'http://www.intellicast.com/weather/';
var
  GIFStream : TMemoryStream;
  Buffer    : String;
  BytesRead : Integer;
begin

  Screen.Cursor := crHourGlass;

  // Launch Netscape Navigator
  if VarIsEmpty(Netscape) then
  begin
    WeatherForm.StatusPanel.Caption := 'Please wait. Loading Netscape '+
      'for the first time';
    WeatherForm.StatusPanel.Refresh;
    try
      Netscape := CreateOLEObject('Netscape.Network.1');
    except
      ShowMessage('Could not start Netscape 2.0. Please exit.');
      Screen.Cursor := crDefault;
      Exit;
    end; //try
    WeatherForm.StatusPanel.Caption := '';
  end; // if VarIsEmpty()

  try
    WeatherForm.StatusPanel.Caption :='Downloading weather information';
    WeatherForm.StatusPanel.Refresh;

    // attempt to open the URL for the weather forecast GIF
```

```
  if Netscape.Open(BaseURL + FCityAbbrev+'/4day.gif', 0, 0, 0, 0) then
    begin
      GIFStream := TMemoryStream.Create;
try
        while Netscape.GetStatus = 0 do
        begin
          // Set size of Buffer
          SetLength(Buffer,2048);
          // Read a chunk
          BytesRead := Netscape.Read(Buffer, 2048);

          if BytesRead = -1 then
            break // Nothing left to read
          else
          begin
            // Correct the Buffer size
            SetLength(Buffer,BytesRead);
           // Netscape.Read does not update it correctly
            // Store GIF segment into stream
            GIFStream.WriteBuffer(Pointer(Buffer)^,Length(Buffer));

            continue; // Loop up to read more...

          end; // if BytesRead else...
        end; // while Netscape.GetStatus = 0 do

        // convert the GIFStream to a BMP so that
        // we can display it in a TImage
        with TGIF.Create do
          try
            SetIndicators(WeatherForm.Gauge1,
               WeatherForm.StatusPanel);

            Stream := GIFStream;

            // Reset position of GIF stream to origin
            Stream.Seek(0,0);

            GIFConvert;
          finally
            Free;
          end; // try

      finally
        GIFStream.Free;
      end; // try
    end //if Netscape.Open()
  else
  begin
```

```
      // Any one of several problems may have occurred here.
      // The DNS server may be having trouble locating the URL or
      // The connection is bad or
      // The URL has moved or is no longer there.

      WeatherForm.StatusPanel.Caption := '';
      ShowMessage('Sorry! The URL for the Intellicast '+
        'weather site can not be located.');
      Exit;
    end; //if Netscape.Open() else...

  finally
    Screen.Cursor := crDefault;
    WeatherForm.StatusPanel.Caption := '';
    WeatherForm.Gauge1.Progress := 0;
  end; // try

end;

end.
```

This project also includes an About box. This About box is displayed when the user selects Help | About. The unit for this form is named WEATH3.PAS. The code for this unit is not remarkable, so it is not reprinted here.

NOTE: *When you compile this application, the Delphi compiler will display a warning and several hints. These messages are associated with the GIF2BMP.PAS file, which was developed on earlier versions of Delphi. The unit compiles correctly, however, so you can safely ignore these messages.*

Conclusion

OLE Automation is a powerful capability that is relatively easy to use. This capability lets you create an integrated solution that uses the services of other applications. You can now use the objects of other applications as programmable objects and concentrate on the core functionality of your system.

References

NOTE: The following references are for Chapters 14, 15, and 16.

- Brain, Marshall, *Win32 System Services,* Prentice Hall, Upper Saddle River, NJ, 1996.
- Brockschmidt, Kraig, *Inside OLE2,* Microsoft Press, Redmond, WA, 1994.
- Edson, Dave, *Dave's Book of Top Ten Lists for Great Windows Programming,* M&T Books, New York, 1995.
- Goodman, Kevin J., *Building Windows 95 Applications,* M&T Books, New York, 1995.
- Kipping, David, *Migrating to Windows 95: A Programmer's Guide to Win32 Applications for the New Generation of Windows,* Prima Publishing, Rocklin, CA, 1995.
- *The Microsoft Windows 95 Resource Kit,* Microsoft Press, Redmond, WA, 1995.
- *OLE2 Programmer's Reference Volumes 1 and 2,* Microsoft Press, Redmond, WA, 1994.
- *Programmer's Guide to Microsoft Windows 95,* Microsoft Press, Redmond, WA, 1995.
- *Programming Windows 95 Unleashed,* Sams Publishing, Indianapolis, IN, 1995.
- Richter, Jeffrey, *Advanced Windows: The Developer's Guide to the Win32 API for Windows NT 3.5 and Windows 95,* Microsoft Press, Redmond, WA, 1995.
- Schulman, Andrew, *Unauthorized Windows 95: A Developer's Guide to Exploring the Foundations of Windows "Chicago,"* Programmers Press, San Mateo, CA, 1994.
- *The Windows Interface Guidelines for Software Design,* Microsoft Press, Redmond, WA, 1995.

Chapter Fifteen

Using Multithreading in Delphi 2

The code for the examples presented in this chapter can be found in the \CODE\CH15 subdirectory on the CD-ROM that accompanies this book. Please refer to Appendix A for information on using the code files for this chapter.

The Windows 32-bit API (Application Programming Interface) introduces the concept of multithreading to Windows 95 and Window NT programs. Using multithreading, you can improve performance by partitioning an application into multiple paths of execution. Although multithreading is very powerful, it adds a whole new level of complexity to an application. Fortunately, this complexity is moderated by Delphi 2, which provides the TThread class so that you can work with threads and the VCL (Visual Component Library) in a thread-safe manner. This chapter discusses how to create and manage threads.

Since this chapter focuses on a capability that is not available in Windows 3.x, and consequently not in the Delphi 16-bit version, all examples demonstrated in this chapter are designed explicitly for Delphi 2.

Introducing Multithreading

In Windows 95 and Windows NT (referred to here as Win32), an application consists of a *process* and one or more *threads*. A process is an instance of the application and has its own virtual address space, global variables, and operating system resources. By itself, a process does not execute. Instead, each process has a primary thread of execution that gets time slices from the CPU (central processing unit). This primary thread executes the code in the application. When this thread terminates, the process ends.

Win32 allows you to create additional threads, or simultaneous paths of execution, within an application. Each of these threads shares the address space of the parent process, so they have access to the same global variables and resources. Also, the operating system gives each of these additional threads *time slices* so that they appear to execute concurrently. A time slice is a portion of the CPU's execution time. In other words, each thread is allocated some percentage of the processor's capacity. In a multiprocessor machine under Windows NT, each thread may even have its own dedicated CPU.

In effect, threads allow *preemptive multitasking* within a single application. Preemptive multitasking simply means that more than one process can proceed simultaneously, executing its commands during its allocated time slices. By comparison, Windows 3.x offers only *cooperative multitasking*. In a cooperative multitasking environment, a second process can execute only when the currently executing process pauses or otherwise permits the second process to use some of the processing capability of the CPU. The main drawback to cooperative multitasking is that if any process takes all of the processing power of the CPU or does not yield, the second process cannot continue.

The advantage of threads is that they permit you, as the developer, to use the computer's CPU more efficiently by partitioning an application across threads. In other words, while preemptive multitasking permits two or more applications to share the CPU, threads permits a single application to simultaneously pursue two or more operations. For example, within a single application you can create one thread that performs lengthy processing in the background while the user continues to interact with the primary thread of the application.

The Win32 API provides facilities for you to create and use additional threads in your application. However, these facilities alone do not permit you to use VCL components in a *thread-safe* manner without corrupting data. (Thread-safe means that two or more simultaneous processes are designed in such a way that the code being executed in one thread does not interfere with the execution of the other.) Fortunately, Delphi provides a TThread class that encapsulates the threading mechanism and works with the VCL. You can use the TThread class along with Win32 API functions to add powerful multithreading capabilities to your application.

When to Use Additional Threads

Following are some situations in which multithreading can be very useful:

- *When a user initiates some operation that requires lengthy processing.* With Windows 3.x and other single-threaded applications, the user interface is unresponsive during processor intense operations because Windows messages are not processed while the CPU is busy with the primary task. This leaves the user in an unproductive state while waiting for the task to complete. In Win32 you can prevent this by creating an additional thread to finish the task in the background. This keeps the main user interface very responsive and available to handle user interaction while the work is being completed in the background.
- *In MDI (multiple document interface) applications where you have multiple documents represented by child forms.* For these applications you can give each child form its own thread. If one of the child forms initiates a lengthy process, the user can move to one of the other child forms and continue working.
- *When building applications for multiprocessor Windows NT applications.* As this implies, Windows NT supports machines with more than one processor. Furthermore, threads can be distributed efficiently across these processors. When you run a single-threaded application on a machine with multiple processors, you may not be utilizing the additional processing power efficiently. By partitioning the application using threads, you can balance the load and significantly increase the performance of the application.
- *When upgrading a Windows 3.x application in which you have used a Windows timer to perform periodic background work.* When recoding such an application in Win32, these background processes are often excellent candidates for multiple threads.

- *Windows 95 supports both 16-bit and 32-bit Windows applications.* To provide compatibility with 16-bit Windows applications and to maintain a good level of performance, Windows 95 contains a significant portion of the old 16-bit Windows API system code. This code is called by all Windows 3.x applications *and* by Windows 95 applications that make certain Win32 API calls, including those to the GDI and USER modules. This 16-bit code was never designed to be used simultaneously by multiple threads, so access to it is protected. Windows 95 internally uses *Win16Mutex*, a system-wide mechanism for guaranteeing exclusive access to the code. Essentially, whenever a thread makes a call to a 16-bit API function, any other thread attempting to call any 16-bit API function waits until the first thread yields to Windows or releases control. If an application doesn't yield or stops processing window messages for a long time, these other applications will be tied up. Unfortunately, this can leave Windows 95 applications unresponsive because many 32-bit API functions, including those that handle the user interface, actually call the 16-bit code base. To minimize this effect, you can create additional threads to perform the work in the background, while the primary thread is waiting on the user interface.

An Example Where Multithreading Is Needed

The following example illustrates how a single threaded application can tie up the user. A well-designed Windows application should let the user stay productive if a long task is underway. (The key is to keep the user busy, or at least able to continue work on other things!)

In this example, the application begins a long operation when you press the Start button as shown in Figure 15-1. The work the application performs is simply to loop to 5000 and update a ProgressBar, named ProgressBar1, and a Label, named Counter, with the progress. In your particular situation, the operation might represent a long calculation or some other lengthy task. After the button is pressed, its caption changes to read "Stop" so that you can cancel the operation.

Since the primary (and only) thread is working on completing the task, it cannot process any user interaction or any other window messages. In this example, you

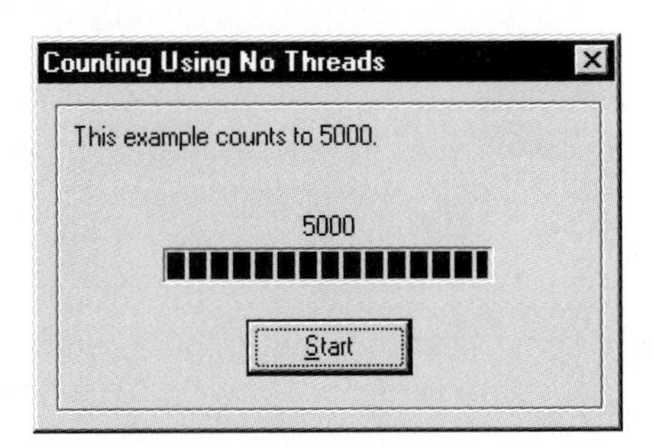

Figure 15-1. *The NOTHREAD project counts to 5000 in a single process*

cannot move the form around, click on the button if you wanted to cancel the operation, or try to close the form. You can't even close the form if you inserted code into the loop to let the application process some of the window messages.

```
program nothread;

uses
 Forms,
 nothreau in 'nothreau.pas' {CountForm};

{$R *.RES}

begin
 Application.CreateForm(TCountForm, CountForm);
 Application.Run;
end.
```

The listing for NOTHREAU.PAS shows the code for StartButtonClick. The StartButtonClick method is executed each time the user presses the button. Initially, the button's caption shows "Start." When you press it, the method resets the caption to show "Stop" and then initializes ProgressBar1 and Counter controls with 0. Next, it begins a loop from 0 to 5000 and, finally, resets the button's caption to "Start" upon completion. At any time the button's caption displays "Stop" you can press it to cancel the operation—that is, if the application could respond to the mouse click.

```
unit nothreau;

interface

uses
 Windows, Messages, SysUtils, Classes, Graphics, Controls, Forms, Dialogs,
 StdCtrls, Menus, ExtCtrls, ComCtrls;

type
 TCountForm = class(TForm)
  Panel1: TPanel;
  StartButton: TButton;
  Label1: TLabel;
  ProgressBar1: TProgressBar;
  Counter: TLabel;
  procedure StartButtonClick(Sender: TObject);
 private
  { Private declarations }
 public
  { Public declarations }
 end;
```

```
var
 CountForm: TCountForm;

implementation


var
 i: Integer;

{$R *.DFM}

procedure TCountForm.StartButtonClick(Sender: TObject);
begin
 with Sender as TButton do
  if Caption = '&Start' then
  begin
   Caption := 'S&top';
   ProgressBar1.Position := 0;
   Counter.Caption := '0';

   i:= 0;
   while i <= 5000 do
   begin
    Counter.Caption := IntToStr(i);
    ProgressBar1.Position := i;
    Inc(i);
   end;

   Caption := '&Start';
  end
  else
  begin
   Caption := '&Start';
   ProgressBar1.Position := 0;
   Counter.Caption := '0';
  end;
end;

end.
```

When you run the example, you can see how unresponsive the user interface is. Even the label caption is not updated as long as the while loop is executed. This is, admittedly, a very simplistic example. Furthermore, it would not be much work to alter this project to get it to work without using additional threads. However, in more complex, real world applications, you'll want to use multithreading.

A multithreaded version of this example is presented later in this chapter in the section "Multithreading Using Child Forms and Worker Threads." The basic techniques for creating threads are introduced in the following sections.

Creating Threads Using the TThread Class

The Delphi 2 TThread class encapsulates the multithreading mechanism so that you don't have to rely solely on Win32 API function calls to create threads. More importantly, the TThread class provides a facility to work with VCL components in a thread-safe manner. The TThread class also supplies a simpler alternative to *thread local storage*, which is a technique used to associate data with individual threads.

Although you can work entirely with threads using the Win32 API, doing so requires you to work at a lower level. In other words, it is a lot more work. Furthermore, working with the API directly also requires that you supply your own framework for synchronizing access to the VCL. If you do not synchronize your thread's access to VCL properties and methods, you run the risk of corrupting shared data and generating access violations. The TThread class in Delphi 2 provides this framework for you.

The TThread class does not completely hide all the details of working with the Win32 API but instead is a thin wrapper that removes the drudgery of VCL synchronization and thread local storage. When you instantiate a Thread, the class creates a new thread and stores its handle internally. Table 15-1 lists the protected and public properties of the TThread class. Table 15-2 lists the protected and public methods of the TThread class.

NOTE: The TThread class is defined in the CLASSES unit. Consequently, you will need to ensure that this unit is included in a uses statement for any unit instantiating a Thread object.

Property	Description
FreeOnTerminate	Specifies whether the VCL automatically destroys the thread upon termination. Defaults to False
Handle	The thread handle
OnTerminate	An event property for the event handler that is executed when the thread terminates
Priority	A variable that lets you get and set the thread's relative priority
ReturnValue	Returns the value of the thread
Suspended	A Boolean variable that lets you get and set the thread's suspended state
Terminated	A read-only Boolean that indicates if the thread should terminate
ThreadID	The thread's ID

Table 15-1. *TThread Class Properties*

Method	Description
Create	Create is the thread constructor
Destroy	Destroy is the thread destructor
DoTerminate	DoTerminate calls the OnTerminate event handler, if one exists. DoTerminate executes as part of the thread, as opposed to OnTerminate, which executes as part of the process. It is unusual to override this method
Execute	Execute is a virtual, abstract method that you override to specify the threads behavior. Do not call this method—it is automatically called by the constructor
Resume	Resumes execution of a suspended thread
Suspend	Suspends execution of a thread
Synchronize	Synchronizes access to VCL properties or methods
Terminate	Sets a flag that tells the thread to end
WaitFor	Suspends execution until a specified thread becomes signaled

Table 15-2. *TThread Class Methods*

NOTE: The TThread class provides both a Handle property and a ThreadID property. These properties supply the thread handle and thread ID values that are needed when calling certain Win32 API functions, such as WaitForSingleObject. There is no danger in mixing Win32 API functions with TThread methods. However, it is always advisable to use the TThread version of the function if it provides one. You should not, for example, suspend the thread using the Win32 API function SuspendThread. Instead, you should use the TThread class Suspend method. In addition to suspending the thread, the Suspend method maintains an internal field indicating the suspended state.

Using the TThread Class

The steps required to add multithreading to your Delphi 2 application are fairly straightforward. First, for each new thread, you derive a new TThread class from the base TThread class, and then you add code to instantiate this new object. You can define the new thread class by adding the TThread type declaration into an existing unit or by creating a separate unit to hold the TThread definition from the repository. To create a new thread unit for an existing project using the repository, select File | New. Delphi displays the New Items dialog box as shown in Figure 15-2.

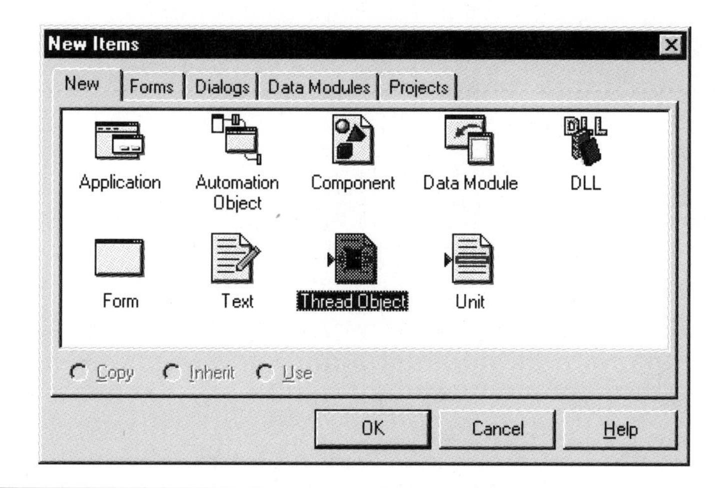

Figure 15-2. *The New Items dialog box*

When you select the Thread Object icon from this dialog box and then click OK, the New Thread Object dialog box appears, prompting you for the name to call the new class.

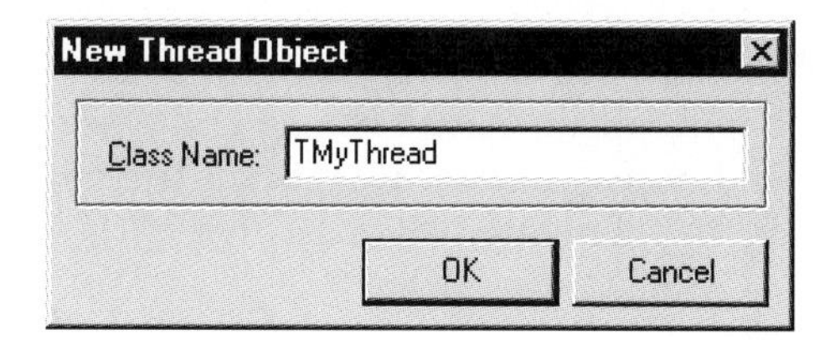

After you fill in the name, a new unit appears containing a basic TThread class declaration. For example, if you have a new project, and then used the repository to add a second unit for a thread class named TMyThread, your screen will look like the one shown in Figure 15-3.

NOTE: *The New Thread Object dialog box uses the name that you enter to create a type declaration for a new thread. Although you can enter any name here, it is appropriate to enter a name that begins with a T. By convention, all type declarations in Delphi should be identified by an initial T in the type name.*

After declaring the new class, you need to define the code that goes into the TThread's member functions. At a minimum, you should place the thread's main worker code into the TThread's Execute method, the place reserved for this code. For instance, if your code performs a background calculation, you should place this calculation in Execute. Next, you should add code to store the TThread variable in a

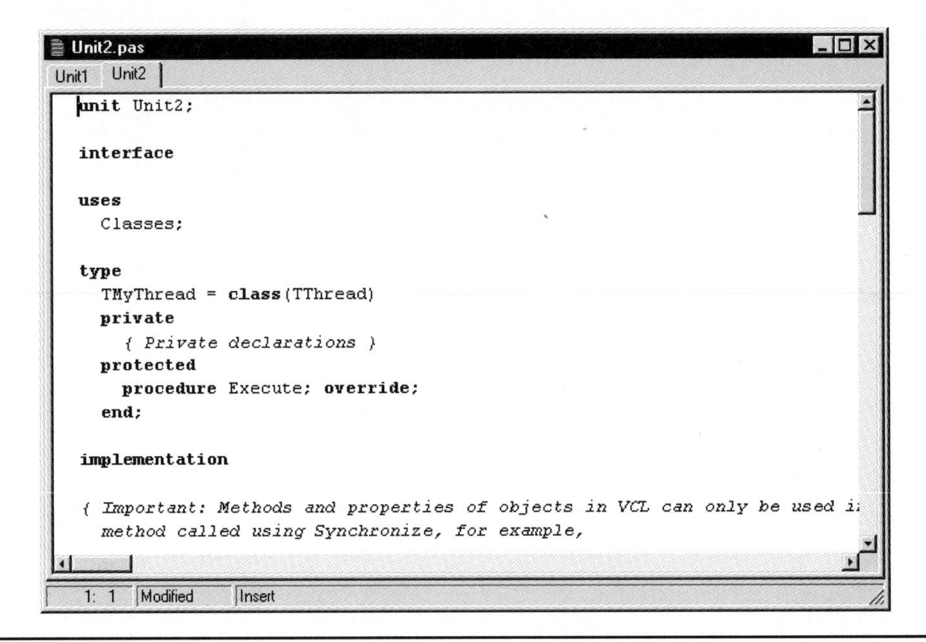

Figure 15-3. *The default unit created for your new TThread type*

global or member variable so that you can reference it in your code. Finally, you should add the actual code to create the new TThread and work with it. This code may perform functions to suspend or resume execution of the thread or even terminate it. These steps are described in the following sections.

Creating a Thread

To create a new TThread, you declare a TThread class, a variable or member variable of this class, and then call its Create constructor. A constructor of the TThread type has the following syntax:

```
Create(Suspended: Boolean);
```

When you call the constructor you pass to it a single Boolean parameter, Suspended, that indicates if the thread should be created in a suspended state. Normally, you would pass a value of False so that the thread begins execution immediately.

Assuming that you have declared an object named MyThread of the type TThread, the following code segment would create and execute it:

```
MyThread.Create(False);
```

If you want to set a custom thread priority, or if you want to delay execution of the thread, you will want to pass a value of True. This creates the thread and leaves it in a suspended state. To begin execution, you call the TThread's Resume method to resume it. The following code demonstrates how you would create the MyThread object, set its priority, and then commence its execution:

```
MyThread.Create(True)
MyThread.Priority := tpHighest;
MyThread.Resume();
```

Placing the Code for the Background Work

The TThread class defines a virtual, abstract method, Execute, that is overridden in order to implement the code for your background task. The constructor for TThread calls Execute immediately after creating the thread so that you do not need to explicitly run it. When Execute is finished running, the thread terminates and sets a return value that you can query using the ReturnValue property.

The code that you place into Execute may perform some background task such as a lengthy calculation or repagination of a document. If the code resides in a loop, the loop should contain some predefined condition that breaks out when it is True, such as when a certain number of iterations has passed. You should also place a test inside this code to see if the Terminated property is True. If it is True, your code should immediately exit the Execute method. The reason why you need this additional piece of code is explained in the next section, "Terminating a Thread." The following is an example of the implementation code for an Execute method:

```
procedure TMyThread.Execute;
begin
 while MoreWork do
 begin
  CalculateSpreadsheet; {perform some work}
  if Terminated then
   Exit;
 end;
end;
```

Terminating a Thread

There are two recommended ways to terminate a thread when using the TThread class: You can call Exit from the TThread's Execute method or you can call the TThread's Terminate method. Although you might be tempted to also use the Win32 API function TerminateThread to terminate the thread, this is not recommended. TerminateThread terminates the thread in such a way that neither the Thread object nor the TThread class knows that this termination has occurred. The two consequences of this are that any valuable resources used by the thread are not released, and you have no opportunity to execute any code of your own upon the thread's termination.

Calling Exit to Terminate a Thread

The bulk of the code responsible for performing your background task resides in the Execute method. When this code finishes running, it should exit the Execute method. This can happen implicitly as the last action of the method finishes or if you call Exit. When Execute finishes, the thread terminates and the TThread class takes care of any cleanup.

Calling Terminate from Another Thread

A second way to terminate a thread is to call the Thread's Terminate method. Typically, you do this when you want to terminate a specific thread from the main thread or from another thread. Terminate does not actually terminate the thread but rather sets the Terminated property to True. It is then up to your code to check the value of Terminated from inside the Thread's methods, and to act appropriately to exit the Execute method. If you do not have any code that does this, calling Terminate is ineffective. The following code segment illustrates how this code might appear:

```
procedure TMyThread.Execute;
begin
 while SomeCondition do
 begin
  {Do some work here}
  DoSomeWork;
  if Terminated then
   Exit;
 end;
end;
```

After performing a unit of work, the if statement checks the value of Terminated, and exits the method if it is True.

TIP: Before terminating a thread, make sure that the thread has released any resources, such as memory, that it specifically allocated. Otherwise, the resources are not released and will remain unavailable for other applications.

NOTE: The TThread's destructor also calls Terminate for you, as long as the thread is not suspended at the time.

Using VCL Components from Within a Thread

There are special considerations to be made if you plan to access any of the VCL components from within your thread. This is because the VCL is not implicitly thread-safe. In other words, any unprotected access of a component from within a thread may corrupt data or cause an access violation. This includes calling any methods and/or reading or writing from any of a component's properties.

Access to the VCL needs to be protected because multiple threads may try to work with the same component simultaneously, possibly leading to data corruption or other unwanted side effects. Also, for performance and efficiency, the VCL caches Windows GDI (Graphics Device Interface) objects that handle screen painting. Windows does not allow two or more threads simultaneous access to a GDI object. This may happen because the VCL stores and reuses GDI objects—in this case, you can get an access violation with multithreaded access.

With these caveats in mind, you may conclude that your code is still safe if you avoid *writing to* any of the properties of a component. However, this is not the case. Recall that a property of a component may have an access method that gets executed when you attempt to read the value. This access method may perform some operation that changes data or may attempt to read from one or more fields or properties that are being changed by another thread.

But even if there was no access method associated with the reading of a property, you could still have problems. For example, even if a property used direct access, another thread may be in the middle of updating that same property or some other property using an access method that creates side effects. As a result, there is no guarantee that a given property would be in a valid or consistent state when your thread attempts to read it. Even if your code does not generate an access violation, it may receive invalid data.

Using Synchronize with the VCL

To address the issue of thread-safe VCL access, the TThread class provides a Synchronize method. If your thread needs to access a VCL component, the thread should not do it directly. Instead, you should put this code into a separate method and then execute this method by calling Synchronize. Synchronize has the following syntax:

```
Synchronize(Method: TThreadMethod);
```

When you call Synchronize, you pass to it a method by value. Synchronize then executes this method in a thread-safe manner.

In most cases, you will want the method that you pass to Synchronize to be a member of the same derived Thread object. Doing so provides the method with access to the object's private interface and variables. The following code segment shows you what your code might look like:

```
// This method accesses the caption of a Label component.
method TMyThread.UpdateDisplay
begin
 MyForm.ProgressLabel.Caption := 'Up to ' + IntToStr(Count);
end;
```

```
method TMyThread.Execute;
begin
 while WorkToDo do
 begin
  DoSomeWorkMethod;

  Synchronize(UpdateDisplay);

  if Terminated then
   Exit;
 end;
end;
```

The preceding code demonstrates how you can update a component's property from a thread. First, a method named UpdateDisplay is implemented for the TMyThread class. Within this method, a Label component's Caption property is updated.

Within the Execute method for the thread object, a while loop continues to execute so long as a variable named WorkToDo evaluates to True. Within this loop, a call is made to a method named DoSomeWork. Next, this thread needs to update the display of the Label component. To do this it calls UpdateDisplay. However, it does so by passing the name of the UpdateDisplay method to the Synchronize method, permitting the update to the Caption in a thread-safe manner.

How Synchronize Works

Synchronize works by *synchronizing*, that is, coordinating your thread with other threads so that any shared access to the VCL is protected. It does this by *delegating* the execution of your method to the primary thread. This delegation means that the primary thread executes this code instead of your own thread having to do so. Since the primary thread is the *only* thread accessing the VCL, there is no chance of corruption. Synchronize guarantees that only one thread is in the Synchronize call at any one time, and consequently, only one thread can access the VCL at any given time.

Internally, this is what happens when you use Synchronize: When you create your first thread using the TThread class, the TThread creates an invisible window that responds to a private message. This window is owned by the *primary* thread so that any code it runs is executed on the primary thread's time slice. When you call Synchronize and pass it your method as an argument, it in turn packages your method (pointer) into a Windows message and sends it off to the invisible window. When the invisible window receives it, it executes your method. Synchronize waits for the invisible window to complete execution of the method, and then continues to the next line of code in your thread.

Special Considerations

The following sections describe special considerations that you should take when working with VCL components in a multithreaded situation.

MINIMIZE THE CODE CALLED BY SYNCHRONIZE You should minimize the amount of code called by Synchronize and the number of calls to Synchronize. When you call Synchronize, your thread is no longer executing independently "in the background." This is because execution has been deferred to the primary thread. The primary thread may currently be processing its own messages or messages from other threads at the time that you call Synchronize. If this is the case, your thread waits for the primary thread to complete its processing so that it can get a turn. Your thread is not running while it waits.

BACKGROUND DATA ACCESS The data access objects such as Tables and Queries are VCL components. Does this mean that you must use Synchronize to access them? The answer is no. The general rule is that you should not access data through DataSet objects from multiple threads within a single Session. If you want to access data from a separate thread, you must define a new session, and then create the DataSet object from within that session.

For example, if you want to perform a query in the background, from within a second thread, your thread must create a new Session object, and then define the Query object for that Session. When you do this, all access to data using that Query will be as though a second, independent user is accessing the data. Consequently, the standard table and record locking mechanisms of the BDE (Borland Database Engine) will be responsible for all concurrency issues.

Note that this exception does not cover the visual data controls such as DBEdits. To access those controls, you should still use Synchronize.

TERMINATING FROM INSIDE SYNCHRONIZE You should not use Terminate if you want to terminate your thread from within the Synchronize call. Instead, in the TThread's Execute method, place a check for the Terminated property. If it is True, your code should exit the thread. In the method passed to Synchronize, you should set Terminated to True, and then immediately exit the method. This is demonstrated in the following code segment:

```
procedure MyThread.UpdateDisplay;
begin
 {do VCL work here}

 if TimeToEnd then
 begin
  Terminated := True;
  Exit;
 end;

 {do more VCL work here}
end;

procedure MyThread.Execute;
```

```
begin
 while (SomeCondition = True) and (not Terminated) do
 begin
  {do work here}
  Synchronize(UpdateDisplay)
end;
end;
```

SYNCHRONIZE AND THE USER INTERFACE The user interface may appear to be less responsive each time you call Synchronize. This is because the primary thread is responsible for handling window messages associated with the user interface. If the primary thread is currently performing work on behalf of your Synchronize call, it does not have the opportunity to process other messages. This is another reason to pay attention and avoid putting unnecessary code into a Synchronize call.

This section covered how to synchronize access to the VCL between threads. Chapter 16 describes how you can use synchronization and Win32 kernel objects to protect multithreaded access to other shared resources.

Example of a Simple Thread

The project SIMPTHRD.DPR is a multithreaded version of the example presented earlier. Unlike the project NOTHREAD, this project counts using a second thread. In both examples, the application performs simulated work by counting to 5000 and updating the user on its progress as shown in Figure 15-4.

In this version, the user interface remains fully responsive. You can move the form around, close it, and even press the button to cancel the operation. Furthermore, once you press the Start button, the label caption is updated visibly. If this were a more

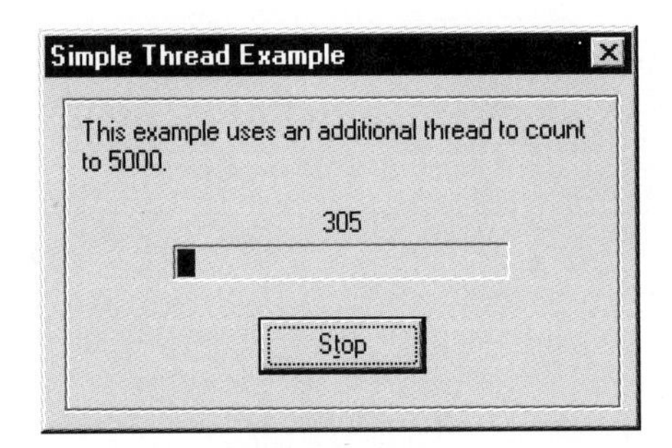

Figure 15-4. *The running SIMPTHRD.DPR project*

complex application, you could also interact with other parts of the form to work on different tasks. The following is the listing of the project source code:

```
program Simpthrd;

uses
  Forms,
  simthdu1 in 'simthdu1.pas' {CountForm},
  simthdu2 in 'simthdu2.pas';

{$R *.RES}

begin
  Application.CreateForm(TCountForm, CountForm);
  Application.Run;
end.
```

The following is the code for SIMTHDU1.PAS, the unit associated with the main form. If you compare this code to the unit for the NOTHREAD project, you will notice that the code for the lengthy operation (the loop) has been replaced by code to create a new thread, CountThread. CountThread performs all the work of counting and updating the visual controls with the progress. CountThread is a variable of class TSimpleThread stored in a global variable so that it can be freed when the user cancels the operation or when the thread's work is completed.

```
unit simthdu1;

interface

uses
  Windows, Messages, SysUtils, Classes, Graphics, Controls, Forms, Dialogs,
  StdCtrls, Menus, ExtCtrls, ComCtrls;

type
  TCountForm = class(TForm)
    Panel1: TPanel;
    StartButton: TButton;
    Label1: TLabel;
    ProgressBar1: TProgressBar;
    Counter: TLabel;
    procedure StartButtonClick(Sender: TObject);
  private
    { Private declarations }
  public
    { Public declarations }
  end;
```

```
var
  CountForm: TCountForm;

implementation

uses Simthdu2;

var
  CountThread : TSimpleThread;

{$R *.DFM}

procedure TCountForm.StartButtonClick(Sender: TObject);
begin
  with Sender as TButton do
    if Caption = '&Start' then
    begin
      Caption := 'S&top';
      ProgressBar1.Position := 0;
      Counter.Caption := '0';

      if CountThread <> nil then {free any previous instance of
CountThread}
        CountThread.Free;

      CountThread := TSimpleThread.Create(False)

    end
    else
    begin

      CountThread.Free;
      CountThread := nil;

      Caption := '&Start';
      ProgressBar1.Position := 0;
      Counter.Caption := '0';
    end;
end;

end.
```

The real work is done by the thread class, TSimpleThread, that is declared in the unit SIMTHDU2.PAS:

```
unit simthdu2;

interface
```

```
uses
  Classes, SimThdu1, dialogs;

type
  TSimpleThread = class(TThread)
  private
    { Private declarations }
    i: Integer;

    procedure UpdateCounts;
    procedure ResetStartButton;
  protected
    procedure Execute; override;
  end;

implementation

uses sysutils, forms, windows, messages;

{ TSimpleThread }

procedure TSimpleThread.UpdateCounts;
begin
  CountForm.Counter.Caption := IntToStr(i);
  CountForm.ProgressBar1.Position := i;
end;

procedure TSimpleThread.ResetStartButton;
begin
  CountForm.StartButton.Caption := '&Start';
end;

procedure TSimpleThread.Execute;
begin
  i:= 0;

  while i <= 5000 do
  begin
    if not Terminated then
      Synchronize(UpdateCounts) // Update the progress bar
    else
      Exit; // User pressed Stop, Exit immediately
    Inc(i);
  end;

  Synchronize(ResetStartButton);
end;

end.
```

The new thread class is named TSimpleThread, and it is derived from the base TThread class. TSimpleThread has a private variable, *i*, that stores the counter for the loop. It also has two private methods, UpdateCounts and ResetStartButton, that will be called by Sychronize since these methods work with components. UpdateCounts reads the value of *i* and then updates the progress bar (ProgressBar1) and the label (Counter). ResetStartButton simply resets the button's caption to display "Start."

The while loop increments the value of *i* until it reaches 5000. Inside the loop, the code also checks to see if the thread's Terminated property is True. If so, it immediately returns out of Execute; otherwise, UpdateCounts is called by Synchronize. When the loop terminates, ResetStartButton is called by Synchronize, and then the Execute method ends.

This example shows how easy it is to adapt a single threaded application and convert it into a multithreaded version.

Suspending and Resuming Threads

The TThread class provides the Suspend and Resume methods to suspend and resume execution of a thread. When a thread is suspended, it is idle and no CPU cycles are given to it. To suspend a thread, just call the TThread object's Suspend method from another thread (primary or otherwise). A thread can even suspend itself by calling its own Suspend method. However, you should not do this unless you expect another thread to reawaken the suspended thread. To resume execution, just call the TThread's Resume method.

Setting Thread Priority

The TThread class defines the Priority property so that you can dynamically change the *priority* of a thread. A thread's priority determines when and how often it is scheduled for execution by the operating system. By setting one thread's priority higher than another, you give it more CPU time. A thread's priority level ranges from 0 to 31, with 31 being the highest level. By default, a newly created thread adopts the same priority level as its parent process.

How Windows Schedules Thread Execution

The system's thread scheduler schedules time slices to threads in a round-robin fashion based on the thread's priorities, skipping over all suspended threads. It starts with the threads with the highest priority and schedules each a time slice. The scheduler continues until none of these highest priority threads needs the CPU, perhaps because some have suspended and others are not doing any work. Next, the scheduler works its way down to the threads at the next highest level of priority and gives them all time slices. This continues until the lowest priority threads get their share of the CPU, or until a higher priority thread needs to execute. If the latter case occurs, the lower priority thread is preempted and execution is passed to the higher priority thread.

Setting a Thread's Priority

You use the TThread's Priority property to set the priority level for a thread. A thread's priority is set relative to the priority of its process. The VCL defines seven priority levels that you can use to set the thread's relative priority. They are part of the TThreadPriority enumerated type. The five main priority levels are: tpLowest, tpLower, tpNormal, tpHigher, and tpHighest. A thread with a relative priority level of tpNormal has a priority level equal to its process. With priority levels of tpHigher and tpHighest, the thread's relative priority is 1 higher and 2 higher than its process, respectively. With priority levels of tpLowest and tpLower, the thread's relative priority is 2 lower and 1 lower than its process.

There are two special priority levels: tpIdle and tpTimeCritical. If a thread's priority is tpIdle, its priority is always set to 1, unless its process is 24 or higher (real time). In this case, the thread's priority level is set to 16. If the thread's priority is tpTimeCritical, its priority is always set to 15, unless its process is 24 or higher. In this case, the thread's priority is set to 31.

Starting a Thread with a Desired Priority

To start a thread's execution with a specified relative priority, you must create it in a suspended state. You then set the TThread's Priority to one of the TThreadPriority values. Afterwards, you can call the Resume method to begin execution of the thread. You cannot specify a priority when creating the thread because Windows does not allow you to do so. The following code segment shows how to set a Thread's Priority to the TThreadPriority value tpIdle:

```
MyThread := TWorkThread.Create(True);
MyThread.Priority := tpIdle;
MyThread.Resume;
```

Example of Setting a Thread's Priority

The project PRIORITY.DPR illustrates how to start new threads with a specified priority and how to dynamically change the priority as the thread is running. In the example shown in Figure 15-5, there are three glasses. Each glass has its own thread that is responsible for filling its glass with liquid. When the Start button is pressed, each thread begins filling a glass, until one of the glasses is filled. The priority for each thread is controlled by a progress bar and can be set to one of the relative priority levels. By controlling the priority, you can influence which glass is filled first.

The following is the project source:

```
program Priority;

uses
  Forms,
  prioriu1 in 'prioriu1.pas' {MainForm},
  prioriu2 in 'prioriu2.pas';{TFillGlass thread}
```

```
{$R *.RES}

begin
  Application.CreateForm(TMainForm, MainForm);
  Application.Run;
end.
```

The liquid and glasses are actually implemented by colored Shape and Panel components, respectively. These objects are defined in unit PRIORIU1.PAS, which is the unit for the form MainForm. This unit also supplies several important methods and event handlers: SetWinner, InitGlasses, StartButtonClick, and GlassTrackBarChange. There are also some important properties: WinningGlass and the FillGlassThread*x* thread variables ($x = 1,2,3$).

When the user clicks on the Start button, StartButtonClick is executed. This method first disables the button so that it cannot be pressed while the "race" is on. It then calls InitGlasses to "empty" the glasses (leaving just a little liquid for show). Next, it creates the three threads in a suspended state so that each can be started with the relative priority specified by each progress bar. It sets the priorities by directly calling the GlassTrackBarChange event handler for each of the progress bars. Finally, each thread is started by calling its Resume method.

The GlassTrackBarChange method takes care of setting the Priority of each thread. Each track bar has a valid range of Positions from –2 to 2. When you change the Position, the method converts this value into a TThreadPriority and assigns it to the thread's Priority.

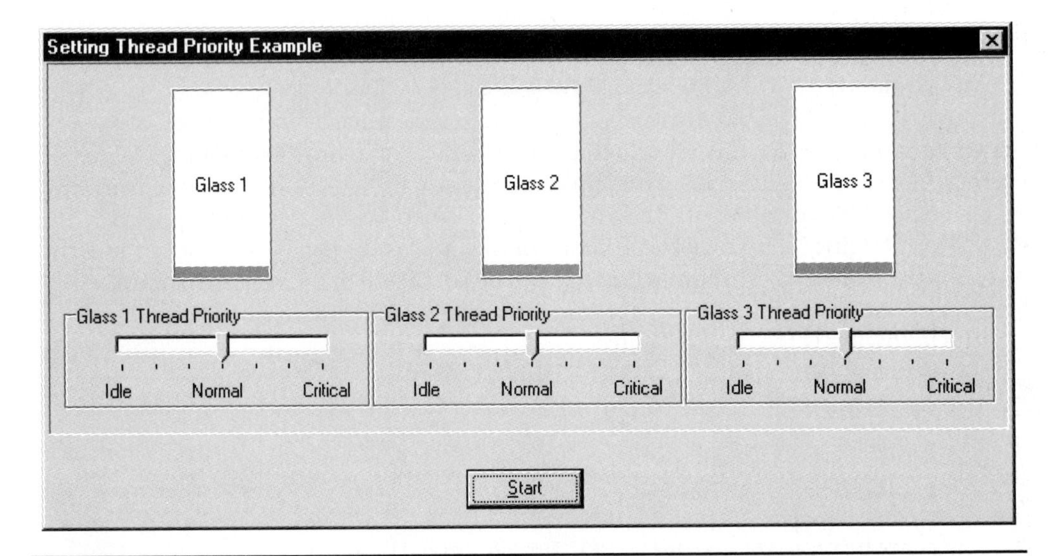

Figure 15-5. *The Setting Thread Priority example, found in project PRIORITY.DPR*

The last important method is SetWinner. SetWinner is a property procedure that is executed when the WinningGlass property is written to. The threads are numbered from 1 to 3. The winning thread assigns its number to the WinningGlass property when it is finished filling the glass. This triggers SetWinner, which displays a dialog announcing the winner. SetWinner also frees the threads and re-enables the Start button. The following is the code for the PRIORIU1.PAS unit:

```
unit prioriu1;

interface

uses
  Windows, Messages, SysUtils, Classes, Graphics, Controls, Forms, Dialogs,
  StdCtrls, Buttons, ExtCtrls, ComCtrls, Prioriu2;

type
  TMainForm = class(TForm)
    Panel1: TPanel;
    GroupBox1: TGroupBox;
    Label1: TLabel;
    Label2: TLabel;
    Label3: TLabel;
    GlassTrackBar1: TTrackBar;
    Glass1: TPanel;
    Liquid1: TShape;
    GroupBox2: TGroupBox;
    Label4: TLabel;
    Label5: TLabel;
    Label6: TLabel;
    GlassTrackBar2: TTrackBar;
    Glass2: TPanel;
    Liquid2: TShape;
    StartButton: TButton;
    GroupBox3: TGroupBox;
    Label7: TLabel;
    Label8: TLabel;
    Label9: TLabel;
    GlassTrackBar3: TTrackBar;
    Glass3: TPanel;
    Liquid3: TShape;
    procedure StartButtonClick(Sender: TObject);
    procedure GlassTrackBar1Change(Sender: TObject);
    procedure GlassTrackBar2Change(Sender: TObject);
    procedure GlassTrackBar3Change(Sender: TObject);
  private
    { Private declarations }
    FWinningGlass: Integer;

    procedure InitGlasses;
```

```
    procedure SetWinner(Winner: Integer);

  public
    { Public declarations }
    FillGlassThread1 : TFillGlass;
    FillGlassThread2 : TFillGlass;
    FillGlassThread3 : TFillGlass;

    property  WinningGlass: Integer read FWinningGlass write SetWinner;

  end;

var
  MainForm: TMainForm;

implementation

{$R *.DFM}


procedure TMainForm.SetWinner(Winner: Integer);
begin

  // announce the winner
  FWinningGlass := Winner;
  MessageDlg('Glass '+ IntToStr(FWinningGlass) +
    ' was filled first',
    mtInformation, [mbOk], 0);

  // reset StartButton
  StartButton.Enabled := True;

  // destroy threads
  FillGlassThread1.Free;
  FillGlassThread2.Free;
  FillGlassThread3.Free;
end;

procedure TMainForm.InitGlasses;
begin

  FWinningGlass := 0;
  Liquid1.Height := 8;
  Liquid1.Top := 112;
  Liquid2.Height := 8;
  Liquid2.Top := 112;
  Liquid3.Height := 8;
  Liquid3.Top := 112;
end;
```

```
procedure TMainForm.StartButtonClick(Sender: TObject);

begin

  (Sender as TButton).Enabled := False;
  // disable the Start button

  InitGlasses;

  FillGlassThread1 := TFillGlass.Create(True);
  FillGlassThread1.FLiquid := Liquid1;
  // tell thread where to fill
  FillGlassThread1.FGlassNo := 1;

  FillGlassThread2 := TFillGlass.Create(True);
  FillGlassThread2.FLiquid := Liquid2;
  // tell thread where to fill
  FillGlassThread2.FGlassNo := 2;

  FillGlassThread3 := TFillGlass.Create(True);
  FillGlassThread3.FLiquid := Liquid3;
  // tell thread where to fill
  FillGlassThread3.FGlassNo := 3;

  // Start each thread with priority set by its trackbar.
  GlassTrackBar1Change(GlassTrackBar1);
  GlassTrackBar2Change(GlassTrackBar2);
  GlassTrackBar3Change(GlassTrackBar3);

  FillGlassThread1.Resume;
  FillGlassThread2.Resume;
  FillGlassThread3.Resume;

end;

procedure TMainForm.GlassTrackBar1Change(Sender: TObject);
begin
  if FillGlassThread1 <> nil then
    FillGlassThread1.Priority :=
      TThreadPriority((Sender as TTrackBar).Position + 3);
  { TThreadPriority is an enumerated type
  that maps to the priority levels}
end;

procedure TMainForm.GlassTrackBar2Change(Sender: TObject);
begin
  if FillGlassThread2 <> nil then
    FillGlassThread2.Priority :=
```

```
      TThreadPriority((Sender as TTrackBar).Position + 3);
  end;

procedure TMainForm.GlassTrackBar3Change(Sender: TObject);
begin
  if FillGlassThread3 <> nil then
    FillGlassThread3.Priority :=
      TThreadPriority((Sender as TTrackBar).Position + 3);
end;
end.
```

The class for the threads, TFillGlass, is defined in PRIORIU2.PAS. This class defines some member variables, FNewHeight, FNewTop, and FGlassNo. FNewHeight and FNewTop are used in drawing the dimensions of the liquid as it is filling the glass. FGlassNo identifies the number of the glass that the thread is responsible for filling. The class also has a property that stores a reference to the Shape component, the liquid, the thread is responsible for drawing. The class also defines Fill, the method responsible for the actual drawing. Since this method works with the VCL, it is called by Synchronize.

The Execute method fills the glass by changing the Top and Height properties of the Shape component representing the liquid. To minimize the code required in the Synchronize call, Execute doesn't actually write to the Top and Height properties. It changes the values of the FNewTop and FNewHeight variables that Fill uses to draw the TShape. If this was not done, most of the code would reside inside Fill, leaving little for the thread to perform in the background.

Finally, when the first thread finishes, it sets the WinningGlass property to its glass number, stored in FGlassNo. This causes the primary thread to display the winner and conclude that the race is over. The following is the code for PRIORIU2.PAS:

```
unit prioriu2;

interface

uses
  Classes, ExtCtrls;

type
  TFillGlass = class(TThread)
  private
    { Private declarations }
  protected
    procedure Fill;
    procedure Execute; override;
  public
    FLiquid: TShape;
    FNewHeight : Integer;
```

```
    FNewTop : Integer;
    FGlassNo : Integer;
  end;

implementation

uses Windows, Prioriu1;

procedure TFillGlass.Fill;
begin
  FLiquid.SetBounds(2,FNewTop,62,FNewHeight);
end;

procedure TFillGlass.Execute;
var
  i: Integer;
begin

  // Initialize internal height and top variables
  FNewHeight := 8;
  FNewTop := 112;

  while (FNewHeight < 120) do
  // 120 is the Height property of the glass - 1
  begin

    // Resize "liquid"
    Inc(FNewHeight);
    Dec(FNewTop);
    {Instruct the OS to give CPU to next thread
    regardless of any remaining time slice.
    This is need because the threads finish too quickly.}
    Sleep(0);

    if not Terminated then
      Synchronize(Fill)
    else
      Exit;

    if MainForm.WinningGlass <> 0 then
      Exit;
  end; // while (FNewHeight < 120)

  MainForm.WinningGlass := FGlassNo;
end;

end.
```

Multithreading Using Child Forms and Worker Threads

In an MDI (Multiple Document Interface) application, or in an application that displays a form for each task, multithreading may be appropriate. With multithreading, you can let each form have its own thread. This way the user can initiate a background task in one form, and then continue to interact with other forms while the background work is progressing. In such a scenario, the primary thread handles all the work of managing the user interface and responding to window messages. Each time the user initiates a new task, the primary thread creates a new form and gives it its own "worker" thread.

Multithreading Example Using Child Forms

This next example illustrates how you can open new forms, each owning its own worker thread. Again, the lengthy task in this example is represented by iterating through a long loop and updating a track bar to show the progress. When you run the example in project WORKR.PAS, the Worker Thread Examples form appears. Each time you press the New Thread button on this form, a new child form is created with its own thread and immediately begins its work. Each new form has a unique caption indicating which worker it is. Also, each form contains a Suspend/Resume button letting you suspend and resume the thread. Finally, if you close the form before the thread is finished, the form closes and the thread terminates. Figure 15-6 depicts the main form surrounded by several working forms.

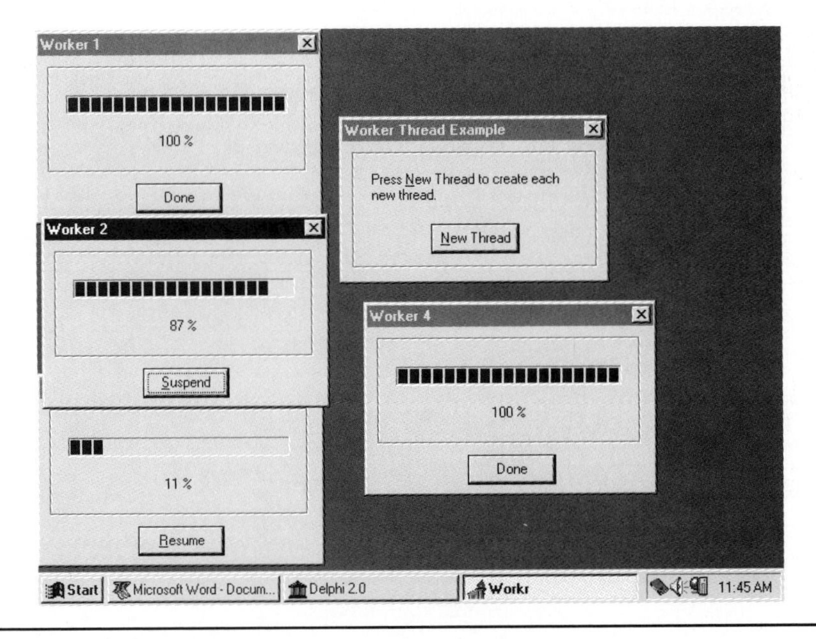

Figure 15-6. *The Main form and several worker forms*

The following is the project file code for WORKR.DPR:

```
program Workr;

uses
  Forms,
  workru1 in 'workru1.pas' {LaunchForm},
  workru2 in 'workru2.pas' {MDIChild},
  workru3 in 'workru3.pas';{WorkerThread}

{$R *.RES}

begin
  Application.CreateForm(TLaunchForm, LaunchForm);
  Application.Run;
end.
```

The main form class, TLaunchForm, is defined in WORKRU1.PAS. This form defines a thread counter, Workers, that is incremented and displayed in the caption of each new worker form. Workers is initially set to 0 in the form's FormCreate method. The New Thread button has a method, NewThreadButtonClick, that creates a new form of type TWorkerForm. The NewThreadButtonClick method then calls its StartWorking method to initiate the work. The following is the source code for WORKU1.PAS:

```
unit workru1;

interface

uses
  Windows, Messages, SysUtils, Classes, Graphics, Controls,
  Forms, Dialogs, StdCtrls, Buttons, ExtCtrls;

type
  TLaunchForm = class(TForm)
    Panel1: TPanel;
    NewThreadButton: TButton;
    Label1: TLabel;
    procedure NewThreadButtonClick(Sender: TObject);
    procedure FormCreate(Sender: TObject);
  private
    { Private declarations }
  public
    { Public declarations }
    Workers: Integer;
  end;

var
```

```
  LaunchForm: TLaunchForm;


implementation

uses Workru2;

{$R *.DFM}

procedure TLaunchForm.NewThreadButtonClick(Sender: TObject);
begin
  with TWorkerForm.Create(Self) do
  begin
    try
      Inc(Workers);
      Caption := 'Worker ' + IntToStr(Workers);
      Show;
      StartWorking;
    except
      Free;
    end;
  end;
end;

procedure TLaunchForm.FormCreate(Sender: TObject);
begin
  Workers := 0;
end;

end.
```

The TWorkerForm class is defined in WORKRU2.PAS. The form has a member variable, WorkerThread, that belongs to the class TWorkerThread (declared in WORKRU3.PAS). There are two important event handlers: FormCreate and FormClose. The FormCreate method initializes the Position of the progress bar to 0 when the form is created. The FormClose method frees the thread when the form is closed.

The form also has a method, StartWorking, that is called to create its worker thread. The thread is started in a suspended state so that the form can pass a reference to itself to the thread, and to give the thread an initial priority of tpIdle. This method also passes to the thread a reference to Self that the thread uses to determine which form contains the progress bar to update.

When you click on the Suspend/Resume button, WorkerButtonClick is executed. This method suspends and resumes the thread by calling its Suspend and Resume methods. The following is the code for WORKRU2.PAS:

```
unit workru2;

interface

uses
  Windows, Messages, SysUtils, Classes, Graphics, Controls, Forms, Dialogs,
  StdCtrls, ExtCtrls, ComCtrls, Workru3;

type
  TWorkerForm = class(TForm)
    Panel1: TPanel;
    WorkerButton: TButton;
    WorkProgressBar: TProgressBar;
    WorkProgressLabel: TLabel;
    procedure FormCreate(Sender: TObject);
    procedure FormClose(Sender: TObject; var Action: TCloseAction);
    procedure WorkerButtonClick(Sender: TObject);
  private
    { Private declarations }
  protected
    FWorkerThread : TWorkerThread;
  public
    { Public declarations }
    procedure StartWorking;
  end;

var
  WorkerForm: TWorkerForm;

implementation

{$R *.DFM}

procedure TWorkerForm.StartWorking;
begin
  FWorkerThread := TWorkerThread.Create(True);
  with FWorkerThread do
  begin
    OwnerForm := Self;
    Priority := tpIdle;
    {Setting the thread to tpIdel makes the primary thread
     more responsive. Note that the OS can also dynamically
     boost the main thread if the user is interacting with it.}
    Resume;
  end;
end;

procedure TWorkerForm.FormCreate(Sender: TObject);
```

```
begin
  WorkProgressBar.Position := 0;
end;

procedure TWorkerForm.FormClose(Sender: TObject; var Action: TCloseAction);
begin
{If the thread is currently suspended, a call to
FWorkerThread.Free would not terminate the thread,
free FWorkerThread. This would leave the suspended
thread orphaned from FWorkerThread and result in
the loss of a tiny amount of resources. To prevent
this, first ensure that the thread is not suspended.}
  if FWorkerThread.Suspended then
    FWorkerThread.Resume;
  //Now safe to free FWorkerThread.
  FWorkerThread.Free;
end;

procedure TWorkerForm.WorkerButtonClick(Sender: TObject);
begin
  with (Sender as TButton) do
  begin
    if Caption = '&Suspend' then
    begin
      FWorkerThread.Suspend;
      Caption := '&Resume';
    end
    else
      if Caption = '&Resume' then
      begin
        FWorkerThread.Resume;
        Caption := '&Suspend';
      end
      else
        //Caption must be equal to &Done
        Close;
  end;
end;

end.
```

TWorkerThread is defined in WORKRU3.PAS. TWorkerThread stores a Boolean variable, MoreWork, that indicates whether there is more work to perform. Also, a reference to the owning form is stored in FOwnerForm.

There are two methods: Execute and UpdateDisplay. Execute pretends to do work by calling Sleep to put the thread to sleep for 100 milliseconds (1/10th of a second). Execute then executes UpdateDisplay in a call to Synchronize. UpdateDisplay updates the progress bar and sets the MoreWork Boolean if the progress bar is completely filled. The following is the code for WORKRU3.PAS:

```
unit workru3;

interface

uses
  Classes, Forms;

type
  TWorkerThread = class(TThread)
  private
    { Private declarations }
    MoreWork: Boolean;
    FOwnerForm: TForm;
  protected
    procedure Execute; override;
  public
    property OwnerForm: TForm read FOwnerForm write FOwnerForm;
    procedure UpdateDisplay;
  end;

implementation

uses Workru2, Windows, SysUtils;

{ TWorkerThread }


procedure TWorkerThread.UpdateDisplay;
begin
  with (FOwnerForm as TWorkerForm) do
  begin
    with WorkProgressBar do
      if Position < Max then
      begin
        Position := Position + 1;
        WorkProgressLabel.Caption := IntToStr(Position)+' %';
        if Position = Max then
        begin
          MoreWork := False;
          WorkerButton.Caption := 'Done';
        end;
      end;
  end;
end;

procedure TWorkerThread.Execute;
```

```
begin
  //Initialize MoreWork variable.
  MoreWork := True;
  while MoreWork do
  begin
    {Do some work here. In this example we will
    simulate work by putting thread to sleep 100 ms.}
    Sleep(100);

    if not Terminated then
      Synchronize(UpdateDisplay)
    else
      Exit;
  end;
end;

end.
```

In the thread in this example, there is more work being performed in UpdateDisplay than in Execute. In the projects in which you employ this technique, you will want to assign a very useful task to the thread.

General Recommendations

Here are some general recommendations to follow when using the TThread class:

- If you access any of the properties or methods of a VCL component from inside your thread, make sure to use the Synchronize facility to execute this code. If you don't, you are not working with the VCL in a thread-safe manner and may trigger an access violation.
- If your TThread's Execute implementation uses a loop to perform your background task, be sure that the loop contains a condition that terminates the loop when the task is completed. Also, be sure to include code that tests the value of the Terminated property and exits the Execute method if the property is True. This lets you use the TThread's Terminate method to terminate the thread from the primary thread or another thread.
- Do not use the TerminateThread Win32 API function to terminate a thread that is created using a Thread object. This immediately terminates the thread without allowing you to execute any post-termination code that cleans up resources. The Thread object, also, is unaware that the thread has terminated. This may cause your code to act in unexpected ways. TerminateThread should only be used as a last resort to terminate a runaway thread.

- Generally, in a VCL-based application, additional threads do not create their own forms. Instead, new forms may create their own threads. Recall that if a thread needs to create its own form, it must do so in a call to Synchronize. This is because forms are part of the VCL. Synchronize creates the form using the primary thread.
- Any access to using Tables and Queries from an additional thread must be made from a Session other than that used by the primary thread. Doing so permits the BDE's table and record locking mechanisms to control concurrency.

Conclusion

The TThread class allows you to add powerful multithreading capability to your applications by:

- encapsulating the threading process
- providing a facility to work with the VCL in a thread-safe manner
- offering a way to associate local data with each thread

The next chapter, Chapter 16, goes into detail on how to protect shared resources when using multithreading and how to prevent various fatal and, often, subtle problems that may arise. You may also want to refer to the references listed at the end of Chapter 14.

Chapter Sixteen

Thread Synchronization in Delphi 2

The code for the examples presented in this chapter can be found in the \CODE\CH16 subdirectory on the CD-ROM that accompanies this book. Please refer to Appendix A for information on using the code files for this chapter.

Multithreading is a welcome feature to Win32 (Windows 95 and Windows NT) applications, but it can add complexity and unique problems of its own. Although you can use additional threads to add power and flexibility to an application, you must be prepared to think with a new mindset. Whenever an application has more than one thread accessing a shared resource, bugs that are often subtle and hard to track down can be introduced into the program. Even worse, these types of bugs may be difficult to repeat and may appear at seemingly random occasions.

This chapter discusses *synchronization*, a way to coordinate threads so that you can use multithreading effectively to create robust, defect-free applications. In particular, examples using two synchronization objects, critical sections and mutexes, are covered. Two other synchronization objects, semaphores and events, are discussed briefly, but an in-depth coverage of these is left to an advanced Win32 reference.

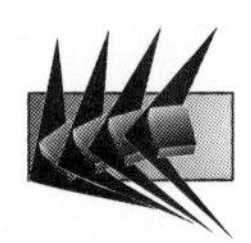

NOTE: *In Chapter 15 you learned about the TThread class' Synchronize method, which is used only to protect access to the VCL (visual component library). The synchronization discussed in this chapter is a more general approach and is used to access resources outside of the VCL such as global variables.*

Protecting Resources Using Synchronization

Synchronization is a technique to coordinate the execution of threads. Frequently it is used to protect access to shared resources, such as global data or files, or to signal one or more other threads that an event is completed. For example, whenever an application has two or more threads accessing a nonstatic global variable, it is an immediate candidate for using synchronization. In a multithreaded application without synchronization, it is possible for one thread to be preempted by a second thread while the first is in the middle of updating a variable. This second thread might then read the value of the variable and obtain data that is inconsistent or invalid.

This problem is compounded when there are multiple threads trying to simultaneously read or write to the same data. In fact, there is a situation called a *race* condition, in which two or more threads race for control of a variable. The thread that gets preempted first is the loser. Since this depends on the current system state, such a problem is often so subtle that it surfaces unexpectedly when not planned against. Fortunately, several synchronization techniques are available to protect your application.

To implement synchronization in a Delphi 2 program, you use your Thread object with some Win32 API functions and synchronization objects. Synchronization objects include critical sections, events, processes, mutexes, and semaphores. These objects act like flags and exist in one of two states: signaled or unsignaled. When an object is *signaled,* it means that it is available. When an object is *unsignaled,* it is unavailable.

To protect a resource so that only one thread can have access at a time, you create a synchronization object in the beginning of your program. When one thread needs access to the resource, it sets the object to the unsignaled state and then begins working with the resource. When the thread is finished, it resets the object to the signaled state, thereby signaling the object, and then continues execution. While the synchronization object is unsignaled, no other thread can access the resource. If another thread attempts to access that resource while the object is unsignaled, this thread is put on hold until the object becomes available again.

The synchronization objects discussed in this chapter are critical sections, mutexes, semaphores, and events:

- *Critical sections* are used within a single process to protect access to shared resources.
- *Mutexes* are like critical sections, but they also work across processes.
- *Semaphores* are used to limit concurrent access of a resource to a certain number of threads.
- *Events* are used to signal the completion of an event.

Using Critical Sections

One of the simplest ways to add synchronization to a multithreaded application is to create and use a critical section object with Win32 API functions. A critical section lets you ensure that only one thread can access a shared resource at a time. To program a critical section, you place a call to enter the critical section at the start of the code that is accessing the shared resource. After the last line that accesses the shared resource, you place a call to leave the critical section.

You can think of using a critical section as "marking" the code you're trying to protect. If one thread has the critical section active, any other thread that attempts to enter the critical section will be blocked and "put to sleep" by the operating system. Only when the critical section is available again will the second thread be "awakened" and allowed to enter the critical section.

This might be easier to visualize if you think of a critical section as a wall around your code. The wall has a door with a single key that hangs on a hook next to the door. If the key is available when a thread approaches, it enters, shuts the door, and begins working with the resource. Other threads that arrive cannot get in until the first thread exits and replaces the key on the hook.

Declaring and Initializing a Critical Section

For each critical section you have, you must declare a critical section variable, which is usually implemented as a global variable. You can have as many critical section variables as you need, but you should not reuse the same variable for different areas in your code. The following code segment shows a typical declaration for a critical section object:

```
var
 CritSect1: TRTLCriticalSection;
```

After declaring a critical section object, but before using it, you must initialize the object in a call to InitializeCriticalSection. You should do this before any additional threads are created; otherwise, a thread might enter a critical section before it has been initialized. One place you may want to perform the initialization is in the form's OnCreate method as follows:

```
procedure TForm1.FormCreate(Sender: TObject);
begin
 InitializeCriticalSection(CritSect1);
end;
```

You must make a call to InitializeCriticalSection for each critical section variable you intend to use.

Using a Critical Section

At the start of the code that you want to protect, place a call to EnterCriticalSection, passing it a critical section object as an argument. When a thread executes this function, the operating system first checks to see if any other thread is in the critical section. If not, this thread *owns* the critical section object and is allowed to proceed. If another thread attempts to enter the same critical section, the operating system determines that it is already owned by the first thread and suspends the second thread. The second thread remains suspended until the first thread releases the critical section object. As new threads arrive, they are queued up and are put to sleep. These waiting threads receive no CPU (central processing unit) time as long as the critical section object is owned by a thread.

When the code is no longer accessing the shared resource, you can place a call to LeaveCriticalSection, again passing it the critical section object as an argument. After this function is executed, the critical section object is released. The next thread that is waiting for the critical section object is resumed and given ownership.

Deleting a Critical Section

When you no longer need to use a critical section object, you should delete it so that the operating system can deallocate any resources associated with it. You delete a critical section object by passing it as an argument in a call to DeleteCriticalSection. The obvious place to do this is in the form's OnClose method as shown here:

```
procedure TForm1.FormClose(Sender: TObject; var Action: TCloseAction);
begin
 DeleteCriticalSection(CritSect);
end;
```

NOTE: The TRTLCriticalSection object and the EnterCriticalSection, LeaveCriticalSection, and DeleteCriticalSection procedures are declared in the Windows unit. To use these you must have this unit listed in your unit's uses clause.

A Simple Counter Example

The following three projects show you the effects of using multithreading in an application with and without synchronization. Each project is a variation of the same example. Common to all these example projects is a form with a list box and a button on it. The form has a routine that increments a global integer variable 100 times. Each time it increments the global variable, the routine also adds the value of the variable as an entry in the list box. When you press the button, the code will call the routine four times. The list box lets you visualize the effects of the program on the shared resource, that is, the global variable, when you run it.

A Single Threaded Version of the Example

The first example project, CSDEMO1.DPR, is a single threaded version that does not create any additional threads, so no synchronization is needed. It shows you what the correct behavior of the program is since only one thread (that is, the *only* thread) will be reading and writing the variable at any one time. (This thread belongs to the process.) The routine that increments the global variable is called IncCount100Times. When you press the button, this procedure is executed four times. When you do this, the list box is filled with 400 entries sequentially numbered from 1 to 400. If you run this project, and then click the Start button, the screen will look like that shown in Figure 16-1.

```
program CSDEMO1;

uses
  Forms,
  CSEXu1 in 'CSDEMO1U.pas' {CounterForm};

{$R *.RES}

begin
  Application.CreateForm(TCounterForm, CounterForm);
  Application.Run;
end.
```

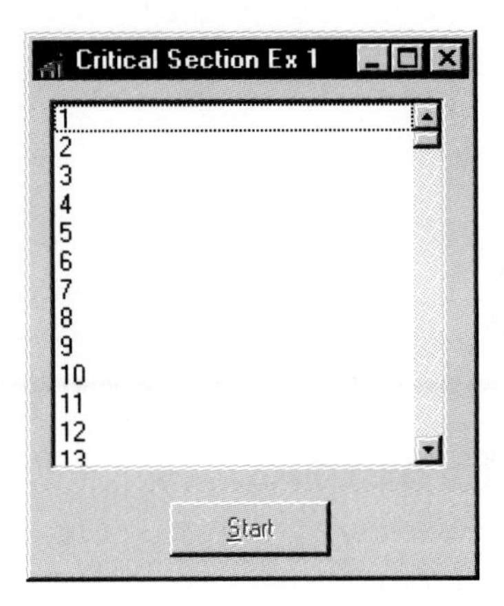

Figure 16-1. *Main form for CSDEMO1.DPR*

The following is the code for the form's unit, CSDEMO1U.PAS:

```
unit CSDEMO1U;

interface

uses
  Windows, Messages, SysUtils, Classes, Graphics, Controls, Forms, Dialogs,
  StdCtrls;

type
  TCounterForm = class(TForm)
    StartButton: TButton;
    ListBox1: TListBox;
    procedure StartButtonClick(Sender: TObject);
  private
    { Private declarations }
  public
    { Public declarations }
  end;

procedure IncCount100Times;

var
  CounterForm: TCounterForm;
  Counter: Integer;
```

```
implementation

{$R *.DFM}

procedure IncCount100Times;
var
  i: Integer;
begin

  for i:= 1 to 100 do
  begin
    Counter := Counter + 1;
    CounterForm.ListBox1.Items.Add( IntToStr(Counter) );
  end;

end;

procedure TCounterForm.StartButtonClick(Sender: TObject);
begin
  (Sender as TButton).Enabled := False;

  Counter := 0;

  IncCount100Times;
  IncCount100Times;
  IncCount100Times;
  IncCount100Times;
end;

end.
```

Notice that the IncCount100Times method has a loop that steps from 1 to 100. Each time it iterates through the loop, the global variable Counter is incremented once and is added to the list box ListBox1 as a string. The StartButtonClick event handler first disables the button by setting its Enabled property to False and then executes IncCount100Times four times.

A Multithreaded Example Without Using Synchronization

This next example, CSDEMO2.DPR, introduces multithreading into the program, but without the protection of synchronization. The following is the project source:

```
program CSDEMO2;

uses
  Forms,
```

```
  CSDEMO2u in 'CSDEMO2u.pas' {CounterForm},
  CSDEMO22 in 'CSDEMO22.pas';{CountThread}

{$R *.RES}

begin
  Application.CreateForm(TCounterForm, CounterForm);
  Application.Run;
end.
```

The following is the unit for the form, CSDEMO2U. The OnClick event handler for the button creates four thread objects. Since a Boolean false is passed to the Create method for the threads, each thread begins executing immediately. Each thread operates by incrementing the global variable Counter and updating the list box 100 times.

```
unit CSDEMO2u;

interface

uses
  Windows, Messages, SysUtils, Classes, Graphics, Controls, Forms, Dialogs,
  StdCtrls;

type
  TCounterForm = class(TForm)
    StartButton: TButton;
    ListBox1: TListBox;
    procedure StartButtonClick(Sender: TObject);
  private
    { Private declarations }
  public
    { Public declarations }
  end;


var
  CounterForm: TCounterForm;
  Counter: Integer;

implementation

uses CSDEMO22;

{$R *.DFM}

procedure TCounterForm.StartButtonClick(Sender: TObject);
```

```
begin
  (Sender as TButton).Enabled := False;

  Counter := 0;

  TCounterThread.Create(False);
  TCounterThread.Create(False);
  TCounterThread.Create(False);
  TCounterThread.Create(False);
end;

end.
```

The unit CSDEMO22.PAS contains the type definition for the thread. The TCounterThread class contains two methods, Execute and UpdateListBox. Execute is the multithreaded counterpart to IncCounter100Times and contains the loop that iterates 100 times. Each time the loop is executed, the code increments the global variable Counter and then calls UpdateListBox to update the list box. Note that the Synchronize call to UpdateListBox does *not* protect the global variable and is unrelated to the synchronization techniques discussed in this chapter. Recall also that Synchronize is the mechanism TThread uses to protect access to the VCL, as described in Chapter 15.

The following is the code for the CSDEMO22 unit:

```
unit CSDEMO22;

interface

uses
  Classes;

type
  TCounterThread = class(TThread)
  private
    { Private declarations }
  protected
    procedure UpdateListBox;

    procedure Execute; override;
  end;

implementation

uses CSDemo2U, SysUtils, Windows;

{ TCounterThread }
```

```
procedure TCounterThread.UpdateListBox;
begin
  CounterForm.ListBox1.Items.Add( FloatToStr(Counter) );
end;

procedure TCounterThread.Execute;
var
  i: Integer;
begin
  for i:= 1 to 100 do
  begin
    Counter := Counter + 1 ;

    if not Terminated then
      Synchronize(UpdateListBox)
    else
      Exit;
  end;
end;

end.
```

Figure 16-2 shows you what happens when you run this form and then click the Start button. In this figure, the list box has been scrolled to reveal a problem with the counting. Notice that the entry 233 appears twice and 234 is missing altogether. (Exactly which numbers are repeated and which are skipped may differ every time this project is executed.) This occurs because the threads are not synchronized. In this case, while one thread was in the middle of updating and displaying the variable Count, others were also reading or writing it.

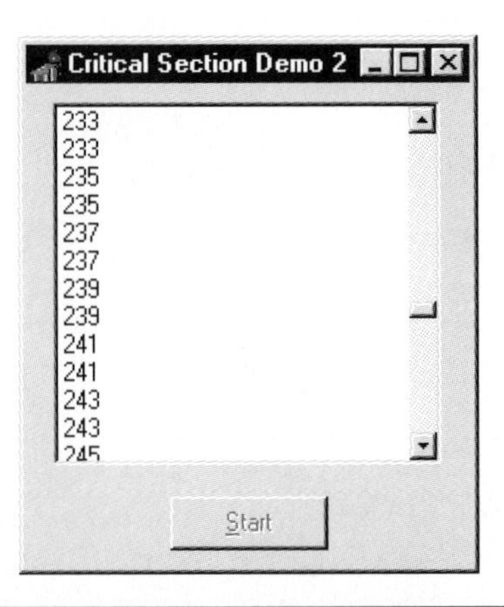

Figure 16-2. *Form for counter example CSDEMO3.DPR*

This application is wide open to problems because each thread may compete for access to the shared resource, the variable Counter. For example, suppose that the first thread has just executed the line to increment the counter:

```
Counter := Counter + 1;
```

Counter now has a value of 100. The thread now wants to update the list box with a new entry of 100 and is about to continue to the next section of code to do this:

```
if not Terminated then
 Synchronize(UpdateListBox)
else
 Exit;
```

What happens if the thread is preempted (by the CPU) immediately before this happens? Another thread could increment Counter so that it is now 101. This problem is compounded if CPU time is now given to yet another thread that also increments Counter. By the time the first thread gets a chance to update the list box, the value of Counter is no longer 100, but 101 or higher, throwing off the display order in the list.

A Multithreaded Example Using Synchronization

This last project, CSDEMO3.DPR, shows you how to protect a shared resource using synchronization. This version takes the previous example and adds a critical section object to guarantee that only one thread can access Counter at a time. The example now works properly because the global variable is protected.

```
program CSDEMO3;

uses
  Forms,
  CSDEMO3u in 'CSDEMO3u.pas' {CounterForm},
  CSDEMO32 in 'CSDEMO32.pas';{CountThread}

{$R *.RES}

begin
  Application.CreateForm(TCounterForm, CounterForm);
  Application.Run;
end.
```

The code for the main form, CSDEMO3U.PAS, is identical to CSDEMO2U.PAS except that a critical section object is introduced. This critical section object, CritSect, is of type TRTLCriticalSection. It is declared as a global variable so that the system allocates memory for it when the application is run. The form's OnCreate event handler, FormCreate, takes care of initializing the critical section by calling

InitializeCriticalSection. Before the form is destroyed, FormDestroy calls DeleteCriticalSection to free it. The following is the code for this unit:

```
unit CSDEMO3u;

interface

uses
  Windows, Messages, SysUtils, Classes, Graphics, Controls, Forms, Dialogs,
  StdCtrls;

type
  TCounterForm = class(TForm)
    StartButton: TButton;
    ListBox1: TListBox;
    procedure StartButtonClick(Sender: TObject);
    procedure FormCreate(Sender: TObject);
    procedure FormDestroy(Sender: TObject);
  private
    { Private declarations }
  public
    { Public declarations }
  end;


var
  CounterForm: TCounterForm;
  Counter: Integer;
  CritSect: TRTLCriticalSection;

implementation

uses Counthd;

{$R *.DFM}

procedure TCounterForm.StartButtonClick(Sender: TObject);
begin
  (Sender as TButton).Enabled := False;

  Counter := 0;

  TCounterThread.Create(False);
  TCounterThread.Create(False);
  TCounterThread.Create(False);
  TCounterThread.Create(False);
end;

procedure TCounterForm.FormCreate(Sender: TObject);
```

```
begin
  InitializeCriticalSection(CritSect);
end;

procedure TCounterForm.FormDestroy(Sender: TObject);
begin
  DeleteCriticalSection(CritSect);
end;

end.
```

The critical section is entered inside the Execute method of the thread because this is where Counter is used and needs to be protected. Immediately before Counter is first accessed, a call to EnterCriticalSection is made. (You do not place this call outside of the loop because this will prevent other threads from incrementing the variable until after the loop is finished.) When the use of Counter has been completed, a call to LeaveCriticalSection is made, releasing the critical section object. Notice also that a try-finally resource protection block is used to guarantee that LeaveCriticalSection is executed. This ensures that the critical section is exited even if an exception is generated during it. The following is the source code for the thread unit:

```
unit CSDEMO32;

interface

uses
  Classes;

type
  TCounterThread = class(TThread)
  private
    { Private declarations }
  protected
    procedure UpdateListBox;
    procedure Execute; override;
  end;

implementation

uses CSDemo3u, SysUtils, Windows;

{ TCounterThread }
procedure TCounterThread.UpdateListBox;
begin
  CounterForm.ListBox1.Items.Add( IntToStr(Counter) );
end;
```

```
procedure TCounterThread.Execute;
var
  i: Integer;
begin
  for i:= 1 to 100 do
  begin
    EnterCriticalSection(CritSect);
    try
      Counter := Counter + 1;
      if not Terminated then
        Synchronize(UpdateListBox)
      else
        Exit;
    finally
      LeaveCriticalSection(CritSect);
    end;
  end;
end;

end.
```

Figure 16-3 shows this final example project running. Notice that the use of the critical section prevents the problems associated with the multiple threads.

Coordinating Threads Using WaitForSingleObject

The remaining techniques in this chapter synchronize an application by causing a thread to wait until an indicator announces that it is safe to proceed. The go-ahead

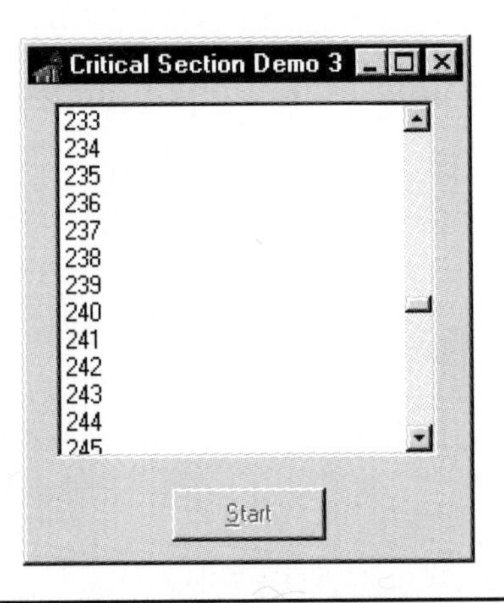

Figure 16-3. *Form for counter example CSDEMO3.DPR*

signal may occur when another thread is finished accessing a shared resource. Alternatively, the signal may result from a change in a state in your system. Consequently, these techniques have value that extend beyond simply the issues of synchronization.

A traditional, single-tasking approach to programming this technique would be to use a global Boolean variable as the indicator. A loop would be programmed to poll the variable so that the thread doesn't proceed until it is okay to do so.

The following code has a thread that performs such an operation. In the loop, ProcessMessages is called so that the application continues to process window messages while looping; otherwise, the application will be unresponsive. When SafeToProceed is set to True (presumably by another thread), this thread leaves the loop and proceeds:

```
while not SafeToProceed do
 Application.ProcessMessages;
```

This approach may work; however, it is very inefficient. While the thread is waiting, it is using up valuable CPU time as it executes the loop. The Win32 API provides an alternative, the WaitForSingleObject function and its variations.

Waiting for an Object to Be Signaled

The WaitForSingleObject function lets you tell a thread to wait until a system object becomes signaled. While the thread is waiting, it is consuming very little CPU time. The system puts the thread in a wait state and reawakens it when the object is signaled or after a specified time-out period. WaitForSingleObject can be used with several objects, including some of the synchronization objects discussed earlier (for example, mutexes, semaphores, and events).

WaitForSingleObject, which is imported by the Windows unit, has the following syntax:

```
WaitForSingleObject(hHandle: THandle;
         dwMilliseconds: DWORD): DWORD; stdcall;
```

To use WaitForSingleObject, you pass it a THandle to an object and a time-out period. To wait indefinitely, you can pass a predefined constant, INFINITE, as a value for the time-out period. WaitForSingleObject returns one of four constants to indicate the results of the call:

- WAIT_TIMEOUT is returned if the object does not become signaled within the time-out period.
- WAIT_OBJECT_0 is returned if the object becomes signaled.
- WAIT_ABANDONED is returned if the object is a mutex and its owning thread terminates before the mutex becomes signaled.

- WAIT_FAILED is returned if the function failed.

If you want to determine the current state of an object, you can pass WaitForSingleObject a time-out value of nil, and then check the return value for WAIT_OBJECT_0.

The following system objects can be used with WaitForSingleObject:

- Change Notifications
- Console Inputs
- Mutexes
- Semaphores
- Events
- Processes
- Threads

You create these objects using an appropriate Win32 API function, such as CreateFile, CreateMutex, CreateProcess, and so forth. Each of these functions returns a handle identifying the object. This handle lets you work with the object, for example, passing it to WaitForSingleObject. Furthermore, each of these system objects can exist in a signaled or unsignaled state. For instance, mutexes, semaphores, and events are signaled when they become available. Threads become unsignaled when they terminate.

Monitoring File Changes—A WaitForSingleObject Example

The project VIEWDIR.DPR illustrates how to use WaitForSingleObject with a change notification object to monitor changes to a directory. A change notification object becomes signaled whenever a specified change occurs, such as when a file is created or deleted.

When you run this application, a dialog box appears prompting you for a directory to monitor as shown in Figure 16-4.

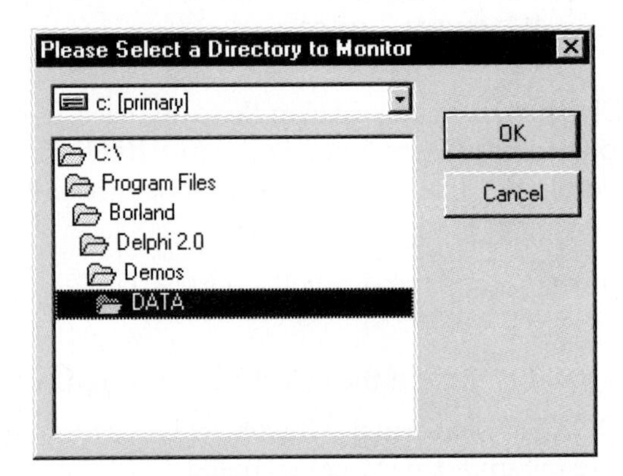

Figure 16-4. *Main form for VIEWDIR.DPR*

After you select a directory, another form appears containing a list of the files in that directory as shown in Figure 16-5. As long as this form is open, this list will automatically update whenever a file is created, deleted, or renamed. If you use an application to change the contents of the directory you are viewing, such as the Windows Explorer, you will observe that this form refreshes the list of files.

The following code is the project source:

```
program VIEWDIR;

uses
  Forms,
  VIEWDIR2 in 'VIEWDIR2.pas' {FileChangeForm},
  VIEWDIR1 in 'VIEWDIR1.pas' {SelectDirForm},
  VIEWDIR3 in 'VIEWDIR3.pas';{NotifyFileChange}

{$R *.RES}

begin
  Application.CreateForm(TSelectDirForm, SelectDirForm);
  Application.Run;
end.
```

The following unit, VIEWDIR1.PAS, contains the definition for TSelectDirForm, the dialog box that appears when you first launch the application. This dialog box contains a directory list box, a drive combo box, and OK and Cancel buttons. If you press the Cancel button, the application terminates. If you press the OK button after selecting a a directory, a second form of the type TFileChangeForm is created, and the

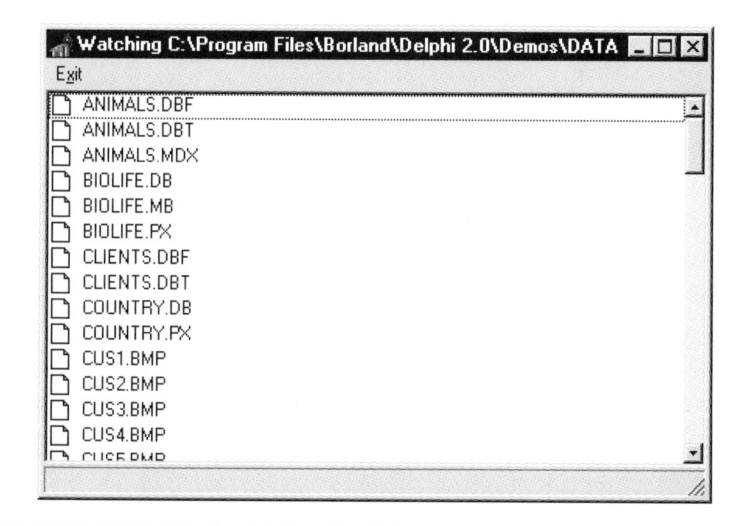

Figure 16-5. *Results of selecting a directory in VIEWDIR.DPR*

directory is passed as an argument to one of the form's methods, BeginMonitoring. Finally, the TFileChangeForm is displayed with ShowModal.

The following is the code for VIEWDIR1.PAS:

```
unit VIEWDIR1;

interface

uses
  Windows, Messages, SysUtils, Classes, Graphics, Controls, Forms, Dialogs,
  StdCtrls, FileCtrl;

type
  TSelectDirForm = class(TForm)
    DirectoryListBox1: TDirectoryListBox;
    DriveComboBox1: TDriveComboBox;
    OKButton: TButton;
    Button2: TButton;
    procedure Button2Click(Sender: TObject);
    procedure OKButtonClick(Sender: TObject);
  private
    { Private declarations }
  public
    { Public declarations }
  end;

var
  SelectDirForm: TSelectDirForm;

implementation

uses ViewDir2;

{$R *.DFM}

procedure TSelectDirForm.Button2Click(Sender: TObject);
begin
  Close;
end;

procedure TSelectDirForm.OKButtonClick(Sender: TObject);
begin
  with TFileChangeForm.Create(Self) do
  begin
    try
      Self.Hide; // hide the selection dialog.

      BeginMonitoring(FileListBox1.Directory);
      ShowModal;
```

```
    finally
      Free;
      Self.Close;
    end;
  end;
end;

end.
```

TFileChangeForm is defined in VIEWDIR2.PAS. The form contains a file list box that displays the files. The BeginMonitoring method creates a TNotifyFileChange thread in a suspended state in order to pass it a handle to the TFileChangeForm. The thread needs to know about the form in order to access the form's file list box to refresh it. After assigning this information to a property of the thread, BeginMonitoring resumes the thread. The following is the code for VIEWDIR2.PAS:

```
unit VIEWDIR2;

interface

uses
  Windows, Messages, SysUtils, Classes, Graphics, Controls, Forms, Dialogs,
  ComCtrls, FileCtrl, StdCtrls, Menus;

type
  TFileChangeForm = class(TForm)
    FileListBox1: TFileListBox;
    StatusBar1: TStatusBar;
    MainMenu1: TMainMenu;
    Exit1: TMenuItem;
    OpenDialog1: TOpenDialog;
    procedure Exit1Click(Sender: TObject);
  private
    { Private declarations }
  public
    { Public declarations }
    procedure BeginMonitoring(const MonitorDirectory: string);
  end;

implementation

uses ViewDir3;

{$R *.DFM}

procedure TFileChangeForm.Exit1Click(Sender: TObject);
begin
  Close;
end;
```

```
procedure TFileChangeForm.BeginMonitoring(const MonitorDirectory: string);
begin
  with TNotifyFileChange.Create(True) do
  begin
    Caption := 'Watching ' + MonitorDirectory;
    MasterForm := Self;
    Resume;
  end;

end;

end.
```

The TNotifyFileChange thread class is defined in VIEWDIR3.PAS. The thread contains a public variable, MasterForm, that points to the owning form. The thread's UpdateFileList method uses a reference to the form to update some controls on it whenever a file change is detected. The thread's Execute method takes care of detecting the file changes.

When the Execute method is run, it first creates a change notification object. This object is created in a call to the Win32 function FindFirstChangeNotification. A handle to the object is returned by the function and is stored as a local variable, HFileChange. FindFirstChangeNotification has the following syntax:

```
FindFirstChangeNotification(lpPathName: PChar;
       bWatchSubtree: BOOL; dwNotifyFilter: DWORD): THandle; stdcall;
```

When you call FindFirstChangeNotification, you pass it a directory path, a Boolean value for monitoring the directory or directory tree, and a predefined constant indicating the type of activity to watch. The TNotifyFileChange thread passes in the name of the directory to monitor and also passes the value False, indicating that only the directory should be monitored. A predefined constant, FILE_NOTIFY_CHANGE_FILE_NAME, is passed as the argument for dwNotifyFilter so that file creations, deletions, and renames are monitored. A list of valid constants is defined in the WINDOWS.PAS RTL (Run-Time Library) unit.

After creating the change notification object, the thread enters a loop. The condition of the loop is determined by comparing the return value of WaitForSingleObject to WAIT_FAILED. The call to WaitForSingleObject has as its arguments a handle to the change notification object and a time-out value of INFINITE. When the thread encounters this call to evaluate the condition, it enters a wait state and does not continue until either the object is signaled or the function fails.

If the function fails, WAIT_FAILED is returned, so the condition of the loop is False and execution falls to the end of the method. If the object is signaled, it means that a file change has occurred, so the body of the loop is entered. This code calls UpdateFileList through a call to Synchronize to update the status bar and refresh the file list box.

Finally, it resets the change notification object by calling the Win32 function FindNextChangeNotification so that it can be used again to monitor another change.

```
unit VIEWDIR3;

interface

uses
  Classes, Windows, ViewDir2;

type
  TNotifyFileChange = class(TThread)
  private
    { Private declarations }
    procedure UpdateFileList;

  protected
    procedure Execute; override;
  public
    MasterForm: TFileChangeForm;
  end;

implementation


{ TNotifyFileChange }


procedure TNotifyFileChange.Execute;
var
  HFileChange: THandle;
begin

  HFileChange :=
    FindFirstChangeNotification(PChar(MasterForm.FileListBox1.Directory),
    False, FILE_NOTIFY_CHANGE_FILE_NAME);

  while WaitForSingleObject(HFileChange, INFINITE) <> WAIT_FAILED do
  begin
    Synchronize(UpdateFileList);
    FindNextChangeNotification(HFileChange);
    if Terminated then
      Exit;
  end;
end;

procedure TNotifyFileChange.UpdateFileList;
begin
```

```
    with MasterForm do
    begin
      StatusBar1.SimpleText := 'Changes detected';
      Update;

      with FileListBox1 do
      begin
        // Delay updating screen until after file list is built.
        Items.BeginUpdate;
        // Rebuilt file list
        Update;
        Items.EndUpdate;
      end;

      StatusBar1.SimpleText := '';

    end;
  end;

  end.
```

As you can see from this example, using WaitForSingleObject is much more efficient than polling for a condition. In the next section, you will see how to use WaitForSingleObject to synchronize threads.

NOTE: You might be tempted to think that polling is going on in VIEWDIR3.PAS due to the use of the while loop. In polling situations, the purpose of the loop is to repeatedly test a condition, with the repeated executions of the loop acting to produce the delay. In the current example, the WaitForSingleObject function, not the execution of the loop, produces the delay. The purpose of the while loop as it is used here is to update the directory list after repeated changes.

TThread and WaitFor

The TThread class has encapsulated the WaitForSingleObject for a special circumstance. If your thread needs to wait for completion of a second thread to terminate, it can call the second thread's WaitFor method. The WaitFor method simply calls WaitForSingleObject and passes it the thread handle of the second thread. The following code example demonstrates the use of this method:

```
procedure TFirstThread.DoSomething;
begin
  // finish some work here

  // now wait for the second thread to finish
```

```
  SecondThread.WaitFor;

end;
```

A thread should not call its own WaitFor since it would be waiting for *itself* to terminate—which will never happen.

The WaitForMultipleObjects Function

You should be aware of a very important variation of WaitForSingleObject. This function, WaitForMultipleObjects, allows you to wait on the completion of any one or all of a set of specified objects. This function helps avoid *deadlock,* a situation in which two threads are waiting on each other for a resource that the other owns. Neither thread will continue until it has control of both resources, so both are caught in a deadlock. WaitForMultipleObjects has the following syntax:

```
WaitForMultipleObjects(nCount: DWORD;
     lpHandles: PWOHandleArray; bWaitAll: BOOL;
     dwMilliseconds: DWORD): DWORD; stdcall;
```

WaitForMultipleObjects accepts an array of object handles. The nCount object handle indicates the number of objects. The lpHandles object handle is a pointer to the array. The bWaitAll object handle specifies if the function should return only when all the objects are signaled. The dwMilliseconds object handle is the time-out value. For more information on using WaitForMultipleObjects, see Delphi's online help.

Using Mutexes

A mutex is a synchronization object that you can use in place of a critical section object. Like a critical section object, a mutex allows you to synchronize access to a shared resource. However, a mutex has some advantages over a critical section. A mutex can be used to synchronize threads not only within a single process but also *across* processes. Recall that in Chapter 15 a *process* was defined as an instance of an application. Each process has its own virtual address space, global variables, and operating system resources.

By naming the mutex, the object can be referenced by multiple processes and, consequently, can be used to coordinate them. Even though this entails greater overhead, using a mutex adds flexibility when you need to synchronize across processes. A mutex also allows you to set a time-out value because it is used in a call to WaitForSingleObject. A thread waiting on a mutex can specify the time-out value as infinite or a specified number of milliseconds, wherease a thread waiting on a critical section must always wait indefinitely.

Before you can use a mutex, you must create it using a call to CreateMutex and store its handle in a global variable. Afterwards, you can pass the mutex to WaitForSingleObject whenever you need to synchronize access with another thread.

Creating a Mutex

To create a mutex, you use the CreateMutex Win32 API function. This function has the following syntax:

```
CreateMutex(lpMutexAttributes: PSecurityAttributes;
     bInitialOwner: BOOL; lpName: PChar): THandle; stdcall;
```

CreateMutex takes several arguments and returns a handle to a mutex. A PSecurityAttributes value called lpMutexAttributes specifies the NT security attributes and (process) inheritability of the mutex. To use default security and non-inheritability, you can use nil as a value. The argument bInitialOwner indicates whether the mutex is immediately owned by the thread (signaled) or is left unowned (unsignaled).

The argument lpName lets you give a name to the mutex. This name is used to share a common mutex across multiple processes. When a mutex is used in this fashion, you give it a name. When CreateMutex is called the first time, the system creates the mutex. Subsequently, each process that calls CreateMutex with this name receives a process relative handle to the same mutex.

Using the Mutex

Once you have created the mutex, you can use it to synchronize your threads by passing its handle to WaitForSingleObject, which blocks the thread until the mutex becomes signaled or available. When the mutex becomes available again, the system gives ownership of the mutex to the blocked thread and then resets the mutex state to unsignaled. The thread signals the mutex when it no longer needs it by calling ReleaseMutex. A mutex is signaled when it is owned by a thread and unsignaled when it is not. ReleaseMutex has the following syntax:

```
ReleaseMutex(THandle)
```

When you are finished with the mutex, you free it by passing its handle to CloseHandle. CloseHandle has the following syntax:

```
CloseHandle(THandle)
```

Using a Mutex Example

The project MUTEX.DPR is a variation of the critical section example shown earlier, but it has been adapted for use with mutexes. Recall that a mutex can behave similarly to a critical section. By specifying an infinite time-out value, the mutex can block indefinitely just like a critical section. The following is the project source code:

```
program MUTEX;

uses
  Forms,
  MUTEXU1 in 'MUTEXU1.pas' {CounterForm},
  MUTEXU2 in 'MUTEXU2.pas';{CounterThread}

{$R *.RES}

begin
  Application.CreateForm(TCounterForm, CounterForm);
  Application.Run;
end.
```

The mutex is created in the form's FormCreate method through a call to CreateMutex. In the call to CreateMutex, zero is passed as the value for the security attributes and mutex name. The form's FormDestroy takes care of releasing the mutex by calling CloseHandle. The following is the code for the main form's unit:

```
unit MUTEXU1;

interface

uses
  Windows, Messages, SysUtils, Classes, Graphics, Controls, Forms, Dialogs,
  StdCtrls;

type
  TCounterForm = class(TForm)
    StartButton: TButton;
    ListBox1: TListBox;
    procedure StartButtonClick(Sender: TObject);
    procedure FormCreate(Sender: TObject);
    procedure FormDestroy(Sender: TObject);
  private
    { Private declarations }
  public
    { Public declarations }
  end;

var
  CounterForm: TCounterForm;
  Counter: Integer;
  CounterMutex: THandle;
```

```
implementation
uses MutexU2;

{$R *.DFM}

procedure TCounterForm.StartButtonClick(Sender: TObject);
begin
  (Sender as TButton).Enabled := False;

  Counter := 0;

  TCounterThread.Create(False);
  TCounterThread.Create(False);
  TCounterThread.Create(False);
  TCounterThread.Create(False);
end;

procedure TCounterForm.FormCreate(Sender: TObject);
begin
  CounterMutex := CreateMutex(nil,False,nil);
end;

procedure TCounterForm.FormDestroy(Sender: TObject);
begin
  CloseHandle(CounterMutex);
end;

end.
```

The thread that increments the global variable Counter is defined in METEXU2.PAS. Again, UpdateListBox takes care of updating the list box. Execute contains the code that implements the mutex. Instead of using EnterCriticalSection to block the thread, WaitForSingleObject is used. The mutex handle, along with an INFINITE time-out value, is passed to the function. The if condition compares the return value of WaitForSingleObject to WAIT_OBJECT_0 to see if the mutex becomes signaled. You must explicitly check the return value because WaitForSingleObject returns not only if the mutex becomes signaled, but also if it is abandoned. A mutex can be abandoned if the thread that owns it terminates before signaling the mutex.

The protected code takes care of incrementing Counter and calling UpdateListBox. When the mutex is no longer needed, it is signaled by a call to ReleaseMutex and the thread no longer owns it. The following is the code for MUTEXU2.PAS:

```
unit MUTEXU2;

interface
```

```
uses
  Classes;

type
  TCounterThread = class(TThread)
  private
    { Private declarations }
  protected
    procedure UpdateListBox;
    procedure Execute; override;
  end;

implementation

uses MutexU1, SysUtils, Windows;

{ TCounterThread }

procedure TCounterThread.UpdateListBox;
begin
  CounterForm.ListBox1.Items.Add( IntToStr(Counter) );
end;

procedure TCounterThread.Execute;
var
  i: Integer;
begin
  for i:= 1 to 100 do
  begin
    if WaitForSingleObject(CounterMutex, INFINITE) = WAIT_OBJECT_0 then
    begin
      try
        Counter := Counter + 1;
        if not Terminated then
          Synchronize(UpdateListBox)
        else
          Exit;
      finally
        ReleaseMutex(CounterMutex);
      end;
    end
    else
      Break; // Wait failed - mutex abandoned?
  end;
end;

end.
```

Semaphores and Events

Two other synchronization objects that can be used with WaitForSingleObject are semaphores and events. A semaphore object is used to limit the number of threads that can access a shared resource. An event is used by multiple threads that are working on separate but dependent tasks. Suppose one thread must wait for the other thread to finish. An event can be used to signal the completion of this task. Both semaphores and events can be used between multiple processes.

To use a semaphore object, you specify a maximum count when you create it (using the CreateSemaphore function). The semaphore maintains an internal usage counter based on this value. Each time a thread calls WaitForSingleObject and gains access to a resource, the counter is increased. When the thread is finished with the resource, it calls a function (ReleaseSemaphore) to decrement the count. WaitForSingleObject blocks incoming threads until the semaphore becomes signaled. This happens when the counter is greater than zero. The semaphore is unsignaled when the count is zero.

To use an event object, you create an event object and specify its initial state (signaled or unsignaled) and its reset event type. There are two types of reset events: manual-reset and auto-reset. An *auto-reset event* is automatically reset to unsignaled by WaitForSingleObject after satisfying the first waiting thread. This ensures that only one waiting thread wakes up when the event is signaled. With a *manual-reset event,* the event is not reset until ResetEvent is called. This lets many threads reawaken. When a thread wants to signal an event, it calls SetEvent.

For more information on semaphores and events, use Delphi's online help. To obtain in-depth coverage of these objects and other synchronization issues, you should consult an advanced Win32 API reference. Chapter 14 provides a list of references that you might consult.

Conclusion

Combined with the TThread class, synchronization lets you create powerful and robust multithreaded applications. Using the Win32 API, you have a variety of synchronization objects to coordinate your threads. Each of these objects has a special purpose that can be used to meet the needs of your particular situation. You may also want to refer to the references listed at the end of Chapter 14.

PART THREE

Case Study: Delphi and the Web

Throughout this book you have seen examples of how to solve many different programming problems with Delphi. The remaining chapters in this book take a somewhat different approach by providing you with a "behind the scenes" look at the issues behind real-world development. Much of the material in these chapters takes the form of a case-study—an in-depth look at the issues and technique involved in delivering a commercial-quality application built in Delphi.

The focus of much of the material in this section revolves around WebHub, a commercially available product from HREF Tools Corporation. WebHub started as a set of freeware and shareware components (primarily TCGIEnvData and TCGIDB) that were initially designed to prove that you can use Delphi to write CGI programs to serve dynamic pages over the World Wide Web. The initial proof-of-concept components had several major limitations, and WebHub was designed to cut through all those and to add many significant layers of functionality—truly providing a CGI *framework*.

In order to create WebHub as a robust and extendible tool in a particularly short time frame, HREF Tools had to solve several complex problems specific to the Web, as well as some pertaining to Delphi development in general.

The World Wide Web, in addition to being a fast growing and exciting area to work in, includes some subtle, and some not so subtle, complexities. Building a commercial-quality application like WebHub meant addressing and overcoming a number of new obstacles. Among these are:

- How to support multiple Web servers so that developers can build portable modules
- How to break the fundamental speed limitations of the traditional CGI framework
- How to build a system that would make Web applications not only easy to build, but easy to maintain
- How to support remote administration
- How to pass data to Java applets
- How to handle the various UI (User Interface) improvements offered over time by Netscape browsers, such as frames

The issues related to building WebHub are not solely related to the Web itself. In order for it to be supportable, extensible, and usable, many issues that apply to all application development in Delphi had to be addressed as well. These issues include:

- How to write code for 16- and 32-bit Delphi
- How to build components for a complex environment while keeping programming simple
- How to develop core functionality and a user interface

Chapter 17 takes a look at the Internet in general, and the Web in particular. It also provides a basic introduction to WebHub. WebHub is a sophisticated and powerful set of components that are designed to work together, be easily supportable, and are a pleasure to use. This required careful planning, as well as the development of several new techniques. Chapter 18 considers some of the important issues that all developer's of commercial quality products need to consider, and it demonstrates how some these issues were addressed when creating WebHub.

Chapter 19 focuses on many of the complex issues involved in building Delphi applications for the World Wide Web in particular. Here you will learn some of the unique problems that the Web poses, as well demonstrations on how to solve them.

Finally, Chapter 20 demonstrates how to interface Delphi, Java applets, and JavaScript. What roles these various tools play, and how to integrate them, is demonstrated.

Chapter Seventeen

Introduction to the Internet and the World Wide Web

This chapter is intended to provide you with an introduction to the Internet and the World Wide Web, as well as a basic understanding of what WebHub is and what it does. If you are already familiar with terms like ISP, HTTP, HTML, URLs, FTP, CGI, and Java you can skip the first part of this chapter and go immediately to the introduction to WebHub in the section "What Is WebHub?"

Overview of the Internet

The Internet is many things to many people. It's a dynamic network of between 70,000 and 30,000,000 computers (depending on who and when you ask) connected around the globe. It's a 24-hour worldwide culture with its own ethics and traditions. It's an unspoken collaboration for global peace and communication in the garb of a military expenditure to protect U.S. communication lines from nuclear war. It's the hottest new marketplace for software, as well as just about anything else, from insurance to cars. It's the new singles scene. It's an alternative to driving to work. It's a research library of vast size, with some extremely odd areas of expertise.

The Internet is all these things and more. But the only way to really find out what the Internet is about is to get yourself connected.

Getting Connected

The first thing you need in order to get connected to the Internet is an ISP (Internet service provider). Just like you need a local phone company to get your telephone connected in a useful way to the national switching network, you need an ISP to connect your modem to the Internet. Your ISP will give you an IP address somewhat like your local telephone number in that you can connect with other people on the network. You'll pay a monthly fee for this connectivity, and it's best to pay the extra fee associated with a dedicated IP number that doesn't change each time you connect. This way, you can advertise your IP number and other people can connect to you in a predictable way.

By the time you read this, there will probably be some national and perhaps worldwide players that make Internet services available to everyone. Most small ISPs advertise in local newspapers and online. But not all ISPs are the same. In fact, like any developing market, there is a full range of offerings at many price levels. And not surprisingly, you do not always get what you pay for.

You should do your homework before choosing an ISP, since it's likely you will be paying a chunk of money, possibly for a long time. Following are some common questions concerning ISPs and services that are available:

Q: How much should it cost, monthly?

A: Usually about $12 to $35, but it can be much, much higher if you need a high-speed connection, such as an ISDN (Integrated Services Digital Network) or a T1 line. ISDN can support speeds of up to 128 Kbps (kilobytes per second); a T1 line can support speeds of up to 1.544 Mbps (megabytes per second).

Q: Does the ISP provide you with a fixed IP (Internet Protocol) address?

A: An IP address is an explicit address in the form of four numbers, each between 0 and 255, separated by periods (for example, 199.4.118.45). Most ISPs do not provide you with a fixed IP but instead generate one for you each time you log on.

Without a fixed IP, you cannot run your own Web site, because people cannot reliably connect to your machine. Even with a fixed IP, it is generally desirable to register a domain name (for example, borland.com or href.com) with Internic (a worldwide authority) and rely on Domain Name Servers (DNSs) to resolve the names to IP addresses. Then you can publicize your address using a name instead of a number, which is easier for people to remember and also leaves you free to change providers (and even your IP address). The DNS performs the service currently provided by telephone information, by which you can dial 411 to get a phone number based on a company name. DNS gives you the IP number based on the domain name.

Q: How many hours of usage do you get per month?

A: This varies widely. Some ISP provide something on the order of 20 hours per month, with additional fees for more hours. Others give you unlimited access. You want unlimited access!

Q: How many megabytes (MB) of storage space should you get?

A: This will depend on your needs and is relevant only if you plan to post your Web site on the ISP's server. Many ISPs provide users with between 10 and 30 MB. Some ISPs charge per megabyte.

Q: Will your ISP even permit you to post a Web site?

A: Most small companies do. It's often a matter of their capabilities and whether they consider Web-site posting part of their value-added package.

Q: Will your ISP permit you to run Web applications, including CGI (Common Gateway Interface) programs, which enable you to create dynamic database-driven Web sites?

A: Most do not allow this on their own servers but may permit you to attach your own machine to their network.

Q: What operating system do Web servers run on, and does this matter?

A: Most run on Unix or Linux (a Unix-based operating system). Some run on Macintosh and Windows systems. If you want to use Delphi to create dynamic Web sites, you'll need a Web server that runs on Windows. This should be one of your first questions to your potential ISP. If you're planning to deploy an Intranet (i.e., an internal corporate LAN) solution, you'll have control over the hardware and the operating system, and your task is simplified to find the most appropriate Web server software.

Q: Will you be able to add your own Windows machine to the ISP's network if they don't let you run Windows-based programs on one of their machines?

A: Not with the large, commercial ISPs. With the smaller ones, it's possible. Not only will you want to connect a server, but you will also want 24-hour physical access to it.

Q: Will you be able to post files in an anonymous FTP (File Transfer Protocol) area?

A: It depends on the ISP.

Q: Are there other charges?

A: Yes. Here is a list of what some ISPs offer, as well a range of prices you might expect to pay:

- Setup fee for the account (free to $50)
- Setting up a domain name ($45 to $200)
- Setting up an automatic e-mail reply "Infobot" ($0 to $100)

NOTE: An Infobot is a one-line entry provided by your ISP that says if I get mail at this address, send back this text file.

- Running a listserv (varies, though not widely available)

NOTE: A listserv is an e-mail-based discussion group that is administered automatically by a software program. Participants can subscribe and unsubscribe as they have interest in the discussion, and the administrator can moderate content if necessary. ISPs that are using LINUX or UNIX can most likely provide this service for free.

- Subscribing to newsgroups (usually free)
- ISDN connectivity (varies around a few hundred dollars per month)
- Partial T1 ($800 to $2000 per month, depending largely on how many miles you are from a main line)

For more information about evaluating Internet service providers, see *Connecting to the Internet* by Susan Estrada (O'Reilly and Associates, 1993).

Online Services Versus Direct Internet Connection

CompuServe (CIS) has some advantages over the "raw" Internet. Some of these advantages include better security of transmitted messages; easy binary file transfer between CIS members; unparalleled technical support in forums, especially Borland forums; and excellent research facilities.

America Online (AOL) seems most appealing for its social nature; however, it doesn't compete with CompuServe on technical or cost-saving points.

It is quite useful to have more than one type of connectivity. If you work with people who have CompuServe accounts, you will be able to trade files easily only if you are on that network. For other purposes such as e-mail, FTP, Web surfing, and certainly Web-site hosting, a direct Internet connection is far preferable in terms of cost and speed.

The Internet Is Just a Network

The Internet was originally explicitly non-commercial in nature—it was the domain of academicians and the military. That all changed in 1990, with the development of the World Wide Web. You can think of the Web as the graphical, user-friendly, commerce and transaction-oriented part of the Internet. Because the barriers to entry to publishing on the Web were so low, and the relative benefits were so high, by 1995 the growth of the Internet was nothing short of explosive.

During its brief history, the Internet has gone through many growth spurts and so far has always managed to bring the latest flood of newcomers on board without losing its essence of fast, open communication among interested parties. That communication occurs based on a networking protocol called TCP/IP (Transmission Control Protocol/Internet Protocol). TCP/IP drivers are available for Windows 3.11, and it's included with Windows 95 and NT. TCP/IP is also available for Unix, Linux, and Macintosh, enabling users to keep their favorite platform and still connect in order to send messages and files.

Intranet: the Non-Public Internet

Although a lot of attention is being focused on shopkeepers on the public Internet, much of the important growth of TCP/IP as a standard, and of the Web as a widespread publishing platform, is happening on internal corporate LANs, increasingly referred to as *Intranets.*

Corporations are discovering the key factors that make the Intranet an ideal platform for deploying information publishing as well as data-entry-enabled applications: the simplicity of HTML as a presentation style, the intuitive use of Web browsers and their cross-platform nature, as well as the relatively low cost of reusing existing (legacy) databases rather than constantly creating new information systems.

For example, a hardware repair company was running a Paradox for Windows application used by seven employees to track orders for customers. Before the Web, a customer service representative answered the phone to provide order status information; now customers are able to connect to the company's Web site and check on orders directly for better service at lower cost to both parties.

On the Intranet, corporations can use the Web to publish a variety of information, even databases in multiple file formats. The challenges for Intranet Web site developers are in reworking existing applications to make the user interface appropriate for the Web. As with all software development, an investment in design and a focus on reusability yields the most robust and lowest cost systems. As a developer, you will want to find a Web publishing framework that meets your needs; you will learn about one such framework, WebHub, in the next three chapters.

Hackers, Cyberpunks, and Lurkers in Cyberspace

The Internet has its own culture, based largely on a love of knowledge and technology. To get some quick insights into some of the minds on the Internet, drink some Jolt cola and watch some Monty Python movies! It's the quick mind and the often sarcastic sense of humor that enable one to survive the miles of technical micro-facts that most Internet denizens are supposed to master. On the Internet, no one sees your face or your business suit; your writing and your work must speak for themselves. Of course, even that's changing already with some of the new video-based technology that is becoming available.

Many entertaining tales have been written about hackers, the people who take on established bastions of security to point out their vulnerabilities. A site of historical importance on the Web is the "Hack Netscape, Win a T-shirt" page; this Web site organizes the international group of programmers who are actively double-checking Netscape's security plans. And an equally important force are the cyberpunks, who not only value personal privacy but are willing to do something about it. And then there are the lurkers, those who just read messages, typically from newsgroups, but rarely contribute anything original.

All joking aside, the core values that keep the Internet alive are technical excellence, the general lack of censorship, and the fairly level playing field, which allows for plenty of new ideas (and an admittedly large number of bad ones).

TIP: *To find out exactly how the Internet promotes these values, you should check out the IETF (Internet Engineering Task Force) or review some RFC (Request for Comment) documents. A classic RFC from October 1985 is the specification for FTP (File Transfer Protocol), which we now take for granted completely. It can be seen at http://www.cis.ohio-state.edu/htbin/rfc/rfc959.html.*

Internet standards and policies are generally very well documented—always with the goal that someone else could pick up the documentation and offer a newer, better implementation of the basic protocol.

Meet Your Mate on the Internet

The Internet can also be a place for international romance, with near-instant e-mail, IRC (Internet Relay Chat), and Internet Phone eliminating the cost of long-distance communication. IRC provides a real-time online chat environment, which enables low-budget worldwide communication. As with any communication technology, humans are using the Internet to find themselves and each other.

Location-Independent Lifestyles

Because the cost of living is so high around the technology cities, the appeal of a home-based business that relies on the Internet for connectivity to customers and colleagues is growing stronger. With more and more dial-in options, individuals are planning lives based on this model, while sales reps and other travelers tap in remotely on a daily basis.

The Internet Is a Wide Area Library

If you can find your favorite topic on the Web at all, you can probably find a few facts that you hadn't encountered elsewhere. The Web doesn't do a good job of covering all subjects, but as institutions and individuals take responsibility for more and more areas of interest, the overall global knowledge base is growing into a surprisingly useful research library. For instance, if you want to find all the hot Java resources, visit http://www.gamelan.com.

A number of Web sites are devoted specifically to locating information on the Web. For example, Yahoo! (www.yahoo.com) is a very popular site that can assist your search. Another powerful search site is Digital's Alta Vista (www.altavista.digital.com). Most Web browsers include features for access to one or more search sites.

The Internet Is Up to You

If you want to participate, you'll need to start with an e-mail account and then add a direct connection so that you can browse the Web. If you want to become a provider of Web-site CGI programs, continue reading—the upcoming chapters will go into much more detail on using Delphi for CGI programming.

E-mail: A Basic Necessity

Certainly it's true that the Internet is a global network of computers that are tied together not only with hardware and software protocols, but with human agreements that make amazing things happen. E-mail (electronic mail) was one of the first applications on the Internet and remains one of the top three most popular. It's the communication vehicle that enables collaboration among the people who build the Internet—who build its new software, invent its new protocols, and maintain the parts that already work.

E-mail messages travel from California to New York in seconds, and from California to Poland often in less than an hour. E-mail is quicker to process than voice mail, easier to search than a pile of faxes, faster than Federal Express, and fells fewer trees than a postcard. A small business can send an electronic newsletter to thousands of subscribers for almost no cost; and the recipient can easily file the information for later use. In fact, this book, a collaboration among seven authors from across the United States, was written by passing the electronic versions of the manuscript across e-mail. For those who use it, e-mail is changing the nature of business—information travels faster, less formally, and often in a more useful format.

A few other traditional Internet software applications deserve mention: FTP can be thought of as "Federal Express for files"—it lets you move files from one place to another. Usenet News is an organized discussion area where people can read and post messages under thousands of topic headings. IRC (Internet Relay Chat) is a CB-like chat experience based on typing, rather than talking. Telnet connects you to a server, through a port, and you can do whatever that port allows. Of all these options, the must-master items are e-mail, FTP, and Telnet.

The World Wide Web

The latest tidal wave of traffic on the Internet is, of course, the World Wide Web. The Web is a hypertext-based experience that lets the surfer (that is, reader or client) read information, view graphics, listen to sound files, and follow hyperlinks that lead everywhere from Capitol Hill to New Zealand. The Web is based on the HTTP protocol (Hypertext Transfer Protocol). This is a very simple protocol that enables the surfer to request a file from a Web server, and for that file to contain links that lead to other files. Files are typically displayed in a browser (Netscape and Mosaic are the most popular browsers). Add-on software modules are used to play the audio files, run the Java applets, handle the electronic commerce transactions, and so forth. These add-on modules are invoked based on the file extension and a simple header in the file that indicates its type. Many new browsers incorporate these capabilities into one product.

NOTE: Did you say "surfer?" Yes. The person who uses the browser software (often the Netscape browser) is called the "surfer," a term coined early on because of the sensation of surfing around the world on a generally self-directed wave of information. The term is useful because it always refers to the user at the browser, as opposed to the Web master (the user maintaining the Web server) or any other role.

An Unrestricted Free Market

Seemingly overnight, the Web has made global electronic commerce a reality, and it seems as though everyone is getting involved in some way. Thousands of businesses have built themselves Web sites, in hopes of either selling more goods to a wider audience, or of saving customer service costs by providing information online with no operator involvement. Thus far it seems that the businesses that are succeeding on the sales side are those that offer a unique product that cannot be obtained elsewhere, a significantly lower price, or an extremely valuable search system combined with a smooth "checkout stand" so that shoppers find the store truly convenient.

From an advertising and public relations point of view, the Web is an ideal medium. Instead of being confined to a four-inch square in a magazine, you have unlimited space to tell your story—as long as you can keep the surfer's attention. Most software and hardware companies are moving their technical information from private BBSs (Bulletin Board Systems) to the Web, and many maintain a second presence on CompuServe.

One of the ways that the early Web sites started making money was by selling links. Any site that naturally attracted traffic had the option of selling hypertext links to other businesses, for anything from $25 to $1500 per month. Many sites trade links as a courtesy, rather than charging a fee.

Web-Related Terms

There are some basic terms and concepts that you need to understand about the Web as an application development arena. This section provides key definitions and gives you an overview of how things work:

Surfer: The person surfing the Web with a browser. The surfer could be on any operating system.

Browser: The software used during surfing. The most popular and full-featured browser is Netscape. Mosaic is another one. It's now possible (and easy, too) to write your own browser with Delphi using HTML rendering components. (One option is ThtmlViewer, an HTML viewer for Delphi, available for $129 from http://www.startups.com/.)

Web page: A single document displayed in the browser, in response to an HTTP request.

HTTP (Hypertext Transfer Protocol): The surfer uses a browser to make HTTP requests for documents.

URL (Uniform Resource Locator): The request is expressed as a URL, that is, a request for a specific resource at a specific location. An example of a URL is:

```
http://www.href.com/index.html
```

The first portion of the URL defines the program to be used to get to the resource (http). The **://** is a required separator. The www.href.com portion is the fully qualified name of the server containing the resource. The index.html portion is the filename, which in this case is an HTML document. URLs also apply to resources other than Web pages, such as FTP, gopher, e-mail, and so forth.

Server names: In the previous example, href.com is the domain name and www is an alias that is mapped to the server machine. Servers do not have to be named www. An alternative example is http://xxx.href.com where xxx is the server name.

IP addresses and domain names: URLs can also reference IP addresses directly. For example:

```
http://127.0.0.1/
```

This is a reserved IP address, which loops you back to your local machine—a technique that is essential for local prototyping (testing your CGI applications on a local machine, without loading them onto a "live" Web server). If you have a domain name, you would use that name instead of a number.

Web server: Also known as an HTTP server, this is the software that answers the HTTP requests. Requests are sent to one or more IP addresses and the Web server software "listens" on a port, usually port 80, and responds with the appropriate document.

TIP: If you're evaluating Web servers, you should know that you can tell each server to listen on a separate port, For instance, you can have Microsoft's IIS listening on port 80, and O'Reilly's WebSite on port 81, and both servers will work simultaneously. The different server products have their own strengths, and you may want to deploy more than one Web server on a single machine.

Generally, the Web server responds with a static file (for example, a graphics, audio, HTML, or Java file), and sometimes it runs a Web application, which takes responsibility for creating the output document on the fly.

Initially all Web servers were on Unix machines; one of the first Web servers priced for the Windows market was WebSite from O'Reilly and Associates, which shipped in June 1995. Other major Web servers are available on the NT platform from Microsoft, Netscape, and Spry.

CGI (Common Gateway Interface): A category of programs that follow certain rules, rather than a programming language. It's incorrect to ask, "How do I program in CGI?" The better question is, "How do I write a program that follows the rules of CGI?" The rules vary from one Web server to another, but essentially the Web server invokes the CGI program, passing it some parameters that tell it what to do. Then the CGI program runs and creates an output document with an agreed-upon filename or memory location. When the CGI program terminates, the Web server sends the document back to the surfer. A CGI program can be written in any language that can follow those rules. Common languages are Perl, C and C++, Visual Basic, and Delphi.

NOTE: As of April 1996, the specific rules of CGI are giving way to Web-server-specific APIs, which promise much higher performance. It's increasingly important to choose a Web application framework that provides a layer between the Web server and your work in Delphi, thus ensuring that your application is portable.

Perl: A scripting language initially used on Unix but since ported to Windows NT. It is good for writing short (less than 100 lines) CGI scripts.

Dynamic Web pages: This refers to using a CGI program to create an output document in response to the surfer's request. In contrast, a static file is retrieved by the Web server with no CGI action necessary.

HTML (Hypertext Markup Language): Web pages are built using HTML. If you can learn something as sophisticated as Delphi, you can easily learn the basics of HTML in a few hours. It's a very simple markup language with tags for bold, italic, minimal page layout, and hypertext links. The links create the "web" of pages.

Database-driven Web pages: This refers to having the CGI program consult a database in order to generate the content of the output document. Database-driven

Web sites offer far better features than simple, static sites. Because Delphi has a strong database connection, CGI programs built with Delphi can easily pull data from the full range of desktop and SQL databases.

NOTE: A database-driven Web page simply means that the database can play a role in creating the content of that output document.

Java: A cross-platform development environment that lets you supplement the browser with custom features for the surfer. By combining Java with a set of database-aware server-side components, it is possible to produce a platform on which sophisticated, globally accessible, database-aware applications can be built. (It is anticipated that Borland will release a version of a Java compiler shortly after the publication of this book.)

JavaScript: The Netscape Navigator browser's scripting language, which is designed to make Web sites more interactive.

TIP: For anyone deploying Web sites on the public Internet, you should carefully consider the cost and benefits of any browser-specific add-ons, since by definition you will shut out those surfers who don't use the given browser. It may be advantageous to focus on features that can be used by all surfers. Using a Web-page publishing framework such WebHub, you can dynamically generate pages that are customized based on browser type.

Building Web-Based Applications with Delphi

In many ways, writing a Web application in 1996 is like writing an old mainframe, terminal-based application. The Web browser software (for instance, Netscape) is a "dumb" terminal in the sense that it knows absolutely nothing about your application. Most important, there is no continuous connection between the surfer and the application software; it's more of a planned dialogue, and the surfer can hang up at any time.

If you study HTML and HTTP, you'll see that the possibilities are fairly limited in terms of user interface, data exchange, and application features. In particular, HTML limits the screen layout, and HTTP limits the application features by keeping the surfer's request completely separate from the server's response. The "line" is not held open. It is a "stateless" protocol, with no intrinsic way of connecting a surfer's first request to the second. (See Chapter 19 for further discussion of these limitations and how to work around them.)

To learn more about HTTP and HTML, refer to the following Web sites as a starting point.:

- http://home.netscape.com/home/how-to-create-Web-services.html
- http://www.microsoft.com/windows/ie/ie20html.htm

Traditional CGI Framework

In general, there is a well-defined flow of information on the Web. The request starts with the surfer, who issues an HTTP request. The URL is resolved to an IP number by a DNS (which the surfer had to configure correctly based on data supplied by the ISP), and then the request speeds on its way to the Web server machine located at that IP address.

The Web server could be running any operating system and Web server, but for the sake of this discussion, let's assume that it is a Windows 95 or NT machine running a Web server such as IIS, WebSite, Netscape, or Spry. If the request is one for CGI or ISAPI, the Web server will run the requested program, passing in a set of input data that further defines the request. That program will do whatever it is designed to do based on the request (connecting to a database, perhaps), and it will create an output document that the Web server feeds back to the surfer.

For example, if you use the Yahoo! search engine and request information about HTML, the CGI program will run a query and dynamically generate an HTML document with a set of links for you. This entire process is depicted in Figure 17-1.

Even among the four Web servers mentioned, there are important implementation differences in terms of how Web applications are called. WebSite and Netscape both use a WinExec call to run an executable (.EXE) file. Microsoft and Spry allow you to use a dynamic link libray (DLL) instead of an .EXE file and do not require that the output document be communicated as a file (it can be a global memory object). It's clear that the DLL interface offers a five to tenfold increase in speed, and you can expect optimizations in the near future from all vendors.

As the CGI program loads and unloads with each request, it takes tremendous performance hits—especially if it is also connecting to a database each time. Clearly, there is a fundamental bottleneck with .EXE-based CGI calls.

You may also see something more subtle in Figure 17-1, which is that HTTP is a stateless protocol. Chapter 19 discusses more fully the drawbacks of this type of protocol and how to work around them.

Passing Data from the Surfer to the CGI Program

To have an interactive Web site in which a Web application responds to a surfer's request, you need to have a way to communicate data from the surfer to the application. There are two ways to get data from the surfer to your program.

One method is by passing information on the URL, typically after a question mark, which separates the file request from the so-called CGI query string. For example,

```
http://www.href.com/cgi-win/hubws.exe?hrefsite:toco
```

The hrefsite:toco string is considered part of the CGI environment data and is made available by the Web server to the CGI program for its use.

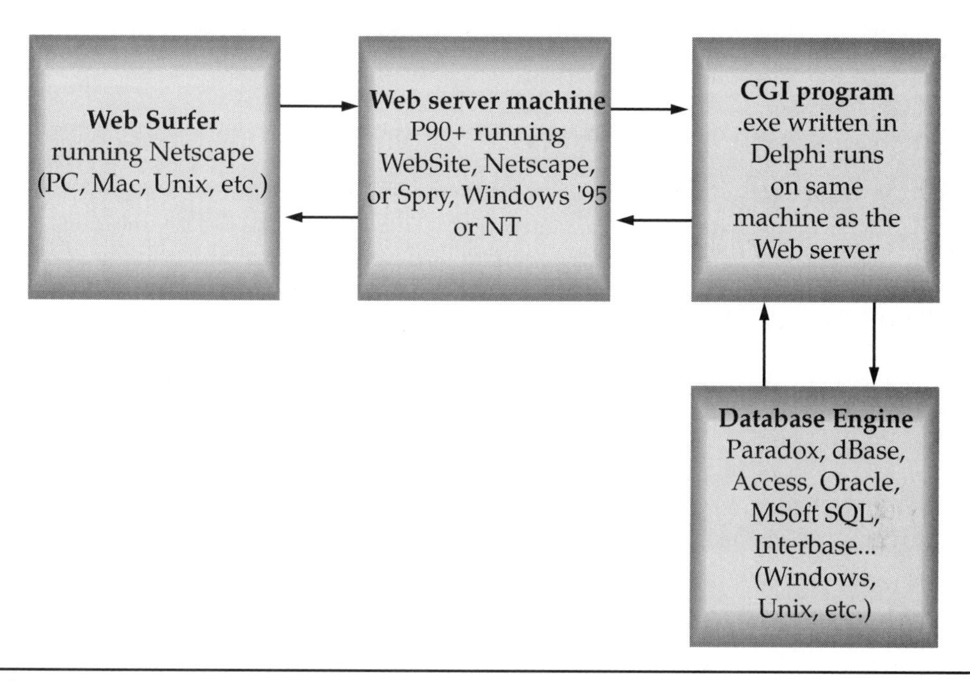

Figure 17-1. *How a request is processed by a server*

The second way is when the surfer actually fills out an HTML form and posts that data over the Web. In this case, all of the form data is made available to the Web application. Implementation details vary among Web servers, and an important consideration for Internet sites is whether the data can be sent securely. Typically, security is implemented with the Secure Sockets Layer (SSL) encryption method.

Although some sites, such as Yahoo!, send the surfer's query criteria on the URL, that is not always the best approach, as there are some obvious limits to the complexity that can be expressed on a single line.

What Is WebHub?

WebHub is a Web-publishing framework for building dynamic, database-driven Web sites with Delphi for deployment on Windows-based Web servers. One of the major benefits of WebHub is that Delphi programmers can build applications that are portable across the variety of Web servers, leaving the Delphi developer free to focus on the core application features. The complete WebHub package for Delphi programmers includes the Hub System, approximately 40 base classes (from TPack), and over 30 Web-specific components.

By leveraging Delphi's component capability, WebHub eliminates the need for extensive custom programming. Contrast Figure 17-2 with Figure 17-1 to see how WebHub's fundamental architecture is quite different from the traditional CGI paradigm and offers higher performances and process control. The WebHub System architecture consists of three layers: the Web-server-specific runner, WEBHUB CENTRAL, and custom .EXE files that are built with the WebHub components.

Solving the Performance Bottleneck

The rules of CGI require that the CGI program load and unload with every request, as a signaling mechanism for the Web server. (Microsoft and Spry servers are currently more sophisticated and require that a module in a DLL be invoked each time.) WebHub satisfies this requirement by providing a small (less than 50K) runner program that loads and unloads—while the HUB.EXE and your custom .EXE stay running for optimal performance.

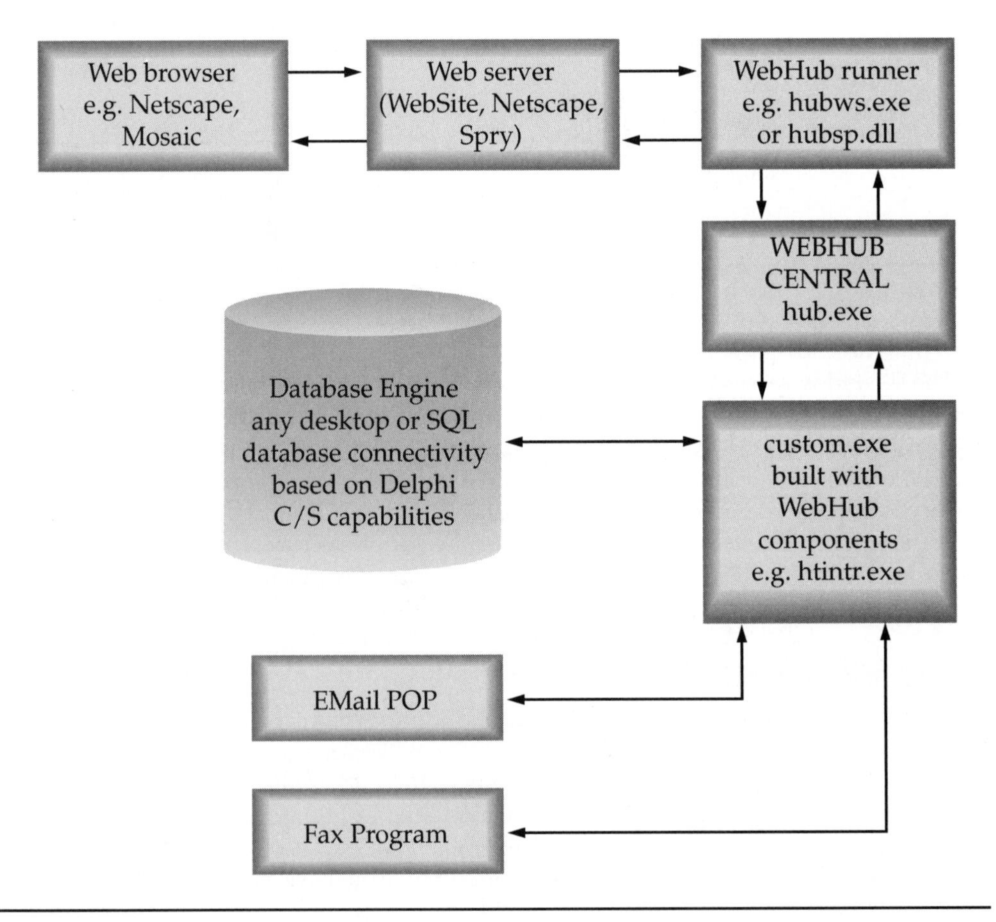

Figure 17-2. *WebHub data flow diagram*

Data Flow Analysis

The following is a description of the flow of data when WebHub is involved:

1. As usual, the data flow starts with the surfer making an HTTP request.
2. Let's assume that the request requires CGI. The Web server will notice this and call the CGI program—in this model, the WebHub runner.
3. The WebHub runner passes the command line information to WEBHUB CENTRAL (HUB.EXE). The runner has a customizable timeout to abort requests after a given period; the default is 15 seconds. If the runner times out, a customizable response file is returned instead of the regular output document.

   WebHub URLs exhibit a special form that has placeholders for four pieces of information. Three of these pieces are needed in all applications; the fourth is optional. This URL standard promotes reusability and makes it easy to build multiple applications with flexibility and consistency.

   There are advantages to adopting this standard. After the question mark (?) that separates the basic request from the so-called CGI query string, WebHub URLs always include an AppID followed by a PageID. The AppID is needed to support multiple Web applications on the same server.

   The first time a surfer requests a page from a WebHub application, a Session# is assigned. Thereafter, that Session# follows the surfer on all links within the site, so that the URL contains:

   ```
   ?AppID:PageID:Session#
   ```

   Thus for all subsequent connections, the application knows who the surfer is. (At the same time, the surfer is anonymous; no personal information is required.) See Chapter 19 for a full discussion of how the WebSession component handles saving state.

   Following the Session#, there is an optional command string, which is used for custom processing inside the application. Consequently, there are four standard pieces to the CGI query string:

   ```
   AppID:PageID:Session:Command
   ```

4. The HUB.EXE has two modes: regular Hub and Maître d'Hub. In regular mode, the Hub determines the AppID and will either process the page request internally or pass the request to a custom .EXE. If the custom .EXE is busy, the request will go into a queue. Page requests are processed based on priority (which is configurable).

WebHub addresses scalability in two ways. You can run multiple instances of the custom .EXE on the same machine to service multiple, simultaneous page requests, or you can expand to use a cluster of machines. Use the Maître d'Hub mode to direct surfers to other machines in a cluster. This means the Delphi developer can respond to a high-traffic situation by running the Web application on multiple machines. The essential task of the Hub is process control, whether on one or multiple machines.

5. The custom .EXE (or HUB.EXE in the special case of a HubApp) now generates the requested page, one section at a time. Unlike regular HTML, WebHub supports macro expansion on the fly. The combination of macro support with Delphi's runtime-type information (RTTI) gives WebHub many features not found elsewhere.

   Because of RTTI, WebHub action components can be invoked by name as a page is constructed. For example, creating an HTML table from a database requires connecting the proper components and then calling that grid component (TWebDataGrid) by its name within a page section (for example, %=grid1=%). Other action components enable e-mail, PGP (pretty good privacy), interactive outlines, and graphics generation. WebHub is designed to enable Delphi component authors to easily build additional action components that plug in smoothly.

   WebHub provides a simple solution to the common problem of the throughput bottleneck associated with large media files. Links to graphics, audio, shockwave, Java, and CAD-CAM files can be enhanced by using the media macro, which provides cycling across multiple machines to distribute the Web server load. This capability was added to support a site being built with WebHub for the Air Force, in which the Air Force is serving up files as large as 35 MB after searching through an Interbase database of approximately 10 million file descriptions.

6. Once the last page section is complete, the custom .EXE is finished with its job, and an output document is ready for the surfer. The runner shuts down, signaling completion of the CGI process, and the Web server passes the document back to the surfer.

Teamwork

Another vital point about the overall WebHub framework is that the basic file structure separates the HTML text from the Object Pascal work. Consider that HTML programmers cost significantly less than do Delphi programmers, and the skills required are quite different. It is much better to have one person work on page layout while someone else works on the Delphi application. Furthermore, by keeping the HTML outside the Delphi project, you can make changes to your page without recompiling and often without "taking down" your Web site. This facilitates remote administration and dramatically lowers the cost of site maintenance.

This separation of HTML from Object Pascal is accomplished in WebHub with simple text files that store HTML "chunks" and can be easily maintained outside the Delphi application and managed remotely, as well as reused across pages and applications.

The macro expansion and page definition features make it possible for HTML authors to do all the page layout while Delphi programmers focus on the work of providing searches, e-mail, and so forth.

Conclusion

This chapter provided you with a brief overview of Internet and Web terms, as well as an introduction to WebHub. In the next chapter you will learn about the underlying components that comprise WebHub and techniques that are relevant for Delphi projects in general and Web applications in particular. The TPack base classes made it possible to rapidly develop this commercial-grade product, which has relevance to developers everywhere.

Chapter Eighteen

Core WebHub Technology

WebHub includes a large collection of components that share a common ancestry, in an object-oriented sense. In the process of producing WebHub as a commercial product, HREF Tools Corp. developed a related series of capabilities in the ancestor classes of WebHub. The capabilities introduced in these base classes are applicable across Delphi applications, on and off the Web. They enable you to make application development truly fast and solid. You may want to use these techniques when building your own Delphi components, and a thorough understanding of them will enable you to leverage this core technology when building Web applications.

NOTE: *These base classes are called TPack. They were written by Michael Ax and are marketed by HREF Tools Corp.*

The key goal in designing WebHub was to build components that were easy for the developer to use and test, while making all the code as reusable as possible. Delphi is ideally suited for this kind of thinking and investment.

Projects and source code shown in this chapter are available on the CD-ROM that comes with this book with the exception of TPack. A shareware version of TPack, including its complied units and installation program, is on the CD-ROM. The source code for TPack can be purchased from HREF Tools Corp. Please refer to Appendix A for information on using the code files for this chapter.

Building the Ideal Component

Many of the issues for Web component design are the same as for other non-visual components. In this book, you've already learned about the benefits of object-oriented design. Now we're going to go several steps farther, looking first at some general principles and then using them to create specific features.

From the beginning, the organizing principle of WebHub was related to Delphi's object model. It was essential for the components to have clear tasks and properties. The user interface naturally evolved out of these tasks and properties. Following concepts applied by Delphi with TDataSource and TDBGrid, where the components are testable inside the Delphi IDE (Integrated Development Environment) so that you don't have to compile an entire project to check your work, HREF Tools built a set of base classes enabling the other 70+ components to have certain core features. The central characteristics that are critical to these components are:

- Clear identity
- Ready status, and the ability to get ready
- Cooperation with other components

- Reusable user interface
- The principle of verbs

The remainder of this chapter discusses these characteristics and how they are implemented. Once this groundwork has been covered, Chapter 19 continues with a discussion of Delphi in the context of the Web.

Clear Identity

Start by envisioning components as if they were actors on a stage. The key word here is *actors.* Actors are differentiated by how they look and sound and, in the context of a given production, by what they do. Components are likewise differentiated by their properties and their methods.

Like good characters in a play, good components need to have clearly defined roles. Otherwise the story becomes muddled, and you can't tell who is doing what, or why. The annoying bugs in our programming lives come from typos and tired eyes. The devastating bugs come from a lack of clarity about the purpose of our code and about the larger context in which the code must function.

Any developer can tell you that clear design is important. But how are you supposed to do the thinking required? How are you supposed to test your ideas? The exercise of formulating and testing components forces a better design process than does writing traditional procedural code because the very language makes you think in terms of boundaries: what exactly does this object do and how exactly is it described?

We can borrow another insight from the *actors on a stage* metaphor. We don't care so much about what a component "is"—we care what it "does." An actor has a role to play; a component has a *function* to provide. A developer faced with a new component for the first time thinks, Show me what I can do with it. The emphasis is on the action, and the properties and overall structure are important only inasmuch as they support that action.

As we continue with a slightly less philosophical checklist of desirable features, keep in mind the overriding importance of clear identity—as expressed by what a component does. The best components do one thing well while cooperating with the rest of the environment.

The theme of clear identity runs throughout TPack and WebHub. This is partially observable using the Object Browser, shown in Figure 18-1, where you can see the object hierarchy. Functionality is added on layer by layer, and the clear boundaries between components provides for optimal code reuse. Global functionality is defined at the higher levels (objects that appear more to the left in the object pane), while more granular behavior is instantiated in the descendant components (objects that appear more to the right in the object pane).

Readiness

A well-designed component should know when it is ready and how to get ready. A component is ready when it is initialized thoroughly enough to do its job. Sometimes a

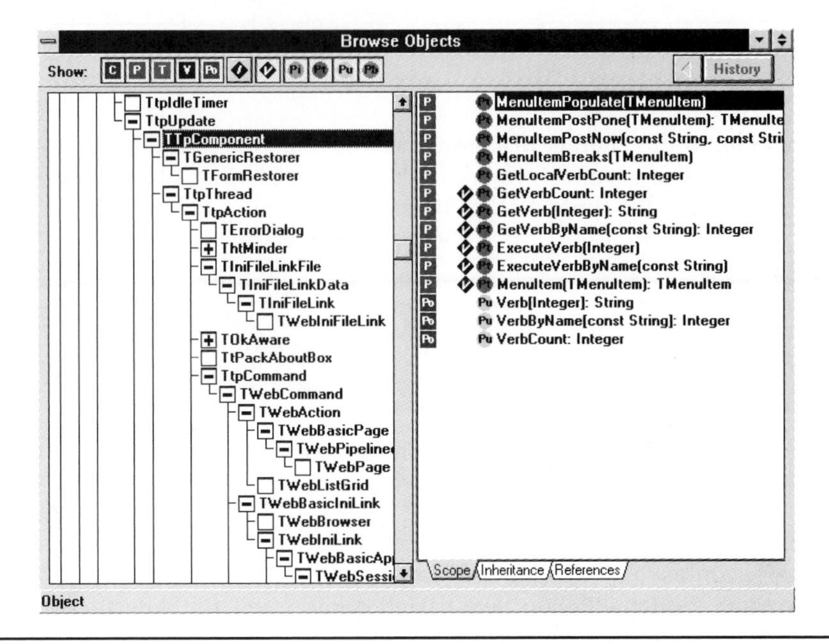

Figure 18-1. *The Object Browser displaying the relationship between TPack and WebHub*

component is ready as soon as it is loaded. Another component, however, may have data allocation and initialization issues that need to be handled before it can do its job accurately. For a component that requires initialization, this might take time. Furthermore, a particular component might lose its readiness status when properties are changed, and must be updated (made ready) again.

Imagine how changing two numbers affects the result of an addition. When a number changes, you should only need to tell the "sum component" that it is inaccurate (not ready) and write your code in such a way that the sum is only recomputed when next utilized. In a nutshell, that is supposed to be how you encapsulate rules in OOP (object-oriented programming) theory.

TPack handles readiness by publishing a simple Boolean property and hiding the complexity inside the component. The published property is named tpUpdated. The underlying private field is named ftpState and is a set that comprises one or more of these values: tpUpdating, tpUpdateOk, or tpLoaded. The component can be in none or any combination of these states. The read access procedure of tpUpdate properties not only looks at the current state flags but also calls the update mechanism. This permits a TPack component to perform additional tasks when you look at its Updated property in the Object Inspector. In other words, by performing a read, you are triggering the Update mechanism.

The action of this update mechanism depends on the particular component. In TPack, the component that adds the layer of "doing something" on update is called TtpUpdate.

NOTE: Sometimes you'll want to check whether a component is updated without triggering the "get ready" code. TPack includes an IsUpdated property to provide this information.

Following is the code for the TtpUpdate.GetUpdated method:

```
function TtpUpdate.GetUpdated: Boolean;
begin
  if (tpYieldTime in ftpOptions) then
  Application.ProcessMessages;
  if tpUpdateOnGet in ftpOptions then
  Update; {trigger autoupdate on read}
  Result:=tpUpdateOk in ftpState;
end;
```

To leverage the concept of readiness, components need to be able to communicate their readiness. The published property tpUpdated can serve this purpose. But there is also a benefit to communicating state information to the programmer and the end user in an easier-to-notice way. TPack therefore includes a TtpStatusBar component that is active at design time and runtime and is shared by most of the components as a place to put messages. You can see this component in Figure 18-2, where a component has changed the caption of this status bar to indicate its readiness.

To understand how this component works, you have to look at how the functionality is layered on. The following listing shows the interface for TtpUpdate. Notice the virtual methods that are meant to be overridden by subsequent layers (such as TtpAction). Some of the code is protected because it's never called from the outside.

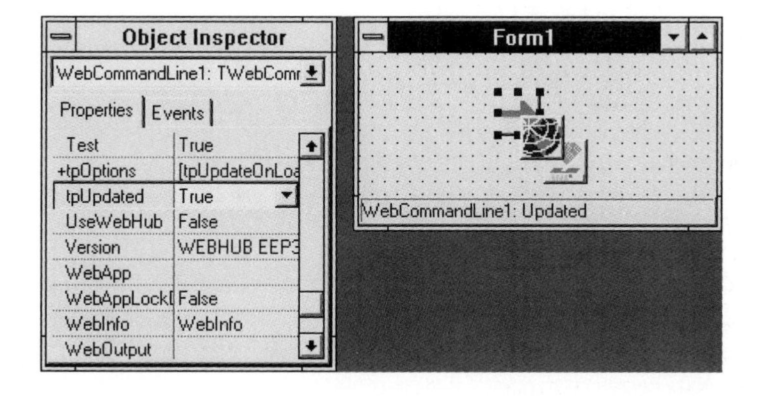

Figure 18-2. *In this figure, the WebCommandLine1 object is using the status bar to signal that it has been updated*

The purpose of the pedantic breakdown is explicitly to enable the layering of functionality as encouraged by the Delphi object model.

```
const
 TtpUpdateCapabilities =
   (tpUpdateOnLoad,tpUpdateOnGet,tpYieldTime,tpStatusPanel,tpQuiet);
 TtpUpdateStates    = (tpUpdating,tpUpdateOk,tpLoaded);
 TtpUpdateOptions   = set of TtpUpdateCapabilities;
 TtpUpdateState     = set of TtpUpdateStates;

 TtpUpdate = class(TComponentExtended)
 private
  ftpState: TtpUpdateState;
  ftpOptions: TtpUpdateOptions;
  fOnUpdate: TNotifyEvent;
  fOnUnUpdate: TNotifyEvent;
 protected
  function GetUpdated: Boolean;
  procedure SetUpdated(Value:Boolean);
  function CallDoUpdate: Boolean; Virtual;
  function DoUpdate:Boolean; Virtual;
  procedure DoUnUpdate; Virtual;

  function GetTpState:TtpUpdateState;
  procedure SetTpState(Value:TtpUpdateState);
  function GetTpYield: Boolean;
  procedure SetTpYield(Value:Boolean);

 public
  Constructor Create(aOwner:TComponent); Override;
  procedure Loaded; Override;

  function Update: Boolean; virtual;
  function IsUpdated: Boolean;
  function Refresh: Boolean;

  property tpOptions: TtpUpdateOptions read ftpOptions
    write ftpOptions;
  property tpState: TtpUpdateState read ftpState
    write SetTpState stored False;
  property tpYield: Boolean read GetTpYield
    write SetTpYield {default true};
  property tpUpdated: Boolean read GetUpdated
    write SetUpdated stored false; {if we did}
  property OnUpdate: TNotifyEvent read fOnUpdate write fOnUpdate;
  property OnUnUpdate: TNotifyEvent read fOnUnUpdate write fOnUnUpdate;
 published
  end;
```

The following code shows how the core functionality of TtpUpdate is implemented:

```
function TtpUpdate.Update: Boolean;
begin
  Result:=True;
  if ([tpUpdating,tpUpdateOk]*ftpState)<>[] then
    {either updating or updated}
    exit;
  ftpState:=ftpState+[tpUpdating];
{Must access field to change this member}
  try
    Result:=CallDoUpdate;
  finally
    ftpState:=ftpState-[tpUpdating];
    end;
  if Result then begin
    ftpState:=ftpState+[tpUpdateOk];
    if (csDesigning in ComponentState)
    and (Owner<>nil) and (Owner is TForm)
    and (tForm(Owner).Designer<>nil) then
      tForm(Owner).Designer.Modified;
    end;
  if assigned(fOnUpdate) then
    fOnUpdate(self);
end;
procedure TtpUpdate.DoUnUpdate;
begin
  ftpState:=ftpState-[tpUpdateOk];
  if assigned(fOnUnUpdate) then
    fOnUnUpdate(self);
end;

function TtpUpdate.CallDoUpdate:Boolean;
begin
  Result:=False;
  if (decUpdate in DebugFlags) then
    with cx do try
      DebugLog(Self,'+Update');
      Result:=DoUpdate;
      finally
      DebugLog(Self,'-Update= '+BoolString[Result]);
      end
  else
    Result:=DoUpdate; {finally we see if it's ok to update now}
end;

function TtpUpdate.DoUpdate:Boolean; {The 'Ancestor'}
begin
  Result:= True;
end;
```

Notice how the ftpState field is modified around CallDoUpdate so that the tpUpdating flag is appropriately added to and subtracted from the set. Before the update can take place, the ftpState field is flagged as including the state of Updating. This is done in the following statement:

```
ftpState:=ftpState+[tpUpdating];
```

In the finally clause, the state of Updating is over and is subtracted from the set of flags. This technique of adding and subtracting flags—rather than direct assignment—means there is no conflict with other parts of the system that may be manipulating other aspects of the set. In this example, direct assignment of ftpState:=tpUpdating might have worked, at least in the short term.

NOTE: *The calls to DebugLog in the CallDoUpdate function are for use with TDebugControl. All the components that inherit functionality from TtpUpdate will already know how to fill in the log as they load, update, and so forth. This information is particularly valuable when prototyping; during deployment, the debug flags would be turned off.*

The following TtpAction component overrides the Update method to add integration with the status bar. If you change the status property, the string will be displayed on the status bar.

```
function TtpAction.Update: Boolean;
begin
  if (([tpUpdating,tpUpdateOk]*ftpState)<>[]) then begin
  Result:=True;
  Status:='Updated';
  exit;
  end;
  Result:=inherited Update;
end;

function TtpAction.CallDoUpdate:Boolean;
begin
  Result:=False;
  try
  Status:='Updating '+Name;
  Result:=Inherited CallDoUpdate;
  finally
  if fStatusPanel<>nil then
    if Result then
    Status:='Updated'
    else
    Status:='Not Updated';
  end;
end;
```

Delphi 2 includes the Update property, which enables a component to reflect the Update state of all the components it owns (for example, the parent reports on the combined update state of all its children). That sense of depth is a second important step toward the overall expression of readiness.

What can you do with these features? The Updated concept is essential when, for example, you are working on encapsulating concepts and creating clear boundaries in code. These self-reflective state properties (TPack's tpUpdate and Delphi 2's Update property) let you concentrate on refining the actors and improving the "play" you use them in. This methodology enables you to rapidly customize the required logic and begin building multithreaded applications wherein all the actors can receive attention and "do their own thing" without the need for a centralized controller object and without the need for a linear representation of the program's flow.

By building sets of components to model a process, you can write down all the assumptions and intricacies of the process by using Delphi's property access methods. Beware, though. Developing a solution is never an inexpensive or rapid process. You can expect to work about 5 to 10 times as long and hard on an OOP solution as compared to a procedural one. However, the benefits of total encapsulation and clearly defined problem representation that result from the process should always lead to higher quality output and more adaptable systems.

Of course, you can write multithreaded applications without tpUpdated; it's just harder. The basic issue is that in a multithreaded environment, code is more likely to be called out of turn, and a component needs a simple (low overhead) way of indicating readiness for a task.

To pursue this topic more, look specifically at the TtpUpdate and TtpAction components in TPack. Download links are available at http://www.href.com/software/.

Cooperation

Out of a sense of clear identity comes the ability to cooperate—in our context, to cooperate with other components on the form. Soon you'll see that not only can a component be aware of its required properties and complain when they are not filled in, but it can automatically link to other components on the form when they are of the correct class, and can even create them if they are not yet in place. TComponentExtensions provides these features in a portable component that you can use in your own code.

Furthermore, a component should, where applicable, respond to the creation, existence, and removal of other components in the TForm neighborhood. In the first TShapes example, presented later in this chapter, the Notification procedure is overridden to provide this responsiveness.

Reusable User Interface

The task of building a Web application is best supported by a set of components that work together, flexibly and powerfully. Both the programmer and the end user need to interact with the components, although in different ways. Although both the programmer and end user will want to view and set properties, only the programmer can customize event handlers. Nonetheless, the benefit of enabling the end user to interact with the properties and to invoke component actions should not be underestimated. This raises the issue of user interface: how exactly should this happen?

Delphi already includes the ability to create custom property editors, which was discussed in Chapter 4. In this chapter you will learn how to allow the user interface to literally grow out of the object model, so that custom property editors become the interface not only for the programmer in the Delphi design environment, but also for the end user at runtime. There are two enormous benefits of this approach: code re-usability and learning curve leverage. Instead of having a completely unrelated user interface, the end-user product can have features that are identical to those experienced by the programmer. Any time you provide enhancements to one, you improve both.

Verbs

A *verb* is an action that a component can perform. The design of WebHub employs the notion of verbs to capture the possible actions of a component and make them part of the object model, thereby providing both the developer and the end user access to the component's behaviors. Some common methods shared by many of the TPack components and made available through verbs are items such as Test (do the main action), Update (become ready if possible), and Refresh (the environment has changed; please reinitialize). The special treatment of verbs by TPack leads directly to the user interface through the use of automatic menus and automatic verb bars. *Verb bars* are what most users call toolbars or speed bars. The difference is that verb bars are surfaced through the presence of verbs.

Figure 18-3 demonstrates the effect of using verbs for automatic menus. This figure includes a menu that was generated automatically based on the components in the TForm neighborhood by means of those components' verbs. Figure 18-4 shows a verb bar, with automatic buttons for the current object. (This is also a great way to conserve screen space in an application with hundreds of features.) Because the object model anticipates and supports verbs, it's possible to have auto-generating user-interface elements such as these.

Summary of Design Goals

The principles of clear identify, readiness, cooperation, interface reusability, and verbs provide a sound foundation upon which powerful, intelligent, and easily maintainable components can be constructed. The remainder of this chapter presents examples to show you how these principles are employed.

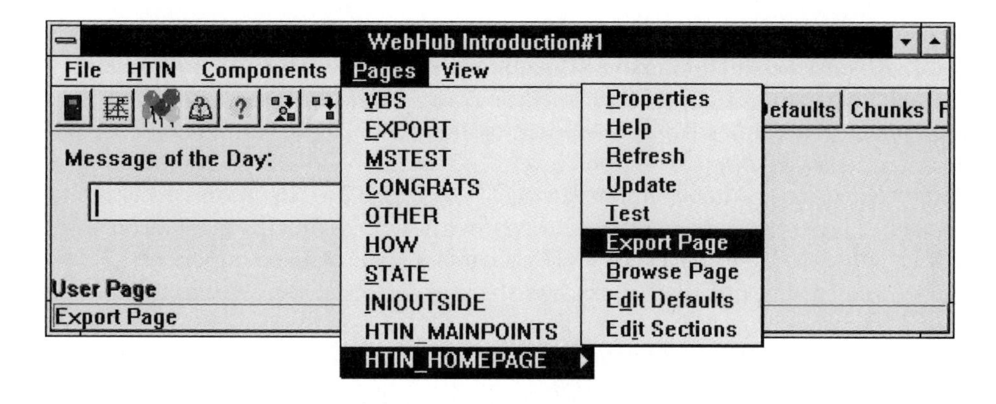

Figure 18-3. *A menu created from the published verbs of the components on the form*

TComponentExtensions—Components that Auto-link and Auto-create

Imagine a component that knows it must be connected, through its properties, to another component of a particular class in order for it to do its job. When asked whether it's tpUpdated (ready), that component can look around on the form and see whether the required component exits, and if so, connects to it. If not, the component can be assertive—creating the prerequisite component on the fly and then connecting to it. Such a component relieves you from the mundane task of placing each individual component and setting individual properties. It also reduces the likelihood of errors resulting from omitting required components.

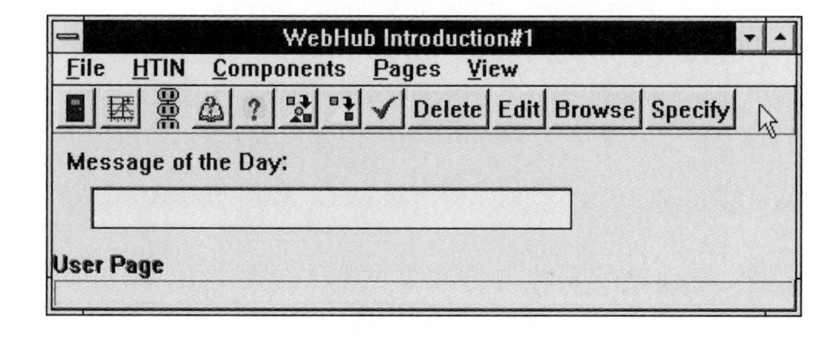

Figure 18-4. *A verb bar that includes automatic buttons for the current object*

The auto-link and auto-create abilities are found in TComponentExtensions. It leads to the experience that you have when building applications with the WebHub components, where placing a single TWebApp component on a form and double-clicking it to request an update leads to the immediate instantiation of several other components. This can be seen in Figure 18-5, where a TWebApp component has been placed on a form. After double-clicking TWebApp, it creates several additional components, and links to them. Figure 18-6 shows how this same form looks once TWebApp is updated. As this example demonstrates, making the components aware of what they need simplifies the process for the developer.

A Simple Example Using Circles and Frames

To illustrate these principles of readiness, auto-link, and auto-create, let's try a couple of examples. First is an example that focuses on auto-linking using two visual components. At the end of the chapter is an example that focuses more on readiness and includes a reusable property editor.

NOTE: To follow along with this example, you must first install the demo version of TPack from the CD-ROM. TryTP16.EXE installs the compiled units for the 16-bit version of TPack (Delphi 1.0), whereas TryTP32.EXE installs the 32-bit version (Delphi 2). Once you have run the installation, you must add the directory in which you have installed TPack to your component library search path (defined on the Library page of the Environment Options dialog box). Finally, add the REGTPACK.PAS unit to your component library and compile it. REGTPACK registers all of the TPack components with the component library.

The first example involves two components, a red circle and a black hollow frame. The red circle requires the frame. In fact, it requires that the frame appear surrounding the circle.

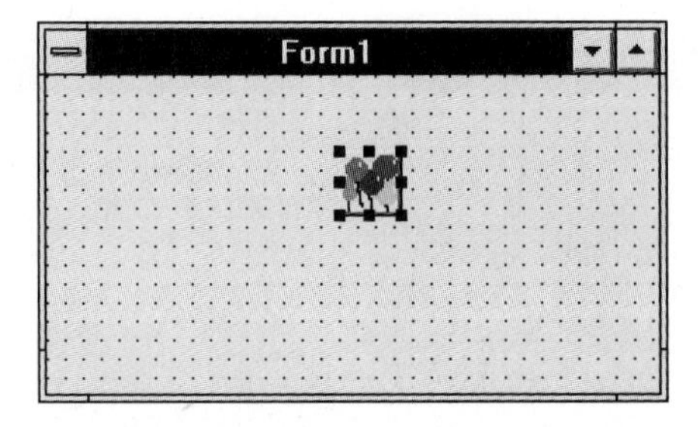

Figure 18-5. *A form with a single TWebApp component on it. This component requires additional components, which will be added when the TWebApp component updates itself*

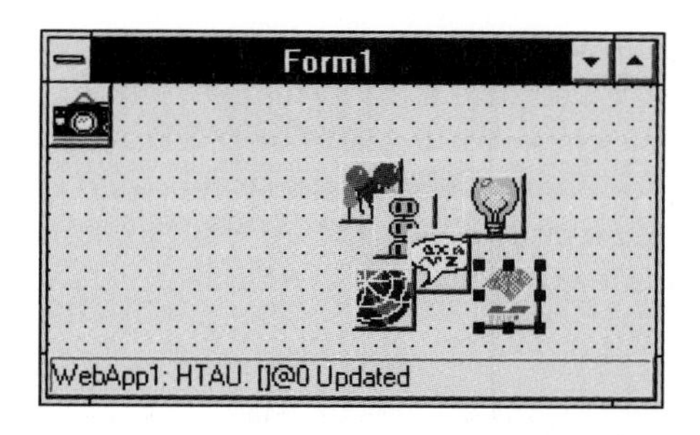

Figure 18-6. *Double-clicking the WebApp component causes it to update*

This example is demonstrated with TFramedRedCircle. This component looks for a Frame object and either connects to an existing one (if it already appears on the form) or creates a new one, if necessary.

NOTE: You run into very different issues when applying these ideas to visual versus non-visual components. The WebHub components are almost all non-visual. This visual example was chosen so that you can see what happens, but it requires some extra work that is not needed for non-visual components.

Figure 18-7 shows a new project with the addition of a FramedRedCircle; the black rectangle, a frame, was created on the fly by the FramedRedCircle.

Defining TFrame

The next step is to start building the components. In Object Pascal, TFrame needs to be declared before TFramedRedCircle because TFramedRedCircle will reference TFrame. Look at the definition for TFrame first. It is derived from TShape and has only a few

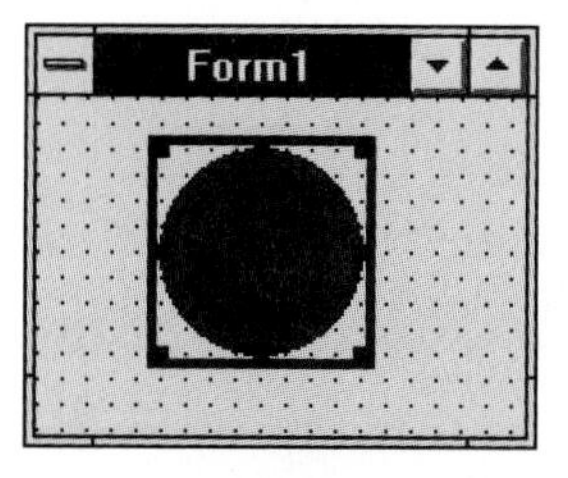

Figure 18-7. *The FramedRedCircle component will create a Frame component if a Frame does not already exist on the form*

customized properties, including the ability to make the frame hollow (or clear), have a wider edge, and be of the correct size to fit the circle. (If this frame also needed to respond to the resizing of the circle, the declaration of TFrame would be more complex.) The following code shows the type declaration and the constructor for the TFrame class (the entire code listing for the TSHAPES.PAS unit appears later in this chapter in the section "Summary of TSHAPES.PAS Example"):

```
unit Tshapes;
interface
uses
  SysUtils
  {$IFDEF WIN32}
  , Windows
  {$ELSE}
  , WinTypes
  {$ENDIF}
  , Messages, Classes, Graphics, Controls, ExtCtrls
  , Xtension {needed for TComponentExtensions};
const
  perfectFrameWidth=3; {used by TFrame}

{Customizing TFrame to make it 'clear' and have a perfect width}
type
  TFrame = class(TShape)
  public
  { Public declarations }
  Constructor Create(aOwner:TComponent); Override;
  end;
{more code here...}
implementation
{more code here...}
Constructor TFrame.Create(aOwner:TComponent);
begin
  inherited Create(aOwner);
  Brush.Style:=bsClear; {to be a 'frame' it has to appear hollow}
  Pen.Width:=perfectFrameWidth; {anything > 1 is noticeable}
end;
```

The only non-Delphi file mentioned in the uses clause is xtension. The xtension unit is part of TPack and is included on the CD-ROM. The xtension unit will in turn require the updateok unit from TPack.

As mentioned in earlier chapters of this book, the {$IFDEF WIN32} is a conditional compiler directive. If you are compiling with Delphi 2, include the unit Windows, otherwise use WinTypes (and often WinProcs). Using an $IFDEF enables you to have one source code file that compiles under both Delphi 1.0 and Delphi 2 environments, which is an obvious advantage.

The constant perfectFrameWidth is set once at the top so that you can quickly notice and easily change it. Because it's only used in the implementation section, it could (and probably should) be declared in the implementation section of this unit instead.

The type declaration of TFrame tells you two things immediately: TFrame is descended from TShape, and the only change we are making is to override the Create method. This new constructor calls the inherited Create method to take advantage of all the programming already done for TShape, and then sets two properties, Brush.Style and Pen.Width, to make this shape a frame.

Defining TFramedRedCircle

Once TFrame has been defined, the real task is making a self-aware component. It would be nice to inherit from *both* TComponentExtensions and TShape—but that is not possible since Delphi does not support multiple inheritance. The solution is to inherit from TShape, and "graft on" the TComponentExtension feature set. This can be accomplished by adding a member variable "cx" to TFramedRedCircle. This is shown in the following code segment from TSHAPES.PAS:

```
type
  TFramedRedCircle = class(TShape)
  cx: TComponentExtensions;
  private
  { Private declarations }
  fFrame:TFrame;
  public
  { Public declarations }
  Constructor Create(aOwner:TComponent); Override;
  Destructor Destroy; Override;
  procedure Notification(AComponent: TComponent; Operation: TOperation);
verride;
  procedure Loaded; Override;
  procedure Paint; Override;
  published
  { Published declarations }
  property Frame:TFrame read fFrame write fFrame;
  end;
procedure Register;
```

Notice exactly where the TComponentExtensions is added on to the type—above the private section. This makes it a public variable by default (unless the unit is compiled in the {$M+} state, in which case it would be published). This is done so that whenever you are within the scope of TFramedRedCircle you have access to all the methods of TComponentExtensions.

Two other topics are handled within the type declaration. The first is that the connection is made between the circle and its frame. This is accomplished via the combination of the private fFrame pointer (the real connection) and the published Frame property (which just refers back to fFrame). The published Frame property will be visible in the Object Inspector. The cx graft will take care of creating the frame object and making the link. Figure 18-8 displays both the form with the components on it, as well as the Object Inspector for the TFramedRedCircle component. Notice that the Frame property points to the Frame object; the assignment of this property was done by cx rather than by an explicit developer selection at design time.

The final task of the type declaration in this example is to itemize all the methods that will be overridden. Create, Destroy, and Notification must be overridden in all cases where you graft on cx because of the additional memory allocated for cx. The following code segment from TSHAPES.PAS shows how the Create method allocates the memory, Destroy frees it, and Notification handles the disconnect (of the frame from the circle) in the case where the programmer decides to delete the frame first.

NOTE: *The Loaded method in NAME.PAS is only relevant at runtime, and its code is commented out. You can experiment with turning off the Paint method and using Loaded instead; what you'll find is that the frame can't be moved in the designer, but at runtime it will jump into position. The Paint method turns out to be one of the few TShape methods that can be overridden and still has an effect in the designer.*

```
implementation
{------------------------------------------------------------------}
Constructor TFramedRedCircle.Create(aOwner:TComponent);
begin
  inherited Create(aOwner);
  cx:= TComponentExtensions.Create(Self);
  if aOwner.Name<>'' then begin {aOwner is the Form}
  Shape:=stCircle;
  Brush.Color:=clRed;
  cx.SetIfFoundExactly(fFrame,TFrame);
  cx.MakeIfNil(fFrame,TFrame); {create TFrame if none found on form}
  end;
end;
Destructor TFramedRedCircle.Destroy;
begin
  cx.free; {what we create, we must destroy}
  inherited Destroy;
end;

procedure TFramedRedCircle.Notification(AComponent: TComponent;
  Operation: TOperation);
begin
  inherited Notification(AComponent, Operation);
  if Operation = opRemove then begin
  {disconnect if fFrame is being removed}
  cx.NilIfSet(fFrame,AComponent);
  end;
end;
```

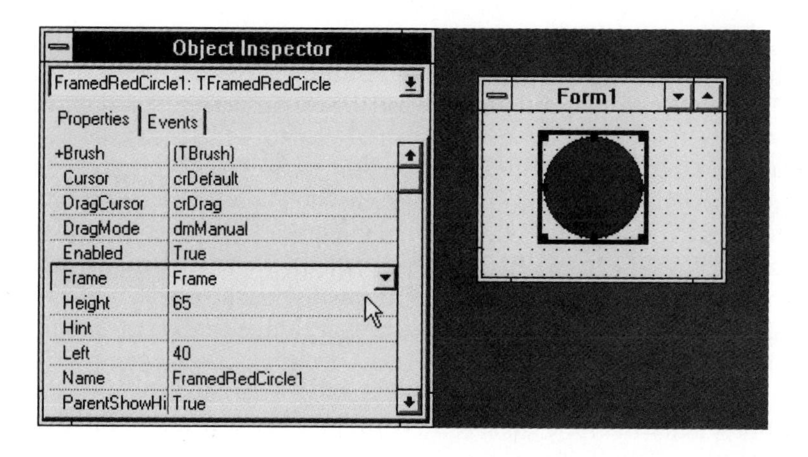

Figure 18-8. *The TFramedRedCircle component automatically assigns its Frame property to the available Frame object*

A number of gems are hidden in the Create method. Of course, you start by inheriting the Create method from the TShape object, as was done for TFrame. Next the cx object is created—essentially, allocating memory for it and initializing it. The rest of the code is supposed to be run if and only if you are in the designer. If the statement

```
aOwner.Name<>''
```

returns True, the component is being created at design time.

You might be tempted to use the following statement to test whether you are in the designer:

```
if csDesigning in ComponentState then ...
```

Unfortunately, inside the Create method of a component, Delphi has not yet set the ComponentState property—its value is False even though you are in fact in the designer. So how can you tell whether you are in the designer? It turns out that the TForm Name property is only set while you're in the designer (to avoid duplicate names with multiple instances of the form). This lets you sneak in some design-time-only code into a component's constructor *before* Delphi gets around to setting the ComponentState property.

Setting the shape and brush color is straightforward enough. The two lines following the setting of these properties draw on functionality provided in the xtension unit. The method setIfFoundExactly searches through the components on the form, looking for an instance of a Frame object. If one is found, it connects fFrame to that instance. (Try creating a new project and putting a TFrame on the form first. Then add a TFramedRedCircle and you will see the frame captured and moved into position.)

The makeIfNil method is responsible for creating the TFrame component on the fly. After creating the component, it also sets the connection between the fFrame property and the new object, producing the effect shown in Figure 18-8.

If you were writing TSHAPES.PAS yourself, you might be tempted to set the location of the Frame right after creating it. You can do this; however, you would probably want to set the location of the frame *relative* to the location of the circle. That is not possible because from inside the constructor Delphi has not yet moved the circle to its destination on the form; it is instead sitting at 0,0. Consequently, any attempts to position the frame relative to the circle from within the constructor would end up setting it to a position like –4,–4.

This brings up the need for the Paint procedure, shown in the following code listing. Overriding the Paint method *does* work. Our new Paint method's code is straightforward and amounts to calculating how large the frame should be, where the frame should be placed, and then setting the appropriate values.

```
procedure TFramedRedCircle.Paint;
var
  goHereLeft, goHereTop:integer;
  thisDiameter:integer;
  offset:integer;
begin
  inherited Paint;
  if fFrame<>nil then begin
  {offset=how much displacement between frame and circle}
  offset:=FFrame.pen.width+1;
  goHereLeft:=Left-offset;
  goHereTop :=Top-offset;
  {base the frame size on circle width}
  thisDiameter:=width+(offset*2);
  with fFrame do begin
    left:=goHereLeft;
    top :=goHereTop;
    height:=thisDiameter;
    width :=thisDiameter;
    end;
  end;
end;
```

As mentioned earlier, the Loaded procedure is optional; it is shown here to demonstrate an easy way to have features applied at runtime only, when the component is loaded into memory:

```
procedure TFramedRedCircle.Loaded;
begin
  inherited Loaded;
  {if fFrame<>nil then
  with fFrame do begin
    left:=self.Left-(pen.width+1);
    top :=self.Top -(pen.width+1);
    end;}
end;
```

Registering the Components

To make components available on the palette, you have to register them with the component library. The following code contains the registration procedure, which will place these components on the Samples palette page:

```
procedure Register;
begin
  RegisterComponents('Samples', [TFramedRedCircle, TFrame]);
end;
end.
```

Summary of TSHAPES.PAS Example

The TSHAPES unit demonstrates a simple case of grafting TComponentExtensions onto a visual component. There is one known problem with this simplistic implementation. If you add a second TFramedRedCircle to your project, you can see the two fight over the single frame. To work around this problem, you could add some additional code to be sure that each circle gets its own frame.

The following is the entire code listing for the TSHAPES.PAS unit:

```
unit Tshapes;
interface
uses
 SysUtils
 {$IFDEF WIN32}
 , Windows
 {$ELSE}
 , WinTypes
 {$ENDIF}
 , Messages, Classes, Graphics, Controls, ExtCtrls
 , Xtension {from TPack; needed for TComponentExtensions}
 ;

const
```

```
 perfectFrameWidth=3; {used by TFrame}

{Customizing TFrame to make it 'clear' and have a perfect width}
type
 TFrame = class(TShape)
 public
  { Public declarations }
  Constructor Create(aOwner:TComponent); Override;
 end;

{ TFramedRedCircle is the "real example." }
type
 TFramedRedCircle = class(TShape)
  {Add a variable, cx, to "graft on" the functionality. See
   xtension.pas for source to TComponentExtensions. }
  cx: TComponentExtensions;
 private
  { Private declarations }
  fFrame:TFrame;
 public
  { Public declarations }
  Constructor Create(aOwner:TComponent); Override;
  Destructor Destroy; Override;
  procedure  Notification(AComponent: TComponent;
    Operation: TOperation); Override;
  procedure  Loaded; Override;
  procedure  Paint; Override;
 published
  { Published declarations }
{Here is the pointer to the other object to create automatically.}
  property Frame:TFrame read fFrame write fFrame;
 end;

procedure Register;

{-----------------------------------------------------------------------}

implementation

Constructor TFrame.Create(aOwner:TComponent);
begin
 inherited Create(aOwner);
 Brush.Style:=bsClear;
 {it wouldn't be a frame if you couldn't see through it}
 Pen.Width:=perfectFrameWidth; {anything > 1 is noticable}
end;

{-----------------------------------------------------------------------}
```

```
Constructor TFramedRedCircle.Create(aOwner:TComponent);
begin
 inherited Create(aOwner);

 cx:= TComponentExtensions.Create(Self);

{Perform following if and only if we are in the designer.}
{Here's some code that does NOT work because Delphi hasn't
 set this yet: if csDesigning in ComponentState }
{This alternative works. The tForm Name property is only set while
in the designer to avoid duplicate names with multiple instances of the
form. Design-time only code is placed into a component's constructor
*before* Delphi sets the 'ComponentState' property.}
 if aOwner.Name<>'' then begin {aOwner is the Form}
  Shape:=stCircle;
  Brush.Color:=clRed;
  cx.SetIfFoundExactly(fFrame,TFrame);
  cx.MakeIfNil(fFrame,TFrame); {create TFrame if none found on form}

  {It is NOT POSSIBLE to set the location of fFrame here because
   in this moment, our circle is sitting at 0,0 and has not yet
   been moved to its real location, as determined by your click.
   Paint is used to accomplish this instead.}

  end;
end;

procedure TFramedRedCircle.Paint;
var
 goHereLeft, goHereTop:integer;
 thisDiameter:integer;
 offset:integer;
begin
 inherited Paint;
 if fFrame<>nil then begin
  {offset=how much displacement between frame and circle}
  offset:=FFrame.pen.width+1;
  goHereLeft:=Left-offset;
  goHereTop :=Top-offset;
  {base the frame size on circle width}
  thisDiameter:=width+(offset*2);
  with fFrame do begin
   left:=goHereLeft;
   top :=goHereTop;
   height:=thisDiameter;
   width :=thisDiameter;
   end;
  end;
end;
```

```
Destructor TFramedRedCircle.Destroy;
begin
 cx.free; {what we create, we must destroy}
 inherited Destroy;
end;

procedure TFramedRedCircle.Notification(AComponent: TComponent;
  Operation: TOperation);
begin
 inherited Notification(AComponent, Operation);
 if Operation = opRemove then begin
  {disconnect if fFrame is being removed}
  cx.NilIfSet(fFrame,AComponent);
  end;
end;

procedure TFramedRedCircle.Loaded;
begin
 inherited Loaded;
{If you run the form, the frame moves into place. This works even if
you remove the Paint method. With paint overridden, there is no need for
this piece.}
 {if fFrame<>nil then
  with fFrame do begin
   left:=self.Left-(pen.width+1);
   top :=self.Top -(pen.width+1);
   end;}
end;

{-----------------------------------------------------------------------}

procedure Register;
begin
 RegisterComponents('Samples', [TFramedRedCircle, TFrame]);
end;
end.
```

Learning More About Auto-linking and Auto-creation

If you want to pursue the topic of auto-linking and auto-creation, you should study the xtension.pas unit. In particular, examine the following methods: setIfFoundExactly, makeIfNil, makeNewComponent, CreateComponent, and NameComponent.

Property Editors and the User Interface

If components provide the functionality of an application, and setting properties invokes features (through the use of write methods), then configuring the properties is the essence of controlling the application and is the shortest path to a complete user interface. This is "organic" user interface design in the sense that the interface grows directly out of the structure.

Property editors are reused throughout WebHub. You will see the same forms in the Delphi IDE that the end user sees at runtime. Briefly, to implement this feature yourself, you need only one insight: a property editor is a form and can be easily invoked in the second context of runtime use.

NOTE: *As described in Chapter 4, property editors do not have to be dialog box-based, although the property editors discussed in this chapter are all based on dialog boxes.*

This technique of using property editors as end-user interface elements is demonstrated in the following code extracted from the classic Delphi component TSmiley, created by Nick Hodges. (This code appears here and on the CD-ROM with permission of the author.) The following code shows a property editor being used at design time. The component being modified is TSmiley, the property is Smiley's mood, and its type is an ordinal value. The property editor provides a nice user interface to allow the selection of a value.

The following is the Edit method of the TSmileyMoodProperty property editor. This method is called when the user clicks the ellipses (...) button for the Mood property at design time. Within this method, the TSmileyMoodDlg dialog box is created and displayed, permitting the user to select a value for the Mood property. The use of this property editor at design time is shown in Figure 18-9.

```
procedure TSmileyMoodProperty.Edit;
{here's where we run the property editor at design time}
begin
  with TSmileyMoodDlg.Create(Application) do
try
  Mood:=TSmileyMood(GetOrdValue);
  {small difference only to MoodDialog above}
  if ShowModal=mrOk then
    SetOrdValue(Ord(Mood))
  finally
  Free
  end;
end; {Edit}
```

Now consider the MoodDialog method for the TSmiley class. This method, which is called when the user right-clicks on a Smiley component at runtime, also displays

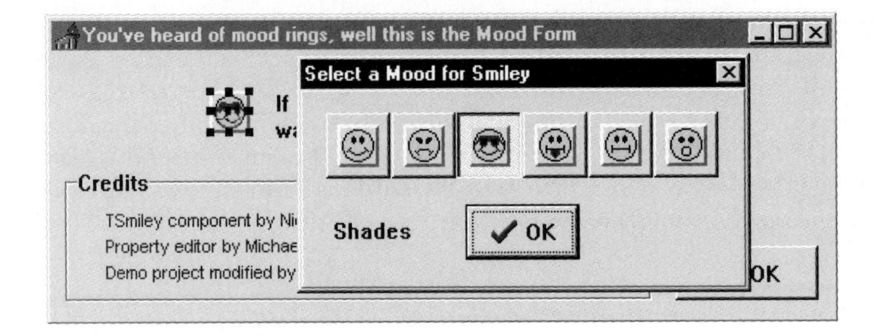

Figure 18-9. *The Property Editor for the Mood property of the TSmiley class. Property editors are generally displayed at design time*

the TSmileyMoodDlg dialog box. The use of this dialog box at runtime is shown in Figure 18-10.

```
procedure TSmiley.MoodDialog;
{here's where we run the property editor at runtime}
begin
  with TSmileyMoodDlg.Create(Application) do try
  Mood:=Self.Mood;
  if ShowModal=mrOk then
    Self.Mood:=Mood;
  finally
  Free
  end;
end;
```

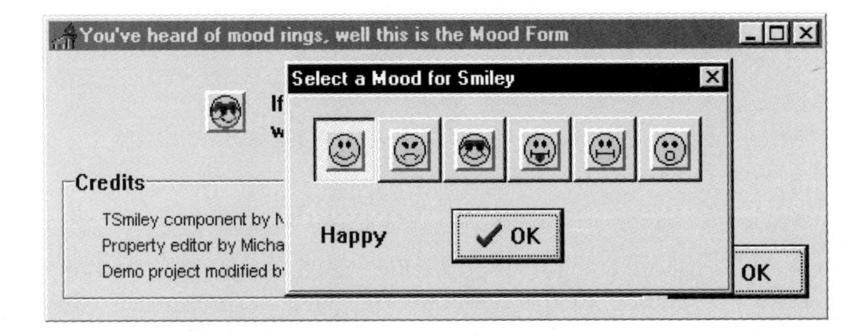

Figure 18-10. *The Property Editor for the Mood property of the TSmiley class is being surfaced for use by the end user at runtime, allowing the single dialog box to serve both design time and runtime duties*

You can try the project by copying the TSMILE.PAS unit to a directory listed in your library search path. You must also add the appropriate resource file, TSMILE16.RES or TSMILE32.RES to this directory, depending on whether you are running Delphi 1.0 (16-bit) or Delphi 2 (32-bit). You will also need to copy TSMILE.DCR to this directory, but only if you are working with Delphi 1.0. The *.DCR file is a resource file containing the bitmap displayed by the component on the component palette. The CD-ROM with this book only has the 16-bit version of this resource. Once you have copied the files, add the TSmile unit to your component library and compile it. Finally, open and run the project file SMILEYP.DPR.

The following is the complete code listing for the TSMILE.PAS unit:

```
{  The TSmiley component is Copyright © 1995  }
{     by Nick Hodges All Rights Reserved    }
{     email: 71563.2250@compuserve.com     }
 MODIFIED by Michael Ax, ax@href.com, to demonstrate a few things
 about property editors...
{ Reprinted with permission from the authors}

unit TSmile;

interface

uses
  SysUtils
{$IFDEF WIN32}
, Windows
{$ELSE}
, WinProcs, WinTypes
{$ENDIF}
 , Messages, Classes, Graphics, Controls,
  Forms, Dialogs, Buttons, ExtCtrls, StdCtrls, DsgnIntF, TypInfo;

type
  TSmileyMood = (smHappy, smSad, smShades, smTongue,
  smIndifferent, smOoh);

const
   smInitialMood = smHappy;
   smClickedMood = smSad;
   MoodString : array[TSmileyMood] of PChar = ('smHappy', 'smSad',
    'smShades', 'smTongue', 'smIndifferent', 'smOoh');
   MaxHeight = 26;
   MaxWidth = 26;

type
    TSmiley = class(TImage)
    private
    { Private declarations }
```

```
    Face: TBitmap;
    FMood: TSmileyMood;
    procedure SetBitmap;
    procedure SetSmileyMood(NewMood: TSmileyMood);
    procedure WMSize (var Message: TWMSize); message wm_paint;
    procedure MouseClicked(up:boolean);
    procedure MaxSize;
  public
    { Public declarations }
    constructor Create(AOwner: TComponent); override;
    destructor Free;
    procedure Toggle;
    procedure MoodDialog;
    procedure MouseDown(Button: TMouseButton;
      Shift: TShiftState; X, Y: Integer); override;
    procedure MouseUp(Button: TMouseButton;
      Shift: TShiftState; X, Y: Integer); override;
  published
    property Mood: TSmileyMood read FMood write SetSmileyMood;
  end;

  TSmileyMoodDlg = class(TForm)
    BitBtn1: TBitBtn;
    Panel1: TPanel;
    SpeedButton1: TSpeedButton;
    SpeedButton2: TSpeedButton;
    SpeedButton3: TSpeedButton;
    SpeedButton4: TSpeedButton;
    SpeedButton5: TSpeedButton;
    SpeedButton6: TSpeedButton;
    Label1: TLabel;
    procedure SpeedButton1Click(Sender: TObject);
  private
    { Private declarations }
    FMood: TSmileyMood;
    procedure SetSmileyMood(NewMood: TSmileyMood);
  public
    { Public declarations }
    property Mood: TSmileyMood read FMood write SetSmileyMood;
  end;

  TSmileyMoodProperty = class( TEnumProperty )
    function GetAttributes: TPropertyAttributes; override;
    procedure Edit; override;
  end;

procedure Register;
```

```
{-------------------------------------------------
         implementation
--------------------------------------------------}

implementation

{$R *.DFM}
{$IFDEF WIN32}
{$R TSmile32.res}
{$ELSE}
{$R TSmile16.res}
{$ENDIF}

{-------------------------------------------------
            TSmiley
--------------------------------------------------}

constructor TSmiley.Create(AOwner: TComponent);
begin
  inherited Create(AOwner);
  Face := TBitmap.Create; {Note dynamic allocation of the pointer}
  SetSmileyMood(smInitialMood);
end; {Create}

destructor TSmiley.Free;
begin
  Face.Free; {Use Free rather than Destroy,
    as Free checks for a nil pointer first}
  inherited Free;
end; {Free}

procedure TSmiley.Toggle;
begin
  if fMood = high(TSmileyMood) then {Don't allow fMood to overflow}
    Mood := low(TSmileyMood)
  else
    Mood := Succ(fMood);
end; {Toggle}

procedure TSmiley.SetSmileyMood(NewMood: TSmileyMood);
begin
  if (face.handle=0) or (fMood<>NewMood) then begin
    FMood := NewMood;
    SetBitmap;
    end;
end; {SetSmileyMood}

procedure TSmiley.SetBitmap;
begin
```

```
  Face.Handle := LoadBitmap(hInstance, MoodString[fMood]);
  {Use RTTI to cast face as TGraphic, needed by TImage}
  Self.Picture.Graphic := Face as TGraphic;
  MaxSize;
end; {SetBitmap}

{This method will respond to a mouse push on the Smiley by storing the
old face for later use and giving the "Sad" face.}
procedure TSmiley.MouseDown(Button: TMouseButton;
  Shift: TShiftState; X, Y: Integer);
begin
  inherited MouseDown(Button, Shift, X, Y);
  if Button=mbRight then
    {Here's where we run the property editor at runtime}
    MoodDialog
  else
    MouseClicked(false);
end; {MouseDown}

{This method restores the old face when the mouse comes back up}
procedure TSmiley.MouseUp(Button: TMouseButton;
 Shift: TShiftState; X, Y: Integer);
begin
  inherited MouseUp(Button, Shift, X, Y);
  if Button<>mbRight then
    MouseClicked(true);
end; {MouseUp}

procedure TSmiley.MouseClicked(up:boolean);
const {the proc uses a constant rather than a field.}
  OldMood: TSmileyMood=smInitialMood;
begin
  if up then          {button back up.}
    SetSmileyMood(OldMood)     {restore prior mood}
  else             {button now down}
    if Mood<>smClickedMood then begin {store if different!}
      {windows/delphi can loose the up sometimes so we must
      not just act on any down but must see what it'd do first}
      OldMood:= Mood;     {store mood in local constant}
      SetSmileyMood(smClickedMood); {express clicked-on mood}
      end;
end;

procedure TSmiley.WMSize(var Message: TWMSize);
{This method keeps the user from sizing the Smiley at design time.
(You can use the 'csDesigning in ComponentState' to control what
the user can do at design time.}
begin
  inherited;
```

```
  if (csDesigning in ComponentState) then
    MaxSize;
end;

procedure TSmiley.MaxSize;
begin
  Width := MaxWidth;
  Height := MaxHeight;
end;

{Here's where we run the property editor at runtime}
procedure TSmiley.MoodDialog;
begin
  with TSmileyMoodDlg.Create(Application) do try
    Mood:=Self.Mood;
    if ShowModal=mrOk then
      Self.Mood:=Mood;
  finally
    Free
  end;
end;

{--------------------------------------------------
         TSmileyMoodDlg
---------------------------------------------------}

procedure TSmileyMoodDlg.SetSmileyMood(NewMood: TSmileyMood);
var
  Counter: Integer;
begin
{ if (fMood<>NewMood) or (label1.caption='Label1') then }
    for Counter:= 0 to ComponentCount - 1 do
      if (Components[Counter] is TSpeedButton) then
        with TSpeedButton(Components[Counter]) do
          if Tag= Ord(NewMood) then begin
            Down:= True; {sets fMood vis click}
            fMood:= NewMood;
            with Label1 do begin
              Caption:= copy(strpas(MoodString[fMood]),3,255);
              Update;
              end;
            end;
end;

procedure TSmileyMoodDlg.SpeedButton1Click(Sender: TObject);
begin
  Mood := TSmileyMood((Sender as TSpeedButton).Tag);
end; {SpeedButton1Click}
```

```
{---------------------------------------------------
         TMoodProperty
---------------------------------------------------}

function TSmileyMoodProperty.GetAttributes: TPropertyAttributes;
begin
  Result:=[paDialog];
end;

{here's where we run the property editor at design time}
procedure TSmileyMoodProperty.Edit;
begin
  with TSmileyMoodDlg.Create(Application) do try
    {small difference only to MoodDialog above}
    Mood:=TSmileyMood(GetOrdValue);
    if ShowModal=mrOk then
      SetOrdValue(Ord(Mood))
  finally
    Free
  end;
end; {Edit}

{---------------------------------------------------
       Smiley ends, keep smiling.
---------------------------------------------------}
procedure Register;
begin
  RegisterComponents('SAMPLES', [ TSmiley ] );
  RegisterPropertyEditor( TypeInfo( TSmileyMood ),
    TSmiley, 'Mood', TSmileyMoodProperty );
end;

end.
```

As pointed out earlier, the primary advantage of this technique is that the one dialog box you create adds features both in design time and runtime. If you later need to update the dialog box, your updates automatically apply to both the design time and runtime interfaces.

Using Verbs to Automate the Creation of the User Interface

Delphi already implements the concept of verbs. This notion is represented in speed menus—the pop-up menus that appear when you right-click something in the Delphi IDE. TPack takes this concept farther and makes the same verbs available for automatic menus and on verb bars at runtime. Furthermore, TPack does it in object-oriented fashion where verbs are inherited. Prior verbs sometimes need to be suppressed as well. (In WebHub, see TtpMainMenu and TtpComboBar for general use, and TWebMenu in the Web context.)

The following code listing shows the declaration of a TtpComponent. This is the layer in which verb capability is added into the object hierarchy. You should pay particularly close attention to the functions GetLocalVerbCount and GetVerbCount.

```
type
  TTpComponent = class(TtpUpdate)
  private
  protected
  procedure MenuItemPopulate(Item:TMenuItem);
  function MenuItemPostPone(Item:TMenuItem):TMenuItem;
  procedure MenuItemPostNow(const aCaption,aHint:String;
      DeleteOnSet:Boolean);
  procedure MenuItemBreaks(Item:TMenuItem);
  function GetLocalVerbCount: Integer;
  function GetVerbCount: Integer; Virtual;
  function GetVerb(Index: Integer): string; Virtual;
  function GetVerbByName(const Value: String):integer; Virtual;
  procedure ExecuteVerb(Index: Integer); Virtual;
  procedure ExecuteVerbByName(const Value: String); Virtual;
  function MenuItem(Item:TMenuItem):TMenuItem; Virtual;
  public
  property Verb[Index: integer]:String read GetVerb;
  property VerbByName[const Value:String]:integer read GetVerbByName;
  property VerbCount: integer read GetVerbCount;
  end;
```

The idea is that for any component, its verbs are those of its ancestor plus its own local verbs. The following code shows how this idea works using the inherited GetVerbCount:

```
function TtpCommand.GetVerbCount: Integer;
begin
  Result := inherited GetVerbCount + GetLocalVerbCount;
end;
```

Of course, the verbs have to be listed somewhere and called at some time. The next listing shows how you do this. The WebHub components are descended from TtpComponent, and your components can also descend from TtpComponent. Notice the definition of verb 0, the Update verb.

```
{what is the verb's name}
function TTpComponent.GetVerb(Index: Integer): string;
begin  {ancestor}
  case Index of
  0: Result := 'Update';
```

```
    1: Result := 'Refresh';
    2: Result := 'Help';
    3: Result := 'Properties';
    end;
end;

procedure TTpComponent.ExecuteVerb(Index: Integer);   {do the verb}
begin  {anchestor}
  case Index of
  0: Update;
  1: Refresh;
  2: Help;
  3: EditProperties;
  end;
end;
```

To try out this code, make a new project and drop in these three components from TPack: TtpAboutBox, TtpMainMenu, and TtpComboBar. The TtpAboutBox displays a quick dialog with version information. The TtpMainMenu builds the main menu on the fly. The TtpComboBar combines a verb bar with a more traditional Tool Bar, plus an Idle Dot. (See the QUIKMNU.DPR project on the code disk.)

To make the verb bar display icons, add these extra $R lines to the implementation section:

```
implementation
{$R *.DFM}
{$IFDEF WIN32}
{$R TPack32.RES}
{$ELSE}
{$R TPack16.RES}
{$ENDIF}
```

Figure 18-11 displays the main form for the project QUIKMNU. As you can see, these defined verbs can be used to build a menu. Another way to look at this process is that the menu builds itself based on the components on the form.

NOTE: *To open, work with, and compile the QUIKMNU project you must first install the demo version of TPack from the CD, as described earlier in this chapter. TryTP16.EXE installs the compiled units for the 16-bit version of TPack, whereas TryTP32.EXE installs the 32-bit version. Once you have run the installation, you must add the directory in which you have installed TPack to your component library search path. Finally, add the REGTPACK.PAS unit to your component library and compile it. REGTPACK registers all of the TPack components with the component library.*

It takes one more step to connect the verb bar to a valid component. Set the TtpVerbBar.tpComponent to point to the TtpAboutBox. Figure 18-12 shows how

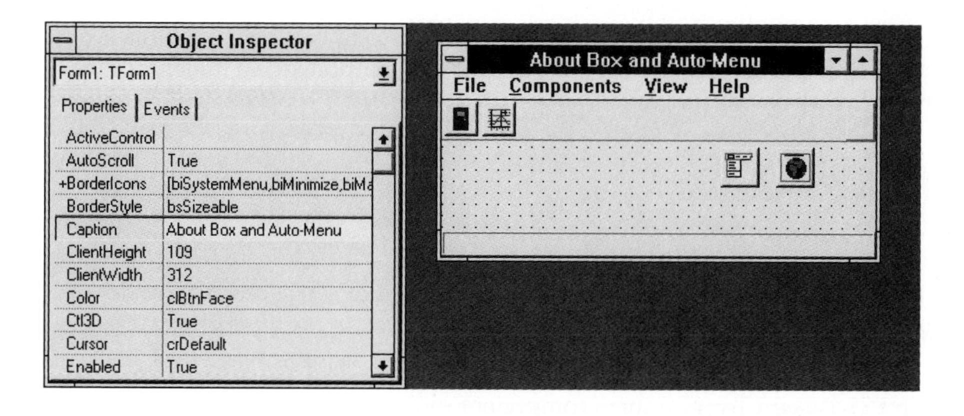

Figure 18-11. *The main form for the QUIKMNU project. The components placed on this form are responsible for the contents of the displayed menu and the behavior of the verb bar*

default buttons will be created for the TtpAboutBox component, with their icons and correctly spaced on the verb bar.

To see what the About box is going to do, right-click it and select Test. Then run the form and try selecting Components | tpAboutBox | Test, and also try clicking the Test button on the verb bar. Code reuse! You can also play with the Run Time Type Information dialog box, which is available under the Properties verb.

OOP Calculator

This final example ties together a number of the main concepts from this chapter. The example in this section builds a component that knows how to add two numbers, setting its "readiness" flags and also making use of a custom property editor to allow

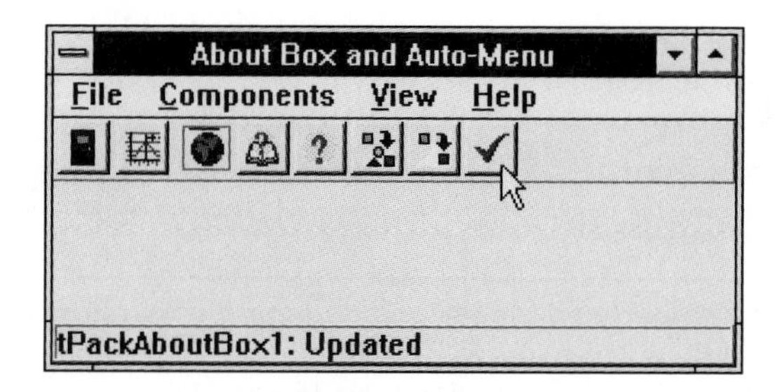

Figure 18-12. *By pointing a verb bar to a component, the verbs for that component become buttons on the verb bar. The current component can be toggled at design time and runtime*

data entry changes. The code is heavily commented, so only the main points are reviewed here. The component is derived from TtpComponent, so it includes the TComponentExtensions functionality.

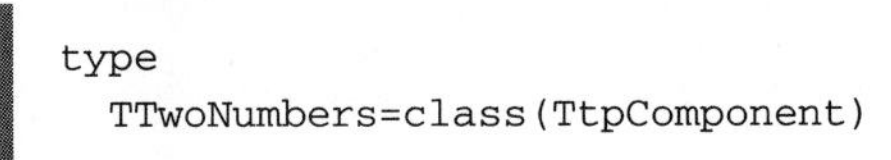

```
type
  TTwoNumbers=class(TtpComponent)
```

NOTE: To run this project, you must have installed TPack, as described in the preceding section, as well as TTWONUM.PAS, to your component library.

READINESS The TTwoNumbers component's job is to add together two numbers, NumberOne and NumberTwo, putting the result into the published property TheResult. Following OOP principles, the Get and Set procedures hide the complexity of the readiness issue. Figure 18-13 shows the application at runtime.

The Set procedure is predictable enough—unUpdate the component and set the value.

```
procedure TTwoNumbers.SetNumberOne(Value:Longint);
begin
  if Value<>fNumberOne then begin {New Value}
    tpUpdated:=false;  {un-update}
    fNumberOne:=Value; {store}
    end;
end;
```

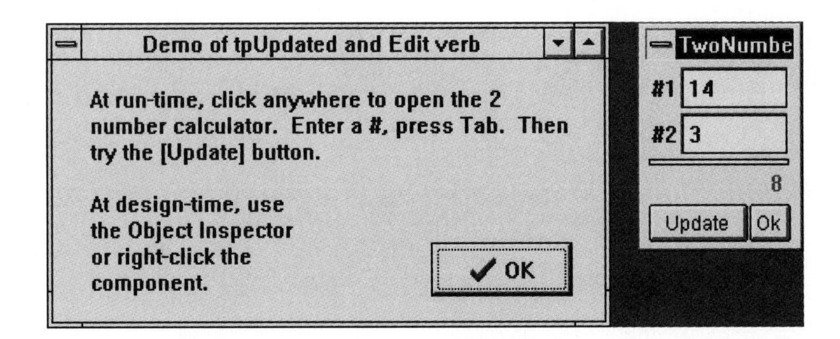

Figure 18-13. *The property editor lets you change the two numbers. Clicking the Update button causes a recalculation. Notice the separation between setting the values and getting the result*

The Get procedure needs more careful study—at first glance, it would appear that TheResult would always be –1 since the code above always unUpdates the component.

```
function TTwoNumbers.GetTheResult:Longint;
begin
  if tpUpdated then
    Result:=fTheResult
  else
    Result:=-1;
end;
```

The reason GetTheResult *does* work is that just checking the flag tpUpdated says, "Are you updated? If not, try to get updated." which calls the recalculation as follows:

```
function TTwoNumbers.DoUpdate:Boolean;
begin {recalculate}
  Recalc;
  Result:=True;
end;
procedure TTwoNumbers.Recalc;
begin
  fTheResult:=fNumberOne+fNumberTwo;
end;
```

VERBS Most of the verbs handled by this component are done by its ancestors. This component only does custom processing for the Edit verb.

```
procedure TTwoNumbers.ExecuteVerb(Index: Integer);
begin
  case Index of
    0: Edit;
  else
    Inherited ExecuteVerb(Index - GetLocalVerbCount);
    end;
end;
```

The core work for handling the Edit verb is set up in TComponentExtended, where a provision is made for overriding the Edit method as well as EditFormClass, the class of the form to be used for editing.

```
 TComponentExtended = class(TComponent)
  protected
    fHelpContext: Byte;
    cx: TComponentExtensions;
```

```
    function EditFormClass:TComponentEditFormClass; virtual;
    procedure SetUniqueName(const Value:String);
    procedure SetNoByte(Value:Byte);
    procedure SetNoBoolean(Value:Boolean);
    procedure SetNoLongint(Value:Longint);
    procedure SetNoString(const Value:String);
  private
  public
    Constructor Create(aOwner:TComponent); Override;
    Destructor Destroy; Override;
    procedure Edit; virtual;
{remainder omitted}
```

This code flows into TtpComponent, which has a few key lines that enable the polymorphic use of the Edit verb.

```
procedure TComponentExtended.Edit;
begin
  with EditFormClass.Create(nil) do try
    fPersistent:=Self;
    Execute;
  finally
    free;
    end;
end;
```

The line that sets the fPersistent pointer (with fPersistent being an admittedly poor choice of field name) is essential. Since this line is used in descendant components, fPersistent will be set to point to the component itself. The form appropriate to the component (based on the EditFormClass) will then be executed—providing the right form at the right time.

In the calculator example, the right form is TTwoNumbersForm.

```
{this proc determines the form used by the edit method}
function TTwoNumbers.EditFormClass:TComponentEditFormClass;
begin
  Result:=TTwoNumbersForm;
end;
```

The code for that form is able to reference the values of the component because fPersistent is available as a pointer. The integration of user-typing with field-posting is rather straightforward at the end—this code is called when the user exits either edit field:

```
procedure TTwoNumbersForm.ExitNumberField(Sender: TObject);
begin
  with TTwoNumbers(fPersistent),tEdit(Sender) do begin
    case tag of {tag of the last item in the with-list}
      1: begin  {oh yes.. the edit boxes have tag=1}
          NumberOne:=StrToIntDef(Self.NumberOne.Text,-1);
          Self.NumberOne.Text:=IntToStr(NumberOne);
          end;
      2: begin  {and tag=2.. no error checking here.}
          NumberTwo:=StrToIntDef(Self.NumberTwo.Text,-1);
          Self.NumberTwo.Text:=IntToStr(NumberTwo);
          end;
      end;
    Self.TheResult.Enabled:=IsUpdated; {show result state!}
    end;
end;
```

With all this scaffolding in place, implementing the onClick method for the recalc button is the simplest of all.

```
procedure TTwoNumbersForm.Recalculate(Sender: TObject);
begin {button1.OnClick}
  with TTwoNumbers(fPersistent) do begin
    Self.TheResult.Caption:=IntToStr(TheResult); {might! recalc}
    Self.TheResult.Enabled:=IsUpdated; {show result state!}
    end;
end;
```

The following is the complete source code for the TTWONUM.PAS unit:

```
unit TTwoNum;

{ Author: Michael Ax, ax@href.com, http://www.href.com/.
  Copyright (c) 1996 HREF Tools Corp. All Rights Reserved.
  Reprinted with permission from the author}

{ This unit implements a sample updating component, incorporating
  an edit form and verb. }

interface

uses
  SysUtils, WinTypes, WinProcs, Messages, Classes, Graphics, Controls,
  Forms, Dialogs, StdCtrls, ExtCtrls
, UpdateOk {tPack edit,update,verb,action,command levels}
, utForm; {tPack slightly extended tform base classes for edit level}
```

```
type
  TTwoNumbersForm = class(TtpDocForm)
    {these three controls are named after the matching properties}
    NumberOne: TEdit; {standard edit control for #1}
    NumberTwo: TEdit; {standard edit control for #2}
    TheResult: TLabel; {label to show the result of the addition}
    {these controls play supporting roles}
    Button1: TButton; {calls Recalculate method}
    Button2: TButton; {set to mrOk}
    Label1: TLabel;  {#1}
    Label2: TLabel;  {#2}
    Shape1: TShape;  {line}
    procedure Recalculate(Sender: TObject); {button1.click}
    procedure UpdateForm(Sender: TObject); {form.activate}
    procedure ExitNumberField(Sender: TObject); {sync properties}
    end;

{Step zero: pick your base class. Define the class as derived from one
of [TtpUpdate, TtpComponent, TtpAction, TtpCommand, TWebAction]
depending on your goal. The rest of the steps don't necessarily happen
top-down so read through to the end.}

type
 TTwoNumbers=class(TtpComponent)
  private   {step two: define the storage fields}
    fNumberOne: Longint; {first stored field}
    fNumberTwo: Longint; {second stored field}
    fTheResult: Longint; {buffer the result to make a point!}
  protected  {step three: define the access procedures}
    procedure SetNumberOne(Value:Longint);
    procedure SetNumberTwo(Value:Longint);
    function GetTheResult:Longint;
    {step five: list the procedures to override}
    function DoUpdate:Boolean; Override; {update the result}
    function EditFormClass:TComponentEditFormClass; override;
    {so far so good, lets add the edit verb with these procs:}
    function GetLocalVerbCount: Integer;
    function GetVerbCount: Integer; Override;
    function GetVerb(Index: Integer): string; Override;
    procedure ExecuteVerb(Index: Integer); Override;
    {the recalc code is only called internally. We've now
    met the goal of encapsulating the actual business rules.}
    procedure Recalc; {adds the two numbers}
    {you can go from here and look through the webhub source
    code samples which will build on the principles shown here
    and introduce you to additional concepts and possibilities.}
  public
  published  {step one: define the published interface}
    property NumberOne:longint read fNumberOne write SetNumberOne;
```

```
    property NumberTwo:longint read fNumberTwo write SetNumberTwo;
    property TheResult:longint read GetTheResult
      write SetNoLongInt stored false;
    end;

procedure Register;

implementation

{$R *.DFM}

{step four: implement the access procedures. Hint: access procedures
should be simple. Consider adding public properties as intermediaries.}

procedure TTwoNumbers.SetNumberOne(Value:Longint);
begin
  if Value<>fNumberOne then begin {New Value}
    tpUpdated:=false;  {un-update}
    fNumberOne:=Value; {store}
    end;
end;

procedure TTwoNumbers.SetNumberTwo(Value:Longint);
begin
  if Value<>fNumberTwo then begin {New Value}
    tpUpdated:=false;  {un-update}
    fNumberTwo:=Value; {store}
    end;
end;

function TTwoNumbers.GetTheResult:Longint;
begin
  if tpUpdated then
    Result:=fTheResult
  else
    Result:=-1;
end;

{-------------------------------------------------------}
{step seven: implement the business rules code. This might include
DoExecute and SetCommand procedures and code to implement verbs}


procedure TTwoNumbers.Recalc;
begin
  fTheResult:=fNumberOne+fNumberTwo;
end;

{-------------------------------------------------------}
```

```
{step six: implement the overridden procedures}

function TTwoNumbers.DoUpdate:Boolean;
begin {recalculate}
  {in this case you can simply write:}
  Recalc;
  Result:=True;
  {or be more elaborate:}{
  Result:=inherited DoUpdate;
  if Result then
    Recalc;
  {or add errorchecking:}{
  if Result then try
    Recalc;
  except
    Result:=false;
    raise;
    end;{}
end;

{-----------------------------------------------------}
{this proc determines the form used by the edit method}

function TTwoNumbers.EditFormClass:TComponentEditFormClass;
begin
  Result:=TTwoNumbersForm;
end;

{-----------------------------------------------------}
{the next four procs add a verb to the component}

function TTwoNumbers.GetLocalVerbCount: Integer;
begin
  Result := 1;
end;

function TTwoNumbers.GetVerbCount: Integer;
begin
  Result := inherited GetVerbCount + GetLocalVerbCount;
end;

function TTwoNumbers.GetVerb(Index: Integer): string;
begin
  case Index of
    0: Result := 'Edit Numbers';
 else
    Result:=inherited GetVerb(Index - GetLocalVerbCount);
  end;
end;
```

```
procedure TTwoNumbers.ExecuteVerb(Index: Integer);
begin
  case Index of
    0: Edit;
  else
    Inherited ExecuteVerb(Index - GetLocalVerbCount);
    end;
end;

{-----------------------------------------------------}
{these are the procedures used by the edit form to
link to the actual component at design and runtime}

procedure TTwoNumbersForm.UpdateForm(Sender: TObject);
begin {form.OnActivate}
  with TTwoNumbers(fPersistent) do begin
    {prepare the form}
    Self.NumberOne.Text:=IntToStr(NumberOne);
    Self.NumberTwo.Text:=IntToStr(NumberTwo);
    Self.TheResult.Caption:=IntToStr(TheResult);
    end;
end;

procedure TTwoNumbersForm.ExitNumberField(Sender: TObject);
begin
  with TTwoNumbers(fPersistent),tEdit(Sender) do begin
    case tag of {tag of the last item in the with-list}
      1: begin  {oh yes.. the edit boxes have tag=1}
           NumberOne:=StrToIntDef(Self.NumberOne.Text,-1);
           Self.NumberOne.Text:=IntToStr(NumberOne);
           end;
      2: begin  {and tag=2.. no error checking here.}
           NumberTwo:=StrToIntDef(Self.NumberTwo.Text,-1);
           Self.NumberTwo.Text:=IntToStr(NumberTwo);
           end;
      end;
    Self.TheResult.Enabled:=IsUpdated; {show result state!}
    end;
end;

procedure TTwoNumbersForm.Recalculate(Sender: TObject);
begin {button1.OnClick}
  with TTwoNumbers(fPersistent) do begin
    Self.TheResult.Caption:=IntToStr(TheResult); {might! recalc}
    Self.TheResult.Enabled:=IsUpdated; {show result state!}
    end;
end;

{-----------------------------------------------------}
```

```
procedure Register;
begin
  RegisterComponents('Samples',[TTwoNumbers]);
end;

end.
```

Conclusion

This chapter has explored some of the core technology that makes the development of commercial-grade applications such as WebHub possible, and perhaps shows why Delphi itself inspires such work.

The final section on verbs ties back to the Web directly, as verbs become something that an HTML (Hypertext Markup Language) author can invoke within the WebHub framework, further empowering flexible, powerful Web applications with Delphi.

Chapter Nineteen

Tracking Surfers and Their Data

The source code shown in this chapter, with the exception of TPack, is available on the CD-ROM that comes with this book. A shareware version of TPack, including its complied units and installation program is on the CD-ROM. The source code for TPack can be purchased from HREF Tools Corp. Please refer to Appendix A for information on using the code files for this chapter.

In the previous chapter you learned about some general issues facing Delphi developers who want to create reusable components in the context of a commercial application. This chapter discusses Web-related application issues. The topics covered here include one of the key challenges to creating a surfer-friendly, interactive Web application—saving state. This chapter begins with a discussion of interactive Web sites and what is required to make them happen. Next, various ways of saving state with Delphi in general are considered. Finally, you will learn how dynamic sites are implemented by WebHub.

NOTE: This chapter, like the others in this section, refers to the Web client as the "surfer." This term has been generally accepted to represent the user who is using a browser to view a Web site.

Overview of Interactive Web Technology

With respect to Web sites, there is a clear distinction between static sites and dynamic, or interactive, sites. A static Web site gives the same experience to each surfer: a given set of files may be retrieved by following links, and, although each person may view different pages in a different order, the presentation and content is identical for all surfers.

At a dynamic site, the content of one or more pages is created on the fly (by a CGI—common gateway interface—program or by utilities provided with the Web server). This permits for a great amount of flexibility. For example, a given page may look entirely different to two surfers loading the page. This technology even allows your site to adjust the content of a page for the same surfer, depending on the time of day, information tracked by the CGI program, or just about any other criteria. In other words, dynamic pages can be tailored to the surfer's needs.

Internet Examples

The ability to create dynamic Web sites opens the door to many possibilities that are unachievable with static sites. The following are some examples of currently active dynamic Web sites:

- Yellow page searches, including places like www.yahoo.com. This popular Web site lets you quickly find most resources on the Web. You enter a search topic, and the response page tells you about sites on the Web that cover the topic.

- Catalog stores, including places like www.mofi.com (a store for high-quality music records and CDs). Such stores generally allow you to search their merchandise and place orders.
- A creativity center, such as lanark.jf.intel.com/. You can manipulate graphical images at this Intel site.
- A help desk, such as the tech support BBS available at spry.com.
- A customer service center, such as the tracking facilities at www.fedex.com.
- Public kiosks based on a browser for a user interface, such as the Jobs system, which will become a pilot study of the State of California Employment Development Department in July 1996 (using WebHub).

Intranet Examples

Although the examples just presented are all related to the Internet, dynamic Web sites are not solely the domain of the public network. In fact, dynamic Web sites will likely have their greatest impact on the *Intranet*—the internal networks established within companies. Here, greater control of the network and the need to distribute sometimes sensitive data to selected individuals make dynamic Web sites a powerful solution. For internal networks, bandwidth and connectivity problems are much less of an issue than they are for the public Internet, where some users still connect with 14.4 bps (bits per second) modems.

The following are examples of Intranet applications of dynamic Web site technology:

- Groupware projects (such as schedulers or contact management systems), implemented for virtual teams that use the Internet to work together.
- Document management systems, enabling corporate users to search and retrieve a variety of legacy file formats.
- Reporting systems for companies that have users on a variety of hardware and software platforms and that can easily use a browser as a common end-user interface to access required data.

What does it take to implement a dynamic site? To start with, you need a CGI program that will create the pages on the fly, such as Delphi, Perl, C, or Visual Basic. You may also need a mechanism inside the CGI program that tracks the surfer and saves state. (Saving state is discussed in detail later in this chapter.) The next sections explore how to differentiate those sites that require this extra work of tracking the surfer and saving state, and then show how these tasks are accomplished.

Understanding HTTP

HTTP is by nature a stateless protocol. What this means is that each HTTP request comes into the Web server and then on to the CGI program independently. There is no connection between one HTTP request and another. Consequently, without taking additional steps, it is also impossible to tell whether two different HTTP requests originated from the same surfer.

An additional problem results from HTTP's stateless nature. Specifically, without significant effort, it is impossible for the CGI program to respond to anything but the most recent request. Thus, more work is often needed to build a dynamic Web site. In many cases, the CGI program needs to have a way to connect page requests with an individual surfer, and it must have data structures that store that surfer's data between requests. (This is covered later in this chapter in the section "Object-Oriented State Saving Technique.")

Under normal conditions, without the ability to save state, the following steps transpire during a typical HTTP request:

1. The surfer requests a file using a browser such as Netscape. The request is in the form of a URL (Uniform Resource Locator), which has the general form http://serverName/cgiPath/cgiProgramName. For example, the surfer may tell the browser to issue the command http://www.href.com/cgi-win/hubws.exe, which is sent out over TCP/IP.
2. The surfer's Domain Name Server resolves the name to an IP address. For example, in February 1996, the name href.com resolved to 199.4.118.45. (By the time you read this, href.com will likely resolve to a different IP.) The request is then sent to the IP address by TCP/IP.
3. The request arrives on the Web server identified by the IP address. This server listens on a port of the IP address (usually port 80). The HTTP specification defines the form of the request. In this case, the requested resource is cgi-win/hubws.exe on the href.com server.
4. The Web server looks for certain keywords in the path of the requested resource. Based on these keywords, the Web server is able to distinguish between requests for static pages from requests based on CGI calls. Specifically, each Web server has its own CGI path that is used to indicate that the file (hubws.exe) is actually a CGI program. The on-disk location of the program is configured using the Web server's administration program. Each server has a default location that you can usually modify, if necessary. For example, with WebSite server, the default location for CGI programs is c:\website\cgi-win\. For Spry, it is c:\spry\cgi-bin\. If the server identifies the requested resource as a CGI program, it runs that program. In this example, it would run hubws.exe.
5. What happens at this point is the responsibility of the CGI program. Typically, this program creates an output document, after which the program shuts down. For example, a CGI program may run based on the CGI environment data. The CGI program then builds the output HTML document (or any other kind of file, such as a graphics file), and then returns control to the Web server—by shutting down.

NOTE: See Chapter 17 for a comparison of the traditional CGI framework to WebHub's strategy for bypassing the performance problems usually associated with CGI programs.

NOTE: CGI environment data includes about 25 standard items, including the IP address of the surfer, authentication information for the surfer, the resource requested, and the CGI Query String.

6. The Web server returns the output document to the surfer by simply passing it through with no changes. In other words, the CGI program has to create a correctly formatted file, containing proper HTML or a valid .GIF graphics file. The server simply sends that file to the requesting surfer.
7. The surfer, having received the document, may be done. Alternatively, the surfer may now wish additional information and would then generate another request. Thus this process returns to step 1.

The critical issue here, and the point of this discussion, is that this new request is completely independent of the first request. The HTTP specification does not include any information that uniquely connects two or more requests from a given individual. Although the CGI environment data will include the surfer's IP address (as the CGI Remote Address), this is not sufficient because there is not a one-to-one correspondence between the surfer and the IP. For example, surfers coming in from large providers such as America Online share only a few IPs.

Therefore, to say that HTTP is stateless means that it does not provide a mechanism for the CGI program to engage in a continuous conversation with an individual surfer. But why does this stateless issue matter? It all depends on how complex a Web application you want to build.

Interactive Sites that Do Not Need to Save State

When modeling a Web site, it is important to look at it in terms of pages. The surfer will issue a page request, and the CGI program will respond with a document for that page. Once you have a flowchart that outlines the various pages, it becomes easy to determine whether a saving-state framework is required.

The easy sites are the ones in which the result page immediately follows *all* the relevant input, with no intermediate pages. A diagram of such a site is shown in Figure 19-1. The site in this example represents one where there is only one search screen leading to a result page. The search page could be either a static .HTML file or one generated dynamically. The result page is generated dynamically by the CGI program. Before considering a more complex example, let's first consider how this simple site can be implemented.

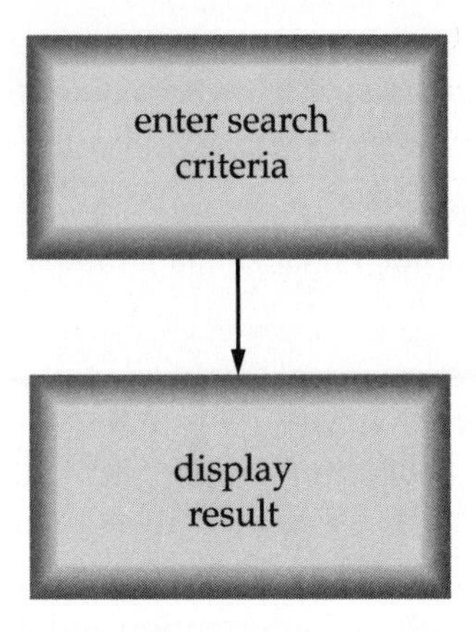

Figure 19-1. *An example where the CGI program does not need to save state in order to respond with the result page*

NOTE: The page that links to a CGI program can be called the launch page. This launch page can be either a static .HTML file or one that is itself dynamically created. Most people make launch pages static because they don't have an easy way to do otherwise. However, with a dynamic launch page, you can add some nice user interface features, such as remembering the prior search conditions so that the surfer doesn't have to re-enter the question. WebHub combines the ease of maintaining HTML in ASCII files with the benefits of dynamic page generation. If you are building your own CGI framework, you should consider this carefully.

A Simple Web Page Example

The search page would be built using the HTML <FORM> tag, and any data entered by the surfer on that page would be sent to the Web server and made available to the CGI program. For example, the following listing contains a simple HTML form:

```
<FORM METHOD=POST ACTION="/cgi-win/webapp.exe">
Enter customer ID: <INPUT TYPE=TEXT NAME=CUSTID><p>

<INPUT TYPE=SUBMIT>

</FORM>
```

The <FORM> tag tells the browser that an input form is being defined. The method can be GET or POST (and it's not case sensitive). POST is preferred. If you use POST, the data is passed to the Web server as form literals, and there is no limit on the number of fields you can have. The ACTION specifies the program that should run when the user clicks the Submit button. ACTION must always be a call to a CGI program.

The <INPUT> tags define the input fields. These fields may consist of edit boxes, combo boxes, radio buttons, check boxes, and memo fields. The TYPE= tag indicates the type of field. Refer to an HTML reference guide to find out all your options. A good free one is at http://www.microsoft.com/windows/ie/ie20html.htm.

<INPUT TYPE=SUBMIT> creates the Submit button, which the surfer must click to transmit the data. You can customize the caption on the label by saying <INPUT TYPE=SUBMIT VALUE="Caption Here">. There are only two types of buttons: Submit and Reset. A Reset button just clears all the input fields.

The specifics of how the form data is made available to the CGI program vary among Web servers. The WebSite server prepares an .INI file that contains all the CGI environment data (e.g., surfer IP, CGI query string, and authentication information). In the case of forms processing, that .INI file will also contain a [Form Literals] and the form data will be itemized as convenient name=value entries, such as CUSTID=2345.

Web Page: Display Result

What happens next depends entirely on the CGI program. The webapp.exe program might look at the form data and generate the HTML output file based on this information. For example, the CGI program might use this data to execute a SQL (structured query language) query, and then generate the HTML output page based on the query result. Because all the information needed to construct the query is coming from the prior page, the CGI program (webapp.exe) does not need to save state.

Although some significant Web sites do fall into this simpler category, most interactive sites do not. In the next section, we'll look at real world examples of sites that do need to save state.

Interactive Sites that Need to Save State

In general, whenever the data from one page is required on a page other than the next one that will be displayed, the CGI program needs to be able track the surfer and the surfer's data. A site that requires this capability is shown in Figure 19-2. The capability represented in this diagram requires state information to be saved from the first page, on the left, and used in the third page, on the right. (You can view this site at http://airtravel.com/.)

In the example shown in Figure 19-2, the information from both pages 1 and 2 is needed to generate information on page 3. This Web application is only possible if:

- The surfer's identity is tracked. The identity being tracked is not the surfer's name, but some sort of unique identifier. (In WebHub, this identifier is called the Session ID.)
- The surfer's data from page 1 is saved after page 2 is generated and reloaded again for use when page 3 is generated.

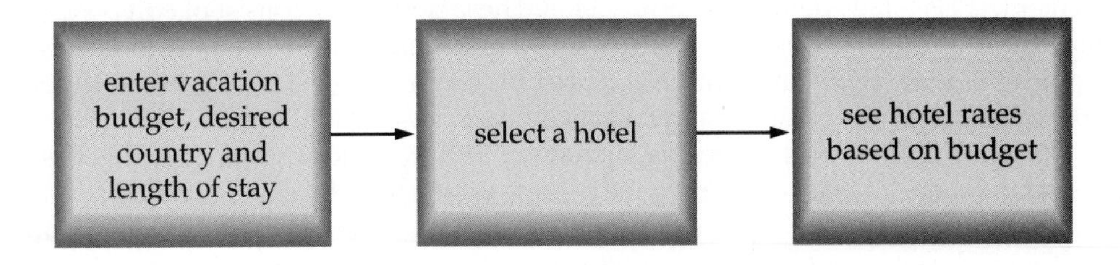

Figure 19-2. *A Web application that needs to remember the information from page 1 and 2 in order to create page 3*

Figure 19-3 shows another common situation that requires saving state—the building of *cyberstores.* A cyberstore is a Web site that can conduct electronic commerce. In order to build a "shopping cart interface," where purchases are remembered until the surfer proceeds to the checkout counter, the CGI program must track the surfer and the surfer's data. When the surfer tags an item for purchase, it is saved in the surfer's "shopping cart" and then recalled at the checkout stand.

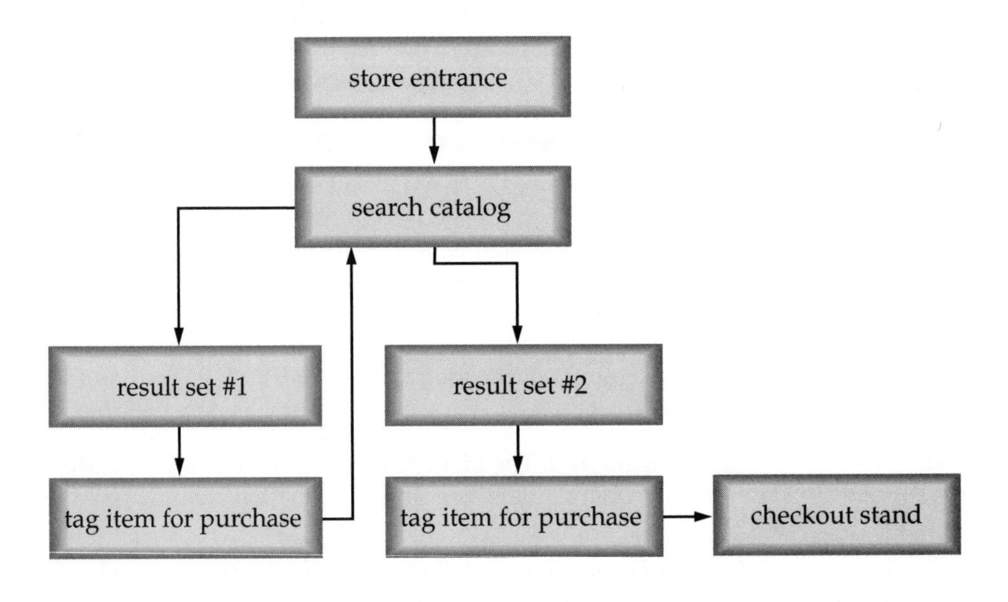

Figure 19-3. *A simple model of a cyberstore*

In the shopping cart scenario, it is quite clear that the CGI framework again needs to track the surfer's identity and data. By making a similar model of the Web application that you want to build, you should be able to see whether your dynamic pages always follow the input forms (as shown in Figure 19-1), or whether you will need to save state (as shown in Figures 19-2 and 19-3).

When building Web applications, developers must provide a solution as quickly as possible to provide a prototype or prove the feasibility of an application. It is tempting to take shortcuts and write code that handles only the current site's specification. This is short-sighted, as it often limits what type of modifications can be made as business needs change. The WebHub components give a developer the best of both worlds: the ability to build prototypes quickly, while taking care of tracking the surfer as well as the surfer's data.

The remainder of this chapter discusses what is meant by saving state—in general, and on the Web in particular.

Saving State: Overview

To help you think about saving the state of something in your application, ask yourself, "What information would I need to be able to come back to this same point next time?" The details vary by application, but this is an extremely common theme for application development. Let's begin by considering the general issue of saving state.

In Delphi, the state of a component is equivalent to the cumulative values of its properties. Remember that a Delphi TForm is a component, and that the .DFM file (Delphi form file) contains the information needed to reconstruct the form each time you reload the project, either into the designer or at runtime. If you open a .DFM file, you will see that for each component Delphi tracks the values of each published, stored property. The following listing shows a partial example of the .DFM file used in the CLCKCALC.DPR project introduced in Chapter 18:

```
object Form1: TForm1
  Left = 200
  Top = 96
  Width = 357
  Height = 187
  Caption = 'Demo of tpUpdated and Edit verb'
  Font.Color = clWindowText
  Font.Height = -13
  Font.Name = 'System'
  Font.Style = []
  PixelsPerInch = 96
  OnClick = FormClick
  TextHeight = 16
object TwoNumbers1: TTwoNumbers
    NumberOne = 16
    NumberTwo = 3
    Left = 188
```

```
      Top = 54
    end
  end
```

When Delphi loads the project, it sets the properties of the components according to the saved-state information in the .DFM file.

NOTE: *The .DFM file is a resource and is linked into the executable (.EXE) file during compilation. Consequently, the .DFM file does not need to be shipped with the .EXE file.*

Of course, the .DFM file does include enough saved information for many applications. For example, you might want to save a form's location at runtime, the contents of edit fields, or the status of menu options between two invocations of the same .EXE. If you are developing more than one application, you would want a generic, component-based solution that you can reuse across applications.

Three TPack components are worth studying in this context:

- TFormRestorer
- TEditRestorer
- TtpComboBar

The TFormRestorer component remembers form size and location and can be used in just about any Delphi application. The form window coordinates are saved to an .INI file when the user closes the form and are restored when the form activates.

TEditRestorer adds the ability to remember the values of TEdit, TComboBox, TCheckBox, and TTabbedNotebook page settings. This component looks at all the controls on the form and saves information for those classes.

The TtpComboBar (which combines a toolbar and a verb bar) remembers which bar was visible and notes the current component for the verb bar. (TPack verbs are described in Chapter 18.) This component enables the end user to customize the work environment. (A parallel feature in Delphi would be if it remembered which palette you last used and kept that palette current instead of always resetting to the first one.)

If you have installed TPack into your component library, you can see how this works. (TPack is available on the CD accompanying this book.) Follow these steps to perform this demonstration:

1. Create a new Delphi project.
2. From the TPack3 palette, add in TFormRestorer.
3. From the same palette, add in TEditRestorer.
4. From the Delphi standard palette, add in a TEdit box. An example of this form is shown in Figure 19-4.

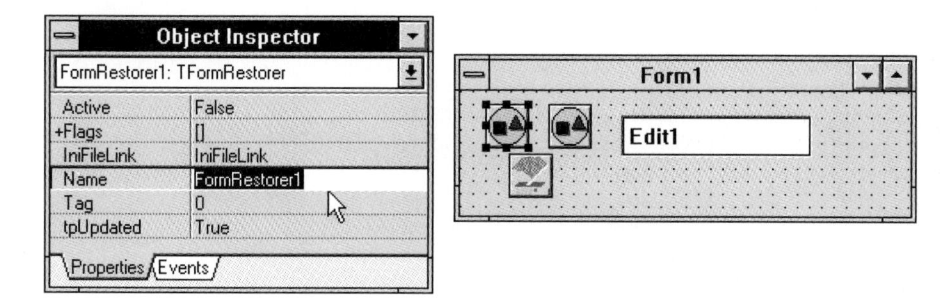

Figure 19-4. *Forms using TFormRestorer will automatically remember their size and location between use*

5. Run the application.
6. Resize and move the form.
7. Type some text into the edit field.
8. Close and restart the application. When you do so, the form will come back as you left it with the data intact.

How TPack Saves State

The TPack components remember values by storing them in an .INI file between sessions. The following listing shows the structure of the TGenericRestorer and the TFormRestorer. Notice in particular the Save and Load methods, which are called from the DoUpdate method. The DoUpdate method takes care of initialization in the Delphi designer and at runtime. At runtime, the saved code is called because the onSave handler is hooked into the form's onClose event.

```
type
 TRestorerFlag = {these contain elements used by descendants}
    (resLoad,resSave,resDefaultIni    {Generic}
    ,resUseCaption                    {Form}
    );

 TRestorerFlags = set of TRestorerFlag;

type
  TGenericRestorer = class(TtpComponent)
  private
    fFlags: TRestorerFlags;
    fFormClose: TCloseEvent;
```

```
    fIniFileLink: TIniFileLink;
  protected
    function  GetLocalVerbCount: Integer;
    function  GetVerbCount: Integer; Override;
    function  GetVerb(Index: Integer): string; Override;
    procedure ExecuteVerb(Index: Integer); Override;
    function GetActive: Boolean;
    procedure SetActive(Value: Boolean);
      {will save when setting true in designmode}
    function DoUpdate:Boolean; Override;
  public
    constructor Create(AOwner: TComponent); override;
    destructor Destroy; override;
    procedure Notification(AComponent: TComponent;
      Operation: TOperation); Override;

    procedure Save; virtual; abstract;
    procedure Load; virtual; abstract;
    procedure Reset; virtual; abstract;
    procedure FormClose(Sender: TObject; var Action: TCloseAction);
  published
    property Active: Boolean read GetActive
      write SetActive stored false;
    property Flags: TRestorerFlags read fFlags
      write fFlags default [resLoad,resSave];
    property IniFileLink: TIniFileLink read fIniFileLink
      write fIniFileLink;
     end;

 TFormRestorer = class(TGenericRestorer)
 private
   fOnSave,
   fOnLoad: TNotifyEvent;
 protected
   procedure SetFile; virtual;
 public
   constructor Create(AOwner: TComponent); override;
   procedure Save; Override;
   procedure Load; Override;
   procedure Reset; Override;
 published
   property OnLoad: TNotifyEvent read fOnLoad write fOnLoad;
   property OnSave: TNotifyEvent read fOnSave write fOnSave;
   end;

function TGenericRestorer.DoUpdate:Boolean;
begin
  cx.MakeIfNil(fIniFileLink,TIniFileLink);
```

```
  Result:= inherited DoUpdate;
  if not Result then
    exit;
if (resSave in fFlags) and cx.Designing then
    Save;
  if (resLoad in fFlags) then
    Load;
  if not cx.Designing then begin  {when initializing at runtime}
    with TForm(Owner) do begin    {hook the save proc into }
                                  {the form's OnClose handler}
      fFormClose:=OnClose;
      OnClose:=FormClose;
      end;
    end;
end;
```

The following key problems need to be addressed in order to save state:

- When to save and restore the data
- Where to save the data
- What data to save
- What format to save the data in

Deciding when to save and restore the data requires a clear understanding of the order of the events. In the case of saving the size and location of a form, you have to save the values when the user closes the form and restore the values after the form has been created, but before it is made available to the user.

Where to save the data depends on the operating system and how much trouble you want to go to. In Windows 3.x, .INI files are the preferred place for initialization data. Alternate choices include the registry (in Windows 95 and Windows NT only), a custom text file, or even a database. In many cases, using an .INI file is the most convenient solution. It is available for all versions of Windows and is very easy to implement.

Deciding what data to save depends on the application. Some applications may only need to save the size and location of the form. For others, the contents of many edit fields may need to be saved.

Choosing the format in which to save the data often depends on where you are saving that data. Since .INI files are text based, all non-text data needs to be translated when the data is being saved, and again when it is being restored. Boolean values, for example, can be translated to single-character zeros and ones.

NOTE: *The TIniFile class permits three data types to be saved: String, Boolean, and Integer; however, the representation of all three of these types is simply textual.*

These same four problems also need to be addressed when considering the process of saving state on the Web. Fortunately, many of the answers are the same as those just presented.

Let's return our attention to TFormRestorer. The following listing shows how the TFormRestorer component saves the form's window position. It uses the TIniFileLink component to facilitate writing those coordinates. (One of the enhancements in TIniFileLink is the convenience of handing non-string data such as window coordinates.)

```
procedure TFormRestorer.Save;
var
  wp: TWindowPosValue;
begin
  SetFile;
  with tForm(Owner) do
    if WindowState=wsNormal then begin
      wp.Top:=Top;
      wp.Left:=Left;
      wp.Height:=Height;
      wp.Width:=Width;
      with fIniFileLink do
        WindowPosEntry['WindowPos']:=wp;
      end;
  if assigned(fOnSave) then
    fOnSave(Self);
end;
```

The following two lines do the work of saving the four window coordinates to the .INI file:

```
with fIniFileLink do
        WindowPosEntry['WindowPos']:=wp;
```

The TIniFileLink component hides all the complexity of saving the window position. For example, the set procedure for TIniFileLink.WindowPosEntry writes out the four numbers as strings. On the loading side (for reloading the form), there is a parallel set of two lines for the restoration. These lines are demonstrated in the following procedure:

```
procedure TFormRestorer.Load;
var
  wp: TWindowPosValue;
begin
  SetFile;
  with fIniFileLink do
    wp:=WindowPosEntry['WindowPos'];
```

```
  if (wp.Width>0) and (wp.Height>0) then
    with tForm(Owner) do begin
      Top:=wp.Top;
      Left:=wp.Left;
      Height:=wp.Height;
      Width:=wp.Width;
      end;
  if assigned(fOnLoad) then
    fOnLoad(Self);
end;
```

The entire window position comes in from the .INI file with these two lines:

```
with fIniFileLink do
    wp:=WindowPosEntry['WindowPos'];
```

The discussion so far has covered the topic of saving state in general. The next section examines how these basic principles of saving state apply to the Web. Keep in mind that there are really two problems that need to be solved: The first is how to connect multiple HTTP requests from the same surfer, and the second is how to save that surfer's data across multiple page requests.

Tracking the Surfer

Clearly, for many applications, being able to have a continuous conversation with the user is essential. For example, an ATM (automated teller machine) would be completely useless if it forgot the account number as a user progressed through a transaction. But this is exactly what goes on with HTTP. As the developer, you need to do the equivalent of assigning customer numbers (sometimes called a Surfer ID or Session ID) to each surfer so that you can make each page fit the surfer's needs.

This raises the question of how the Session ID gets assigned. The CGI program has to notice when a surfer first comes in with no ID, and then give the surfer a unique number. Exactly what's involved in "noticing the absence of an ID" depends on the solution chosen. WebHub uses the URL to pass the Session ID around, so it looks at the URL to find out whether a Session ID has already been assigned.

The Session ID basically provides a key into the "database" of saved state information. In other words, there will be saved-state data for each surfer, keyed by Session ID. Once the ID has been assigned, it is used to create and maintain a set of data for the surfer. (WebHub does this with a TWebSession component, which is discussed in detail in the "Object-Oriented State Saving Technique" section later this chapter. There are ways to control whether the state data is kept only in RAM, saved to binary disk files, or saved in a database, for example.)

TIP: A substantial side benefit to tracking surfers is that it becomes possible to analyze site traffic in terms of individuals, instead of just page hits. You can tell that a given surfer requested n *pages and even how long the surfer spent looking at each page—except the last one, because you never know when a surfer leaves your site.*

Whichever solution you choose for passing the Session ID, you need to do it consistently throughout your site—otherwise you lose contact with the surfer and have to start over. In other words, the Session ID needs to be made part of every page request.

One Solution: Using Hidden Fields

Some people use hidden fields on HTML forms as a place to put a Surfer ID. To do this, a page that includes the hidden field is generated dynamically. When the form is submitted, the Surfer ID is available to the CGI program through this field.

The following listing shows the simple search form with a hidden field added to track surfer ID#1234:

```
<FORM METHOD=POST ACTION="/cgi-win/webapp.exe">

Enter customer ID: <INPUT TYPE=TEXT NAME=CUSTID><p>
<INPUT TYPE=HIDDEN VALUE="1234" NAME=SURFERID>
<INPUT TYPE=SUBMIT>
</FORM>
```

The problem with this approach is that you can only save state if all of the pages include HTML forms, which severely limits the user interface. Think back to the flowchart for the cyberstore shopping cart interface shown in Figure 19-3. If the user interface had to use an HTML form, the result set (that is, the answer to the search question) would have to be presented with a list of check box or radio button items for the user to make a selection and then click the Submit button to move on to the next page. Although this solution works, it is a more limiting and clumsy interface.

Preferred Solution: Using the URL to Pass Key Facts

One technique bypasses the need to use the <FORM> tag everywhere. This technique is to pass the Session ID on the URL.

One common example from a real store on the Web is shown in Figure 19-5. This figure shows an HTML table with the result of searching for "Blues albums." Each album is a hot link. You can see this in the HTTP link shown in the status bar of the browser. This interface is clearly better for the surfer than that presented using a <FORM> tag because with this interface, the surfer only has to click once to get to the desired data.

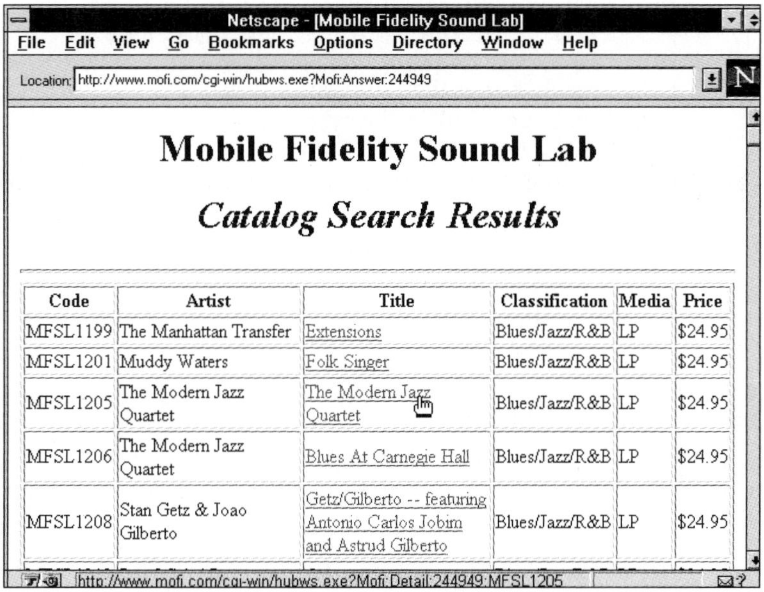

Netscape - [Mobile Fidelity Sound Lab]

File Edit View Go Bookmarks Options Directory Window Help

Location: http://www.mofi.com/cgi-win/hubws.exe?Mofi:Answer:244949

Mobile Fidelity Sound Lab

Catalog Search Results

Code	Artist	Title	Classification	Media	Price
MFSL1199	The Manhattan Transfer	Extensions	Blues/Jazz/R&B	LP	$24.95
MFSL1201	Muddy Waters	Folk Singer	Blues/Jazz/R&B	LP	$24.95
MFSL1205	The Modern Jazz Quartet	The Modern Jazz Quartet	Blues/Jazz/R&B	LP	$24.95
MFSL1206	The Modern Jazz Quartet	Blues At Carnegie Hall	Blues/Jazz/R&B	LP	$24.95
MFSL1208	Stan Getz & Joao Gilberto	Getz/Gilberto -- featuring Antonio Carlos Jobim and Astrud Gilberto	Blues/Jazz/R&B	LP	$24.95

http://www.mofi.com/cgi-win/hubws.exe?Mofi:Detail:244949:MFSL1205

Figure 19-5. *HTML table displaying the result of a search*

NOTE: A hot link is simply a hypertext link, created with an <A HREF> tag in HTML. Because you can pass data on the command line (via the CGI Query String), you can request individual items from the CGI program. The URL for The Modern Jazz Quartet in Figure 19-5 is http://www.mofi.com/cgi-win/hubws.exe?Mofi:Detail:244949: MFSL1205. Everything after the ? is the CGI Query String. "Mofi" indicates which application to run. "Detail" is the page requested. "244949" is the session ID. "MFSL1205" is the primary key of the album to show detail on, if the surfer clicks that hot link.

WebHub lets the Session ID as well as any optional command (such as MFSL1205) travel on the URL. As you can see, the HTTP request can pass not only the name of the CGI program to execute, but also additional information. The Session ID can be part of this information. Typically this information would be sent as the CGI Query String, which is to say that it would be sent after a question mark in the URL. (The information could also be passed after a forward slash (/) separator; in which case it is referenced as PathInfo instead of as CGI Query String.) The following is a simple example:

```
cgi-win/webapp.exe?123
```

Each CGI program can have its own use for the string "123." There are no general standards. WebHub uses a standard of putting the following four items into the CGI Query String: Application ID, Page ID, Session ID, and an optional command. As a general rule, you can employ this technique to pass whatever string your CGI program needs.

In the URL-based approach, rather than dynamically sending hidden fields, the CGI program makes sure that every link in the system contains the current Session ID. Instead of sending out simple <A HREF> links, the CGI program would always append the Session ID as part of the CGI query string. The following table shows this comparison:

Simple "A HREF" link	<A HREF="http://www.href.com/cgi-win/hubws.exe?hrefinfo:announce">Announcements</A>
with Session ID added	<A HREF="http://www.href.com/cgi-win/hubws.exe?hrefinfo:announce:**123456**">Announcements</A>

The second approach (the URL-based approach) ensures that every page request includes the Session ID so that the CGI program can easily stay in conversation with the surfer.

In a traditional CGI programming environment, the developer needs to write a procedure that stuffs the Session ID into each link. This can be done, but it is inconvenient in the long term. The WebHub framework supports the notion that HTML should be maintained separately from Object Pascal, since two different skills are required to maintain HTML and Object Pascal code. The separation also makes application maintenance more convenient since modifying the HTML does not necessitate changes in the program logic.

WebHub's architecture provides for the use of HTML *chunk files,* which are assembled at page-generation time. A chunk file is merely a file that holds the various chunks of HTML. For example, a typical page might have several sections, including a page header chunk at the beginning and a page footer chunk at the end. Those chunks can be defined once and then reused throughout the site. The HTTP request tells the CGI program which page to create and, within WebHub, each page is defined in terms of its required sections. Page sections can bring in HTML from a chunk file, or invoke a component such as TWebDataGrid (to create a grid as shown in Figure 19-4) or TWebMail (to send e-mail).

As part of that dynamic assembly, WebHub supports macro expansion, which means that certain expressions are expanded according to certain rules. In WebHub, %= indicates *begin macro,* and =% indicates *end macro.* The TWebApp component will attempt to expand text within those markers. The expansion can handle various types of items, including simple text substitution (e.g., turn %=ImageDir=% into /mofi/img/ for the graphics images) as well as properties on the Delphi components. The result is that macros lead to dynamically generated HTML.

The TWebApp component has a property that holds the current Session ID inside the application. The %=session=% macro will therefore expand to that ID. Thus the HTML author can build links more or less as usual, requesting the session macro without worrying about how the ID gets filled in.

NOTE: In actual practice with WebHub, one generally uses an additional shortcut, called the JUMP macro, for links within a WebHub site. Example syntax would be %=JUMP|feedback|Go to Feedback Page=%. This would be expanded to something like <A HREF="/cgi-win/hubws.exe?appID:Feedback:123">Go to Feedback Page</A>.

Tracking the Surfer's Data

So far, the need for tracking the surfer and the surfer's data has been described as well as how the Session ID for the surfer can be passed as part of the URL. This section examines exactly what data needs to be stored for the surfer and discusses how this can best be done using Delphi. There are four categories of data that you might want to track for a surfer:

- Data entered on HTML forms
- Cross-application surfer attributes
- Application-specific surfer data
- Component state data

Each of these categories of data is described in the following sections.

Data Entered on HTML Forms

Form data is the information collected on HTML forms, as mentioned earlier in this chapter. From a CGI program standpoint, this data is an array of string values that comes from surfer data entry on an HTML form. The key into the array is the NAME of the field as set in the HTML command. In the following example, which creates an edit field, the NAME tag is CUSTID:

```
<INPUT TYPE=TEXT NAME=CUSTID>
```

Cross-Application Surfer Attributes

Cross-application surfer attributes are facts that your application needs to know about a surfer in general, such as the capabilities of the surfer's browser. This information can often be derived from the CGI environment data sent by the Web server to the CGI application.

You can find out about CGI environment data interactively on the Web. For an example, go to http://www.href.com/sample/, go into The Fish Store, and follow the link to Set Preferences. Check the Show System Info check box, and you will see data for your situation, similar to the screen shown in Figure 19-6.

The User Agent (at the bottom of the screen in Figure 19-6) tells which browser is being used. Mozilla is the name for the Netscape browser. (The early versions of Netscape had Mozilla, a green dragon, as an icon.)

The most important browser capability to know about is whether the browser can handle TABLE syntax. If not, your page presentation options are strictly limited. Many sites say that you must be using a "modern" browser to see the site properly and generally recommend using the Netscape browser for its feature set. Netscape supports TABLE syntax, as do some versions of Mosaic.

There are two other important considerations:

- Whether the browser supports the META tag, which is required if you want to be able to force a page request. For example, you can use this tag for creating self-running slide shows.
- Whether the browser supports FRAME syntax. This is a Netscape invention (version 2.0 and higher) that allows for more sophisticated page layouts and, generally, better user interfaces.

Application-Specific Surfer Data

Application-specific surfer data are items that are needed for the given application. In a cyberstore situation, this could be fields such as the order total, and sales tax, as well as a list of the items ordered.

Component State Data

Component state data is more abstract, and it applies specifically to Delphi. WebHub has a set of components, all descended from TWebAction, that handle basic Web tasks

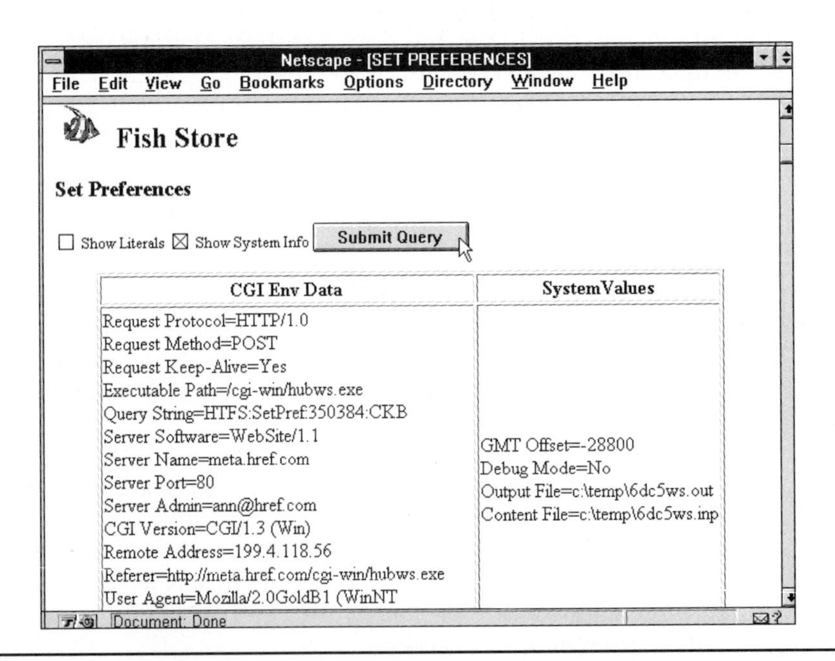

Figure 19-6. *A Web page displaying current CGI environment data*

such as generating table syntax from TDataSets, enabling data entry into TTables, sending e-mail, and managing an outline. Each of these components has properties that need to be uniquely maintained for each surfer. For example, the TWebOutline component needs to store the state of expansion/compression of each outline node uniquely for each surfer.

Object-Oriented State Saving Technique

WebHub implements state saving for the Web by using a session object, TWebSession, which provides a structured data area for each surfer and saves the four types of data discussed in the "Tracking the Surfer's Data" section of this chapter.

To use this technique, you place one copy of the TWebSession component into the Delphi project at design time. At runtime, a separate copy of TWebSession is instantiated for each surfer who comes in to your Web site.

NOTE: Of course, there are limits as to how many copies should be instantiated. WebHub can keep up to a defined number of copies in memory, or it can swap the data to binary or .DB files on disk between page requests. By default, the number of copies held in memory is 300, but this is configurable on the TWebInfo component. If you choose to swap the session data to disk, the data can be shared by multiple instances of your Web application .EXE file. You can run multiple instances in order to serve simultaneous surfers. A full discussion of how to handle high-traffic sites is beyond the scope of this chapter.

Let's examine how the structure of TWebSession supports the four categories of data that need to be stored, and then look at when TWebSession does the restore and save steps. The following listing defines the class hierarchy:

```
type
  TWebBasicSessionOptions =(sfChanged,sfStreaming,sfImagesOk,
         sfBackGroundOk,sfHtml3Ok,sfMetaRefreshOk,sfFramesOk);

  TWebBasicSessionFlags = set of TWebBasicSessionOptions;

  TWebBasicSession = class(TWebExtended)
  private
    fSessionFlags: TWebBasicSessionFlags;
    fPriorAppPage: pString;
    fWebApp: TWebBasicApp;
    fChecked: TWebValueList;
    fLiterals: TWebValueList;
    fPending: TWebValueList;
    fImageMaps: TWebValueList;
    fSaveStates: TWebStateList;
  protected
    function  GetLocalVerbCount: Integer;
    function  GetVerbCount: Integer; Override;
```

```
    function  GetVerb(Index: Integer): string; Override;
    procedure ExecuteVerb(Index: Integer); Override;

    function  GetSaveStates:TWebStateList;
    procedure SetSaveStates(Value:TWebStateList);
    procedure SetChecked(Value:TWebValueList);
    procedure SetLiterals(Value:TWebValueList);
    procedure SetPending(Value:TWebValueList);
    procedure SetImageMaps(Value:TWebValueList);
    procedure SetNoWebApp(Value: TWebBasicApp);

    function  GetChanged:Boolean;
    procedure SetChanged(Value:Boolean);
    function  GetStreaming:Boolean;
    procedure SetStreaming(Value:Boolean);

    function  GetPriorAppPage:String;
    procedure SetPriorAppPage(Const Value:String);
    function  GetPriorAppId:String;
    procedure SetPriorAppId(Const Value:String);
    function  GetPriorPageId:String;
    procedure SetPriorPageId(Const Value:String);

    function  GetImagesOk: Boolean;
    procedure SetImagesOk(Value:Boolean);
    function  GetBackGroundOk: Boolean;
    procedure SetBackGroundOk(Value:Boolean);
    function  GetHTML3Ok: Boolean;
    procedure SetHTML3Ok(Value:Boolean);
    function  GetMetaRefreshOk: Boolean;
    procedure SetMetaRefreshOk(Value:Boolean);
    function  GetFramesOk: Boolean;
    procedure SetFramesOk(Value:Boolean);

  public
    constructor Create(AOwner: TComponent); override;
    destructor Destroy; override;
    function  Activate(aWebApp:TWebBasicApp;
      Const PageId:String):Boolean; virtual;
    procedure SaveStates;
    procedure RestoreStates;
    procedure Changed;
    function  SessionFileName:String;
    procedure SaveToDisk;
    function  LoadFromDisk:Boolean;

    property HasChanged: Boolean read GetChanged write SetChanged;
    property Streaming: Boolean read GetStreaming write SetStreaming;
```

```
  published
    property WebApp: TWebBasicApp read fWebApp
      write fWebApp stored false;
    property SessionFlags: TWebBasicSessionFlags read fSessionFlags
      write fSessionFlags;
    property Checked: TWebValueList read fChecked
      write SetChecked;
    property Literals: TWebValueList read fLiterals
      write SetLiterals;
    property Pending: TWebValueList read fPending
      write SetPending;
    property ImageMaps: TWebValueList read fImageMaps
      write SetImageMaps;
    property SavedStates: TWebStateList read GetSaveStates
      write SetSaveStates;

    property PriorAppId: String read GetPriorAppId
      write SetPriorAppId stored false;
    property PriorPageId: String read GetPriorPageId
      write SetPriorPageId stored false;
    property PriorAppPage: String read GetPriorAppPage
      write SetPriorAppPage {stored NoInfo};
    property BackGroundOk: Boolean read GetBackGroundOk
      write SetBackGroundOk stored false default true;
    property ImagesOk: Boolean read GetImagesOk
      write SetImagesOk stored false default true;
    property HTML3Ok: Boolean read GetHTML3Ok
      write SetHTML3Ok stored false;
    property MetaRefreshOk: Boolean read GetMetaRefreshOk
      write SetMetaRefreshOk stored false;
    property FramesOk: Boolean read GetFramesOk
      write SetFramesOk stored false;
    end;

{---------------------------------------------------------------------}
type
  TWebSession = class;

  TWebSessionVars = class(TPersistent)
  private
    fWebSession:TWebSession;
  protected
  public
    constructor Create(Value:TWebSession); virtual;
    property WebSession: TWebSession read fWebSession;
    end;
```

```
TWebSessionVarsClass = class of TWebSessionVars;

TWebSession = class(TWebBasicSession)
private
  fVars: TWebSessionVars;
  fPageCost: Longint;
  fPageCount: Longint;
  fMacroCost: Longint;
protected
  function  GetLocalVerbCount: Integer;
  function  GetVerbCount: Integer; Override;
  function  GetVerb(Index: Integer): string; Override;
  procedure ExecuteVerb(Index: Integer); Override;

  function  Activate(aWebApp:TWebBasicApp;
    Const PageId:String):Boolean; override;
  function  VarsClass:TWebSessionVarsClass; virtual;

  function  GetSessionCost: Longint;
  procedure SetNoLongint(Value:Longint);

  function  Designing: Boolean; {true in designer}
  function  DontOutput: Boolean; {true if no file or designing}
public
  constructor Create(AOwner: TComponent); override;
  destructor Destroy; override;

published
  property Vars: TWebSessionVars read fVars write fVars;
  property PageCount: Longint read fPageCount write fPageCount;
  property PageCost: Longint read fPageCost write fPageCost;
  property MacroCost: Longint read fMacroCost write fMacroCost;
  property SessionCost: Longint read GetSessionCost
    write SetNoLongInt stored false;
  end;

TWebSessionClass = class of TWebSession;
```

Data Entered on HTML Forms

Data that the surfer enters on HTML forms is stored in the Literals property, which is basically a TStringList. Specifically, it is a TWebValueList, which is inherited as follows: TStringList -> TpStringList -> TWebStringList -> TWebValueList. The data in the Literals array always takes this form:

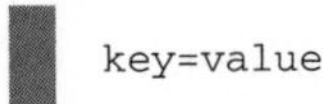

```
key=value
```

For example,

```
custID=123987
```

Whenever form literal data is posted, WebHub adds those values to the Literals array. Entries are not removed, so you end up with a wealth of data from the surfer. Individual entries in the Literals array can be accessed using a statement like the following:

```
WebSession.Literals.Values['custID']
```

This statement retrieves a single value, custID. Values is a property of the TStringList class in Delphi. It works with key=value pairs. You pass in the key and get back the value.

WebHub has a mechanism for storing the TWebSession object. Since the Literals property is part of this object, it is also saved. The Checked property of the TWebSession also assists in the saving of data from HTML forms. This array tracks check box values as Booleans.

Check boxes are always a bit tricky in CGI, since they are only reported when they are checked. If the surfer does not check the box, no information is sent to the Web server about the field. In order to track check box settings throughout a session, WebHub tracks check box field names "on the way out" in the Pending array property, and then compares the submitted values against that list. From that information, it makes True/False entries in the Checked array for each Pending item.

Cross-Application Surfer Attributes

Most of the published TWebSession properties fall into the category of information that is generically useful to know about surfers in all Web applications. Table 19-1 contains a brief description of each of these properties.

It is important to think about how these properties should be generically set for the session. Some of the properties can be determined based on rules about the surfer's browser software. HTML3Ok, FramesOk, and MetaRefreshOk are in this category. WebHub maintains a list of browsers and their capabilities so that it can set these properties automatically when a surfer arrives.

Some of the properties have defaults that can be overridden on surfer preference pages. BackgroundOk and ImagesOk are in this group. These properties default to True so that the surfer will see graphics, but they can be turned off for someone on a slow 14.4-Kbps modem connection.

The other properties are maintained by WebHub as the session progresses. For example, PageCount and the MacroCost amounts are tallied after the page is complete.

Application-Specific Surfer Data

It is quite likely that you'll want to have some application-specific values stored for each surfer. For example, in a shopping cart scenario, you may need to track the list of

Property	Description
PriorAppId	The ID of the application that the surfer was just in. This is useful when you break your Web application into several modules that all work together but that have separate AppIDs.
PriorPageId	The ID of the page the surfer was on prior to the current page. This is useful if you want to generate "go-back" links.
PriorAppPage	A combination of prior AppID:PageID.
BackgroundOk	A Boolean flag to indicate whether the surfer would like to see backgrounds.
ImagesOk	A Boolean flag to indicate whether the surfer would like to see graphics images.
HTML3Ok	A Boolean flag to indicate whether the surfer's browser supports HTML 3, which is useful when deciding whether grids should be created with TABLE syntax or using <pre> tags. Older browsers can not display TABLES, so it's necessary to send out the information using a fixed-size font with the data strings set to the correct width. This can be used to create a column effect. The HTML <pre> tag tells the browser to use such a fixed-size font, typically a Courier font.
MetaRefreshOk	A Boolean flag to indicate whether the surfer's browser supports the Meta Refresh tag, which is required for slide-show effects.
FramesOk	A Boolean flag to indicate whether the surfer's browser supports FRAME syntax.
PageCount	The number of pages requested by the surfer during the current session.
PageCost	The cumulative charge run up by the surfer based on the TWebPage.PageCost. (This defaults to zero, but this can be used to charge surfers for viewing pages, for instance, a "micro-charge" of $.01 or less per page.)
MacroCost	The cumulative micro-charge run up by the surfer based on the use of macros, typically associated with downloading media files such as graphics or audio files.
SessionCost	The combination of page and macro costs.

Table 19-1. *TWebSession Properties*

items ordered so far, the order total, the billing information, and so on. You might store this information long term in a database, or you might want to keep it around only for the duration of the session.

WebHub enables you to keep track of this kind of information in the Vars layer of the component. Look carefully at the following listing. You will see that it defines TWebSessionVars as derived from TPersistent. The TWebSession component has a published Vars property that is of type TWebSessionVars. You can create your own TWebSessionVars and TWebSession classes. By overriding the VarsClass function, you let the component know about your custom TWebSessionVars class.

```
TWebSessionVars = class(TPersistent)
  private
    fWebSession:TWebSession;
  protected
  public
    constructor Create(Value:TWebSession); virtual;
    property WebSession: TWebSession read fWebSession;
    end;

  TWebSessionVarsClass = class of TWebSessionVars;

protected
  function  VarsClass:TWebSessionVarsClass; virtual;

published
    property Vars: TWebSessionVars read fVars write fVars;
```

By studying this part of the WebHub architecture, you can see the object-oriented way of adding a customized data structure to something that is reused throughout a much larger system. The VarsClass function lets the outside world know the exact structure of the customized data structure. The following code listing shows how you can do this:

```
unit Tshowme;

interface

uses
  SysUtils, WinTypes, WinProcs, Messages, Classes, Graphics
  , Controls
  , WebTypes
  , WebApp, WebVars
  ;

type
  TShowMeSessionVars = class(TWebSessionVars)
  private
```

```
    fOrderTotal : double;
    fFramesOk : boolean;
    fAList : TStringList;
  protected
    function  getAList : TStringList;
    procedure setAList( value : TStringList );
  public
    Constructor Create(aWebSession:TWebSession); override;
    Destructor Destroy; override;
  published
    property OrderTotal : double read fOrderTotal
      write fOrderTotal stored false;
    property FramesOk : boolean read fFramesOk
      write fFramesOk stored false;
    property AList : TStringList read getAList
      write setAList stored false;
  end;

  TShowMeSession = class(TWebSession)
  protected
    function VarsClass:TWebSessionVarsClass; override;
    end;

type
  TShowMeApp = class(TWebApp)
  private
    fLogo : string;
  protected
    function SessionClass:TWebSessionClass; override;
  public
    constructor Create(AOwner: TComponent); override;
    destructor  Destroy; override;
  published
    property Logo:string read fLogo write fLogo stored false;
  end;

procedure Register;

implementation

{---------------------------------------------------------------------}

Constructor TShowMeApp.Create(aOwner:tComponent);
begin
  inherited Create(aOwner);
  {placeholder in case you need to do something else later}
end;
```

```
Destructor TShowMeApp.Destroy;
begin
  inherited Destroy;
  {placeholder}
end;

function TShowMeApp.SessionClass:TWebSessionClass;
begin
  Result:= TShowMeSession;
end;

function TShowMeSession.VarsClass:TWebSessionVarsClass;
begin
  Result:= TShowMeSessionVars;
end;

{---------------------------------------------------------------------}

Constructor TShowMeSessionVars.Create(aWebSession:TWebSession);
begin
  inherited Create(aWebSession);
  fAList:=TStringList.create;
end;

Destructor TShowMeSessionVars.Destroy;
begin
  fAList.free;
  inherited Destroy;
end;

{---------------------------------------------------------------------}

function TShowMeSessionVars.GetAList:TStringList;
begin
  result:=fAList;
end;

procedure TShowMeSessionVars.SetAList(value:TStringList);
begin
  fAList.assign(value);
end;

{---------------------------------------------------------------------}

procedure Register;
begin
  RegisterComponents('WebApps', [TShowMeApp, TShowMeSession]);
```

```
end;

end.
```

Let's examine this process step-by-step:

1. First, you define the custom variables on a class derived from TWebSessionVars. You can use any data type here. You can even use custom classes as long as they are derived from TPersistent so that their contents can be streamed, in other words, stored, such as in memory or written to a file:

```
type
  TShowMeSessionVars = class(TWebSessionVars)
```

2. Define the custom session class, derived from TWebSession. Override the VarsClass function to indicate the type:

```
type
TShowMeSession = class(TWebSession)
  protected
    function VarsClass:TWebSessionVarsClass; override;
    end;

function TShowMeSession.VarsClass:TWebSessionVarsClass;
begin
  Result:= TShowMeSessionVars;
end;
```

3. Define the custom application object:

```
type
 TShowMeApp = class(TWebApp)
 private
  fLogo : string;
 protected
  function SessionClass:TWebSessionClass; override;
 public
  constructor Create(AOwner: TComponent); override;
  destructor Destroy; override;
 published
  property Logo:string read fLogo write fLogo stored false;
 end;
```

4. At this point we move into the connection between the Session data and the Web application object. A full discussion of TWebApp is outside the scope of this chapter. However, suffice it to say that each application connects to one

session object, and if the session object is customized, the application object must be also. The SessionClass function is overridden on the application object to indicate the connection to the custom session object:

```
function TShowMeApp.SessionClass:TWebSessionClass;
begin
  Result:= TShowMeSession;
end;
```

5. The rest of the code is "plumbing" to take care of initializing and freeing the data. Custom constructors and destructors are required because a TStringList is involved. (TStringLists require explicit memory allocation and de-allocation.)

The beauty of the object-oriented approach is that each Web application can have a completely customized data structure set up for the surfers. The rest of the components can interact generically with the TWebSession component because of the overridden VarsClass and SessionClass methods. This means that in terms of saving state, WebHub can load and restore the TWebSession component generically without having any strict limits on the contents.

Component State Data

The fourth category of data that needs to be saved for each surfer is probably a surprise for most developers. This is the need to save the state of relevant components within the Delphi project. Remember that the running .EXE file will be shared by many surfers. One surfer at a time uses the .EXE file to create a complete dynamic Web page. Then the next surfer in line uses the file. Certain components have properties that you might want to set for each surfer individually. For example, the TWebDataGrid component (which is used to display scrolling grids based on TDataSet records) tracks the unique identifier of the row at the top of the displayed set of records.

In WebHub, the relevant components are those derived from TWebAction. These components are meant to handle a specific task on the Web, such as creating a grid, sending e-mail, or managing an outline. TWebAction components all have a SaveState property like the following:

```
property SaveState: String read GetSaveState
    write SetSaveState stored False;
```

This string contains the state information for the component. If the ancestor class saved any state data, that is separated out by the | character so that the single string can hold contributions from more than one level in the object hierarchy. See the call to inherited GetSaveState in the code listing for TWebOutline.GetSaveState.

The TWebSession component has a SavedState property that combines the SaveState strings for all the TWebAction components in the project. Thus, each

TWebAction component is responsible for setting its SaveState string, and the TWebSession stores the collected set.

The final piece of the puzzle involves determining when this saved state data should be restored and saved. Recall that TFormRestorer, discussed earlier in this chapter, saved state when a form closed and loaded it when the form opened again. That was a simpler case because the user has control of the .EXE file continuously from load time to close time. In the context of the Web, the data should be restored just before a page starts, and saved after the page ends. This fits with the overall paradigm of a Web site as a set of TWebPages.

Since a single surfer has the use of the .EXE file while a complete page is built, it is a good idea to load the data just prior to beginning the page and to save it at the end. There can be no interruptions between the time the state data is loaded and when it is released.

TWebOutline: An Example of a TWebAction Component

To make this more concrete, let's look at an example of a TWebAction component. TWebOutline is a component that enables you to put interactive outlines for data, such as a table of contents, on a Web page. The surfer can click icons to expand and compress the outline, just as can be done in a regular stand-alone Delphi application that uses TOutline. In this case, each click is an HTTP request, and the page with the outline is redrawn accordingly. You can see this effect on the Table of Contents page at http://www.href.com/.

The complete code for the TWebOutline component is included on the CD. Following are just the code segments that are relevant for saving state. First, is the declaration of the component:

```
Const
  toCollapsed='C';
   toExpanded='E';
  cStateCode:array[false..true] of char=(toCollapsed,toExpanded);
  cOutlineMagic=3;

Type
  TWebOutlineCommands = (ocGoto,ocCut,ocTop,ocLess,ocMore,ocAll);

Const
  WebOutlineCommands: array[ocGoto..ocAll] of string[4]
                    = ('Lvl','Cut','Top','Less','More','All');
Type
  TOnNode= procedure (aNode:TOutlineNode;NodeNr:integer;
    var Value:OpenString) of object;
  TOnFolder= procedure (aNode:TOutlineNode;NodeNr:integer;
    var Value:OpenString;Expanded:Boolean) of object;
  TOnDocument= procedure (aNode:TOutlineNode;NodeNr:integer;
```

```
    var Value:OpenString) of object;

  TNodeNamePrefix= string[10];

Type
  TWebOutline = class(TWebAction)
  private
    fCut,
    fLevel,
    fLevels,
    fIndent: byte;
    fNodeNamePrefix: TNodeNamePrefix;
    fOutline : TOutline;
    fOnNode: TOnNode;
    fOnFolder: TOnFolder;
    fOnDocument: TOnDocument;
  protected
    function  DoUpdate : boolean; override;
      {make sure outline is hooked up}
    procedure DoExecute; override;
      {send the html for the outline}

    procedure SetSaveState(const State:String); override;
      {restore the outline's state}
    function  GetSaveState:String; override;
      {get the outline's state}

    procedure StringToOutline(Const Value:string);
      {set the outline from the state}
    function  OutlineToString:string;
      {convert the outline to the state}

    procedure PerformCommand;
    procedure SetLevel(Value:Byte);
    function  GetLevels:Byte;
    procedure SetToZero(Value:Byte);

    procedure SetExpanded(Node:Integer;Value:Boolean);
    function  GetExpanded(Node:Integer):Boolean;
  public
    constructor Create(aOwner:TComponent); override;
    procedure Notification(AComponent: TComponent;
      Operation: TOperation); override;
     property Expanded[Node:Integer]:Boolean read GetExpanded
      write SetExpanded;
  published
    property Level: Byte read fLevel write SetLevel;
    property Levels: Byte read GetLevels write SetToZero;
```

```
    property Indent: Byte read fIndent write fIndent;
    property Outline : TOutline read fOutline write fOutline;
    property NodeNamePrefix: TNodeNamePrefix read fNodeNamePrefix
      write fNodeNamePrefix;
    property OnNode: TOnNode read fOnNode write fOnNode;
    property OnFolder: TOnFolder read fOnFolder write fOnFolder;
    property OnDocument: TOnDocument read fOnDocument
      write fOnDocument;
    end;
```

The two methods that apply to saving state are GetSaveState and OutlineToString. (There are parallel methods for loading state that perform the reverse process.) The GetSaveState is called when one requests the SaveState property from the component. It incorporates any saved state information from its ancestor (using inherited GetSaveState) and then includes its own information. The OutlineToString function goes through the outline and represents the expand/compress state of each node as a single character, creating a string that completely defines the state of the outline. These methods are shown in the following listing. The SetSaveState can later use this same string to reset the outline to the most recent configuration.

```
function TWebOutline.GetSaveState:String;
begin
  Result:='|'+inherited GetSaveState;
  if tpUpdated then
    Result:=OutlineToString+Result;
end;

function TWebOutline.OutlineToString:string;
var
  i:integer;
begin
  Result:='';
  with fOutline do
    for i:=1 to ItemCount do
      Result:=Result+cStateCode[items[i].expanded];
end;
```

Additional Considerations

When developing Web applications, you may need to consider the following issues regarding tracking a surfer and saving that surfer's data:

Q: When should you purge session data, and how should you purge it?

A: You might want to purge the session files after 24 or 48 hours. This ensures that a surfer is very likely to have a coherent, complete session without leaving an unmanageable pile of surfer variables on your hard drive. Files can be purged with a simple utility that looks at the time stamp.

Q: Where should you draw the boundaries between data that is stored by the TWebSession and data stored in a table?

A: This relates to when the data is purged, and whether you want users to login in some fashion in order to reconnect with data they may have entered more than 24 to 48 hours ago. It also depends on what other processes need to access the data. Information about ordering should probably be kept in a separate table so that other parts of an integrated system can utilize it easily.

Q: What happens when you have a high-traffic site that requires a cluster of machines, all running Web servers and Web applications? How can session data be shared across these instances on different machines?

A: As long as there is a shared directory that all the machines can utilize, they can all share the same session files. In this way, a surfer can be served by an .EXE file on any of the machines within the cluster.

Q: How do you prevent two surfers from accidentally sharing a Session ID?

S You can make sure that there is no change in the IP address between page requests. This is not a guaranteed solution, but it is fairly likely to separate surfers the vast majority of the time. As long as the pool of Session IDs is large (greater than one million), the chances of two surfers randomly bumping into each other in a 24-hour period is quite small.

Conclusion

This chapter discussed the two related topics of tracking a surfer during a session and saving that surfer's data. It covered how the four categories of data are saved in object-oriented fashion using TWebSession, and how a TWebAction component uses a simple string to represent its own state. The basic techniques of loading and saving state data apply not only on the Web, but to programming in general. The biggest difference is that with a Web application, multiple users are sharing the same components within the same .EXE file, so there is the added issue of saving data for each surfer instead of just for each .EXE file.

Once the basic save-state mechanism is in place in the CGI framework, you can begin to build really useful, interesting Web applications. The next chapter explores one such application, in which surfer data is passed to a Java applet.

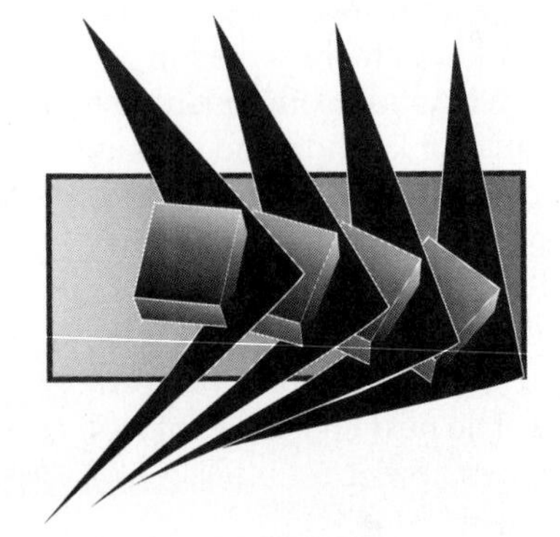

Chapter Twenty

Integrating Delphi CGI, Java, and JavaScript

The code for the Java applets (testfora.jav and receipt.jav) presented in this chapter can be found in the \CODE\CH20 subdirectory on the CD-ROM that accompanies this book. Please refer to Appendix A for information on using the code files for this chapter.

This chapter explores two sample Web applications. Both touch on some basic design issues that come up when building a Web site for electronic commerce. The first example shows how client-side Java applets and JavaScripts can enhance the user interface and how the CGI environment can contribute dynamically to both of these. The second example shows the basics of a shopping cart interface, where surfers can select items and the list is remembered by the CGI program.

After looking at Java applets and JavaScript in context, we'll come back to The Fish Store example to pull together the concepts from the last three chapters. In particular, we'll see how the reusable WebHub components that handle state saving make it quite easy to enable surfer shopping.

NOTE: The examples presented here were built with WebHub, a commercial product built in and for Delphi, from HREF Tools Corp. If you would like to work with these examples, please go to http://www.href.com/ and download a free, trial version of WebHub. The source code to both the Java and Fish Store examples are included with the trial version. The trial version always ships with an expiration date because features are added on a frequent basis, and you are encouraged to download and use the current version. WebHub is not included on the CD-ROM for this book.

What Are Java and JavaScript?

Java and JavaScript have two things in common: they both have the word "Java" in their names, and they have application to the World Wide Web. But the similarity ends there. They are, in fact, two completely separate and unrelated products.

Sun Microsystems, Inc., the originator of Java, describes it as "a simple, object-oriented, distributed, interpreted, robust, secure, architecture neutral, portable, high-performance, multithreaded, and dynamic language." From the standpoint of this chapter, what you need to know about Java is that it is a cross-platform programming language, similar to C in syntax, and similar to Delphi in its object orientation. Using Java, you can create applets that, like other resources, are downloaded to the surfer's browser. What make these applets remarkable, is that once they arrive at the surfer's browser they are executed, using an interpreter supplied by the browser. Furthermore, this execution is platform independent, meaning that it can occur on PCs, Macintoshes, and Unix-based machines. Regardless of the platform, however, the downloading browser must be *Java-enabled*. Currently, Netscape 2.0+ browsers are Java-enabled, and most other browsers should be soon.

Java is certainly one of the fastest growing areas of Internet programming. It seems that new books on Java are coming out every week, and the list of public domain samples is growing daily. (Visit http: / / www.gamelan.com/ for over a thousand Java resources.) Rather than try to cover such a vast subject, this first part of this chapter will focus on how server-side CGI programs can interact with client-side Java applets to significantly enhance their usefulness to the surfer. (For additional information on Java, visit Sun's Java Site at http://www.javasoft.com. See also Borland's site at http://www.borland.com, for information on Latte, Borland's new Java development tool.)

JavaScript, although similar in name, is not related to Sun's Java programming language. Instead, JavaScript is Netscape's scripting language that allows Web page developers to enhance the user interface with elements such as dialog boxes and other interactive controls. JavaScript is not an object-oriented language.

In this chapter, both Java and JavaScript are covered because, from a user-interface point of view, they both provide ways to add graphical features to the surfer's experience. They are competitive approaches but can both benefit from the key idea here, which is to let the Delphi CGI program enhance the client-side application by passing data to it.

NOTE: *Java* applets *are precompiled and are sent to the surfer as .class files. A .class file contains Java Virtual Machine object code, which is then interpreted on the client side, for instance, by the Netscape browser. JavaScripts scripts, by comparison, are sent as source code in-line in the HTML document and are then interpreted by the Netscape browser.*

In this chapter you will learn how you can use Delphi for server-side CGI programming and simply *pass* data to a generic Java applet. For many programmers, and certainly until Java has the database connectivity that the Delphi Client/Server edition has, it is easier to implement this technique of passing data than it is to build everything in Java.

In other words, this chapter proposes that you use Delphi for its strengths and Java when you need a fancy user interface. Delphi has a wealth of features, including database connectivity. If a Delphi-based executable (.EXE) file is running on the Web server, it can already talk to virtually any database. That .EXE can generate HTML pages on the fly and can pass data to Java applets to make them database driven.

Passing Data to the Client

A Delphi-based CGI program can enhance the functionality of either a Java applet or a JavaScript, albeit in different ways. With a Java applet, you can only pass in parameters. These parameters, in turn, can affect how the applet executes. Consequently, your Delphi CGI program can have a profound influence on the execution of the client-side applet.

A JavaScript, unlike a Java applet, is not compiled. Instead, it is embedded directly in the HTML and is executed by the Netscape browser. Instead of merely being able to pass parameters to influence a JavaScript program, the CGI program can write JavaScript from scratch, giving the CGI program complete control over the contents of the JavaScript instructions.

The next two sections demonstrate the basic techniques for controlling Java applets and JavaScript from a CGI program.

Passing Parameters to Java Applets

Let's start by looking at how a CGI program can pass parameters to a Java applet. The following code is an excerpt from a dynamic HTML page that is discussed in detail later in this chapter. This code is generated by WebHub, and it passes one string parameter to the Java applet called "TestForAnn.class." The string value in this case is "Go Delphi!"

```
<applet code="TestForAnn.class" width=450 height=50>
<param name=text value="Go Delphi!">
</applet>
```

This string value is not hard coded as it would first appear. The CGI program is filling in the value dynamically as the <applet> tag is generated. In this particular example, the string is actually entered by the surfer to create a banner. The Java applet, upon receiving the parameter, then creates the following graphical banner:

This Java applet will be discussed in much more detail after the next section takes a brief look at a JavaScript sample.

Creating JavaScript Dynamically

Unlike Java applets, JavaScripts are handled by sending complete source code in-line in the HTML document. If the CGI program is creating the HTML document dynamically, it can also create the JavaScript instructions. Since this content is being created dynamically, there is complete flexibility in what the JavaScript will contain. For example, in one instance the CGI program may create JavaScript instructions that permit the surfer to request additional information. If circumstances are different, the JavaScript instructions may display a dialog box indicating that a process is complete.

The following code is a small excerpt of a complete JavaScript script, presented in full in the section "Java Demo Web Page HTML Source." This script might be sent to a surfer in response to an http request with the response document containing some HTML plus the JavaScript definition. The script then runs on the surfer's machine as the browser interprets the JavaScript.

```
<script language="JavaScript">
<!-- Time of day display.
 //Make right justified textbox for time.
```

```
 document.write(
         "<table border align=right>"
        +"<tr><td align=center><b></b></td></tr>"
        +"<tr><font size=-4><form></font>"
        +"<td><input type=text size=8></td>"
        +"</form></tr></table>"
 );
...code excerpted here...
</script>
```

Whether JavaScript or Java is being used, the basic idea is the same: A CGI program has a tremendous benefit over a static HTML page in terms of launching a Java applet or sending JavaScript commands. A static HTML page can not pass data dynamically.

Once the Java applet or JavaScript program is running for the surfer, the benefit over simple HTML is obvious. Java in particular can generate a full-featured graphical user interface and can continue to interact with the surfer locally, long after the HTTP request has been fulfilled. When necessary, the Java applet can make additional HTTP requests back to the CGI program to further fine-tune the process.

Why Integrate Delphi CGI, Java, and JavaScript?

Java applets and JavaScript scripts are limited in what they can do. Without information about the surfer's actions on the Web site, the Java applet must do the same thing for all surfers. Although some sites, such as www.gamelan.com, have Java applications that connect directly to databases over TCP/IP, most Java applets are much more isolated and can benefit immediately from the inputs that are easily available in the CGI arena.

A concrete example is an online shopping store (cyberstore). As the surfer moves through the store and finds items of interest, the CGI program knows exactly what is going on. Still it is desirable to have an elegant user interface that shows the contents of the order, collects payment, and perhaps even conducts electronic commerce in an automated fashion. The client-side (Java- or HTML-based) application must be informed about the surfer's choices, and it makes sense for the server-side (CGI) application to assist.

A JavaScript Example

Before getting into how to do this, let's take a quick tour of a sample application that uses both Java applets and JavaScript. This example is running on the Web at http://www.href.com/sample/, and its implementation is discussed in detail in the next section.

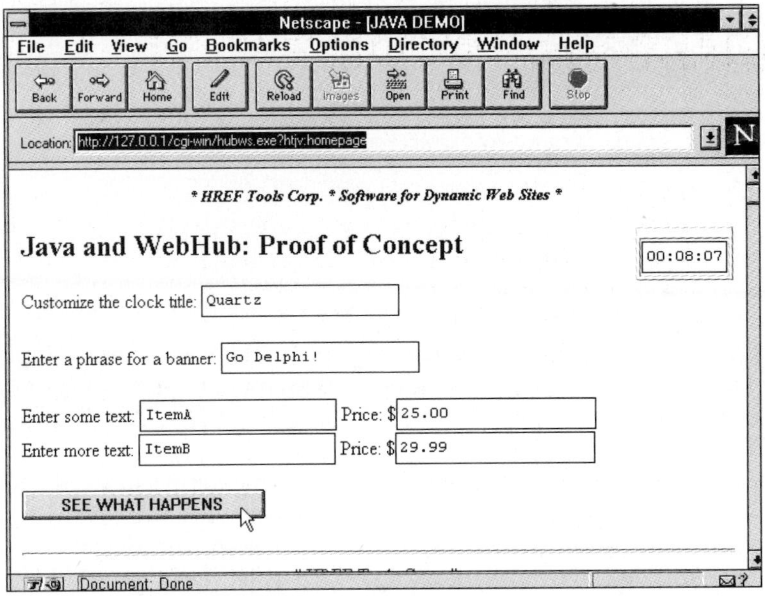

Figure 20-1. *A Web page that is running a JavaScript clock and that is about to dynamically call two Java applets*

Figure 20-1 shows the launch page for this demo, with some data filled into the edit fields. This particular HTML page is generated dynamically by an application built with WebHub. Although you cannot tell from this figure, the JavaScript application continuously updates the time on the clock.

Java Demo Web Page HTML Source

If you use Netscape's View | Source feature to see the HTML document source for this page, you would see the following code:

```
<HTML><HEAD>
<TITLE>JAVA DEMO</TITLE>
</HEAD>
<BODY>

<CENTER>
<h5><i>* HREF Tools Corp. * Software for Dynamic Web Sites *</i></h5>
</CENTER>
<p>

<script language="JavaScript">
<!-- Time of day display.
 //Make right justified textbox for time.
 document.write(
        "<table border align=right>"
```

```
        +"<tr><td align=center><b></b></td></tr>"
        +"<tr><font size=-4><form></font>"
        +"<td><input type=text size=8></td>"
        +"</form></tr></table>"
 );

function showTime() {
        var now = new Date();
        var s = "";
        if (now.getHours() < 10) s="0";
        s = s + now.getHours() + ":";
        if (now.getMinutes() < 10) s = s + "0";
        s = s + now.getMinutes() + ":";
        if (now.getSeconds() < 10) s = s + "0";
        s = s + now.getSeconds();
        document.forms[0].elements[0].value = s;
        setTimeout( "showTime()", 1000 );
 }//TOfunc()
 showTime(); //kickstart time display.
//Show if no javascript--

</script>

<h2>Java and WebHub: Proof of Concept</h2>
<FORM METHOD=POST ACTION="/cgi-win/hubws.exe?HTJV:homepagep:707682">
Customize the clock title: <INPUT TYPE=TEXT NAME=CLOCKTITLE
MAXSIZE=15 VALUE="">
<p>
Enter a phrase for a banner: <INPUT TYPE=TEXT NAME=BANNER
MAXSIZE=25 VALUE="">
<p>
Enter some text: <INPUT TYPE=TEXT NAME=ITEM1 MAXSIZE=20 VALUE="">
Price: $<INPUT TYPE=TEXT MAXSIZE=6 NAME=PRICE1 VALUE=""><BR>
Enter more text: <INPUT TYPE=TEXT NAME=ITEM2 MAXSIZE=20 VALUE="">
Price: $<INPUT TYPE=TEXT MAXSIZE=6 NAME=PRICE2 VALUE="">
<p>
<INPUT TYPE=SUBMIT VALUE="SEE WHAT HAPPENS">
</FORM>
<hr>
<center>|| <A HREF="http://www.href.com/">HREF Tools Corp.</A> ||</center>
<HR>
<ADDRESS>Copyright &copy 1995-1996 HREF Tools Corp.  All Rights Reserved.
</ADDRESS>
</BODY></HTML>
```

HTML Documents that Contain JavaScript Scripts

To clarify the preceding listing in terms of the transitions between HTML and JavaScript and where the CGI program fits in, let's look at a few key phrases:

Tags	Purpose
<HTML><HEAD>	The document starts with regular HTML.
<script language="JavaScript">	The JavaScript portion starts here.
</script>	The JavaScript portion ends here and HTML begins.
<FORM METHOD=POST ACTION="/cgi-win/hubws.exe?HTJV:homepagep:707682">	The <FORM> tag starts the definition of an HTML form, and the ACTION tag defines the CGI program to be called. The CGI Query String is "HTJV:homepagep:707682." The balance of the document contains HTML.

You might wonder what happens for surfers who don't have a Netscape 2.0+ browser and therefore can't interpret the JavaScript code. HTML was designed to ignore expressions that it doesn't understand, so it will ignore the tags <script language="JavaScript"> and </script>. If you look closely at the rest of the example, you will see that the JavaScript code is contained within comment-on (<!–) and comment-off (-->) tags. An HTML rendering system that does not understand JavaScript will ignore this section of code.

Analysis of the JavaScript

The JavaScript code uses the document.write command to create an HTML table that contains a form with one input field. JavaScript is able to write directly into the HTML document in this way:

```
document.write(
         "<table border align=right>"
        +"<tr><td align=center><b></b></td></tr>"
        +"<tr><font size=-4><form></font>"
        +"<td><input type=text size=8></td>"
        +"</form></tr></table>"
 );
```

Of course, there is no advantage to generating HTML embedded inside JavaScript unless you are going to address that area further—which is what happens in the showTime() function. The showTime() function creates a string, *s*, which contains the current time. That string is then placed into the only input field (elements[0]) inside the only HTML form (forms[0]) with the line

```
document.forms[0].elements[0].value = s;
```

NOTE: JavaScript comments start with // and continue to the end of the line.

If you want to display something for non-JavaScript-aware browsers, you can put something in the blank area after the comment-end and the </script> tag:

```
//Show if no javascript--
Clock not available.
</script>
```

All browsers except Netscape (for example, Mosaic) would display "Clock not available."

Dynamically Generating the JavaScript Code

Any CGI program can dynamically send out a JavaScript script as demonstrated in this chapter. It's particularly easy with WebHub because you can define a *chunk* (called JavaClock in this example), and then reuse that chunk on as many pages as desired throughout an application. As you might recall from the preceding chapters, a WebHub chunk is often just a segment of predefined HTML that the CGI program can use to piece together a larger HTML document. (More precisely, a chunk is the smallest element in WebHub that can be conditional; it can also be the name of a component.)

Chunks are a convenient technique for building HTML documents because they are maintained in ASCII files outside the Delphi project, instead of in-line in the Object Pascal (or Perl, or C) source code. Consequently, you do not need to recompile your application when you change a particular chunk. Furthermore, with WebHub's ability to "refresh" components at runtime, you can post a new chunk file, tell TWebApp to refresh itself, and the changes will be in effect from then on. There is no need for recompilation or system downtime just because you want to try a variation in your Java code. (See Chapter 18 for a discussion of "readiness" and the Update verb. Refresh is a related verb used to indicate that "the outside environment has changed. Re-initialize from disk.")

The following listing shows what the JavaClock chunk looks like when defined in WebHub. The parts highlighted in bold are the only portions that vary from the exact code sent to the surfer, as listed in the previous section "Java Demo Web Page HTML Source."

```
%=chunkBegin=%javaclock%=endInfo=%
<script language="JavaScript">
<!-- Time of day display.
 //Make right justified textbox for time.
```

```
 document.write(
         "<table border align=right>"
        +"<tr><td align=center><b>%=CLOCKTITLE=%</b></td></tr>"
        +"<tr><font size=-4><form></font>"
        +"<td><input type=text size=8></td>"
        +"</form></tr></table>"
 );

function showTime() {
        var now = new Date();
        var s = "";
        if (now.getHours() < 10) s="0";
        s = s + now.getHours() + ":";
        if (now.getMinutes() < 10) s = s + "0";
        s = s + now.getMinutes() + ":";
        if (now.getSeconds() < 10) s = s + "0";
        s = s + now.getSeconds();
        document.forms[0].elements[0].value = s;
        setTimeout( "showTime()", 1000 );
 }//TOfunc()
 showTime(); //kickstart time display.
//Show if no javascript--
</script>
<!-- *********************** --
```

The %=chunkBegin=% line defines the chunk name for WebHub, and the rest of the information up to the comment containing the row of asterisks is the content for the JavaClock chunk.

The only part of this chunk definition that is not straight JavaScript is the use of %=CLOCKTITLE=%, which you can see in the definition of the HTML table that appears in the seventh line of the preceding listing. The "%=" characters invoke WebHub macro syntax. When the text is sent to the output document, TWebApp will expand CLOCKTITLE dynamically according to its macro expansion rules. By a process of elimination, TWebApp will determine that CLOCKTITLE refers to a TWebApp.Literal value, thereby replacing %=CLOCKTITLE=% with the appropriate value before sending the HTML document to the requesting surfer.

If you look back at the HTML in the section " Java Demo Web page HTML Source," you will see that the NAME tag of one of the fields on the launch page is CLOCKTITLE. Within the WebHub CGI framework, when the surfer's data is posted, a key=value string goes into the TWebApp.Literal array and can be referenced immediately from HTML with macro syntax. In this case the key would be CLOCKTITLE and the value Quartz. Because WebHub saves state, that value will not only be available on the page immediately following the launch page, but also on any other page within the site. (See Chapter 19 for a discussion of state saving.)

From this clock example you may already see how a CGI program can dynamically influence the HTML environment. Although you can easily generate the entire

JavaScript program, it's more likely that you'll simply substitute key phrases here and there, as is done in the clock example.

Dynamically Passing Data to Java Applets

When working with precompiled Java applets, the CGI program does not have the option to write and compile the Java applet in the same way that it can write a JavaScript from scratch. However, it can still influence the Java application by passing parameters to it. This applet can then use the values passed to direct its execution.

Continuing with this same example, let's now see exactly how to dynamically pass parameters to a Java applet. First you need to get some input from the surfer. If you refer back to Figure 20-1, you will see that there are several input fields, including one for requesting a phrase for a banner, and two items that we are purchasing in this cyberstore. (Remember, this is just a simple demonstration. In a real cyberstore Web site, the procedure for choosing items would be much more elaborate. The Fish Store example shown later in this chapter is a more realistic demonstration.)

When you click on the button labeled SEE WHAT HAPPENS in Figure 20-1, the HTTP request that is sent by the browser to the Web server is defined by the HTML FORM ACTION tag, which is set to

```
<FORM METHOD=POST ACTION="/cgi-win/hubws.exe?HTJV:homepagep:707682">
```

The file HUBWS.EXE referenced in this request is a WebHub *runner* that communicates the page request to the Hub. (A runner is a small .EXE file that is quickly loaded and unloaded, while the Hub stays resident in memory. See Chapter 18 for a more detailed discussion of the role of HUBWS.EXE in WebHub.) The Hub (HUB.EXE, also known as WEBHUB CENTRAL) will look at the AppID (HTJV in this case) and queue the page request to the custom Web application. Although you cannot see the name of the custom Web application in the URL, it happens to be HTJAVA.EXE in this example. The HTJAVA.EXE program then dynamically creates the homepagep page, based on the predefined sequence of chunks for that page. It will do a bit of work to total up the order and to create strings that are formatted correctly for the Java applet. Those strings will be stored in the TWebApp.Literals array so that they can be substituted easily into the chunk using macro syntax. We'll look at that step in just a moment. First, let's see the result from the surfer's perspective. The homepage that is returned by the CGI program is shown in Figure 20-2.

The homepage displayed in Figure 20-2 includes both JavaScript and Java applets. JavaScript was used to create the clock. Two separate Java applets create the banner and the receipt graphics. The CGI program was responsible for dynamically sending the variables for the clock heading, the data within the banner, and the data on the receipt.

If you compare Figures 22-1 and 22-2, you will see that the word Quartz has been added as a clock title. This occurred because the CLOCKTITLE form literal was sent as part of the JavaClock chunk (the JavaScript).

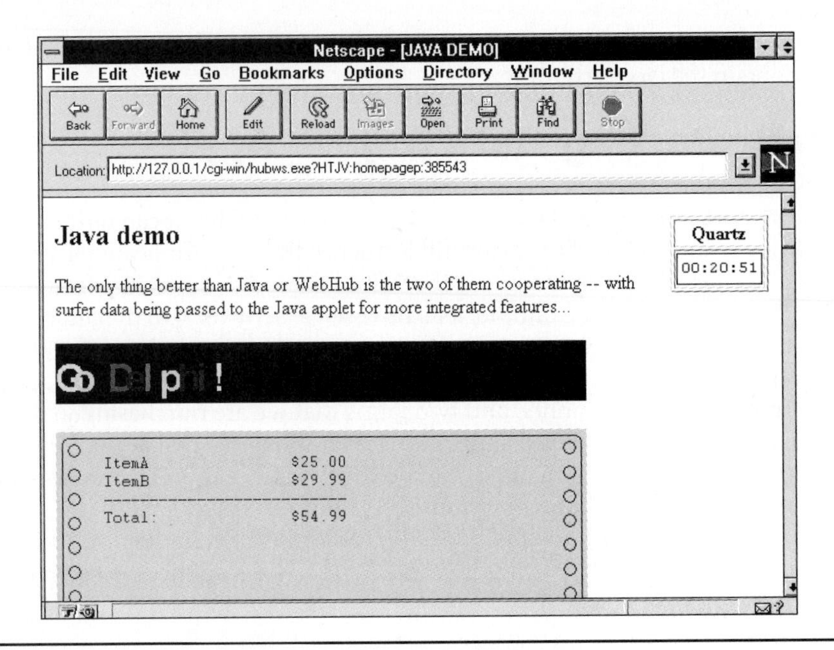

Figure 20-2. *The homepage returned by the Delphi CGI program*

You should also note that the banner text came directly from surfer input. The four strings of text on the receipt were created dynamically within the CGI program, stored in the TWebApp.Literals array, and then filled into the correct spots in the applet call as the output document was created.

It will help to consider the document source in detail to see how it creates the display shown in Figure 20-2, and then we'll step back to see exactly how the Delphi program created the four strings. The following is the source of the page shown in Figure 20-2. You can see this source from this page if you select View | Source from a Netscape browser.

```
<HTML><HEAD>
<TITLE>JAVA DEMO</TITLE>
<BASE HREF="http://meta.href.com/htdemo/java/">
</HEAD>
<BODY>

<CENTER>
<h5><i>* HREF Tools Corp. * Software for Dynamic Web Sites *</i></h5>
</CENTER>
<p>

<script language="JavaScript">
<!-- Time of day display.
 //Make right justified textbox for time.
```

```
 document.write(
         "<table border align=right>"
        +"<tr><td align=center><b>Quartz</b></td></tr>"
        +"<tr><font size=-4><form></font>"
...code excerpted here...

</script>
<h2>Java demo</h2>
The only thing better than Java or WebHub is the two of them
cooperating -- with surfer data being passed to the Java applet
for more integrated features...
<p>

<applet code="TestForAnn.class" width=450 height=50>
<param name=text value="Go Delphi!">
</applet>
<p>

<applet code="Receipt.class" width=450 height=600>
<param name=Parameter1 value="ItemA               $25.00">
<param name=Parameter2 value="ItemB               $29.99">
<param name=Parameter3 value="-------------------------">
<param name=Parameter4 value="Total:              $54.99">
</applet>

<hr>
Thanks to <A HREF="mailto:73170.1423@Compuserve.com">Dan Dumbrill</A>
for writing the two Java applets that take parameters.
<hr>

<CENTER>|| <A HREF="/cgi-win/hubws.exe?HTJV:HomePage:707682:">Try Again</A>
||</CENTER>
<hr>
<center>|| <A HREF="http://www.href.com/">HREF Tools Corp.</A> ||</center>
<HR>
<ADDRESS>Copyright &copy 1995-1996 HREF Tools Corp.  All Rights Reserved.
</ADDRESS>
</BODY></HTML>
```

Highlights of the Output Document

Let's again clarify the listing in terms of the transitions between HTML, JavaScript, and Java:

Tag	Purpose
<HTML><HEAD>	The document begins with HTML
<BASE HREF="http://meta.href.com /htdemo/java/">	This dynamically created HTML statement is required so that the .class files can be found in the htdemo\java path on the Web server machine.
<script language="JavaScript">	Here we see the JavaScript clock application covered earlier.

Tag	Purpose
<h2>Java demo</h2>	HTML resumes here.
<applet code="TestForAnn.class" width=450 height=50>	This marks the beginning of the Java applet that makes the banner. The browser will issue a separate request for the .class file and download it for the surfer.
</applet>	This marks the end of the Java applet definition.
<p>	HTML paragraph break.
<applet code="Receipt.class" width=450 height=600>	Receipt.class is the Java applet that draws the receipt.
</applet>	This marks the end of the second Java applet. The remainder of the code is HTML.

The Banner Applet

The job of the banner applet (TestForAnn.class) is very simple: create a banner with multi-colored letters that flash on and off like a neon sign. As far as we are concerned, the banner applet is a black box—it takes one parameter, which is the text to display. The CGI program does not need to know anything about how the applet builds the banner.

NOTE: *The source code for the banner applet is presented later in this chapter, but a detailed discussion of it is beyond the scope of this chapter. For information on Java, read* The Java Handbook *(Osborne/McGraw-Hill, 1996).*

The banner applet is called with these lines from within the HTML document:

```
<applet code="TestForAnn.class" width=450 height=50>
<param name=text value="Go Delphi!">
</applet>
```

When this part of the HTML document gets to the surfer's browser, the browser will send another HTTP request for the TestForAnn.class file, just as it would do if a graphic or multimedia file had been referenced in the document. When this Java applet file comes back from the Web server, it will be interpreted by the browser and executed.

You probably already noticed how the string "Go Delphi!" is passed in as a parameter to the TestForAnn class. If we look at the portion of the chunk used to create that effect, you'll see that it's again done with macro syntax, dynamically passing in the banner value from the TWebApp.Literal property.

```
<applet code="TestForAnn.class" width=450 height=50>
<param name=text value="%=banner=%">
</applet>
```

Referring back to the section "Java Demo Web Page HTML Source," you will see that the HTML source for the launch page defines an input field with NAME of banner. If you use the WebHub CGI framework, you don't need any custom Delphi programming in order to pass through such form literals.

Building the Receipt

The receipt is a bit more complicated, because the CGI program has to manipulate the data (totaling two numbers and formatting the strings for the receipt) before passing it out to the Java applet.

Calling the Applet

First let's review the WebHub chunk that calls the Java applet (receipt.class). It passes four strings using the Value tag.

```
<applet code="Receipt.class" width=450 height=600>
<param name=Parameter1 value="%=value1=%">
<param name=Parameter2 value="%=value2=%">
<param name=Parameter3 value="-------------------------">
<param name=Parameter4 value="%=Total=%">
</applet>
```

When WebHub sends this chunk to the output document, it expands the portions inside macro syntax (the %=ID=% segment) based on the contents of the Literal array property, and thereby publishes the form literals named value1, value2, and total. The following section demonstrates how Delphi code defines those entries in the Literal array used by WebHub.

Loading the WebHub Literal Array from Delphi

The procedure HTJV_HOMEPAGEPExecute is an event handler that is called when the HOMEPAGEP page executes, that is, before any page sections are sent to the output document. It is from this event handler that the entries in the Literals array that are needed for the application are initialized.

This event handler contains two embedded functions: itemFormat and priceFormat. These simple, unoptimized helper functions create strings of the proper length and layout for use in the graphical receipt displayed by the Java receipt.class applet. The important code is at the end, where the entries in the Literals array are created.

```
Literal['total']:=itemFormat('Total:')+priceFormat(total);
```

This line creates (or overwrites) TWebSession.Literals.Values['total'] with the text "Total:" plus the total dollar amount for the receipt. The following is the complete procedure listing:

```
procedure TJavaDemo.HTJV_HOMEPAGEPExecute(Sender: TObject;
  var Continue: Boolean);
function itemFormat( const s:string ):string;
begin
  result:=copy(s,1,16);            {shorten in case it's too long}
  result:=format('%-16s',[result]);    {then widen, left justify}
end;

function priceFormat( const value:real ):string;
begin
  result:=formatCurrency(value);
  result:=copy(result,1,10);  {shorten in case it's too long}
  result:=format('%10s',[result]);
end;

var
  p1,p2,total:real;
  s:string;

begin
  {now we jump in and create some literals
   which will flow into the output stream}
  {as the macros are expanded}

 with TWebPage(Sender).WebApp do begin
    try
      s:=WebServer.FormLiterals.Values['price1'];
      if s<>'' then
        p1:=StrToFloat(s);
      s:=WebServer.FormLiterals.Values['price2'];
      if s<>'' then
        p2:=StrToFloat(s);
    except
      p1:=0;
      p2:=0;
      end;
    total:=p1+p2;
    s:=WebServer.FormLiterals.Values['item1'];
    if s='' then s:=defaultItem1.text;
    Literal['value1']:=itemFormat(s)+priceFormat(p1);
    s:=WebServer.FormLiterals.Values['item2'];
    if s='' then s:=defaultItem2.text;
    Literal['value2']:=itemFormat(s)+priceFormat(p2);
    Literal['total']:=itemFormat('Total:')+priceFormat(total);
    end;
end;
```

Once the entries have been established in the Literals array, they are available for publication to the Web from chunk files. To reiterate, these values are included in the delivered HTML by replacing the macros in the stored chunk files with the corresponding data from TWebSession's Literal array property.

More About the Java Applet

Of course you also have to build the .class files by writing them in Java and then compiling them. The .class files need to be installed on the Web server in a directory that is accessible to surfers, just as you need to make bitmaps, or other similar downloadable resources, available to surfers. (The difference is that, at the time of this writing, you cannot use a path name when referencing the .class files. By comparison, path names are quite common for image and audio files.)

If you are using WebSite server, the path might be c:\website\htdocs\java\. To work around the no path name restriction, the generated document uses the <BASE HREF> tag at the beginning of the document to point to the location of the files. (<BASE HREF> is an HTML tag that tells the browser that all links in the current document should be resolved relative to the specified directory.) You can define the base directory manually, within a static chunk, or you can calculate it at runtime based on the CGI Referer variable. The next code example shows how you can do this.

Calculating the BASE HREF

In the HTJAVA demo, the <BASE HREF> is calculated dynamically so that this application will run on any Web server. When building dynamic pages, the default BASE would be the /cgi directory, which never works for graphics, audio, or Java files. Instead you need to get back either to the root / or perhaps a subdirectory below. For our situation, we want to get back to /htdemo/java/ for the current Web server location.

First we should look at the WebHub "headerwithbasehref" chunk that calls the Delphi code:

```
%=chunkBegin=%headerwithbasehref%=endInfo=%
<HTML><HEAD>
<TITLE>%=PageDesc=%</TITLE>
<BASE HREF="%=getBaseHREF=%">
</HEAD><BODY>

<CENTER>
<h5><i>* HREF Tools Corp. * Software for Dynamic Web Sites *</i></h5>
</CENTER>
<p>

<!-- ******************************************** --
```

The phrase getBaseHREF is listed as a custom event macro for the HTJAVA application, in effect, setting it up as a special keyword. When WebHub encounters any custom macro name within macro syntax, it calls the OnEventMacro event handler for TWebApp (the Application object). The first parameter passed to this event handler is a pointer to the object calling the event handler (Sender). The second parameter, the one in which we are particularly interested, is aMacro, which is a string containing the current macro name. (The third and forth parameters permit additional information to be sent to this event handler.) Normally, the critical information is the name of the macro being called; however, in this application only one custom macro is defined, so it's not necessary to check this parameter's value.

```
procedure TJavaDemo.WebAppHTJVEventMacro(Sender: TWebOutputApp;
  const aMacro, aParams, aID: String);
var
  w:word;
  s:string[128];
begin
{getBaseHREF}
  s:=Sender.WebServer.cgiReferer;
  w:=pos('/cgi',s);
  Sender.SendString( copy(s,1,w)+'htdemo/java/' );
end;
```

Let's look at this code line by line.

```
s:=Sender.WebServer.cgiReferer;
{for example: http://123.123.123.123:81/cgi-win/hubws.exe}
```

Sender is the TWebApp object. TWebServer is the component that publishes all the CGI environment data, including cgiReferer, which contains the URL that called us and would be something like http://123.123.123.123:81/cgi-win/hubws.exe.

```
w:=pos('/cgi',s);
```

The variable *w* tells us the position of /cgi within the cgiReferer string. We need to use the Referer information up to that byte.

```
Sender.SendString( copy(s,1,w)+'htdemo/java/' );
```

This final line sends the IP address (and any port information) to the output document. It does so using SendString, which is a method of the TWebApp class.

This completes the discussion of how CGI programs can enhance Java applets and JavaScripts by dynamically passing data to them. The next section focuses on a portion of a demonstration shopping site, where surfers get to select fish from Borland's biolife table.

The Fish Store Example

You can see the Fish Store online starting at http://www.href.com/sample/index.html. You will need to use a browser that can display HTML 3.0 tables with borders. The latest version of Netscape is recommended. The Fish Store demonstrates many of WebHub's features; however, this discussion focuses only on one that clearly utilizes the WebHub capability to save state. The next section looks at the site from the perspective of a surfer. Finally, the Delphi code that permits Web sites like the Fish Store is discussed.

Surfing the Fish Store

The homepage is a dynamically generated page. By the time that page is visible in your browser, you have already been noticed by the HTFISH application, and you have your own Session ID assigned and your own TWebSession object allocated. (Sessions are discussed in Chapter 19.)

The homepage has a link labeled "Look at Fish," which is the first link we will follow. If you look at the URL for that link, you will see embedded in it the CGI query string, which is HTFS:lookfish:270503. HTFS is the WebHub application ID, and lookfish is the PageID that you are requesting. The number at the end is the Session ID. In this example, the session ID is 270503. It is this Session ID that enables the Fish Store to respond to you as an individual, without confusing your requests with those of other surfers who may be accessing the site simultaneously.

Once you follow the link, you will see the lookfish page shown in Figure 20-3. The main attraction on this page is an HTML table displaying three records from the BIOLIFE.DB table (from the DBDEMOS alias).

The TWebDataGrid component is responsible for creating the HTML table display. One of its properties is PageHeight, which determines the number of records to show. Rather than display all records in the result set, the TWebDataGrid shows a small amount, and then uses links to enable the surfer to scroll to the next set. In this example, the user selects the More Fish link to display the next set of three records.

The multiline grid shown in Figure 20-3 is possible because, as discussed in general in Chapter 19, the TWebDataGrid is a TWebAction component, and its state is saved in the SaveState string on the TWebSession object. This permits surfers to request their own pageHeight and be at their own position in the table.

NOTE: The TWebDataGrid connects to a TWebDataSource, which connects to a TDataSource, which then connects to a TTable or TQuery. In the Fish Store application, a TTable is used and is connected to the BIOLIFE.DB table from the DBDEMOS alias that ships with Delphi. Besides handling pageHeight, the TWebDataGrid also respects DisplaySets (list of fields to show) and IndexOrders (sorting).

For the purpose of the discussion, we need to follow one of the links within the grid to see a detail page for one of the fish. We'll choose the Red Emperor link. Notice in Figure 20-3 that the CGI query string for this link is HTFS:Detail.270503:90030. The final number of this query string, 90030, is the primary key of the record to be

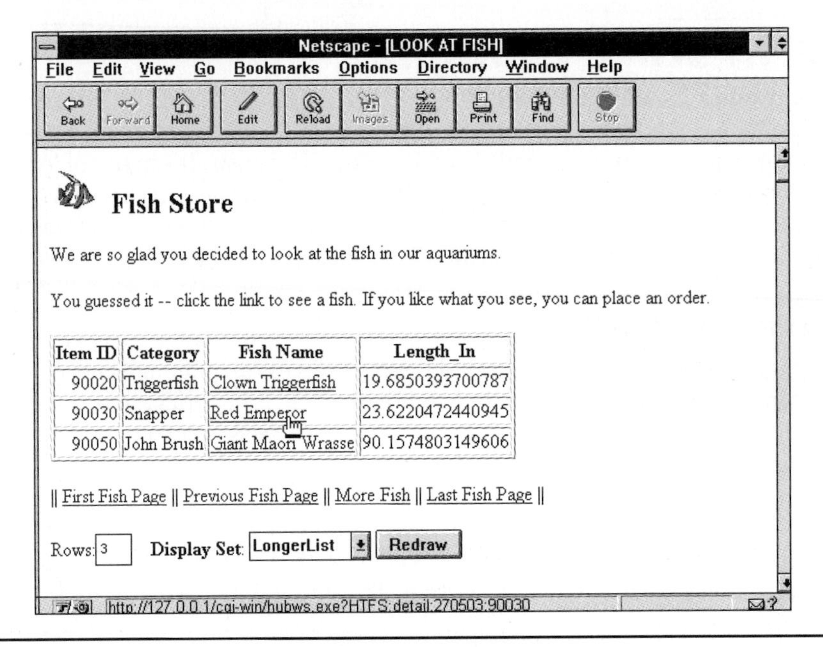

Figure 20-3. *The lookfish page from the Fish Store*

retrieved. When following this link, the page shown in Figure 20-4 is delivered by WebHub.

After the detail information about the fish, there is a link that lets you initiate the "purchase" of the fish. It is labeled Put Fish in Cart. (This link is on the page shown in Figure 20-4, but it is below the viewable area. From the page shown in Figure 20-4, you can scroll down to see the link Put Fish in Cart.) When you click this link, you invoke the grabfish page, and the Web application adds your fish request to a TStringList that it tracks internally. This TStringList is the metaphorical shopping cart.

Imagine that you go through these steps of selecting a fish and putting it in the cart one more time, so that now there are two fish, #90030 and #90050, in the cart. If you are now following the link labeled Go to Checkout Counter, the checkout page shown in Figure 20-5 dynamically displays the contents of the current order.

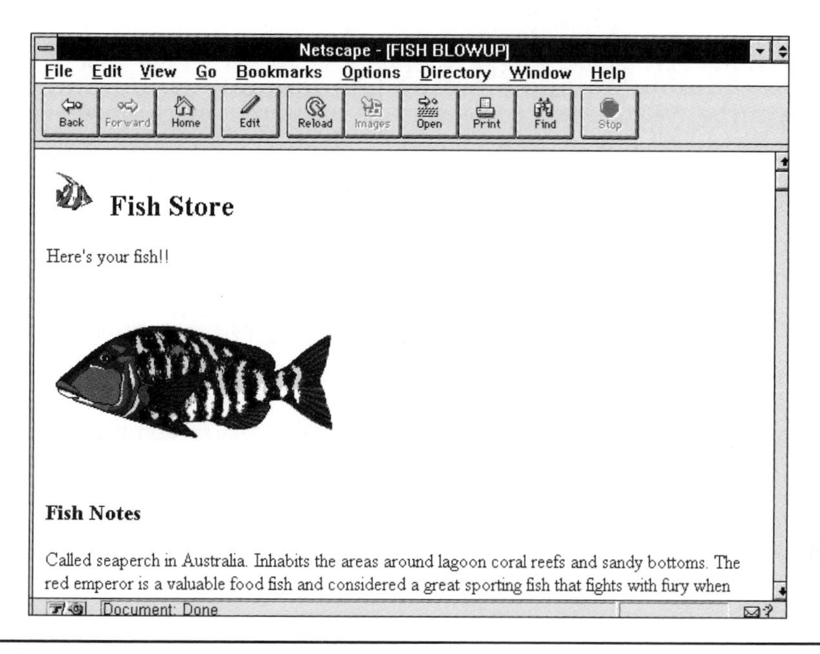

Figure 20-4. *Detail about the Red Emperor fish*

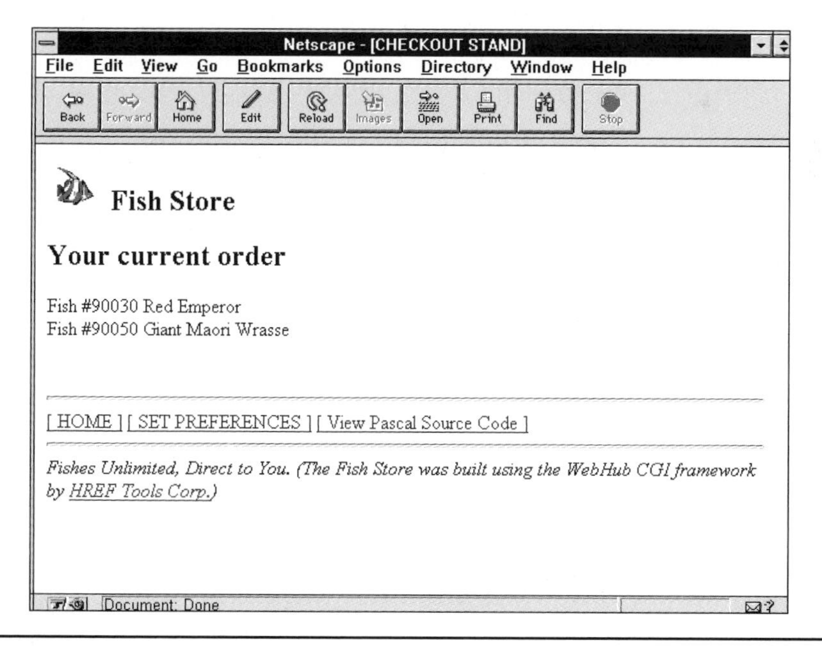

Figure 20-5. *The checkout counter, which lists the selected items*

Key Elements of the Fish Store

That the fish can be selected and then taken to the checkout counter is proof that the CGI application has saved state. The CGI program remembers each fish that was selected and is able to present the complete list when needed. Let's now look at the key elements to the Delphi solution.

The TWebSession object remembers the shopping order. The Fish Store uses a component called TFishSessionVars, which is derived from TWebSessionVars and adds three published properties. As discussed in Chapter 19, the custom Vars layer is grafted onto the TWebSession by overriding the VarsClass function. The custom session component is connected to the Application object by overriding the SessionClass function.

The following code shows the definition of the all the custom components used in the Fish Store application. Of the three additional published properties, the two of greater interest are CurrentFish (a Double that is set to the active fish) and FishList, which is a TStringList used to hold the order.

```
type
  TFishSessionVars = class(TWebSessionVars)
  private
    fCurrentFish : double;
    fFishList : TStringList;
    fPrefReturnsTo : string;
  protected
    function getFishList : TStringList;
    procedure setFishList( value : TStringList );
  public
    Constructor Create(aWebSession:TWebSession); override;
    Destructor Destroy; override;
  published
    property CurrentFish : double read fCurrentFish write fCurrentFish;
    property FishList : TStringList read getFishList write setFishList;
    property PrefReturnsTo : string read fPrefReturnsTo
      write fPrefReturnsTo;
  end;
  TFishSession = class(TWebSession)
  protected
    function VarsClass:TWebSessionVarsClass; override;
    end;
  TFishApp = class(TWebApp)
  private
    fPathForTempGifs:string;
  protected
    function SessionClass:TWebSessionClass; override;
  public
  published
```

```
    property pathForTempGifs:string read fPathForTempGifs
      write fPathForTempGifs;
  end;
```

Remember that the basic model of a Web site is that it comprises distinct pages, which in WebHub are broken down further into sections (called chunks), perhaps conditionally. The page is represented by the component TWebPage, which has a PageSections property that itemizes the sections of the page. As seen earlier in the Java example, event handlers get called when the page starts, as well as before each section. In the Fish Store, when the surfer goes to the grabfish page to put the current fish in his or her cart, the following procedure is called because it was defined as the TWebPage.OnSection event handler:

```
procedure TFishStoreForm.HTFS_GRABFISHSection(Sender: TObject;
  Section: Integer; var Chunk, Options: String);
var
  item:double;
  desc:string;
  theList:TStringList;
  vp:TFishSessionVars;  {vars pointer}

begin
  if section=1 then begin
    vp:=TFishSessionVars(WebAppHTFS.WebSession.Vars);
    item:=vp.currentFish;

    with TableBiolife do begin
      findKey([item]);
      desc:=fieldByName( 'Common_Name' ).asString;
      end;

   desc:='Fish #' + FloatToStr(item) + ' ' + desc;

   { Put the Fish In the Shopping Cart !!! }
    vp.fishList.add( desc );
    end;
end;
```

Let's look at this code in more detail. The variables are common enough, except for vp. The variable vp, defined in the following code segment, is a pointer to the type TFishSessionVars. It provides a typing shortcut as well as a slight optimization of referencing the items within the Vars layer. This should be clear when the procedure code is reviewed later on.

```
vp:TFishSessionVars;  {vars pointer}
```

The same event handler is called for each page section (that is, page header section, body, and footer). The fishList array needs to be touched only once, so a simple if statement ensures that the steps are executed only once.

```
if section=1 then begin { only do this once! }
```

The variable vp points to the correct spot by casting the long expression to TFishSessionVars in this line:

```
vp:=TFishSessionVars(WebAppHTFS.WebSession.Vars);
```

In this line, WebAppHTFS is the Web Application object of type TFishApp. WebHub Application objects have a WebSession property that is declared as type TWebSession. The component will always point to the current surfer's session data; no extra steps are required to make WebSession connect to the right data.

To understand the casting, remember that although at runtime the SessionClass function can tell us that WebSession is TFishSession rather than TWebSession, the compiler doesn't know that. Therefore, in order to refer to a custom property of TFishSession, WebSession is cast as TFishSession. However, we really want to get to the Vars layer, and that is not a custom property. Both the generic TWebSession and the custom TFishSession have a Vars layer. By the same logic, because we want to access the custom properties within the Vars property, it is also necessary to cast Vars as TFishSessionVars. In this case, there is no danger in performing this casting because we know that the Vars of TFishSession is really a TFishSessionVars object.

The next line defines a local variable to have a copy of the currentFish value:

```
item:=vp.currentFish;
```

This next code segment locates the current fish and remembers the Common_Name in a string variable called desc, which stands for description:

```
with TableBiolife do begin
      findKey([item]);
      desc:=fieldByName( 'Common_Name' ).asString;
      end;
```

The desc variable is then redefined to include a prompt, the item number and the description.

```
desc:='Fish #' + FloatToStr(item) + ' ' + desc;
```

Once the description is prepared, it is added to the fishList array on the Vars layer of the current session object.

```
vp.fishList.add( desc );
```

To summarize what just happened, first, the surfer clicked a link to indicate selection of an item. That link led to the grabfish page. In the OnSection event handler for that page, a string was created that represented the selected item and then added that string to a custom TStringList called fishList. Because fishList is stored on the session object, it is automatically saved between page requests.

The final question is, how does that string list appear on the checkout page? This is done with WebHub's macro syntax. Using macro syntax, you can publish certain properties of certain WebHub components in-line in the HTML—in this case, a TStringList property on the TWebSession component. The WebHub chunk file for the Fish store includes this HTML for the checkout page:

```
<h2>Your current order</h2>
%=fishList=%
```

When this chunk file is sent to the output document, fishList is expanded and prints the entire TStringList. Thus the Delphi programmer's job is clearly defined as storing the item selections, and the HTML author's job is clearly defined as deciding how and where to present that data.

Conclusion

There are dozens of features that people want to build into interactive, database-driven Web sites. This chapter demonstrated several of them, including Java applets, JavaScript, hot links within tables, and a rudimentary shopping-cart interface. The advantage of building Web applications using or incorporating Delphi is that Delphi is such a rich environment. With its database capability, it is quite reasonable to use Delphi to build sophisticated, feature-rich Web sites. It is also possible to do so in a fraction of the time required with other platforms.

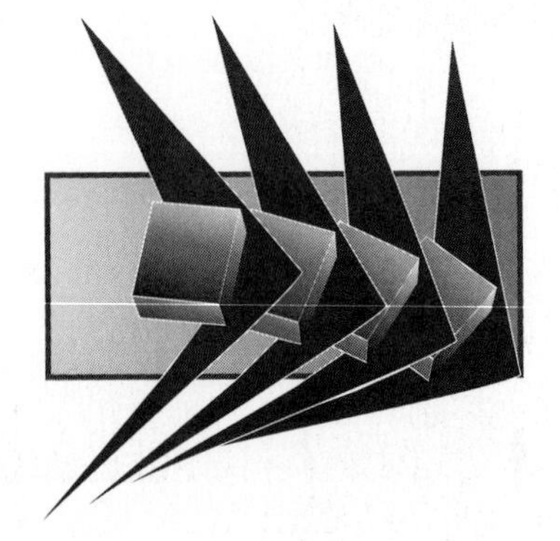

PART FOUR

Appendixes

Appendix A

Code Files and the CD-ROM

This book is accompanied by a CD-ROM that contains the code presented in the book, along with a variety of other utilities and fun Windows multimedia files (.AVIs). This appendix describes how to use the files on the CD-ROM as well as how to get additional information about this book on the Internet.

Using the CD-ROM

For your convenience, all code presented in this book is located on the CD-ROM. These code files can be found in the CODE subdirectory of the disk. Under this subdirectory you will find one subdirectory for each chapter in the book (excluding those chapters for which there is no code). These subdirectories are named using a four-letter naming convention. Each subdirectory name begins with the letters CH and ends with two digits that identify the chapter. For example, the subdirectory for Chapter 3 is named CH03 and the subdirectory for Chapter 15 is named CH15.

Within the subdirectory for a given chapter, there are one or two additional subdirectories. The chapter code is located within these subdirectories. For each chapter containing material that applies to Delphi 1.0, there is a subdirectory named DELPHI16 (16-bit Delphi). Since every chapter includes code examples that apply to Delphi 2, there is also a subdirectory named DELPHI32.

The following are examples of where you will find the code you want. If you want to access the Delphi 1.0 version of code for Chapter 4, look in the following subdirectory on the CD-ROM:

```
\CODE\CH04\DELPHI16
```

If, however, you want to locate the Delphi 2 code for Chapter 14, look in the following subdirectory:

```
\CODE\CH14\DELPHI32
```

Using the Code Examples

To use the code examples for a particular chapter, copy the files from the specified subdirectory on the CD-ROM to your hard disk. Once the files are on your hard disk, you can compile the project and run it. (The code disk does not include .EXE files or .DCU files. The .DCU files are compiled units.)

Some code examples require that you first install one or more components into your component library. The chapter in which a given example is discussed contains instructions on whether you need to install additional components to work with the example. If needed, use the following steps to add a component to your component library:

1. Close all open projects.
2. From the Delphi main menu, select Components | Install (Delphi 2) or Options | Install Components (Delphi 1.0). Delphi displays the Install Components dialog box.
3. From the Install Components dialog box, select the Add button. Delphi displays the Add Module dialog box.
4. From the Add Module dialog box, enter the path and name of the unit (.PAS file) or compiled unit (.DCU) that registers the new component, and then select OK.
5. Delphi adds the selected unit (or compiled unit) to the Install units list of the Install Components dialog box. If you still want to add another unit, repeat steps 3 and 4 until all required units have been added. When done adding units, click the OK button on the Install Components dialog box. This causes the component library to be recompiled, and your installed components will now appear in the component palette.

In addition to ensuring that all required components have been installed, you must also have correctly installed Delphi and its necessary files. For example, in order to run some of the example files in Chapter 9 for ReportSmith 2.5 (from Delphi 1.0), the ReportSmith directory must be on the DOS path.

NOTE: With some network operating systems, if you copy a file from a CD-ROM onto your hard disk, the file will be assigned the read-only attribute, since the source the files were copied from is a read-only device (the CD drive). If you are working with such a system, you will need to use the DOS ATTRIB command, or either the Windows Program Manager or Windows 95 Explorer, to turn off the read-only attribute of any files you copy from the CD-ROM.

Other Material on the CD-ROM

In addition to the code examples, the CD-ROM contains other materials, divided into four subdirectories: UTILS, INFORMNT, NEWSLETR, and VIDEOS. The UTILS subdirectory contains the subdirectories for the various demoware and shareware provided by some of the top third-party developers of Delphi products. Within this subdirectory, you will find a separate subdirectory for each included utility. The INFORMNT subdirectory contains three issues of *Delphi Informant*, as well as an issue of the *Delphi PowerTools Catalog*. These materials may be viewed using the Adobe Acrobat Reader. If you have not already installed the Adobe Acrobat Reader, you can do so from the files available in the ACROREAD subdirectory, located under the INFORMNT subdirectory.

In the NEWSLETR subdirectory you will find twelve issues of the Delphi Unofficial Newsletter, edited and published by Robert Vivrette, one of the authors of this book. The Delphi Unofficial Newsletter is published in the Windows Help File format, and therefore can be accessed using the Windows Help system. Finally, the VIDEOS subdirectory contains five Borland videos, including the thrilling Delphi 2 Launch video. These videos are in .AVI format and can be viewed using the Windows multimedia viewer or the MediaPlayer component in Delphi. You can only view these videos if your computer is multimedia enabled.

The *Delphi In Depth* Web Site

A Web site has been established for this book. The URL (Uniform Resource Locator) for this site is http://gramercy.ios.com/~jdsi/did.html. This Web site contains current information on this book. Also, if updated code examples or corrections to the text are available following the publication of this book, this Web site will contain a description of how you can obtain (download) the updates. This site also includes links to other Delphi sites of interest.

A Web site for this book will remain active at least until May 1998. However, we cannot guarantee that the site will be active beyond that date. Also, we regret that we will be unable to provide general technical support for Delphi through this page. We suggest you try Borland International's Web site at http://www.borland.com or contact Borland via CompuServe by typing GO BORLAND.

If You Cannot Find the Web Site

So many changes are occurring on the Internet that it is not possible to ensure that the Web site listed in the preceding section will remain at the given URL. If for some reason this site is moved, you will need to use a Web search utility to find it. You can use the search facility surfaced by your Web browser. Alternatively, check out the search sites at http://www.yahoo.com or http://www.altavista.digital.com. Use the search string "Delphi In Depth Book." The Web site for this book will contain that text. Alternatively, you can search for the names of the co-authors of this book. Most of the co-authors of this book have their own Web sites, and these sites will likely contain a link to the page for this book.

Appendix B

Acronyms

Acronym	Definition
AOL	America Online
API	Application Programming Interface
BBS	Bulletin Board System
BDE	Borland Database Engine
CGI	Common Gateway Interface
CIS	CompuServe
CORBA	Common Object Request Broker Architecture
DCE	Distributed Computing Environment
DDE	Dynamic Data Exchange
DLL	Dynamic Link Library
DNS	Domain Name Servers
DRDA	IBM's Distributed Relational Database Access architecture
FTP	File Transfer Protocol
GDI	Graphics Device Interface
GUI	Graphical User Interface
HTML	Hypertext Markup Language
IDAPI	Independent Database Application Programming Interface
IDE	Integrated Development Environment
IETF	Internet Engineering Task Force
IP	Internet Protocol
IRC	Internet Relay Chat
ISDN	Integrated Services Digital Network
LAN	Local Area Network
LIBS	Local InterBase Server
MDI	Multiple Document Interface
MOM	Message-oriented middleware
OCX	OLE Control
ODBC	Open Database Connectivity
OLE	Object Linking and Embedding
OODBMS	Objected Oriented Database Management System

Acronym	Definition
PGP	Pretty good privacy
RAD	Rapid Application Development
RAM	Random Access Memory
RDBMS	Relational Database Management System
RFC	Request for Comment
RPC	Remote Procedure Call
RTL	Run-Time Library
RTTI	Run-Time Type Information
SDI	Single Document Interface
SQL	Structured Query Language
SSL	Secure Sockets Layer
TCP/IP	Transmission Control Protocol/Internet Protocol
TP	Transaction Processing
UDF	User-Defined Function
URL	Uniform Resource Locators
VB	Visual Basic
VB4	Visual Basic 4.0
VBX	Visual Basic Extension
VCL	Visual Component Library
Win32	Windows 95 and Windows NT (32-bit operating systems)
3GL	Third generation language
4GL	Fourth generation language

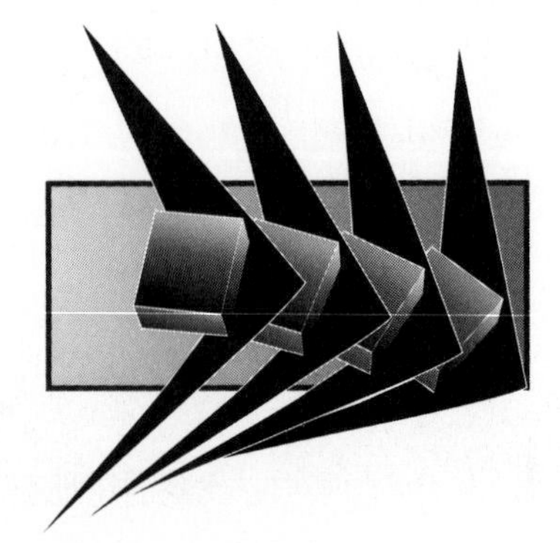

Index

B

C

D

E

K

L

M

N

R

S

T

U

V